Business & Financial Literacy
Spring 2019/2020

Week	Topic	Pages from Text
1	Classifying and Characterizing Businesses	pp. 1-25
	Prepare a written response to Student Problem 1-1	pp. 25
	Financial Statement Basics	pp. 32-50
2	Prepare a written response to Student Problem 3-2	pp. 79
	Core Quantitative and Leveraging Concepts	No reading
	Corporations: Basic Business Considerations	pp. 104-114
3	Corporations: Basic Business Considerations	pp. 114-142
	Prepare a written response to Student Problem 4-4	pp. 125
4	Shareholder Rights and Activism	pp. 143-191
	Prepare a written response to Student Problem 5-1	pp. 152
5	Partnership and LLC Entity and Design Options	No reading
	Funding the Enterprise	pp. 228-258
	Business Enterprise Taxation	pp. 259-279
6	Prepare a written response to Student Problem 7-1	pp. 241
	Business Enterprise Taxation	pp. 280-290
	Choosing the Best Entity Form	pp. 291-304
	Owners of Closely Held Businesses	No reading
7	Fights for Control in Public Corporations	pp. 354-377
	Prepare a written response to Student Problem 11-1	pp. 374
	Employee Benefits and Executive Perks	pp. 378-394
8	Employee Benefits and Executive Perks	pp. 394-420
	Prepare a written response to Student Problem 12-1	pp. 400
9	Important Historical and Planning Perspectives 14-11	pp. ~~421-465~~
	Prepare a written response to Student Problem ~~13-2~~	pp. 432
10	Review & 466-480 INTLCT PRUF	439-455

WEST ACADEMIC PUBLISHING'S LAW SCHOOL ADVISORY BOARD

BUSINESS AND FINANCIAL LITERACY FOR LAW STUDENTS

■ ■ ■

by

Dwight Drake

University of Washington School of Law

AMERICAN CASEBOOK SERIES®

Mat #41654451

444 Cedar Street, Suite 700
St. Paul, MN 55101
1-877-888-1330

Printed in the United States of America

ISBN: 978–1–62810–244–4

In memory of my parents,
Charles and Leola Drake

*

PREFACE

Many law students graduate today with little or no understanding or appreciation for what they do not know about the world of business and how that deficiency in their education might hamper their professional development and their effectiveness in serving others. In its report issued in January 2014, the ABA's Task Force on the Future of Legal Education concluded that law schools must devote "more attention to skills training, experiential learning, and the development of practice-related competencies." Given the pervasive links between business and law practice, it's hard to imagine a practice-related competency more in need of attention than business and financial literacy.

This book is my attempt to help address this gap in legal education. I wrote the book for a course on business and financial literacy that I teach at the University of Washington School of Law. The book's emphasis is on breadth and real-world relevance and promoting awareness and a basic understanding (not expertise) of foundational business concepts and terms, financial statements, quantitative concepts, how markets function, core business factors, entity concepts, and practical, business-related challenges often faced by lawyers. The book is designed for students who have not had any significant business training, but any student who uses the book, even the more business-savvy student, will be better prepared to understand the world of business and interface with business owners and executives and professionals who serve the business community.

When I sat down to design the course and write this book, I knew that the course would not work if the range of topics was too narrow, the discussions were too complicated, or the book was too long. I ended up asking myself two fundamental questions: (1) If I was still in practice and hiring new associates, what business and financial literacy topics would I like to see included in the training of our new associates? (2) How can I pack those topics into a reader-friendly, 500-page book designed for use in a short course targeted at smart students who are business neophytes?

My answer to the first question encompassed a broad range of topics that fall into three categories. The first category includes quantitative concepts that are often associated with financial literacy: understanding and reading financial statements; leveraging basics and strategies; core business factors, measures, and performance ratios; time value of money concepts; business valuation techniques; and basic microeconomics concepts that are often used to justify or explain a specific event, decision, or course of action.

The second category was the most difficult and in many respects is the most important. There are key features of this book that significantly distinguish it from the works of others, but none is more significant than this second category of topics. It includes numerous business factors that directly impact core legally-related challenges faced by businesses. I am continually amazed at how often a law student is introduced to a technical concept of business law without ever being exposed to the related business challenges and the all-important business factors that must be considered in applying the concept. The student, for example, is taught how to form a corporation with no mention of the numerous business operational factors that co-owners of the new business should consider in the organizational process. This book introduces students to over 180 business factors that directly impact 22 important legally-related business challenges. A grasp of these business factors and challenges defines business literacy and is the key to bridging the gap between legal concepts and business objectives and priorities. The best lawyers instinctively bridge that gap with their core business knowledge.

The third category includes foundational knowledge about business and how elements of the business world function. Some subjects are not specifically law-related: the audit process; business plans; stock market basics; trading strategies; going public realities; start-up funding sources; letters and lines of credit; key business characteristic differences; derivatives; global tax trends; bond markets; and the like. Other subjects are focused on legal developments: business entity tax concepts; transfer pricing; the role of antitrust; securities law liabilities; intellectual property protections; employment and executive compensation practices and developments (e.g., Affordable Care Act, say-on-pay); fights for corporate control; multi-entity planning; and business-related ethical challenges.

Once identified, the topics needed to be presented in a concise, understandable manner that would work for a law school course. I have tried to do this by keeping the discussions focused on core concepts, avoiding nonessential complexities, using many illustrative examples, incorporating problems that test student comprehension, and being stingy with my words.

As an example, the discussion on time-value-of-money concepts has various elements: defines the subject matter and how it relates to specific business challenges; illustrates with examples the seven different factors and related computation challenges that often surface (from the simplest present value calculation to a complicated internal rate of return calculation); explains and shows how the calculations can be made in seconds with an online calculator; and presents a problem that tests a student's comprehension of the discussion and challenges the student to make a semi-difficult calculation with an online calculator. What the discussion lacks is the traditional lengthy and complicated explanation of the exponential formulas that are the basis of the calculations and the voluminous tables that summarize specific computation factors. The formulas are presented in footnotes, but the reader is advised that, in today's world, a lawyer can easily navigate time-value-of-money challenges with no understanding of the mathematic formulas and no tables. The key for this book-related challenge is that this entire discussion on time-value-of-money concepts consumes less than six pages.

The book includes 45 mini-case-study student problems that enable students to daily analyze and apply the substance of what they are reading to specific fact situations. The book is supported by a teacher's manual that provides answers to the student problems and explains how I use the book and the student problems to promote the development of analytical, writing, presentation, and teamwork skills in my course. There is also a companion website that provides sample exam questions and a PowerPoint slide library that can help in providing answers to the student problems.

I thank the Seattle firm of Foster Pepper PLLC for use of the four forms included in Chapter 15, Professor Scott Schumacher for his discussion of business-related ethical issues in Chapter 14, the University of Washington School of Law for allowing me to teach business and tax courses, the University of Washington Executive MBA Program for giving me the opportunity to teach corporate executives for many years, and attorney Michael Heatherly for his assistance with the manuscript. Above all, I am grateful for the many business owners, executives and professionals who I have had the opportunity to work with and serve for over four decades.

DWIGHT DRAKE
Fall City, Washington
June 2014

SUMMARY OF CONTENTS

Page

TABLE OF CONTENTS

Page

PART II: CORE ENTITY CONCEPTS

PART IV: FOUNDATIONAL INFORMATION

CHAPTER 1

Classifying and Characterizing Businesses

A. THRESHOLD CHALLENGE

A lawyer needs to appreciate the breadth of the word "business." The term encompasses a huge range of enterprises that differ in many respects. The differences are important. For any lawyer, a threshold challenge is to have an understanding of core business differences. At the most basic level, such an understanding will help any person communicate and work with others and better comprehend the significance of developments and trends that are reported daily.

The importance of understanding core business differences escalates for the lawyer who wants to assist business owners or executives at any level. It is a prerequisite to developing the capacity to meaningfully assist clients in the processes of identifying and prioritizing specific business objectives. And it is that capacity that is often the difference between good and mediocre (or worse) legal services.

Many business owners and executives, even some of the brightest, are incapable of identifying and articulating specific objectives without the aid of a knowledgeable advisor. They often need help in understanding the significance of an issue and eliciting facts and considerations that will impact the identification of their specific objectives relative to the issue. Then a prioritization challenge often surfaces because of conflicts and inconsistencies triggered by competing business objectives. It's a balancing analysis that requires an understanding of the strategic options and trade-offs. In nearly every situation, this understanding is impossible without the knowledgeable input of a legal advisor who understands the uniqueness of the business. The biggest mistake a legal advisor can make is to assume that businesses are essentially the same and owners and executives share the same basic objectives and require the same essential structural plans. Business is never a "one-size-fits-all" game.

This opening chapter focuses on core business differences by explaining owner and entity differences, illustrating different ways businesses are characterized and contrasted, and describing the tool used by a business to explain how and why it is unique. This is not a comprehensive discussion of all significant business differences; it's hard to imagine what such a discussion would entail. The hope is that this short, introductory discussion will provide a useful starting point and foundation for what follows in later chapters and help narrow knowledge gaps between business novices and more business-savvy students.

One important, fundamental business difference needs to be indentified up front. It's the difference between for-profit businesses and non-profit businesses. The former are organized, funded, and operated with a goal of generating a profit for the owners. As we will see, a for-profit enterprise usually has other important stakeholders, including employees, creditors, vendors, communities, taxing authorities and more, but the ever-present driving force (for good or bad) is the profit motives of the owners.

A non-profit business has no owner profit motive. It is organized, funded, and operated to accomplish specifically-identified community or charitable objectives. Although it lacks profit-seeking owners, it can raise capital, own property, employ people, perpetually exist, and operate on a grand scale. Virtually every state has a statutory scheme that authorizes the creation and governs the operation of non-profit entities. And, of course, important provisions of the Internal Revenue Code exempt qualifying non-profit organizations from the federal income tax[1] and specify requirements for donors to receive an income tax charitable deduction for amounts contributed to a charitable entity.[2]

This book is focused only on for-profit businesses. It's not that non-profits are not important; they play vitally important roles in every community. They are just outside the scope of this effort.

B. OWNER DIFFERENCES

Businesses differ based on the type, mix, and number of their owners. Following are brief descriptions of nine business owner classifications. These classifications are not perfect; overlaps, exceptions and omissions regularly surface in the real world. But they work for purposes of explaining different owner expectations and illustrating and analyzing the different and competing objectives that often must be addressed in evaluating options for resolving a specific business challenge. The first eight relate to the 27 million privately owned businesses in America that represent more than 99 percent of all employers, historically produce 65 percent of all net new jobs, and produce 16.5 times more patents per employee than their public company counterparts.[3]

1. *SINGLE-OWNER ENTITIES*

A single-owner entity is a true soloist. No partners. No co-shareholders. It may be a corporation, a limited liability company, or a sole proprietorship. Whatever the form, the planning focus is on a single owner. The soloist has no need for buy-sell agreements, control strategies, or the complexity of Subchapter K (the partnership provisions) of the Internal Revenue Code. But he or she must

---

1. See, generally, I.R.C. §§ 501 through 505.
2. I.R.C. § 170.
3. See "Small Business Fact Sheet," U.S. House of Representatives Committee on Small Business (May 21, 2013).

still be concerned about entity forms and structures, motivating and retaining key employees, funding and growing the enterprise, developing exit and transition strategies, controlling and managing risks, taxes, and other critical challenges. The business and planning challenges usually are easier only because they are lonelier; there is no need to grapple with the competing objectives and perspectives of co-owners. The focus is always on the hopes, dreams, and risks of a single individual.

2. EMPLOYEE-OWNED ENTITIES

These businesses are owned by individuals who work fulltime for the business. The owners toil in their businesses every day. To them, the business is much more than an investment; it is their job, their career, and often their sole or primary means of support. They cherish the independence of working for themselves. They long for stability; above all, the business must continue to provide the owners their needed cash flows. The owners know that if the business folds, they likely will end up working for another or standing in an unemployment line.

Among the owners, there often is a "democracy" spin on control issues, with minority rights being protected only on the most sensitive issues. The admission of a new owner is a carefully controlled event because any new owner will become a true day-to-day colleague who will have the capacity to directly impact the success of the business. When one leaves the group, the survival and health of the ongoing entity always trumps the interests of the departing owner.

3. INVESTOR-OWNED ENTITIES

These organizations are owned by investors who do not work for the business. The owners often are heavily involved in the highest-level management decisions while others sweat out the day-to-day challenges of the business. For most investors, the business is not their primary or sole means of support; it's an investment. They are looking for a return on that investment – the sooner the better. Compared to employee owners, investors usually are less risk averse and less concerned with the identity of their co-owners or ownership changes.

4. HYBRID ENTITIES

The hybrid organization has both employee-owners and investor-owners. Often it is the most difficult organization for planning purposes. The employee-owners usually put their careers, but not their checkbooks, on the line. They want to do all in their power to protect their paychecks for the long run and control the operations of the business. The investors are concerned about the money they have at risk and the potential of having to put up more if things don't go as planned. They want equity growth and the flexibility to exit and cash out at the most opportune time.

5. DOMINANT-OWNER ENTITIES

This organization has one majority owner and a few small minority owners. The dominant owner may be an employee-owner or an investor-owner. The minority owners are usually employees. The dynamics are very different with this type of enterprise. In almost every situation of this type, the dominant owner will want and expect special treatment. It's not about democratic votes or minority rights.

From the dominant owner's perspective, real damage can be done by trying to create a level playing field to treat all the owners the same. The dominant owner usually will want exclusive control rights that can be passed onto chosen successors and special buy-out rights and liquidity protections to ensure that his or her position always can be preserved. Often the minority owners maintain their equity interests at the will of the dominant owner, who possesses broad rights to terminate and buy out their interests at any time.

6. FAMILY-DOMINATED BUSINESSES

Many businesses are owned and controlled by a single family. All planning issues are complicated by estate planning challenges and the dynamics among the family members. Usually the parents have family objectives that take priority over business issues, and often the children have special agendas. In many cases, the objectives of children who work in the business collide with objectives of the "outside children." Liquidity issues often are magnified by estate tax realities. Control issues usually are impacted by family considerations unrelated to the business.

Family-dominated businesses compose more than 80 percent of U.S. enterprises, employ more than 50 percent of the nation's workforce, and account for the bulk (some estimate as much as 64 percent) of America's gross domestic product.[4] Although more than 80 percent of senior family owners claim that they want the business to stay in the family, less than 30 percent acknowledge having a transition plan.[5] The result is that most family businesses remain in the family, but at a dear cost. Best estimates are that less than 30 percent of family dominated businesses survive a second generation, and the survival rate is even uglier for those businesses that make it to generation three.[6]

Although many successful family business owners enjoy a net worth that rivals or exceeds that of other well-heeled clients, the planning dynamics usually are much different when a family business takes center stage. In a recent survey, a startling 93 percent of senior business owners acknowledged that the business is their primary source of income and security.[7] With little or no diversification, everything gets tougher. And more often than not, business and planning challenges are further complicated by strong emotional ties to the business as

4. See generally R. Duman, "Family Firms Are Different," Entrepreneurship Theory and Practice, 1992, pp. 13–21; and M. F. R. Kets de Vries, "The Dynamics of Family Controlled Firms: The Good News and the Bad News," Organizational Dynamics, 1993, pp. 59–71; W. G. Dyer, Cultural Change in Family Firms, Jossey–Bass, San Francisco, 1986; and P. L. Rosenblatt, M. R. Anderson and P. Johnson, The Family in Business, Jossey–Bass, San Francisco, 1985; Arthur Anderson/Mass Mutual, American Family Business Survey, 2002.

5. Family to Family: Laird Norton Tyee Family Business Survey 2007, page 5. The survey also indicated that (1) only 56 percent of the respondents have a written strategic business plan, (2) nearly 64 percent do not require that family members entering the business have any qualifications or business experience, and (3) 25 percent do not believe that the next generation is competent to move into leadership roles.

6. J. I. Ward, Keeping the Family Business Healthy, Jossey–Bass, San Francisco, 1987. This study suggests that the survival rate to generation three is less than 15 percent.

7. Family to Family: Laird Norton Tyee Family Business Survey 2007, page 5 (Executive Summary).

well as historical perceptions regarding essential bonds between the family and the business.

7. PERSONAL SERVICE ORGANIZATIONS

These are organizations that generate income by their owners providing services in fields such as healthcare, law, engineering, accounting, actuarial science, performing arts and consulting. It's actually a type of employee-owned organization that warrants its own classification for a few reasons.

First, the owners are the instruments of production of the business; their talents generate the fees that drive everything. The owners are well educated, independent and have the flexibility to make a move at any time. Typically, their large incomes are exceeded only by their larger egos. As a result, these organizations tend to be fragile. Their existence is tied to professional talent that can die, become disabled, or just decide to walk if an ego is bruised. Transitions in and out always are a challenge. Often new blood must be recruited to replenish or expand the talent base.

Second, professional service corporations have been a popular target of Congress. The have their own tax provisions, most of which are not friendly.[8] These include a unique tax avoidance and evasion provision that empowers the government to allocate income, deductions, credits and exclusions between a personal service corporation and its employee-owners.[9] There are severe limitations on a personal service corporation's ability to defer earnings by using a fiscal year.[10] But perhaps the harshest provision is the tax rate structure. Unlike all other C corporations, even other employee-owned organizations, a personal service corporation cannot benefit from the favorable graduated corporate tax rate structure that starts at 15 percent. All income accumulated in a personal service corporation is taxed at the maximum corporate rate of 35 percent.[11]

8. EMERGING PUBLIC COMPANIES

Only a tiny fraction of businesses will ever consider "going public" – having their stock owned and regularly traded by a large number of public shareholders. All other closely held businesses are just too small or not suited for public ownership and the associated regulatory hassles and horrendous expenses. But for those select few that are destined for the big time, going public is the ballgame; it is their mission, their purpose, and a prerequisite to their success. Their closely held status is merely preparatory to their real life as a public company. Typically, these companies are developing and preparing to exploit

---

8. The exception is the right afforded qualified personal service corporations to use the cash receipts and disbursements method of accounting under I.R.C. § 448(b). Any other corporation (unless in the farming business) may not use the cash method of accounting once its annual gross receipts hit $5 million.

9. I.R.C. § 269A. Allocations may be made when the services of the personal service corporation are performed for another corporation, partnership or entity, as is the situation where a professional uses a corporation to hold his or her interest in a broader organization of professionals.

10. I.R.C §§ 441(i). Use of an accounting period other than a calendar year is permitted only upon a showing of a business purpose for the different accounting period. The desire to defer income is not such a valid business purpose. A personal service corporation may adopt a fiscal year with a deferral period of no more than three months under I.R.C. § 444(b)(2), but in such event, the corporation is required to comply with the minimum distribution requirements of I.R.C. § 280H, which eliminate most deferral benefits.

11. I.R.C. § 11(b)(2).

intellectual property rights and are financed and controlled by professional investment funds. All planning is focused on the unique objectives of the deep pockets that are writing the checks and calling the shots in preparation for the big day when the public is invited to the party.

9. *PUBLIC COMPANIES*

Stocks of these companies are traded daily and available to the public. These are the largest companies, those that populate the pages of the Wall Street Journal. Their primary challenges are building shareholder value and income streams that, in the eyes of all, are viewed as solid and growing. A strong public image is supreme. Staying out of trouble with the SEC and other regulators is a must. Competitive intelligence and strategic planning are essential. A focus and place in the globalization of the world's economy are top priorities. A solid, committed executive management team and board of directors are fundamental to the company's success.

At the end of 2013, the stocks of slightly more than 45,000 public companies traded throughout the world. Since 1997, the number of companies whose stock trades on a U.S. exchange has been declining. The total number stood at 5,008 at the end of 2013, a far cry from the 8,884 that traded on U.S. exchanges at the end of 1997. There was a modest bump up in 2013 (92 companies), the first annual increase since 1997.[12]

Public companies have been dramatically impacted by the growth of institutional investors: mutual funds, state pension funds, hedge funds, labor union pension funds, corporate pension funds, and the like. From 1900 to 1945, the percentage of public company stocks owned by institutional investors always hovered in the 5 percent range. After World War II, institutional ownership ballooned. By 1980, institutions held $473 billion, 34 percent of the total market value of U.S. common stocks. By 2010, institutional ownership had grown to $11.5 trillion, 67 percent of all U.S. stocks.[13]

A further complicating factor is that an estimated 70 to 80 percent of the outstanding stock of public corporations is held in "street name" through custodians, such as banks and brokerage firms.[14] The custodians, in turn, hold the shares through accounts at Depository Trust Company (DTC), a depository institution and the record owner registered on the books of the company. The result is that it is difficult, often impossible, for a public company to ascertain the identity of the beneficial owners of its outstanding stock at any given time.

Public companies have always been classified by the size of their market capitalization ("market cap"), which is determined by multiplying the number of the company's total shares outstanding by the market share price for the company's stock. The historical three categories of large-cap, mid-cap, and small-cap have generally been expanded as follows:

---

12. World Federation of Exchanges Statistics Report for December 2013.

13. Working paper of Wharton Professors Marshall E. Blume and Donald B. Keim entitled "Institutional Investors and Stock Market Liquidity: Trends and Relationships."

14. See, generally, M. Kahan & E. Rock, *The Hanging Chads of Corporate Voting,* 96 The Georgetown L. J. 1227 (2008).

- Mega-cap (over 200 billion market cap)
- Large-cap (from 10 billion to 200 billion market cap)
- Mid-cap (two billion to 10 billion market cap)
- Small cap (250 million to two billion market cap)
- Micro-cap (below 250 million market cap)
- Nano-cap (below 50 million market cap)

Public companies also are slotted into sectors based on the nature and scope of their respective products and services. These sectors are further divided into industry groups, industries, and sub industries. The performance standards of the companies included in a particular category become the yardstick for measuring the performance for a specific company in the category and for sizing up the relative strengths of various sectors and industries in the overall economy. Key sectors include:

- Materials (everything from chemicals to steel)
- Consumer discretionary (example industry groups include apparel, auto, leisure, media)
- Consumer stables (example industry groups include food and stables, household and personal products, and beverage and tobacco)
- Healthcare (example industry groups include healthcare equipment and services and pharmaceuticals)
- Energy (all types)
- Utilities
- Technology (example industry groups include computers, software, office equipment, semiconductors)
- Financials (example industry groups include banks, real estate, insurance, diversified financials)
- Industrials (example industry groups include capital goods, transportation, commercial and professional services)
- Information technology (example industry groups include software, hardware, semiconductors);
- Telecommunication service

C. ENTITY DIFFERENCES

Businesses operate through different entity forms. A lawyer must understand the basics of these various forms. Many of the following chapters focus on important core details regarding these various entity forms, including tax differences and factors that should be considered in selecting the best entity form for a particular business. Following are brief descriptive recaps of the most common forms.

1. SOLE PROPRIETORSHIP

Sole proprietorships are for single owners who operate simple businesses and do not want the hassles of dealing with a separate entity, such as a corporation or a limited liability company. Tax-wise, everything is reflected through the individual owner's tax return. This form's greatest virtue is its simplicity, but it offers few other benefits. For this reason, it generally is confined to small businesses that create no significant liability concerns for their owners.

2. C CORPORATION

The C corporation is a regular corporation that pays its own taxes. It is a creature of state law and is recognized as a separate legal and taxable entity. Public companies and many closely held businesses are C corporations. The earnings and losses of a C corporation are taxed at the entity level, not passed through to the shareholders. The result is that C status often triggers a double tax burden - one at the entity level and another at the shareholder level when dividends or liquidating distributions are paid. The tax basics of C corporations are reviewed in Chapter 8.

A C Corporation may have different classes of stock and any number of shareholders. It offers its shareholders personal protection from the debts and liabilities of the business and a host of tax benefits. It is a popular choice for many service organizations, emerging public companies, operating companies that need to retain modest earnings each year, and owners who do not want to endure the administrative and tax hassles of a pass-through entity. Any corporation that does not qualify and elect to be taxed as an S corporation will be taxed as a C corporation.

3. S CORPORATION

The S corporation is the preferred choice for many. It is organized as a corporation under state law and offers the same corporate limited liability protections as a C corporation. But unlike a C corporation, it is taxed as a pass-through entity under the provisions of Subchapter S of the Internal Revenue Code. The taxable income and losses of the entity are passed through and taxed to the shareholders, eliminating the double tax consequences of a C corporation. These S tax provisions are similar, but not identical, to the partnership provisions of Subchapter K. The tax basics of S corporations are reviewed in Chapter 8.

The S corporation is particularly attractive to shareholders of a corporate entity that makes regular earnings distributions or that may be sold for a substantial profit in a taxable exchange. And usually conversion to S status is the only viable option for a C corporation that wants to eliminate future double tax bites by converting to a structure that offers pass-through tax benefits.

There are certain limitations and restrictions with an S corporation that often pose problems. Not every corporation is eligible to elect S status. If a corporation has a shareholder that is a corporation, a partnership, a non-resident alien or an ineligible trust, S status is not available.[15] Banks and insurance companies cannot elect S status.[16] Also, the election cannot be made if the corporation has more than 100 shareholders or has more than one class of stock.[17] For purposes of the 100-shareholder limitation, a husband and wife are counted as one shareholder and all the members of a family (six generations deep) may elect to be treated as one shareholder.[18] The one-class-of-stock requirement is not violated if the corporation has both voting and nonvoting common stock and the only difference is voting rights.[19]

In defining S status eligibility, trusts have received serious Congressional attention over the years. There has been a constant expansion of the trust eligibility rules, but many commonly used trusts still cannot qualify as S corporation shareholders.[20]

Electing in and out of S status requires attention to important details. An election to S status requires the consent of all shareholders.[21] A single dissenter can hold up the show. For this reason, often it is advisable to include in an organizational agreement among all the owners (typically a shareholder agreement) a provision that requires all owners to consent to an S election if a designated number of the owners at any time approve the making of the election. The election, once made, is effective for the current tax year if made during the preceding year or within the first two and one-half months of the current year.[22] If made during the first two and one-half months of the year, all shareholders who have owned stock at any time during the year, even those who no longer own stock at election time, must consent in order for the election to be valid for the current year.[23]

Exiting out of S status is easier than electing into it; a revocation is valid if

---

15. I.R.C. § 1361(b).
16. I.R.C. § 1361(b)(2).
17. I.R.C. § 1361(b)(1)(A) & (D).
18. I.R.C. § 1361(c)(1).
19. I.R.C. § 1361(c)(4). Also, there is an important straight debt safe harbor provision that easily can be satisfied to protect against the threat of an S election being jeopardized by a debt obligation being characterized as a second class of stock. I.R.C. § 1361(c)(5). To fit within the safe harbor, there must be a written unconditional promise to pay on demand or on a specified date a sum certain and (1) the interest rate and payment dates cannot be contingent on profits, the borrower's discretion, or similar factors; (2) there can be no stock convertibility feature; and (3) the creditor must be an individual, an estate, a trust eligible to be a shareholder, or a person regularly and actively engaged in the business of lending money. For planning purposes, it is an easy fit in most situations.

20. Trusts that are now eligible to qualify as S corporation shareholders include: voting trusts; grantor trusts; testamentary trusts that receive S corporation stock via a will (but only for a two-year period following the transfer); testamentary trusts that receive S corporation stock via a former grantor trust (but only for a two-year period following the transfer); "qualified subchapter S" trusts (QSSTs), which generally are trusts with only one current income beneficiary who is a U.S. resident or citizen to whom all income is distributed annually and that elect to be treated as the owner of the S corporation stock for tax purposes; and "electing small business" trusts (ESBTs), which are trusts that elect to be treated as an S corporation shareholder and whose beneficiaries are qualifying S corporation shareholders who acquired their interests in the trust by gift or inheritance, not purchase, and who are willing to pay the highest individual marginal income tax rates on all S corporation income allocated to them. I.R.C. §§ 1361 (e)(1)(A), 1361(c)(2)(b)(v).
21. I.R.C. § 1362(a). See generally Reg. § 1.1362-6.
22. I.R.C. § 1362(b)(1).
23. I.R.C. § 1362(b)(2). For potential relief on a late election where there is reasonable cause for the tardiness, see I.R.C. § 1362(b)(5) and Rev. Proc. 2004-48, 2004-2 C.B. 172.

approved by shareholders holding more than half of the outstanding voting and nonvoting shares.[24] For the organization that wants to require something more than a simple majority to trigger such a revocation, the answer is a separate agreement among the shareholders that provides that no shareholder will consent to a revocation absent the approval of a designated supermajority. The revocation may designate a future effective date. Absent such a designation, the election is effective on the first day of the following year, unless it is made on or before the fifteenth day of the third month of the current year, in which case it is retroactively effective for the current year.[25]

4. *PARTNERSHIP OPTIONS*

A partnership form often is used for a venture that holds appreciating assets, such as real estate or oil and gas interests. Historically, partnerships also have been effective family planning tools to shift income to family members, freeze estate values, and facilitate gifting of minority interests at heavily discounted values. Often partnerships are used in conjunction with one or more other business entities. Their use with operating businesses has diminished in recent decades as the limited liability company has taken center stage.

Generally, there are four types of partnerships: general partnerships, limited liability partnerships, limited partnerships, and limited liability limited partnerships. Details of these various partnership forms are reviewed in Chapter 6.

In a general partnership, each partner is personally liable for the debts and liabilities of the entity and has a say in the management of the business. No formal documentation is required to form a general partnership. All that is required is for two or more persons to manifest an intention to carry on a business for a profit.

A limited liability partnership ("LLP") is a partnership that, pursuant to applicable state law, has filed a statement of qualification (sometimes called an "application") with the state's secretary of state to eliminate the personal liability exposure of the partners. The name of an LLP must end with the words "Registered Limited Liability Partnership," "limited liability partnership," or the abbreviation "R.L.L.P," "RLLP," "L.L.P.," or LLP."

A limited partnership is an entity that has one or more general partners ("GPs") and one or more limited partners ("LPs") and is formed under a state's limited partnership act. GPs have the authority to manage and conduct the business of the partnership and are personally liable for the debts and obligations of the partnership. LPs typically are investors who have no or minimal control over business decisions of the partnership and have no personal liability for the obligations of the partnership beyond their capital contributions to the partnership.

The limited liability limited partnership ("LLLP") is to a limited partnership

24. I.R.C. § 1362(d)(1).
25. I.R.C. § 1362(d)(1)(C) & (D).

what an LLP is to a general partnership. Its role is to eliminate the personal liability exposure that general partners have for the obligations of a limited partnership. It's a relatively new entity form that has been adopted in roughly half the states. An LLLP must elect LLLP status in the limited partnership's filed certificate and use a name that includes the phrase "limited liability limited partnership," "LLLP," or "L.L.L.P." With LLLP status, a general partner is not personally liable for an obligation of the limited partnership incurred while the partnership is an LLLP, whether arising in contract, tort, or otherwise. This limited liability protection exists even if the partnership agreement contained inconsistent provisions before making the election to become an LLLP.

Although partnerships file separate returns, they are not taxpaying entities. The profits and losses of the partnership are passed through and taxed to the partners under the provisions of Subchapter K of the Internal Revenue Code. The tax basics of partnership-taxed entities are reviewed in Chapter 8.

5. *LIMITED LIABILITY COMPANY*

The limited liability company ("LLC") is a relatively new candidate. All states now have statutes authorizing LLCs, most of which were adopted during the 1980s. Many advisors claim that the LLC is the ultimate entity, arguing that it offers the best advantages of both corporations and partnerships and few of the disadvantages. It's an overstatement, but not by much in some situations.

As discussed in Chapter 9, there is no question that the arrival of the LLC has made the choice-of-entity challenge easier in many cases. Like a corporation, the LLC is an entity organized under state law. It offers liability protection to all owners, making it possible for its owners to fully participate in the management of the business without subjecting themselves to personal exposure for the liabilities of the business. LLCs are classified as either "member-managed" (managed by all members) or "manager-managed" (managed by designated managers).

Although similar to a corporation for state law purposes, a limited liability company is taxed as a partnership for federal income tax purposes unless it elects otherwise. As such, it offers better pass-through benefits than an S corporation and completely avoids all the S corporation eligibility and election hassles. It can have more than 100 owners, and partnerships, corporations, nonresident aliens, and any kind of trust can be included as owners. For these reasons, many wrongfully conclude that the LLC eliminates the need to consider S corporations and partnerships as viable pass-through entity candidates. As we will see in Chapter 9, there are still many situations where an S corporation or a partnership will be the best entity choice.

The professional limited liability company ("PLLC") is a state-chartered entity that allows licensed professionals (e.g., doctors and lawyers) to enjoy the benefits of a limited liability company. A PLLC does nothing to reduce a professional's personal liability for his or her own mistakes or malpractice, but it eliminates a professional's liability for the errors, omissions, negligence, incompetence or malfeasance of other professionals who are not under his or her supervision and control. It also eliminates personal exposure for contract liabilities that the professional has not personally guaranteed. States often require that a PLLC register with the applicable state licensing board before filing its organizational documents with the state.

D. CHARACTERISTIC DIFFERENCES

Every business has specific characteristics that define the nature and role of the business and reveal its uniqueness, strengths, weaknesses, market position, vulnerabilities, and a host of other important factors. These characteristics are key indicators of the business' growth potential, most significant risk factors, and long-term survival prospects. The following fifteen factors illustrate some of the common ways businesses are characterized and contrasted. In no sense is it an all-inclusive list.

1. PRODUCT VS. SERVICE

Whether a business is product-based or service-based is a core defining factor. Generally, a product-based operation is more complicated, poses greater downside risks, and offers the potential of higher yields for the owners of the business. The initial challenges of designing the product, developing manufacturing processes and relationships, and assessing and creating demand for the product set the stage for success or failure. Key operational challenges include managing inventory levels, developing supply chains to efficiently get the product to end-users, monitoring competitive conditions and other product life-cycle factors, and making smart pricing decisions that reflect market realities and preserve profit margins. It usually takes substantial capital and a talented management team. And, of course, the challenges are magnified many times when there is a group of products, as is so often the case.

Getting the product to end-users is a threshold, strategic consideration. Often the only viable option is traditional brick-and-mortar retail that requires a supply chain of regional and national distributors, local wholesalers, and a wide variety of retail outlets. Smart management is required to ensure product availability without ballooning inventories to risky levels, to protect and police the incentives and profit margins of all players in the chain, and to maintain the image of the product and the manufacturer. For example, wholesalers typically are prohibited from cutting out retailers by selling directly to end-users, and often there are manufacturer-imposed prohibitions on selling to businesses outside the approved chain of players or unreasonably discounting the product.

Every manufacturer must assess the role of the Internet in getting product to consumers. For many, it is a powerful tool to enhance product demand, educate potential consumers, and drive end-users into approved retail outlets. For others, the Internet is the sole and ultimate answer to their product delivery challenge, enabling direct communication and shipping to end-users while ignoring or eliminating the hassles and costs of traditional middleman players. The technological advances of e-commerce and ballooning popularity of online shopping have opened opportunities for many manufactures that could not otherwise effectively complete for retail shelf space or reach distant markets.

The profit potential for a product-based business often trumps by many times those of a service business. The driving factors are demand for the product, volume, and profit margins. The traditional service-constraints of time spent and hourly yields do not apply.

A service-based business is a very different and often a simpler enterprise. The focus is on defining the service, identifying and reaching a market, and generating a profit. In some situations, owner-investors can generate a yield by imposing price points that exceed the costs of running the business, including amounts paid to those who actually provide the services. In many others, the business is used to generate an income for employee-owners. Take, for example, the typical law firm that collects fees (usually based on hourly rates) for professional services rendered by members of the firm. Key challenges include professional training and recruiting, developing and exploiting a smart marketing plan and firm reputation, and implementing efficient office (or multiple office) procedures. Such challenges are very different from those required for a successful product-based company.

2. ASSET-BASED VS. OPERATIONAL-BASED

Some businesses are asset-based. The business exists because of an asset or group of assets. It may be a tract of real estate, a group of oil wells, a movie script, a valuable intellectual property right, a proprietary manufacturing process, or some other valuable, unique asset. Without the asset, there is no business or, at the minimum, a much different business. The useful life of the asset often defines the life cycle of the business.

The defining asset for some businesses is their brand. Often a brand has been developed over decades and has a perceived unshakeable stability, although there are brands that develop and fade quickly. The strength of a brand often is the supreme factor that enables the business to secure a strong market share and generate substantial profit margins by avoiding the competitive pressures of less profitable players. Such a brand can work for a multinational product-based company, a local service business, and everything in between. That's why the development of a strong brand is an overriding goal of many businesses, although very few succeed in enjoying the profitable benefits of a strong brand over the long-term. In 2013, the top five on Forbes' list of the world's most valuable brands (brand value only) were Apple (104.3 billion), Microsoft (56.7 billion), Coca-Cola (54.9 billion), IBM (50.7 billion), and Google (47.3 billion).[26]

However, a unique, valuable asset or strong brand often is not a prerequisite for success. Many successful businesses have neither. They succeed long-term by delivering services or moving products through operations that profitably exploit a defined niche in a market. Their value is measured by the strength, growth potential, and stability of their earnings. Their asset base often is not substantial and has little or nothing to do with their goodwill and going concern values. They often have a reputation for quality, but not the kind of brand

---

26. Kurt Badenhausen, "Apple Dominates List Of The World's Most Valuable Brands," Forbes (November 6, 2013).

identity that drives demand or transcends competitive pressures.

3. *STAND-ALONE VS. AFFILIATED*

Most businesses are stand-alone enterprises that are able to operate free from any direct controls by another system or company. They usually have important strategic relationships, but the business itself is not controlled by another entity or dependant on an affiliated system that the business does not control.

Other businesses are part of a broader affiliated group or system. Their success is tied directly to key decisions of the broader group and factors that impact the broader group. The most common examples are holding companies that have layers of subsidiaries, the control and ownership of which can be traced to a common parent holding company. The business of some of the subsidiaries often serves a niche function or market of a product line or service operation that reaches across the whole or a major segment of the affiliated group. Other subsidiaries may operate self-contained businesses that simply diversify the operations of the holding company and add to its consolidated earnings. One of the biggest examples of such a holding company is General Electric, whose multinational affiliated group includes hundreds of companies throughout the world, purchases dozens of companies each year, and maintains huge integrated operations in power and water, oil and gas, aviation, healthcare, transportation, home and business solutions, and capital formation. It is believed that GE files the largest tax return in the U.S.; its return for 2010, for example, totaled more than 57,000 pages.[27]

Franchising is an affiliated business expansion strategy that has spawned thousands of new companies since the 1950s. Although independently owned, each of these companies is tied to and dependant on a franchisor. Fast food outlets are the best example, but there are many other large franchise operations. The franchisor develops a specific business strategy, usually supported by a distinctive trade name and trademark, a broad-based consumer marketing and advertising campaign, detailed operating procedures, approved vendor sources, site approval procedures, and various other support systems. Expansion is funded by franchisees putting up money to establish their own franchise outlet businesses that are governed by a detailed franchise agreement. The agreement mandates operating requirements and imposes royalty obligations, usually a percent of gross revenues. The strength of the franchisor's control varies among different franchise operations, but it is always a crucial factor that limits flexibility and creates conflict potentials. For these reasons and the fact that franchisees usually must spec investment capital against the promises of a business plan developed and sold by the franchisor, the Federal Trade Commission has rules and many states have statutes that specify disclosure requirements, sometimes require advance registration, and often mandate the inclusion of specific franchisee-protection provisions in the franchise agreement.

---

27. John McCormack, "*GE Filed 57,000-Page Tax Return, Paid No Taxes on $14 Billion in Profits*," The Weekly Standard (November 14, 2011).

Multilevel marketing is another form of affiliated business expansion that has resulted in the creation of thousands of small businesses over the past five decades. Sometimes it is referred to as network marketing or referral marketing, and legally defective programs are often referred to as pyramid schemes. The typical multilevel marketing program recruits salespeople, each of whom receives commissions through the direct sale of products and direct sales generated by others in the "downline" that he or she recruits. Each salesperson operates as an independently owned business. Such marketing programs have often been criticized for their high entry costs, tendency to promote unrealistic profit expectations, price fixing risks, aggressive sales practices, and more. But the fact remains that highly successful multilevel marketing programs operate in all 50 states and have done so for decades. Examples of large, successful programs include Amway and Shaklee. Products that meet a consumer demand independent of any business opportunity factors are the key to long-term success and legality. If product sales predominately occur only as an incidental part of the salesperson recruitment process, the FTC and state regulators will likely deem the program an illegal pyramid scheme that is doomed to fail. Plus, many states have adopted business opportunity statutes that impose disclosure requirements on those who seek to sell business opportunities to others.

4. MARKET POWER OR NOT?

Some businesses have real market power, which is the power to control or influence the price or availability of a product or service in a given market. The best example is a monopolist, defined as the exclusive seller of a product or service for which there is no close substitute. Being a monopolist is not illegal per se, and even a very small business can enjoy the benefits of a monopolist if that business is the only provider of a product or service that has a demand in the relevant market. The sole plumber or newspaper in a small town may each have strong market power.

Market power is not limited to monopolists. Some markets have a few key sellers, each of whom may easily cue off the actions of the others so that the collective group, without any agreement or understanding, maintains prices and output levels that maximize profits. It's called an "oligopoly," and the expected behavior is called "oligopolistic interdependence."

At the opposite end of the spectrum are atomism markets that have many sellers, none of whom are large enough to influence the market price. The withdrawal of a given seller's entire supply from the market will not affect the market price. Often this is referred to as pure competition. Each seller accepts that it will sell its share of the market at the price established by the market, and that any attempt to exceed the market price will quickly halt sales.

5. GEOGRAPHIC EXPANSION POTENTIAL OR NOT?

The geographic reach of a business is always an important factor. A multinational business is defined as a business that maintains offices or assets in at least one country other than its own. Although some multinationals have budgets that exceed those of many small countries, a relatively small business that maintains inventories and sales personnel in a foreign land may meet the definition of a multinational business. Technological advances and world market conditions are pushing many businesses of all sizes to seriously explore the benefits of international expansion.

A PwC family business survey in 2013 found that nearly half (47 percent) of U.S. family businesses were selling goods and services outside the country and even more (54 percent) anticipate they will be selling internationally by 2017. This represented a major increase from two years earlier when only 30 percent of surveyed family businesses were intending to develop markets abroad and a huge jump from 2007 when only 21 percent planned on exploring international markets. As for the most likely targeted markets, 30 percent of the surveyed companies are eyeing the Americas (primarily Brazil, Canada, and Mexico), 25 percent have their sights on the Asia Pacific region (China alone garnered 14 percent), and 14 percent are focused on Europe.[28]

Any geographic expansion increases complexities and costs. In addition to new employee and management challenges, there are a host of planning issues, including increased risk-management assessments, enhanced regulatory burdens, cultural differences, and the need for an expanded multi-entity business structure. Often a separate subsidiary company needs to be formed to conduct operations in a different state and certainly a different country. It usually makes no sense to expose the main business entity to the regulatory, tax, and liability risks of a new jurisdiction.

6. *HIGH VS. LOW LEVERAGE*

Leverage refers to the use of debt in financing a business. The yield realized on the capital invested by the owners of a business can be increased by leveraging the borrowed dollar to finance a portion of the business. For example, if the business can grow its earnings by borrowing funds at a 6 percent interest cost and generating a return of 12 percent on the borrowed funds, the spread between the cost and the yield directly boosts the return to the owners. It's Business 101. In nearly all businesses, smart leveraging makes sense. It's not a question of whether. It's a question of how much.

The risks of too much leverage are real. When leverage is overused, a significant drop in asset values or earnings may wipe out the equity capital in the business, leaving the company with liabilities that exceed its asset base and the inability to service its ever-ballooning debt load. The company will be headed for bankruptcy absent one or more of three remedies. The first is a quick reversal of values and earnings, which often becomes progressively less likely as others in and out of the company react to the company's deteriorating condition. The second is an infusion of new equity capital, which usually becomes much tougher when debt takes over. The third is a government bailout, the "too large to fail" answer for the grossly over-leveraged financial institutions that found themselves upside down with debt when their asset values crumbled in the fiscal crisis of 2008.

---

28. PwC Family Business Survey 2012/2013 (US Findings). PwC is a network of firms in 158 countries with more than 180,000 employees that provide assurance, tax, and advisory services.

The risks of no or too little leverage are just as real, but not as severe. Owners of successful businesses eventually face a basic decision regarding the profits generated by the business. Are the profits going to accumulate in the company or be distributed to the owners of the company? The easy answer for many is to stockpile. Keep the profits in the company. Let them ride as the business expands and matures.

During the building period of most businesses, stockpiling usually is the only viable alternative. The earnings are needed to finance inventories, receivables, facilities, better technology, and new personnel. More debt isn't possible or prudent. As the business begins to mature, the retained profits are used to retire debt and the pressure to accumulate begins to fade and often disappears completely. But in many cases, this accumulation pattern has been set. The owners enjoy watching the net worth of the business expand every year with a corresponding increase in the value of their equity. Their success is measured and quantified by the accumulations. As time goes on, the balance sheet of the business becomes rock solid – lots of equity, little or no debt – while the balance sheets of the owners become lopsided – a large net worth and a big taxable estate, the bulk of which is represented by a single business equity interest. Concentrating wealth in the business can be risky, imprudent, and damaging in the long run. Beyond diluting the owner's yield, it can hike risk management pressures (too much of the owners' wealth is exposed to business risks), make it harder to transition the business, and reduce the benefits of income and estate tax planning.

There is no stock answer to the "How much leverage?" question. As explained in Chapter 3, a debt-to-equity ratio is often used as a measure of a business' leverage. Generally speaking (and I do mean "generally"), a ratio of under 5-to-1 is considered reasonable for a profitable, mature business while a ratio in excess of 10-to-1 is usually suspect. The gap between five and 10 often is a grey area. This ratio may be a measure, but often is not a sole determining factor. For example, two businesses may each reasonably use a bank line equal to 90 percent of their current collectible accounts receivable and 50 percent of the cost of their current salable inventories. Because of differences in the asset mixes of the two businesses, the bank line produces a 6-to-1 ratio in one business and a 4-to-1 ratio in the other. For many businesses, various factors must be considered in setting a smart leverage level, including industry standards, the asset base of the business, the stability of earnings, current banking practices, and more.

7. SCALABLE OR NOT?

Scalability is an important factor in assessing the growth potential of a business. A scalable business is one that can maintain or increase its profit margins as the volume of the business expands to higher levels. The operations, asset requirements, and market conditions easily accommodate a growth in volume without a hit to profit margins. Many non-manufacturing businesses are scalable. A service business often can continually increase its profitability by adding more personnel to service a growing demand. So too, a product-based company that continually distributes a higher volume of finished goods that it sources from others may preserve or enhance its margins and thereby increase its profitability as it continues to grow.

A non-scalable business is one that cannot handle a higher volume without making investments or other changes that currently reduce margins. Higher volumes may require significant infrastructure improvements, expensive expansion into new markets, and more. Assume, for example, that a company has the capacity to produce 100,000 units. A production level of 50,000 units results in a cost per unit of $7.00. As volumes increase and production moves upwards towards 100,000 units, positive economies of scale kick in, high equipment fixed costs are spread over more units, and the cost per unit eventually drops to $5.00. Production beyond 100,000 units requires a significant new investment in equipment and systems that drives up the cost per unit to $8.00, resulting in a corresponding decrease in profit margins.

8. SMALL VS. LARGE EMPLOYEE BASE

Few businesses can survive without the loyal support of dedicated employees. But nearly all business owners appreciate (or certainly should appreciate) that the challenge goes beyond motivation and management. Laws have continually evolved to give employees more rights; and these rights pose risks for the uninformed business owner who is determined to run the show just as he or she did 20 years ago.

The role of a company's employment base often is a defining factor for a business. In many businesses, it's everything. The existence, profitability, and growth potential of the business is dependent on an ever-evolving base of rank-and-file and management employees. Every expansion requires, at a minimum, a proportional increase in the employee base.

Other businesses are able to grow with disproportionately small increases in their employment ranks. Technology and management innovations and personal incentives are designed to enhance the productivity of each employee. The focus is higher productivity, not just more employees. Often this is coupled with strategic outsourcing relationships that enable the company to shift specific operations and functions to outside independent contractors.

There are reasons why a company may want to explore options for reducing its dependence on an ever-growing employee base. Recruiting, retaining and motivating a work force usually get progressively more difficult as the base grows. Required cutbacks are painful and expensive. The uncertainties and ballooning costs of employee benefits often put pressure on the bottom line and create ongoing expectation challenges and cost sharing conflicts.

Employee terminations are always a challenge. While most employers believe they operate under the "at will" doctrine as regards their employees, the company takes a risk every time it terminates an employee. Wrongful discharge suits have popped up with increasing frequency throughout the country. Many employee victories have been publicized. New laws have been made in the courts and the legislatures, chipping away at the old "at will" standard. Each victory and law change has provided incentives to aggrieved, discharged employees and lawyers who are willing to fight their cases. Many companies have had to endure the pain of paying big legal fees to defend the termination, only to pay more when the employee prevails. The operative word is "caution" when terminating an employee.

Employees pose potential liability risks that should be mitigated with smart planning. In general, a company is responsible and liable for those acts of its employees that are carried out within the scope of their employment. This is a true vicarious liability. It is one of the broadest forms of vicarious, third-party liability in the law. The company may be fully liable, even though it had no direct involvement with, or knowledge of, the event creating the problem. In most instances, the liability pops up because an employee has committed one of four wrongs: (1) the employee exceeds his or her authority in making a deal on behalf of the company; (2) the employee, in the process of carrying out his or her duties, negligently or recklessly injures another party; (3) the employee ignores or violates a black letter law that has been established for the good of all; or (4) the employee engages in intentional misconduct that, in some cases, may rise to the level of criminal conduct. Businesses usually need to take specific steps to reduce or mitigate the scope of the liability that may be created by employees

9. UNION VS. NON-UNION

A relatively small percentage of employees in the private (as opposed to government) sector are represented and protected by union relationships. The percentage of private sector union employment has consistently fallen for decades. In 2013, for example, the private sector percentage was 6.7 percent, about one-fifth of the percentage for public sector employees. In the private sector, industries with high unionization rates included utilities (25.6 percent), transportation and warehousing (19.6 percent), telecommunications (14.4 percent), and construction (14.1 percent).[29]

Union employees usually are subject to contracts that offer various protections. Examples: employee discipline and discharge often are subject to grievance procedures and binding arbitration; wages, benefits and working conditions are subject to negotiation; hiring and promotion decisions may be governed by contractual provisions that impose seniority and other requirements; labor and management are contractually obligated to listen and negotiate and pursue reasonable compromises; contractual changes require the consent of both labor and management.

10. HEAVY REGULATION OR NOT?

Increasing government regulation is a fact of life for business. According to the Congressional Research Service, over 13,000 final rules were published in the Federal Register from 2009 to 2012. Small businesses are hit the hardest by increased regulation. Small businesses now bear a regulatory cost of $10,585 per employee, estimated to be 36 percent higher than the regulatory per-employee compliance cost for large businesses. Small business environmental compliance

29. News Release, Department of Labor Statistics, U.S. Department of Labor (January 24, 2014).

costs exceed by more than four times the corresponding costs for large firms.[30]

The highest three regulated sectors are financial, healthcare, and energy. Any business in these industries must continually be tuned in to government regulators. But since nearly all businesses need energy, want healthcare benefits for their employees, and require financing, the positive benefits and associated increased costs and burdens of ever-growing regulation in these and other industries are ultimately felt across the economy.

11. INTERNET-DEPENDENT OR NOT?

The Internet is the most powerful communication tool that has ever been available to business enterprises. For business purposes, it has shrunk the world and created countless entrepreneurial opportunities that couldn't possibly exist without it.

Many businesses are not inherently dependent on the Internet. They use the Internet to promote their businesses and educate their customers, but their core operations are not directly tied to their use of the Internet. Generally, they need not fear that a new or expanding company from anywhere in the world may threaten their market share with an Internet-based strategy.

Other businesses exist because of the Internet. These include those that provide Internet support services, such as website design, optimization, and app development services. It also includes businesses that must use the Internet to conduct their businesses. Take Dena, for example, a stay-at-home mom of three young children who imports her custom designed infant parasols from a China manufacturer, takes orders principally from European and African buyers who want quality parasols that bear the names of their children or grandchildren, and customizes and ships the parasols from a garage in a small Northwest town. A tiny business of this type that reaches from China to Africa would be impossible without the Internet, the tool that attracts customers in a foreign land at an insignificant cost. Dena is able to compete heads-up with her competition, but understands that anyone from anywhere could use the same tool she uses to challenge her market share.

12. LOW–TECH VS. HIGH–TECH

A low-tech business is one that does not rely heavily on new technology to sustain its market position. It does not have to keep coming up with new technology concepts to support the viability of its product mix. It offers a group of products that are readily recognized as non-technical. In contrast, a high-tech business is dependent on its ability to create new ideas and new products. Often the success of the high-tech business is tied directly to the talent of individuals who work in the business. The overriding, ongoing challenge is to secure and recruit new talent.

From a profit perspective, seldom will a low-tech business be able to match the upside potential of a successful high-tech operation. High-tech usually poses

30. Small Business Fact Sheet, U.S. House of Representatives Committee on Small Business (May 21, 2013).

greater risks, and offers the potential of larger and faster rewards. A successful high-tech start-up can quickly secure the financial future of its founders. As we have seen many times, the age and business acumen of the innovators often are not limiting factors.

Regarding risk and stability, often a low-tech business will be in a much stronger position than a struggling high-tech business. Today's high-tech business can quickly end up being tomorrow's defunct no-tech business if it cannot keep pace by producing new products that play well in the marketplace. The competition in high-tech businesses progressively grows at a rapid pace as players from around the world continue to surface and expand. The past 30 years suggests that no one can comfortably predict who will be the dominant high-tech players in the following decades.

13. STRATEGICALLY–BASED VS. RELATIONSHIP–BASED

The strength of some businesses is primarily attributable to key personal relationships that have been developed over many years. The relationships may be with suppliers, customers, key employees or all three. These relationships give the business its advantage and make it possible for the business to succeed. In contrast, there are other businesses that are strategically-based. They have identified and filled a market niche that is not dependent or tied to personal relationships. The business succeeds because it is strategically situated to competitively deliver goods or services in its identified market niche.

Obviously, a strategically-based business has a better chance of surviving long-term than a relationship-based business. Relationships are often difficult, if not impossible, to transfer. A child, for example, may develop a friendly interface with a crucial vendor, but that interface may never match the strength of the personal relationship that the child's father had with the vendor. The challenge becomes even more difficult when the vendor's successor takes charge. The reality is that, over time, the strength of personal relationships often breaks down and fizzles out as attempts are made to transition relationships. As this occurs, there is a substantial risk that the business activity between the parties will diminish unless both parties identify a strategic business advantage for maintaining the relationship.

Often it is assumed that a business is strategically-based, when, in fact, the basis of its success is personal relationships that have been developed over many years. Similarly, there are some businesses that appear to be propped up by relationships, but that could be strategically strengthened with some careful analysis, restructuring and public relations. The ongoing challenge is to identify key personal relationships, assess the importance of those relationships to the overall success of the business, and evaluate the capacity of the business to enhance its strategic base.

14. INSTITUTIONALIZATION OR NOT?

A central challenge for many businesses is to begin the process of institutionalization. In this context, an institutionalized business is one that is bigger than any one individual. Its operations and growth do not primarily depend on the person who started it all. It has developed systems, personnel, management structures, and expertise to allow it to function like an institution. Usually, this condition is easily recognized by the employees of the company and outsiders who deal with the company on a regular basis. The contrast is the business that is operationally dependent on one individual. That individual is the key to all that happens. Without the daily presence of that individual, the business lacks direction and suffers. The systems, support personnel, and expertise are absent.

Often founders of a business do not want to invest the time or capital required to build systems and personnel that will allow the business to effectively function on its own. In some cases, it takes a financial commitment that the owners are unwilling to make. In others, it's an issue of control or ego. The owner enjoys the importance of his or her invaluable presence. The challenge is to fairly assess whether appropriate steps are being taken to institutionalize the business. Usually these steps are critical if the business is going to survive long term.

15. High vs. Low Margin Tolerance

Does the business have the capacity to survive and prosper if it is faced with some tough price competition? A helpful question: What would be the impact if the business was forced to cut its gross margin by 3 or 4 percent to remain competitive? If the response is a roll of the eyes and a "No way" exclamation, this may suggest that the long-term survival prospects for the business are weak.

In most businesses, price competition is intensifying. Others have found better ways of producing the same products or delivering comparable services at lower prices. New manufacturing techniques and operating systems are being developed to allow businesses to operate more efficiently. Businesses are "right sizing" to cut out the fat and to have the capacity to operate on lean, tough margins. New players are not tied to old systems and old investments.

Often a business finds itself at an extreme competitive disadvantage as bigger and stronger players, sometimes from foreign lands, enter the market. It does not have the capital or the sales volume to justify the development of the economies of scale and operating systems that would allow it to remain tough on price. This condition prompts may to consider selling while the company's market share is still intact. If the opportunity is missed, the owners may be forced to sacrifice or eliminate profitability by cutting margins to preserve the business. This has been the fate of many businesses that have been unable to survive a second generation.

E. Business Plans

A business plan is a written document created and used by entrepreneurs and others who desire to develop or expand a business. It's much more than just a marketing plan. It explains in detail all the key aspects (sometimes called the "DNA") of the business. A well-conceived and written business plan takes time, research, analysis, and an intellectual honesty that continually questions base assumptions and core underpinnings of the proposed business. Plus, the writing must reflect quality – a style that is clear, concise, and convincing and avoids overstated adjectives, convoluted sentences, and sloppy grammar. The role of legal advisors usually never goes beyond select technical aspects of the plan, such as entity choice, tax, and securities law considerations. Although lawyers do not write business plans for their clients, it often helps to have a basic understanding of the purposes and elements of a plan and what separates the good from the bad.

1. PURPOSE AND ROLE

Is a business plan always necessary? There are countless blogs and articles that try hard to make the case that detailed written business plans often are a waste of time and effort and that business schools should scrap their business plan courses and competitions. Although there are examples of successful company launches without a business plan and virtually no guarantees that a business plan itself will turn an idea into a successful business, the value of a business plan to two vital groups is hard to deny in the real world.

The first group is the organizers of the enterprise, those who must create the plan. The process of creating a plan and reducing it to writing often pushes everything and everybody to a higher level: better critical thinking, deeper market knowledge, smarter risk factor strategies, better understanding of funding needs and expectations, and more. The result is that the key players are more capable and confident to tackle the new enterprise. If done right, the plan becomes a living, evolving document that is continually used as a tool to define and measure performance and success.

The second group that benefits from and needs the document is the potential investors who often are essential to funding and jumpstarting the enterprise. While a few ideas may be sufficiently attractive on their face to attract investor interest without a written business plan, the great bulk of ideas will go nowhere unless the details are fleshed out and the case for success is made in a smartly crafted business plan.

2. PLAN ELEMENTS

A business plan typically includes the following elements:

- **Executive Summary** – Brief review of plan that sparks interest by recapping mission statement, product or service, relevant markets, key customers, financial requirements, management's background and expertise, and potential yield to investors.

- **Product or Service** – Detailed description, potential of different versions, why needed and valued by customers, status of development and readiness for market, intellectual property elements, any licensing and royalty requirements, future enhancement potentials, and challenges to volume growth.

- **Market and Competition** – Definition of relevant market(s), size of market, market growth potential, market profitability potential, technology and regulatory impacts on market, customer descriptions and customer segmentation criteria, competitor strengths and weaknesses, positioning opportunities against existing competitors, future competitor risks, anticipated competitor and market reactions.

- **Sales and Marketing** – Pricing considerations and challenges, volume expectations, consumer education needs and risks, selling process, strategies for reaching customers and getting product or service to customers, advertising strategies and risks, reliance on third parties in supply chain, Internet role and options, launch and ongoing budget needs.

- **Business Organization** – Form of entity, organizational chart, lines of authority, key outside company relationships, needed technical expertise and sources, quality assurance challenges, risk management measures, location of business.

- **Management Team** – Description of key players and their backgrounds, common vision of group, complementary attributes and strengths, staying power and individual commitments to enterprise, prior history working together.

- **Plan Implementation** – Implementation schedule, investment timing and variables, human resources planning, key milestones, bottleneck risks.

- **Financial Elements** – Detailed financial projections (three to five years) under three alternative scenarios, key assumptions and their reasonableness, breakeven timing and key factors, cash flow analysis and risks, setback impacts and alternatives, investor return potentials.

- **Risks** – Description of key market and delivery risks, technology challenges, interest rate risks, key human resources risks, strategies and options for mitigating risks.

- **Appendix** – Management resumes, organization chart, supplemental market and competitor information, key articles, other relevant outside sources.

3. *APPEALING TO INVESTORS*

Many business plans contain all the requisite elements, read like a novel, and completely fail to capture the interest of investors. Often they resemble a canned "paint-by-numbers" project that was approached and executed as a chore. They look complete on their face, but lack genuineness, a demonstrated expertise, and smart, thoughtful analysis. A superficial review by an experienced investor will quickly trigger concerns about management's vision, passion, and understanding of what lies ahead.

In order to appeal to experienced investors, a plan usually must persuasively explain why and how the proposed company will profitably meet a definable need and be relevant. It must demonstrate that the proponents, through tough analysis and research and their development of market expertise, know their customers, the competition, industry trends, and how specific competitors will be impacted or eliminated. The plan must convincingly describe how a quality team has come together to develop a vision, priorities, and processes that will convert a smart idea into an efficient, well-managed, profitable business.

STUDENT PROBLEM 1-1

Jennifer, a lawyer who works with many businesses, is having lunch with Jeff, a client who owns and operates a successful trucking company. Jeff explains that his brother-in-law Sam has given him the opportunity to invest in a company ("Twilight") that operates retirement homes in two states. Sam, Twilight's chief financial officer, has explained to Jeff that Twilight is owned by five individuals (including Sam), has become very profitable, plans on expanding into six more states, and is seeking expansion capital from a small group (no more than 10) of new investor-owners. Sam characterized the investment opportunity as "a no-brainer windfall." Jeff has set up a meeting with Sam and other key Twilight officers.

After explaining this background, Jeff states to Jennifer, "I know trucking, but retirement homes and this type of an investment are completely foreign to me. I would like to be able to ask some smart questions at this upcoming meeting in order to assess the opportunity and, perhaps most importantly, to dispel any notion held by my brother-in-law that I am a soft-touch fool who happens to have some money. If you were in my shoes, what are the key questions you would ask?"

Assume that you are Jennifer. Based on what you have read in the prior 24 pages and your general instincts, list the top 10 questions that you would recommend to Jeff.

F. BRIEF LOOK BACK AND THE ALLURE OF ENTREPRENEURSHIP

Although America's businesses differ in many respects, most of them share a compelling common interest – the strength of the American economy. We have experienced major shakeups to our economy over the past few decades that have permanently impacted the business environment and different ways (referred to here as "money doors") in which people generate income to meet their needs and build capital. Many biases and preconceptions exist about the relative values of the different doors and huge differences in the ability, desire, and aptitude of different people to walk through different doors. But few dispute the significance of the traumas we've experienced in the recent past and their impact on the various doors. That's why all lawyers should have a basic understanding of the resulting changes.

Everyone understands the first door. It's income that people earn by working for someone else. They either get a paycheck or fees from clients. It's pay for service. For most Americans, this is the easiest and most comfortable way to earn a living. That's not necessarily because it's the best way. It's because from day one, we've all been conditioned for, prepared for – virtually pointed at – this way of earning rewards. As a child, you pick up your toys and get a prize. In school, you do your assignments and get good grades. As an adult, you do your work and get a paycheck; get a good job; then a better job. Then the best job you can handle.

The employment world has changed dramatically over the past few decades. The risks, rewards and challenges have all escalated. The gap in rewards and security between those who have real skills and expertise and those who have none is forever growing wider. No longer is it reasonable to expect that one will get a job and then cruise on autopilot to get promoted, wait for the right older colleague to retire, and then get promoted again. There are no longer vows of permanence or long-term commitments. There are new guiding words: outsourcing, downsizing, streamlining, consolidating, efficiency. Many employees who once thought they had solid, secure jobs were shocked and dismayed to find themselves on the outside, looking back and saying, "I can't believe this." All age brackets have been hit. No class has been immune. Today's employees need to be prepared to adjust expectations. The challenge is to develop the will, talent, and ability to shift gears along the way, perhaps many times.

Ask any employee what he or she wants in a job and you'll get some combination of four objectives: A job that's interesting and challenging; a job that develops skills and expertise; a job that's rewarding; and a job that's secure. As our economy has languished, many have been denied any opportunity to focus on, let alone maximize, any of these objectives. They've been forced to scramble in taking what they can get. The ideal of being able to pick and choose from real options to improve one's plight has been limited to a select few. Most now understand that a good job should be cherished and that all working Americans have a vested interest in the strength and stability of the American economy and the capital that feeds it.

The second door is the money one earns from investments. A person invests earnings and collects income from the investments or watches the investments grow, or both. Or the person watches the investments shrink or disappear. Some people immerse themselves in the environment of this financial door; they learn how the inside works and the details necessary to play the game. Most are led to this door by others, stand at the threshold, and throw their money in.

Most individuals have their Door One job and their Door Two investments and never go further. In fact, prior generations didn't have to go this far. In their day, the universal plan was to just enter Door One and walk on to the end of his or her career. When the end was reached, the company paid the worker an honest-to-goodness pension for life. But a few decades ago, things started changing for all future generations. The idea of private companies funding complicated, actuarially driven, life-long pension plans for ever-aging employees and ex-employees began to disappear and quickly became a dinosaur for nearly all except a few private individuals and many government employees. For the rest, the money formula for life had changed. It used to be: work, retire, collect a pension, and die. It has become: work, save, invest, pray your investments grow, retire, live off your savings, don't outlive your money, die.

This change in who assumes the risk of funding retirement changed Door Two in a big way forever. For prior generations, pros entered this door, knowing they had to perform because if they didn't, the company, not the employee, would suffer the consequence. The employee's monthly pension would be paid like clockwork in any event. The company would have to contribute more if the investments didn't perform as expected. Now, with the big change, masses of uninformed, financially illiterate employees were heading for Door Two, often led by self-proclaimed professionals who had only a half-tablespoon more knowledge than the flocks they were herding.

During the '90s, America enjoyed a powerful economic expansion that began in March 1991 and ended in March 2001. Door Two ballooned with excitement. The driving force behind this extraordinary expansion was the technology and dot.com boom and an associated abundance of confidence and optimism about the future. This force transcended all politics and parties. It produced plentiful capital that fueled all our markets, allowed innovators to innovate, and empowered businesses to increase productivity. Many, both inside and outside of government, believed and proclaimed that we had experienced a major structural change to a "new economy."

Americans benefited big time. Unemployment was down; wages were up; inflation was low; and individual portfolios were skyrocketing. The paper net wealth of Americans grew an astounding $18.3 trillion. The ratio of net wealth to disposable income grew from 4.9 percent to 6.4 percent, the highest level since 1952. Price/earnings ratios began to move out of sight – then often out of existence because there were no earnings on which to calculate the ratios. Everyone's monthly investment statement showed growth each month. The only question was: how much growth? The Internet was becoming a reality and promised the future. Companies with an Internet strategy, but no earning and meager revenues, could attract investors, then more investors, and then watch their stock prices balloon as the demand fed on itself.

During the boom, Americans grew confident with their ever-escalating investment portfolios and were anxious to spend. Consumer spending outstripped all disposable income. As a result, Americans solidified their position as the worst savers in the industrial world. Experts estimate that the personal savings rate in America dropped from 8 percent to less than zero, and the share of Gross Domestic Product that households consumed rose 6 percent.

So a big question was: If Americans were spending all their income, where was the capital coming from – the capital that made everything possible? The answer: Offshore. Foreign money flooded into our stock markets, our financial institutions, and our government. The importing of foreign dollars allowed America to expand in the short run while its citizens progressively fueled demand by spending everything they earned. In 1993, net foreign investment was less than 5 percent of growth investments in the United States. By the end of the '90s, it had spiked to 23 percent.

The high employment and escalating income levels of the '90s heyday produced a bonanza for federal government coffers. By 1999, there was actually an on-budget surplus, something we hadn't seen since 1960. Higher earnings had pushed annual income tax revenues past the $1 trillion mark for the first time, and the government's public debt had actually dropped. In early 2000, the Congressional Budget Office projected ever-escalating on-budget surpluses through the year 2010, which would reduce the total public debt to under $1 trillion by 2010. Every year into the future was projected to just get better.

Of course, the surpluses never came. The new economy never materialized. Everything began to shift in 2000 as the realization set in that this joyride was not a *bona fide* boom, but rather an over-hyped bubble that was about to burst. The difference between a boom and a bubble is the aftermath; the first retracts to something that resembles an acceptable norm, while the latter produces across-the-board misery. The burst began as some, then many, and then all concluded that the future profitability expectations of new investments were grossly overoptimistic, particularly those related to the technology and dot.com boom. Foreign capital began to disappear, which triggered a big drop in the value of the dollar.

All Americans witnessed that, just as capital giveth, the lack of capital taketh away. Unemployment skyrocketed. Our capital markets crashed. Monthly investment statements became something to hide from, not hang on the fridge. Companies quickly found themselves swimming in excess manufacturing capacity. Venture capital for new growth and innovation was nearly impossible to find.

As the equity markets crashed, the huge historic gains in the ratio of consumer wealth to disposable income completely disappeared, retracting to pre-1993 levels. The tech-heavy Nasdaq Composite lost 78 percent of its value, and even the stalwart S&P 500 got hammered, losing 49 percent of its value during the same time frame. Trillions of dollars in equity value had vanished in a few short years following the bubble's burst.

But for those who sucked up the hit, it wasn't about a trillion dollars. It was about having the nerve to open and look at monthly statements to see the losses that mounted every month. For many older players, it was about dashed retirement dreams or, at best, long-delayed retirement hopes. For younger players, who anxiously entered the market in the '90s, with expectations of riding the upward momentum to riches, it was about getting KO'd in their first round.

The pumping up and ultimate burst of the '90s bubble reminded us of the power of optimism and confidence about the future, our dependence on foreign capital, the importance of sound investing discipline, and the positive impact robust private sector growth can have on government coffers and employment and income levels.

Slowly, the return began and then strengthened, strongly prodded by big tax cuts and the lowest interest rates most could ever remember. Foreigners fueled the recovery with serious capital, and all was back on track again until everything crashed again in 2008.

Since then, our economy has been struggling to slowly crawl out of a protracted recession and anemic recovery that have delivered chronically high unemployment numbers, brought our largest financial institutions to their knees, and forced many businesses to close their doors. Million have given up their job-seeking efforts and are no longer even included in the unemployment calculation. The labor force participation rate continues to hover at a 40-year low. And millions who do have jobs consider themselves grossly underemployed as they net only a fraction of what they used to earn.

What got us to this point? For more than two decades, the world markets have been fueled by consumers in developed countries progressively spending at a faster pace. It was done with leverage – debt backed by assets that were supposed to continually grow in value and support perpetual borrowing and spending increases. The leverage occurred at all levels: government debt escalated; financial institutions leveraged derivative-based securities to the hilt; subprime mortgages and government mandates pushed millions of families to buy homes they couldn't afford; and households pumped up debt through refinanced home mortgages and the use of easily available credit card leverage. Then the momentum shifted. Asset values turned and headed in the wrong direction, spiraling down as demand shrank and fire sales escalated the descent. The largest financial institutions – those "too big to fail" – were grossly overleveraged and saw their balance sheet values crumble. They were soon on life support, begging the government for a lifeline. The value of just about every home in America plummeted, leaving millions of Americans underwater, with more debt than assets.

The private sector was forced to deleverage by reducing debt and cutting spending. The resulting massive drop in demand forced employers to slash payrolls, which further accelerated the drop in demand. The government and the Federal Reserve kept money flowing by cutting short-term interest rates to nearly zero, driving up annual federal deficits to unprecedented trillion-dollar levels from 2009 to 2012 that no one could have imagined just a few years ago, and pumping trillions into the economy through the Federal Reserve's "quantitative easing" programs. The big question now is whether these measures can offset the effects of the private deleveraging that drove buyers to the sidelines without doing untold damage in the long term.

These experiences of the recent past have once again confirmed some tough realities. All Door Two players must understand that the past is not an automatic blueprint for the future and that values are fragile, capable of being rapidly driven down by many external forces and artificially propped up by aggressive monetary policies. We have witnessed again that unrestrained, irresponsible asset-based leveraging is a double-edged sword; it has the capacity to either fuel wonderful growth or quickly put large financial institutions and millions of businesses and families on their backs. Debates will forever rage over the effectiveness of various government actions designed to help offset the massive private sector de-leveraging and the debilitating drop in global demand. But there is little doubt that when it comes to job creation, aggressive, creative government monetary policies are no substitute for new technologies and market opportunities that push American companies to build products and deliver services that the world wants and is capable of buying. And to that end there appears to be widespread agreement on one basic point: America's private business sector is the best hope for any real recovery. Which brings us to Door Three.

Years ago as a planning lawyer entrenched in my Door One position, trying regularly to toss money into Door Two, I began to witness firsthand something that really impressed me. I observed that the happiest, most financially secure, most energetic, most interesting, most fun-to-be with people were not Door One people. Please note that I did not say the most educated. These individuals had more freedom, financial independence, and flexibility. They didn't have to worry about a pink slip. But they had to think. They got to think. They were smart at what they did. They experienced the endless joy and wonder of self-discovery. A few were really educated - PhD types - but many never graduated college and some never finished high school. These people built businesses, which is Door Three, along with their Door Two activities.

Most successful Door Three players could not have possibly imagined they'd end up owning a business when they entered the work force. They may have had some fuzzy notions about the world of Door Three, thinking, as many do, that Door Three is only for hard-nosed business types and risk-taking entrepreneurs. It couldn't possibly be a smart place for a person concerned about financial security and a life dedicated to those things that are more important than money.

As these individuals pursued their Door One jobs, they kept their eyes wide open, perpetually learned more, and stayed flexible. They viewed their career as a journey of self-discovery and reaching higher. They were not fixated on one path, a forty- or fifty-year blueprint, that shut out other possibilities. Each found a niche, something that he or she could do well and that others wanted. This triggered an effort to learn everything about that niche and how to run a business. The next step was a written business plan that trusted others critiqued and that forced a brutally honest analysis of every assumption, success factor, and risk. Through this process, a genuine confidence in their plan was developed through hard, objective, factually-sound analysis, not just wishful dreaming. Actions were then taken to assemble the money, the people, and the organization to bring the business to life. For many, the money side of their lives surpassed all their expectations, and often the most important non-money elements improved as well.

Beyond the benefits to the owners, each of these closely held business success stories helps drive our economy. These enterprises create jobs, commerce, and opportunities for everyone. Historically, they have created 65 percent of all net new jobs.[31] Yet today, business owner perceptions are negative, and robust growth is stalled. Surveys of successful business owners in 2013 confirmed that 79 percent believe that we are on the wrong track, 87 percent want more certainty, less than 15 percent intend to hire full time employees over the next year, and only four percent intend to significantly expand their business over the next year.[32] Average per-employee regulatory compliance costs for small businesses are estimated to be 36 percent higher than the per-employee average for large companies.[33] And as for the ease of starting a new business in

31. Small Business Fact Sheet, U.S. House of Representatives Committee on Small Business (May 21, 2013).

32. See April 2013 Chamber of Commerce Survey, 2013 BNA Economic Outlook Survey, and 2013 National Federation of Independent Business Survey.

33. Impact of Regulatory Costs on Small Firms, SBA Study (2010). This study found that the average

the U.S. as compared to other leading nations, the U.S. world ranking descended from third in 2007 to 13th in 2013.[34]

Ask any owner of a successful business what the two largest outside threats are to the business and you'll likely get two responses: shortage of capital and a lousy economy. The inability to secure enough capital is the primary reason many good business ideas never make it, never reach their potential, or never get off the ground. And as we have witnessed since 2009, an unstable economy discourages risk-taking and promotes tentativeness and contraction.

In order to aggressively play to win, businesses need to know the rules of the game and have confidence that market forces are headed in the right direction. Today, the rules and forces are anything but certain. Far-reaching, unpredictable legislation and regulations have frightened many who must meet a payroll. Unprecedented government deficits and recent tax increases have discouraged many business owners and investors, who fear that more bad news is inevitable. Congress is deadlocked, with half our leaders screaming for more regulation on all fronts while the other half proclaim that downsizing government and unleashing free market forces is our only hope. Meanwhile, the long-term business impact of massive federal spending, unprecedented deficits, and extreme monetary policies remains unknown, as we witness the economies of some nations shake and the entire global economy struggle to find a solid footing.

---

annual per-employee regulatory compliance cost for small businesses was $10,585.

34. 2013 Word Bank and IFC Doing Business Study.

CHAPTER 2

Financial Statement Basics

A. THE LANGUAGE OF BUSINESS

Accounting is the language of business. It's the primary source of quantitative information in every enterprise. A quality accounting system is a prerequisite to long-term success. It produces internal reports that management must have to effectively manage the enterprises and external reports designed to meet the needs and demands of owners, government agencies, and other third parties. A substandard or defective accounting system often results in poor strategic decisions, the inability to effectively plan, and inaccurate and misleading documents. In many situations, such a system can lead to broken careers and serious legal problems that threaten the survival of the enterprise.

The primary external outputs of a company's accounting system are its financial statements. These are the scorecards of every business. They are the ultimate measures of success and failure, important trends, and management quality.

A lawyer should have a basic understanding of financial statements and the ability to read them. They routinely surface in all types of legal disputes and challenges. A lawyer who must rely on others for the basics usually will be at a significant disadvantage. There is no need to master the art of debits and credits or to know the detailed requirements for a quality accounting system. But there is a need to understand core concepts that underlie financial statements, the components of each of the key financial statements, how the statements relate to one another, how key transactions impact financial statements, and the role and limits of standard safeguards.

B. UNDERLYING CONCEPTS

1. OBJECTIVITY – GAPP AND IFRS

Objectivity is a threshold goal of the accounting process. It requires freedom from bias and adherence to principles, standards, and procedures that are designed to promote conformity and produce reasonable, objectively determined results. In the United States, these standards are known as generally accepted accounting principles (GAAP), which are a flexible set of principles and rules that, in large part, define the outer limits of reasonableness for reporting specific transactions. US public companies must comply with GAAP requirements in reporting their results of operations, and generally (although not always) GAAP requirements are followed in the preparation of financial statements for closely held enterprises.

GAAP standards are primarily determined by the Financial Accounting Standards Board (FASB), a seven-member board created with the support of the premier accounting organization in the Unites States (the American Institute of Certified Public Accountants (AICPA)) and the Securities and Exchange Commission. The AICPA and the SEC also have the authority to promulgate GAAP standards. FASB board members serve fulltime for five-year terms, and a member may serve no more than two terms. To promote objectivity and independence, members are required to sever connections with any firms or institutions they worked with prior to becoming a board member. The members have diverse backgrounds in accounting, finance, business, accounting education, and research, and each must have a demonstrated concern for users of financial statements and the public interest in matters of accounting and financial reporting.

GAAP standards are not the controlling authority outside the United States. The International Financial Reporting Standards (IFRS) are the primary international standards. Designed to meet the demands of expanding international trade and shareholder ownership, the IFRS requirements have become a common global language for business affairs, promoting accounting uniformity across international boundaries and progressively replacing national accounting standards. They are important to any company that has significant dealings in several countries. IFRS reporting requirements have been adopted by many countries, including Australia, Canada, European Union, India, Japan, Russia, Taiwan, and more.

Although efforts are continually being made to unify ("converge" is the term often used) GAAP and IFRS reporting requirements, significant differences remain. These differences are important to U.S. companies that engage in cross-border mergers and acquisitions, report to major non-US shareholders and institutions that demand IFRS compliant information, and own and manage non-U.S. subsidiaries that must comply with IFRS requirements. The differences are also important to the growing number of U.S. investors who invest in non-U.S. public companies that comply only with IFRS standards.

2. *ENTITY FOCUS*

An accounting system is designed to record the transactions of a specific entity and report the results of operates for that entity. The nature of the entity defines the scope of the accounting system. It may be a large conglomerate of multiple companies, a component company of such a conglomerate, a division of a company, a small stand-alone business, or any other definable economic unit. Transactions that are part of the specific entity fall within the scope of the accounting system. Outside transactions do not. For example, the sale of a company's truck would be a recordable accounting transaction for the company while the purchase of a new truck for personal use by the company's owner would not be a recordable transaction for the company.

3. *GOING CONCERN*

The accounting process assumes that an entity is a going concern that will continue to operate and carry on its business indefinitely. The process makes no attempt to measure the impacts of a shutdown in the near term that would result in a liquidation of the company's assets. This going concern assumption necessarily is based on the premise that assets and resources will be consumed and replenished during the ongoing operation of the business and that liabilities and debts will be paid and incurred in due course.

4. *MONETARY MEASURE*

The dollar is the measuring unit for recording transactions in an accounting system. But except in very limited circumstances, no attempt is made to account for changes in the value of the dollar. Inflation is ignored. Thus, for example, a $30,000 equipment purchase in 1999 is recorded the same as a $30,000 equipment purchase in 2014 even though a 1999-dollar was worth considerably more than a 2014-dollar. As Henry Sweeney stated decades ago in his book *Stabilized Accounting* (Harper & Bros 1936), "The truthfulness of accounting depends largely on the truthfulness of the dollar, and the dollar is a liar."

Constant dollar accounting is an accounting method that is used in select situations to provide supplemental information. It adjusts financial statements for changes in the value of the dollar, using a price index such as the consumer price index (CPI). The premise is that such information may facilitate better comparisons of companies that had significant asset transactions in different years. But a fundamental weakness is that the index used (CPI for example) often will not reflect actual price changes in the underlying assets.

5. *HISTORICAL DOLLAR COST*

The accounting process generally records and carries assets at their historical dollar cost, adjusted for depreciation and amortization as appropriate. Thus, if an asset purchased in 2005 for $100,000 is now worth $150,000, the $50,000 appreciation will not be reflected in the accounting system until the asset is sold and the gain is recognized. There are exceptions for liquid investment assets that have readily ascertainable market values and are capable of being sold into established markets. These assets are "marked-to-market" to reflect their current values.

Many claim that a major cause of the subprime mortgage and banking crisis of 2008 was aggressive, irresponsible mark-to-market accounting by financial institutions. These institutions supported extreme borrowing levels by marking up mortgage-backed securities and other assets to levels that many in hindsight characterized as unsustainable and not reflective of true market conditions. When the markets for these securities crashed in the face of rapidly declining real estate prices, values plummeted and many institutions were buried in debt with no equity. They were forced to fire sell assets at distressed prices. The fire sales accelerated the rapid descent of values and the ongoing deterioration of balance sheets. The federal government ultimately stepped in with favorable loans to bailout many, including those deemed "too big to fail."

6. *REALIZATION*

Realization is the concept that defines when revenue is realized and recorded by an accounting system. For every sale of a product or service, there are various key events in the transaction process: when the order is received; when the inventory is produced or acquired; when the order is processed; when the goods or services are delivered; and when the revenue is collected in the form of cash. Under the realization concept, the event that triggers the realization of revenue is the delivery of the goods and services. In most businesses, a completed legal right to be paid for the goods and services is created at that time. Except in very limited situations, such as long-term construction contracts, no attempt is made to allocate the realization of revenue to various events that occur during the process of completing an order or project.

7. *ACCRUAL*

Closely related to the realization concept is the accrual concept. A cash method of accounting recognizes income when cash is collected and recognizes expenses when they are paid in the form of cash. For example, under such a system a lawyer would recognize income when fees are actually collected and recognize rental expense when the rent is paid. An accrual method recognizes income when it is realized (the delivery of the product or service) and recognizes an expense when a liability is created for costs incurred. Thus, under this system a lawyer would recognize income when services are completed and billed and would recognize rental expense when the applicable rental period expires. Financial statements nearly always reflect the accrual method, although there are limited exceptions.

Depreciation and amortization are expenses that receive like treatment under cash and accrual methods of accounting. For example, the cash method would not currently expense $100,000 paid to acquire a piece of equipment that has a useful life of 10 years. As under the accrual method, the cost of the equipment would be expensed (depreciated) in allocable shares over its useful life.

The accrual method of accounting is more complicated and demanding than the cash method. Special entries (often called adjusting journal entries) must be made to reflect accrual elements that are not picked up by transaction journals maintained daily. Examples include accrued wages, prepaid income, accrued interest, prepaid expenses (e.g. insurance), and the like.

8. *CONSERVATISM*

Conservatism is a fundamental accounting concept. In the broadest sense, it means that the accounting process prefers to run the risk of erring on the side of understating, rather than overstating, results and values. When in doubt, yield to the downside. The concept often surfaces in determining balance sheet asset values. Three common examples:

- **Accounts Receivable.** These are the amounts that a company is legally entitled to collect for services and goods previously delivered. The total of the amounts due must be reduced for estimated bad debt amounts that won't be collected (usually called an "Allowance for Doubtful Accounts), discounts, returns and price allowances. The bad debt allowance is based on the company's prior history. For example, if the company generally has failed to collect five percent of its accounts receivable, conservatism requires that the balance sheet accounts receivable balance be reduced by a 5-percent bad debt contra-asset account.

- **Inventories.** Inventories are goods that are being processed and held for future sale to customers. The cost of the inventories is carried as an asset on the balance sheet. Since goods with varying cost levels are continually being added to and pulled from the inventories, the accounting system must have a method for determining, at any given time, the cost of goods actually sold and the cost of the remaining inventory. There are various costing methods: (1) a moving average method, which continually combines new and old inventory costs to arrive at a moving average that is used to value sold and unsold goods; (2) a first-in, first-out (FIFO) method, which assumes the first items acquired are the first items sold at their cost; and (3) a last-in, first-out (LIFO) method, which assumes the last items acquired are the first items sold at their costs. Whichever costing method is used, conservatism requires that the inventory value on the balance sheet does not exceed the lower of the cost determined under the applicable costing method or the market value of the inventory. This lower-of-cost-or-market requirement is designed to protect against inflated inventory values. On the flip side, there is no capacity to write up the inventory if the market value exceeds the cost determination. For purposes of the requirement, market value usually is defined as current replacement cost, but it may not exceed what the company expects to realize from the inventory (net of selling costs) and may not be less than such net realized amount reduced by a normal profit margin.

- **Depreciable and Amortizable Assets.** The cost of tangible and intangible fixed assets that have a useful life beyond one year generally must be incrementally written off and expensed over the useful life of the asset. Conservatism requires this even if the underlying value of the asset remains constant or appreciates.

9. CONSISTENCY

The consistency concept recognizes that companies have discretion and flexibility in selecting alternative accounting methods, all of which may comply with generally accepted accounting principles. Examples include alternative inventory costing and depreciation methods. The consistency concept encourages use of the same methods from year to year in the financial statements of the company. Year-to-year comparisons are an important element of financial statements. That is why key statements typically set forth, side-by-side, results for the last three years. Absent this consistency concept, year-to-year comparisons may be difficult or impossible, and the potential for year-to-year manipulation and abuse would escalate. Departures from this consistency concept have to be carefully considered and often require special disclosure in the footnotes to the financial statements.

10. *DISCLOSURE*

The disclosure concept establishes a simple working rule: when in doubt disclose. Basic financial statements generally won't do the job of adequately disclosing the results of a company's operations. Footnotes are the answer. Often the footnotes are long and carefully crafted. They provide vitally important, clarifying details that enable the user of the financial statements to understand important elements of the statements and the financial condition of the company. Any critical analysis of a company's financial statement should include a thorough review of the accompanying footnotes.

In addition to the footnotes, a document entitled "Management's Discussion and Analysis of Financial Condition and Results of Operations" (MD&A) will accompany the financial statements of a public company. In this document, the top executives of the company express their views of the company's financial performance and condition; discuss important trends, events or uncertainties known to management; and provide management perspectives and information to investors.

C. READING FINANCIAL STATEMENTS

SEC Guide to Financial Statements[1]

The Basics

If you can read a nutrition label or a baseball box score, you can learn to read basic financial statements. If you can follow a recipe or apply for a loan, you can learn basic accounting. The basics aren't difficult and they aren't rocket science.

This is designed to help you gain a basic understanding of how to read financial statements. Just as a CPR class teaches you how to perform the basics of cardiac pulmonary resuscitation, this will explain how to read the basic parts of a financial statement. It will not train you to be an accountant (just as a CPR course will not make you a cardiac doctor), but it should give you the confidence to be able to look at a set of financial statements and make sense of them.

Let's begin by looking at what financial statements do.

"Show me the money!"

We all remember Cuba Gooding Jr.'s immortal line from the movie *Jerry Maguire*, "Show me the money!" Well, that's what financial statements do. They show you the money. They show you where a company's money came from, where it went, and where it is now.

There are four main financial statements. They are: (1) balance sheets; (2) income statements; (3) cash flow statements; and (4) statements of shareholders' equity. Balance sheets show what a company owns and what it owes at a fixed point in time. Income statements show how much money a

1. U.S. Securities and Exchange Commission, Beginners' Guide to Financial Statements (February 5, 2007).

company made and spent over a period of time. Cash flow statements show the exchange of money between a company and the outside world also over a period of time. The fourth financial statement, called a "statement of shareholders' equity," shows changes in the interests of the company's shareholders over time.

Let's look at each of the first three financial statements in more detail.

Balance Sheets

A balance sheet provides detailed information about a company's assets, liabilities and shareholders' equity.

Assets are things that a company owns that have value. This typically means they can either be sold or used by the company to make products or provide services that can be sold. Assets include physical property, such as plants, trucks, equipment and inventory. It also includes things that can't be touched but nevertheless exist and have value, such as trademarks and patents. And cash itself is an asset. So are investments a company makes.

Liabilities are amounts of money that a company owes to others. This can include all kinds of obligations, like money borrowed from a bank to launch a new product, rent for use of a building, money owed to suppliers for materials, payroll a company owes to its employees, environmental cleanup costs, or taxes owed to the government. Liabilities also include obligations to provide goods or services to customers in the future.

Shareholders' equity is sometimes called capital or net worth. It's the money that would be left if a company sold all of its assets and paid off all of its liabilities. This leftover money belongs to the shareholders, or the owners, of the company.

The following formula summarizes what a balance sheet shows:

ASSETS = LIABILITIES + SHAREHOLDERS' EQUITY

A company's assets have to equal, or "balance," the sum of its liabilities and shareholders' equity.

A company's balance sheet is set up like the basic accounting equation shown above. On the left side of the balance sheet, companies list their assets. On the right side, they list their liabilities and shareholders' equity. Sometimes balance sheets show assets at the top, followed by liabilities, with shareholders' equity at the bottom.

Assets are generally listed based on how quickly they will be converted into cash. Current assets are things a company expects to convert to cash within one year. A good example is inventory. Most companies expect to sell their inventory for cash within one year. Noncurrent assets are things a company does not expect to convert to cash within one year or that would take longer than one year to sell. Noncurrent assets include fixed assets. Fixed assets are those assets used to operate the business but that are not available for sale, such as trucks, office furniture and other property.

Liabilities are generally listed based on their due dates. Liabilities are said to be either current or long-term. Current liabilities are obligations a company expects to pay off within the year. Long-term liabilities are obligations due more than one year away.

Shareholders' equity is the amount owners invested in the company's stock plus or minus the company's earnings or losses since inception. Sometimes companies distribute earnings, instead of retaining them. These distributions are called dividends.

A balance sheet shows a snapshot of a company's assets, liabilities and shareholders' equity at the end of the reporting period. It does not show the flows into and out of the accounts during the period.

Income Statements

An income statement is a report that shows how much revenue a company earned over a specific time period (usually for a year or some portion of a year). An income statement also shows the costs and expenses associated with earning that revenue. The literal "bottom line" of the statement usually shows the company's net earnings or losses. This tells you how much the company earned or lost over the period.

Income statements also report earnings per share (or "EPS"). This calculation tells you how much money shareholders would receive if the company decided to distribute all of the net earnings for the period. (Companies almost never distribute all of their earnings. Usually they reinvest them in the business.)

To understand how income statements are set up, think of them as a set of stairs. You start at the top with the total amount of sales made during the accounting period. Then you go down, one step at a time. At each step, you make a deduction for certain costs or other operating expenses associated with earning the revenue. At the bottom of the stairs, after deducting all of the expenses, you learn how much the company actually earned or lost during the accounting period. People often call this "the bottom line."

At the top of the income statement is the total amount of money brought in from sales of products or services. This top line is often referred to as gross revenues or sales. It's called "gross" because expenses have not been deducted from it yet. So the number is "gross" or unrefined.

The next line is money the company doesn't expect to collect on certain sales. This could be due, for example, to sales discounts or merchandise returns.

When you subtract the returns and allowances from the gross revenues, you arrive at the company's net revenues. It's called "net" because, if you can imagine a net, these revenues are left in the net after the deductions for returns and allowances have come out.

Moving down the stairs from the net revenue line, there are several lines that represent various kinds of operating expenses. Although these lines can be reported in various orders, the next line after net revenues typically shows the costs of the sales. This number tells you the amount of money the company spent to produce the goods or services it sold during the accounting period.

The next line subtracts the costs of sales from the net revenues to arrive at a subtotal called "gross profit" or sometimes "gross margin." It's considered "gross" because there are certain expenses that haven't been deducted from it yet.

The next section deals with operating expenses. These are expenses that go toward supporting a company's operations for a given period – for example, salaries of administrative personnel and costs of researching new products. Marketing expenses are another example. Operating expenses are different from "costs of sales," which were deducted above, because operating expenses cannot be linked directly to the production of the products or services being sold.

Depreciation is also deducted from gross profit. Depreciation takes into account the wear and tear on some assets, such as machinery, tools and furniture, which are used over the long term. Companies spread the cost of these assets over the periods they are used. This process of spreading these costs is called depreciation or amortization. The "charge" for using these assets during the period is a fraction of the original cost of the assets.

After all operating expenses are deducted from gross profit, you arrive at operating profit before interest and income tax expenses. This is often called "income from operations."

Next companies must account for interest income and interest expense. Interest income is the money companies make from keeping their cash in interest-bearing savings accounts, money market funds and the like. On the other hand, interest expense is the money companies paid in interest for money they borrow. Some income statements show interest income and interest expense separately. Some income statements combine the two numbers. The interest income and expense are then added or subtracted from the operating profits to arrive at operating profit before income tax.

Finally, income tax is deducted and you arrive at the bottom line: net profit or net losses. (Net profit is also called net income or net earnings.) This tells you how much the company actually earned or lost during the accounting period. Did the company make a profit or did it lose money?

Earnings Per Share or EPS

Most income statements include a calculation of earnings per share or EPS. This calculation tells you how much money shareholders would receive for each share of stock they own if the company distributed all of its net income for the period.

To calculate EPS, you take the total net income and divide it by the number of outstanding shares of the company.

Cash Flow Statements

Cash flow statements report a company's inflows and outflows of cash. This is important because a company needs to have enough cash on hand to pay its expenses and purchase assets. While an income statement can tell you whether a company made a profit, a cash flow statement can tell you whether the company generated cash.

A cash flow statement shows changes over time rather than absolute dollar amounts at a point in time. It uses and reorders the information from a company's balance sheet and income statement.

The bottom line of the cash flow statement shows the net increase or decrease in cash for the period. Generally, cash flow statements are divided into three main parts. Each part reviews the cash flow from one of three types of activities: (1) operating activities; (2) investing activities; and (3) financing activities.

Operating Activities

The first part of a cash flow statement analyzes a company's cash flow from net income or losses. For most companies, this section of the cash flow statement reconciles the net income (as shown on the income statement) to the actual cash the company received from or used in its operating activities. To do this, it adjusts net income for any non-cash items (such as adding back depreciation expenses) and adjusts for any cash that was used or provided by other operating assets and liabilities.

Investing Activities

The second part of a cash flow statement shows the cash flow from all investing activities, which generally include purchases or sales of long-term assets, such as property, plant and equipment, as well as investment securities. If a company buys a piece of machinery, the cash flow statement would reflect this activity as a cash outflow from investing activities because it used cash. If the company decided to sell off some investments from an investment portfolio, the proceeds from the sales would show up as a cash inflow from investing activities because it provided cash.

Financing Activities

The third part of a cash flow statement shows the cash flow from all financing activities. Typical sources of cash flow include cash raised by selling stocks and bonds or borrowing from banks. Likewise, paying back a bank loan would show up as a use of cash flow.

Read the Footnotes

A horse called "Read The Footnotes" ran in the 2004 Kentucky Derby. He finished seventh, but if he had won, it would have been a victory for financial literacy proponents everywhere. It's so important to *read the footnotes*. The footnotes to financial statements are packed with information. Here are some of the highlights:

- Significant accounting policies and practices – Companies are required to disclose the accounting policies that are most important to the portrayal of the company's financial condition and results. These often require management's most difficult, subjective or complex judgments.

- Income taxes – The footnotes provide detailed information about the company's current and deferred income taxes. The information is broken down by level – federal, state, local and/or foreign, and the main items that affect the company's effective tax rate are described.

- Pension plans and other retirement programs – The footnotes discuss the company's pension plans and other retirement or post-employment benefit programs. The notes contain specific information about the assets and costs of these programs, and indicate whether and by how much the plans are over- or under-funded.

- Stock options – The notes also contain information about stock options granted to officers and employees, including the method of accounting for stock-based compensation and the effect of the method on reported results.

Read the MD&A

You can find a narrative explanation of a company's financial performance in a section of the quarterly or annual report entitled, "Management's Discussion and Analysis of Financial Condition and Results of Operations." MD&A is *management's* opportunity to provide investors with its view of the financial performance and condition of the company. It's management's opportunity to tell investors what the financial statements show and do not show, as well as important trends and risks that have shaped the past or are reasonably likely to shape the company's future.

The SEC's rules governing MD&A require disclosure about trends, events or uncertainties known to management that would have a material impact on reported financial information. The purpose of MD&A is to provide investors with information that the company's management believes to be necessary to an understanding of its financial condition, changes in financial condition and results of operations. It is intended to help investors to see the company through the eyes of management. It is also intended to provide context for the financial statements and information about the company's earnings and cash flows.

Financial Statement Ratios and Calculations

You've probably heard people banter around phrases like "P/E ratio," "current ratio" and "operating margin." But what do these terms mean and why don't they show up on financial statements? Listed below are just some of the many ratios that investors calculate from information on financial statements and then use to evaluate a company. As a general rule, desirable ratios vary by industry.

- *Debt-to-equity ratio* compares a company's total debt to shareholders' equity. Both of these numbers can be found on a company's balance sheet. To calculate debt-to-equity ratio, you divide a company's total liabilities by its shareholder equity, or

Debt-to-Equity Ratio = Total Liabilities / Shareholders' Equity

If a company has a debt-to-equity ratio of 2 to 1, it means that the company has two dollars of debt to every one dollar shareholders invest in the company. In other words, the company is taking on debt at twice the rate that its owners are investing in the company.

- *Inventory turnover ratio* compares a company's cost of sales on its income statement with its average inventory balance for the period. To calculate the average inventory balance for the period, look at the inventory numbers listed on the balance sheet. Take the balance listed for the period of the report and add it to the balance listed for the previous comparable period, and then divide by two. (Remember that balance sheets are snapshots in time. So the inventory balance for the previous period is the beginning balance for the current period, and the inventory balance for the current period is the ending balance.) To calculate the inventory turnover ratio, you divide a company's cost of sales (just below the net revenues on the income statement) by the average inventory for the period, or

Inventory Turnover Ratio = Cost of Sales / Average Inventory for the Period

If a company has an inventory turnover ratio of 2 to 1, it means that the company's inventory turned over twice in the reporting period.

- *Operating margin* compares a company's operating income to net revenues. Both of these numbers can be found on a company's income statement. To calculate operating margin, you divide a company's income from operations (before interest and income tax expenses) by its net revenues, or

Operating Margin = Income from Operations / Net Revenues

Operating margin is usually expressed as a percentage. It shows, for each dollar of sales, what percentage was profit.

- *P/E ratio* compares a company's common stock price with its earnings per share. To calculate a company's P/E ratio, you divide a company's stock price by its earnings per share, or

P/E Ratio = Price per share / Earnings per share

If a company's stock is selling at $20 per share and the company is earning $2 per share, then the company's P/E Ratio is 10 to 1. The company's stock is selling at 10 times its earnings.

- *Working capital* is the money leftover if a company paid its current liabilities (that is, its debts due within one-year of the date of the balance sheet) from its current assets.

Working Capital = Current Assets – Current Liabilities

Bringing It All Together

Although this discusses each financial statement separately, keep in mind that they are all related. The changes in assets and liabilities that you see on the balance sheet are also reflected in the revenues and expenses that you see on the income statement, which result in the company's gains or losses. Cash flows provide more information about cash assets listed on a balance sheet and are related, but not equivalent, to net income shown on the income statement. And so on. No one financial statement tells the complete story. But combined, they provide very powerful information for investors. And information is the investor's best tool when it comes to investing wisely.

D. SAMPLE FINANCIAL STATEMENTS

Following are the primary financial statements (without accompanying notes) of Caterpillar Inc. for the year ending December 31, 2012. These statements were filed with the SEC on February 19, 2013. They are offered as examples of financials of a successful public company. Caterpillar was selected solely because your author is a big fan of CAT products. The notes to these financial statements (not included here) are long and very detailed. The following clarifying points (a tiny fraction of what are in the official notes) are offered solely to help a reader understand a few basics of these statements.

- These consolidated statements include the accounts of Caterpillar Inc. and all subsidiaries in which Caterpillar has a controlling financial interest.

- Inventories are stated at the lower of cost or market, and cost is primarily determined using the last-in, first-out (LIFO) method. If the first-in, first-out (FIFO) method had been used, inventories would have been $2.75 billion higher at the end of 2012.

- The balance for property, plant and equipment at the end of 2012 ($16.461 billion) reflects the difference between the historical cost of $29.932 billion and the accumulated depreciation of $13.471 billion.

- The balances for receivables are net of allowances for bad debts and impaired loans and financial leases. A bad debt allowance for a Machinery and Power System receivable is established when it becomes probable that a receivable will not be collected. The allowance for such bad debts is not significant.

- Intangible assets consist principally of purchased customer relationships (with a weighted amortizable life of 15 years) and intellectual property (with a weighted amortizable life of 12 years).

- Goodwill represents the excess of the cost paid to acquire businesses over the fair value of the assets acquired in the acquisitions.

- Long-term debt consists principally of medium-term notes in the financial products segment of the business and notes and debentures (with maturities stretching from 2014 to 2097) in the machinery and power systems segment of the business.

- The $11 billion liability for postemployment benefits at the end of 2012 includes $4.9 billion for US pensions, $1.4 billion for non-US pensions, and $4.7 billion for benefits other than pensions.

- Note that the amounts paid by Caterpillar over time to acquire its own treasury stock ($10.074 billion) exceed by more than two-to-one the amounts received by Caterpillar from the sale of its stock ($4.481 billion).

- Note the substantial increase in stockholders' equity from 2011 ($12.929 billion) to 2012 ($17.582 billion) and cumulative retained earnings at the end of 2012 ($29.558 billion).

- The accumulated other comprehensive loss in the stockholders' equity section reflects cumulative losses from currency gains and losses resulting from translating the financial statements of foreign subsidiaries, unrealized gains and losses on securities available for sale, gains and losses on derivatives held as cash flow hedges, and actuarial gains and losses on defined benefit retirement plans. In 1997, FASB issued Statement on Financial Accounting Standards No. 130 that required that the cumulative balance of such items, which impact the value of stockholders' equity but are not treated as normal income statement items that are closed to retained earnings each period, be reflected in the stockholders' equity section of the balance sheet. Effective January 1, 2012, FASB permitted companies to show such items in a statement (typically called a "consolidated comprehensive income" statement) that is separate from and supplemental to the income statement. Like many public companies, Caterpillar opted to use this separate statement. Note that the items reflected on this statement, which directly follows the income statement, are also listed in the stockholders' equity statement.

- The provision for income taxes on the income statement ($2.528 billion) for 2012 equals 30.7 percent of consolidated pretax net income. The difference between this percentage and the 35 percent US corporate tax rate is principally attributable to non-US subsidiaries that are taxed at a lower rate, nondeductible goodwill, and prior year interest and tax adjustments.

- Note the cash dividends per share ($2.02) in 2012 as compared to the earnings per share ($8.71). The difference represents the addition to the retained earnings for 2012 that is reflected in the changes in the stockholders' equity statement.

- Note that depreciation expenses for the current year are reflected in the consolidated cash flow statement, as are goodwill charges, annual changes in non-cash asset amounts, and investing and financial activity cash impacts.

- Note how the consolidated profit on the income statement ($5.722 billion for 2012) becomes the starting point for the cash flow statement and the first reconciling item on the changes to stockholders' equity statement.

- Note how the accrued dividends shown on the 2011 balance sheet as a liability ($298 million) exactly equals the difference between the total dividends paid in 2012 ($1.617 billion) as reflected in the cash flow statement and the dividends declared in 2012 ($1.319 billion) as reflected in the changes to stockholders' equity statement.

Caterpillar Inc. – Sample Balance Sheet

Consolidated Financial Position at December 31
(Dollars in millions)

Assets	**2012**	**2011**	**2010**
Current assets:			
Cash and short-term investments	**$ 5,490**	$ 3,057	$ 3,592
Receivables - trade and other	**10,092**	10,285	8,494
Receivables - finance	**8,860**	7,668	8,298
Deferred and refundable income taxes	**1,547**	1,580	931
Prepaid expenses and other current assets	**988**	994	908
Inventories	**15,547**	14,544	9,587
Total current assets	**42,524**	38,128	31,810
Property, plant and equipment - net	**16,461**	14,395	12,539
Long-term receivables - trade and other	**1,316**	1,130	793
Long-term receivables - finance	**14,029**	11,948	11,264
Investments in unconsolidated affiliated companies	**272**	133	164
Noncurrent deferred and refundable income taxes	**2,011**	2,157	2,493
Intangible assets	**4,016**	4,368	805
Goodwill	**6,942**	7,080	2,614
Other assets	**1,785**	2,107	1,538
Total assets	**$ 89,356**	$ 81,446	$ 64,020
Liabilities			
Current liabilities:			
Short-term borrowings:			
Machinery and Power Systems	**$ 636**	$ 93	$ 204
Financial Products	**4,651**	3,895	3,852
Accounts payable	**6,753**	8,161	5,856
Accrued expenses	**3,667**	3,386	2,880
Accrued wages, salaries and employee benefits	**1,911**	2,410	1,670
Customer advances	**2,978**	2,691	1,831
Dividends payable	—	298	281
Other current liabilities	**2,055**	1,967	1,521
Long-term debt due within one year:			
Machinery and Power Systems	**1,113**	558	495
Financial Products	**5,991**	5,102	3,430
Total current liabilities	**29,755**	28,561	22,020
Long-term debt due after one year:			
Machinery and Power Systems	**8,666**	8,415	4,505
Financial Products	**19,086**	16,529	15,932
Liability for postemployment benefits	**11,085**	10,956	7,584
Other liabilities	**3,182**	3,583	2,654
Total liabilities	**71,774**	68,044	52,695
Commitments and contingencies (Notes 20 and 21)			
Redeemable noncontrolling interest (Note 24)	—	473	461
Stockholders' equity			
Common stock of $1.00 par:			
Authorized shares: 2,000,000,000			
amount	**4,481**	4,273	3,888
shares			
and 2010 - 176,071, 910 shares) at cost	**(10,074)**	(10,281)	(10,397)
Profit employed in the business	**29,558**	25,219	21,384
Accumulated other comprehensive income (loss)	**(6,433)**	(6,328)	(4,051)
Noncontrolling interests	**50**	46	40
Total stockholders' equity	**17,582**	12,929	10,864
Total liabilities, redeemable noncontrolling interest and stockholders' equity	**$ 89,356**	$ 81,446	$ 64,020

Caterpillar Inc. – Sample Income Statement

Consolidated Results of Operations for the Years Ended December 31 (Dollars in millions except per share data)	2012	2011	2010
Sales and revenues:			
Sales of Machinery and Power Systems	**$ 63,068**	$ 57,392	$ 39,867
Revenues of Financial Products	**2,807**	2,746	2,721
Total sales and revenues	**65,875**	60,138	42,588
Operating costs:			
Cost of goods sold	**47,055**	43,578	30,367
Selling, general and administrative expenses	**5,919**	5,203	4,248
Research and development expenses	**2,466**	2,297	1,905
Interest expense of Financial Products	**797**	826	914
Goodwill impairment charge	**580**	—	—
Other operating (income) expenses	**485**	1,081	1,191
Total operating costs	**57,302**	52,985	38,625
Operating profit	**8,573**	7,153	3,963
Interest expense excluding Financial Products	**467**	396	343
Other income (expense)	**130**	(32)	130
Consolidated profit before taxes	**8,236**	6,725	3,750
Provision (benefit) for income taxes	**2,528**	1,720	968
Profit of consolidated companies	**5,708**	5,005	2,782
Equity in profit (loss) of unconsolidated affiliated companies	**14**	(24)	(24)
Profit of consolidated and affiliated companies	**5,722**	4,981	2,758
Less: Profit (loss) attributable to noncontrolling interests	**41**	53	58
Profit 1	**$ 5,681**	$ 4,928	$ 2,700
Profit per common share	**$ 8.71**	$ 7.64	$ 4.28
Profit per common share — diluted 2	**$ 8.48**	$ 7.4	$ 4.15
Weighted-average common shares outstanding (millions)			
- Basic	**652.6**	645	631.5
- Diluted 2	**669.6**	666.1	650.4
Cash dividends declared per common share	**$ 2.02**	$ 1.82	$ 1.74

Caterpillar Inc. – Sample Statement of Consolidated Comprehensive Income

Consolidated Comprehensive Income for the Years Ended December 31
(Millions of dollars)

	2012	2011	2010
Profit of consolidated and affiliated companies	**$ 5,722**	$ 4,981	$ 2,758
Other comprehensive income (loss), net of tax:			
Foreign currency translation, net of tax (expense)/benefit of: 2012 - $9; 2011 - $3; 2010 - ($73)	**60**	(312)	(34)
Pension and other postretirement benefits:			
Current year actuarial gain (loss), net of tax (expense)/benefit of: 2012 - $372; 2011 - $1,276; 2010 - $214	**(731)**	(2,364)	(540)
Amortization of actuarial (gain) loss, net of tax (expense)/benefit of: 2012 - ($243); 2011 - ($221); 2010 - ($173)	**458**	412	310
Current year prior service credit (cost), net of tax (expense)/benefit of: 2012 - ($12); 2011 - ($51); 2010 - $3	**23**	95	(8)
Amortization of prior service (credit) cost, net of tax (expense)/benefit of: 2012 - $17; 2011 - $11; 2010 - $12	**(31)**	(21)	(17)
Amortization of transition (asset) obligation, net of tax (expense)/benefit of: 2012 - ($1); 2011 - ($1); 2010 - ($1)	**1**	1	1
Derivative financial instruments:			
Gains (losses) deferred, net of tax (expense)/benefit of: 2012 - $29; 2011 - $12; 2010 - $29	**(48)**	(21)	(50)
(Gains) losses reclassified to earnings, net of tax (expense)/benefit of: 2012 - ($10); 2011 - $21; 2010 - ($18)	**16**	(34)	35
Available-for-sale securities:			
Gains (losses) deferred, net of tax (expense)/benefit of: 2012 - ($13); 2011 - $2; 2010 - ($25)	**26**	(5)	37
(Gains) losses reclassified to earnings, net of tax (expense)/benefit of: 2012 - $1; 2011 - ($1); 2010 - $2	**(3)**	1	(4)
Total other comprehensive income (loss), net of tax	**(229)**	(2,248)	(270)
Comprehensive income	**5,493**	2,733	2,488
Less: comprehensive income attributable to the noncontrolling interests	**(24)**	(82)	(78)
Comprehensive income attributable to stockholders	**$ 5,469**	$ 2,651	$ 2,410

Caterpillar Inc. – Sample Cash Flow Statement

Consolidated Statement of Cash Flow for the Years Ended December 31
(Millions of dollars)

	2012	2011	2010
Cash flow from operating activities:			
Profit of consolidated and affiliated companies	$ 5,722	$ 4,981	$ 2,758
Adjustments for non-cash items:			
Depreciation and amortization	2,813	2,527	2,296
Net gain from sale of businesses and investments	(630)	(128)	—
Goodwill impairment charge	580	—	—
Other	439	585	469
Changes in assets and liabilities, net of acquisitions and divestitures:			
Receivables - trade and other	(173)	(1,345)	(2,320)
Inventories	(1,149)	(2,927)	(2,667)
Accounts payable	(1,868)	1,555	2,570
Accrued expenses	183	308	117
Accrued wages, salaries and employee benefits	(490)	619	847
Customer advances	241	173	604
Other assets - net	252	(91)	358
Other liabilities - net	(679)	753	(23)
Net cash provided by (used for) operating activities	5,241	7,010	5,009
Cash flow from investing activities:			
Capital expenditures - excluding equipment leased to others	(3,350)	(2,515)	(1,575)
Expenditures for equipment leased to others	(1,726)	(1,409)	(1,011)
Proceeds from disposals of leased assets and property, plant and equipment	1,117	1,354	1,469
Additions to finance receivables	(12,010)	(10,001)	(8,498)
Collections of finance receivables	8,995	8,874	8,987
Proceeds from sale of finance receivables	132	207	16
Investments and acquisitions (net of cash acquired)	(618)	(8,184)	(1,126)
Proceeds from sale of businesses and investments (net of cash sold)	1,199	376	—
Proceeds from sale of available-for-sale securities	306	247	228
Investments in available-for-sale securities	(402)	(336)	(217)
Other - net	167	(40)	132
Net cash provided by (used for) investing activities	(6,190)	(11,427)	(1,595)
Cash flow from financing activities:			
Dividends paid	(1,617)	(1,159)	(1,084)
Distribution to noncontrolling interests	(6)	(3)	—
Common stock issued, including treasury shares reissued	52	123	296
Excess tax benefit from stock-based compensation	192	189	153
Acquisitions of redeemable noncontrolling interests	(444)	—	—
Acquisitions of noncontrolling interests	(5)	(8)	(132)
months):			
- Machinery and Power Systems	2,209	4,587	216
- Financial Products	13,806	10,873	8,108
Payments on debt (original maturities greater than three months):			
- Machinery and Power Systems	(1,107)	(2,269)	(1,298)
- Financial Products	(9,992)	(8,324)	(11,163)
Short-term borrowings - net (original maturities three months or less)	461	(43)	291
Net cash provided by (used for) financing activities	3,549	3,966	(4,613)
Effect of exchange rate changes on cash	(167)	(84)	(76)
Increase (decrease) in cash and short-term investments	2,433	(535)	(1,275)
Cash and short-term investments at beginning of period	3,057	3,592	4,867
Cash and short-term investments at end of period	$ 5,490	$ 3,057	$ 3,592

Caterpillar Inc. – Sample Changes in Stockholders' Equity Statement (2011 to 2012)

Changes in Consolidated Stockholders' Equity for the Years Ended December 31
(Dollars in millions)

	Common stock	Treasury stock	Profit employed in the business	Accumulated other comprehensi income (loss)	Noncontrol interests	Total
Balance at December 31, 2011	$ 4,273	$ (10,281)	$ 25,219	$ (6,328)	$ 46	$ 12,929
Profit of consolidated and affiliated companies	—	—	5,681	—	41	5,722
Foreign currency translation, net of tax	—	—	—	83	(23)	60
Pension and other postretirement benefits, net of tax	—	—	—	(285)	5	(280)
Derivative financial instruments, net of tax	—	—	—	(32)	—	(32)
Available-for-sale securities, net of tax	—	—	—	22	1	23
Change in ownership from noncontrolling interests	—	—	—	—	(4)	(4)
Dividends declared	—	—	(1,319)	—	—	(1,319)
Distribution to noncontrolling interests	—	—	—	—	(6)	(6)
Common shares issued from treasury stock for stock-based compensation: 7,515,149	(155)	207	—	—	—	52
Stock-based compensation expense	245	—	—	—	—	245
Net excess tax benefits from stock-based compensation	192	—	—	—	—	192
Cat Japan share redemption 2	(74)	—	(23)	107	(10)	—
Balance at December 31, 2012	$ 4,481	$ (10,074)	$ 29,558	$ (6,433)	$ 50	$ 17,582

E. SAFEGUARDS

1. *THE AUDIT PROCESS*

False and misleading financial statements are dangerous. They can lead to bad management actions, poor investment decisions, deceptive business practices, and a lack of confidence in the accounting process. When a serious problem surfaces, the root cause usually is some combination of incompetence, a reckless disregard of protocol, cronyism fueled by mutual greed, pressures to meet expectations, or willful misconduct. And, of course, we have witnessed time and again the power of using bad statements as a tool to fuel outright fraud.

The audit process has always been the primary safeguard against false and misleading statements. An accounting firm that stands independent of the company spends many hours applying established auditing standards to test the transactions and internal controls of the company and verify account balances. The desired end product is a document from the firm (sample below) that opines that the company's financial statements "present fairly, in all material respects" the financial condition and operating results of the company in accordance with generally accepted accounting principles and that the company has "maintained, in all material respects, effective internal controls over financial reporting."

Any company whose stock is publicly traded is required to annually file audited financial statements with the SEC. Closely held businesses generally are not required to have audited financial statements, and most don't. However, there are many situations where a private company will need to have audited statements in order to meet the demands of investors, lenders, key customers, or other important players or to prepare for the potential of going public in the future.

Audits are detailed, time consuming, and expensive. According to the 2013 audit survey of Financial Executives International, the average audit fee paid by public companies in 2012 was $4.5 million, a four percent increase over the previous year. In 2012, it took an average of 16,737 audit hours to complete a public company audit.[2] The corresponding averages for private company audits were a fraction of these public company averages, but still significant and beyond the reach of most small businesses. Audit fees of private companies in 2012 averaged $147,800, a three percent increase over the prior year, and the number of audit hours expended averaged 1,769.

In the audit of a public company, the auditing firm must comply with standards established by the Public Company Accounting Oversight Board (PCAOB), a private-sector, non-profit corporation created by the Sarbanes-Oxley Act of 2002 (SOX). This board oversees the audits of public companies and public company auditors through registration, inspection, standard-setting, and enforcement processes. The creation of the PCAOB put an end to the accounting profession's self-regulation of its public company auditing activities. Headquartered in Washington, D.C., the PCAOB has five board members, no more than two of whom may be certified public accountants. The members are

---

2. Financial Executives International (FEI) Audit Survey 2013 (July 30, 2013).

appointed by the SEC, after consultation with the Chairman of the Board of Governors of the Federal Reserve System and the Secretary of the Treasury.

An audit of a non-public company must be in accordance with the Statements on Auditing Standards promulgated by the Auditing Standards Board of the American Institute of Certified Public Accountants. These statements provide guidance to auditors on generally accepted auditing standards.

The internal control element of the audit process is usually based on criteria established by the Committee of Sponsoring Organizations of the Treadway Commission (COSO) through its Internal Control - Integrated Framework. First released in 1992 and continually refined, this framework has gained broad acceptance throughout the world and is recognized as a leading framework for designing, implementing, and conducting internal control and for assessing the effectiveness of an internal control system. An effective internal system includes policies and procedures that provide reasonable assurance that (1) records are maintained to accurately and fairly reflect transactions and permit preparation of financial statements in accordance with generally accepted accounting principles, (2) receipts and expenditures are made in accordance with authorizations of management and directors, and (3) protections are in place to prevent or timely detect the unauthorized acquisition, use, or disposition of assets.

The audit of a public company requires a firm with substantial expertise and personnel. The result is that 87 percent of public companies use one of the "Big Four" for their auditing needs.[3] The Big Four include Deloitte, PwC, Ernst & Young, and KPMG. Each is a group of multinational companies that employ in excess of 150,000 people and generate annual revenues ranging from $23 billion to $32 billion. Only one of the Big Four (Deloitte) is headquartered in the United States, but each maintains substantial offices throughout the country.

The audit process must necessarily depend on materiality concepts and conclusions drawn from examinations that occur on a test basis. No matter the magnitude and massive expense of the process or the pedigree of those orchestrating the process, there is no guarantee that the process will accomplish the ultimate goal of preventing false and misleading statements. That is why every lawyer should know something about the Enron debacle and its aftermath.

2. *ENRON AND SARBANES-OXLEY*

The Enron scandal is one of the darkest stories in American corporate history. The root cause of the tragedy was not a function of bad market conditions. It was greed and the power to manipulate financial statements and reports, facilitated by a host of players who benefited by assuming the best and never demanding answers to tough, obvious questions. The collapse of giant Enron was triggered in 2001 when Lynn Brewer, an Enron executive, notified members of the U.S. government of her witness to corrupt dealing including bank fraud, espionage, unlawful price manipulation, and gross overstatements to the press and public. It eventually led to the bankruptcy of the Enron Corporation and the *de facto* dissolution of Arthur Andersen, one of the largest accounting

3. Id.

firms in the world. Enron was the largest bankruptcy reorganization in American history at that time.

Enron was organized in 1985, when it started operations as an interstate pipeline company. It was the product of a merger of Houston Natural Gas and Omaha-based InterNorth. Kenneth Lay, the former chief executive officer of Houston Natural Gas, became the CEO and chairman of Enron. A sign in Enron's Houston headquarters announced that Enron was to become "the World's Greatest Company." Lay was widely hailed as a visionary, a man with strong political connections, and a friend of President George W. Bush, who referred to Lay as "Kenny boy."

In 1999, Enron launched EnronOnline, an Internet-based trading system for electricity, natural gas, crude oil, and a wide range of other products. It soon became the largest business site in the world, with 90 percent of Enron's income coming from trades over EnronOnline. It was a perfect fit for the dot.com-driven stock market boom of the '90s. As Enron mushroomed on the Internet, Wall Street propelled its stock upward. At its peak, Enron was worth about $70 billion, with its shares trading in the $90 range.

Enron enjoyed spectacular growth with its revenues tripling from 1998 to 2000, reaching $100 billion in 2000. Enron had become the seventh-largest Fortune 500 company and the sixth-largest energy company in the world.

When things began to unravel, it was revealed that Enron had formed a dozen "partnerships" with companies it had created to hide huge debts and heavy trading losses. Chief Financial Officer Andrew Fastow and others were successful in misleading Arthur Anderson and Enron's board of directors and audit committee on high-risk accounting practices. Everything crashed when Enron admitted that it had misstated its income and that its equity value had been significantly overstated. Enron's natural gas trading desk, which dominated its business, was shut down. Soon credit rating agencies downgraded Enron to "junk bond" level, Enron stopped paying its bills, and others halted all business with Enron. Enron's stock plunged from a high of $90 a share to less than 61 cents in less than a year. Thousands of Enron employees were thrown out of work and, together with thousands of investors, lost billions as Enron's shares shrank to penny-stock levels.

Enron's collapse pulled down the stocks of Citigroup Inc. and J.P. Morgan Chase & Co., who had granted Enron several hundred million dollars of unsecured loans within weeks of the collapse. The hit to Citigroup and J.P. Morgan Chase, both Dow Jones companies, knocked more than 30 points off the Dow. The collapse also triggered widespread selling on Wall Street, with both the Standard & Poor's 500 and the Nasdaq composite index experiencing significant Enron-related declines.

Enron executives were indicted on a variety of charges and were later sentenced to prison. Arthur Andersen, Enron's auditor, was found guilty in a United States District Court, but the ruling was eventually overturned by the U.S. Supreme Court. Nevertheless, the firm lost the bulk of its clients during the scandal and was forced to close its doors. Enron employees and shareholders received limited returns in lawsuits, nothing close to the billions that had been lost in pensions and stock prices.

Enron wasn't the only corporate scandal during the dot.com bust period. Other corporate accounting scandals surfaced at Tyco International, WorldCom, and other companies, none quite as sensationally sinister as Enron, but all bad. These failures eventually led to new regulations and legislation designed to improve the quality of financial reporting for public companies, including the Sarbanes-Oxley Act of 2002 ("SOX"). SOX had huge bipartisan support, with 423 approving votes in the House and 99 in the Senate. When signing the bill, President George W. Bush heralded it as "the most far-reaching reforms of American business practices since the time of Franklin D. Roosevelt." Bush claimed, "The era of low standards and false profits is over; no boardroom in America is above or beyond the law."[4]

SOX ushered in a number of important changes, all designed to improve confidence in the capital markets of the U.S. and the veracity of corporate financial statements. Key provisions of SOX include the following:

- The Public Company Accounting Oversight Board was established to provide independent oversight of public accounting firms providing audit services. It also was tasked with registering auditors, defining the specific processes and procedures for compliance audits, inspecting and policing conduct and quality control, and enforcing compliance with specific SOX mandates.

- SOX enhanced reporting requirements for financial transactions, including off-balance-sheet transactions, pro-forma figures, and stock transactions of corporate officers. It required internal controls for assuring the accuracy of financial reports and disclosures, and mandated both audits and reports on those controls. It also required timely reporting of material changes in financial condition and enhanced reviews by the SEC or its agents of corporate reports.

- Standards were established for external auditor independence, to limit conflicts of interest, to address requirements for new auditor approval, audit partner rotations, and auditor reporting, and to restrict auditing companies from providing non-audit services (e.g., consulting) for the same clients.

- SOX mandated that senior executives take individual responsibility for the accuracy and completeness of corporate financial reports. It defined the interaction of external auditors and corporate audit committees, and specified the responsibility of corporate officers for the accuracy and validity of corporate financial reports. It enumerated specific limits on the behaviors of corporate officers and mandated forfeitures of benefits and civil penalties for non-compliance.

- SOX included measures designed to help restore investor confidence in reporting by securities analysts by defining a code of conduct for securities analysts and requiring disclosure of knowable conflicts of interest.

---

4. Bumiller, *"Bush Signs Bill Aimed at Fraud in Corporations,"* The New York Times (July 31, 2002).

• SOX defined the SEC's authority to censure or bar securities professionals from practice and defined conditions under which a person can be barred from practicing as a broker, advisor, or dealer.

• SOX required the Comptroller General and the SEC to perform various studies and report their findings.

• SOX included sections called the "Corporate and Criminal Fraud Accountability Act of 2002" that mandated specific criminal penalties for manipulation, destruction or alteration of financial records or other interference with investigations and provided certain protections for whistle-blowers.

• SOX's sections called "White Collar Crime Penalty Enhancement Act of 2002" increased criminal penalties associated with white-collar crimes and conspiracies, recommended stronger sentencing guidelines, and specified that the failure to certify corporate financial reports is a criminal offense.

• SOX required a company's Chief Executive Officer to sign the company's tax return.

• SOX's sections called "Corporate Fraud Accountability Act of 2002" identified corporate fraud and records tampering as criminal offenses, revised sentencing guidelines, strengthened penalties, and enabled the SEC to temporarily freeze transactions for payments deemed "large" or "unusual."

In looking back at the Enron tragedy, it's hard to comprehend how a company could grow so fast and promise so much to so many and then completely collapse even faster. A useful insight as to how it happened was provided by Lynn Brewer, the Enron executive who blew the whistle, in the following passage from her foreword to a book written in 2003:[5]

> I know crisis. I've felt it breed through an organization one office, one individual at a time. I've seen how the presence of opportunity with supporting pressures and available validation creates an environment ripe for self-serving acts with unfathomable consequences.
>
> I know crisis. I've watched leaders so preoccupied with short-term appearances and the security of their current power base that they lose all capacity to distinguish what is right from what they believe may be justifiable. I've experienced the inertia of a large institution hurling itself into destruction as the fight to make right dies with determined avoidance of any conflict or murmur of transgression.
>
> I know lies. I've witnessed the posturing and manipulation of numbers, reports and financial records to defensibly mislead uninformed masses. I've observed first-hand how the need for money and capital can force subordination of intellectual honesty to practical pressures of delivering on expectations of empty promises. I've worked alongside good intentioned people who lose all capacity to acknowledge past blunders and wrongdoings for fear of what they know is inevitable.

5. Dwight Drake, "*Gutless Neglect: America's Biggest Money Crisis*" (Enterprise Actions 2003), p. i.

> I know these things. In fact, I have lived them. It was my abhorrence of these realities that prompted me to do what I did at Enron. It is the continued presence of these realities that has driven me to devote my career to improving the position and practice of integrity in our corporate world and capital markets.

3. RESPONSIBLE PARTIES

There are many who play a role in the audit process. Each bears some responsibility for the quality of the process and the ultimate outcomes.

a. Shareholders

Although not required, most public companies give their shareholders the right to ratify the board's selection of the outside auditor. It's generally considered a best practice of corporate governance. Although the dynamics of the proxy process nearly always result in a near unanimous ratification, many claim that the process of seeking ratification promotes the all-important independence perception and establishes a stronger accountability link between investors and the company's auditor.

b. Board Members

The board of directors is the ultimate management authority in a corporation and is charged with playing a key oversight role in the audit process. This is done through an audit committee of the board, which consists of board members (usually no more than six) who are independent outside directors. At least one audit committee member must qualify as a financial expert. The responsibilities of the audit committee typically include overseeing and monitoring of various audit-related challenges, including:

- The financial reporting and disclosure process
- The selection of accounting policies and principles
- Outside auditor issues (hiring, performance, and independence)
- Regulatory compliance
- Internal control issues and challenges
- Internal audit practices, procedures and personnel
- Risk management practices and procedures
- Ethics and whistleblower issues

While the oversight duties assigned to an audit committee are impressive on their face, the tough question in nearly every situation is: How much can realistically be expected from a group of independent outsiders who are engaged fulltime in unrelated activities? Robert Jaedicke, chairman of Enron's audit committee, provided a sobering, insightful answer to this question in his Congressional testimony before the Subcommittee on Oversight and Investigations on February 7, 2002. Jandicke stated:

> I am the Chairman of the Audit Committee of the Board of Directors of Enron Corporation. I have held that position since the mid-1980s.
>
> Let me tell you about my background. I joined the faculty of the Stanford Graduate School of Business in 1961. I served as Dean of the Business School from 1983 until 1990. At that time, I returned to the faculty of the Business School, and retired in 1992.
>
> What happened at Enron has been described as a systemic failure. As it pertains to the Board, I see it instead as a cautionary reminder of the limits of a director's role. We served as directors of what was then the seventh largest corporation in America. Our job as directors was necessarily limited by the nature of Enron's enterprise—which was worldwide in scope, employed more than 20,000 people, and engaged in a vast array of trading and development activities. By force of necessity, we could not know personally all of the employees. As we now know, key employees whom we thought we knew proved to be dishonest or disloyal.
>
> The very magnitude of the enterprise requires directors to confine their control to the broad policy decisions. That we did this is clear from the record. At the meetings of the Board and its committees, in which all of us participated, these questions were considered and decided on the basis of summaries, reports and corporate records. These we were entitled to rely upon. Directors are also, as the Report recognizes, entitled to rely on the honesty and integrity of their subordinates and advisers until something occurs to put them on suspicion that something is wrong.
>
> We did all of this, and more. Sadly, despite all that we tried to do, in the face of all the assurances we received, we had no cause for suspicion until it was too late.

Each Enron director was paid approximately $350,000 in annual compensation benefits for services as a director. Many questioned the plausibility of the directors' "see-no-evil, hear-no-evil" defense. The directors were charged with ignoring many red flags, including multiple warnings from Enron's outside auditors that Enron's accounting practices were "high-risk," "pushing the limits," and "at the edge" of acceptable practice. Ultimately, the directors settled the shareholders' legal claims by contributing $13 million to a $168 million settlement. It was widely reported that the Enron directors' $13 million personal contribution to the settlement represented about 10 percent of the profits realized by the directors from trading in Enron stock in the months leading up to the energy giant's collapse.

c. Officers

The officers of the company are in a much stronger position than the audit committee of the board to influence, for good or bad, the effectiveness of a company's accounting system and internal controls. As stated above, SOX recognized this by expanding the responsibilities and personal liabilities of company officers, principally the chief executive officer (CEO) and chief financial officer (CFO).

SOX section 302 requires such officers to submit a statement that accompanies the audit report and certifies that "based on such officer's knowledge, the financial statements, and other financial information included in the report, fairly present in all material respects the financial condition and results of operations of the issuer as of, and for, the period presented in the report." Certification of false or inaccurate statements can result in harsh personal consequences for such officers, including substantial fines, penalties, criminal sanctions (including jail time), costly civil and criminal litigation, and potentially being barred by the SEC from ever serving as an officer or director of a public company. The rationale for such SOX provisions is that enhanced responsibilities and personal risks for the top executives will create strong top-down pressure on officers, managers, operating personnel, and internal auditors to maintain quality accounting systems and internal controls.

d. Auditors

An auditing firm that issues a clean opinion in connection with false or misleading statements often has legal exposure to others who suffer losses in the course of trading the company's stock. In the case of Enron, such exposure ended up toppling Arthur Andersen, one of the premier firms of its time. The primary source of liability is the securities laws. Since the auditors often had no prior knowledge of the defects in the statements, the threshold question in many cases is: What level of culpability must a plaintiff prove to establish auditor liability when the auditor is duped or unknowingly fails to detect a material defect in the statements?

In *Ernst & Ernst v. Hockfelder*,[6] the Supreme Court held that something more than ordinary negligence was required in an action by investors under SEC Rule 10b-5[7] who alleged that they were injured as a result of trading in the company's stock in reliance on false statements. The case did not involve a proxy or registration statement. In that case, the victims of a fraudulent Ponzi scheme alleged that Ernst & Ernst had aided and abetted the perpetrator of the fraud by negligently conducting audits over many years. In rejecting the SEC's argument for a negligence standard, the Court stated:

> The argument simply ignores the use of the words "manipulate," "device," and "contrivance," terms that make unmistakable a congressional intent to proscribe a type of conduct quite different from negligence. Use of the word "manipulate" is especially significant. It

6. 425 U.S. 185 (1976)

7. Chief Justice Rehnquist once described Rule 10b-5 as "a judicial oak which has grown from little more than a legislative acorn." Blue Chip Stamps v. Manor Drug Stores, 421 U.S. 723, 737 (1975). The Rule makes it "unlawful for any person, directly or indirectly, by the use of any means or instrumentality of interstate commerce, or of the mails or of any facility of any national securities exchange, (a) To employ any device, scheme, or artifice to defraud, (b) To make any untrue statement of a material fact or to omit to state a material fact necessary in order to make the statements made, in the light of the circumstances under which they were made, not misleading, or (c) To engage in any act, practice, or course of business which operates or would operate as a fraud or deceit upon any person, in connection with the purchase or sale of any security."

> is and was virtually a term of art when used in connection with securities markets. It connotes intentional or willful conduct designed to deceive or defraud investors by controlling or artificially affecting the price of securities. 425 U.S. at 193.

Although the Court in *Ernst & Ernst* left open the issue of whether recklessness would support a 10b-5 claim, the federal circuit courts have answered the question by uniformly holding that reckless behavior by an auditing firm is actionable under 10b-5.[8]

A negligence standard will apply when the defective financial statements are part of a registration statement for a securities offering. Rule 10b-5 is not the governing source of liability when a registration statement is involved. Section 11 of the Securities Act establishes negligence as the applicable test in such a situation.

The question is open on whether the 10b-5 scienter requirement disappears – that is, will ordinary negligence work? – when a claim is made under section 14(a) of the Securities Exchange Act based on a false or misleading proxy statement. In footnote 5 of its decision in *Virginia Bankshares, Inc. v. Sandberg,*[9] the Supreme Court stated that it was reserving the question of "whether scienter was necessary for liability generally under § 14(a)." Lower courts are split on the issue. In *Gould v. American-Hawaiian S. S. Co.*,[10] the Third Circuit held that ordinary negligence was the requisite standard by comparing a section 14(a) violation to a false or misleading registration statement claim under section 11 and concluding that the "parallel between the two sections would strongly support adoption of negligence as the standard." In contrast, the Sixth Circuit has held that 10b-5 scienter was the appropriate standard for an accountant who aided in the preparation of misleading financial statements in a proxy statement.[11] After observing that an "accountant's potential liability for relatively minor mistakes would be enormous under the negligence standard," the Sixth Circuit said that it saw "no reason for a different standard of liability for accountants under the proxy provisions than under 10b-5."[12]

4. EXAMPLE AUDIT AND INTERNAL CONTROLS OPINION

Following is the opinion that PricewaterhouseCoopers LLP issued in connection with Caterpillar Inc.'s financial statements for the year ending 2012. Note how it describes the scope of the opinion and references generally accepted accounting principles, the materiality concept, inherent internal control limitations, test basis examinations, the standards of the Public Company Accounting Oversight Board, and the internal control criteria of the *Internal Control - Integrated Framework* issued by the Committee of Sponsoring Organizations of the Treadway Commission.

---

8. See *Hollinger v. Titan Capital Corp.*, 914 F.2d 1564 (9th Cir. 1990), and various circuit cases cited in footnote 6 of that opinion.

9. 501 U.S. 1083 (1991).

10. 535 F.2d 761 (3rd Cir. 1976).

11. Adams v. Standard Knitting Mills, 623 F.2d 422 (6th Cir. 1980).

12. 623 F.2d at 429.

REPORT OF INDEPENDENT REGISTERED PUBLIC ACCOUNTING FIRM

To the Board of Directors and Stockholders of Caterpillar Inc.:

In our opinion, the accompanying consolidated statement of financial position and the related consolidated statements of results of operations, comprehensive income, changes in stockholders' equity, and of cash flow, including pages A-5 through A-97, present fairly, in all material respects, the financial position of Caterpillar Inc. and its subsidiaries at December 31, 2012, 2011 and 2010, and the results of their operations and their cash flows for each of the three years in the period ended December 31, 2012 in conformity with accounting principles generally accepted in the United States of America. Also in our opinion, the Company maintained, in all material respects, effective internal control over financial reporting as of December 31, 2012, based on criteria established in *Internal Control - Integrated Framework* issued by the Committee of Sponsoring Organizations of the Treadway Commission (COSO). The Company's management is responsible for these financial statements, for maintaining effective internal control over financial reporting and for its assessment of the effectiveness of internal control over financial reporting, included in Management's Report on Internal Control Over Financial Reporting appearing on page A-3. Our responsibility is to express opinions on these financial statements and on the Company's internal control over financial reporting based on our integrated audits. We conducted our audits in accordance with the standards of the Public Company Accounting Oversight Board (United States). Those standards require that we plan and perform the audits to obtain reasonable assurance about whether the financial statements are free of material misstatement and whether effective internal control over financial reporting was maintained in all material respects. Our audits of the financial statements included examining, on a test basis, evidence supporting the amounts and disclosures in the financial statements, assessing the accounting principles used and significant estimates made by management, and evaluating the overall financial statement presentation. Our audit of internal control over financial reporting included obtaining an understanding of internal control over financial reporting, assessing the risk that a material weakness exists, and testing and evaluating the design and operating effectiveness of internal control based on the assessed risk. Our audits also included performing such other procedures as we considered necessary in the circumstances. We believe that our audits provide a reasonable basis for our opinions.

A company's internal control over financial reporting is a process designed to provide reasonable assurance regarding the reliability of financial reporting and the preparation of financial statements for external purposes in accordance with generally accepted accounting principles. A company's internal control over financial reporting includes those policies and procedures that (i) pertain to the maintenance of records that, in reasonable detail, accurately and fairly reflect the transactions and dispositions of the assets of the company; (ii) provide reasonable assurance that transactions are recorded as necessary to permit preparation of financial statements in accordance with generally accepted accounting principles, and that receipts and expenditures of the company are being made only in accordance with authorizations of management and directors of the company; and (iii) provide reasonable assurance regarding prevention or timely detection of unauthorized acquisition, use, or disposition of the company's assets that could have a material effect on the financial statements.

Because of its inherent limitations, internal control over financial reporting may not prevent or detect misstatements. Also, projections of any evaluation of effectiveness to future periods are subject to the risk that controls may become inadequate because of changes in conditions, or that the degree of compliance with the policies or procedures may deteriorate.

As described in Management's Report on Internal Control Over Financial Reporting, management has excluded ERA Mining Machinery Limited, including its wholly-owned subsidiary Zhengzhou Siwei Mechanical Manufacturing Co., Ltd., commonly known as Siwei, from its assessment of internal control over financial reporting as of December 31, 2012 because Siwei was acquired by the Company in May 2012. We have also excluded Siwei from our audit of internal control over financial reporting. Siwei is a wholly owned subsidiary of Caterpillar Inc. whose total assets and total sales and revenues represent approximately 1 percent and less than 1 percent, respectively, of the related consolidated financial statement amounts as of and for the year ended December 31, 2012.

/s/PricewaterhouseCoopers LLP

Peoria, Illinois

February 19, 2013

STUDENT PROBLEM 2-1

As the financial statements of Caterpillar Inc. (set forth above) indicate, the book value of the stockholders' equity of Caterpillar Inc. increased from $10.864 billion on December 31, 2010 to $17.582 billion on December 31, 2012, a 62 percent growth in value. Based solely on your review of the statements, what factors contributed most to this impressive (extraordinary?) growth in value over a 24-month period?

STUDENT PROBLEM 2-2

Refer to the financial statements of Caterpillar Inc. set forth above. Assume that Caterpillar Inc. determines that these statements need to be changed to account for the four hypothetical unrecorded transactions or adjustments described below. How would the recording of each transaction change specific line items in each of the financial statements? Treat each transaction separately, assume each transaction is material, and ignore tax considerations.

1. The board of Caterpillar Inc. declared an additional shareholder cash dividend of $1.2 billion in December 2012 that is payable on January 15, 2013.

2. Caterpillar Inc. overstated the amount of its inventories on December 31, 2012 by $3.2 billion and understated its cost of goods sold by a like amount. It must adjust its statements for such error.

3. Caterpillar Inc. failed to record a bonus of $2.5 million earned by its CEO in 2012 and payable in March 2013.

4. Caterpillar Inc. failed to record an equipment cash sale of $1.2 million that occurred in November 2012. The cost of the equipment sold was $900,000. Such cost was included in the inventory balance on December 31, 2012.

CHAPTER 3

Core Quantitative and Leveraging Concepts

A. FUNDAMENTAL BUSINESS FACTORS

A lawyer should understand basic business concepts. Without such an understanding, a lawyer will struggle to comprehend business objectives and participate in intelligent business-focused conversations. Knowledge of sophisticated accounting or financial principles is not necessary. What is required is a working knowledge of those basic concepts that drive all businesses: income, cash flow, leverage, opportunity costs, depreciation, return on equity, etc. The following simple description of a tiny company's first three years of operation is designed to illustrate 10 important business concepts.

Party Time Inc.

Jane knows food and is a party animal. After much thought and analysis, she quit her job at the end of 2008 to start her own catering business in early 2009. She formed a corporation named Party Time, Inc., contributed $60,000 for the stock, and started business on January 1. Initially, Party Time's targeted clients were high-income couples who wanted the very best when they threw a party.

During the first year of operation, Jane was Party Time's sole employee and handled every detail of every event. When she needed assistance, Party Time hired temporary help for a flat hourly rate of $13. Party Time rented a small commercial kitchen and used $50,000 of its capital to buy a van and essential equipment items.

In 2009, Party Time's gross client billings totaled $100,000, of which $80,000 was collected during the year. The uncollected $20,000 represented billings from the busy year-end holiday season that were collected during the first two months of 2010. Party Time's expenses in 2009 totaled $81,700, of which $11,000 remained unpaid at year-end. Key expenses included rent, food, advertising, temporary help, and gas. Jane took no compensation from the company during 2009.

1. INCOME

What was Party Time's income in 2009? Income is an essential concept of business, but it has different meanings based on what it is measuring. The starting point for most business owners is operating income, which is the earnings from the business before any reductions for interest, income taxes, depreciation, and amortization. It is commonly referred to as "EBITDA." EBITDA measures the profitability of the company's operations. Party Time's EBITDA in 2009 was $18,300, the excess of its total billings of $100,000 over its operating expenses of $81,700.

EBITA

Exhibit 1
Party Time Inc. Income Statements

	2009	2010	2011 No-Debt	2011 Debt
Revenues	$ 100,000	$ 180,000	$ 640,000	$ 640,000
Expenses				
Rent	$ 18,000	$ 18,000	$ 18,000	$ 18,000
Food	25,000	39,600	137,300	137,300
Advertising	22,000	22,000	22,000	22,000
Salaries	-	50,000	275,000	275,000
Payroll Taxes	-	4,500	24,750	24,750
Gas	1,100	1,900	7,500	7,500
Help	14,000	22,000	4,800	4,800
Misc. Expenses	1,600	2,900	3,400	3,400
Total	$ 81,700	$ 160,900	$ 492,750	$ 492,750
Operating Income	$ 18,300	$ 19,100	$ 147,250	$ 147,250
Depreciation	10,000	10,000	42,000	42,000
Interest Expense	-	-	-	13,500
Income Before Taxes	$ 8,300	$ 9,100	$ 105,250	$ 91,750
Income Taxes	1,245	1,365	24,297	19,445
Net Income	$ 7,055	$ 7,735	$ 80,953	$ 72,305

The next income definition is net income before taxes. This definition factors in all expenses except the income taxes that the company must pay on its earnings. It is calculated by reducing the EBITDA by expenses for interest, depreciation, and amortization. Party Time had no interest expense in 2009 because it had no debt, nor did it have any amortizable assets. But it did own a van and equipment that will wear out over time and will need to be replaced. This wearing out cost is referred to as depreciation. It is not an expense that is based on a cash outlay; it reflects the diminution in value of assets owned by the business. Since the equipment purchased by Party Time for $50,000 at the beginning of 2009 was expected to wear out over a useful life of five years, Party Time's annual depreciation expense for that equipment was $10,000. Thus, Party Time's net income before taxes in 2009 was $8,300, its EBITDA of $18,300 less its depreciation expense of $10,000.

The third income component is net income after taxes. This component factors in the income taxes that need to be paid on the company's income. At a federal corporate tax rate of 15 percent on the first $50,000 of earnings, Party Time's income tax liability on its $8,300 of earnings in 2009 was $1,245. Thus, its net income after taxes equaled $7,055. All three of the income concepts described above are reflected in Party Time's income statement for 2009 (Exhibit 1, 2009 column).

2. *CASH FLOW*

Cash flow is a concept different than income, although it is heavily influenced by the income of the business. Cash flow is just what its name implies; it measures the cash that goes in and out of the business. The starting point for the cash flow analysis is the net income after taxes of the business, which was $7,055 in 2009.

Exhibit 2
Party Time Inc. Cash Flow Summary

Beginning Cash	$ 60,000
Plus:	
Net Income	$ 7,055
Accounts Payable Increase	11,000
Income Tax Payable Increase	1,245
Depreciation	10,000
Total Additions	$ 29,300
Less:	
Equipment Purchases	$ 50,000
Accounts Receivable Increase	20,000
Total Reductions	$ 70,000
Net Change	(40,700)
Ending Cash	$ 19,300

To arrive at the cash flow, this income number must be increased for expenses that did not require any cash outlay during 2009, which for Party Time included the depreciation expense of $10,000, the $11,000 of operating expenses that remained unpaid at the end of the year (typically referred to as accounts payable increase), and the income tax liability of $1,245 that was not paid until the following year.

For cash flow purposes, the net income must be decreased by the $20,000 of gross billings that were not actually collected during the year (the accounts receivable increase) and the $50,000 that was used to purchase the van and equipment. Exhibit 2 is Party Time's Cash Flow Summary for 2009.

As Exhibit 2 indicates, even though Party Time showed a net after-tax income of $7,055 in 2009, its cash resources plummeted from $60,000 at the beginning of the year to $19,300 at year-end. This is why many say "cash is king" in start-up operations and why undercapitalization is the reason so many promising businesses fail. The income statement and cash flow summary show the activity of the company over a given period, here calendar year 2009. This activity is reflected in the balance sheets of Party Time at the beginning and end of the year (Exhibit 3), each of which provides a snapshot of the assets and liabilities of the company at a specific time.

Exhibit 3
Party Time Inc. Balance Sheet

	As of 1/1/2009	As of 12/31/2009
Assets		
Cash	$ 60,000	$ 19,300
Accounts Receivable		20,000
Total Current Assets		$ 39,300
Equipment		50,000
Less: Accum. Depreciation		(10,000)
Total Assets	$ 60,000	$ 79,300
Liabilities		
Accounts Payable		$ 11,000
Taxes Payable		1,245
Total Current Liabilities		$ 12,245
Owner Equity		
Contributed Capital	$ 60,000	$ 60,000
Retained Earnings		7,055
Total Owner Equity		$ 67,055
Total Liabilities and Equity	$ 60,000	$ 79,300

3. *CURRENT AND QUICK ASSET RATIOS*

A business needs to be able to meet its obligations as they become due. A popular technique for measuring a business' capacity to timely fund its obligations is to compare the company's current assets with its current liabilities. Current assets are those assets that will be converted to cash within one year, and current liabilities are those debts that must be paid within a year. The number obtained by dividing the current assets by the current liabilities is known as the "current ratio." Party Time's current ratio at the end of 2009 was 3.2, strong by any standard.

Another ratio that is often used is known as a "quick ratio" or "acid test" ratio. It is the same as the current ratio, except that inventories are excluded from current assets in making the calculation. Since Party Time had no inventories, its quick ratio would be the same as its current ratio. A company that carries substantial inventories typically will have a quick ratio that is much smaller than its current ratio. Depending how quickly such a company sells and replenishes ("turns" is the verb often used) its inventories, the quick ratio may be the best indicator of the company's capacity to timely discharge its cash flow obligations.

4. *Opportunity Costs*

Beyond the costs actually incurred in operating the business, business owners must always consider the opportunity costs of any decision they make. Opportunity costs are the benefits that are lost because a particular course is pursued.

In this case, Jane chose to form a new business that generated a bottom line profit of $7,055 in 2009 and consumed a large portion of the $60,000 that she contributed to the business. She worked hard in 2009, but drew no salary or income from the business. This course of action triggered at least three opportunity costs. First, if she had left the $60,000 that she invested in the company in a bank certificate of deposit that earns five percent annually, she would have earned $3,000 of interest in 2009, and she would have had all of her cash at year end. Second, if she had stayed at her old job, she would have earned a salary and other benefits valued at $75,000 in 2009. Third, if she had remained at her old job, she would have racked up another year of experience and seniority. These are significant opportunity costs that she incurred in starting the business.

Smart business decisions are made by factoring in all costs, both real and opportunity. Standard financial statements do not reflect or account for opportunity costs. And often it isn't advisable to approach an opportunity cost analysis based solely on specific numbers. For example, when Jane decided to make her move in 2009, she knew that she would risk $60,000 of capital, would work hard in 2009 for no pay, and would give up her secure job and all the benefits that it promised. Any short-term quantitative analysis of those opportunity costs likely would have encouraged Jane to sit tight and count her blessings. Many business plans never come to fruition because the short-term pain of making the move and taking the risks (the opportunity costs) is perceived as being too great. But in this case, Jane weighed these known opportunity costs against the opportunity benefits of doing something she loved and potentially building a valuable going concern that she would own. Although her numbers in 2009 were nothing to write home about, she knew momentum was building and the numbers would improve going forward. And they did.

5. *Fixed vs. Variable Expenses*

Through word of mouth, the demand for Party Time's custom catering services grew rapidly in 2010. By mid-year, Jane was regularly turning away more business than she accepted. As her revenue (her top line) number grew, she noticed that her bottom line income number grew at a faster rate. This was because certain key expenses – rent and advertising – were fixed in amount and did not increase with the growth in revenues. Other expenses, such as food and temporary labor, were variable with the revenues.

The ability to leverage fixed expenses is very important in the growth cycle of any business. Proportionately high fixed costs permit a greater leveraging as the costs are spread over a greater number of units with volume increases and the fixed cost per unit drops. In 2010, Jane grew Party Time's total revenues to $180,000, but profitability grew fast enough to allow Jane to draw personal compensation benefits of $50,000 from the business and still drop $7,735 to the bottom line as income. Party Time's income statement for 2010 is in Exhibit 1, 2010 column.

6. ECONOMIES OF SCALE

Although Jane was pleased with the activity in 2010, she was frustrated with the work she was being forced to turn away. Many of her clients owned or ran businesses or professional practices, and she was constantly being offered lucrative opportunities to cater business events. She was forced to turn down all but the smallest of these jobs because of her limited personnel and her one-truck operation. She soon discovered that the economy of scale of her business was not large enough to accommodate the kind of growth she wanted.

Every business must be geared to operate at a given level of activity. Its resources and planning are based on a defined level of activity, commonly referred to as its economy of scale. Some businesses are very "scalable," which means they can easily adjust their economy of scale to accommodate more volume. On the other end of the scalability spectrum are those businesses that must make significant additional investments and take on much greater risks to build an expanded economy of scale.

Jane quickly determined that she needed to build a new economy of scale to meet the expanded demand for her services. After careful analysis, she decided to purchase and outfit three large trucks and to hire three full-time "event lieutenants," each of whom would be paid compensation and benefits equal to $50,000 a year. Jane easily identified the best candidates from a talented pool of temporary assistants. She knew that each of the three candidates adored the business, would work hard, and would jump at the opportunity to have a full-time job that paid well. Jane's new economy of scale required an additional investment of $180,000 to cover the costs of the trucks and equipment and the necessary working capital to fund the expansion. Jane dipped deeper into her savings and made the additional investment.

Jane's expanded economy of scale was in full swing by the start of 2011. It all worked. Jane was able to effectively use her lieutenants to leverage her personal touch across all major events. As Party Time began catering larger corporate events, its reputation ballooned in all markets. Its gross revenues grew to $640,000 in 2011.

7. LEVERAGE AND RETURN ON EQUITY

Jane's expansion plan required an additional investment of $180,000, bringing her total investment in Party Time to $240,000. And it all paid off. In 2011, she was able to pay herself $75,000 from the business and still generate a bottom line net profit of $80,953, as indicated by Party Time's 2011 income statement (See Exhibit 1, 2011 No-Debt column). This net profit represented a

33.73 percent annual return on her total equity investment of $240,000.

Suppose that Jane did not fund her expansion plan with more private investment capital. Assume instead that she went to her local bank, presented her operating history and future plans, and secured a bank line of credit for $180,000 at an annual interest cost of 7.5 percent. Jane would be spared the burden of having to come up with more personal capital, but Party Time would have a new annual interest expense of $13,500.

This interest expense, net of income tax impacts, would reduce Party Time's net income in 2011 to $72,305, as illustrated in Party Time's revised income statement for 2011 (see Exhibit 1, 2011 Debt column). Although the net income would be reduced by the net after-tax cost of the interest expense, the yield on Jane's equity investment would skyrocket. With this debt leverage, her original equity investment of $60,000 would generate an annual yield in 2011 of $72,305, more than 120 percent. This is known as positive leverage. The business operations created the opportunity to leverage the existing equity by generating a yield off borrowed funds that far exceeded the cost of the funds. This leverage often is the key to maximizing business equity. It's business 101.

8. DEBT-TO-EQUITY RATIO

The potential of debt leverage encourages some to overdo it. The ratio of the debt to the equity of the business must be reasonable for business and tax purposes. Reasonableness is measured by a debt-to-equity ratio, which is determined by dividing the company's debt by the equity of the business. Sometimes the ratio is based on all the debt of the business; other times it includes only the long-term debt.

There is no mandated acceptable ratio. Debt-to-equity ratios vary widely among industries and particular businesses. Generally (and I really mean generally), a ratio of less than 5-to-1 is considered reasonable, and any ratio in excess of 10-to-1 is usually suspect. If Jane had used the bank line to finance her expansion plan, the book value of the owner's equity on the company's balance sheet at the end of 2011 would equal $147,095. This is calculated by increasing the owner's equity balance at the end of 2009 (Exhibit 3) by the net retained income in 2010 and 2011 (Exhibit 1, Debt Column). Thus, even with a bank line of $180,000, her debt-to-equity ratio would have been less than 2-to-1, reasonable by any standard.

9. GROSS MULTIPLIERS AND CAPITALIZATION RATES

By the end of 2011, many were aware of Jane's success. Party Time had a superb reputation, and Jane was known as the inspiration behind its success. A profitable high-end regional restaurant chain (Chain) had been planning a move into the corporate catering business. Chain was faced with a choice. It could endure the start-up expense and hassle of trying to compete with Party Time's reputation and Jane's golden touch, or it could try to buy Party Time and make Jane part of its team.

Chain's management decided that a purchase would make sense if the purchased operation would generate a pre-tax operating yield of 13 percent on the price paid for the business. This is known as the capitalization rate, the rate used to determine the purchase price based on a known EBITDA.

Party Time's EBITDA in 2011 was $147,250 (Exhibit 1, 2011 Debt column). Dividing this amount by the desired capitalization rate of 13 percent produced a purchase price of $1,132,692. If Jane accepted Chain's offer of this amount for the business, she would pay off the $180,000 bank line, pay her tax hit, put the rest in her pocket, and negotiate a lucrative employment contract with Chain. Sometimes the capitalization rate is expressed as an equivalent income multiple. They are two sides of the same coin. In this case, an EBITDA income of $147,250 was the basis of a purchase price of $1,132,692 based on a 13 percent capitalization rate. This represents an income multiple of 7.69 (147,250/1,132,692). Thus, specifying an EBITDA income multiple of 7.69 is the equivalent of specifying a capitalization rate of 13 percent.

10. Goodwill and Going Concern Value

Under the foregoing analysis, the corporate equity owned by Jane at the time of sale had a value of approximately $953,000, after the purchase price of $1,132,692 was reduced by the $180,000 bank line of credit balance. But, as indicated above, the book value of Jane's equity on the company's balance sheet at the end of 2011 was only $147,095. Valuing the business' equity on the basis of the earnings power of the operation produced a value that was many times greater than the equity book value derived from the assets and liabilities of the company. This excess value, which is huge for many companies, is known as goodwill and going concern value. It recognizes that Jane has built an ongoing, profitable operation that has valued customers and employees and a coveted market reputation. A large, ever-growing goodwill and going concern value is the ultimate goal of all operating businesses.

Student Problem 3-1

Refer to the financial statements of Caterpillar Inc. in Section D of Chapter 2 and the related clarifying points included in that section.

1. Based on such financial statements, what was Caterpillar Inc.'s:

- Current ratio at the end of 2012?
- Quick ratio at the end of 2012?
- Increases or decreases in its cash position in 2010, 2011 and 2012.
- Total debt-to-equity ratio at the end of 2012?

2. What was Caterpillar's EBITDA for 2011 and 2012? Refer to its Income Statements and Cash Flow Statements for these periods and assume that Goodwill Impairment Charges are a relevant factor in computing its EBITDA.

3. Assume Caterpillar Inc. could be sold for a price determined by applying a 12.5 percent capitalization rate to the average of its EBITDA for 2011 and 2012. What would be the purchase price?

B. LEVERAGING DEBT

1. BUSINESS DEBT BASICS

As we saw with Jane's catering business above, bank debt enabled her to expand her business to a new level without any additional capital out of her pocket. Although the interest cost of the debt reduced the bottom line net income of her enterprise, the debt catapulted the yield on the capital that she had invested in the business and freed her other capital to be diversified into other investments or businesses. Ongoing debt leverage is the norm for nearly all successful businesses. Creditor-debtor relationships are created regularly to fund the enterprise, finance specific transactions, and generate a yield on investable assets.

Each such relationship triggers an interest cost. Interest is the cost that is paid for the temporary use of another party's money. The amount of the interest cost depends on the interest rate charged and the length of time the money is used. Although advertisements often tout interest-free financing, it's usually just a signal that the interest burden of the financing has been buried in the cost of the product. In business, something for nothing doesn't work. The use of money is no exception.

A lawyer should understand the basic concepts and vocabulary of common creditor-debtor business transactions. Following are descriptions of five transactions that illustrate many such concepts and the related vocabulary. Bonds, a powerful debt tool for major corporations and government entities, are discussed separately in the following subsection.

Carla's Certificate of Deposit

Carla's business has generated $100,000 of cash that she wants to safely invest for the next twelve months. She plans to use the cash in the following year to finance an expansion of her office and the hiring of an additional salesperson. She purchases a one-year, $100,000 certificate of deposit from her bank that will pay interest at an annual rate of 3 percent. In this transaction, Carla is the creditor and her bank is the debtor.

Certificate of Deposit (CD). This is a time deposit that is payable at the end of a specific length of time ("term"). Terms can range from seven days to ten years. A CD typically pays a fixed rate of interest that usually is higher than rates paid on other types of deposit accounts. The CD requires Carla to pay a penalty to withdraw funds from the CD before the end of the designated term.

Simple Interest. This is the interest paid only on the principal amount deposited by Carla. It does not reflect any interest that is earned on any interest accumulated in the account. A straight 3 percent on Carla's $100,000 deposit would generate $3,000 of simple interest over the twelve month term.

Compound Interest. This is interest paid on both the principal deposited by Carla and interest accumulated in the account. For example, if Carla's CD specified that interest would be compounded semiannually, Carla's CD would earn $1,500 of interest ($100,000 at 3 percent annual rate for half a year) during the first six months and would earn $1,522.50 of interest (($101,500 at 3 percent annual rate for half a year) during the second six months of the CD. The amount of the compound interest is a function of the designated compounding period and the length of the deposit. A two-year deposit that compounds interest quarterly will generate more interest than one that compounds semiannually.

Nominal or Quoted Rate. This is the rate quoted by the bank on the deposit, irrespective of any compounding impacts. This would be 3 percent in Carla's situation.

Effective or Annual Percentage Rate (APR). This is the rate at which interest is earned over the term, inclusive of all compounding impacts. With semiannual compounding, Carla would earn a total of $3,022.50 of interest, an effective rate of 3.023 percent.

Accumulated Interest vs. Accumulated Balance. The accumulated interest is the total interest earned on the deposit over a given time. The accumulated balance is the total of the principal deposit and accumulated interest at a point in time. At the end of six months, Carla's CD would have $1,500 of accumulated interest and an accumulated balance of $101,500. Determining the accumulated balance via a formula[1] can be challenging when there are multiple compounding periods. The easiest approach is to ignore the formula and just use a compound interest table (they are all over the Internet) or an Internet compound interest calculator (e.g., www.calculator.net).

Maturity Value. This is the accumulated balance at the end of the designated term of the CD, the time at which the CD matures and is paid. The maturity value in Carla's CD at the end of the one-year term would be $103,022.50.

Federal Deposit Insurance Corporation (FDIC). This is an independent agency of the United States government that protects depositors against the loss of their insured deposits (checking, savings and money market accounts and CDs) if an FDIC-insured bank fails. Protection is available for each depositor up to $250,000 (per bank). This protection is backed by the full faith and credit of the United States.

Ned's Equipment Note

Ned needs to buy a $200,000 piece of equipment to expand his business. He has secured from his bank a loan for $200,000, payable in equal payments of principal and interest over a sixty-month term. The loan is secured by a perfected security interest on the equipment and Ned's personal guarantee.

Promissory Note. This is a written, signed, unconditional promise to pay a stated sum of money in accordance with the terms specified in the note. The note signed by Ned would set forth the terms that govern the loan he has secured from the bank.

Principal Balance. This is the amount that Ned borrows from the bank -

1. The common formula is $P \times (1\text{-}i)^t$ where P is the principal, i is the interest rate, and t is the number of time periods.

$200,000.

Unpaid Principal Balance. This is the portion of the loan's principal balance that remains unpaid at a specified time. For example, at the end of twenty months, the unpaid balance on Ned's note would be $144,046. At the end of forty months, the unpaid balance would be $74,565.

Fixed Rate. This means that the rate on the loan is fixed (7 percent in Ned's case) for the life of the loan.

Installment Payment or Periodic Payment. This is the fixed amount that Ned will have to pay each month for sixty months to fully repay the principal balance of the loan and the monthly interest that is charged each month on the unpaid balance at the fixed rate during the term of the loan. In Ned's case, the required monthly payment will be $3,960. This payment can be easily calculated with a financial or online calculator (just input the principal balance, interest rate, and number of monthly payments). A portion of each $3,960 monthly payment will represent the repayment of the principal balance, and the remaining portion will represent the interest charge for the last month on the unpaid balance. Since the unpaid principal balance declines each month, the interest element will decline each month, and there will be a corresponding increase in the principal repayment element each month. For example, in month one, $1,167 of Ned's $3,960 payment will be interest and $2,793 will be principal; in month 30, $653 will be interest and $3,307 will be principal; and in month 50, $246 will be interest and $3,714 will be principal.

Amortization Schedule. This is a schedule that shows the interest and principal component of each payment over the term of the loan and the unpaid principal balance after each payment has been made. Ned will have sixty rows (one for each monthly payment) on his amortization schedule. An amortization schedule can easily be prepared on an Excel worksheet or through an online calculator, such as www.calculator.net. Ned's amortization schedule is set forth in Section F. of Chapter 15.

Fully Amortizing Loan. This term means that the payments on the loan have been structured to pay off the entire principal balance and all interest charges over the term of the loan. Ned has such a loan.

Balloon Payment Loan. This term means that the payments on the loan have been structured to not pay off the entire principal balance and all interest charges over the term of the loan. At the end of the loan term, a portion of the principal balance will remain unpaid and will need to be paid in full at that time (hence, a balloon payment). Suppose in Ned's case that the bank would not agree to a loan in excess of 36 months, but agreed that Ned could make monthly payments based on an amortization schedule of sixty months. Ned's payment would still be $3,960 and this would help his current case flow situation. But Ned's amortization schedule confirms that he must plan for a balloon payment of $88,462 at the end of 36 months.

Debt-to-Value Ratio. This ratio measures the principal balance of the loan against the value of the collateral (in this case, the $200,000 equipment). A loan of $200,000 in Ned's situation would produce a ratio of 100 percent. A loan of

$120,000 would yield a ratio of 60 percent, which would be considered safer from the bank's perspective and might provide a basis for a lower interest rate, a longer term, or no need for a personal guarantee (see below). The value of an equipment item generally will decline over time, but, so too, the principal balance of the loan will be declining in accordance with the amortization schedule as payments are made. The sharpness of these comparative descents often is a factor in setting the term of the loan

Default Events. These are designated events in the promissory note that constitute a default by the borrower. In Ned's case, these events likely would include failure to make any required payment, any bankruptcy or assignment for the benefit of creditors, and any sale or impairment of the equipment. Often the note specifies a cure or grace period, a limited period for the borrower to remedy the default. A penalty or extra interest charge is typical for any late payment.

Acceleration. This term refers to the creditor's right to accelerate the debt and demand that the unpaid principal balance and all accrued interest be paid immediately in the event of a default that is not timely cured. The debtor loses the right to pay the loan in installments.

Perfected Security Interest. Ned would grant to the bank a security interest in the equipment to secure his obligations under the promissory note. This would give the bank preferential rights to the equipment, including the right to seize and sell the equipment in the event of Ned's default. The bank's security interest would "attach" when the bank has given value (made the loan), Ned has acquired the equipment or the right to transfer the equipment as collateral for the loan, and the security interest has been "authenticated" by Ned signing a security agreement that grants the security interest (with all associated details) and defines the collateral. In order to protect its priorities to the collateral against third parties or in the event of Ned's bankruptcy, the bank would "perfect" its security interest in the equipment by filing a U.C.C. financing statement (which names the debtor and the secured party and defines the collateral) with the appropriate public office, usually a department in the Secretary of State's office.

Personal Guarantee. Suppose Ned operates his business through a corporation or a limited liability company (LLC). In such event, the corporation or LLC would be the party that buys the equipment, secures the loan, and grants the security interest, with no personal exposure for Ned. In order to more fully protect itself, the bank might require that Ned personally guarantee the entity's obligations under the promissory note. This guarantee would expose Ned's personal assets to the bank's rights under the loan and, as to the loan, would effectively override any liability protection provided by the corporation or LLC. Whether such a personal guarantee will be required in a given situation is a function of negotiation, which often is influenced by the financial strength of the entity, the debt-to-value ratio, and the relative bargaining power (based on competitive market conditions) of the parties.

Martha's Mortgage

Martha owns an LLC that is going to buy a building to house its growing business at a cost of $1.6 million. The LLC will put up $400,000 (25 percent) of the purchase price. The balance will be funded by a $1.2 million loan from a mortgage lender. The loan carries a fixed rate of 6 percent, requires monthly payments based on a 240-month (20 year) amortization schedule, and balloons (the balance comes due) at the end of ten years. Most of the concepts and terms described above in Ned's situation are directly applicable to this loan. But mention of a few additional concepts and terms is warranted because Martha's loan involves real estate.

Mortgage vs. Deed of Trust. Mortgages or deeds of trust, while technically different, share a common purpose: to grant the lender an interest in the real estate to secure the loan. If Martha defaults, the lender has the right to foreclose on the property – secure and sell the property and apply the sales proceeds to fully pay off its loan and recover any costs associated with the default. The balance of the sales proceeds (if any) would be paid to the debtor, Martha's LLC. Because of this common purpose, the term "mortgage" is often used to refer to both mortgages and deeds of trust. Technically, a mortgage is a document between two parties, where the owner of the real estate transfers an interest in the real estate to a lender to secure the performance of a debt. The document spells out the terms and conditions of the interest and the lender's rights with respect to the real estate. In contrast, a deed of trust is a document that involves three parties, the real estate owner who transfers an interest in the property to a neutral third-party trustee (e.g., a title company), who in turn exercises the rights under the deed of trust for the benefit of the designated beneficiary, the lender. The trustee is the legal owner of the property while the loan is outstanding, but the debtor remains the equitable owner. The mortgage or deed of trust must be recorded as a real estate document in the county in which the property is located in order to protect the interests of the lender against third parties. In comparing the two forms (mortgage vs. deed of trust), the deed of trust is the most common (only a handful of states remain mortgage-only states), a deed of trust often makes foreclosure possible without judicial involvement (a mortgage typically requires judicial foreclosure), and a deed of trust often grants broader rights for a debtor to pay all amounts due and "redeem" the property for a limited period following the foreclosure sale.

Recourse vs. Nonrecourse. Unlike Ned's equipment, Martha's real estate may go up in value over time. Although there are countless exceptions, historically real estate has been viewed as a growth asset, an effective hedge against inflation. In recognition of this reality, sometimes a nonrecourse real estate loan can be obtained. With such a loan, the lender looks solely to the real estate for protection in the event of default. If the proceeds from a foreclosure sale are insufficient to pay the amount due under the loan, the shortfall (often called a "deficiency") is not recoverable from the debtor on the loan. With a recourse loan, the debtor (Martha's LLC in this case) would remain liable for any deficiency, along with Martha if she has provided a personal guarantee. Obtaining nonrecourse financing typically requires some combination of a low loan-to-value ratio, a quality piece of real estate, a strong ownership team, and favorable market conditions.

Adjustable Rate. Some real estate loans are structured for the interest rate to change at a given time. In Martha's situation, the rate may remain fixed for the first five years and then adjust annually for the next five years based on changes in the twelve-month Treasury Average Index (MTA). There are various indexes that are commonly used. An adjustable rate loan often provides an opportunity for a lower rate during the initial term because the lender's long-term rate risk is reduced. Thus, if Martha anticipates that she may sell or refinance the building within the first five years or shortly after the five-year mark, an adjustable rate loan with a lower initial rate may be the preferred choice.

Closing Costs. The costs to close a real estate loan typically are much higher than other loans. Such costs usually include, among others, a title insurance premium (to insure the lender's interest in the real estate), appraisal fees, escrow fees, loan origination fees, potentially upfront points to the lender, document preparation fees, and recording fees.

Refinance. As a real estate property appreciates in value, often the owners will have the capacity to refinance the property for higher amounts. The refinancing proceeds are first used to pay off the unpaid balance on the old loan, and the remaining proceeds are distributed to the owners, usually tax free.

Construction Financing. Often a construction real estate loan is used to finance the construction of a new building. This loan permits the owner of the property to "draw" against the loan as needed to fund construction costs as they are incurred. Typically interest is charged monthly at a variable rate based on the amount of the loan drawn to date. This construction period interest is usually treated as a cost of the project that is rolled into the loan. When the building is completed, a "permanent" loan is obtained to pay off the construction loan. In some situations, the construction loan is designed to convert to a permanent loan.

Lucy's Line of Credit

In order to finance the growth of its business, Lucy's corporation obtains a line of credit from its bank that allows it to borrow at any time up to 90 percent of its current outstanding accounts receivable. If sales are strong and accounts receivable escalate to $3 million, the available line would grow to $2.7 million. If sales drop and outstanding accounts receivable contract to $2 million, the available line would drop to $1.8 million. The credit line is available for one year, with the parties anticipating that the line will be renewed ("rolled") annually if the business remains strong. Interest charges adjust monthly based on changes in the bank's prime lending rate. Payments of interest only are required each month. The bank's interest in the accounts receivable is protected by a security agreement and a properly filed U.C.C. financing statement (see Ned's note above).

Room on Line. This refers to the difference in the amount that may be drawn on the line and the amount that has actually been drawn at any point in time. This is the amount (the room) that remains to finance working capital needs of the business.

Lockbox. This refers to a service where the customers of a business send their payments to a post office box that is under the direction of the lending bank. It is sometimes called a "Remittance Service" or a "Remittance Process." Through this process the bank is assured that all accounts receivable collections will be applied to reduce the line of credit balance, thereby freeing up more room on the line or making certain that the outstanding balance on the line is reduced in accordance with any decline in receivable balances. The company manages its cash flow needs through fluctuations in the room on the line.

Covenants. Covenants are used in commercial loan agreements to require that the borrower take certain actions and perform at designated levels. Breach of a covenant can result in a termination of the line and a demand that the outstanding line balance be paid. Covenants can cover a host of items, including repayment terms, collateral protection obligations, reporting requirements, officer salary and owner distribution (or dividend) limitations, working capital requirements (current ratio or quick-asset ratio standards), debt limitations (debt-to-equity ratio standards), and more. Covenants are a function of negotiation, which is impacted by the strength of the business, the relative leverage of the parties, market conditions, and the policies of the lender.

Debt Service Coverage (DSC) Covenant. This covenant focuses on how the cash flow of the business for a given time frame compares to the business' total debt service obligations during the same time frame. For example, the covenant may require that the DSC ratio (cash flow divided by debt service) not be less than 1.15-to-1.

Prime Rate. The prime rate is the interest rate that a bank charges its most creditworthy customers. Often, a line of credit will charge a variable rate that is a few percentage points higher than its prime rate at a given time. Lucy's line, for example, mandated a rate equal to the bank's prime rate plus 2 percent. There is a general perception that the prime rate of most banks is about 3 percent (300 basis points) above the Federal Funds Rate (see below), which is the interest rate banks charge each other for overnight loans needed to meet reserve funding requirements.

Wall Street Journal Prime Rate. This is the base rate on corporate loans charged by at least 70 percent of the ten largest banks in the United States. Many lenders set their prime rates according to the Wall Street Journal prime rate. Interest rates on credit cards, auto loans and other consumer debt often fluctuate based on changes in this rate because so much consumer debt is tied to this rate. Changes in this rate are a function of decisions made by the largest banks and, thus, occur at regular intervals.

LIBOR. The is the London Interbank Offered Rate, which is the average interest rate that leading banks in London estimate they would be charged for borrowing from other banks. LIBOR is calculated for ten currencies and fifteen borrowing periods ranging from overnight to one year. It is published daily at 11:30 am (London time). Many financial institutions, mortgage lenders and credit card agencies set their rates based on LIBOR. Most believe that LIBOR is the primary benchmark for short-term interest rates throughout the world.

Federal Funds Rate. Federal funds transactions refer to short-term transactions in immediately available funds (balances at the Federal Reserve) between depository institutions (banks and others who maintain funds primarily from deposits by investors) and other institutions that maintain accounts at the Federal Reserve. The Federal Funds rate is the interest rate charged on such transactions, which can vary among depository institutions from day to day.

Duke's Letter of Credit

Duke's corporation (D Corp) has decided to buy its raw materials from a foreign supplier. Each shipment will be large, but the price per unit will be far better than any alternative available to D Corp. The foreign seller is unwilling to ship goods overseas on D Corp's promise that it will pay for the goods when they arrive. So too, D Corp is not willing to pay the price of a shipment until it has received confirmation that the goods have been properly finished and shipped. A bank letter of credit is the answer in this situation and countless others like it.

A letter of credit (LC) is a written promise from D Corp's bank to pay the foreign seller the price due on a shipment when the seller satisfies the conditions of the LC by presenting the documentation specified in the LC. D Corp initiates the process by a having its bank (often called the "opening" or "issuing" bank) approve the issuance of the LC based on D Corp's creditworthiness and willingness to pay the bank's fees for the LLC. When the issuing bank selected by the buyer (D Corp in this case) is unknown to the seller, a confirmed LLC is often required. This is an LLC where a second bank (often called the "prime bank") approved by the seller guarantees the obligations of the issuing bank under the LC.

Conditions. LC payment conditions typically specify delivery dates, product specifications, and the timely delivery of specific documents, such as bills of lading, inspection certificates, commercial invoices, and packing lists. A bill of lading is a written document of title issued by a carrier or transport company and confirming its receipt of merchandise in transit and its contractual obligation to deliver the merchandise to a specified party at a specified location. A negotiable bill of lading (one that is "to the order of a specified party") permits the title of the property to be transferred by the issuing party.

Payment of LC. The documents presented to the paying bank include a draft, which resembles a check and is sometimes called a "bill of exchange." The draft is the seller's formal demand for payment. A sight draft requires the bank issuing the LC to pay the amount indicated on the draft when it has received the proper documentation (usually within no more than seven days). A time draft requires payment within the time specified in the LC (e.g., 60 days after receipt of proper documentation). Payment of a sight draft or accepting a time draft is often called "honoring the draft."

Revocable vs. Irrevocable. An irrevocable LC accepted by a seller cannot be altered or cancelled without the consent of the seller. Any change requires the consent of all parties, including the issuing and any confirming banks. With a revocable LC, the issuing bank (the buyer's bank) may alter or cancel its obligations at any time before payment of a sight draft or acceptance of a time draft. Revocation is permitted even if goods have been shipped in reliance on the LC.

Stand-By LC. This is a letter of credit that is not expected to be the primary source of payment from the buyer to the seller. It "stands by" to pay amounts due the seller if the buyer fails to make the payments contemplated by the parties.

If Duke's company becomes an exporter of goods to buyers in foreign countries and wants payment protection, it should instruct the foreign buyers to open irrevocable letters of credit, payable 100 percent at sight, fully negotiable, and confirmed by a bank in the United States acceptable to Duke.

STUDENT PROBLEM 3-2

Refer to the financial statements of Caterpillar Inc. in Section D of Chapter 2. Assume that the management of Caterpillar Inc. has decided to raise an additional $4 billion to finance its growth plans. It has identified three options for securing the needed capital:

1. A term loan for $4 billion, with the principal and interest at a fixed annual rate of 5.5 percent on the unpaid balance being paid and fully amortized in equal monthly installments over a ten-year period.

2. A $4 billion line of credit, requiring interest-only payments each month calculated on the average line balance during the month at the Wall Street Prime Rate (currently 3.25 percent) as of the last business day of the preceding month. The line would be available on such terms for two years, and thereafter could be renegotiated and renewed for successive two-year terms.

3. The issuance of $4 billion of additional common stock.

What factors would Caterpillar Inc.'s management likely consider important in evaluating and comparing these three options?

If the management would consider issuing more stock only on a basis that values the company's existing outstanding common stock at a capitalization rate of 8 percent on its 2012 after-tax profit of consolidated and affiliated companies, what percentage of the total outstanding stock of Caterpillar Inc. would be issued for the $4 billion of new equity capital?

2. *BONDS*

A bond is a debt security that allows institutions to borrow money directly from investors. The issuer of the bond promises to pay a fixed rate of interest over the life of the bond and to repay the principal amount on the designated maturity date. The description of a corporate bond generally includes the corporation's name, the coupon rate, and the maturity date. For example: "General Motors (GM) 5.25% due 12/31/2015" would mean the bond was issued by General Motors, pays an annual interest rate of 5.25 percent, and matures on December 31, 2015.

According to the Securities Industry and Financial Markets Association (SIFMA), the United States bond market as of September 2013 totaled $39.519

trillion. Of this total, $3.685 trillion represented debt of municipalities, $11.590 trillion represented debt of the federal treasury, and $9.561 trillion represented corporate debt.

Corporate bonds offer investors a consistent fixed-income yield, long-term capital preservation, and liquidity – the capacity to sell the bond at any time. Bonds are often used by investors to hedge against the higher risks of stock investments. Some corporate bonds have a call option that allows the issuing corporation to redeem the bond before its maturity date. Other bonds offer a conversion feature that allows an investor to convert the bond into equity stock of the company.

A bond's interest rate, as compared to current interest rate levels, is usually the most important factor that influences a bond's market price and total return. Changes in the overall level of interest rates will cause the price of a bond owned by an investor to move in the opposite direction. If interest rates fall, an existing bond's value will move up, all other factors being equal. If interest rates rise, a bond's value will drop.

Creditworthiness is always a factor in valuing bonds. Rating agencies, such as Moody's and Standard & Poor's, rate bonds based on their credit strength. The value of the bond moves in the same direction of any rating change. Corporate bonds often are listed on major exchanges, although the bulk of the trading volume in corporate bonds is done through decentralized, dealer-based, over-the-counter markets.

Bonds have their own language. Following are the definitions of some of the key bond terms:[2]

Ask Price (or Offer Price): The price at which a seller offers to sell a security.

Basis Point: Smallest measure used in quoting yields on bonds and notes. One basis point is 0.01 percent of yield. For example, a bond's yield that changed from 6.52 percent to 7.19 percent would be said to have moved 67 basis points.

Bid: Price at which a buyer is willing to purchase a security.

Bond year: An element in calculating average life of an issue and in calculating net interest cost and net interest rate on an issue. A bond year is the number of twelve-month intervals between the date of the bond and its maturity date, measured in $1,000 increments. For example, the "bond years" allocable to a $5,000 bond dated April 1, 2014, and maturing June 1, 2014, is 5.830 [1.166 (14 months divided by 12 months) x 5 (number of $1,000 increments in $5,000 bond)]. Usual computations include "bond years" per maturity or per an interest rate, and total "bond years" for the issue.

Call: Actions taken to pay the principal amount prior to the stated maturity date, in accordance with the provisions for "call" stated in the bond. Another term for call provisions is redemption provisions.

2. See Sifma, Investing in Bonds.com/Glossary

Call Premium: A dollar amount, usually stated as a percentage of the principal amount called, paid as a "penalty" or a "premium" for the exercise of a call provision.

Call Price: The specified price at which a bond will be redeemed or called prior to maturity, typically either at a premium (above par value) or at par.

Coupon: The rate of interest payable annually.

Covenant: The issuer's pledge, in the financing documents, to do or to avoid certain practices and actions.

Current Yield: The ratio of interest to the actual market price of the bond, stated as a percentage. For example, a $1,000 bond with a current market price of $900 that pays $60 per year in interest would have a current yield of 6.67 percent.

Junk Bond: A debt obligation with a rating of Ba or BB or lower, generally paying interest above the return on more highly rated bonds, sometimes known as high-yield bonds.

Premium or Discount Price: When the dollar price of a bond is above its face value, it is said to be selling at a premium. When the dollar price is below face value, it is said to be selling at a discount.

Treasury Bond: A long-term debt instrument issued by the U.S. Treasury, having a maturity of 10 years or more, issued in denominations of $1,000 or more, and paying interest semiannually. In contrast, a Treasury note has a maturity of one year to 10 years, is issued in $1,000 denominations, and pays interest semiannually. A Treasury bill is a short-term debt that has a maturity of less than a year and is sold at a discount (the yield is the difference between the price paid and the amount paid at maturity).

Yield to Maturity: A yield on a security calculated by assuming that interest payments will be made until the final maturity date, at which point the principal will be repaid by the issuer. Yield to maturity is essentially the discount rate at which the present value of future payments (investment income and return of principal) equals the price of the security.

Zero-Coupon Bond: A bond for which no periodic interest payments are made. The investor receives one payment at maturity equal to the principal invested plus interest (compounded semiannually) earned through the date of maturity.

STUDENT PROBLEM 3-3

Julie has $100,000 that she wants to invest in a safe fixed-income investment that will pay her interest on a regular basis for ten years and repay her the $100,000 upon maturity at the end of year 10. She is trying to decide between two options: (1) ten-year municipal bonds issued by the City of Denver that offer a tax-free annual coupon rate of 4.15 percent and (2) corporate bonds issued by Caterpillar Inc. that offer a coupon rate of 6.65 percent.

What factors should Julie consider in making her decision between these two options? Assume Julie's marginal federal income tax rate is 33 percent and that the state of her residence does not have an income tax.

3. LEVERAGED REAL ESTATE – AN EXAMPLE

A drive through any significant town in America will reveal warehouses, apartments, storefronts, office buildings, strip malls, and other commercial properties that are an income source for someone. Typically these buildings perpetually generate income with favorable tax breaks.

Some powerful positives come with real estate. Everyone needs it, and there's only so much of it. High quality real estate often goes up in value as it ages. It can be a wonderful hedge against inflation, that force that constantly devalues our dollars. And the escalating value prospects of good real estate encourage lenders to provide money to help make an income real estate play happen. Positive leverage is the name of the game in real estate.

Then add to this leverage potential the tax breaks of real estate. The interest payments on the debt are currently tax deductible. More importantly, for income tax purposes, depreciation deductions are available all along the way based on the premise that the building's cost must be written off over time, even though everyone knows that the building's value is likely inching upward. It's the best real estate fiction in the Internal Revenue Code. As time goes on, the gap between the building's true value and its undepreciated cost (the cost that has not yet been written off) is forever widening. When the building is sold, that gap, which is the profit on the sale, is usually taxed at favorable capital gain rates. And if the building's owner can pull out tax-free cash through refinancings predicated on ever-growing values and thereby hold onto the building until death, the taxable income hit on the gap disappears at death.[3]

Let's illustrate how it can work with a simple example.

Linda's Triumph

Linda, a 30-year old who likes numbers, went to work as an assistant in a mortgage brokerage firm. In her job of reviewing mortgage deals for commercial properties, she learned how the lending world of real estate works. Plus she learned all about appraisals, capitalization rates, lease rates and terms, and other information that makes for a good real estate play. She learned her market, the hot spots and where the action in town was trending. She learned the identity of the best contractors in town and how real pros work with contractors to get the best deals. With this information, Linda started snooping around for valuable pieces of raw land, dreaming that one day she might go for it.

Shortly thereafter, Linda attended a holiday party with friends and relatives. She overheard her Uncle Pete, the owner of a solid, fast growing manufacturing business, tell her husband Frank that he would need more space in the upcoming year, about 30,000 square feet of warehouse and 10,000 square feet of office space. Linda got excited because she spotted the opportunity.

---

3. Under I.R.C. § 1014, a decedent's basis in property (that portion that can be recovered tax free on a sale) is increased to the property's fair market value at death.

Within seven days, Linda presented Uncle Pete with a proposal. She would provide his company with a new building, finished to his specifications, on a choice parcel that she had already tied up for sixty-days on a feasibility contingency. Pete's monthly rent would be 50 cents a square foot for warehouse and $1.00 per square foot for office space, triple net. These prices were slightly less than existing market rental prices. Triple net (very standard) means that the tenant, Uncle Pete's company, would pay all taxes, insurance and upkeep on the building (which, in this case, were estimated to collectively equal 2.23 percent of the value of the building).

As an incentive kicker to get the deal done and secure a long-term lease from Pete, Linda offered Pete a 10 percent equity interest in any sale or refinancing proceeds realized from the building.

When Pete agreed to the deal, Linda knew that she had the two most valuable ingredients to a smart deal – a lease with a solid, long-term tenant and a quality parcel of land. Based on the lease that would initially pay a monthly rental of $25,000 ($300,000 a year) and her plans for the building, she secured an appraisal on the to-be-built building, which came in at $3,340,000. With the strength of the lease and this appraisal, Linda was able to secure a commitment for a 6.5 percent mortgage loan for $2,666,000, roughly 80 percent of the appraised value. The monthly payment, based on a twenty-year amortization period, would be $19,900.

Linda then went to work on the contractors in town. Working hard to eliminate soft costs and negotiate the best deals, she ended up with a total project cost of $2,900,000. The result was that she needed a cash infusion of $234,000 to cover the difference between the total cost and her loan amount. She went to her dad, Pete's brother, who had an investment nest egg that was bouncing up and down in the markets. She showed her dad her projections and then made her offer: If he'd put up the $234,000, she'd pay him an annual 8 percent yield until his capital was returned, would repay the loan in full at the end of year 10, and would give him a 20 percent interest in all sale and refinancing proceeds for as long as she owned the building. Her dad looked at her numbers and asked: "You can do this?" Her response: "Just watch".

Linda formed a limited liability company (LLC) and went to work to implement her plan. The building was built, and Pete's company moved in and started paying a triple net rent of $25,000 a month. Out of this amount, Linda's LLC made the mortgage payment of $19,900 and paid Linda's dad $1,560 a month, the 8 percent yield on his investment. That left $3,540 for Linda each month. Her husband, Frank, shook his head and exclaimed, "Not bad?" Linda's pat response: "Just watch."

At the end of year 3, the rents on the building jumped to 60 cents a month for warehouse space and $1.10 a month for office space under the lease. This netted Linda a monthly cash flow of over $7,540. Now husband Frank was very excited.

At the end of year 6, the monthly rents went to 70 cents a foot warehouse and $1.25 office under the lease. A new appraisal valued the building at

$5,025,000. The principal balance on the loan had been paid down to $2,190,000. Linda showed Frank the numbers, an owner equity value of over $2,800,000. Frank screamed "Sell, Sell." Linda smiled and responded, "And what, pay a big sales commission and a bunch of closing costs and income taxes and kill the golden goose for the future? Just watch."

Linda's LLC refinanced the building – a new loan for $3,750,000 (75 percent of the new appraised value). Based on a twenty-year amortization period, the monthly loan payment increased to $27,900. The monthly cash flow from the building dropped back to $5,600. But the LLC generated $1,560,500 cash, the excess of the new loan over the balance due on the old loan. Uncle Pete got a check for $156,000. Linda's dad got back his initial $234,000, which to this point had been yielding 8 percent like clockwork, plus a kicker for $312,000. Both Uncle Pete and Dad were ecstatic with their yield and the realization that a new round was just beginning. Frank fell off his chair when he saw Linda's share of the tax-free refinancing proceeds ($780,000), learned that $5,600 a month would keep coming from the building, and discovered that bigger numbers would be realized in the future as the rents and values continued to slowly move upward.

Experiences like these make real estate an attractive investment for many. Note that a key element of Linda's success was that she had a strong tenant under a long-term lease. This is the reason so many successful business owners invest in the real estate their business needs. The business is the golden tenant, the most precious ingredient to success. Beyond the benefits of the real estate itself, the business owner doesn't have to worry about a third-party landlord terminating an important lease to favor a more valued client or to unreasonably hike renewal rates. Plus, reasons the owner, why give my precious lease to some third party? Keep it in the family and make it pay for the long term.

STUDENT PROBLEM 3-4

Assume in Linda's example above that Uncle Pete's company becomes a victim of a lousy economy and ends up shutting its doors and going bankrupt in year 4. Linda's LLC ends up with an empty building.

1. Estimate the impact on the LLC's monthly cash flow while the building sits empty and Linda scrambles to find a new tenant.

2. Assume that two options emerge for Linda's LLC. The first is to transfer the building to the bank that holds the debt and walk away from the whole deal with no residual liability. The second is to move forward with a new tenant who demands (remember, the economy is now hurting) six months of free rent and thereafter seven years of fixed, triple-net rents at 40 cents warehouse and 80 cents office. What factors should Linda consider in assessing these two options?

C. TIME-VALUE-OF-MONEY CONCEPTS

A dollar in the future is worth less than a dollar today. Today's dollar can be invested to create a positive yield, and yield is a function of time. It's a simple concept that is understood by everyone. Business owners and executives often have to make decisions that require a comparison of dollar values at different points in time. Those decisions require an application of basic concepts related to the time value of money.

Conceptually, such principles are relatively easy to understand. The complicating factor in many time-value-of-money discussions is the formulas, the equations with exponential functions that are used to calculate key numbers. Readers often get lost in trying to comprehend how particular formulas work, and soon everything seems very difficult. The key for most lawyers and executives is to ignore the formulas. Focus on the relevant concept, the numbers necessary to apply the concept, and the elements needed to produce such numbers. Leave the formulas to a calculator. Handheld financial calculators are easy to use, and online calculators (see, for example, www.calculator.net) are even easier. Simple technology has stripped away the mathematical challenges of decisions that incorporate time-value-of-money concepts. A user-friendly online calculator (www.calculator.net) was used to generate the numbers in the following illustrations in a few seconds.

1. PRESENT VALUE

Bob is a talented operating officer whom Petro Inc. badly wants to recruit. Bob and Petro have tentatively agreed to a deal that includes a $500,000 signing bonus. If Bob voluntarily leaves Petro within the first four years, he must repay $300,000 of the bonus. When Petro's chief financial officer (CFO) reviewed the deal, he didn't like the idea of Petro having to chase Bob for $300,000 if Bob has a change of heart during the first four years. As an alternative, he proposed paying Bob a $200,000 bonus on signing and a deferred $350,000 signing bonus at the end of four years. Bob's voluntary departure would be the only circumstance that would prevent payment of the deferred bonus.

Bob understands the basis of the CFO's proposed alternative. He has no concerns about Petro's capacity to pay the deferred bonus or willingness to honor its commitments. His concern is how $350,000 four years from now stacks up against $300,000 right now. After considering all variables, Bob has determined that an annual yield factor of 8 percent is fair. If he had the money now, he might be able to generate an annual yield of 8 percent. This is usually called an "interest rate," the factor used to calculate a yield going forward. But, in this case, what Bob needs to know is the present value of $350,000 four years down the road, using the eight percent as a discount factor. Think of a "discount rate" as an interest rate looking back. It is used to derive the present value of future amounts by "discounting" such amounts.

Bob's question now: What sum invested now at an annual compounded yield of 8 percent would produce a value of $350,000 in four years? Inserting the future value ($350,000), the discount factor (8 percent), and the number of time periods (four) into the online calculator generates a present value of only $257,260.[4] Bob now knows that the CFO's proposal falls far short of the original deal that would pay Bob the $300,000 forfeitable portion of his bonus upfront.

---

4. The relevant formula is $PV = FV/(1+r)^n$ where PV is the present value, FV is the future value, "r" is the discount rate, and "n" is the number of periods.

2. *FUTURE VALUE*

Bob and the CFO need to get their deal back on track. The CFO accepts Bob's 8 percent interest/discount factor. To find an acceptable solution, they change the underlying question. No longer would it focus on the present value of $350,000 in four years. The question would now focus on the future value of $300,000 right now. Simply stated: What would be the future value in four years of $300,000 invested now at an annual compounded yield of 8 percent?

Inserting the present value ($300,000), the discount factor (8 percent), and the number of time periods (four) into the online calculator generates a future value of $408,147.[5] Bob and the CFO settle on a deferred bonus of $410,000, each understanding that, given Bob's 8 percent yield factor, this future payment fairly equates to the payment of $300,000 right now.

3. *FUTURE VALUE FROM PERIODIC PAYMENTS*

Bob joins Petro and does a superb job. He has become the chief operating officer of the company (COO), is approaching his 50th birthday, and is constantly being courted by other companies. In order to provide Bob with a powerful incentive to stay with Petro, the chief executive officer (CEO) of Petro has proposed that Bob be given a supplemental retirement plan designed specifically for him. Such executive retirement plans (called "SERPs") are discussed in Chapter 12.

Bob's plan would require the company to accrue on the first day of each year a $50,000 credit that would be used to fund a retirement benefit for Bob at age 65. These annual accruals (15 in total) would grow at a compounded annual rate of 7 percent. If Bob voluntarily terminates his employment with Petro before reaching age 65, he would forfeit all accrued benefits. If Bob's employment with Petro terminated before age 65 as a result of death or disability, the accrued balance at time of termination would be paid to Bob or his designated heirs, as appropriate.

When told of the CEO's proposal, Bob had one overriding question: How much will accumulate in the plan by age 65? The question requires a calculation of the future value of the annual accruals that Petro will make for Bob's benefit. This is not the future value of a fixed sum today, as was the case with Bob's deferred signing bonus. This is the future value of a series of annual accruals that occur over a fixed period of time.

Inserting the number of time periods (15), the interest factor (7 percent), and the amount of each annual accrual ($50,000) into the calculator generates a future value of $1,344,000.[6] This is the total amount that would accrue under the CEO's plan for Bob's benefit by age 65.

---

5. The relevant formula is $FV = PV \times (1+r)^n$ where FV is the future value, PV is the present value, "r" is the discount rate, and "n" is the number of periods.

6. The relevant formula is $FV = P \times [(1+r)^n - 1/r]$ where FV is the present value, P is the periodic payment, "r" is the interest rate, and "n" is the number of periods.

4. PERIODIC PAYMENT FROM A PRESENT VALUE

Bob is initially impressed with the future value of $1,344,000 that will accumulate by the time he reaches 65. But as he thinks more about the situation, he concludes that a lump sum figure at age 65 doesn't fully answer his key retirement question. He really needs to know the amount of the monthly retirement income that he and his spouse can plan on receiving during the 20 years following his retirement (from age 65 to 85).

The answer to this question requires the calculation of a future monthly benefit based on a known present value and an assumed interest factor. Given that this will be a retirement nest egg that is conservatively invested, Bob decides to use an annual interest yield of 5.4 percent from age 65 to 85. Note that the future value from the previous calculation ($1,344,000) has become the present value in this calculation because the relevant time periods have shifted from pre-age-65 to post-age-65. Inserting the present value ($1,344,000), the annual interest factor (5.4 percent), and the number of monthly payments (240) into the calculator produces a monthly payment of $9,169.[7]

5. PRESENT VALUE FROM FUTURE PERIODIC PAYMENTS

Bob is dismayed to learn that his special retirement plan will generate a monthly retirement payment of only $9,169. Considering the impacts of inflation and taxes (every payment will constitute taxable income), he figures that he is going to need much more. He wants the plan structured to pay a monthly benefit of $15,000 for the 20 years following his retirement, based on his retirement yield assumption of 5.4 percent.

The first step is to calculate the amount needed at age 65 to fund such a benefit. This is a present value calculation based on a known future payment stream and a given discount factor. Inserting the number of monthly payments (240), the annual discount factor (5.4 percent), and the desired monthly payment ($15,000) into the calculator produces a present value of $2,208,500.[8] This is the amount that would need to be accrued by age 65 to fund a $15,000 monthly benefit for 20 years.

6. PERIODIC PAYMENT FROM A FUTURE VALUE

Bob presents his analysis to Petro's CEO. The CEO's appreciates Bob's concerns, but wants to know how much will have to be annually accrued over the next fifteen years to accumulate a total accrued balance of $2,208,500 by the time Bob reaches age 65. This requires the calculation of a periodic payment based on a future value and a given interest factor. Note that here the present value from the prior calculation ($2,208,500) becomes the future value in this calculation because the relevant time period has shifted from post-age-65 to pre-age-65. Inserting the number of annual periods (15), the annual interest factor (7

---

7. The relevant formula is $P = (r \times PV) / (1 - (1 + r)^{-n})$ where P is the periodic payment, PV is the present value, "r" is the interest rate, and "n" is the number of periods.

8. The relevant formula is $PV = P \times ((1 - (1 + r)^{-n}) / r)$ where PV is the present value, P is the periodic payment "r" is the interest rate, and "n" is the number of periods.

percent), and the future value ($2,208,500) into the calculator produces a required periodic payment of $82,136.[9] This is the principal amount that Petro would need to accrue each year for the next fifteen years in order to accumulate $2,208,500 at an annual compounded yield of 7 percent.

7. *ANNUITIES*

In the foregoing analysis, the amount accumulated for Bob's benefit at age 65 would be paid to Bob over a 20-year period in equal monthly installments. This is often referred to as "annuitizing" a fixed sum. In Bob's case, the assumption was that Petro would calculate and pay the annuitized amount each month.

In many situations, a person decides to purchase an annuity contract from an insurance company. Such an annuity can shift investment and other risks to the company, depending on how the annuity is structured. Plus, it can eliminate the hassles of tracking and monitoring investments and mitigate temptations to deviate from an established spending program. Of course, the strength and creditworthiness of the insurance company and the specific terms of the annuity contract, including commissions paid, are always important considerations. Lawyers should have an understanding of basic annuity terms and the related vocabulary.

Immediate Annuity. An immediate annuity triggers periodic payments as soon as the contract is executed. There is no accumulation period. A sum is deposited, and the company immediately starts making payments pursuant to the terms of the annuity.

Deferred Annuity. A deferred annuity delays the commencement of payments. The owner of the annuity decides when the annuitization of the contract commences. The period preceding the annuitization is often called the accumulation period. The annuity may be funded with a single premium or multiple deposits to the contract at various times during the accumulation period. All yields that accumulate inside the contract are tax deferred until they are actually paid. The size of the periodic payment when annuitization commences is predicated on the balances generated during the accumulation period.

Fixed-Term vs. Life Annuity. A fixed-term annuity guarantees periodic payments for a defined period. A life annuity guarantees periodic payments for the life of the individual (often called the "annuitant") or so long as one of a designated group (e.g., husband and wife) is living. The insurance company takes an added mortality risk with a life annuity and, therefore, the periodic payments are often less than what would be received under a fixed annuity. An annuity contract may incorporate both mortality and fixed elements by requiring payments for the greater of a defined term or the life of one or more individuals. For example, the annuity contract could mandate a payout period of at least 20 years if the annuitant dies within 20 years.

---

9. The relevant formula is $P = (r \times FV) / ((1+r)^n - 1)$ where P is the periodic payment, FV is the future value, "r" is the interest rate, and "n" is the number of periods.

Fixed vs. Variable Annuity. With a fixed annuity, the insurance company promises a guaranteed rate of return during the accumulation and annuitization periods. The investment risk is born by the company. With a variable annuity, the owner of the contract determines the investments within the contract and bears all the associated investment risks. The deferred tax benefits remain the same. Typically, the owner of a variable annuity must select from a pre-defined list of investments (often called "sub-accounts") that offer a wide range of risk/reward options.

8. INTERNAL RATE OF RETURN

Internal rate of return ("IRR") is a concept that helps compare the profitability of investments, particularly when one or more of the investments have irregular cash flows in or out of the investment. Sometimes IRR is referred to as the "economic rate of return" or "discounted cash flow rate of return." Technically, the calculation of an investment's IRR is designed to determine the discount rate at which the net present value of all amounts put into the investment (the negative cash flows) equals the net present value of payments (positive cash flows) that come from the investment. A simple example will help illustrate the function of an IRR analysis.

Let's go back to Bob, our stellar COO. Bob's neighbor has a "hot real estate" deal for Bob. Bob would invest $60,000 in year 1, $50,000 in year 2, and $40,000 in year 3. The venture is projected to start paying off in year 6. The projections show that Bob would receive $30,000 in year 6, $50,000 in year 7, $60,000 in year 8, and $120,000 in year 9 when the project sells out. Bob wants to know how the projected yield from this investment stacks up against his other more traditional investments that historically have yielded Bob an average of 7 percent annually.

Bob needs an IRR calculation that is based on the projected cash flows (both positive and negative) of the venture. An online calculator (www.pine-grove.com/) confirms that his neighbor's projected cash flows would generate an IRR of 9.36 percent. If by chance the actual cash flow benefits (the returns in years 5 through 9) turn out to be 15 percent less than the projections, the IRR plummets to 6.5 percent. Similarly, if the amount of the annual projected payments turns out to be accurate but is delayed two years because of unforeseen obstacles, the IRR drops to 7.55 percent. With these IRR calculations, Bob is now in a much better position to compare this opportunity against other available investment options.

STUDENT PROBLEM 3-5

Lauren is the sole owner of Belts Galore, Inc. ("Belts"), a successful C corporation. Morse Inc. ("Morse") has offered to buy all of the assets and business of Belts for a price that has Lauren very excited. The big obstacle is that Morse wants to buy the assets of Belts, which (as discussed in Section C. of Chapter 10) will trigger a costly double income tax for Lauren and her company. The tax burden would be substantially reduced if Morse bought Lauren's stock in Belts, as opposed to the assets of Belts. But such a stock purchase would result in Morse having smaller tax deductions in each of the next fifteen years (about

$100,000 a year), and thus higher taxes ($35,000 a year) in each of such years. Lauren thinks that her after-tax yield from the sale will be higher if she entices Morse to do a stock (as opposed to an asset) deal by reducing the stock price by an amount equal to the present value of the $35,000 additional tax costs that Morse is projected to incur in each of the next fifteen years with a stock deal.

1. In making such present value calculation, will Lauren prefer to use a high discount rate or a low discount rate? What will Morse prefer?

2. Assume that Lauren and Morse agree that the price reduction should be based on a discount factor of 9 percent. Calculate the amount of the price reduction. I suggest using the finance calculator at www.calculator.net

D. VALUING A BUSINESS ENTERPRISE

1. THE LAWYER'S NON-ROLE

A primary objective of nearly all business owners is to continually increase the value of the business. There are many situations where a business owner wants or needs third party verification of the enterprise's value. In these situations, experts are called upon to express an opinion as to the value of the business as a going concern.

Foolish is the lawyer who attempts to value a client's business or even express an opinion on its value. It's not the job of the lawyer. It is beyond the lawyer's expertise or training. Other professionals are trained to tackle the tough job of pinning a value on an ever-evolving bundle of assets and income-generating operations. Let them take the heat. Avoid any temptation to start sounding like a valuation expert with clients.

This does not mean that a lawyer should not understand the vocabulary and basic techniques of business valuations. Such an understanding is essential to being a good legal advisor to business owners. At the most basic level, it makes intelligent conversation possible with those business owners who regularly analyze and ponder the importance of events, both internal and external, that may impact the value of the business they have devoted their working lives to building. They regularly talk of intangible asset indicators, capitalization and discount rates, EBITDA multipliers, and the like.

But the need to know goes beyond client relationships. The issue of value goes right to the heart of the planning effort in many situations. It, for example, is center stage in buy-sell planning among co-owners, new owner admission challenges, executive-based equity incentives, insurance planning, estate planning and related family planning challenges, and all exit strategy planning. Valuation challenges are always present in major transactions, including acquisitions, mergers, leveraged buy-outs, and initial public offerings. Also, business valuation issues often arise in a broad range of litigation contexts, including marital dissolutions, bankruptcies, breach of contract battles, dissenting shareholder and minority owner oppression disputes, economic damages computations, and many other situations.

While the lawyer is not the valuation expert in these situations, the lawyer's working knowledge of the relevant factors and techniques can strengthen the quality of the entire planning or dispute-resolution effort. It facilitates dialogue with the experts that may help identify or eliminate sloppy valuations. It enables the lawyer to spot unreasonable client valuation expectations. Often it makes it possible for the lawyer to assist the client in understanding the factors that impact the valuation determination and to explain the valuation to other parties who are impacted by the determination. And in most situations, it helps the lawyer lead the planning process.

Knowledge of valuation factors and techniques also can make a lawyer a much better negotiator. Most business negotiations are about value. A primary challenge in the negotiation process is to convince the other side that it is being offered a fair deal based on the values. The lawyer who is equipped to use valuation lingo and measurement techniques to make the case is often very effective. This is one situation where the lawyer can become a valuation advocate by applying favorable factors, drawing comparisons, and expressing "heat-of-battle" opinions. The difference here (and it is huge) is that the lawyer is not seeking to advise a client, but rather is seeking to prevail in a negotiation with one who is not a client. Often the lawyer who gets on a valuation soapbox in a tough negotiation is well advised to privately remind any client who witnessed the show that negotiation dialogue is no substitute for quality advice from a valuation expert.

2. *SCOPE OF THE CHALLENGE*

Revenue Ruling 59-60[10] is a useful starting point in assessing the nature of the business valuation challenge. Although ancient, this ruling continues to provide relevant guidance. In the context of business valuations, it states the classic definition of "fair market value" as "the price at which the property would change hands between a willing buyer and a willing seller when the former is not under any compulsion to buy and the latter is not under any compulsion to sell, both parties having reasonable knowledge of the relevant facts." In lieu of prescribing a specific mathematical valuation formula, the ruling discusses the following factors that should be considered in arriving at a fair market value determination:

1. The nature of the business and the history of the enterprise from its inception.

2. The economic outlook in general and the condition and outlook of the specific industry in particular.

3. The book value of the stock and financial condition of the business.

4. The earning capacity of the company.

5. The dividend-paying capacity of the business.

6. Whether or not the enterprise has goodwill or other intangible value.

10. 1959-1 C.B. 237. Years later in Revenue Ruling 68-609, 1968-2 C.B. 327, the Service stated that the valuation principles of 59-60 also would apply to partnership interests.

7. Sales of the stock and the size of the block of stock to be valued.

8. The market price of stocks of corporations engaged in the same or a similar line of business that have their stocks actively traded in a free and open market, either on an exchange or over-the-counter.

Although the fair market value standard has been around forever and nearly a half century ago the Internal Revenue Service provided guidance on how it should be applied in valuing business interests, serious valuation disputes routinely erupt. These disputes teach two important lessons. First, secure the services of a professional appraiser. Valuing a business interest requires judgment calls that must be made by a professional. Second, get the best appraiser available. If a dispute breaks out, the quality, reputation, and competence of the appraiser may be the ultimate deciding factor. The Tax Court, for example, has consistently refused to accept an appraisal on its face; it has followed a practice of carefully examining the underlying details and assumptions and the quality of the appraiser's analysis.[11]

Revenue Ruling 59-60 also recognized that the size of the block of stock is a relevant factor in valuing an interest in a business enterprise, specifically noting that a minority interest would be more difficult to sell. In many situations, valuation discounts become the name of the game and play an essential role in the valuation process. The two most significant discounts associated with an interest in a closely held business enterprise are the minority interest (lack of control) discount and the lack of marketability discount. The minority interest discount recognizes that a willing buyer will not pay as much for a minority interest; there is no control. The lack of marketability discount reflects the reality that a willing buyer will pay less for an interest in a closely held business if there is no ready market of future buyers for the interest. Usually both discounts are applied in valuing the transferred interest.[12] Often the two discounts total as much as 35 to 40 percent when a minority interest is being valued.[13]

Of course, publicly traded companies and closely held enterprises present different valuation challenges. A public company's value is impacted by the demand for its stock, which can be heavily influenced by general market conditions and factors that are unrelated to the company's performance. A closely held enterprise's value tends to be more closely tied to specify industry factors and the company's track record. Stockholders of public companies generally have no significant influence on how the company is managed; owners of closely held enterprises usually run the whole show. And whereas profit maximization is the premier objective in publicly traded companies, income maximization often takes a back seat to tax planning for the owners of closely held businesses.

When it comes to business valuations, nothing is easy and uncertainty abounds. William Yegge, an experienced business valuation expert and author of

---

11. See, for example, Rabenhorst v. Commissioner, 71 TCM(CCH) 2271 (1996) and Estate of Kaufman v. Commissioner, 77 TCM (CCH) 1779 (1999).

12. See, for example, Dailey v. Commissioner, 82 TCM 710 (2001); Janda v. Commissioner, 81 TCM 1100 (2001); Barnes v. Commissioner, 76 TCM 881 (1998); Litchfield v. Commissioner, T.C. Memo 2009-21.

13. Id.

books on business valuation practices, summed it as follows:

> For nearly 30 years I have wrestled with the question: What is business value? And to this day, assignment of intangible value in business remains the more perplexing task. There simply is no "pat" answer or formula. My way is neither right nor wrong, and the task is not really made easier with experience. If I have learned one common essential, it is to exercise caution in assigning intangible value throughout the whole process. There will always be reams of theory and flames of discussion, because scientific formulas developed for intangible value can do no more than "attempt" to measure the art form of human enterprise.[14]

3. ALTERNATIVE VALUATION METHODS

It helps to have a basic understanding of the various methods that are used to value a business. The most appropriate method in any given situation depends on the nature and history of the business, market conditions, and a host of other factors. Often a combination of methods is used. In Section A of this chapter (concept number 9), the capitalized earnings method was illustrated. The business' value was determined by applying a capitalization rate to EBITDA or some other designated measure of income. Following is a brief description of select other methods.

Book Value Method. The book value method bases the value on the company's balance sheet. It is total assets less total liabilities, using the balance sheet's historical dollar cost numbers. No attempt is made to account for the fair market value of the assets or the going concern value of the enterprise. For that reason, it is usually a poor measure of a company's real value. Its only virtue is its simplicity.

Adjusted Book Value Method. This is the same as the Book Value Method, with one important twist. Under this method, the assets are adjusted to reflect their current fair market values. The balance sheet is still the driving force, but asset values are restated. It works best in those situations where asset values are the key to the company's value. But it is a poor measure for an operating business whose value is predicated on its earning capacity and going concern value.

Hybrid Method. The hybrid method, in most situations, is a combination of the Adjusted Book Value Method and the capitalized earnings method illustrated in Section A above (Item 9). A value is determined under each method and then the two values are weighted to arrive at a value for the business. For example, if a determination is made to base 20 percent of the value on the Adjusted Book Value Method and 80 percent on the capitalized earnings value, an amount equal to 20 percent of the Adjusted Book Value method would be added to an amount equal to 80 percent of the capitalized earnings value. The Hybrid Method works best in those situations where the business' value is attributable to a combination of asset values and its earning capacity.

---

14. Yegge, A Basic Guide to Valuing a Company (John Wiley & Sons Inc. 2002).

Excess Earnings Method. This method incorporates the features of the Hybrid Method, but factors in the cost of carrying the assets of the business and financing impacts. The starting point is to multiply the "Net Tangible Assets" (aggregate fair market value of the tangible assets less liabilities) by a relevant applied lending interest rate to arrive at the annual cost of carrying the assets ("Cost of Money"). The designated income measure (EBITDA, for example) is reduced by the Cost of Money, and the result is divided by the designated capitalization rate to arrive at the business' "Intangible Value." The Intangible Value is then added to the Net Tangible Assets to arrive at the total value.

Discounted Cash Flow of Future Earnings. This method calculates the company's value by looking to the future. The applicable earnings measure (EBITDA, for example) is projected to increase at a given rate for a designated period of time, such as 10 years. The present value of the projected EBITDA in each of such years is then calculated by applying a discount rate that reflects the level of risk and uncertainty associated with the business and the time value of money. The present value determinations for each of the years are then added together to arrive at the business' value. When this method it used, often it is done to confirm the reasonableness of conclusions under one or more other methods.

STUDENT PROBLEM 3-6

Refer to the financial statements of Caterpillar Inc. set forth in Section D of Chapter 2, but ignore the reference that they are expressed in millions of dollars (that is, assume they are dollars only). Calculate the company's value as of December 31, 2012 under the following methods:

A. Book Value Method

B. Adjusted Book Value Method, assuming the following assets have the following values and each other asset has a value equal to its book value:

Inventories: $ 19,500

Property, Plant and Equipment: $ 26,000

Investments in Unconsolidated Affiliated Companies: $ 7,500

Goodwill: $ 49,000

Intangible Assets: $ 8,000

C. Capitalized earnings method based on the average consolidated profits before taxes for the last three years (2010 thru 2012) and a capitalization rate of 12.5 percent (equivalent to a multiplier of 8).

D. Hybrid of B and C, with 30 percent allocated to B and 70 percent allocated to C.

E. Excess earnings method based on consolidated profits before taxes in 2012, a 6.5 percent applied lending rate, and a 12.5 percent yield rate (capitalization rate). Assume the Net Intangible Assets total $ 23,500.

F. Discounted cash flow of future earnings method based on projections of consolidated profits before taxes for the next ten years, assuming consolidated profits before taxes increase 8 percent each year and the risk-level return requirement is 18 percent.

E. BASIC MICROECONOMICS CONCEPTS

Most lawyers should have at least a rudimentary understanding of elementary neoclassical microeconomics concepts. These are the supply and demand concepts that are so often used to justify or explain a specific event, decision, or course of action. For those who study antitrust, such an understanding is a must. But the need to know reaches far beyond those who seek a deeper knowledge of market inefficiencies and anticompetitive conduct. It extends to any lawyer who wants a basic understanding of how certain market forces work and how many business owners approach decisions to maximize profitability. The following short discussion explains and illustrates certain key concepts and the related vocabulary.

1. THE DEMAND SIDE

The law of demand is simple: if the price of a product increases, the demand for the product will decrease. Similarly, if the price is driven down, more consumers will be drawn to the product and the demand will increase. Anyone who shops understands this basic law. Of course, there are exceptions. Some products are so essential or attractive that certain consumers will pay whatever it takes to get them. Utilities are an example. The term used to describe the demand for these products is "inelastic" – price changes do not precipitate significant demand changes. In contrast, the demand for many products is deemed to be "elastic" – a change in price will trigger a significant change in demand. Many factors can impact the elasticity of a product, including the nature of the product (is it essential or a staple?), competitive products, the availability of substitutes, the strength of the brand, fads, and a host of other potential considerations.

A demand curve is commonly used to illustrate the demand for a seller's product at different price points at a fixed point in time. It assumes the seller has sufficient information to develop the curve and make rational profit-maximizing decisions based on the curve. Exhibit 4 is an example of three demand curves. The vertical axis in each curve reflects escalating prices, and the horizontal axis reflects increases in quantities. The curve represents the quantity demand at various price points. Given the law of demand itself, the curve generally has a negative slope.

Note the differences in the demand curves in Exhibit 4. The curve in the right margin is nearly vertical to reflect an inelastic demand and strong market power. With this curve, the seller knows that it can increase prices significantly and suffer only minor losses in volume. This is the monopolist's dream. The curve in the center reflects an elastic demand and limited market power. If the seller chooses to increase the price, there will be a significant drop in demand. Consumers will either opt for competitor products or substitutes or choose to go without.

Exhibit 4
Demand Curves

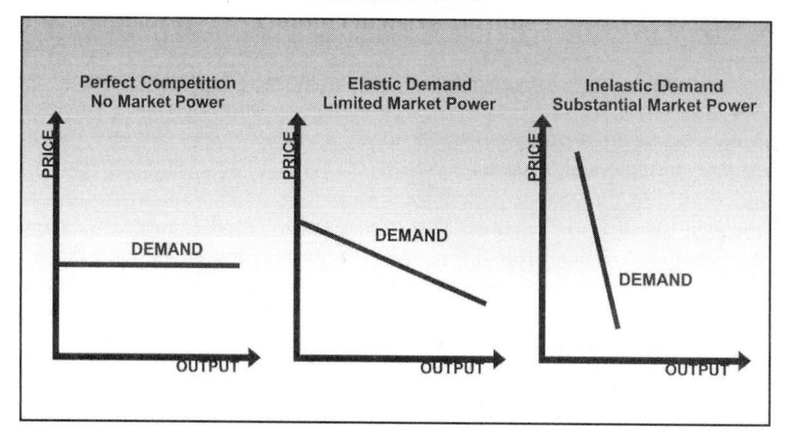

The curve to the far left reflects a state of pure competition and no market power. In this situation, the seller has no control over price because there is so much competition. The seller's entrance and exit from the market would have no impact on price. The price is established by the market and is not impacted by the seller's volume. Hence, a horizontal line is used to reflect the market price at all volumes. If the seller tries to sell at any price above the line, there will be no demand because other sellers will satisfy all demands of consumers at the market price. As described below, even in such a pure-competition condition, the model may still be used to identify the volume that will maximize profits for the seller.

In many situations, the demand curve is not a straight line. Exhibit 5 illustrates such a demand curve.

Exhibit 5
Market Power Hypothetical Market

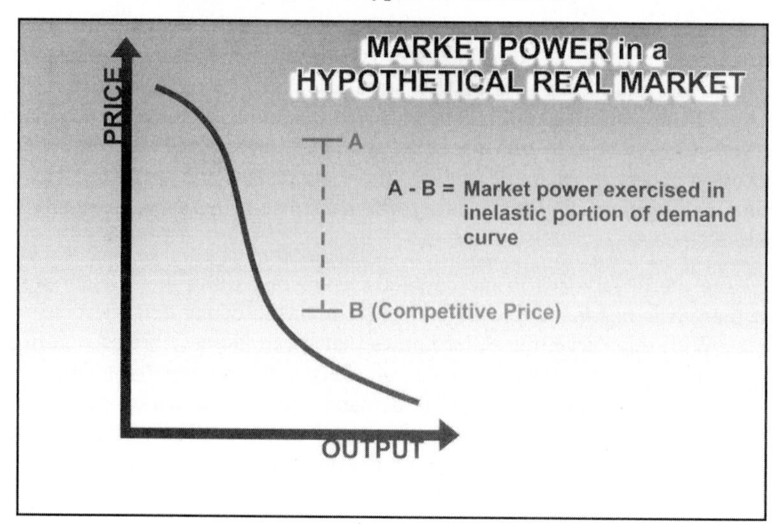

At lower volumes, there may be significant market power, little elasticity, and thus a more vertical demand curve. A certain volume of customers may be willing to pay any price within a broad range to get the product. For example, it may be a niche market condition geared to a limited audience of discriminating buyers. In order to move to higher volumes, the seller will have to compete with many more competitors or substitute products and attract customers who are far less discriminating and far more price conscious. The result is greater elasticity and a more horizontal curve at these higher volume levels.

Marginal revenue is an important concept associated with demand curves. It can best be illustrated with an example. Assume that Judy has developed a new computer case and has determined that she can sell 10,000 units during a designated time frame if she prices the case at $100. Higher volumes will be realized as she lowers the price. Her findings are summarized in Exhibit 6.

Exhibit 6
Judy's Revenue Analysis

Total Unit Sales	**10k**	**13k**	**16k**	**19k**	**22k**	**25k**
Price Per Unit	$100	$90	$80	$72	$64	$57
Total Dollar Sales	**1,000,000**	**1,170,000**	**1,280,000**	**1,368,000**	**1,408,000**	**1,425,000**
Marginal Revenue Per Unit		$57	$37	$29	$13	$6

As the Exhibit indicates, a decrease in the price to $80, for example, would increase the sales volume to 16,000 units, and a price of $57 could push volumes to as high as 25,000 units. The last row on this exhibit reflects the marginal revenue per unit that would result from each price reduction and volume increase. The marginal revenue for each price change is calculated by dividing the projected increase in total sales by the projected increase in units sold (here 3,000 units).

Note, for example, that a reduction in price from $100 to $90 increases sales from 10,000 to 13,000 units and increases total revenues from $1 million to $1,170,000. This additional $170,000 of revenue translates to a marginal yield of $57 per unit (170,000/3,000) for each of the additional 3,000 units sold. The marginal revenue per unit number is far less than the sales price of $90 because all units, not just the additional 3,000 units, would be sold at the lower price of $90.

Note the impact of price and volume changes on marginal revenue per unit yields, as reflected on the last line of Exhibit 6. The marginal revenue per unit drops rapidly as prices decrease and volumes increase. This is because, as volumes increase, there is a disproportionately larger increase in the percentage of units that could be sold at higher price points. Thus, for example, as shown on Exhibit 6, a price reduction from $64 to $57 and a corresponding jump in volume from 22,000 units to 25,000 units generates a marginal revenue yield of only $6 per unit. For these reasons, the marginal revenue curve for a product (as shown on Exhibit 7) typically will descend much faster (be more vertical) than the product's demand curve.

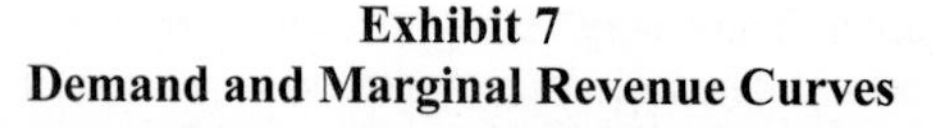

Exhibit 7
Demand and Marginal Revenue Curves

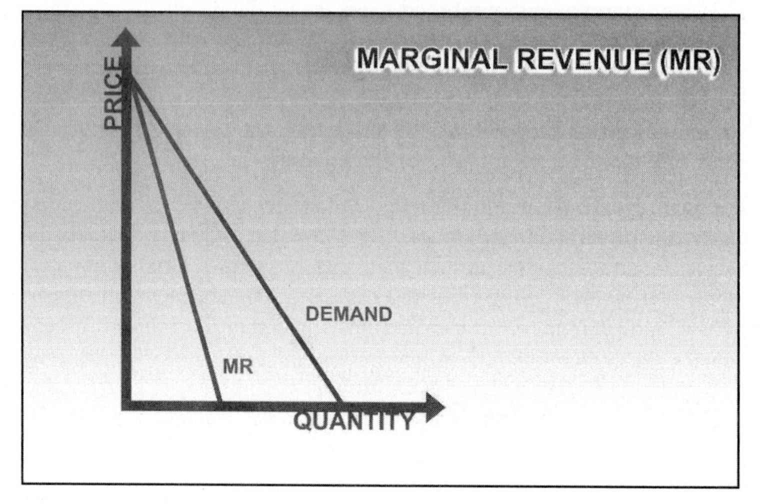

2. *THE COST-SUPPLY SIDE*

Let's turn to the cost side by again looking at Judy's situation. Judy first calculates her total projected costs at each volume level. These are reflected on line 6 of Exhibit 8. Thus, for example, her costs would total $600,000 at a production level of 10,000 units and $980,000 at a projection level of 19,000 units. The average cost per unit at each production level (shown on line 5) is calculated by dividing total costs at that level by the number of units produced. Therefore, at 19,000 units, the average cost per unit is $52 (980,000/19,000).

Exhibit 8
Judy's Revenue and Cost Analysis

Total Unit Sales	**10k**	**13k**	**16k**	**19k**	**22k**	**25k**
Price Per Unit	$100	$90	$80	$72	$64	$57
Total Dollar Sales	**1,000,000**	**1,170,000**	**1,280,000**	**1,368,000**	**1,408,000**	**1,425,000**
Marginal Revenue Per Unit		$57	$37	$29	$13	$6
Average Cost Per Unit	$60	$59	$54	$52	$51	$53
Total Costs	**600,000**	**765,000**	**860,000**	**980,000**	**1,120,000**	**1,330,000**
Marginal Cost Last Unit		$52	$37	$43	$64	$78

The average cost per unit consists of two components. The first component is fixed costs, those costs that do not change as the volume increases. Examples include rent, insurance, professional fees and the like. The total fixed cost per unit drops as volumes increase because the fixed costs are spread over a greater number of units. Thus, as volumes increase, the fixed cost component will drive down the average per-unit cost.

The second component of average cost is the variable costs. These are the additional costs incurred to produce more units; they vary based on volume. Examples include raw materials, labor, and shipping expenses. The variable cost per unit at any production level is calculated by dividing the total variable costs at the level by the number of units produced.

If the variable cost per unit remains relatively constant, the fixed cost component will push average per-unit costs down as volumes increase. But often the variable cost per unit starts to increase at higher levels that stretch capacities and trigger inefficiencies. A host of additional expenses may surface – more overtime pay, expanded rental facilities, more production errors, accelerated shipping needs, higher raw material costs, and the like. If and when increases in the variable cost component exceed the fixed-cost-per-unit benefit, there will be an increase in the overall average cost per unit. Note in Judy's situation (line 5 of Exhibit 8) how the average cost per unit descends until the volume level hits 22,000 units, beyond which the average cost per unit starts to increase. Of course, in some situations the fixed cost component may be so dominant within the relevant volume ranges that variable expense hikes cannot trigger an increase in the average per-unit cost.

Closely related to variable cost is the concept of marginal cost. Marginal cost is the additional cost incurred to produce a single unit. Whereas variable cost focuses on the extra costs incurred to produce a designated quantity of units, marginal cost is focused on the cost of a single unit. In essence, variable cost for a designated number of units is the sum of the marginal costs for each of those units. As efficiencies kick in at higher volumes, the marginal cost per unit will decrease. But as described above, costs may be pushed higher at certain volume levels, triggering increases in the marginal cost per unit. Line 7 of Exhibit 8 reflects Judy's marginal per unit costs at designated volume levels. Note how they descend until the volume level hits 16,000, at which point they start to increase.

Exhibit 9
Average and Marginal Cost Curves

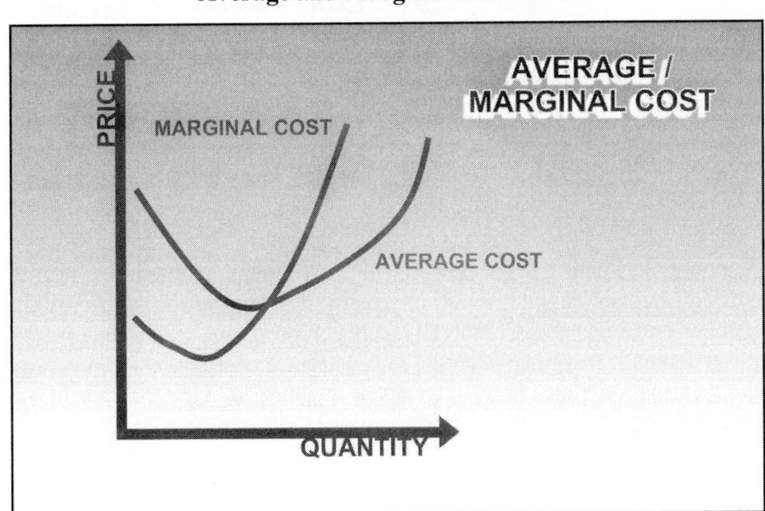

Exhibit 9 reflects average and marginal per-unit cost curves at various price and quantity levels. Note how they descend, bottom out, and then start to increase. Because marginal per-unit costs (unlike average per-unit costs) do not factor in the per-unit benefits of the fixed cost component, the average cost curve bottoms out at a higher volume level and then increases at a more modest pace. This is certainly true in Judy's situation. Compare line 5 (average cost) with line 7 (marginal cost) in Exhibit 8.

3. PROFIT MAXIMIZATION

Judy is now in a position to determine what price point and corresponding sales volume will maximize her profitability. She does this by subtracting her total costs from total revenues at each price point level. The bottom line of Exhibit 10 shows these results. It indicates that her profits will be maximized at a price of $80 and a projected sales volume of 16,000 units.

Note that this profit maximization point is the intersection of Judy's marginal revenue and marginal cost points, both $37 at the 16,000 volume level. Up to this point, each unit sale produced revenue that exceeded the cost to produce the unit, thus adding to the profitability of the enterprise. Any sale beyond this point triggers a marginal cost in excess of the corresponding marginal revenue, thereby reducing overall profits.

Exhibit 10
Judy's Revenue, Cost and Profit Analysis

Total Unit Sales	**10k**	**13k**	**16k**	**19k**	**22k**	**25k**
Price Per Unit	$100	$90	$80	$72	$64	$57
Total Dollar Sales	**1,000,000**	**1,170,000**	**1,280,000**	**1,368,000**	**1,408,000**	**1,425,000**
Marginal Revenue Per Unit		$57	$37	$29	$13	$6
Average Cost Per Unit	$60	$59	$54	$52	$51	$53
Total Costs	**600,000**	**765,000**	**860,000**	**980,000**	**1,120,000**	**1,330,000**
Marginal Cost Last Unit		$52	$37	$43	$64	$78
Profits	**400,000**	**405,000**	**420,000**	**388,000**	**288,000**	**95,000**

Maximized

A monopolist with market power will always seek to maximize profits by selling up to, but not beyond, the point where the marginal per-unit cost equals marginal per-unit revenue. Graphically, this is represented by Exhibit 11, which shows the demand, marginal revenue, and marginal cost curves. The marginal cost and marginal revenue curves intersect at quantity "q" (16,000 units in Judy's situation) and price "p" ($80 in Judy's situation).

Exhibit 11
Market Power Profit Maximization Price and Quantity

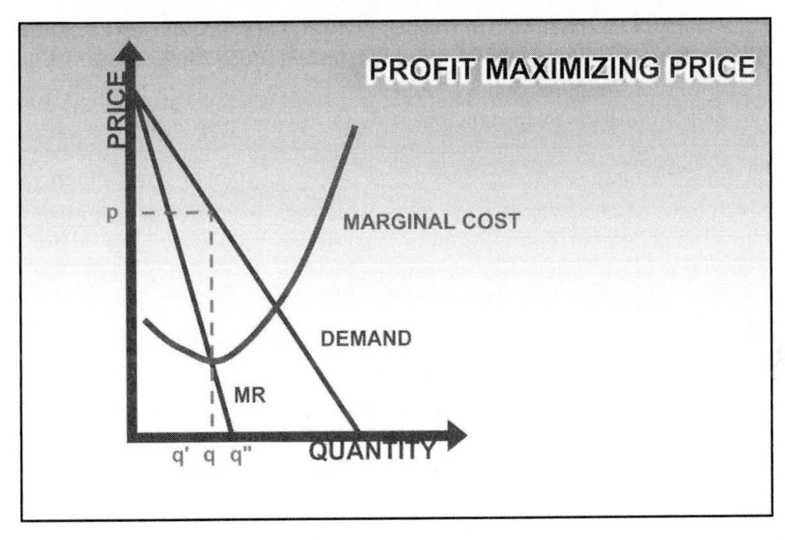

Now let's switch gears and assume that Judy has no real market power. She is in a highly competitive market with many sellers and competing products. Assume further that the established market price for a case is $64, and any attempt to sell above that price will generate no significant demand. Exhibit 12 reflects Judy's situation under this scenario.

Exhibit 12
Judy's Profit Analysis with No Market Power

Total Unit Sales	**10k**	**13k**	**16k**	**19k**	**22k**	**25k**
Price Per Unit	$64	$64	$64	$64	$64	$64
Total Dollar Sales	**640,000**	**832,000**	**1,024,000**	**1,216,000**	**1,408,000**	**1,600,000**
Marginal Revenue Per Unit		$64	$64	$64	$64	$64
Average Cost Per Unit	$60	$59	$54	$52	$51	$53
Total Costs	**600,000**	**765,000**	**860,000**	**980,000**	**1,120,000**	**1,330,000**
Marginal Cost Last Unit		$52	$37	$43	$64	$78
Profits	**40,000**	**67,000**	**164,000**	**236,000**	**288,000**	**270,000**

Maximized (↑ 288,000)

Note that her sales price and marginal revenue will be $64 at all volume levels because her volumes will have no impact on the market price. The only real question for Judy is: What volume will maximize profits? Profit maximization will occur at that volume where her marginal per-unit cost equals the established market demand price (which is also her marginal per-unit revenue). As Exhibit 12 indicates, Judy would maximize profits by selling 22,000 units. Any unit sale beyond this point would reduce profitability by triggering marginal costs in excess of marginal revenues.

We are now ready for a little (very little!) antitrust theory. Most now agree that the social objectives of antitrust are to promote the efficient allocation of goods and services; to prevent "deadweight loss," the loss that results when restricted output limits access to products and services; to stop "wealth transfer," the transfer of wealth from consumers to those who exercise market power to limit or restrict competitive conditions; and to promote "dynamic efficiency," the development of new products, innovations and technologies. Of far less concern, although once deemed the essence of antitrust, are desires to decentralize power and to protect market entry for individual firms. Now all have pretty much accepted the reality that big is not bad when it promotes efficiency and innovation and produces no serious signs of deadweight loss or wealth transfer. It is against these fundamental objectives that each gray issue must ultimately be tested.

The comparative profit maximization conclusions for Judy under the alternative market-power and no-market-power scenarios described above (Exhibit 10 versus Exhibit 12) demonstrate the market inefficiencies of deadweight loss and wealth transfer. With the market power to set her price, Judy will set a price of $80 and restrict output to 16,000 units in order to maximize profits. With no market power and a competitive market price of $64, she will maximize profits by producing 22,000 units. The difference in volumes under the two scenarios (6,000 units) is the deadweight loss, the units that never get to customers under the market power scenario. Exhibit 13 reflects this graphically, with "Qm" being the market power quantity (16,000 units in Judy's situation), and "Qc" being the competitive no-market-power quantity (22,000 units in Judy's situation).

Exhibit 13
Profit Maximization – Deadweight Loss

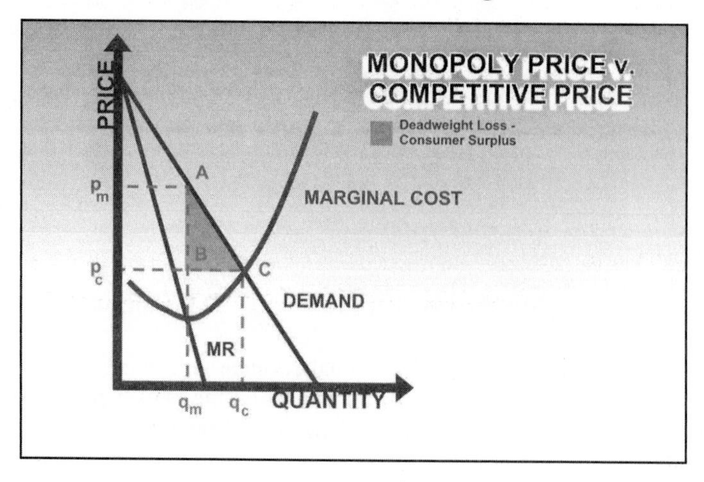

The difference in price under the two scenarios ($16 per unit) is the wealth transfer, the additional transfer of wealth from consumers to the seller with market power. Exhibit 14 reflects this graphically, with "Pm" being the market-power price ($80 in Judy's case) and "Pc" being the competitive no-market-power price ($64 in Judy's situation).

Exhibit 14
Profit Maximization – Wealth Transfer

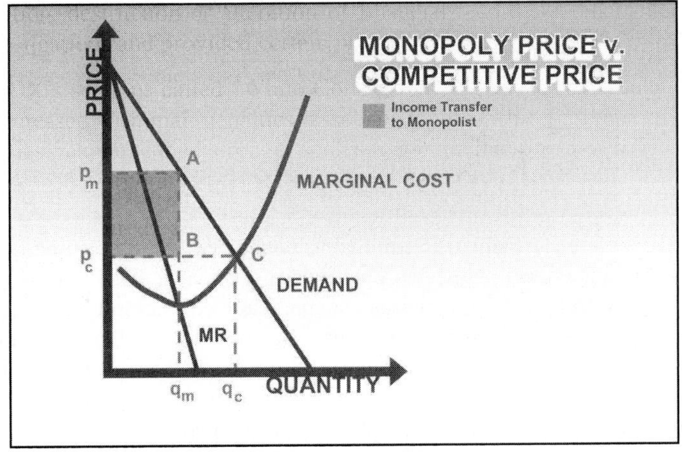

STUDENT PROBLEM 3-7

Judy, our computer case designer, has carefully studied the foregoing discussion and has some questions. Provide her answers to the following:

1. Under the market power scenario, will profits always be maximized at the volume that yields the lowest marginal cost per unit?

2. Is an average variable cost curve the same as a marginal cost curve? If not, how do they differ?

3. Under what conditions will the price of a product be the same as the marginal revenue generated from a sale of the product?

4. Will a seller with market power ever prefer a demand curve that is not highly vertical?

5. What impact will very high fixed costs have on an average cost curve?

CHAPTER 4

Corporations: Basic Business Considerations

A. BENEFITS OF INCORPORATING

The bulk of America's business is conducted through corporations. The stocks of numerous public corporations are traded daily by thousands of shareholders. But most corporations are characterized as closely held because their stock is owned by only a few individuals, often members of the same family. Stock transfers in closely held corporations are a rare event, usually triggered only by a sale of the business or an event that requires a shareholder to cash out, such as death, disability, bankruptcy, or a falling out with other shareholders.

A corporation is a creature of state law. Every corporation is organized under and governed by the laws of a given state. State corporate matters are handled by a separate state division or department that is under the auspices of the attorney general's office of the state.

For legal purposes, a corporation is viewed as a separate being. It can own property; it can sue and be sued; it can enter into contracts; it can borrow money; it can commit a crime or a tort; it must pay taxes. In short, when it comes to property and business, a corporation generally has all the rights and liabilities of a human being.

A corporation can even have offspring. It can create and own subsidiary corporations that can also spawn their own corporate entities. Often this type of multi-tiered holding company structure is used to segregate liabilities and manage risk exposures, reduce expansion-related regulatory and tax hassles, enhance financing opportunities, develop and incent management teams, and facilitate a host of other important business objectives.

A corporation is immortal. Its existence can be perpetual. It can span multiple generations and become an institution that promotes permanence and stability.

A corporation can assemble capital by issuing stock to many individuals and institutions, while centralizing the control of the entire business in the hands of only a few. In a public corporation, stock can be bought or sold with a phone call to a broker or by a computer click. Ownership interests in a closely held enterprise can be transferred by handing over a simple document – a stock certificate – without impacting the assets, liabilities, or operations of the business.

Limited liability is often trumpeted as a supreme benefit of a corporation. If the corporation defaults on a contact or loan, the aggrieved creditor generally has no claim against the shareholders, directors or officers unless they personally guaranteed the obligation. If an employee, while on the job, injures someone in an auto accident, the corporation can be held liable for the employee's actions, but the corporation's shareholders, directors and officers are not exposed personally. As sweet as the corporate shield may appear, it has its limits.

As we will see in Chapter 8, a corporation can offer attractive tax benefits. And business and financial communities, worldwide, understand and accept the preeminent role of corporations.

These factors make the corporate structure a must for many businesses, both large and small.

B. SELECTING THE STATE OF INCORPORATION

1. *DELAWARE OR NOT?*

The starting point for every corporation is to choose the state of incorporation. In the corporate charter game, Delaware is the reigning king, and it is highly unlikely that any other state will ever threaten its crown. For the organizers of most corporations, the question is: Should we incorporate in our home state or Delaware? A number of factors may influence the answer to this threshold question.

The challenge is to focus on the reasons that Delaware is the king and assess whether those reasons are relevant to the specific situation. Delaware's dominance in large part is attributable to its judiciary's demonstrated competence to resolve corporate matters efficiently and fairly. Many of its judges are accomplished former corporate lawyers who have the benefit of a massive body of state corporate case law and a deep appreciation of the importance of Delaware's corporate supremacy to the state. Corporate managers and lawyers generally cherish the predictability offered by Delaware's established case law and its favorable statutory provisions relating to compensation, self-dealing contracts, and indemnification.[1] Decades of doing deals in Delaware have made investment bankers and other money players comfortable with Delaware's corporate mindset. Everyone understands and appreciates the importance of corporate franchise fees in Delaware and the state's strong incentive to remain corporate-friendly on cutting edge issues. Plus, unpopular statutory changes are unlikely given a state constitutional provision that requires a two-thirds vote of both legislative houses to change Delaware's corporation code.[2]

The importance of these factors in a given situation will depend in large part

1. See 8 Del. C. §§ 143, 144, 145.
2. Del. Const. art. IX, § 1.

on the nature of the company's projected operations and ownership structure. If the company is going to do business in many states, it will be required to register as a foreign corporation in all such states and likely will deal with important third parties in multiple states. In such a case, the company may prefer to organize in Delaware to bolster its national or regional image and to remove any "local" taint. Similarly, a company that has any hope of going public or that is, or may become, dependent on capital from established brokerage or venture firms generally would be well advised to incorporate in Delaware from the get-go. The managers who run such firms and their lawyers will be saved the task of asking "Why not Delaware?" and taking necessary corrective actions.

In contrast, a closely held corporation that is going to be owned and controlled by a group of local shareholders often has no need to look beyond its local corporate law.[3] The potential benefits of Delaware's deep body of case law and the trappings of having a Delaware charter may not be worth the added hassle and expense of incorporating in Delaware and registering as a foreign corporation in the company's home state. In this very common situation, franchise fees and any specific oddities of the home state's corporate statutes may need to be factored in. Often, the ultimate conclusion is to "stay local."

2. *THE INTERNAL AFFAIRS DOCTRINE*

The traditional internal affairs doctrine is alive and well in nearly all states, including Delaware.[4] A legal advisor needs to understand the scope and impact of the internal affairs doctrine and potential wrinkles that may be triggered in New York or California under specific conditions. Simply stated, the doctrine provides that the law of the state of incorporation will govern any matter related to the internal affairs of the corporation.[5]

Internal affairs generally include matters involving the relationship between the corporation and its officers, directors, and shareholders. Common examples of internal affairs subject to the doctrine include voting rights, the rights and liabilities of directors and officers, shareholder rights, distributions, indemnifications, mergers, and derivative litigation. The internal affairs doctrine does not apply to matters unrelated to internal corporate relationships or procedures, such as taxes, antitrust, employment matters, environmental issues, securities laws, intellectual property matters, consumer protection, and most tort and contract claims.

Two states – California and New York – have statutes that apply their corporate law to resolve specific internal affairs of a corporation organized in another state (a "pseudo-foreign" corporation) that conducts most of its activities in California or New York, as the case may be, and has most of its outstanding

---

3. Delaware does have a set of provisions in its corporation code that are specifically designed for close corporations, generally defined as corporations with no more than 30 shareholders. See 8 Del. C. §§ 341-356. These provisions, among other things, make it easier for shareholders to manage the affairs of the corporation and facilitate the appointment of a provisional director to help resolve disputes.

4. See, e.g., Rogers McDermott Inc. v. Lewis, 531 A.2d 206 (Del. 1987), and Kozyris, Corporate Wars and Choice of Law, 1985 Duke L.J. 1, 98.

5. For a succinct statement and adoption of the doctrine by the United States Supreme Court, see Rogers v. Guaranty Trust Co. of New York, 288 U.S. 123, 130 (1933).

stock owned by residents of the state.[6] Although these pseudo-foreign corporation statutes often govern the outcome of any litigation in California or New York courts,[7] they are highly unlikely to control in a dispute that breaks out in another state.

A few Delaware Supreme Court cases will help illustrate the importance of this doctrine.

In *McDermott Inc. v. Lewis*,[8] the plaintiffs sought to enjoin or rescind a 1982 reorganization in which McDermott Incorporated, a Delaware corporation ("McDermott Delaware"), became a 92-percent-owned subsidiary of McDermott International Inc., a Panamanian corporation ("International"). McDermott Delaware owned 10 percent of International's voting stock. The Delaware Court of Chancery had granted partial summary judgment for the plaintiffs, holding that McDermott Delaware should not have been able to vote its stock in International to approve the merger because Delaware law (consistent with the corporate law of every state in the United States) prohibits a majority-owned subsidiary from voting stock that it owns in its parent corporation. Relying on the internal affairs doctrine (described as "a major tenet of Delaware law having important constitutional underpinning" and "not merely a principle of conflicts law") and noting that the issue before the court did not involve the internal affairs of McDermott Delaware, the court applied the law of Panama and found that Panamanian law allows a controlled subsidiary to vote shares of its parent company, provided certain conditions are met. Since these conditions had been satisfied, the court reversed the lower court and upheld the reorganization in question. The court noted the importance of the internal affairs doctrine to due process (citing the right of directors, officers, and shareholders to have notice of what laws govern a corporation) and to the commerce clause (claiming that there was no basis for subjecting International to Delaware corporate law). The court concluded, "due process and the commerce clause, in addition to the principles of Delaware conflict laws, mandate reversal."

In *Vantagepoint Venture Partners 1996 v. Examen, Inc.*,[9] the Delaware Supreme Court confronted California's pseudo-foreign corporate statute. VantagePoint, a Delaware limited partnership and the owner of a substantial majority of Series A Preferred shares (more than 83 percent) of Examen, Inc., a Delaware corporation, objected to a merger of Examen and Reed Elsevier. Although the merger was approved by the shareholders in accordance with Delaware law, VantagePoint brought suit, arguing that California's Section 2115 (described as a "narrowly-tailored exception to the internal affairs doctrine to protect important state interests") compelled application of California law to the merger because Examen satisfied the conditions of Section 2115. Under California law, the merger would have required a separate approval of each class of stock.

6. See Section 2115 of the California Corporation Code and N.Y. Bus. Corp. Law §§ 1317-20 (McKinney 1963 & Supp. 1981).

7. See, e.g., Wilson v. Louisiana-Pacific Resources, Inc., 187 Cal. Rptr. 852 (1982).

8. 531 A.2d 206 (Del. 1987).

9. 871 A.2d 1108 (Del. 2005).

The Delaware trial court ruled in favor of Examen, and VantagePoint appealed. The Delaware Supreme Court held that the issue was internal to Examen and that Delaware law and the federal constitution compelled application of Delaware law. The court cited *McDermott* for the due process and commerce clause underpinning of the internal affairs doctrine in refusing to apply California's pseudo-foreign corporate statute to a corporation that was organized in Delaware but had its closest ties to California.

STUDENT PROBLEM 4-1

Jennifer has developed a business plan to purchase a hilltop "mega" estate located in State A and convert it to a luxury "get-away" for affluent couples and corporate retreats. It will be known as "The View" and will be owned and operated by a corporation named "View Inc." Jennifer is a resident of State B, as are the four initial investors she has lined up. The corporation's board will consist of three members: Jennifer, Rod (chief financial officer), and Mary (chief operating officer).

State A has a very high "accommodations tax" that is imposed on any business that rents dwelling units for a period of less than 30 days. State B has no such tax. State A's corporate statutes do not require that a shareholder of a corporation have a preemptive right to purchase a portion of any new stock issued by the corporation in order to preserve the shareholder's percentage interest in the corporation unless the corporation's charter document (the articles of incorporation) provides for such a right. State B's statutes grant such a right unless the corporation's charter expressly denies the right.

Jennifer is confused as to whether View Inc. should be incorporated in State A or B. She fears that future money raising efforts will be harder if her investors have preemptive rights, and she worries (although not certain) that the investors will demand such rights if they are referenced in the articles of incorporation. Yet her greater concern at this point is the prospect of having to pay high state accommodation taxes.

Based only on these facts, how would you advise Jennifer in choosing the state of incorporation for View Inc.

C. THE CORPORATE ACTORS: A PRIMER

A corporation must act through human beings who wear various hats and are given varying degrees of authority to act for and on behalf of the corporation.

Incorporator. The incorporator is the person who actually forms the corporation, signs the articles of incorporation, and does what is necessary to bring the corporation into existence. Usually the incorporator is the driving force behind the new business or an attorney who represents that person.

Registered Agent. The registered agent of a corporation is the person, identified in the state's records, who is authorized to receive service of process in legal proceedings involving the corporation. Any person who wants to sue a corporation may check state records, secure the name and address of the registered agent, and serve that person.

Shareholders. The shareholders are the owners of the corporation's stock. In public companies, there are thousands of shareholders who regularly trade the corporation's stock. In closely held corporations, there may be only one or a few shareholders, and stock transfers are very rare events that are carefully controlled. As described in the following chapter, corporate shareholders have certain rights, including the right to elect the board of directors, approve major transactions (merges and the like), and vote on proposals. Corporate shareholders do not manage the affairs of the corporation, although shareholders in closely held corporations may agree in writing to various deal points relating to the operation of the company that will preempt the management authority of the board.

Board of Directors. The board of directors is the ultimate management authority of a corporation. State law requires that the board manage the affairs of the corporation. Its members are elected by the shareholders. One board member is typically designated as the chairman, the leader of the board. The board members may also be shareholders and officers, although they need not be. All public corporations and many closely held corporations have outside directors who do not work for the company.

The board of directors elects the officers of the corporation and generally manages and approves all important matters relating to the affairs of the business. Often there are sub-committees of the board that are empowered to deal with specific matters. Popular sub-committees include a compensation committee, which deals with all officer-related compensation issues, and an audit committee, which deals with all accounting and audit matters.

Actions taken and approved by the board of directors are reflected in written resolutions. Official resolutions may be adopted by the vote of board members at a meeting or by all of the board members signing a written consent resolution that approves the resolutions.

As discussed in Section F. below, board members have a duty to manage the corporation for the benefit of the shareholders. This is a fiduciary duty that includes a duty of care and a duty of loyalty. The duty of care imposes on each director a responsibility to act in good faith and in a manner that the director reasonably believes to be in the best interests of the shareholders. This duty is softened by the well-established business judgment rule that, absent self dealing or a breach of loyalty, presumes a director acted in good faith and in the best interests of the shareholders. This presumption, of course, can be rebutted. The duty of loyalty requires a director to place the best interests of the corporation above any personal interests. The violation of this duty may surface when a director engages in self-dealing with the corporation or personally usurps business opportunities that should have first been offered to the corporation. A breach of any of these duties may expose a director to a derivative claim brought by a shareholder on behalf of the corporation.

Officers. The officers of the corporation are the ones who actually run the business and work daily to carry out the authority delegated to them by the organization documents of the corporation (the bylaws) and the board. Key officers typically include the President and Chief Operating Officer (CEO), the Chief Operating Officer (COO), the Chief Financial Officer (CFO), the Secretary, and the Treasurer. Often a single person wears multiple hats – the CFO may, for example, be the Secretary and the Treasurer. Plus, the title of vice president is often used with many key players in the company, with various modifying adjectives. Examples: Senior VP in charge of hiring; Executive VP in charge of East Coast operations. In the corporate world, titles are a big deal and the combinations of available options are limitless.

Employees. Employees are those who work for the corporation but are not officers. They are managed by the officers. For most companies, a prerequisite to success is the ability to attract, retain and motivate quality employees. Effective employee motivation often is the key to achieving the company's goals and objectives. New technologies have increased productivity and enabled many companies to do more with fewer people; but, contrary to what some think, they have done nothing to reduce the importance of quality employees. Key challenges for most businesses today include improving employee skill levels, promoting employee stability, enhancing employee training, reducing employee turnover, and developing employees who care about the business.

D. ORGANIZATIONAL MECHANICS AND DOCUMENTS

1. CUSTOMIZATION AND DEFAULT RULES

In order to properly draft organizational documents that will meet a corporate client's objectives, a lawyer must understand the state corporate law that is going to apply to the corporation. This is essential because state corporate statutes specify important default rules that will apply unless the corporate organizational documents provide otherwise. These rules vary by state. In some situations, a particular default rule will be perfectly consistent with a client's objectives, and there will be no need to call attention to the rule in the organizational documents and trigger the possibility of other owners objecting. In such a situation, saying nothing in the documents and letting the default rule kick in may be the best course.

In many other situations, a particular default rule will be inconsistent with the client's core objectives and require special treatment in the organizational documents. This often leads to discussions or negotiations with others who are going to own an interest in the business. In these situations, the organizational documents must be customized to reflect the deal between the owners. Section A of Chapter 10 includes an extensive discussion of co-owner business protection issues and potential solution techniques for dealing with these issues in the organizational documents of a business.

In addition to applicable corporate default rules and the challenge of smart document customization, a lawyer should be aware of tax traps that may trigger an unwanted tax liability when a corporation is organized and stock is issued for non-cash assets or services. These traps are discussed in Chapter 8.

2. *KEY ORGANIZATION DOCUMENTS*

a. Articles of Incorporation

The Articles of Incorporation is the charter document mandated by state statute. The corporation comes into existence when this document is filed with the appropriate state authority. This is a public document that can be easily accessed by anyone. For this reason, often it is drawn to include only the minimum required provisions, which typically include the identity and address of the incorporators, the corporate name (which generally must contain the word "corporation," "incorporated," "company," or "limited," or the abbreviation "corp," "inc," "co," or "ltd."), the registered agent and office of the corporation, and the number of shares of stock that the corporation is authorized to issue. The articles of incorporation may and often does include the number and identity of the initial directors of the corporation and the purpose for which the corporation is organized. In some situations (see the following Section E), the articles of incorporation specify a par or stated value for the authorized common stock.

With this document, it is critically important that the state's default rules regarding certain matters be carefully evaluated. In some situations, a default rule that is ill advised or unacceptable can be negated only in the articles of incorporation. For example, the default rules of many states mandate cumulative voting or preemptive rights (discussed in Section A of Chapter 10) unless such rights are specifically denied in the articles of incorporation. Other states recognize such rights only if they are expressly provided for in the articles of incorporation. Other important issues (all discussed in following sections of this chapter or later chapters) that often require customized treatment in the articles of incorporation include limited liability for directors, the indemnification of directors and related expense advances, shareholder consent voting procedures, the authorization of "blank check" preferred stock, and supermajority shareholder voting requirements. See Section A of Chapter 15 for a sample form of Articles of Incorporation.

b. Bylaws

The bylaws serve as the owners' manual for the corporation. This document describes the roles of the shareholders, directors and officers and the mechanics for calling and holding meetings, approving consent resolutions, and handling other administrative and procedural matters. Key provisions often include:

- The number of directors
- Authorized use of electronic transmissions for shareholder notices
- Special meeting notice requirements
- The time and place of the annual meeting
- Authorized participation via communication equipment
- Authorized board actions through written resolutions without a meeting
- Board of director compensation authorization

- Officers' titles and duties
- Stock certificates and legends
- Stock transfer restrictions
- Indemnification provisions for officers and directors
- Fiscal year designation
- Bylaw amendment procedures
- Special tax elections.

c. Organizational Directors' Resolutions

These resolutions are approved by the board of directors and are essential for the organization and start-up of the business. They may be documented either as written consent resolutions signed by all the directors or as minutes of an organizational meeting where the directors approved the resolutions. The resolutions typically include provisions that:

- Approve the articles of incorporation
- Adopt the bylaws
- Elect the officers
- Authorize the issuance of stock and the receipt of consideration (money, property or services) for the stock
- Authorize the establishment of corporate bank accounts
- Ratify and approve any pre-incorporation business transactions
- Approve credit lines and other financing arrangements
- Authorize the commencement of business operations
- Authorize the execution of documents necessary for the acquisition of assets, leases, licenses and intellectual property rights
- Approve any other significant matters related to the start-up of the business

See Section C of Chapter 15 for a sample form for Organizational Directors' Resolutions.

d. Employment Agreements

These documents govern the employment relationship between the corporation and its key executives, including shareholders who are employed by the corporation. Often employment agreements are used to document important deal points between the owners. See Section B of Chapter 12 for a discussion of these agreements.

e. Stock Register and Stock Certificates

Stock certificates are often issued to the shareholders of closely held corporations. Usually they include legends referencing the provisions of the shareholder agreement (see below) and transfer restrictions under applicable securities laws. The stock register is a record of when specific shares were issued and to whom they were issued.

f. Asset Transfer Documents

Often documents are needed to transfer specific assets to the corporation. Examples include bills of sale, lease assignments, license agreements, and real estate deeds. Sometimes the documents include provisions requiring the corporation to assume liabilities related to the transferred assets.

g. Pre-Incorporation Agreement

In limited situations, the parties desire to document their mutual understandings regarding the formation of the corporation and their approval of the terms and conditions of all the organizational documents before steps are taken to officially form the corporation. This is accomplished with a pre-incorporation agreement, which includes the other organizational documents as attachments. A pre-incorporation agreement may deal with a wide range of issues, depending on the circumstances leading to the corporation's formation and the nature and scope of the understandings reached, and transactions undertaken, before the entity's formation. It is not a required document and is not used in many situations.

h. Required Government Filing

Each state requires that certain documents be filed and fees paid in order to form the corporation. Typically these documents include the Articles of Incorporation, the written consent of the registered agent for the corporation, and an application to obtain a state tax identification number. Also, a Form SS-4 needs to be filed with the Internal Revenue Service to obtain a federal tax identification number, and a Form 2553 is required if an S election (see Chapter 8) is desired. The corporation also must register as a foreign corporation in any other state where the corporation maintains assets or personnel.

i. Shareholder Agreement

An agreement between the shareholders of the corporation is critically important in nearly all situations involving closely held corporations. For planning purposes, this agreement usually is the most important document. It lays out the terms of the buy-sell agreements between shareholders and the details of those operational deal points that the shareholders have chosen to document. This is not a required document, and it is shamefully ignored in far too many situations. It takes more work, dialogue and customization than any other organizational document.

Although the authority to manage a corporation is vested in its board of directors, state corporate statutes generally authorize the use of a shareholder agreement to establish rights among the shareholders of a closely held corporation that preempt the management authority of the board. Many such state statutes are modeled after The Model Business Act, which specifically authorizes any such agreements among the shareholders of a non-public company that "govern the exercise of corporate powers or the management of the business and affairs of the corporation or the relationship among the shareholders, the directors and the corporation, or any of them, and is not contrary to public policy."[10]

The shareholders agreement should be carefully drafted, specify how long it will remain in effect (absent such a term provision, applicable state statutes may terminate the agreement after a specified term, such as 10 years), and be conspicuously referenced in written legends on all stock certificates that are issued by the corporation. See Chapter 10 for an expanded discussion of shareholder agreements.

E. CAPITAL STRUCTURE BUSINESS FACTORS

The capital structure of a corporation reflects how the business has secured funds to finance its assets and operations. A corporation basically has three options for securing funding: sell stock, borrow funds, or reinvest earnings. The capital structure reflects how these sources have been used to create rights and values for different stakeholders. As explained in Chapter 2, these sources appear on the right side of the balance sheet.

1. COMMON AND PREFERRED STOCK Q&AS

What is common stock? It is the foundational stock of a corporation. Every corporation has common stock. Common stockholders are the last in line in a bankruptcy proceeding and usually the big winners when a corporation performs well or is sold at a handsome profit. Dividends are often paid to common stockholders, but only after obligations to debt holders and preferred stockholders have been satisfied. Common stockholders usually have the exclusive right to elect the board of directors, are the primary beneficiaries of fiduciary duties imposed on the board of directors, and must approve major transactions, including substantial mergers and any sale of substantially all of the corporation's assets. Different classes of common stock and non-voting common stock may be issued.

Do common stockholders manage the corporation? No. Management issues are the responsibility of the board of directors, which is elected by the shareholders. However, as previously explained, shareholders in a closely held corporation usually have the statutory right to contractually bind themselves to operational matters in a manner that preempts the authority of the board.

What is the difference between authorized stock and issued stock? Authorized stock refers to the number of shares that the articles of incorporation authorize the board of directors to issue. Issued stock is the actual stock that the board has issued and is outstanding. The authorized stock of a corporation typically exceeds by many times the number of outstanding shares. If a corporation needs additional authorized stock, it must amend its articles of incorporation, and such an amendment requires shareholder approval.

---

10. MBCA § 7.32(a)(8).

What is par or stated value? It is a concept that was popular decades ago to protect creditors of a corporation. A corporation was required to designate a legal par or stated value of its stock and was prohibited from selling stock at a price below that designated par or stated value. The theory was that such a prohibition would protect against the issuance of "watered" stock that provided insufficient asset protection for creditors. The concept lost all its value when the use of very low par stock became the norm. Eventually the corporate laws of most states were amended to permit no-par stock. The Model Business Corporation Act completely rejects the concept of "par" or "stated" value, although a corporation may designate such a value in its articles of incorporation.[11] The official comments to MBCA § 6.21 state, "There is no minimum price at which specific shares must be issued and therefore there can be no 'watered stock' liability for issuing shares below an arbitrarily fixed price."

What is the meaning of the following phrase that often appears on a corporation's balance sheet: "Paid-in capital in excess of par value"? If a corporation's articles of incorporation designate a par or stated value, then the par or stated value of the shares outstanding is disclosed in the owners' equity section of the corporation's financial statements. The amounts in excess of the par or stated value that have actually been paid for the outstanding stock (usually many times the size of the par or stated value) are reflected in this line item in the owners' equity section. If the corporation has no par or stated value, there is no need for this separate line item, and the entire consideration paid for the stock is reflected as "Common Stock."

What constitutes valid consideration for common stock? The Model Business Corporation Act and most states define the scope of valid consideration broadly, permitting any "tangible or intangible property or benefit to the corporation, including cash, promissory notes, services performed, contracts for services to be performed, or other securities of the corporation."[12] Historically, a promise of future services and promissory notes were not authorized consideration for common stock. Residues of these limitations still exist in certain states that have not implemented the expansion provision of the Model Act. Delaware, for example, did not amend its corporate laws to permit stock to be issued for future services until 2004.

Who decides the terms for issuing common stock? The board of directors. State statures typically provide that the board's determination "is conclusive insofar as the adequacy of consideration for the issuance of shares relates to whether the shares are validly issued, fully paid, and nonassessable."[13]

Why would a corporation ever want to use non-voting common stock? Often in closely held corporations, particularly those dominated by a single family, there is a desire to spread the economic benefits of stock ownership to heirs or other individuals without disrupting the existing voting power. Non-voting common stock can be the answer in these situations. The recipients of the stock receive all the economic benefits of common stock, but no voting rights.

---

11. MBCA § 6.21.
12. MBCA § 6.21.
13. MBCA § 6.21(c).

Non-voting stock also may help avoid an estate tax trap that is triggered when a parent transfers stock to a child in a controlled corporation and, through some means, "directly or indirectly" retains the right to vote the stock. When this condition exists, section 2036(b) of the Internal Revenue Code may kick in and bring the stock back into the parent's estate for estate tax purposes. A safe way to avoid this trap is to transfer non-voting stock.

What is treasury stock? It is that portion of a company's issued shares of stock that the company keeps in its own treasury. It may come from a repurchase or buyback of stock from shareholders, or it may represent issued stock that was never sold to the public. Treasury shares have no dividend rights, no voting rights, and should not be included in any calculations that are based on the number of shares outstanding. Why have treasury shares? They may aid in meeting an urgent cash need (just sell the stock) and might help in warding off a hostile takeover (see Chapter 11).

What is preferred stock? It is any stock that has economic rights that are senior to the rights of common stock. The rights may be preferences in the event of liquidation, dividend preferences, call preferences, or any combination of these preferences.

Must preferred stock and its preferential terms be authorized in the articles of incorporation? The different classes of stock and the number of authorized shares in each class must be set forth in the articles of incorporation. Beyond this basic requirement, the articles of incorporation may give the board of directors the right to establish the terms and preferences of any preferred stock at the time it is issued.[14] Such a "blank check" provision promotes flexibility, greatly simplifies the articles of incorporation, enhances the board's authority, and reduces the need for shareholder approval.

What is the difference between cumulative and non-cumulative preferred stock? Preferred stock dividends typically are due on an annual or quarterly basis. Cumulative preferred stock requires the payment of all dividends that have accrued, including any that have been missed, before any dividends can be paid on common stock. The preferred dividends "cumulate." With non-cumulative preferred, a dividend payment obligation lapses once if it is not paid and ceases to be an impediment to common stock dividends. Obviously, cumulative preferred stock is the preference of most investors.

What is the difference between participating and non-participating preferred stock? Participating preferred stock pays the owner the dividend and liquidation preferences of the stock plus permits the owner to share (participate) in dividend and liquidation distributions made on the common stock. Non-participating preferred stock does not offer this sharing right with the common stock.

What is callable preferred stock? It is preferred stock that, by its terms, can be purchased ("called") by the corporation at specified times or under specified conditions. Often, the corporation is required to pay a call premium to

14. See MBCA § 6.02.

exercise this right.

What is convertible preferred stock? It is preferred stock that is convertible into common stock at a specified exchange ratio. This is an attractive option for many investment groups. The preferred stock provides liquidation and dividend preferences while the company's value is being built. The conversion feature ensures a large common stock return when the corporation is sold or goes public.

May preferred stockholders have voting and control rights? Yes. It's a matter of negotiation, and often preferred investors drive a hard bargain, demanding seats on the boards and preferential voting rights on specific matters. Corporate statutes typically provide preferred stockholders with the right to vote on any corporate structural change that would adversely impact their rights or preferences.

What is "subordinated" preferred stock? It is preferred stock that has rights that take a back seat (are subordinated) to the rights of another class of preferred shareholders. Subordination is common when multiple financing rounds are necessary to fund the growth of a business and the risks and stakes change with each round.

Why might a company prefer to issue preferred stock rather than common stock? The issuance of more common stock always dilutes the financial interests of the existing common stockholders in the growth in value of the business enterprise. For an investor who is looking for a fixed income yield, a non-convertible, cumulative, non-participating preferred stock may fit the bill without any serious dilution impacts to the existing common stockholders. Of course, if the preferred stock has a conversion feature, common stock dilution is likely if the business does well.

Why might a company prefer to issue preferred stock rather than debt? A preferred stock often resembles a debt obligation because it offers a fixed periodic yield and may offer the potential of being called ("paid off") at some point down the road. The big difference, though, is that it is not a debt subject to debt legal repayment obligations and default risks. The holder of a debt instrument usually has the right to accelerate payment of the entire obligation if required payments are not made or other covenants in the instrument are not satisfied. Plus, all parties know that the debt must be paid off at a given point in time in accordance with its terms. In contrast, preferred stock usually is far more forgiving. If a dividend payment is missed, it may "cumulate" and move forward as an obstacle to common stock dividends, but it will not trigger the burdens of a default on a debt obligation. With preferred stock, there may be the possibility, and perhaps even an expectation, that it will be retired through redemption at some future point, but usually there is no legal obligation comparable to that included in a debt instrument. The bottom line is that a preferred stock, as compared to a debt, is more flexible for the corporation and offers fewer guarantees to the investor. For that reason, the stated yield on a preferred stock often must be higher than a debt obligation of the same corporation in order to attract investors.

Are actively-traded preferred stocks rated? Yes. As with bonds, actively-traded preferred stocks are rated by the major credit rating companies, such as Standard & Poor's and Moody's. The rating of a company's preferred stock is generally one or two tiers below that of the same company's bonds because preferred dividends do not carry the same guarantees and they are junior to all creditors of the company.

What is a stock option? A stock option is a contract that gives a person, usually an executive, the right to buy stock from the company over a designated period of time on certain specified terms and conditions. With any stock option plan, there are three key points in time: the time the person is given the option (the "grant date"), the time the person acquires the stock through the exercise of the option and payment of the option price (the "exercise date"), and the time that the stock is sold and the sales price is realized in the form of cash (the "sale date").

Why do corporations issue stock options? Typically stock options are used to incentivize executives. They are a form of compensation that can handsomely reward those who cause a company's common stock price to escalate over time. There are two general types of stock options: incentive stock options ("ISOs" and sometimes called "qualified stock options") and non-qualified stock options. The requirements and tax consequences of these two types are very different. Details regarding these option types and the business factors that impact the use of such options are discussed in Section B of Chapter 12.

What is restricted stock? It is stock that is given to an executive as compensation with strings attached – restrictions. If one of the restrictions is violated, the company yanks the string and retrieves all or a portion of the stock. There is broad authority in structuring these restrictions. For example, the restriction may provide that if the executive leaves the company at any time during the following 10 years, he or she will forfeit all the stock. Alternatively, it may allow the stock to "vest" at a designated rate, such as 5 percent, each year or may provide that all or a portion of the stock shall be forfeited if the executive fails to hit certain sales volumes or otherwise fails to satisfy some other objective measure of performance. Details regarding restricted stock and the business factors that impact the use of such stock are discussed in Section B of Chapter 12.

What are retained earnings? They are the portion of a company's net earnings that are not paid out as dividends but rather are retained by the company to finance growth or retire debt. A company's total retained earnings are reflected in a line item in the shareholders' equity section of the balance sheet. Retained earnings are calculated by adding current net income to (or subtracting current net losses from) the beginning retained earnings balance and then subtracting any shareholder dividends declared during the year. Thus, it is possible to have a deficit balance in a retained earnings account. Retained earnings are sometimes referred to as "retained surplus," "earned surplus," or "retention ratio."

What are stock indexes? They are various indexes that track movements of certain public company stock values throughout every business day. Usually one can't avoid hearing of the most popular three indexes: the Dow Jones Industrial Average (an index based on 30 stocks); the NASDAQ (which tracks thousands of stocks, many in the technology and communication sectors); and the S&P 500 (an index based on 500 stocks traded on the New York Stock exchange). Other much less visible, but highly regarded, indexes include the Russell 2000 Index (which tracks 2,000 stocks traded on the over-the-counter ("OTC") market) and the Wilson 5000 Equity Index (which is based on thousands of stocks of varying sizes).

STUDENT PROBLEM 4-2

Reference Jennifer's business plan described in Student Problem 4-1 and her plans to form View Inc., have stock issued to herself and each of her four investors, and to have a three-person board. As Jennifer prepares to form View Inc., she has 12 questions that need answering. Please answer the following for her:

1. As the largest shareholder and chief executive officer of the corporation, does Jennifer have to be identified in the state's records as the registered agent of the corporation or the incorporator of the corporation?

2. Do the names of the directors have to be disclosed in the articles of incorporation?

3. Can the corporation be named "The View"?

4. When does the corporation come into existence?

5. When can the corporation start conducting business?

6. Can Jennifer be issued stock for the services that she has provided in developing the plan and forming the corporation even though she contributes no money or assets to the corporation?

7. Will the terms for issuing stock need to be included in the articles of incorporation?

8. Must the common stock of the corporation have a par or stated value? What are the benefits of having a par or stated value?

9. Can preferred stock be authorized in the articles of incorporation without specifying the preferences provided by the preferred stock?

10. Could Jennifer have the right to elect all five members of the board of directors even though she owns only 40 percent of the stock?

11. Will Jennifer's investors have any management authority with respect to the business?

12. If Jennifer needs to provide her investors with select management rights in order to secure their funding, how could such rights be provided without putting investors on the board?

2. *DIVIDEND CHALLENGES*

There are three ways that a shareholder realizes a yield on an investment in the stock of a corporation. First, the shareholder can hold the stock until the corporations sells its business to a third party and liquidates. Corporate sales are discussed in Section C of Chapter 10.

Second, the shareholder can sell the stock to a third party. An investment in a public corporation whose stock is actively traded can easily be sold at any time. The sale of stock in a closely held corporation presents a much tougher challenge. Usually there is no market for the stock, and the other shareholders do not want stock in the enterprise being shopped to third parties. This is why the buy-sell provisions between the owners of a closely held corporation (discussed in Section B of Chapter 10) are such a big deal. These provisions spell out those situations where a shareholder's stock will be purchased by the corporation or the other shareholders and the terms and conditions of such a purchase. They also lay out the conditions that must be satisfied for a shareholder to sell stock to third parties.

Third, shareholders can receive dividends from the corporation, which represent distributions of the company's earnings, or receive payments from the corporation in redemption of all or a portion of their stock. Preferred stocks often specify periodic dividends that are to be paid before any dividends are paid to those who own the common stock of the corporation. Payment of dividends or redemption payments on common stock are usually at the discretion of the board of directors. The dividend and redemption policies of the board can trigger legal problems if dividends are too low or nonexistent, or if dividends are too large.

a. Oppression Claim Risks

When dividends are too low or nonexistent, minority shareholders of a closely held corporation may complain that they are being treated unfairly by those in control. In many situations, the essence of the claim is that the minority shareholder is being oppressed and squeezed out, with no opportunity to realize any yield on the stock because it can't be sold and no dividends are being paid. Often the claim is accompanied by allegations that the controlling shareholder is able to generate income from the corporation through lucrative compensation payments.

Such oppression claims can result in drastic remedies. For example, in *Bonavita v. Corbo,*[15] Gerald Bonavita, the owner of 50 percent of the stock of Corbo Jewelers, Inc., a New Jersey corporation, brought suit against Alan Corbo, the other 50 percent owner, alleging that the corporation was deadlocked and that he was a victim of oppression by Corbo. The plaintiff established that the corporation paid no dividends even though its financials were strong ($5 million of retained earnings, cash of $1.1 million, and current liabilities of only $12,000), the Corbo family annually withdrew salaries and benefits of over $400,000, negotiations to buy Bonavita's stock had broken down, and only the Corbo family received any benefits from the corporation. Corbo contended that the

15. 692 A.2d 119 (Ch. Div. 1996).

Board's decision to not pay dividends was protected by the business judgment rule presumption and the corporation's need to maintain substantial cash reserves to quickly take advantage of "bargain" purchases. Recognizing that this was not a case of board deadlock (the company had two directors who could act) and that the board's dividend policy would be "unassailable" under the business judgment rule if it impacted the shareholders equally, the court found that Corbo's conduct had "destroyed any reasonable expectation" of benefit from the Bonavita stock and, as a result, such stock had "absolutely no value." The court concluded that such conduct constituted "oppression" under New Jersey law, reviewed the available remedies, and ordered the corporation or Corbo to purchase Bonavita's stock for $1.9 million (other purchase details were to be worked out by a court-appointed fiscal agent). The court reasoned that this was "a less drastic remedy" than dissolution and eliminated the ongoing annual battles that would result with "a lesser remedy."

b. Excessive Dividend Risks

Legal problems also can surface when the board authorizes the payment of dividends or stock redemption payments that are too large. The overriding fear is that the corporation will be stripped of all its assets through generous payments to its shareholders and will not be able to meet its obligations to creditors. There have been legal limitations on the payment of excessive dividends or redemption payments from the beginning.

The old approach adopted a relatively complicated concept of legal capital – a designated minimum amount of capital (usually the par or stated value of the stock times the number of shares outstanding) that a corporation was required to maintain in the enterprise. Any capital or earnings in excess of the minimum capital was considered "surplus" that could be used to pay dividends or repurchase the corporation's stock. This minimum capital approach has proved inadequate over time because a corporation could designate an insignificant par or stated value that had no relationship to its stock's value or the corporation's capacity to honor its obligations. The result was that a corporation could pay large dividends, meet its minimum legal capital obligation, and be left with insufficient assets to pay its creditors. Although admittedly inadequate, this minimum capital approach is still part of the statutory schemes of certain states.

The modern statutory approach to excessive dividends or redemption payments, adopted by the Model Business Corporation Act and many states, imposes a two-prong test: a "Solvency" test and a "Balance Sheet" test.[16] The Solvency test prohibits a corporation from paying dividends or repurchasing its own stock if the corporation is unable to pay its debts as they become due in the ordinary course of business. The Balance Sheet test prohibits a corporation from paying dividends or purchasing its own stock if the corporation's total assets are less than the sum of its total liabilities and any liquidation preferences that would be owed if the corporation dissolved at the time of distribution. State statutes often provide that, for purposes of the Balance Sheet test, asset values may be based on the corporation's financial statements prepared in accordance with

16. MBCA § 6.40(c), (d).

generally accepted accounting principles or a reasonable fair valuation of the assets.

Under the Model Act and many state statutes, these dividend limitations carry three significant consequences. First, board members can be held personally liable for consenting to the payment of any dividend that exceeds the statutory limitation.[17] Second, a corporation may not relieve a board member of such personal dividend liability exposure by a "good faith" exculpatory provision in the corporation's articles of incorporation or bylaws.[18] And third, any shareholder who receives such a dividend with knowledge that it exceeds the limitations may be required to repay the dividend to a director who has been held liable for the unlawful distribution.[19]

How does Delaware, the controlling law for many corporations, deal with the risks of excessive dividends? Delaware still has the old minimum capital/surplus scheme for limiting the payment of excessive dividends. Dividends and share repurchases may be made out of "surplus," defined to mean capital that exceeds the par or stated value of the shares and any additional amounts that the board elects to add to the minimum stated capital. The board has tremendous flexibility in structuring dividends and share repurchases that fit within the limitations of this statutory scheme.

STUDENT PROBLEM 4-3

Reference Jennifer's business plan described in Student Problem 4-1. View Inc. is formed, acquires the real estate, and commences the extensive renovation effort. Unforeseen problems soon cause delays in the approval processes that generated rumblings from the investors. To pacify the investors and show strength, Jennifer's called a board meeting and had the board approve a redemption of 20 percent of the corporation's outstanding stock from all shareholders, pro rata, for the sum of $600,000. At the time of the redemption, Jennifer was convinced that if additional funding was required, it could easily be obtained as the project neared completion. The delays continued, causing construction problems and triggering prohibitively expensive cost overruns. In the eighteenth month following the redemption, Jennifer concluded that the project was "in shambles," the economics of the venture "no longer worked," and the company lacked the funds needed to complete the project and the ability to secure such funds. An emergency board meeting was followed by an announcement that the corporation must abandon the project, the property would be conveyed back to the prior owner pursuant to an outstanding note and deed of trust, and unpaid trade creditors would be paid approximately 40 percent of what they are owed.

Assuming View Inc. was incorporated in a state that had adopted the Model Business Corporation Act, was the redemption payment to the shareholders legal at the time it was made? What additional facts (if any) would help in making this

---

17. MBCA § 8.33.
18. MBCA § 2.02(b)(5).
19. MBCA § 8.33(b)(2).

determination? If the payment was not in compliance with the applicable statute, who would have personal exposure for such redemption payment and under what circumstances would liability be imposed?

3. *SHAREHOLDER DEBT IN CLOSELY HELD CORPORATIONS*

In the course of forming many closely held corporations, the shareholders conclude that it is advantageous from a tax perspective to receive corporate debt in return for a significant portion of the money they contribute to the enterprise. Take Sam, Dick and Joy, each of whom has agreed to contribute $500,000 to a start-up corporation that they believe will "quickly take off." One option is to receive only common stock for their contributions. They would each end up owning one third of the equity, and all cash distributions to them would be taxed as double-taxed dividends (see Chapter 8). Or suppose instead they each receive stock for $150,000 of their contributed capital and corporate notes for the remaining $350,000. They still each own one-third of the equity, with equal voting rights and value appreciation rights. But the tax impacts of cash distributions as the business "takes off" would have changed dramatically if (and it's a big "if") the debt works.

First, there would be no double tax hit on the debt element because the interest payments on the shareholder debt would be deductible by the corporation. Even though interest is taxed to the shareholders at ordinary rates instead of the favorable dividends rates, the net aggregate tax cost for the corporation and the shareholders will still be reduced in nearly all situations. Second (and here's the really big deal), the principal balance of the debt ($350,000 for each shareholder) may be paid off tax free to the shareholders as a return of capital. This gives the corporation the capacity to repay 70 percent of the contributed capital free of any double tax hit.

Will such a shareholder debt plan work? Maybe. Obviously, the IRS has an interest in trying to characterize the shareholder debt as equity for tax purposes. This re-characterization fight has been the subject of countless cases. What has emerged is a body of vague muss, characterized as a "jungle" by one court[20] and a "viper's tangle" by the leading commentator.[21] What we do know is that greed – pushing the concept too far – promises problems. We also know that key factors in assessing the greed include the debt-to-equity ratio (the higher the riskier), the real intent of the parties (as manifested by the terms of the documents and the capacity of the company to service and discharge the debt), proportionality among shareholders (the more proportionality, the more it is suspect), equity conversion rights (usually a killer), and subordination of the debt to other creditors (hurts, but not fatal).[22]

As the courts wrestled with the issue, Congress tried to offer some clarity by enacting Section 385 as part of the comprehensive Tax Reform Act of 1969, heralded as the 1969 Act's "most important" provision[23] because it empowered

---

20. See Commissioner v. Union Mutual Insurance Co. of Providence, 386 F.2d 974, 978 (1st Cir. 1967).

21. Bittker & Eustice, Federal Income Taxation of Corporations and Shareholders ¶ 4.04 (4th ed. 1979).

22. See, e.g., Hariton, "Essay: Distinguishing Between Equity and Debt in the New Financial Environment," 49 Tax L. Rev. 499 (1994).

23. Bittker & Eustice, Federal Income Taxation of Corporations and Shareholders ¶ 4.05 (3rd ed. 1971).

the Treasury to promulgate definitive regulations for determining whether and when a shareholder debt instrument would be treated as debt or equity. Temporary regulations came years later, followed by a second attempt, but then (over the cries of far too many) all was withdrawn and the effort was abandoned in 1983.[24] Nothing has happened since, suggesting that even the Treasury, specifically empowered by Congress, couldn't create acceptable standards that bring certainty to the muss.

So the muss remains. This does not mean that shareholder debt should not be used in planning the capital structure of a closely held enterprise. The advantages are powerful. It means that care and prudence are required, along with a willingness of the clients to live with a little uncertainty and risk. For planning purposes, there are a few semi-bright lights that have emerged from case law and the aborted 385 regulation effort that help in structuring shareholder debt that doesn't cross over the line.

First, any hybrid equity characteristics, such as equity conversion rights, contingent interest obligations, or interest obligations tied to profitability, will kill any debt as debt for tax purposes.[25] They just can't exist.

Second, the debt-to-equity ratio is often the key factor in determining if the debt is "excessive." Under the old 385 regulations, the "excessive" tag was avoided if the outside debt-to-equity ratio (based on all liabilities of the corporation) did not exceed 10-to-1 and the inside debt-to-equity ratio (based only on the shareholder debt) did not exceed 3-to-1.[26]

Third, the intent of the parties to treat the debt as real debt requires that the debt instrument be a commercially "normal" debt instrument (unconditional promise to pay, sum certain, payment dates certain, reasonable interest rate, etc.) and that there is a reasonable basis (hopefully supported by reasonable projections) for concluding that the corporation will have no problem timely making all payments due under the debt instrument.

Fourth, shareholder debt that is proportional among the shareholders is highly suspect, but not necessarily deadly. It may be treated as debt if it is issued for cash or property, bears a reasonable rate of interest, satisfies the old 385 regulation's debt-to-equity safe harbors (10-to-1 and 3-to-1), and has all the appropriate "intent" trappings.[27]

Fifth, subordination of shareholder debt to outside creditors should not be fatal if all other factors are solid, but it can become a big negative if the "intent" issue is equivocal, the debt-to-equity ratios are at or beyond the outer limits, and/or a proportionality condition exists.

Finally, no matter how safely the debt is structured, the client should be advised of the inherent uncertainties and the importance of honoring the terms of the debt and respecting the debt as real debt.

---

24. T.D. 7920, 48 Fed. Reg. 31054 (July 6, 1983). The temporary regulations were published in 45 Fed. Reg. 18957 (1980) and the final regulations in 45 Fed. Reg. 86438 (1980).

25. Prop. Reg. §§ 1.385-3(d), 1.385-0(c)(2).

26. Prop. Reg. §§ 1.385-6(f)(2).

27. Prop. Reg. §§ 1.385-6.

STUDENT PROBLEM 4-4

Reference Jennifer's business plan described in Student Problem 4-1. Each of Jennifer's four investors has agreed to contribute $900,000 to the corporation, provided:

- The investors' contributions are returned first in the event of a sale or liquidation of the company

- The investors receive a priority annual yield equal to six percent of their contributions before any payments are made to other shareholders

- Each investor receives 15 percent of all other distributions made to shareholders, of whatever kind and nature.

1. Explain how preferred stock might be used to meet the demands of the investors? Would Jennifer prefer that such stock be cumulative or non-cumulative? What rights would the investors have if the corporation is unable to make an annual dividend payment? Would the preferred stock need to be convertible into common stock of the company in order to meet the demands of the investors?

2. Assume instead that each investor receives 15 percent of the common stock of the corporation in return for $150,000 and a note from the corporation with a principal balance of $650,000 in return for the remaining $650,000. The loan balance, plus interest at the Wall Street Journal Prime Rate, will be paid off over an eight-year period. No payment will be due for the first 24 months, and then principal and all accrued and current interest charges will be amortized and paid in monthly installments over a six-year period. Projections indicate that View Inc. will be profitable as soon as it commences operations and should have no problem timely servicing such debt obligations to the investors. What are the potential tax advantages of such a plan? Will the plan, as structured, accomplish these objectives? What additional facts would you like to have? What changes to the plan would you suggest?

F. LIABILITY EXPOSURES OF DIRECTORS AND OFFICERS

Director and officers of a corporation are fiduciaries who are subject to duties that are designed to protect the corporation and its shareholders from a host of wrongs, including mismanagement and abusive self-dealing. A breach of these duties often results in a lawsuit, usually a derivative claim brought for the benefit of the corporation by attorneys representing named shareholders who seek to hold the alleged wrongdoers liable. Shareholder lawsuits are discussed in Section D of the following Chapter 5.

These fiduciary duties are the primary accountability link between those who own the corporation and those who manage the enterprise. Every corporate director and officer should be mindful of them. They generally are referred to as the duty of care and the duty of loyalty.

1. DUTY OF CARE

The duty of care requires a director or officer to discharge his or her duties in good faith, with the care that a reasonably prudent person in a like position would exercise under similar circumstances and in a manner reasonably believed to be in the best interests of the corporation. The duty is not premised on any personal benefit realized by the fiduciary; its entire focus is on poor job performance – wanton neglect, shoddy oversight, failure to get informed, defective communications, and the like. Although primarily developed through case law, this definition of the duty of care (or one very similar to it) has been codified as a part of the corporate statutes in most states.

Some states have adopted the latest Model Business Corporation Act definition, which rejects the "reasonably prudent person" standard to ensure that the duty of care is not premised on a negligence or tort law concept that promotes caution and discourages risk-taking.[28] The MBCA definition requires each director to act in good faith and in a manner the director reasonably believes to be in the best interests of the corporation and requires the board (as a whole) to "discharge its duty with the care a person in a like position would reasonably believe appropriate under the circumstances."[29]

Any claim involving an alleged breach of the duty of care must be evaluated in the context of the business judgment rule, a judicially created rule that prevents a court from second guessing substantive decisions made by a board. The rationale for the rule it that it is beyond the expertise and role of courts to meddle in corporate affairs and that a board must be free to make tough decisions and take risks without fear of being legally challenged in hindsight. The rule will not protect dereliction of duty, bad faith, conflicts of interest, and irrational decisions that rise to the level of waste, but it will be a formidable obstacle to many mismanagement claims. In Delaware and many other states, the rule has both a procedural and substantive impact, providing a presumption that the directors were informed, acted in good faith, and reasonably believed that their decision was in the best interests of the corporation. If the plaintiff is unable to sustain the burden of proving why the rule and its associated presumption should not apply, the case will be dismissed.

For example, in *Shlensky v. Wrigley,*[30] the business judgment rule proved insurmountable for a minority shareholder of the corporation that owned the Chicago Cubs baseball team. The shareholder brought a derivative action against the directors for negligence and mismanagement, alleging that the corporation was sustaining losses because, unlike the management of all other major league teams, the board refused to install lights and schedule night games at Wrigley Field in accordance with the dominant shareholder's belief that baseball was a "daytime sport." The appellate court affirmed the lower court's dismissal of the case, noting that the "judgment of the directors of corporations enjoys the benefit of a presumption that it was formed in good faith and designed to promote the best interests of the corporation they serve." While stating that it was beyond its

28. Official Comment to MBCA § 8.30(a).
29. MBCA § 8.30(a).
30. 95 Ill.App.2d 173, 237 N.E.2d 776 (1968)

"jurisdiction and ability" to rule on the correctness of the directors' decision, the court found that the decision did not involve fraud, illegality, a conflict of interest, or negligence. The court stated that "unless the conduct of the defendants at least borders on one of these elements, the courts should not interfere."

An additional obstacle to many claims alleging a breach of the duty of care grew out of the landmark case of *Smith v. Van Gorkom*,[31] in which a board that included four CEOs of large companies and a former dean of the Chicago Business School was held liable for breach of their duty of care for approving a merger on the recommendation of the corporation's CEO (Van Gorkom). In reversing the lower court and holding the director's liable for breach of their duty of care, the Delaware Supreme Court concluded: (1) a business judgment is an informed decision only if a board has all reasonably available material information before making the decision; (2) a standard of gross negligence is applied in determining whether a decision was informed; and (3) the board was grossly negligent because it failed to inform itself of Van Gorkom's role, was uninformed as to the intrinsic value of the company, accepted without scrutiny Van Gorkom's value representation, and deliberated only a few hours. Characterizing the majority opinion as "an advocate's closing address," the dissent argued that the business judgment rule was applicable and pointed to the directors' strong credentials, extensive backgrounds in business, experiences with corporate mergers and takeovers, knowledge of the company ("knew it like the back of their hands"), and inability to be "taken in by a fast shuffle."

The *Van Gorkom* decision was a bombshell. A $23.5 million judgment, rendered in favor of over 12,000 shareholders, was entered against a highly distinguished group of directors for approving a transaction that yielded the aggrieved shareholders a price that was 50 percent higher than the existing market price for their stock. The shock of the decision and the risk it posed for corporate directors drove Delaware to adopt, almost immediately following the decision, Section 102(b)(7) of Delaware's General Corporate Law. This section permits a Delaware corporation to include a provision in its charter that protects directors from personal money damages for any claim alleging a breach of the duty of care, with limited exception. The exceptions are claims based on an alleged breach of the duty of loyalty, acts or omissions not in good faith or which involve intentional misconduct or a knowing violation of the law, the improper payment of dividends, or a transaction from which a director derived an improper personal benefit.

States have now adopted similar duty-of-care protection statutes that authorize a provision in the articles of incorporation that eliminates monetary damages for most breach of duty-of-care claims. Many are patterned after the MBCA's counterpart to Delaware's Section 102(b)(7), which authorizes a provision "eliminating or limiting the liability of a director to the corporation or its shareholders for money damages for any action taken, or any failure to take any action, as a director," except a liability for the receipt of a financial benefit to which the director was not entitled, for an intentional infliction of harm on the

---

31. 488 A.2d 858 (Del. 1985).

corporation or the shareholders, for the approval of an unlawful dividend, or for an intentional violation of criminal law.[32]

The obvious question: Given the limiting impacts of the business judgment rule and charter provisions eliminating money damage claims (which are now the norm), what remains of the duty of care? Breach claims are still possible, but the exposure range is very limited.

A complete dereliction of duty can still be the basis of a valid duty-of-care claim. For example, in *In Re Walt Disney Company Derivative Litigation (II),*[33] Disney shareholders brought a derivative lawsuit against the Disney board members, alleging that they had breached their fiduciary duties by blindly approving an employment contract with Disney's new president that ended up paying the president a severance benefit of more than $350,000 for each day that he had worked at Disney. Delaware's Chancery Court held that the plaintiff's new complaint could withstand a motion to dismiss because its allegations were not limited to "mere" negligence or gross negligence, but claimed that the board members had "made no good faith" effort to fulfill their fiduciary duties, had abdicated all responsibility, and had failed to "meet minimal proceduralist standards of attention." The court reasoned that the provision in the articles of incorporation protecting directors from money damages did not apply to acts or omissions not undertaken honestly or in good faith and that the business judgment rule presumption did not apply when there was no good faith exercise of any business judgment.

A charter provision limiting director liability usually will not protect officers. In *McPadden v. Sidhu,*[34] shareholders brought suit against the directors and a corporate officer (Dubreville) for approving a sale of a subsidiary to a group of investors led by Dubreville, alleging that the price was grossly inadequate. In reply, the directors alleged that they were protected by an exculpatory provision in the corporation's charter limiting the directors' liability for any actions not constituting bad faith. The court held that although the plaintiffs had proven gross negligence on the part of the board, they had not proven bad faith, reasoning that bad faith required either motivation of subjective bad intent or actions amounting to an "intentional dereliction of duty or the conscious disregard for one's responsibilities." Thus, the court ruled that the directors were protected by the corporation's exculpatory provision, and granted defendants' motion to dismiss as to the directors. However, the court ruled that the case against Dubreville could move forward because, as an officer of TSC, he was not shielded by the charter provision that limited directors' liability for money damages.

There are two other common situations that might lead to a finding of bad faith to sustain a duty-of-care-breach claim and render inapplicable a charter provision limiting directors' liability for money damages. The first is a bad faith oversight claim where directors are aware of an existing risk and utterly fail to implement any reporting or information system or controls related to the risk or

32. MBCA § 2.02(b)(4).
33. 825 A.2d 275 (Del.Ch. 2003).
34. 964 A.2d 1262 (Del.Ch. 2008).

consciously fail to monitor or oversee the operation of such a system.[35] The second is a bad faith disclosure claim based on the directors' distribution of false or misleading information to the corporation's shareholders.[36]

2. DUTY OF LOYALTY

The duty of loyalty focuses on self-dealing and other actions where an officer or director acts against the best interests of the corporation or seeks to reap a personal benefit not generally available to the shareholders of the corporation. A claim based on an alleged breach of loyalty typically is more sinister than a duty-of-care claim and, if supported by particularized facts, can often withstand a motion to dismiss. Neither the business judgment rule nor a charter provision limiting directors' liability for money damages will apply to bar such a claim. Generally, breach-of-loyalty claims arise in one or more of three contexts.

a. Undisclosed Benefits

The clearest context is the situation where an officer or director uses his or her position to secretly reap personal profits or kickbacks or misuse corporate assets. A breach-of-loyalty claim can be sustained even if there is no apparent injury to the corporation. For example, in *Hawaiian International Finances, Inc. v. Pablo*,[37] a corporate president and director (who was also a licensed real estate broker) was deemed to have violated his duty of loyalty to the corporation by personally sharing a real estate commission that was paid as a result of the corporation's purchase of a parcel of real estate. The president's personal interest in the commission was not disclosed to the corporation. In rejecting the president's arguments that the size of the total commission in the transaction was customary and that the corporation (not being a licensed broker) could not have legally shared in the transaction, the court held that a director and officer "cannot profit from" the breach of a fiduciary obligation and reasoned that knowledge of the president's personal interest in the commission may have provided the corporation with a basis for negotiating a better price for the real estate.

b. Interested-Fiduciary Transactions

There are a variety of situations where a known conflict of interest is created between an officer or director of a corporation and the corporation itself. It may be a transaction involving the purchase or sale of property, the provision of services, intellectual property contractual rights, and a host of other considerations. The common factor in these situations is that the officer or director has a personal interest in the side of the transaction that sets opposite the corporation.

Historically, courts ruled that such transactions were void because of the inherent risk that the interested fiduciary could misuse his or her position for personal gain to the detriment of the corporation. The harshness of this rigid

35. See, for example, In Re Caremark International Inc. Derivative Litigation, 698 A.2d 959 (Del.Ch. 1996), and Stone v. Ritter, 911 A.2d 362 (Del. 2006).

36. See, for example, Malone v. Brincat, 722 A.2d 5 (Del. 1998) and Gantler v. Stephens, 965 A.2d 695 (Del. 2009).

37. 488 P.2d 1172 (Haw. 1971).

"void" rule soon gave way to realizations that often such interested-fiduciary transactions were in the best interests of the corporation and that many qualified outside directors would refuse to serve if there was a permanent bar to transactions between the corporation and other companies that they owned or served. What followed in most jurisdictions was a judicially created, two-pronged "voidable" rule that required the interested fiduciary to sustain the burden of proving both procedural and substantive fairness. Procedural fairness required a showing of full disclosure and approval of the transaction by disinterested directors or disinterested shareholders. Substantive fairness required a showing that the terms of the transaction were fair and reasonable to the corporation.

California then took the lead in adopting a statute[38] that dealt specifically with transactions involving a director's conflict of interest. Nearly all states, including Delaware, now have statutes dealing with "Directors' Conflicting Interest Transactions." The common element in these statutes, including the MBCA[39] version, is a three-prong approach for removing the taint of the director's interest in the transaction: (1) approval of the transaction by a majority of the disinterested directors after full disclosure of all material facts; (2) approval of the transaction by a majority of disinterested shareholders after full disclosure of all material facts; or (3) the interested director proving that the transaction was just, reasonable and fair to the corporation.

Although state statutes typically incorporate this three-prong structure, differences and ambiguities often surface in determining the impact of an approval by disinterested directors on the scope of the judicial review of the transaction. Some courts have viewed such director approval as only proof of procedural fairness and have still required that the interested director prove substantive fairness.[40] Other courts have held that approval by disinterested directors shifts the burden of proof on the substantive fairness issue to the plaintiffs.[41] And many courts, including those in Delaware[42] and states that have adopted the MBCA version of the statute, significantly elevate the impact of an approval by disinterested directors by holding that such an approval triggers the business judgment rule presumption or otherwise eliminates any substantive fairness inquiry. In these states, the plaintiff's only hope, as a practical matter, is to attack the process of approval and the applicability of the business judgment rule presumption by proving waste (nearly impossible as described below), defective disclosures, a lack of director independence, or a gross dereliction of the duty to be informed.

There is more certainty when the transaction has been approved by a majority of the disinterested shareholders. As a practical matter, the plaintiff has only two limited options. The first is to prove that the disclosures to the shareholders were defective in some material respect. This would nullify the

---

38. California Corporations Code § 310 (present statute).

39. See Subchapter F of the Model Business Corporations Act.

40. See, for example, Cookies Food Products, Inc. v. Lakes Warehouse Distributing, Inc., 430 N.W.2d 447 (Iowa 1988).

41. See, for example, Cohen v. Ayers, 596 F.2d 733 (7th Cir. 1979).

42. Benihana of Tokyo, Inc. v. Benihana, Inc., 906 A.2d 114 (Del. Supr. 2006).

shareholder vote and restore the obligation of the interested fiduciary to sustain the burden of proving the substantive fairness of the transaction. The second option is to prove waste, which requires the plaintiff to show that the consideration received by the corporation in the transaction was so inadequate that no ordinary person with sound business judgment would have approved the transaction. It's an extremely difficult burden of proof, often requiring proof of a gift or no valuable consideration. And logically it's difficult to comprehend how and why a majority of fully informed, disinterested shareholders would ever approve a transaction that meets the definition of waste.[43]

c. Corporate Opportunity Doctrine

The third context that often triggers a breach of loyalty claim is the situation where a director personally appropriates a business opportunity that should have first been offered to the corporation. If the particular venture constitutes a corporate opportunity, the director must fully disclose all material details to the corporation and not act until the corporation rejects the opportunity. If it does not constitute a corporate opportunity, the director is free to proceed without any disclosure or corporate rejection.

The threshold challenge is determining whether a particular opportunity is subject to this corporate opportunity doctrine. Courts have considered various factors in making this determination, including how the director learned of the opportunity, whether the corporation was known to have a special or unique interest in the opportunity (the "interest test"), whether the opportunity fell within the scope of the corporation's line of business (the "line of business test"), whether fairness based on the totality of the circumstances required court intervention to protect the interests of the corporation (the "fairness test"), whether the corporation had the financial capacity to participate in the transaction, and the known expertise and other business interests of the director. The cases of *Farber v. Servan Land Company, Inc.*[44] and *Broz v. Cellular Information Systems, Inc.*[45] illustrate the relevant factors and the difficulty of applying the factors to a given set of facts.

In *Farber*, the board of Servan Land Company ("SLC") had considered the purchase of a parcel of land adjacent to its golf course, but had taken no action. Later, Serianni and Servan, the two majority shareholders of SLC (also directors and key officers), purchased the parcel on their own. A year later the issue of the purchase by Serianni and Servan was raised at a shareholders' meeting, and there was conflicting evidence as to whether the shareholders had ratified and approved their purchase at that meeting. Three years later, SLC, Serianni and Servan sold their adjoining parcels to a third-party for a price that was allocated to produce a yield for SLC's shareholders that was greater as a result of the purchase by Serianni and Servan. Farber, a shareholder in SLC, brought suit, alleging that Serianni and Servan had violated their duty of loyalty by

43. See Harbor Finance Partners v. Huizenga, 751 A.2d 879 (Del. Ch. 1999) for a discuss of the waste standard in the context of an approval by disinterested shareholders and a persuasive argument (in dicta) that the standard is unnecessary and does more harm than good.

44. 662 F.2d 371 (5th Cir. 1981).

45. 673 A.2d 148 (Del. Supr. 1996).

misappropriating a corporate opportunity and that all profits from the joint sale should be paid to the shareholders of SLC.

The trial court (on remand from the Fifth Circuit) ruled in favor of Serianni and Servan, concluding that they had proven the propriety of their purchase because SLC had taken no action to acquire the adjoining parcel, the shareholders had ratified the purchase three years later when they approved the joint sale, and Serianni and Servan had been generous in allocating the sales proceeds. The Fifth Circuit reversed, holding that a corporate opportunity existed (the purchase fit within the activities of SLC and had been previously discussed), the corporation never rejected the opportunity to purchase, there was no effective ratification because Serianni and Servan controlled the vote, and the presumed economic benefit to SLC from the joint sale was irrelevant (a fortuitous sale could not impact the applicability of the corporate opportunity doctrine).

In *Broz*, the outcome was completely different. Robert Broz, president and sole shareholder of RFBC, a cellular telephone service provider, was also on the board of Cellular Information Systems ("CIS"), a separate and competing cellular service provider. Through personal connections unrelated to CIS, Broz became aware of an opportunity to purchase a cellular service license for a portion of northern Michigan. Broz purchased the license for RFBC and did not inform CIS of the opportunity. At the time of Broz's purchase, CIS was emerging from bankruptcy and was not in a financial position to purchase new assets, but was in very preliminary talks with a third company, PriCellular, regarding a potential purchase of CIS by PriCellular. PriCellular was interested in the license that Broz had purchased, but had not been notified of Broz's intent to purchase the license. After Broz's purchase, PriCellular finalized its plan to acquire CIS and executed the buyout.

PriCellular then caused CIS to sue Broz for appropriating the opportunity to purchase the license, arguing that because Broz knew of the potential impending merger between CIS and PriCellular, Broz had a fiduciary duty to present the opportunity to PriCellular even if CIS would not have been able to take advantage of the opportunity. The Chancery Court ruled in favor of CIS, and Broz appealed.

The Delaware Supreme Court reversed. Noting that the corporate opportunity doctrine "arose as a means of defining the parameters of fiduciary duty in instances of potential conflict," the court held the doctrine applies if: (1) the corporation had the financial means to take advantage of the opportunity; (2) the opportunity was within the corporation's line of business; (3) the corporation had an interest or expectation in the opportunity; and (4) taking the opportunity would place the officer or director in a position inimical to his or her duties to the corporation. The court then defined a "corollary" by stating that an officer or director may take advantage of an opportunity if the opportunity is presented to the officer or director in his or her personal capacity, the opportunity is not essential to the corporation, the corporation holds no interest or expectancy in the opportunity, and the officer or director did not wrongfully employ resources of the corporation in pursuing the opportunity.

Noting that no single set of factors are determinative and that corporate opportunity claims "range over a multitude of factual settings," the court held that Broz had not misappropriated a corporate opportunity. The court emphasized that Broze learned of the opportunity in his personal capacity, CIS had no means of pursuing the opportunity, CIS had no expectation in the opportunity, CIS was fully aware of Broz's activities with RFBC, and Broz's purchase of the license for RFBC did nothing to increase potential conflict with CIS. The court rejected claims relating to PriCellular's interest in the license, finding that PriCellular's acquisition of CIS was speculative at the time of Broz's purchase and that it was not reasonable to expect directors and officers to consider potential future mergers or acquisitions.

As the *Farber* case illustrates, an officer or director who improperly usurps a corporate opportunity usually is deemed to hold any profits realized from the opportunity in a constructive trust for the benefit of the corporation. Expenditures made to exploit or develop the opportunity may be recovered by the offending party, along with reasonable compensation for services rendered.

In 2000, Delaware added a provision to its general corporation laws[46] to provide protection against corporate opportunity claims. This protection is particularly helpful to entrepreneurs and investment groups who invest and hold board positions in companies that are in the same or related industries. The provision authorizes a corporation to renounce in its certificate of incorporation or by action of its board of directors any interest or expectancy of the corporation in specified business opportunities or specified classes or categories of business opportunities that are presented to the corporation or one or more of its officers, directors or stockholders.

3. MITIGATING LIABILITY RISKS

Given the nature and scope of the charges that a corporate director might face as a fiduciary, directors want protection against personal liability exposure and the risk of having to incur horrendous litigation costs. Without such protections, many qualified and responsible individuals could never be persuaded to serve on a corporation's board.

The protections come in three forms. The first is corporate statutes that permit a corporation to include in its articles of incorporation a provision that eliminates or limits the liability of a director to the corporation or its shareholders for money damages for any action taken, or any failure to take any action, as a director unless the liability is for (1) the amount of a financial benefit received by a director to which he or she is not entitled, (2) an intentional infliction of harm on the corporation or the shareholders, (3) the approval of an unlawful dividend, or (4) an intentional violation of criminal law. Model Business Act § 202(b)(4) and Delaware General Corporate Law § 102(b)(7) (described above) are examples of such a provision.

The second form of protection is corporate statutes that obligate a corporation to indemnify a director in select situations and permit a corporation

---

46. DGCL § 122 (17).

to include in its articles of incorporation a provision that imposes broader indemnification obligations on the corporation for director liabilities and related costs.

The third form of protection is an errors and omissions insurance policy, funded by the corporation, which provides each director added protection for acts taken in good faith.

Officers and directors typically want all three levels of protection.

a. Indemnification and Advancement Rights

An officer or director generally had no indemnification rights at common law, even if he or she prevailed on the merits. A 1939 landmark case[47] denying such rights sparked a push in New York to provide statutory rights of indemnification. Every other state followed.

Today, each state has statutory provisions that enable a corporation to indemnify its officers and directors under designated conditions.[48] Beyond the basic indemnification rights, and in recognition of the onerous legal expenses that accompany claims against officers and directors, state statutes also authorize corporations to advance funds to cover legal and other expenses that an officer or director incurs to mount a defense in a civil, criminal or regulatory proceeding. Such advances usually are conditioned on a repayment obligation if it is ultimately determined that the officer or director is not entitled to indemnification by the corporation. Often the rights of "indemnification" and "advancement" are not tied together. In many situations, an advancement right turns on the specific provisions of the corporation's bylaws, which may obligate the corporation to advance funds in circumstance where indemnification is permissive or nonexistent.

There are two types of indemnification statutes – mandatory and permissive. A mandatory statute typically requires the corporation to indemnify a director or officer when that person prevails on the merits in defending against an asserted claim of liability. For example, Delaware entitles a present or former officer or director to indemnification for defense expenses "actually and reasonably incurred" when the officer or director "has been successful on the merits or otherwise in defense of" a claim based upon his or her actions on behalf of the corporation or a claim asserted by or on behalf of the corporation.[49]

A permissive statute allows, but does not obligate, a corporation to indemnify directors, officers and other persons if the person ends up settling or paying a claim and certain conditions are satisfied. For example, if a claim is made against an officer, director, employee or agent for actions taken on behalf of a corporation, Delaware's statute permits the corporation to indemnify such person for all defense expenses, fees, judgments, fines and settlements, actually and reasonably incurred, so long as the person acted in good faith, acted in the corporation's best interests; and had no reason to believe that his or her conduct

47. New York Dock Co., Inc. v. McCollom, 16 N.Y.S.2d 844 (N.Y.Sup. 1939).
48. See, for example, Delaware's statute, 8 DGCL § 145.
49. 8 DGCL § 145(c).

was unlawful.[50] The statute specifically provides that an adverse termination or settlement does not create a presumption that the indemnification conditions have not been satisfied. If the threatened or actual claim is based on a charge made by or on behalf of the corporation, the permissive indemnification is conditioned on the same "good faith" and "best interest" requirements, plus a judicial determination that the indemnification is fair and reasonable when liability to the corporation is found to exist.

In Delaware, as is common in most states, there are various ways for determining whether the indemnification conditions have been satisfied. The determination can be made by (a) a majority vote of the directors who are not parties to such action, suit or proceeding, even though less than a quorum, (b) by a committee of such directors designated by majority vote of such directors, even though less than a quorum; (c) by a written opinion of legal counsel if there are no such directors, or if such directors so direct, or (d) by the stockholders.[51]

State indemnification statutes typically include a non-exclusivity provision that allows for additional indemnification and advancement protections through the corporation's articles of incorporation or bylaws or contracts with officers and directors. The specific indemnification and advance provisions in a corporation's charter documents or specific contracts often are an important consideration in recruiting and retaining key people to serve in officer and director positions. Often there are a variety of issues that need to be clarified and dealt with, including:

- Criteria for determining whether the officer or director has acted in "good faith" and "in the corporation's best interests"
- The individuals in the corporation who are entitled to indemnification and advancement rights
- Conversion of permissive indemnification or advancement rights under a state statute to mandatory contractual or charter document rights
- Expanded mandatory advancement rights through contracts with specific individuals
- Procedures for evaluating conflicts of interest that warrant separate defense counsel
- Mandatory liability insurance benefits for directors and officers
- The duration of advancement rights (through appeal?)
- Advancement rights in disputes arising out of or relating to indemnification and advancement rights (fee on fee disputes)
- Protections against indemnification and advancement rights being retroactively eliminated or reduced by subsequent bylaw amendments or other board actions.

---

50. 8 DGCL § 145(a).
51. 8 DGCL § 145(b).

b. Insurance for Officers and Directors

Liability insurance for directors and officers ("D&O insurance") is necessary in many companies and has become a core component of corporate insurance programs. For the great bulk of public companies (some speculate as many as 95 percent), it is considered an essential protection. Many closely held corporations also maintain such policies.

A D&O insurance policy may provide multiple and varied protections. Generally, a policy will provide coverage (often called "A-Side" coverage) directly to the directors and officers for losses (damages, judgments, awards, settlements and defense costs, but not fines, penalties, taxes, and multiplied damages) resulting from claims made against them for wrongful acts. A-Side Coverage usually applies when the corporation does not indemnify its directors and officers.

"B-side" coverage protects a corporation for its loss when the corporation indemnifies its directors and officers for claims against them. B-side coverage does not protect a corporation for its own liability.

Often specific optional coverages are provided to protect against risks from employment practices, securities laws, professional errors and omissions, and more. Many insurers offer multi-line insurance policies that have several "towers" of coverages under one policy and provide huge aggregate dollar protections (hundreds of millions) for the combined risks.

A D&O insurance policy gives the insured the right to select counsel, subject to the insurance company's consent, and often obligates the insurance company to advance defense costs. Coverage typically is provided on a "claims made" basis, which means that the policy must be in force when the claim is made. Policy exclusions usually include: dishonesty and fraud; willful violation of the law; illicit gain claims; claims by one insured against another insured, by a direct or indirect affiliate of the insured, or at the behest of the insured; claims relating to the provision of professional services; and claims arising out of wrongful actions taken before a specified date.

STUDENT PROBLEM 4-5

Reference Jennifer's business plan described in Student Problem 4-1. The plan proceeded as expected, with the facility opening on schedule and on-budget and becoming an instant success. The only negative feedback was the two-hour driving distance from the two largest metropolitan areas closest to The View. Roger, an acquaintance of Jennifer and bona fide helicopter expert, approached Jennifer with a plan to address this issue.

Roger had a line on a superb six-passenger helicopter. Seventy-five percent of its cost could be funded with commercial financing, and the seller would carry a note for the balance. Thus, for no money down, The View could have its own helicopter, operated and maintained by Roger full time. Projections showed that this "chopper operation" would be very profitable, servicing the needs of those who want to quickly and easily get to and from The View and clients of The View who need special helicopter services from time to time.

Jennifer got negative reactions from the corporation's other two directors when she presented Roger's idea. Mary said, "I know how to please rich folks, but I know nothing about helicopters." Todd exclaimed, "I never want to see another chopper after my time in Iraq. They are scary, expensive and dangerous." With this reaction, Jennifer decided to move ahead with Roger's plan on her own.

Jennifer formed a new corporation, ViewCopter Inc., issued all the stock to herself, and implemented Roger's plan. The operation exceeded all expectations, with all "chopper profits" going to Jennifer's new company and completely bypassing View Inc. The View's helicopter soon became the ultimate symbol of The View's success, picking up affluent couples and executives and whisking them away to a heavenly place of unmatched luxury, serious dialogue, or both. Jennifer described the operation as a "flying cash machine."

The investors of View Inc. became irate when they discovered what had happened. They demanded a complete accounting of all profits generated by "Jennifer's chopper gig" and insisted that all profits, past and future, be turned over to View Inc. Jennifer resisted, pointing out that their investment in View Inc. was "paying off better than anyone could have imagined." The investors are now gearing up for litigation.

Assume that View Inc. is incorporated in a state that has adopted the Model Business Corporation Act and that its articles of incorporation include a director liability protection provision authorized by MBCA § 2.02(b)(4).

1. Do Todd and Mary, as directors of View Inc., have any personal liability exposure to the shareholders of View Inc. for their refusal to approve the chopper operation? They have no financial interest in the operations of ViewCopter Inc. What additional facts (if any) would you like to have in assessing their potential liability exposure?

2. On what theory or theories might Jennifer be personally liable to the shareholders of View Inc.? Is her exposure any different than that of Mary's or Todd's? What additional facts (if any) would you like to have in assessing Jennifer's potential liability exposure? How could Jennifer have proceeded differently to mitigate or eliminate the threat of any claims from the shareholders of View Inc.?

G. SHAREHOLDER LIABILITY RISKS

Limited liability is often trumpeted as a supreme benefit of a corporation. If the corporation defaults on a contract or loan, the aggrieved creditor has no claim against the shareholders, directors or officers in their personal capacities unless they personally guaranteed the obligation. If an employee, while on the job, negligently injures another, the corporation may be held liable for the employee's actions, but the corporation's shareholders, directors and officers are not exposed personally.[52] As appealing as the corporate shield may appear, it has its limits.

52. MBCA § 6.22 provides: (a) A purchaser from a corporation of its own shares is not liable to the corporation or its creditors with respect to the shares except to pay the consideration for which the shares were authorized to be issued (section 6.21) or specified in the subscription agreement (section 6.20); (b) Unless

1. CONTRACTUAL, TORT AND STATUTORY EXPOSURES

There are various ways that shareholders of a closely held corporation may have personal liability exposure, including the following:

1. Key creditors, such as banks, other lenders, and important vendors often require the personal guarantees of the shareholders as a condition to extending credit.

2. If a shareholder or any person acting on behalf of a corporation negligently injures another, that person cannot escape personal responsibility for his or her tort even though the corporation is also legally responsible.

3. State corporate statutes personally obligate a shareholder in certain situations to return any dividend or distribution received by the shareholder if the shareholder, at the time of the distribution, knew that the corporation could not pay its creditors or that the corporation's liabilities exceeded its assets.

4. If a shareholder, acting as a promoter before a corporation is organized, enters into contracts on behalf of a soon-to-be formed corporation and the corporation is never properly formed or fails to adopt or perform the contract, the shareholder/promoter may have personal liability for the contract. However, if the corporation was never officially formed and the creditor knew that the corporation was going to be the responsible party, courts have sometimes employed a *de facto* corporation doctrine or a doctrine of estoppels to extend the protection of limited liability and prevent a windfall to the creditor.

5. Corporate directors and officers also face personal liability exposure. As discussed in the previous section, they may be exposed to shareholders if they violate their fiduciary duties of care and loyalty. Plus, there are various statutory liabilities: corporate state laws usually make directors personally liable if they approve payments to shareholders when the corporation cannot pay its debts or is insolvent; securities laws impose liability for insider trading or not properly disclosing facts; antitrust laws impose liability for price-fixing, market division schemes and other competitor-related activities that hurt the competitive process; tax laws impose personal liability for failing to properly handle employee withholdings; the list goes on.

2. PIERCING THE VEIL CLAIMS

Sometimes shareholders of a closely held corporation face a "piercing the corporate veil" or "alter ego" threat from creditors. The creditors seek to pierce the corporate veil to get to the personal assets of the shareholders, arguing that the corporation and shareholders are one and the same and that there would be an unjust or inequitable outcome if the shareholders escaped personal liability. It is never an easy burden of proof for the plaintiff-creditor, and there are a host of factors that often come into play.

---

otherwise provided in the articles of incorporation, a shareholder of a corporation is not personally liable for the acts or debts of the corporation except that he may become personally liable by reason of his own acts or conduct.

With respect to creditor tort claims, the cases of *Walkovszky v. Carlton*[53] and *Soerries v. Dancause*[54] illustrate the difficulty and benefits of sustaining a claim to pierce the corporate veil.

In *Walkovszky*, Carlton owned a fleet of taxicabs through multiple corporations, with each corporation maintaining the statutory minimum amount of insurance and having no assets except for a few leveraged cabs. The plaintiff was struck and injured by a cab owned by a Carlton corporation and sued to pierce the corporate veil and recover from Carlton, alleging that the multiple corporate structure was "an unlawful attempt to defraud members of the general public who might be injured by cabs." The trial court ruled in favor of the plaintiff, and Carlton appealed.

The appeals court held that piercing the veil is limited to cases of fraud or where the corporation has been intentionally undercapitalized to the point that it has insufficient assets to legitimately conduct business. The court found that the plaintiff had not provided "sufficiently particularized statements" of undercapitalization, asset intermingling, shuttling funds in and out of the corporations, or conducting business in a personal capacity. Because Carlton's corporations were sufficiently capitalized to conduct business and the insurance, though minimal, met the statutory requirements, the court ruled that the plaintiff had failed to state a cause of action for piercing the veil.

The dissent argued that the corporations were intentionally undercapitalized, that income was continually "drained out" of the corporations, and that "a participating shareholder of a corporation vested with the public interest, organized with capital insufficient to meet liabilities which are certain to arise in the ordinary course of the corporation's business, may be held personally responsible for such liabilities."

In *Soerries*, a drunken 18-year-old girl was admitted to a club when employees did not check her ID. The girl ordered additional drinks and then left, visibly drunk, with a beer in hand. She died in a car accident caused by her inebriated state on the way home. The girl's father sued the club and its owner in his individual capacity for actual and punitive damages. The trial court allowed the corporate veil to be pierced and found the owner, Soerries, jointly and severally liable with the corporation for actual damages and individually liable for punitive damages. The appeals court affirmed the trial court decision because Soerries had failed to observe basic corporate formalities, comingled personal and business funds, paid employees out of his personal funds rather than business accounts, maintained no payroll records, grossly understated corporate earnings for tax purposes, and failed to maintain and operate the club as a separate entity.

The case of *Kinney Shoe Corp. v. Polan*[55] illustrates the challenges of sustaining a piercing claim in a contract dispute. Polan had incorporated two companies, Polan Industries, Inc. ("Polan Industries") and Industrial Realty Company ("Industrial"), and used Industrial to negotiate a lease of property

53. 18 N.Y.2d 414, 233 N.E.2d 6 (1966)
54. 546 S.E.2d 356 (Ga. App. 2001)
55. 939 F.2d 209 (4th Cir. 1991).

owned by Kinney Shoe Corporation. Industrial then sublet the property to Polan Industries. Industrial issued no stock and received no capital on formation. Industrial's first lease payment to Kinney was made from Polan's personal funds. No further payments were made to Kinney, and Industrial subsequently filed for bankruptcy. Kinney sued Polan personally for the unpaid balance due Kinney on the lease. The trial court refused to pierce the corporate veil, ruling that Kinney had knowledge that Industrial was undercapitalized and had assumed the risk when it entered into the lease agreement.

On appeal, the court held that Kinney's knowledge of the undercapitalization was not controlling and stated a two-prong test for piercing the corporate veil: (1) the separate personalities of the corporation and the individual shareholders no longer existed, and (2) an inequitable result would occur if the veil were not pierced. The court concluded that this was a "classic scenario" for piercing the veil because no corporate formalities had been observed (thus, no separateness) and the structure had been designed to produce an inequitable result by preventing Kinney from being able to pursue a party with assets. The court listed the following factors that may be relevant in assessing whether the two-prong test has been satisfied in a given situation:

- Commingling of funds and other assets of the corporation with those of the individual shareholders
- Diversion of the corporation's funds or assets to noncorporate uses (to the personal uses of the corporation's shareholders)
- Failure to maintain the corporate formalities necessary for the issuance of or subscription to the corporation's stock
- An individual shareholder representing to persons outside the corporation that he or she is personally liable for the debts or other obligations of the corporation
- Failure to maintain corporate minutes or adequate corporate records
- Identical equitable ownership in two entities
- Failure to adequately capitalize a corporation for the reasonable risks of the corporate undertaking
- Absence of separately held corporate assets
- Use of a corporation as a mere shell or conduit to operate a single venture or some particular aspect of the business of an individual or another corporation
- Sole ownership of all the stock by one individual or members of a single family
- Use of the same office or business location by the corporation and its individual shareholder(s)
- Employment of the same employees or attorney by the corporation and its shareholder(s)

- Concealment or misrepresentation of the identity of the ownership, management or financial interests in the corporation, and concealment of personal business activities of the shareholders
- Disregard of legal formalities and failure to maintain proper arm's length relationships among related entities
- Use of a corporate entity as a conduit to procure labor, services or merchandise for another person or entity
- Diversion of corporate assets from the corporation by or to a stockholder or other person or entity to the detriment of creditors, or the manipulation of assets and liabilities between entities to concentrate the assets in one and the liabilities in another
- Contracting by the corporation with another person with the intent to avoid risk of nonperformance by use of the corporate entity; or the use of a corporation as a subterfuge for illegal transactions
- The formation and use of the corporation to assume the existing liabilities of another person or entity

As *Kinney Shoe* illustrates, piercing claims often surface when affiliated or subsidiary corporations are used to manage risk exposures. Contrary to what *Kinney Shoe* might suggest, it's never an easy burden for the plaintiff, as illustrated by the case of *Gardemal v. Westin Hotel Co.*[56]

In *Westin*, Gardemal's husband had stayed at a hotel owned by Westin's Mexican subsidiary. During his stay, Gardemal's husband asked the concierge for advice on where to go snorkeling and was directed to a beach that, unbeknownst to Gardemal's husband, was notorious for rough surf and strong undercurrents. While walking along rocks on the beach, Gardemal's husband was struck by a wave, knocked into the rocks, and subsequently drowned.

Gardemal sued both Westin America and Westin Mexico in a wrongful death suit brought in Texas. The trial court ruled that it was jurisdictionally unable to sustain a suit against Westin Mexico in a Texas court and that Westin America, as a parent entity, was a separate corporation from its subsidiary and could not be held liable for acts of its subsidiary.

Gardemal appealed, claiming that the state's alter ego doctrine and single business enterprise doctrine mandated that the corporate veil be pierced and that Westin America be held liable for the acts of its subsidiary Westin Mexico. The first claim, that Westin Mexico was an "alter ego" for Westin America, was rejected by the court because the facts did not show that Westin Mexico was merely a tool or conduit for Westin America. Full stock ownership by Westin America, shared offices, standard quality control standards, coordinated oversight of advertising and marketing, and similar factors were deemed "common" for a parent/subsidiary corporate relationship and were not sufficient to sustain an alter ego allegation. The court held that undercapitalization may be a key factor with a tort claim, but there was insufficient evidence that Westin

---

56. 186 F.3d 588 (5th Cir. 1999).

Mexico was undercapitalized or underinsured.

The second theory of recovery – the single business enterprise doctrine – was also rejected by the court because there was no evidence that the operations were so integrated as to result in a blending of the two corporations. Sharing trademarks, operation manuals, and reservation systems (all common features of parent/subsidiary structures) were not enough to invoke the doctrine. The court held that the doctrine would only apply when two corporations are not operated as separate entities and have been integrated to achieve a common business purpose.

STUDENT PROBLEM 4-6

Reference Student Problem 4-5, The View's smashing success, and Roger's helicopter plan. Assume that the entire board of View Inc. enthusiastically supported Roger's plan. In order to implement the plan "with no serious risk to The View," the board formed a subsidiary corporation, named ViewCopter Inc, and had all the stock of ViewCopter Inc. issued to View Inc. for $10,000. Roger's plan was executed entirely through ViewCopter, with ViewCopter hiring Roger, acquiring the chopper, securing the commercial financing, and issuing the note to the seller.

On its seventh day of operation, the helicopter crashed during a rain and wind storm, tragically killing Roger and four executives who were on their way to The View. Available insurance proceeds paid off the commercial debt on the helicopter and generated $2 million for the victim's families, a fraction of their claimed losses. The original seller received nothing on his note. The seller knew that the note had been signed only by ViewCopter Inc., a separate subsidiary of View Inc., and each of the passengers had signed a "Waiver" acknowledging the risk of helicopter travel and stating that View Inc. was not the operator or owner of the helicopter and had no legal responsibility for its operations.

ViewCopter Inc. has no assets. The seller (who holds the note) and the families of the victims know that their only hope for any real recovery is to reach the assets of View Inc. or its shareholders. What are their chances? What additional facts (if any) would help in making this assessment?

CHAPTER 5

Shareholder Rights and Activism

A. VOTING RIGHTS

For decades economists and legal scholars have sought to explain and rationalize the role of shareholders in public corporations; or, perhaps better stated, the lack of a role. The roots of modern analysis can be traced to a 1932 publication, *The Modern Corporation and Private Property*, where an economics professor (Gardiner Means) teamed up with a legal scholar (Adolf Berle) to study the 200 largest corporations listed on the New York Stock Exchange.

1. THE CONFLICT BETWEEN CONTROL AND OWNERSHIP

Means and Berle concluded that there is a distinct separation of control and ownership in a public corporation, shareholders have no control of the enterprise, management is a "self-perpetuating body" that runs the whole show, and enhanced legal protections are the only hope of protecting shareholders against the unfettered control and greed of management. As for the power of a shareholder at a meeting to impact the election of a slate of directors handpicked by management, Means and Berle aptly characterize the situation as follows, "As his personal vote will count for little or nothing at the meeting unless he has a very large block of stock, the stockholder is practically reduced to the alternative of not voting at all or else of *handing over his vote to individuals over whom he has no control and in whose selection he did not participate*." (Emphasis original).

No one has ever been able to credibly dispute the bottom line conclusions of Means and Berle. Many have tried to explain or rationalize them be developing various theories of how a public corporation should be viewed – everything from a team of producers that delegates control to a chosen few,[1] to an organization that is driven by political and economic forces,[2] to "nexus of contracts" arising from voluntary decisions of all stakeholders,[3] and more. But whatever the theory, governance issues in a public corporation bear no resemblance to what happens in a closely held enterprise. A public corporation entrusts a small group of players with the power to manage a large pool of capital provided by many

1. See M. Blair and Lynn A. Stout, *A Team Production Theory of Corporate Law*, 85 Va. L. Rev. 247 (1999).
2. See Mark Roe, Strong Managers and Weak Owners: The Political Roots of the Separation of Ownership from Control (1994).
3. See Henry N. Butler, The Contractual Theory of the Corporation, 11 Geo. Mason U. L. Rev. 99 (1989).

others. And as always, persuasive arguments will be advanced for the proposition that this concentration of power is necessary and proper to ensure the most efficient deployment of capital and labor for the common good.[4]

The inherent separation of control and ownership in a public corporation does not mean that the role of the shareholder is dead. Indeed, many factors that didn't exist in the days of Means and Berle continually push and facilitate greater shareholder awareness and oversight. These include the ever-growing concentration of economic power in institutional investors, new low-cost means of mass communication, and a heightened awareness of the dangers of unchecked greed in large organizations that operate on a world stage. Our laws have developed, and will continue to develop, in a direction that promotes management accountability and makes it easier for shareholders to be informed and have a voice. The general notion that enhanced shareholder involvement is good will drive many debates and regulatory changes. Many will applaud and seek to leverage these developments. But always undermining these efforts will be the hard reality that most public company shareholders, out of laziness or a perceived lousy effort-benefit ratio, will not expend an ounce of energy looking beyond the movements in the price of the company's stock.

2. *MEETINGS, NOTICES, CONSENTS*

The Meeting Requirement. The shareholder meeting is the primary tool used for shareholder involvement. The Model Act and corporate statues mandate an annual meeting of the shareholders at a time and place specified in the bylaws.[5] Although an annual meeting of shareholders is required, corporate statutes typically provide that the failure to hold an annual meeting will "not affect the validity of any corporate action."[6] Common actions approved at an annual shareholders meeting include the election of directors, approval of the appointment of the company's auditors, approval of stock option plans and other executive compensation arrangements, ratification of select board actions, and consideration of shareholder proposals that have properly come before the meeting.

Special Meetings. At times a special meeting of the shareholders is necessary to approve a shareholder matter, such as a merger, that cannot await the next annual meeting. The Model Act and corporate statutes typically provide that a special meeting may be called by the board of directors, shareholders who own a designated percentage of the corporation's stock (e.g., 10 percent), and any other person authorized by the articles of incorporation or bylaws to call a special meeting.[7] The statutory percentage needed to call a special meeting usually may be changed by the articles of incorporation or bylaws so long as it does not exceed a stated maximum (25 percent under the Model Act).

Notice. The corporation must set the date of the meeting and a date (the "record date") that will be used in determining the identity of the shareholders

4. See, for example, Stephan M. Bainbridge, *Director Primacy: The Means and Ends of Corporate Goverance*, 97 NW. U. L. Rev. 547 (2003).
5. See, for example, MBCA § 7.01.
6. Id.
7. See MBCA § 7.02.

who are entitled to vote at the meeting. The officers of the corporation control these dates. Notice of the meeting must be sent to all shareholders who are entitled to vote at the meeting, typically 10 to 60 days in advance of the meeting date.[8] For special meetings, the purpose of the meeting must be described in the notice, and matters unrelated to the disclosed purpose may not be considered at the meeting.[9] In Delaware, the board has the option of setting two record dates: one to indentify shareholders who are entitled to receive notice of the meeting, and another one closer to the meeting date to identify shareholders who are entitled to vote at the meeting.[10] Corporate statutes usually provide that notice of a meeting may be waived by a written document signed by the shareholder or by the shareholder attending the meeting and not objecting to lack of notice.[11]

Quorum. The successful passage of a matter at a meeting of shareholders requires the presence of a quorum and the casting of the requisite number of votes in support of the matter. Under the Model Act and most state statutes, the default shareholder quorum requirement usually is defined as a majority of shares entitled to vote, although statutory authorization to establish a different quorum requirement in the articles of incorporation is common.[12] Delaware allows a corporation, by a majority vote of its shareholders, to amend its articles or bylaws to increase a quorum requirement or to decrease it to as low as one-third of the number of shares entitled to vote.[13]

Required Vote. As for the requisite voting requirement, once a quorum is present, corporate statutes usually specify that a matter will be deemed approved if a majority of the shares represented at the meeting vote in favor of the matter.[14] The result is that a shareholder matter often passes based on a favorable vote that is far less than a majority of the absolute number of shares outstanding. For director elections, the Model Business Corporation Act, as well as Delaware and most other states, provide that directors will be elected by a plurality of the votes cast.[15] On select matters, the articles of incorporation may require an approval vote of a majority of the total shares outstanding or may specify a super-majority voting requirement (e.g. two-thirds) based on either the shares represented at the meeting or the total number of shares outstanding. Some corporate statutes mandate such a super-majority requirement as a default rule that may be changed only in the corporation's articles of incorporation. Washington State, for example, has such a two-thirds default shareholder voting requirement for a merger, a share exchange, or the sale of substantially all of a corporation's assets.[16]

Consent Resolutions. In closely held corporations, shareholder matters that would typically require a meeting can often be handled without having an actual meeting. Most state corporate statutes authorize the use of written shareholder

---

8. See MBCA § 7.05.
9. See MBCA § 7.02(d).
10. 8 DGCL § 213(a).
11. See MBCA § 7.06.
12. See MBCA § 7.25.
13. 8 DGCL § 216.
14. See, for example, MBCA § 7.25(c) and 8 DGCL § 216.
15. See MBCA § 7.28 and 8 DGCL § 216(3)
16. RCW §§ 23B.11.030, 23B.12.020.

consent resolutions in lieu of a meeting. But unlike the requirements of director written consent statutes that uniformly require unanimous consent, the requirements of shareholder written consent statutes vary widely. The Model Business Corporation Act, for example, requires the written consent of all shareholders entitled to vote on the matter, determined as of the date the first shareholder consents in writing to the action.[17]

In contrast, Delaware permits approval of an action if shareholders owning a majority of the shares entitled to vote on the matter sign a written consent resolution. Written consents may be obtained over a 60-day period, and prompt notice that a matter has been approved by written consent must be sent to all non-consenting shareholders.[18] Other states permit action by unanimous written consent resolution, but authorize a corporation to include in its articles of incorporation a written consent procedure that requires only the number of votes that would be required at a meeting of the shareholders.[19]

However structured, a shareholder written consent procedure can be a valuable tool for any closely held corporation that wants to ensure that shareholder matters are appropriately approved and documented.

3. *THE INDISPENSABLE ROLE OF PROXIES*

The challenge is completely different for a public company. Shareholder meetings cannot possibly be avoided with written consent resolutions, and usually there is no hope of a quorum physically showing up at the meeting. That is why proxies are the name of the game for executives of a public company.

Every state has a statute that permits a shareholder to appoint another person as a proxy. It is done with a simple written document or electronic transmission authorizing the other person to exercise the shareholder's voting rights at a meeting.[20] The appointed proxy may be granted discretion in voting the covered shares or may be specifically directed as to how the covered shares are to be voted on particular matters.

The appointment of a proxy usually may be revoked at any time unless it is an appointment coupled with an interest. For these purposes, a coupled interest typically includes an appointment to a pledgee, to a person who purchased or agreed to purchase the shares, to a creditor of the corporation who extended credit under terms requiring the appointment, to an employee of the corporation whose employment contract requires the appointment, or to a party of a voting agreement. Death or incapacity of the one appointing a proxy generally will not affect the right of the corporation to accept the proxy's authority unless notice of the death or incapacity is received by the secretary or other officer authorized to tabulate votes before the proxy exercises the authority under the appointment.[21]

The expectation and goal of the management of any public company is to make certain that whenever they walk into a meeting room of stockholders

17. MBCA § 7.04.
18. 8 DGCL § 228.
19. See, for example, Washington States statute, RCW 23B.07.040.
20. See, for example, MBCA § 7.22.
21. Id.

(whether empty or packed) they have sufficient proxies in hand to ensure that a quorum is present and that every action supported by management passes by a wide margin. Huge sums of time and money are spent to get to this point. Proxy statements are carefully drafted, posted, printed, disbursed and filed with the SEC. Procedures and personnel are used to solicit and secure proxy appointments authorizing the company's management to vote the covered shares at the meeting.

Under the SEC's new, ever-evolving e-proxy rules,[22] a public corporation must post its proxy solicitation materials on a website (exclusive of the SEC's site) that is publicly available and "cookie free." The materials include proxy statements, proxy cards, information statements, annual reports to shareholders, notices of shareholder meetings, other soliciting materials, and any related amendments. The proxy materials also explain how a shareholder may vote in person, by mail, by phone (via a control number), or over the internet (via a control number). With this website posting, the corporation has two options, referred to as the "notice only" option and "full set delivery" option.

Many public corporations now use the "notice only" option. This option simply requires the corporation to mail shareholders, at least 40 days in advance of the meeting, a form that, in prominent, bold letters, states, "Important Notice Regarding the Availability of Proxy Materials for the Shareholder Meeting To Be Held on [*meeting date*]." The corporation is spared the expense and hassle of sending paper proxy materials to all shareholders. The notice to the shareholders should include:

1. A statement that the notice is not a form for voting;

2. A statement that the notice presents only an overview of the complete proxy materials, which contain important information and are available via the internet or by mail;

3. A statement that encourages shareholders to access and review the proxy materials before voting;

4. The internet website address where the proxy materials are available; and

5. Instructions on how shareholders may request a paper or email copy of the proxy materials at no charge, along with the date by which the request should be made and an explanation that, absent such a request, a paper or email copy of the materials will not be sent.

The second option available to public companies is "full set delivery." This is the traditional paper model that companies have used for decades. The proxy materials are mailed to all shareholders. The company must still post all proxy materials on a "cookie free" internet website and send shareholders a "Notice of Internet Availability" with the proxy materials.

The proxy challenge is the primary corporate governance intersection of state and federal law. State corporate statutes dictate the circumstances that require proxies (where shareholder action is required) and authorize the use of

22. See generally SEC Rule 14a-16.

proxies. But the regulation of proxies and the proxy solicitation process for all companies that must report under section 12 of the Securities Exchange Act of 1934, which include corporations whose securities are traded on a national exchange, are governed by federal law. Section 14(a) of the Securities Exchange Act makes it "unlawful" for any person "to solicit any proxy or consent or authorization in respect of any security" of a public company "in contravention of such rules and regulations as the Commission may prescribe as necessary or appropriate in the public interest or for the protection of investors." This statute puts the SEC in control of all matters related to public company proxy solicitations.

Of all the proxy rules promulgated by the SEC over the past eight decades, the most important (and frightening) is Rule 14a-9, which states:

> No solicitation subject to this regulation shall be made by means of any proxy statement, form of proxy, notice of meeting or other communication, written or oral, containing any statement which, at the time and in the light of the circumstances under which it is made, is false or misleading with respect to any material fact, or which omits to state any material fact necessary in order to make the statements therein not false or misleading or necessary to correct any statement in any earlier communication with respect to the solicitation of a proxy for the same meeting or subject matter which has become false or misleading.

Although neither section 14(a) of the Securities Exchange Act nor Rule 14a-9 refers to a private right of action for one who is injured by false or misleading proxy materials, the Supreme Court held that such a right existed in the celebrated case of *J.J. Case Co. v. Borak.*[23] *Borak* and its aftermath have created a scope of personal liability that is a concern of every public company executive or director who participates in, or has responsibility for, the solicitation of proxies.

The need to revise and update proxy regulations is an ongoing challenge for the SEC. New rules are needed to keep pace with technology, lessons learned from experiences, and new matters that fall within the scope of shareholder governance. There is little question that many individual shareholders still end up with the same two options described by Means and Berle over 80 years ago – abstain or tender a proxy to those who are calling the shots. But, as discussed in the following section of this chapter, the scope of issues now presented to shareholders in public companies far exceeds anything Means and Berle saw in their survey.

One trend that has dramatically impacted the assessment of shareholder voting in public companies is the growth of institutional investors, such as mutual funds, state pension funds, hedge funds, labor union pension funds, corporate pension funds, and the like. In their working paper, "*Institutional Investors and Stock Market Liquidity: Trends and Relationships*," Wharton emeritus finance professor Marshall E. Blume and finance professor Donald B. Keim review trends in institutional stock ownership, noting that the growth of

---

23. 377 U.S. 426 (1964.

institutional investors in the stock market began after World War II. Before the war, from 1900 to 1945, the proportion of equities managed by institutional investors hovered in the 5-percent range. After the war, institutional ownership ballooned. By 1980, institutions held $473 billion, 34 percent of the total market value of U.S. common stocks. By 2010, institutional ownership had grown to $11.5 trillion, or 67 percent of the market value of U.S. common stocks.

From a shareholder governance perspective, this concentration of equities in institutional investors is a mixed blessing. The sheer size of the amounts invested by an institution would suggest a close attention to detail and a willingness to be active in the affairs of its portfolio companies. And over the years, many institutional investors have been active, at times negotiating with management and, when necessary, using the shareholder proposal rules to fight director entrenchment efforts, the use of poison pills, excessive executive compensation plans, and more. But there are also many institutions that respond to the pressures of having to build their portfolios and perform for their investors by staying focused on short-term yield maximization, paths of least resistance, obedience to the norms of the investment community, liquidity options, avoiding conflicts or the appearance of conflicts, and cost reduction measures. It's not about the mantle of ownership; it's about an investment whose performance must be monitored against a market so that it can be sold at the right time.

For these reasons, pressure is building for more institutional investor transparency on shareholder governance initiatives. SEC Rule 30b1-4, which took effect on August 1, 2004, requires mutual fund managers to disclose how they voted on every shareholder proposal that surfaces in their portfolio companies. This change, which was staunchly opposed by the large mutual fund families, enables investors to see which fund managers, for their own sake, have a tendency to be rubber stamps for the managements of their portfolio companies.

Any attempt to evaluate the effectiveness of the proxy process is further complicated by the fact that 70 to 80 percent of the outstanding stocks of public corporations is held in "street name" through custodians, such as banks and brokerage firms.[24] The custodians, in turn, hold the shares through accounts at Depository Trust Company (DTC), a depository institution and the record owner registered on the books of the company. The result is that it is difficult, often impossible, for a public company to ascertain the identity of the beneficial owners of all its outstanding stock at a given time.

To satisfy the SEC proxy rules,[25] companies use a complicated, multi-tiered, circuitous process that, in theory, is designed to timely get proxy materials to the unidentified beneficial owners of their stock.[26] The process is intrinsically fraught with unknowns in each application and produces results that cannot be verified. A company usually ends up with the proxies it needs, but many are

24. See, generally, M. Kahan & E. Rock, *The Hanging Chads of Corporate Voting,* 96 The Georgetown L. J. 1227 (2008).

25. SEC Rules 14a-13, 14b-1, and 14b-2 mandate that a corporation implement procedures that attempt to communicate with beneficial owners through their nominees.

26. For a thorough description of the process, see M. Kahan & E. Rock, *The Hanging Chads of Corporate Voting,* 96 The Georgetown L. J. 1227 (2008).

signed by brokers who exercised their legal right to vote shares owned by clients who, for whatever reason, never responded to the proxy materials. And in some cases, the tallied results confirm multiple votes on the same shares that have been borrowed or lent to cover short sales.

What practical impact the new e-proxy procedures described above will have on this process and the inherent challenges of "street ownership" is yet to be determined. It will definitely reduce costs and hopefully will result in a higher percentage of beneficial owners actually receiving useful information that leads to a vote by proxy.

4. INADVERTENT PROXY SOLICITATION RISKS

A communication to the shareholders of a corporation may constitute a proxy solicitation that is subject to the proxy rules even though the party responsible for the communication had no intention of moving into proxy territory. The source of this risk is the broad definition of a "solicitation" in Rule 14a-1(l):

> (1) The terms "solicit" and "solicitation" include:
>
> (i) Any request for a proxy whether or not accompanied by or included in a form of proxy;
>
> (ii) Any request to execute or not to execute, or to revoke, a proxy; or
>
> (iii) The furnishing of a form of proxy or other communication to security holders under circumstances reasonably calculated to result in the procurement, withholding, or revocation of a proxy.

If a communication is deemed a "solicitation" under this definition, all the proxy rules kick in, including the proxy statement and information rules,[27] the proxy card format rules,[28] the information disclosure format rules,[29] the filing requirements,[30] the antifraud rule for false or misleading statements,[31] and more.

Many courts have struggled with this inadvertent proxy solicitation risk. In *Union Pacific R.R. Co. v. Chicago & N.W. Ry Co.,*[32] for example, a report of a brokerage firm was sent by the firm to its clients at the same time the company sent copies of the report to its shareholders. The court held that the report constituted a proxy solicitation because, in the opinion of the court, the report was "reasonably calculated" to influence how the shareholders would vote on the matter that was the subject of the report. Similarly, in *Studebaker Corp. v. Gittlin,*[33] the Second Circuit held that a shareholder's written communication to other shareholders requesting that they participate in a demand to inspect the corporation's shareholder list constituted a proxy solicitation. Applicable law

---

27. Rule 14a-3.
28. Rule 14a-4.
29. Rule 14a-5.
30. Rule 14a-6.
31. Rule 14a-9.
32. 226 F.Supp. 400 (N.D. Ill. 1964).
33. 360 F.2d 692 (2nd Cir. 1966).

required that shareholders owning a least 5 percent of the company's outstanding stock participate in such a demand to inspect documents. The court reasoned that the written request to the other shareholders was part of a "continuous plan" to gain control of the board through shareholder action.

The case of *Long Island Lighting Company v. Barbash*, 779 F.2d 793 (2nd Cir. 1985), took the issue to a whole new level. In that case, the court held that newspaper and radio advertisements could constitute proxy solicitations subject to the proxy rules, reasoning that the determination of whether a communication is a proxy solicitation does not turn on whether it is "targeted directly" at shareholders but rather on whether it "in the totality of circumstances is reasonably calculated to influence the shareholders' votes." The dissent characterized the ads as "sheer political advocacy" that fostered public debate on a public issue and claimed that the proxy rules did not apply to such newspaper ads, no matter the motives of those who purchased them, and that to hold otherwise raised constitutional issues of "first magnitude."

The LILCO decision was one of many factors that sparked the SEC into taking a hard look at the need to amend the proxy rules. At the time of the LILCO decision, any communication deemed a proxy had to be preceded or accompanied by a written statement that complied with the federal proxy rules. Many argued that the board "solicitation" definition and the scary potential of violating the proxy rules discouraged shareholder communications, damaged the voting process, and further diminished the corporate governance role of shareholders. The upshot was four congressional hearings and years of debates and comments, all of which culminated in a major reform of the proxy rules in 1992. Following is a brief review of some of the key 1992 changes:

- The proxy rules no longer apply to solicitations conducted by persons ("disinterested parties") who do not seek proxy authority and who do not have a substantial interest in the subject matter of the vote. The antifraud provisions of Rule 14a-9 are still in play and there is a filing requirement for certain written communications, but the exemption eliminates all other proxy requirements. A person who owns more than $5 million of the company's securities must file with the SEC a notice within three days of any written solicitation, disclosing the person's name and address and a copy of the solicitation. The exemption does not apply to the company whose shares are the subject of the solicitation, any person acting on behalf of such company, a competitive bidder who is soliciting in opposition to a merger or other major transaction, persons seeking control of the company, or any person who would receive an extraordinary benefit.

- A definition of "solicitation" no longer includes a public announcement of how a shareholder plans to vote on a particular matter and his or her rationale for doing so. Rule 14a-1. This definition refinement takes all such public communications outside the scope of all the proxy rules, including the antifraud provisions of Rule 14a-9. This refinement protects those, including fiduciaries and company officers and directors, who respond to requests from others about their voting intentions.

• Communications made in public speeches, press releases, newspapers, and other broadcast media do not need to be accompanied by a proxy statement so long as no proxy, consent or authorization accompanies the public statement and a proxy statement is on file with the SEC at the time of the communication. Rule 14a-3. This provision is designed to facilitate the use of public media in proxy contests.

• Most proxy solicitations are no longer reviewed by the SEC's staff and, therefore, are no longer subject to a pre-filing requirement. Rules 14a-6, 14a-11, 14a-12, 14c-5. Such materials may be filed with the SEC and the national exchanges on the same day they are published or delivered directly to the shareholders. Solicitation may commence as soon as the materials are filed. Pre-filing reviews are still required for a company's initial proxy statement and certain transactions.

• A company's management may not group or bundle matters in order to force shareholders to cast a single vote on the bundled matters. Each item must be separately identified and voted on, although issues may be conditioned on one another so long as the voting consequences of the conditions are clearly stated. Rules 14a-4(a),(b).

STUDENT PROBLEM 5-1

Dalton Enterprises Inc. ("Dalton") provides specialized "large-item" shipping and transport services to major companies throughout the world. Dalton has a five-member board, 47 shareholders, and a tyrannical chief executive officer, Wade Long. Long is the largest shareholder, owning 14 percent of the company's outstanding common stock. No other shareholder owns more than 4 percent. The board consists of Long, Linda Smith (the chief financial officer), Pete Moore (the chief engineer), and two outside directors, both handpicked by Long.

The company's initial success was credited in part to Long's form of leadership. Now a group of shareholders (the "Group") has determined that Long is doing more harm than good and that it's time for a change at the top. The Group's members collectively own 29 percent of Dalton's outstanding stock. The Group has approached Diane Wilson, a talented CEO of a smaller competitor, who expressed interest in the "top spot" at Dalton only if "Long is long gone." After interviewing and checking out Wilson, the leaders of the Group dubbed her "the perfect next step for the company."

Linda and Pete are sympathetic with the Group's concerns, adore Wilson, but are unwilling to "buck" Long publicly. The Group anticipates that many shareholders outside the Group would support a change if they do not have to confront Long's wrath in an open meeting. The board of directors will never cross Long.

The Group needs advice on how to proceed. The next annual meeting of the shareholders is 11 months away, and any chance of landing Wilson can't await that meeting. Assume that Dalton is incorporated in a state that has adopted the Model Business Corporation Act, which empowers shareholders to terminate directors with or without cause (MBCA § 8.08).

What are the Group's options for moving forward? What additional facts would you like to have? Would your advice be any different if Dalton was incorporated in Delaware, which also empowers shareholders to remove board members with or without cause? (8 DGCL § 141(k))

B. SHAREHOLDER PROPOSAL TRENDS

1. HISTORY AND CURRENT PROPOSAL ACTIVISM

The first SEC rule relating to shareholder proposals (the predecessor to current Rule 14a-8) was adopted in 1942 on the heels of various laws and regulatory developments that prevented active investors from playing a role in the governance of public corporations. Shareholder proposals aimed at improving corporate performance and governance immediately started showing up, and the volume of proposals mushroomed over the next 30 years. In 1970, the landmark *Dow Chemical* decision[34] opened the door for shareholder proposals focused on social issues and the related impacts on the targeted corporation. The social issue agenda grew in both scope and volume. By 1978, for example, of the 790 shareholder proposals on public company agendas, 179 related to social issues.

Prior to the mid-1980s, individual activists drove the shareholder proposal movement. Often the roots of numerous proposals directed to many different companies could be traced to a handful of activists. In 1982, for example, a startling 29 percent of the 972 proposal requests received by 358 public companies came from three individuals.[35] Collective efforts began to take hold midway through the Reagan years. In 1986, T. Boone Pickens founded the United Shareholders Association for the express purpose of "upgrading shareholder awareness," and, for many years, this association actively targeted specific companies for corporate governance shareholder proposals. Since that time, the movement has been advanced by other coalitions, including the Investors' Rights Association of America founded in 1995 and The Investors for Director Accountability organized in 2006.[36]

Over the years the shareholder proposal agendas for public companies have been heavily influenced by the ever-growing presence of institutional investors. As described above, institutional ownership of public securities ballooned during the post-World War II period from a stable 5 percent of the market in the pre-war years to over 67 percent ($11.5 trillion) of all public stocks by 2010. A major event occurred in 1985 when Jesse Unruh, treasurer of the State of California, founded The Council of Institutional Investors. As California's treasurer, Unruh had direct responsibility for the performance of the California Public Employees

---

34. *Medical Committee for Human Rights v. Securities and Exchange Commission*, 432 F.2d 659 (C.A.D.C. 1970).

35. Remarks of SEC Commissioner James C. Treadway, Jr., *The Shareholder Proposal Rule*, Edison Electric Institute Seminar (June 23, 1983); Donald H Chew, Jr., Stuart L. Gillan, Donald H. Chew, *U.S. Corporate Governance* (Columbia University Press 2009), pp. 204-207.

36. Donald H Chew, Jr., Stuart L. Gillan, Donald H. Chew, *U.S. Corporate Governance* (Columbia University Press 2009), pp. 204-207.

Retirement System and the California State Teachers Retirement System. These funds were substantial investors in Texaco at the time Texaco paid a $137 million premium to redeem Texaco stock from a large investor who had acquired a substantial interest (9.8 percent) in the company. The redemption was a wakeup call for Unruh, who responded by forming the Council to serve as an activist and lobbying force for shareholder rights. The Council is now the vehicle that drives many institutional corporate governance advocates. It comprises more than 140 public, labor, and corporate pension funds whose financial assets collectively exceed $3 trillion.[37]

Another compelling institutional force has been Institutional Shareholder Services (ISS), an organization that studies and provides information on corporate proxy votes, principally for the benefit of institutional investors (pension funds, college endowments, etc.). ISS also makes recommendations as to whether it is in a shareholder's best interest to vote for or against particular matters, and it advises a wide range of companies on corporate governance issues. Over its 25-year history, ISS has built a staff of over 600 professionals and a client base that includes more than 1,700 companies.[38]

A review of the shareholder proposal activity for the S&P 500 companies during the 2013 proxy season illustrates the vibrancy and scope of the shareholder proposal movement. In 2013, the shareholders of these 500 companies considered 358 proposals, 46 of which garnered enough shareholder support to pass. The proposals focused on governance issues, social and political issues, and executive compensation issues.[39]

Governance Shareholder Proposals. The shareholders of the S&P 500 companies considered 142 corporate governance shareholder proposals in 2013, of which 44 passed. These included proposals (a) to separate the roles of the corporation's chief executive officer and chair of the board of directors (44 proposals, three passed), (b) to create a new right for shareholders to call a special meeting or to lower the percentage required to call a special meeting (9 proposals, two passed); (c) to grant shareholders the right to act through written consent resolutions (26 proposals, three passed); (d) to give shareholders the right to include director nominees in the company's proxy materials (nine proposals, two passed); (e) to remove classified boards; (f) to adopt majority voting (instead of plurality voting) in director elections; and (g) to eliminate super-majority shareholder voting requirements for removing directors, amending the corporation's articles or bylaws, or approving major transactions. Many of these were precatory proposals that simply requested the board of directors to take action. Directors who do not implement such a proposal that has passed should expect negative recommendations from proxy advisory firms when re-election time rolls around. ISS policies, for example, mandate a negative recommendation for all incumbent directors if a precatory proposal is approved by holders of a

37. Id.

38. See www.issgovernance.com.

39. For all of the following data on the 2012 proxy filing season and addition information regarding shareholder proposal activity during 2012, see the publication of Sullivan & Cromwell LLP entitled *2013 Proxy Season Review,* dated July 2, 2013.

majority of the company's outstanding shares and the board fails to promptly and responsibly act on the matter.

Social and Political Issue Shareholder Proposals. The shareholders of the S&P 500 companies considered 128 social issue shareholder proposals in 2013, two of which passed. These included proposals dealing with political issues (73, one passed), environmental issues (35 proposals), sustainability reporting issues (six proposals, one passed), labor issues (three proposals), human rights issues (four proposals), animal right issues (two proposals), and various other social issues (five proposals). The political issue proposals related primarily to additional disclosures on political expenditures and lobbying costs and, in select cases, requests for an advisory vote on political spending or the prohibition of such spending. The social and political issue proposals collectively received a total supporting percentage vote of 21 percent, far less than the 44 average percentage vote in favor of governance proposals. The range of support levels for various social and political issue proposals usually varies widely. Many activists argue that the value of a social or political issue shareholder proposal that is doomed to fail is the heightened awareness it creates for all corporate stakeholders, particularly the directors, and the momentum for support that it incrementally builds over many years.

Compensation-Related Shareholder Proposals. The shareholders of the S&P 500 companies considered 78 compensation-related shareholder proposals in 2013, none of which passed. These included proposals dealing with executive stock retention requirements (32 proposals), golden parachute limitations (27 proposals), pay and performance link requirements (three proposals), and other compensation issues (16 proposals). The primary focus of compensation-related proposals in 2013 – executive stock retention policies – requires executives to retain a specified amount (often as much as 75 percent) of shares acquired through compensation plans for a specified period that often extends beyond retirement. The percentage of votes cast in favor of compensation-related proposals averaged only 27 percent.

2. *THE CHALLENGE OF ACCESSING THE PROXY MACHINE*

The threshold challenge of every shareholder proposal effort is to force the company's management to include the proposal in the proxy materials for the next annual meeting of shareholders. This leveraging of the company's proxy machine saves big money and efficiently gets the proposal to the shareholders. Without this proxy help, the proposal's proponents may secure a list of shareholders under Rule 14a-7 and launch a solo effort to get the shareholders informed and excited. But it's an expensive, inefficient alternative that usually doesn't get past the first wave of brainstorming.

The company's management is the gatekeeper of the proxy machine and the agenda of the annual meeting of shareholders. Their natural tendency is to not "junk up" the proxy materials or the meeting agenda with multiple proposals that they often characterize as useless, distracting complaints from shareholder factions that do not understand the company's business and have a unique axe to grind. This is where SEC Rule 14a-8 takes center stage. The function of this rule is to determine which shareholder proposals may be excluded by management and to establish a procedure that requires management to consider proposal requests and fairly assess the grounds for exclusion.

The rule imposes basic requirements on the proponent of a proposal.[40] The proponent must have owned the lesser of $2,000 worth of the company's stock or 1 percent of the company's outstanding stock for at least one year before submitting the proposal. A proponent may submit only one proposal for a meeting, and the proposal may not exceed 500 words. The proposal must be submitted at least 120 days before to the anniversary date of the company's proxy statement for the prior year.

There is no prescribed form for a proposal request. Anything from a one page letter to a full blown memorandum with legal opinion attached will get the attention of the company's management. If a decision is made to include the proposal, the proposal moves forward. It is included in the proxy materials, the proponent gears up to be heard at the shareholders meeting, and the company's management states whether it supports or opposes the proposal and its related rationale.

If the company rejects the proposal, it must send a letter to the SEC that discloses its intention to reject the proposal. The letter is accompanied by a legal opinion that explains the grounds of the rejection. If the staff of the SEC agrees with the grounds for exclusion, it sends a simple letter that acknowledges (with no details) that there appears to be a basis for exclusion. If the SEC rejects the company's grounds for exclusion, the SEC's responsive letter states that it is unable to concur and explains the basis of its decision. On select occasions, the SEC suggests changes in the proposal (usually as to form) that will eliminate the grounds for exclusion.

In nearly all cases, the SEC's response is the final word. Although the proponent of the proposal may seek injunctive relieve to have the grounds of rejection reviewed by a court, the costs and uncertainties of such a proceeding are often prohibitive. And, of course, the company could choose to act contrary to the SEC's response and risk a more aggressive response from the SEC, but it is not something that happens. The SEC's no-action letter does the job in nearly all cases.

The key to the whole process, of course, is the permitted grounds for excluding a proposal, which are set forth in Rule 14a-8(i). Many are obvious and seldom trigger a dispute: the proposal that involves a violation of law, deals with a personal grievance or special interest, conflicts with a proposal of the company, is substantially implemented, is duplicative, or is a resubmission. The four grounds that generally define the battleground are:

1. The proposal is improper under state law because it infringes on the management authority of the board of directors;

2. The proposal is not relevant because it relates to less than 5 percent of the company's assets or less than 5 percent of the company's net income or gross

40. See, generally, SEC Rule 14a-8, which uses a question and answer format.

sales and does not raise significant social policy issues related to the company's business;

3. The proposal relates to ordinary business and management functions that are part of the operating details for running the company's business; and

4. The proposal relates to elections.

The SEC and courts have struggled in applying these grounds for exclusion in many cases.

In the landmark case of *Medical Committee for Human Rights v. SEC*,[41] the Medical Committee for Human Rights ("MCHR"), a Dow Chemical shareholder, sought to include in Dow's 1969 proxy materials a shareholder proposal to protest Dow's manufacturing of napalm to support the Vietnam war. Dow denied MCHR's request, relying on proxy rules that then permitted exclusion of political/social causes (not now an exclusion ground) and ordinary business operation proposals (still a ground for exclusion). The SEC issued a no-action letter, accepting Dow's grounds for exclusion. MCHR sued for a review of the SEC's decision.

Remanding the case to the SEC for a more detailed review, the court reviewed the history of both grounds of exclusion, observed that they could be construed to exclude "practically any shareholder proposal," found that the decisions of Dow and the SEC were conclusory, and held that the purpose of the shareholder proposal rule is to protect shareholder rights and that there is "a strong argument" that Dow's exclusion would "contravene" that purpose. Stating that the "immediate concern" was whether the proxy rules could shield management decisions from shareholder control, the court emphasized that Dow's napalm operations were not driven by profits but (as repeatedly stated by management) were political in nature and done to support management's favorable view of the war effort.

In *Lovenheim v. Iroquois Brands, LTD,*[42] Lovenheim, a stockholder of Iroquois, objected to the production of foie gras on animal rights grounds and sought to include a shareholder proposal in Iroquois' proxy materials calling for Iroquois to form a committee to study and report to shareholders on the process used by its supplier to produce the foie gras that Iroquois imported. Iroquois refused to include the proposal in its proxy materials on the grounds that the proposal was not "significantly related" to Iroquois' business as the importation of foie gras accounted for a mere 0.05 percent of Iroquois' assets (and no profits). The court granted Lovenheim's preliminary injunction, holding that history confirmed that the objective 5 percent test is not the sole basis for the "significantly related" determination and that matters that are of social or ethical significance may be deemed to be "significantly related" to the company's business and warrant inclusion in the proxy materials.

Contrast *Lovenheim* with the holding in *Apache Corp. v. NY City*

---

41. 432 F.2d 659 (C.A.D.C. 1970).
42. 621 F.Supp.2d 444 (S.D.Tax. 2008)

Employees' Retirement System,[43] where the New York City Employees' Retirement System ("NYCERS"), a shareholder of Apache, sought to have Apache include in its proxy materials a shareholder proposal that contained a comprehensive sexual orientation and gender identity non-discrimination policy. The proposal listed seven "principles" of non-discrimination and requested management to adopt policies relating to each of the principles. Apache sought and received a no-action letter from the SEC indicating that the SEC would not challenge Apache's decision to exclude the proposal from its proxy materials. The court upheld Apache's exclusion of the proposal. Finding that an SEC no-action letter represented a nonbinding (but persuasive) interpretive rule (as opposed to a substantive rule), the court independently reviewed the merits of the case and concluded that while the subject matter of the proposal (non-discrimination) generally would not be excludable under the "ordinary business" exception, the breadth of the listed principles in the proposal constituted an impermissible "micro-management" of the board in the day-to-day operations of Apache. The court cited the principles relating to advertising, marketing, the sale of goods, and charitable giving (but not employment discrimination).

3. BYLAW AMENDMENT PROPOSALS

In *CA, Inc. v. AFSCME Employees Retirement Plan*,[44] AFSCME, a shareholder of CA, a Delaware corporation, sought to have included in CA's proxy materials a shareholder proposal that would amend CA's bylaws to require board members to cause CA to reimburse the "reasonable" expenses incurred in a successful bid to secure a board seat in a contested election. CA sought a no-action letter from the SEC and included an opinion from CA's legal counsel that the proposal was not a proper subject for a shareholder action and that the proposal, if adopted, would cause CA to violate applicable Delaware corporate law. AFSCME submitted a letter from its own legal team opining in the contrary. The SEC requested certification from the Delaware Supreme Court on two Delaware law questions: Whether the proposal was a proper subject for shareholder action and whether the proposal, if adopted, would cause CA to violate Delaware corporate law?

On the first question, the court held that the proposal was a proper subject matter for shareholder action, reasoning (1) that the rights of shareholders to amend bylaws are not coextensive with the board's amendment rights, (2) that shareholder bylaw amendments may not interfere or limit the directors' management prerogatives, (3) that a shareholder bylaw amendment, therefore, must be process-related (as opposed to a substantive mandate), and (4) that this proposed bylaw amendment was sufficiently process-related (a process of electing directors to encourage non-board sponsored candidates) even though it required the expenditure of corporate funds.

On the second question, the court held that the proposal, if adopted, would cause CA to violate applicable Delaware law because it would bind directors to provide reimbursement even if in their best business judgment no reimbursement

43. 621 F.Supp.2d 444 (S.D.Tax. 2008).
44. 953 A.2d 227 (Del. 2008).

was justified. This, reasoned the court, would impose an unlawful restraint on the board's ability to exercise its fiduciary duties.

The *AFSCME* opinion led to two important 2009 additions to the Delaware General Corporation Law. Section 112 was added to authorize a bylaw provision that required (subject to certain limitations) a corporation to include in any proxy solicitation materials relating to the election of directors details relating to board candidates nominated by shareholders (in addition to those nominated by the board). Section 113 authorized a bylaw provision requiring (subject to certain limitations) the corporation to reimburse expenses incurred by a stockholder in soliciting proxies in connection with an election of directors.

The SEC tried to follow Delaware's lead in making it easier for shareholders to shake up board member elections. On August 25, 2010, the SEC adopted two changes in furtherance of this goal:

(1) A new Rule 14a-11 that would have permitted shareholders or shareholder groups who own not less than 3 percent in voting power of a public company for at least three years to include their nominees (up to 25 percent of the board) in the company's proxy materials, and

(2) A revision to Rule 14a-8 that requires companies to include in their proxy materials, under certain circumstances, shareholder proposals that seek to establish a procedure in the company's governing documents for the inclusion of one or more shareholder director nominees in a company's proxy materials.

The SEC entered a stay of these changes on October 4, 2010 when a lawsuit was filed in *Business Roundtable And Chamber Of Commerce Of The United States Of America v. Securities And Exchange Commission*, 647 F.3d 1144 (D.C. Cir. 2011), challenging new Rule 14a-11. On July 22, 2011, the District of Columbia Circuit vacated new Rule 14a-11. The court held that the Commission acted arbitrarily and capriciously in failing to adequately assess the economic effects of the new rule and, thus, violated the Administrative Procedures Act and the SEC's obligation to consider the rule's impact on efficiency, competition and capital formation.

The SEC responded to the court's decision with a press release on September 6, 2011, stating that it would not seek a rehearing of the court's decision and vowing to find "a way to make it easier for shareholders to nominate candidates to corporate boards."

The court's decision did not impact the change to Rule 14a-8, which became effective in September 2011. This change required companies, under certain circumstances, to include in their proxy materials shareholder proposals that seek to establish a procedure in the company's governing documents for the inclusion of one or more shareholder director nominees.

The net result of this partially aborted SEC effort is an expanded capacity of shareholders to propose bylaw changes related to director election procedures and a confirmation that the SEC's mission to expand the director-election rights of shareholders will move forward. The lesson for all who have a stake in the matter is obvious: stay tuned.

The *AFSCME* case aptly illustrates the point at which state corporate law becomes the focal point of a shareholder bylaw proposal effort. The inherent right of shareholders under state law to propose bylaw amendments was settled long ago.[45] But as the *AFSCME* case illustrates, the power of shareholders to propose bylaw amendments is limited. The analysis used in the *AFSCME* case provides a helpful framework to test whether a particular proposal is a proper matter for shareholder action under applicable state law and whether the proposal, if approved, would violate applicable law by, for example, triggering a violation of the directors' duty of care or duty of loyalty. This should be a threshold consideration for any shareholder group that is pondering a creative or novel bylaw amendment proposal.

STUDENT PROBLEM 5-2

DataSy Inc. is a public company whose stock is traded on the NASDAQ. It operates through various subsidiaries and divisions that design, sell, and maintain sophisticated, industry-specific data management systems. It has a broad base of executives and managers throughout its organization. Its healthcare division is gearing up to explode over the next decade as all elements of the Affordable Care Act ("ACA" or "Obamacare") kick in.

Judd, a 26-year-old blogger, owns DataSy common stock valued at $25,000. It is part of a stock portfolio valued at $1.2 million that he inherited when his father died three years ago.

Judd would like to submit a shareholder proposal to DataSy that would be included in the proxy materials for the next annual meeting of the shareholders (eight months out) and would be voted on at that meeting. The proposal would "prohibit the management of DataSy from hiring or promoting any executive or manager who publicly shows support, through the Internet, public speeches or otherwise, for the Tea Party or any organization or candidate affiliated with the Tea Party."

Judd's blogging activities leave no doubt that the primary motivation for this proposal is his deep-seated disgust for what he calls the "radical right," but Judd is careful to point out that the Tea Party's goal of "repealing or seriously disabling" the ACA would financially hurt the healthcare division of DataSy.

Please answer the following questions that Judd has asked:

- What is the best way to word and frame his proposal?
- When should he submit the proposal?
- What can he do to help position the proposal for inclusion in DataSy's annual meeting proxy materials?
- Does DataSy's management and board have solid grounds for refusing to include the proposal in the proxy materials?

---

45. See, for example, Auer v. Dressel, 306 N.Y. 427, 118 N.E.2d 590 (1954) and Rogers v. Hill, 289 U.S. 582 (1933), where the Supreme Court rejected as "preposterous" an argument that stockholders, by giving power to the directors to make bylaws, had lost their own power to make bylaw changes.

• What happens if the proposal is rejected by DataSy's management rejects? What recourse, if any, does Judd have in the event of such a rejection?

C. INSPECTION RIGHTS

At common law, the shareholder of a corporation had the right to inspect the corporation's books and records.[46] The source of the right was the shareholder's equitable interest in the entity's assets. Under the majority common law rule, a shareholder was presumed to have a proper purpose in making a demand to inspect corporate documents. The corporation had the burden of proving bad faith or an improper purpose.

1. STATUTORY SPINS ON A COMMON LAW RIGHT

This core common law right has been codified by the corporation statutes of every state. It is an important tool for the activist shareholder who wants to get the attention of management, force a dialogue with top executives, build a case for ousting a director or a slate of directors, submit a proposal for a shareholder vote, or commence a derivative lawsuit against officers or directors. Often it is the primary means by which a shareholder can secure the details and evidence to confirm suspicions and properly frame the allegations or the terms of a proposal.

The statutes of many states follow the Model Business Corporation Act in establishing a two-tier approach to shareholder inspection rights. The first tier provides that any shareholder who gives a corporation written notice of an inspection demand at least five business days in advance may inspect and copy, during regular business hours at the corporation's principal office, core organizational documents which include:

• The articles or restated articles of incorporation, all amendments to the articles currently in effect and any related notices to shareholders;

• The bylaws or restated bylaws and all amendments to them currently in effect;

• The minutes of all shareholders' meetings, and records of all actions taken by shareholders without a meeting, for the past three years;

• Resolutions adopted by its board of directors creating one or more classes or series of shares, and fixing their relative rights, preferences, and limitations, if shares issued pursuant to those resolutions are outstanding;

• All written communications to shareholders generally within the past three years, including financial statements furnished to the shareholders;

• A list of the names and business addresses of its current directors and officers; and

• The corporation's most recent annual report delivered to the secretary of state.

46. See, generally, 5A Fletcher Cyc. Corp. § 2251 (perm. edition).

If a shareholder desires to inspect and copy other documents -- financial records, excerpts from the minutes of any board meetings, records of any action of a committee of the board, minutes of any shareholder meeting or consent resolutions beyond the last three years, or the record of shareholders -- the Model Act requires that the shareholder's demand (1) be made in "good faith and for a proper purpose," (2) describe with "reasonable particularity" the purpose and the requested records, and (3) be limited to records that are "directly connected" with the stated purpose.[47] The Model Act solidifies shareholder inspection rights by expressly stating, "The right of inspection granted by this section may not be abolished or limited by a corporation's articles of incorporation or bylaws."[48]

Some states create a third tier right: the right of any shareholder to inspect a list of shareholders entitled to vote at a meeting within 10 days of the meeting.[49] Other states limit certain inspection rights to shareholders who have owned a designated percentage of stock for a specified minimum period.[50]

2. *ESTABLISHING A "PROPER PURPOSE"*

The common element in all state shareholder inspection statutes is the "proper purpose" requirement. This is the toughest hurdle for shareholders who want access to detailed documents that might expose wrongdoing or faulty judgments. It often triggers disputes and sometimes results in litigation that requires a court to determine whether a "proper purpose" exists.

For example***, in*** *State Ex Rel. Pillsbury v. Honeywell, Inc.*,[51] the petitioner, upon learning that Honeywell was producing fragmentation bombs for the US military for use in the Vietnam war, purchased 100 shares of Honeywell stock and, as a shareholder, requested Honeywell's original shareholder ledger, the then-current shareholder ledger, and all of Honeywell's business records dealing with weapons manufacturing. Honeywell refused the document request, and petitioner sought writs of mandamus to force Honeywell's compliance with petitioner's demands. Petitioner argued that a desire to communicate with other shareholders is per se a "proper purpose" and that a shareholder's right to inspect corporate documents for such a purpose is absolute. Acknowledging that some courts have agreed with this contention, the court held that a "better rule" would require a "proper purpose" for the communication to support a document request. The court noted that inspection is "akin to a weapon in corporate welfare" and emphasized the dangers of allowing shareholders to "roam at will" through corporate records. Since petitioner's sole concern was to impress his opinions regarding Honeywell's war efforts on others without regard to the investment or financial impacts (short- or long-term) on Honeywell or its shareholders, the court held that petitioner did not have a "proper purpose" to support his requests. The court recognized that it may have ruled differently if the request was based on bona fide concerns for impacts of the war munitions efforts on Honeywell's

---

47. MBCA § 16.01 and 16.02.

48. MBCA § 16.02(d).

49. See, for example, Washington State's RCW 23B.07.200.

50. See, for example, N.Y.B.C.L. § 624(b), which limits certain shareholder inspection rights to shareholders who have owned at least 5 percent of a class of outstanding stock for at least six months.

51. 191 N.W.2d 406 (Minn. 1971).

economic welfare or his investment in Honeywell.

In *Saito v. Mckesson*,[52] the court faced the situation were a proper purpose had been established but the requesting shareholder also had an improper purpose for requesting the records and was requesting records that were produced before he became a shareholder. The appellate court held that once a proper purpose has been established, an inspection request may not be denied because the shareholder has a secondary, improper purpose, but the scope of the request must be limited to records that are "necessary and essential to accomplish" the proper purpose. The court also held that the shareholder should have access to documents produced before he became a shareholder provided that such documents were related to wrongdoing that occurred after he first acquired stock in the company.

The issue of the requisite factual showing to sustain an inspection request based on a mismanagement claim was considered in *Seinfeld v. Verizon Communications, Inc.*[53] Seinfeld, a Verizon shareholder, sought to obtain Verizon corporate documents to determine whether Verizon's compensation to three high-level executives was excessive. Seinfeld claimed that the compensation (allegedly totaling $205 million over three years) was excessive and wasteful, but he had no evidence to support a mismanagement claim, a duplicative work allegation, or an argument that the executives "did not earn" the substantial compensation they had been paid. Seinfeld appealed the Chancery Court's adverse ruling, arguing that a requirement that he sustain the burden of proving a "credible basis" for his waste and mismanagement claims amounted to an "insurmountable barrier" for minority shareholders. In affirming the lower court, the appellate court emphasized that the "credible basis" standard sets the "lowest possible burden of proof" while maximizing shareholder value by limiting the range of permitted shareholder inspections to those that might have merit. Noting that any lower standard would allow inspection based on "mere suspicion" (as Seinfeld advocated on appeal), the court emphasized that the "credible basis" requirement had not impeded shareholder inspections in actual practice, referencing "a myriad of cases" in which shareholders presented "some evidence" to establish a "credible basis" to infer possible mismanagement that entitled them to receive "some narrowly tailored" right of inspection.

STUDENT PROBLEM 5-3

Reference Student Problem 5-2, DataSy Inc., and its shareholder Judd. In the course of haggling with the management of DataSy over his shareholder proposal, Judd becomes highly suspicious that there is a strong anti-gay bias throughout the executive and management ranks of DataSy. He knows that the three top executives have openly opposed same-sex marriage, and he suspects that this has sent a message down the line that has impacted key hiring and promotion decisions. Plus, one executive, in commenting on Judd's anti-Tea Party proposal, said, "We don't let current trends like same-sex marriage influence our hiring practices."

52. 806 A.2d 113 (Del. 2002).
53. 909 A.2d 117 (Del. 2006).

Judd thinks that this is an issue that would be of real concern to many shareholders, but he needs solid facts. Plus, Judd knows that this kind of story, if provable, could do wonders for his blogging efforts. The question now is whether he can exercise his inspection rights as a shareholder to obtain corporate reports and records that might confirm his suspicions. He would like to inspect board minutes, hiring directives, statistical hiring data, written employment procedures, relevant employee complaints, and more.

Please advise Judd as to his inspection rights and the likelihood of getting the records he wants. Assume that DataSy is incorporated in a state that has adopted the Model Business Corporation Act.

D. SHAREHOLDER INVOLVEMENT IN MAJOR TRANSACTIONS

State corporate statutes give shareholders the right to approve certain major events that fundamentally change the corporation. At common law, such an event usually required unanimous shareholder consent on a contractual theory because the agreement among the owners of the enterprise was being altered. Corporate statutes have preserved the need for shareholder approval, but the unanimity requirement is long gone. Today, most state corporate statutes require only that the event or transaction be approved by those who hold a majority of the shares represented at a meeting in which a quorum is present. A few states, such as Washington,[54] boost the required approval vote to a higher percentage, such as two-thirds of the shares represented at such a meeting, unless the particular corporation's articles of incorporation specify only majority approval.

Often an event or transaction requires both board and shareholder approval. When approval by the board of directors is required, all issues relating to the board's fiduciary duties are in play, including the duties of care and loyalty, the business judgment rule, and the related challenges discussed in Chapter 4. When shareholder approval is required, the proxy rules discussed above and the associated liability risks for false or misleading disclosures are central challenges for all public corporations. When a fight for control of a corporation breaks out, as discussed in Chapter 11, it's all about the power of the shareholder vote. And often the strategic challenge of how best to structure the purchase or sale of a business or the combination of multiple businesses presents alternatives that require shareholder approval but are driven primarily by tax and other considerations (as discussed in Chapter 10). The point is that much of what is discussed in other chapters of this book is impacted by, or tied directly to, state law requirements that mandate shareholder approval in select situations.

1. AMENDMENTS TO THE ARTICLES OF INCORPORATION

State corporate statutes typically require both board approval and shareholder approval in order to amend a corporation's articles of incorporation, with limited exceptions. Many states have used the Model Business Corporation Act to frame their statutory provisions regarding amendments to a corporation's

---

54. See RCW §§ 23B.11.030, 23B.12.020.

articles of incorporation. The Model Act specifically authorizes such amendments and states, "A shareholder of the corporation does not have a vested property right resulting from any provision in the articles of incorporation, including provisions relating to management, control, capital structure, dividend entitlement, or purpose or duration of the corporation."[55]

The Model Act empowers the board of directors, without shareholder approval, to make the following administrative changes to the articles of incorporation:[56]

1. To extend the duration of the corporation.

2. To delete the names and addresses of the initial directors or the initial registered agent.

3. To make certain authorized share changes if only one class of shares is outstanding.

4. To change the corporate name by substituting the word "corporation," "incorporated," "company," "limited," or the abbreviation "corp.," "inc.," "co.," or "ltd.," for a similar word or abbreviation in the name, or by adding, deleting, or changing a geographical attribution for the name.

5. To reflect a reduction in authorized shares when the corporation has acquired its own shares and the articles of incorporation prohibit the reissue of the acquired shares.

6. To delete a class of shares from the articles of incorporation when there are no remaining shares of the class because the corporation has acquired all shares of the class and the articles of incorporation prohibit the reissue of the acquired shares.

As for other amendments to the articles of incorporation, the Model Act requires[57] that the amendment be adopted by the board of directors and then be submitted to the shareholders for their approval, along with a board recommendation that the shareholders approve the amendment or a statement as to why the board has determined that it cannot make such a recommendation ("conflicts of interest or other special circumstances"). The board of directors may condition its submission of the amendment to the shareholders on any basis. The corporation must then notify each shareholder, whether or not entitled to vote, of the meeting of shareholders at which the amendment is to be submitted for approval. The notice must state that the purpose of the meeting is to consider the amendment and must contain or be accompanied by a copy of the amendment. Unless the articles of incorporation or the board of directors requires a greater vote or a greater number of shares to be present, adoption of the amendment requires an approval vote of shareholders owning a majority of shares represented at a meeting at which a quorum consisting of at least a majority of the votes entitled to be cast on the amendment is present.

---

55. MBCA § 10.01(b).
56. MBCA § 10.05.
57. See, generally, MBCA § 10.03.

Delaware specifies a similar dual process of director and shareholder approvals for all amendments to the articles of incorporation.[58]

2. *BYLAW AMENDMENTS*

State corporate statutes typically provide that a corporation's bylaws may be amended by either the board of directors or the shareholders.[59] Dual approval is not required. This gives the board the authority to make bylaw changes as it sees fit, without having to endure the expense and hassle of a shareholder approval process. Although not required, in many situations the board chooses to seek shareholder ratification of its decision to amend the bylaws in order to promote shareholder goodwill and ward off any potential attacks.

3. *CORPORATE DISSOLUTION*

State corporate statutes (including Delaware's statute[60]) generally provide that the board of directors and shareholders may dissolve a corporation by following a dual board and shareholder approval process similar to that described above for amendments to the articles of incorporation. The Model Act requires[61] that a resolution to dissolve the corporation be approved by the board of directors and then be submitted to the shareholders for their approval, along with a board recommendation that the shareholders approve the dissolution or a statement as to why the board has determined that it cannot make such a recommendation ("conflicts of interest or other special circumstances"). The board of directors may condition its submission of the dissolution resolution to the shareholders on any basis. The corporation must then notify each shareholder, whether or not entitled to vote, of the meeting of shareholders at which the dissolution is to be submitted for approval. The notice must state that the purpose of the meeting is to consider the dissolution of the corporation. Unless the articles of incorporation or the board of directors requires a greater vote or a greater number of shares to be present, adoption of the dissolution proposal requires an approval vote of shareholders owning a majority of shares represented at a meeting at which a quorum consisting of at least a majority of the votes entitled to be cast on the amendment is present.

4. *MERGERS, CONSOLIDATIONS, SHARE EXCHANGES, ASSET SALES*

A statutory merger is a transaction where two or more corporations combine to form a single entity.[62] Typically one corporation (the "Acquirer") is absorbing another corporation (the "Target"). All of the assets, liabilities and rights of the Target pass by operation of law to the Acquirer, and the Acquirer is substituted in any pending litigation of the Target.[63] The Acquirer is the surviving entity, just bigger. The Target disappears. As consideration for their Target shares, the shareholders of Target either receive cash, property, or shares of the Acquirer's

---

58. 8 DGCL § 242(b).

59. See, for example, MBCA § 10.20 and 8 DGCL § 109. In Delaware, the power of the board to amend the bylaws must be set forth in the articles of incorporation. 8 DGCL § 109.

60. 8 DGCL § 275.

61. See, generally, MBCA § 10.02.

62. MBCA § 11.02, 8 DGCL § 251.

63. MBCA § 11.07, 8 DGCL § 259.

stock. The transaction is documented with a merger agreement that spells out the exchange terms and includes provisions that are typically included in an asset purchase agreement: covenants, representations and warranties, conditions, indemnifications, legal opinions, and the like. A document entitled "Articles of Merger" or "Certificate of Merger" is filed with the applicable state corporation divisions to evidence and complete the merger. [64]

A consolidation differs from a merger in one significant respect. With a consolidation, a new corporate entity is formed to be the surviving corporation. The existing corporate entities disappear. Consolidations are a rare event in today's world.

A share exchange is a transaction where one corporation, Acquirer, exchanges its stock for the outstanding stock of another corporation, Target.[65] Target ends up being a wholly owned subsidiary of Acquirer.

With any merger, consolidation or share exchange, there are three threshold questions: Which boards must approve the transaction? Which shareholders must approve the transaction? Which shareholders are entitled to dissenter appraisal rights? The answers to these questions turn on applicable state law, any stock exchange rules that are applicable, and the relative positions of the parties in the transaction. Following are a brief discussion of appraisal rights and a description of six scenarios that illustrate how the answers to these three threshold questions can vary based on the terms and structure of a transaction. These scenarios assume that Acquirer is a Delaware corporation and Target is organized in a state that has adopted the Model Business Corporation Act.

Of course, it goes without saying that the corporate laws of the state of incorporation always must be carefully considered in any transaction. The following scenarios illustrate key requirements by focusing on the provisions of the existing Model Act and Delaware law. In no sense do these provisions fairly represent the scope of corporate statutes dealing with shareholder voting and appraisal rights in major transactions. Some state statutes are modeled after the early version of the Model Act (before 1999), which, unlike the current version, did not mandate voting rights for the shareholders of the acquiring entity in triangular mergers and asset purchases. Other states follow the lead of the American Law Institute Principles § 6.01(b) and have a statutory structure that seeks to grant identical shareholder voting and appraisal rights in all major transactions, no matter the form. There are states that seek to line up voting and appraisal rights so that they always go together and states that do not have the market opt-out exception (described below) for appraisal rights. And, of course, there are those states that impose a super-majority shareholder voting requirement for major transactions. The components of the statutory schemes are varied and mixed.

The bottom line is that assumptions and generalizations in this area are ill advised. The specific statutes of the states in which the parties to the transaction are incorporated must be carefully assessed and satisfied.

---

64. MBCA § 11.06, 8 DGCL § 251.
65. MBCA § 11.03

a. Shareholder Appraisal Rights

The potential of shareholder appraisal rights is a consideration in any merger, consolidation, or share exchange. These rights are designed to provide an objecting shareholder with an opportunity to be paid a "fair value" cash price for his or her stock via a judicial proceeding where the price is determined. Every corporate statute authorizes such appraisal rights in select fundamental transactions, but state laws vary significantly in defining the scope and limitations of such rights.[66]

In 35 states (including Delaware) and under the Model Business Corporation Act, there is a significant market-out exception for public corporations that has the effect of taking appraisal rights off the table in most public company transactions.[67] Under the MBCA exception, dissenter appraisal rights are not available to shareholders who own stock if (1) there is a liquid market for the stock (traded on the New York Stock Exchange, American Stock Exchange, NASDAQ, or the stock is held by at least 2,000 shareholders with a $20 million public float) and (2) the transaction does not involve a controlling shareholder (defined as a shareholder who owns 20 percent or more of the corporation's stock or has the power to elect one-fourth of board) or a deal where officers of the target company yield a financial benefit that is not available to the shareholders. The basis of this exception is that, under such circumstances, there is no need for court involvement to set a fair cash price for such shareholders because every shareholder has a market driven liquidity option that will adjust to reflect the value of the deal. Best estimates are that 91 percent of all public companies and 93 percent of Fortune 500 companies are incorporated in a state that provides this type of market-out exception to shareholder appraisal rights.[68]

Delaware also has a market-out exception to shareholder appraisal rights, but that exception contains a unique, important twist – an "exception to the exception." Unlike the Model Act, a transaction under Delaware law in which shareholders are required to accept cash for their shares will not trigger the market-out exception for such shareholders, and, thus, appraisal rights will be available. The result is that, in Delaware, the target company shareholders will always have appraisal rights in a cash merger. In *Louisiana Municipal Employees' Retirement System v. Crawford*,[69] the court held that this "exception to the exception" would apply to restore appraisal rights in a transaction where shareholders were "required" to receive both stock ***and*** cash, but in *Louisiana Municipal Employees' Retirement System v. Crawford*,[70] the court held it would not apply (and thus the market out exception would apply to eliminate appraisal rights) if all shareholders had an option to receive stock ***or*** cash.

---

66. In select situations, an amendment of the articles of incorporation may trigger shareholder appraisal rights if the articles, bylaws or directors' resolutions provide for such rights or others statutory conditions are satisfied. See, for example, MBCA § 13.02(4),(5).

67. See, generally, MBCA § 13.02(b), 8 DGCL § 262(b), and Jeff Goetz, *A Dissent Dampened by Timing; How the Stock Market Exception Systematically Deprives Public*, 15 Fordham Journal of Corporate and Financial Law 771-806 (2009).

68. See, generally, Lucian A. Bebchuck and Alma Cohen, *Firms' Decisions Where to Incorporate*, 46 J.L. & Econ, 383, 391 (2003).

69. 918 A.2d 1172 (Del. Ch. 2007).

70. 918 A.2d 1172 (Del. Ch. 2007).

Even when appraisal rights are available to dissenting minority shareholders, they trigger administrative details, costs, and uncertainties that must be seriously considered in any decision to assert such rights. Statutory appraisal rights are not a panacea for minority shareholders who believe they have been shortchanged in a major transaction. The procedural requirements are significant, as illustrated by sections 13.21 through 13.30 of the Model Business Corporations Act, and section 262 of the Delaware General Corporation Law. Under the Model Act, a shareholder who wants to trigger appraisal rights must first give written notice of his or her intent to dissent prior to the meeting at which the merger will be voted upon, must not vote in favor of the merger, and, if the merger is approved, must then timely demand payment for his or her shares and deposit the share certificates with the corporation. The corporation must then pay the shareholder the amount that it determines to be the fair value of the shares. If the shareholder disagrees with the corporation's determination of value, the shareholder is then required to notify the corporation of his or her estimate of fair value and demand payment from the corporation. The corporation then has a choice: it can honor the shareholder's demand or initiate a judicial appraisal proceeding. If a shareholder fails to comply with any of the procedural requirements and the related deadlines, the appraisal remedy is lost.

Beyond the procedural hassles is the risk that the whole effort may produce little or nothing. There is always the very real possibility that the shareholder's proposed valuation will be watered down or completely rejected, resulting in no yield or a pittance yield that didn't justify the effort.

Costs must also be factored into any decision to assert appraisal rights. An appraisal proceeding will trigger significant opportunity costs in terms of time, effort, and stress. Added to these opportunity costs are the actual costs for lawyers and valuation experts. Court costs, including compensation and expenses of court-appointed appraisers, will be assigned to the corporation unless the court determines that the shareholders acted arbitrarily or in bad faith. But the expert legal and accounting fees of the shareholders are borne by the shareholders, subject only to a discretionary power of the court to have such fees recovered from the benefits reaped by a broader group of shareholders who benefited from the proceedings.[71] See MBCA § 13.31.

The realities of the technical procedural requirements, the uncertainties of a profitable outcome, and the costs (both opportunity and actual) of pushing forward with a time-consuming appraisal proceeding often cause many minority shareholders to rethink an initial urge to fight for a higher price.

b. Scenario 1: Non-Whale Merger

Acquirer and Target, neither predominately larger than the other, merge with Acquirer issuing two shares of its already authorized shares to the shareholders of Target for every three shares of Acquirer's stock outstanding before the merger. Thus, after the merger, the original shareholders of the Acquirer own 60 percent of the Acquirer's shares and the Target shareholders own the remaining 40 percent.

71. See MBCA § 13.31.

- Under Delaware law, the merger would have to be approved by the board of directors of Acquirer.[72]

- Under Delaware law, the merger would have to be approved by the shareholders of Acquirer because the number of shares issued in the transaction exceeds 20 percent of the number of Acquirer shares outstanding before the merger.[73]

- If the stock of Acquirer is traded on the New York Stock Exchange, the American Stock Exchange or the NASDAQ, exchange rules would require that the transaction be approved by the shareholders of Acquirer because the 20 percent threshold is exceeded.[74]

- Under the MBCA, the board of directors and shareholders of Target would have to approve the merger.[75]

- Dissenter appraisal rights would be available to all shareholders, subject to the market-out exception.[76]

- If the Acquirer was incorporated in a state that had adopted the MBCA, its shareholders would not have dissenter appraisal rights because all of their shares would remain outstanding after the merger.[77]

c. Scenario 2: Whale Merger

Acquirer and Target merge with Acquirer issuing one share of its already authorized shares to the shareholders of Target for every five shares of Acquirer's stock outstanding before the merger. Thus, after the merger, the original shareholders of the Acquirer would own 83.3 percent of Acquirer's shares and Target shareholders would own the remaining 16.7 percent.

- Under the MBCA, the board of directors and shareholders of Target would have to approve the merger.[78]

- Under Delaware law, the merger would have to be approved by the board of directors of Acquirer.[79]

- Under Delaware law, the shareholders of Acquirer would not have to approve the merger if the Acquirer is the surviving entity, there is no need to amend Acquirer's articles of incorporation, each share of Acquirer's existing stock remains unchanged and outstanding, and the number of shares of Acquirer to be issued in the merger does not exceed 20 percent of Acquirer's shares outstanding before the merger.[80] Similarly, because the 20 percent threshold is

72. 8 DGCL §§ 251, 252.
73. 8 DGCL §§ 251, 252.
74. See New York Stock Exchange *Listed Company Manual*, Section 312.03 Shareholder Approval; American Stock Exchange *Company Guide*, Section 712 Acquisitions; NASDAQ *Manual: Marketplace Rules*, Section 4350 Qualitative Listing Requirements for Nasdaq Issuers Except for Limited Partnerships.
75. MBCA § 11.04
76. MBCA § 13.02, 8 DGCL § 262(b).
77. MBCA § 13.02(a)(1).
78. MBCA § 11.04
79. 8 DGCL §§ 251, 252.
80. 8 DGCL §§ 251(f).

not exceeded, stock exchange rules would not require a vote of Acquirer's shareholders.[81]

- The same 20 percent no-shareholder-vote exception would apply if Acquirer was organized in a state that had adopted the Model Act.[82]

- As for dissenter appraisal rights, they would be available to the shareholders of Target, subject to the market exception, but would not be available to the shareholders of Acquirer. The same result would follow if the states of incorporation of Acquirer and Target were switched.[83]

d. Scenario 3: Short-Form Squeeze-Out Merger

Acquirer owns over 90 percent of the outstanding stock of Target and merges Target into Acquirer in a transaction that squeezes out the minority shareholders of Target by paying cash for their shares.

- The merger would have to be approved only by the board of directors of Acquirer.[84]

- No vote of Target's board or shareholders would be required.

- As for dissenter appraisal rights, they would be available to the shareholders of Target, but would not be available to the shareholders of Acquirer.

- The same results would follow if the states of incorporation of Acquirer and Target were switched.[85]

e. Scenario 4: Forward and Reverse Triangular Mergers

3 WM

Acquirer forms a new wholly-owned subsidiary corporation ("Sub"), Sub and Target are then merged, and Acquirer issues its already authorized shares to the shareholders of Target. If Sub is the survivor in the merger, the transaction is called a "forward triangular merger," Target disappears, and Sub (now with all Target's assets) remains a wholly owned subsidiary of Acquirer. If Target is the surviving entity in the merger, the transaction is called a "reverse triangular merger," Sub disappears, and Target ends up as a wholly owned subsidiary of Acquirer. This triangular merger technique is popular because it provides the tax benefits of a merger while allowing the Acquirer to accomplish various non-tax objectives in structuring the transaction. (See Section C of Chapter 10).

- The board of directors and shareholders of Target would have to approve the triangular merger, whether Target is incorporated in Delaware or an MBCA state.[86]

- As a formality, Sub's board and its sole shareholder ("Acquirer") v need to approve the triangular merger.[87]

---

81. See cited authority at note 74, *supra*.
82. MBCA § 11.04(g).
83. MBCA § 13.02, 8 DGCL § 262(b).
84. MBCA § 11.05, 8 DGCL § 253.
85. Id.
86. MBCA § 11.04, 8 DGCL § 251.

• Technically, Acquirer is not a party to the merger, but its board would have to approve the issuance of additional Acquirer stock and all matters related to the formation of Sub and the exercise of Sub rights.

• If Acquirer is incorporated in a state that has adopted the Model Act, Acquirer's shareholders would have to approve the share exchange in the triangular merger unless there is no need to amend Acquirer's articles of incorporation, each share of Acquirer's existing stock remains unchanged and outstanding, and the number of shares of Acquirer to be issued in the transaction does not exceed 20 percent of the Acquirer's shares outstanding before the transaction.[88]

• If Acquirer's stock is traded on the New York Stock Exchange, the American Stock Exchange or the NASDAQ, stock exchange rules would require a vote of Acquirer's shareholders if the 20 percent threshold is exceeded.[89]

• If Acquirer is a Delaware corporation and not subject to exchange rules, Acquirer's shareholders would not have to approve the transaction because Acquirer is not a party to the transaction and Delaware's corporate law does not have a share exchange provision. Thus, in many situations Delaware companies may cut off voting and appraisal rights of Acquirer's shareholders by structuring the transaction as a triangular merger.

• As for dissenter appraisal rights, they would be available to the shareholders of Target, subject to the market exception, but would not be available to the shareholders of Acquirer. This would be the result whether the Model Act or Delaware law applied.[90]

f. Scenario 5: Share Exchanges

Acquirer issues its stock in exchange for all of the outstanding stock of Target. Many states (but not Delaware), including those that have adopted the Model Act, authorize this form of exchange and compel participation of the Target shareholders if the transaction is appropriately approved by the board and shareholders of Target.[91] The parties end up in the same position as a reverse triangular merger (Target becoming a wholly-owned subsidiary of Acquirer), but, as described in Chapter 10, the tax requirements of a reverse triangular merger are much easier and more flexible than a straight share exchange. Also, this type of compulsory share exchange should not be confused with a tender offer transaction (discussed in Chapter 11), where Acquirer offers to buy Target shares directly from the Target shareholders and each shareholder may elect to accept or reject the offer.

• The board of directors and shareholders of Target would have to approve the exchange if Target is incorporated in a Model Act state.[92] This type of [illegible]mpulsory share exchange is not authorized in Delaware.

[illegible]A § 11.04.
92. [illegible] authority at note 74, *supra*.
[illegible]02, 8 DGCL § 262(b).

- Acquirer's board of directors would have to approve the transaction.

- If Acquirer is incorporated in a state that has adopted the Model Act, Acquirer's shareholders would have to approve the share exchange unless there is no need to amend Acquirer's articles of incorporation, each share of Acquirer's existing stock remains unchanged and outstanding, and the number of shares of stock of Acquirer to be issued in the transaction does not exceed 20 percent of the Acquirer's shares outstanding before the transaction.[93]

- If Acquirer's stock is traded on the New York Stock Exchange, the American Stock Exchange or the NASDAQ, stock exchange rules would require a vote of Acquirer's shareholders if the 20 percent threshold is exceeded.[94]

- As for dissenter appraisal rights, they would be available to the shareholders of Target, subject to the market exception, but would not be available to the shareholders of Acquirer, whose shares would remain outstanding after the exchange.[95]

g. Scenario 6: Sale of Assets

The sale of a corporation's assets may also trigger shareholder voting and dissenter appraisal rights in certain situations. State corporate statutes[96] generally mandate such rights in a sale that involves substantially all of a corporation's assets, often referred to as a sale not "in the usual or regular course of business."[97]

In our case above, Acquirer could purchase all of Target's assets in return for cash or stock of Acquirer. In such a transaction, Target doesn't automatically disappear. The sale radically changes the composition of Target's assets, and usually most or all of Target's known liabilities will have been transferred to, or assumed by, the buyer. Target then liquidates by discharging any residual liabilities and distributing the remaining proceeds of the sale to its shareholders. Although the form of such an asset sale/liquidation transaction differs significantly from that of a merger, usually the parties, as a practical matter, end up in the same position: Acquirer has the assets and liabilities, Target is gone, and the shareholders of Target own stock of Acquirer.

In such a transaction, the board of directors and the shareholders of the selling corporation (Target) must approve the transaction.[98] As for dissenter appraisal rights, the Model Act gives the shareholders of the selling corporation such rights, subject to the market-out exception,[99] but no such rights are available to the shareholders of the selling corporation under Delaware law.[100]

As for the purchasing entity (Acquirer), Delaware law provides no shareholder voting or dissenter appraisal rights. It's a straight purchase of assets

93. MBCA § 11.04(g).
94. See cited authority at note 74, *supra*.
95. MBCA § 13.02.
96. See, for example, MBCA § 12.02, 8 DGCL § 271.
97. See, for example, RCW 23B.12.020.
98. MBCA § 12.02, 8 DGCL § 271.
99. MBCA § 13.02(3).
100. 8 DGCL § 262.

that requires only board approval in Delaware. The Model Act also provides no appraisal rights for the shareholders of the Acquirer, but shareholder approval is required unless there is no need to amend Acquirer's articles of incorporation, each share of Acquirer's stock remains unchanged and outstanding, and the number of shares of Acquirer to be issued in the transaction does not exceed 20 percent of the Acquirer's shares outstanding before the transaction.[101] If Acquirer's stock is traded on the New York Stock Exchange, the American Stock Exchange or the NASDAQ, stock exchange rules would require a vote of Acquirer's shareholders if the 20 percent threshold is exceeded.[102]

Shareholder voting and appraisal rights come into play only when there is a sale of assets to a third party. A transfer of assets to a wholly owned subsidiary or as a pledge or security for a loan (via a mortgage, deed of trust or other instrument) won't trigger the rights.[103]

The statutory requirement that the sale involve "substantially all" of the corporation's assets often can be a difficult challenge. The Model Act uses the phrase "significant continuing business activity" and provides that a selling corporation will be "conclusively" deemed to have retained such a continuing activity (and thus no shareholder voting rights kick in) if the retained business activity represents at least 25 percent of total assets and either 25 percent of after-tax operating income or 25 percent of revenues.[104] The quantitative and qualitative dimensions of the requirement are challenging, as illustrated by the leading case of *Gimbel v. Signal Companies, Inc.*[105]

In *Gimbel*, a shareholder of Signal Companies challenged the sale of one of Signal Companies' subsidiaries, arguing that the sale represented "all or substantially all" of the company's assets and, therefore, required shareholder approval. While the subsidiary represented Signal Companies' original line of business, Signal Companies had diversified into several industries and the subsidiary represented less than half of Signal Companies' value at time of sale. Recognizing that every transaction out of the normal routine does not require shareholder approval, the court held that, under Delaware law, a sale is "beyond the powers" of the board of directors if it involves assets vital to the operation of the company, is out of the ordinary, and substantially affects the existence and purpose of the corporation. In applying this test to measure the sale "quantitatively" and "qualitatively," the court concluded the it did not involve "all or substantially all" of the company's assets, noting that it represented less than half of Signal Companies' assets (under any measure) and that Signal Companies had evolved over many years into a diversified conglomerate where acquisitions and dispositions had become part of the business.

Historically, a corporation's sale of substantially all of its assets sometimes ered the consideration of two doctrines, one of which is effectively dead and the other of which is still alive in select situations. The dead doctrine

---

BCA § 6.21(f).

103. cited authority at note 24, *supra*.

104. for example, MBCA § 12.01, 8 DGCL §§ 271,272.

CA § 12.02.

A2d 599 (Del.Ch. 1974), aff'd per curiam 316 A.2d 619 (Del. 1974).

is the "de facto merger doctrine." This doctrine was created to protect shareholder rights that were cut off when a transaction was structured as an asset sale instead of a merger but the end result was the same as a merger.[106] The theory was that, in such a situation, the court should declare the transaction a "de facto merger" and bestow the same shareholder voting and appraisal rights that would be required in a merger under applicable state law.

The doctrine has been heavily criticized as being out of touch with the realities of modern capital challenges and the need to carefully structure the form of transactions to accommodate a host of different tax and non-tax objectives. In the world of major corporate transactions, the form of a transaction does matter and often has a co-equal role with substance in getting a deal done. The doctrine has been legislatively abolished in some states[107] and was effectively rejected by Delaware in *Hariton v. Arco Electronics, Inc.*[108]

The second doctrine is the "Successor Liability Doctrine." The focus of this doctrine is not on the lost rights of shareholders in an asset sale. It is on the plight of the creditor of the selling company whose claim was unknown at the time of sale but is discovered after the sale when the selling entity is long gone. Can such a creditor assert the claim against the purchaser in the transaction? Of course, in a merger the surviving entity inherits by operation of law all of the liabilities of the merging parties, including any such unknown claims. But in an asset sale, typically the purchaser is responsible only for the known liabilities that are specifically assumed in the governing document. Hence, there is a need for an equitable doctrine that gives some relief to the creditor who is left out in the cold after the sale is wrapped up. This doctrine is similar to the de facto merger doctrine in that it seeks to import merger protections into an asset sale, and for that reason the doctrines are often confused or inappropriately linked. The purpose and thrust of the successor liability doctrine are entirely different than those of the de facto merger doctrine.

And, unlike the de facto merger doctrine, the successor liability doctrine still works in select situations,[109] particularly when there is a combination of factors that support relief: there were foreseeable unknown tort claims (such as product liability claims); the same business continued after the sale as before the sale; the creditor had no capacity to recover from the selling entity or its owners; and the purchaser had the opportunity to foresee and insure against the risk. Some courts are more hard-nosed in applying the doctrine, allowing its use only in situations where the end result is tantamount to a merger because the purchaser's stock is the primary consideration in the transaction, the selling corporation disappears, and the business, assets and owners of the selling entity become part of the purchasing entity.[110]

---

106. See, for example, *Farris v. Glen Alden Corp.,* 143 A.2d 25 (Pa. 1958). The de facto merger doctrine was subsequently legislatively abolished in Pennsylvania. 15 Pa. Cons. Stat. § 1904.

107. Id.

108. 182 A.2d 22 (Del. Ch. 1962), aff'd 188 A.2d 123 (Del. 1963).

109. See, for example, *Turner v. Bituminous Casualty Co*., 244 N.W. 2d 873 (Mich. 1976) and *Ray v. Alad Corp.*, 560 P.2d 3 (Cal. 1977).

110. See, for example, Niccum v Hydra Tool Corp., 438 N.W.2d 96 (Minn. 1989).

STUDENT PROBLEM 5-4

Wade Industries, Inc. ("Wade") is a successful manufacturer and distributor of fencing materials. Wade wants to acquire SmithFence, Inc. ("Smith"), a West coast competitor that has been shackled by upper-level management shakeups and owner disputes for the last three years. Wade has 67 shareholders and a strong management team. Smith has 12 shareholders and weak management.

The key drivers for the combination are Wade's strong management team, the desire of Smith's shareholders to end their disputes, the synergies that a nationwide presence may create, and the enhanced potential of higher values and better liquidity options for shareholders.

The boards of Wade and Smith have agreed to the basic terms of the deal. Wade would be the surviving entity in the combination. As consideration for their shares in Smith, the Smith shareholders would receive $15 million in cash and shares of Wade stock that would represent 30 percent of Wade's outstanding stock after the combination. The cash and Wade stock would be distributed pro rata to the shareholders of Smith.

The question now: How best to structure the combination of Wade and Smith? The CEOs of the two companies have identified the following basic business objectives that should be considered in structuring the transaction:

1. They do not want the shareholders of Wade to vote on the combination. They know that certain shareholders would voice loud opposition to the additional $15 million of debt that would be required to fund the deal. They are not concerned about any vote by the Smith shareholders (it's a "lock").

2. They do not want Wade shareholders receiving any appraisal rights.

3. They want to minimize the risk of any "significant cash" having to be spent as a result of Smith shareholders exercising appraisal rights.

4. They want to minimize any disruptions to employees, customers, vendors and others who routinely deal with Wade or Smith.

5. They do not want Wade to be liable for debts and obligations of Smith, known or unknown. They have no problem retaining such debts and liabilities in a subsidiary; they just do not want any exposure for Wade.

How should the combination be structured to accomplish these objectives, assuming Wade and Smith are both Delaware companies?

How would the analysis change, if at all, if both companies are incorporated in a state that has adopted the Model Business Corporation Act?

How would the answers to these questions change if both Wade and Smith are public corporations whose stocks are traded on the NASDAQ?

E. THE IMPACTS OF SHAREHOLDER SUITS

Shareholders may use the courts to protect and enforce their rights as shareholders. Such lawsuits come in two forms. The first is a direct action where a shareholder seeks to enforce personal rights or to recover damages sustained as a result of a third party's breach of a duty (usually an officer, director, or controlling shareholder). Examples include an action to enforce inspection rights, a lawsuit to compel the inclusion of a shareholder's proposal in the company's proxy materials, or a claim based on false or misleading disclosures under the applicable securities laws. The second form, called a derivative action, is a lawsuit that a shareholder brings on behalf of the corporation. Actually, it's two equitable actions - a suit by the shareholder to compel the corporation to sue and a suit by the corporation, asserted by the shareholder, against those liable to the corporation.

As we will see, at times the line between direct and derivative actions is fuzzy. But the line is important for many reasons. A derivative action is a weird duck, created in equity to meet a compelling need. It is regulated by state statutes in varying degrees.[111] It serves an essential purpose and often exposes some hard realities.

1. HARD REALITIES; TOUGH REQUIREMENTS

Absolute Necessity. The right of shareholders to prosecute a derivative claim is an absolute necessity. It's the tool that reconciles the conflict between the fiduciary duties imposed on the officers and directors of a corporation and the board's power to manage the enterprise. Without this right, the duties would mean little or nothing. A board is not going to authorize a suit against itself for its breach of the duties of care or loyalty. A shareholder, as an owner of the enterprise, must have the right to expose and prosecute the wrongdoing on behalf of the corporation. The lawsuit is labeled "Derivative" because it is based on the rights of, and injuries to, the corporation.

Corporation Recovers. Any recovery in a shareholder derivative suit against a wrongdoer goes to the corporation, not the shareholder who prosecutes the lawsuit. This is the fundamental difference between a direct claim and a derivative claim. The beneficiaries of a direct claim are the shareholders making the claim. In a derivative action, the shareholder prosecuting the claim reaps only the indirect proportionate benefit represented by his or her stock in the enterprise. So what's the financial incentive for a shareholder to be the named plaintiff in a derivative case? In a derivative action, it's not about the named plaintiff or the corporation. It's all about the lawyers.

Contingent Fee Bounty Hunters. Shareholder derivative lawsuits are driven by lawyers or, better stated, lawyer fees. The plaintiffs' lawyers know that a recovery on behalf of the corporation will yield a big payday funded out of corporate coffers. The lawyers, in effect, are contingent fee "bounty hunters" for the corporation and control all aspects of the litigation – everything from where and when the case is commenced, to the scope of discovery, to whether and on what terms the case settles. All legal fees, whether triggered by victory or settlement, must be approved by the court. The amount of the legal fees may be a function of the size of the recovery or settlement, a multiple of the attorneys' "lodestar" (actual hours multiplied by a prevailing hourly rate), and a host of

111. See, for example, MBCA §§ 7.40 through 7.47.

other factors: the difficulty of the case, the risks of the litigation, the novelty of the issues, whether the case produced positive corporate governance changes, and other factors deemed important by the court. In some situations, the derivative action is accompanied by multiple private or class action direct claims based on allegations of false or misleading disclosures under proxy Rule 14a-9 or Rule 10b-5 (see Section B of Chapter 13). The consolidation of the cases often results in a separate contest to select the lead counsel for the plaintiffs – the firm that will direct the effort and reap the largest share of the fee award, which may be huge by any standard. As an example, the Southern District Court of New York approved lead counsel attorneys' fees totaling $336.1 million (based on a total lodestar of $83.2 million) in the $6.1 billion settlement of the securities litigation arising out of the collapse of telecommunications giant Worldcom, Inc. In approving the fee award, the court praised "the integral role that competent plaintiffs' counsel play in insuring the integrity of U.S. securities markets and supplementing the enforcement work of the SEC in that regard."[112]

The Named Plaintiff. State statutes typically require that the named plaintiff in a derivative action have owned common or preferred stock of the corporation at the time of the alleged wrongdoing,[113] and some states require that such ownership continue through the commencement and completion of the derivative lawsuit. Beneficial ownership through brokerage "street name" stock or a voting trust usually will qualify.[114] Although statutes typically mandate that the named plaintiff "fairly and adequately" represent the interests of the corporation,[115] the presence of competent legal counsel will usually satisfy this requirement even if the named plaintiff has no clue as to what is happening. For example, in *In re Fuqua Industries, Inc. Shareholder Litigation*,[116] the court refused to disqualify a derivative plaintiff who had lost her memory and faculties during the litigation and "lacked a meaningful grasp of the facts and allegations of the case prosecuted in her name." [117] The court stated:

> The allegation that attorneys bring actions through puppet plaintiffs while the real parties in interest are the attorneys themselves in search of fees is an oft-heard complaint from defendants in derivative suits. Sometimes, no doubt, the allegation rings true...Our legal system has privatized in part the enforcement mechanism for policing fiduciaries by allowing private attorneys to bring suits on behalf of nominal shareholder plaintiffs. In so doing, corporations are safeguarded from fiduciary breaches and shareholders thereby benefit. Through the use of cost and fee shifting mechanisms, private attorneys are economically incentivized to perform this service on behalf of shareholders...
>
> Mr. and Mrs. Abrams retained counsel in an effort to redress their grievances. They placed their trust and confidence in their lawyers as

112. 388 F.Supp.2d at 359.
113. See, for example, MBCA § 7.41(1) and 8 DGCL § 3.27.
114. See MBCA § 7.40(2).
115. See MBCA § 7.41(2).
116. 752 A.2d 126 (Del. Ch. 1999).
117. 752 A.2d at 129.

> clients have always done. Our legal system has long recognized that lawyers take a dominant role in prosecuting litigation on behalf of clients. A conscientious lawyer should indeed take a leadership role and thrust herself to the fore of a lawsuit. This maxim is particularly relevant in cases involving fairly abstruse issues of corporate governance and fiduciary duties.

752 A.2d at 133,135.

Abuse Risks. The lucrative dynamics of derivative litigation invite abuse. An aggressive plaintiff's attorney can cook up a marginal fiduciary claim against the directors of a corporation knowing that, when push comes to shove, the directors (personally named in the lawsuit) are going to favor a quick settlement that is covered by corporate indemnification provisions or insurance. When all is said and done, the interests of the corporation on whose behalf the case was brought are viewed as nothing more than an obstacle to getting the settlement approved. The attorney scores fast and starts looking for another derivative nuisance "strike suit."

There are some safeguards that protect against the risks of such abuse. Beyond the normal litigation complaint verification requirements, some state statutes authorize the shifting of all litigation expenses, including the defendants' attorney fees, to the plaintiff in a strike suit. The Model Act permits such a shifting if the suit is commenced or maintained "without reasonable cause or for an improper purpose."[118] And, of course, statutes usually require that any settlement of a derivative suit be approved by the court.[119] A number of factors may impact the approval, including the uncertainties of litigation, the costs of delay, disruption of business, negative publicity, additional indemnification burdens, the overall terms of the settlement, and any other consideration the court deems relevant. The challenge of the attorneys is to leverage these factors in convincing the court that the settlement is in the best interests of the corporation.

Lasting Impacts. The resolution of a derivative suit, whether by settlement or judgment, is binding on the corporation and any party who seeks to prosecute a derivative action based on the same claims raised in the original proceeding. This *res judicata* effect is significant. It underscores the importance of the court's role in approving any settlement. It sometimes opens up the opportunity for parties who were not involved in the lower court's approval of a settlement to prosecute an appeal of that decision.[120] And it may bar federal claims that arise out of the same facts as the derivative action even though the court that approved the derivative settlement had no jurisdiction over the federal claims.[121]

Weird Corporate Roles. The corporation has split and conflicting roles in a derivative proceeding. The named plaintiff is bringing the action on behalf of the corporation (and thus the corporation is the nominal plaintiff), and the

---

118. MBCA § 7.46(2).

119. MBCA § 7.45.

120. See, for example, *Delvin v. Scardeletti*, 536 U.S. 1 (2002), and *In re PaineWebber Inc. Ltd. Partnerships Litigation*, 94 F.3d 49, 53 (C.A.2 1996).

121. *Matushita Elec. Indus. V. Epstein*, 516 U.S. 367 (1996) and *Marrese v. American Academy of Orthopaedic Surgeons*, 470 U.S. 373 (1985).

corporation also is named as a defendant to compel it to assert its rights against the co-defendant wrongdoers. The weirdness continues because the corporation, controlled by the board, usually joins the other defendants in fighting against the claim that has been filed on its behalf. For this reason, the Supreme Court has held that, although technically a derivative claim is for the benefit of the corporation, the corporation should be treated as a defendant for federal diversity purposes if it joins the cause of the co-defendants.[122]

Given this split role, a practical question that routinely surfaces is whether the same law firm (usually the company's regular outside counsel) can represent both the corporation and the other defendants (typically officers and directors) in fighting the derivative claim. The authority is split on this one: some cases strictly forbid such dual representation to insure protection of the corporation's interests[123] and other authorities permit dual representation unless the case involves charges of serious wrongdoing - fraud, intentional misconduct, or self-dealing.[124] And some argue that dual representation should be allowed if the corporation's disinterested directors conclude that there is no basis for the claims.[125] The safest, and often the most prudent, approach is to have separate counsel for the corporation.

Corporate Control? Whether and how a corporation can exercise control in a derivative action filed on its behalf is the threshold legal challenge in most derivative actions. A sole shareholder, supported by a fee-hungry lawyer, can trigger a process that is destined to consume corporate time, effort and money and potentially damage reputation, momentum, morale, and business relationships. The board of directors, charged with the duty of managing the corporation and acting in the absolute best of faith, may conclude that it's in the best interests of the corporation to have the derivative action end quickly and the named plaintiff (with legal counsel) disappear. This is why statutes impose a demand requirement.

The Demand Requirement. The demand requirement is designed to address the potential conflicting interests between the named plaintiff and the corporation. It requires the plaintiff, before commencing the action, to make a demand on the corporation to prosecute or settle the charges. The demand gives the corporation advance notice of the suit and, in theory, provides an opportunity for a pre-suit settlement and exhaustion of intra-corporate dispute resolution procedures. And it gives the corporation's board an opportunity to exercise its management prerogative in sizing up the situation and deciding whether the case should go forward.

Two Forms. This pre-suit demand requirement comes in two forms. The first form, used in Delaware and most states, allows the plaintiff to skip the

---

122. *Smith v. Sterling*, 354 U.S. 91 (1957).

123. See, for example, *Messing v. FDI, Inc.*, 439 F.Supp. 776 (D.C. N.J. 1977) and *In re Oracle Securities Litigation*, 829 F.Supp. 1176 (N.D. Cal. 1993).

124. See, for example, official comments to Rule 1.13 of the Model Rules of Professional Conduct, *Musheno v. Gensemer*, 897 F.Supp. 833 (M.D. Pa. 1995), and *Bell Atlantic v. Bolger*, 2 F.3d 1304 (3rd Cir. 1993).

125. See Comment to Section 131 of the Restatement (Third) of the Law Governing Lawyers (American Law Institute 2000).

demand by alleging in the complaint that such a demand would be futile because the corporation's board is not disinterested and independent. The second form, used in the Model Act, requires that a demand be made in all cases and that the plaintiff wait a designated time (e.g., 90 days) before filing a lawsuit. When the futility form is in play, a demand is never made because it would be an acknowledgment of the board's capacity to decide the fate of the case. In such a situation, absent a showing that the board was not properly informed (a long shot, at best), a decision of the board would put an end to the case before it is filed. So the strength of the plaintiff's futility claim becomes the deciding factor in determining whether the case can proceed over the objection of the corporation's board. When demand is mandated by statute and the board rejects the claim, the fate of the litigation still turns on the court's determination of whether the board's decision is entitled to protection under the business judgment rule.

Another Option. Even if the demand showdown doesn't put an end to the case, the corporation's board may have another option for terminating a derivative action. It may create what the Delaware Supreme Court has dubbed a "unique creature," a special litigation committee (SLC) comprised of disinterested, independent individuals. The SLC is delegated complete authority to evaluate the merits of the case continuing on behalf of the corporation and to bring a motion (unrelated to the demand requirement) at any time to end the litigation. Of course, an SLC may also be used to bolster a corporation's claim in the demand phase of the litigation. But, as we will see, when this option is used after the demand phase, it often imposes heightened burden of proof challenges and is never a slam dunk for the SLC.

2. *DIRECT OR DERIVATIVE CLAIM?*

The challenge of defining a claim as direct or derivative was illustrated and clarified in *Tooley v. Donaldson, Lufkin, & Jenrette, Inc.*[126] In *Tooley*, Tooley and other minority shareholder of Donaldson, Lufkin, & Jenrette ("DLJ") brought suit alleging that DLJ's extension of a merger agreement improperly benefited the controlling shareholder of DLJ at the expense of the other shareholders. The trial court ruled that Tooley and his co-plaintiffs lost their standing when they tendered their shares in connection with the merger because their claims did not assert any "special injury" to support a direct claim but "at most" were claims of the corporation that had to be asserted derivatively.

On appeal, the appellate court found that the lower court erred in finding that a derivative claim had been asserted because the plaintiffs could not prove "special injury" to support a direct claim. Rejecting "special injury" as a determinative factor for whether a claim is direct or derivative, the court held that the determination should be based solely on who suffered the harm and who would benefit from any recovery. Since the corporation suffered no alleged harm and would not benefit from any recovery, the case did not involve a derivative claim. The court further ruled that the case did not involve a valid direct claim because a claim could not ripen until the merger was fulfilled. Thus, the court affirmed the dismissal on the ground (different than the trial court) that no valid

126. 845 A.2d 1031 (Del. 2004).

claim had been asserted.

The direct-derivative distinction often makes little sense in the context of a closely held corporation where some shareholders desire to bring an action against their co-shareholders, alleging breach of fiduciary duties. In such situations, some courts (but not all) ignore derivative requirements and treat the dispute as a conflict between owners, much the same as a dispute among partners.[127] Any recovery will flow to the prevailing party (not the corporation), there is no pre-suit demand requirement, and the parties can settle their dispute without court approval. However, precautions are sometimes necessary to insure that the resolution of the dispute does not encourage multiple claims, preclude a fair recovery for all interested parties, or unfairly prejudice creditors by compromising the financial viability of the corporation.[128]

3. SUSTAINING A FUTILITY CLAIM

As stated above, often the strength of the plaintiff's futility claim becomes the deciding factor in determining whether the case can proceed over the objection of the corporation's board. What it takes to sustain a futility was clarified in the leading case of *Aronson v. Lewis.*[129]

In *Aronson*, Lewis, a shareholder of Meyers Parking Systems, Inc., a Delaware corporation ("Meyers"), brought a derivative suit against Meyers and 10 Meyers' directors (of whom Aronson was one), alleging that transactions between Meyers and Leo Fink (a director and 47 percent owner of Meyers stock) constituted waste and had no valid business purpose. Lewis made no demand on the board to support the derivative action, claiming it would be futile in view of Fink's domination and control of the board. The challenged transactions included interest-free loans to Fink and an employment contract granting 75-year-old Fink $150,000 a year, five percent of Meyers' profits above $2,400,000, and a lucrative consulting arrangement upon the termination of his employment. The trial court ruled that the facts supported a "reasonable inference" that the actions were unprotected by the business judgment rule and the board, therefore, could not have impartially considered and acted upon a demand. Meyers and the board members appealed.

The appellate court reversed (with instructions permitting an amended complaint), holding that Lewis had not alleged sufficient particularized facts to support a finding that a demand would have been futile. Noting that the business judgment rule is "of paramount significance in the context of a derivative action," the court stated that the rule can only be claimed by disinterest directors who reasonably inform themselves and act with the requisite care (gross negligence standard) in discharging their duties.

---

127. See, for example, *Crosby v. Beam*, 548 N.E.2d 217 (Ohio 1989), *Barth v. Barth*, 659 N.E.2d 559 (Ind. 1995), and ALI Principles § 7.01(d). In *Barth,* the court observed: "Because shareholders of closely-held corporations have very direct obligations to one another and because shareholder litigation in the closely-held corporation context will often not implicate the principles which gave rise to the rule requiring derivative litigation, courts in many cases are permitting direct suits by shareholders of closely-held corporations where the complaint is one that in a public corporation would have to be brought as a derivative action." 659 N.E.2d at 561.

128. See ALI Principles § 7.01(d).

129. 473 A.2d 805 (Del. 1984).

The court held that a plaintiff who makes a demand futility allegation to sustain a derivative actions must allege particularized facts to raise a reasonable doubt regarding (1) the directors' ability to act as disinterested and independent parties (divided loyalty or personal benefit), or (2) the challenged transaction was not a result of valid exercise of business judgment (not informed or bad faith). Neither the threat of personal liability from approving the questioned transaction nor general claims of dominance and control would support a lack-of-independence claim (the particularized facts must show a willingness to direct the corporation to "comport" with the interests of controlling person). Similarly, the plaintiff's generalized lack-of-consideration claims regarding the transactions with Fink were not sufficient to raise a reasonable doubt that the directors had not reasonably informed themselves or otherwise breached their fiduciary duties. The court stated: "a bare claim of this sort raises no legally cognizable issue under Delaware law."

Aronson's "particularized facts" pleading requirement presents a formidable challenge for the plaintiff in a derivative action. Facts need to be identified and alleged about the corporation's board before there has been any discovery. General conclusions and speculations won't cut it. The word "particularized" has the same import as the word "facts."

In recognition of this challenge, the Delaware courts have consistently encouraged derivative-action plaintiffs to develop their futility claims by exhausting their inspection rights before the derivative action is commenced. *In Beam ex rel. Martha Stewart Living Omnimedia, Inc. v. Stewart*,[130] for example, the court affirmed the Chancery court's dismissal of plaintiff Beam's derivative case for failure to prove demand futility. The court ruled that Beam had not alleged sufficient particularized facts to raise a reasonable doubt of the independence of outside directors by virtue of Martha Stewart's dominance. The court effectively chastised the plaintiff for not exhausting her inspection rights by stating, "Beam's failure to seek a books and records inspection that may have uncovered the facts necessary to support a reasonable doubt of independence has resulted in substantial cost to the parties and the judiciary."[131]

4. Special Litigation Committee Defensive Tactic

In hopes of putting an end to a derivative action, often a corporate board will appoint an independent special litigation committee ("SLC") to thoroughly investigate the merits of the plaintiff's claim and then initiate a motion on behalf of the corporation to dismiss the action if it determines that the claim has no merit. Courts have taken different approaches in evaluating an SLC non-demand motion to end a derivative lawsuit. For example, in *Auerbach v. Bennett*,[132] the court held that once it was determined that the committee was independent and disinterested in the matter at hand, its conclusions were protected by the business judgment rule. The court ruled that absent a showing of bad faith or fraud, a court may not "trespass into the domain of business judgment."

---

130. 845 A.2d 1040 (Del.Supr. 2004).
131. 845 A.2d at 1057.
132. 393 N.E.2d 994 (N.Y. Ct. App. 1979).

The leading Delaware case of *Zapata Corp. v. Maldonado*,[133] imposed a far tougher dual procedural and substantive standard for SLC actions. In *Zapata*, Maldonado brought a derivative suit against ten officers and directors of Zapata, a Delaware corporation, alleging security law violations and common law claims, and established demand futility. Subsequently, Zapata appointed an independent committee of the board (comprising new, outside directors) with "final" authority to determine whether the derivative litigation should continue on behalf of the corporation. Following an investigation, the committee determined that the suit was not in the best interest of the corporation and caused Zapata to move for dismissal though summary judgment. The trial court denied Zapata's motion to dismiss, holding that the business judgment rule is not a grant of authority for dismissing a derivative suit when a shareholder has established the right to maintain the suit. Zapata appealed.

The appellate court reversed the lower court and remanded for further proceedings consistent with its opinion. Finding as "erroneous" the concept that a shareholder has an absolute right to maintain a derivative action over the objection of the corporation, the court pursed a "middle course" when futility has been established and the corporation, though independent board action, seeks to terminate a derivative case filed on its behalf. The middle course rejected the opposing arguments that the business judgment rule should apply in determining whether a court must yield to the independent committee's determination or that (as held below) the court must yield to the "unbridled" right of a shareholder to maintain the litigation. The court established a two-part test for such a situation: (1) The corporation must prove (perhaps with limited discovery) that the committee is independent, exercised good faith, and conducted a reasonable investigation; and (2) If the first test is met, the court should determine, applying its own independent business judgment, whether the case should continue or be dismissed. The court reasoned that the second prong would thwart instances where the independence and good faith of the committee are established, but dismissal may not serve the best interests of the corporation or may result in a premature termination of a grievance that deserves further consideration.

Some have criticized the *Zapata* standard as adding an unnecessary complexity, fraught with uncertainty, that over complicates the litigation process (adds a suit within a suit) and stalls discovery on the merits while discovery proceeds on the independence of the special litigation committee that seeks to end it all. In the 2004 demand futility case of *In Beam ex rel. Martha Stewart Living Omnimedia, Inc. v. Stewart*,[134] the Delaware Supreme Court took the opportunity to explain the *Zapata* standard that had been established 23 years earlier. The court stated:

> An SLC is a unique creature that was introduced into Delaware law by *Zapata v. Maldonado* in 1981... Unlike the demand-excusal context, where the board is presumed to be independent, the SLC has the burden of establishing its own independence by a yardstick that must be "like Caesar's wife"—"above reproach." Moreover, unlike the presuit

133. 430 A.2d 779 (Del. 1981).
134. 845 A.2d 1040 (Del.Supr. 2004).

> demand context, the SLC analysis contemplates not only a shift in the burden of persuasion but also the availability of discovery into various issues, including independence... Because the members of an SLC are vested with enormous power to seek dismissal of a derivative suit brought against their director-colleagues in a setting where presuit demand is already excused, the Court of Chancery must exercise careful oversight of the bona fides of the SLC and its process.[135]

Under *Zapata*, the burden of having to prove independence can be difficult for any SLC. In *In re Oracle Corp Derivative Litigation,*[136] 824 A.2d. 917 (Del.Ch. 2003), the SLC seemed to have it all and still couldn't get past the independence hurdle.

In that case, a special litigation committee established by Oracle Corporation's board of directors moved to dismiss a derivative action filed by Oracle shareholders against certain officers and directors of Oracle. The complaint alleged illegal insider trading. Noting that the Zapata two-part test applied, the court held that the committee had failed to sustain its burden of proving that there was no material issue of fact regarding the committee's independence. In support of its claim of independence, the committee emphasized that: its members were two distinguished Stanford University professors; the SLC members had agreed to forfeit their compensation should a court determine that the receipt of compensation impeded their objectivity; the committee had met with its own legal counsel at least 35 times for a total of 80 hours; and the committee had produced a report of 1,110 pages. Recognizing that the "law should not ignore the social nature of human beings," the court held that these facts did not satisfy the committee's burden of proof because of the extensive ties (longtime associations, huge contributions, and more) between the committee members, the named defendants, and Stanford. The court reasoned that, "human nature being what it is," neither committee member could be expected to make decisions "without pondering his own association" with the named defendants.

STUDENT PROBLEM 5-5

Reference Student Problem 5-3 and Judd's concern regarding an anti-gay bias in making hiring and promotion decisions at DataSys. As Judd digs deeper, he discovers that the primary source of the bias is DataSy's CEO, a strong-willed leader with a commanding presence and the ability to get whatever he wants from a board of directors that he has handpicked. The CEO was rightfully credited with DataSys's ballooning success in years past, but performance levels have leveled off over the past three years. Judd now believes that the CEO's personal bias has become an obsession, known to the board members and many others, that is hurting the company. Judd has documents suggesting that the bias played a key role in the loss of several lucrative contract opportunities, at least two expansion acquisition opportunities, and many chances to hire talented individuals throughout the industry.

135. 845 A.2d at 1055.

136. 824 A.2d. 917 (Del.Ch. 2003).

Judd has hired a lawyer, Walter, who is excited that Judd, as a shareholder, may have legitimate breach of fiduciary claims against the CEO and the members of DataSy's board. The claims would allege waste and associated breaches of the duties of care and loyalty. Assume DataSy is a Delaware corporation. Advise Judd on the following questions and, where relevant, indicate what additional facts you would like to have in answering the questions:

1. Would the claims against the CEO and DataSy's directors need to be asserted as direct or derivative claims?

2. What are the impacts to Judd if the claims are asserted in a derivative action?

3. What risks does Judd take if the claims are dismissed as being frivolous?

4. Who pays the legal fees if Judd is victorious?

5. Would a formal demand of DataSy's board be required before commencing a lawsuit?

6. If DataSy's board determines that the claims are not meritorious, can Judd still proceed with the lawsuit?

7. What steps should Judd anticipate that the CEO and DataSy's board will take to prevent the case from ever getting to a decision on the merits?

How would your answers to these questions change if DataSy is incorporated in a state that has adopted the Model Business Corporation Act?

F. SAY-ON-PAY RIGHTS

In the world of shareholder core rights, "say-on-pay" is the hot new kid on the block. Since January 21, 2011, section 951 of the Dodd-Frank Wall Street Reform and Consumer Protection Act ("Dodd-Frank") has required a public corporation to submit its executive compensation arrangements to a "yes" or "no" non-binding advisory vote of its shareholders. It's an up or down vote that gives the shareholders an opportunity to officially go on record as to whether they like or dislike the pay packages for the top executives in the company. The significance of the right is heightened by the ever-growing presence of institutional investors who have the will and capacity to evaluate compensation packages, influence the results of the shareholder vote, and leverage the impact of a negative anti-management vote.

1. HISTORY AND PURPOSE

The say-on-pay concept was imported from the United Kingdom. Its roots can be traced to a 1999 announcement by U.K. officials, stating that they were considering a policy for shareholders to review executive "remuneration" reports. In 2002, the U.K. adopted its "Directors' Remuneration Report" regulations that mandated a shareholder vote on the company's remuneration report at each annual meeting. In 2005, the idea first gained attention in the U.S. when Escala Group, Inc.'s proxy statement put the compensation packages of its top two officers to a shareholder vote. In 2007, the shareholders of roughly 50 companies considered proposals that would require a regular say-on-pay vote. The number jumped to 90 in 2008. Although these proposals received average shareholder support of only about 40 percent, they signaled a trend. In 2009, the SEC joined the movement, exercising rights under the American Recovery and Reinvestment Act to require a say-on-pay vote in companies (about 400) that received financial support from the federal government.

Early signs suggested say-on-pay might yield little or nothing, even for companies that made big headlines by promoting controversial executive pay packages amidst claims of abuse. The Merrill Lynch bonus headline mess did not prevent Bank of America from garnering a favorable say-on pay vote that exceeded 70 percent. Goldman Sachs' favorable number hit 98 percent, and Verizon's approval number was over 90 percent. Even Citigroup did well with a favorable vote of over 85 percent.

Meanwhile, pressure was building in Congress for a broader say-on-pay mandate, with specific bills being introduced by Representative Barney Frank and Senator Charles Schumer and heat coming from the Treasury Department, the SEC, and the White House. So when Congress developed Dodd-Frank to address the abuses that contributed to the financial crisis of 2008, the inclusion of say-on-pay was pretty much a legislative no-brainer.

Although the law calls for only a nonbinding vote, it's hard to overstate the significance of say-on-pay. It has quickly become the spotlight proxy issue, and all signs suggest that its impact will continue to grow. Although the tax code has always required shareholders to approve qualified stock option plans and the securities laws have mandated disclosures related to executive compensation, historically shareholders haven't had an official voice in the overall compensation packages for a corporation's top executives. That challenge has been delegated to a compensation committee of the board, comprised solely of outside directors, that receives professional expert advice from an outside consulting firm. The theory, of course, is that the committee and the consulting firm, both cloaked in objectivity, will act in the best interests of the corporation. But, in practice, everyone knows that the members of the compensation committee often are handpicked by the executives whose compensation is at issue and the consulting firm's ongoing involvement is predicated on delivering results that please those same executives. And then there is the sheer size of the numbers that often grab the headlines and put many CEO's in a league that movie stars and star athletes can only dream of. A recent study by Ernst & Young confirmed that escalating executive compensation levels is the highest cost burden of becoming a public company.[137]

Say-on-pay provides a new challenge for all those involved in the executive compensation process. A company's executives, directors, compensation committee, and outside advisors cannot ignore the consequences of the shareholder vote. A failing shareholder vote may ensure conflict and trigger a need for changes. Often a passing grade won't be good enough. Norms are

---

137. Ernst & Young IPO Cost Survey, November 2011. Ernst & Young is a global leader in assurance, tax, transaction and advisory services that employs 141,000 people worldwide.

already developing that suggest that anything short of a 70 percent approval vote shows weakness and signals growing shareholder discontent in the future. The real goal is a solid approval vote north of 90 percent.

There are at least three dimensions to the say-on-pay challenge: (1) an analytical effort to ensure that the corporation's compensation arrangements stack up against the key peer measures and make sense in light of the company's performance; (2) a political and sales effort to develop shareholder support for management's recommendations; and (3) smart responsive strategies to a bad shareholder vote that promise improved future vote outcomes and mitigate exposures for any enhanced legal risks. Obviously, everything is easier if the company is performing strong and hitting its benchmarks for the shareholders. But when the company's performance is stalled in a chronically sluggish economy, say-on-pay will often be the overriding consideration in any effort to inflate executive pay packages.

2. *THE LEGAL REQUIREMENTS*

Section 951 of Dodd-Frank mandated say-on-pay for all public companies by adding new Section 14A(a) to the Securities Exchange Act of 1934. The SEC is authorized under Section 14A(e) to exempt certain classes of issuers. There are three basic requirements of the new section 14A(a).

1. Section 14A(a)(1) requires that all public companies, at least once every three years, provide shareholders with an opportunity to vote on a non-binding basis on the compensation of named executive officers. This same requirement is set forth in newly-adopted Rule 14a-21(a). Although the rule does not specify the form of the "say-on-pay" resolution to be voted on by shareholders, the SEC has provided the following "non-exclusive example" of a resolution that would satisfy the requirements of the rule:

> "RESOLVED, that the compensation paid to the company's named executive officers, as disclosed pursuant to Item 402 of Regulation S-K, including the Compensation Discussion and Analysis, compensation tables and narrative discussion, is hereby APPROVED."

The SEC has indicated that companies may use a resolution that substitutes plain English for the phrase "pursuant to Item 402 of Regulation S-K." The SEC provided the following as an acceptable example: "pursuant to the compensation disclosure rules of the Securities and Exchange Commission, including the compensation discussion and analysis, the compensation tables and any related material enclosed in this proxy statement."

2. Section 14A(a)(2) requires a "say-on-frequency" vote at least once every six years. This vote gives shareholders the opportunity to decide if the safe-on-pay vote is going to be required every year, every second year, or every third year. The first say-on-pay and say-on-frequency votes were required at the first annual or other shareholder meeting occurring on or after January 21, 2011. Rule 14a-21(b) requires that the proxy card for the "say-on-frequency" vote include four choices: every 1 year, every 2 years, every 3 years, or abstain. The "say- on-

frequency" doesn't have to be in the form of a resolution; a narrative explanation of the proposal is permitted.

3. Section 14A(b)(2) requires a separate vote to approve "golden parachute" compensation whenever a public company seeks shareholder approval for "an acquisition, merger, consolidation, or proposed sale or other disposition of all or substantially all the assets of an issuer." Disclosure is required for any agreements or understandings with any "named executive officer...concerning any type of compensation (whether present, deferred or contingent)" that is "based on or otherwise relates to" the transaction. This vote, also non-binding, is only required for golden parachute agreements that have not previously been subject to a shareholder say-on-pay vote under Section 14A(a). New SEC Rule 14a-21(c) requires such a vote for a golden parachute arrangement for "each named executive officer," which generally includes the company's principal executive officer (usually, the CEO), its principal financial officer (usually, the CFO) and the three other most highly-compensated executive officers for the year in question.

3. *EARLY RESULTS*

Say-on-pay was the buzz topic during the 2012 and 2013 proxy seasons. When all was said and done, the median level of shareholder approval was just about 90 percent (91 percent in 2012 and 92 percent in 2013), and less than three percent of all U.S, public companies (2.5 percent in 2012 and 1.8 percent in 2013) had a failed vote. Many believe that these early rounds of say-on-pay taught two important lessons.

First, the Institutional Shareholder Services ("ISS") Proxy Advisory Services' recommendations and methodology must be taken very seriously.[138] Companies with a negative ISS recommendation received an average shareholder support vote of only 68 percent in 2013, compared to a 95 percent approval vote for those that had a positive ISS recommendation. An ISS negative recommendation is usually a strong indicator that there is a "pay for performance disconnect" – the CEO's pay is out of alignment with total shareholder return, as compared to the company's peer group performance. There is no question that the methodology of ISS for making its say-on-pay recommendations is quickly emerging as a threshold compensation consideration for many public companies.

Second, a smart shareholder communication program can seriously boost the odds of securing a favorable say-on-pay vote from shareholders. Such a program will hone the message, communicate frequently, promote feedback (company listening), carefully use the best messengers, target the right people in each significant institutional investor, and proactively anticipate and thwart negative spins.[139]

---

138. See, generally, Sullivan & Cromwell LLP publication entitled *2013 Proxy Season Review,* dated July 2, 2013; David A. Katz and Laura A. McIntosh, *"Say on Pay" in the 2012 Proxy Season*, (The Harvard Law School Forum on Corporate Governance and Financial Regulation 2012); Semler Brossy, "*2012 Say on Pay Results, Russell 3000*," July 18, 2012; and John D. England, *"Say on Pay Soul Searching Required at Proxy Advisory Firms,"* Pay Governance, June 20, 2012.

139. See, generally, David A. Katz and Laura A. McIntosh, *"Say on Pay" in the 2012 Proxy Season*, (The Harvard Law School Forum on Corporate Governance and Financial Regulation 2012).

4. *BAD VOTE LEGAL RISKS*

Does a negative or poor shareholder say-on-pay vote increase the personal legal exposure of officers and directors who ignore the non-binding vote and take actions that on their face appear to be contrary to the expressed desires of the shareholders? New Section 14A(c) of the Exchange Act expressly provides that the say-on-pay and say-on-parachutes votes are not to be construed as "overruling a decision by such issuer or board of directors," "to create or imply any change to the fiduciary duties," or to "create or imply any additional fiduciary duties for such issuer or board of directors." So is that the end of it? Probably not.

The neglect of a negative say-on-pay vote may be evidence to help support a claim that directors or officers have breached their duties of care or loyalty. But the statutory language is specific enough to negate the possibility of a separate private right of action based solely on a non-response to a failed say-on-pay vote. In *Assad v. Hart*,[140] the plaintiff tried just that. In dismissing the complaint, the court stated that Dodd Frank "did not create a private right of action or create new fiduciary duties" and the statutory language "expressly states" that it may not "be construed to create or imply any change to fiduciary duties."

Might a failure to respond to a negative or poor say-on-pay vote help a plaintiff who brings a derivative action and needs to satisfy the *Aronson* demand futility test (see previous section) in order to keep the lawsuit alive? Is it evidence that raises a reasonable doubt concerning the directors' independence and business judgment? The 2012 case of *Laborer's Local v. Intersil*,[141] considered the issue, and more cases will undoubtedly follow. As to the first prong of the *Aronson* test (particularized facts to raise a reasonable doubt as to the directors' independence and disinterest), the *Intersil* court held that the mere threat of personal liability on the part of directors for the failure to respond is insufficient alone to create reasonable doubt as to the directors' independence and disinterest. As to the second prong (particularized facts to raise a reasonable doubt as to the directors' good faith or adequate information), the court held that the negative say-on-pay vote had "substantial evidentiary weight" but, standing alone, was not enough to rebut the presumption of the business judgment rule. Noting that the Dodd-Frank Act does not "change" fiduciary duties or "create or imply" new duties, the court reasoned that Congress "must have intended for the shareholder vote to have some weight."

STUDENT PROBLEM 5-6

Falcon Industries, Inc. ("Falcon") is a Delaware corporation whose stock is traded on the American Stock Exchange. Falcon's primary business is providing customized inventory management and distribution systems to multi-national companies in various industries.

Last year, Falcon hired a new CEO, Jake Moss, to "bring a renewed energy and focus to Falcon." Falcon's board had determined that Jake's hiring was an

140. 2012 WL 33220 (S.D.Cal. 2012).
141. 2012 WL 762319 (W.D.Cal. 2012).

"essential step to break a string of disappointing years for Falcon shareholders." To land Jake, who has a stellar reputation for being one of the absolute best CEO's in the industry, Falcon had to provide Jake a five-year contract that guaranteed an annual salary and cash bonuses of not less than $2.5 million and cash and stock performance incentives that potentially could pay up to an additional $5 million a year. Falcon's board understood at the time that this was the most generous arrangement provided to any CEO in the industry.

Jake has been the leader of Falcon for a year. He's discouraged. A successful turnaround of Falcon is going to take longer and be much tougher than he originally anticipated. Jake sees little hope of earning his incentive compensation, and another opportunity has surfaced, offering Jake a more lucrative contract with a much more realistic upside potential.

Falcon's board is pleased with Jake and badly wants to keep him at the helm. They are convinced that Jake is the key to Falcon's future. In discussions with Jake, they've concluded that they can "hold onto Jake" if Falcon agrees to Jake's demand to convert's $1.5 million of Jake's annual incentive compensation payment to a guaranteed payment each year.

Falcon's board is concerned about its say-on-pay requirements if it agrees to Jake demand, particularly in view of the company's slow turnaround. It has five preliminary questions:

1. Must it condition Jake's demand on a favorable say-on-pay vote? Should it?

2. How can it minimize the number of say-on-pay votes until Jake has had an opportunity to get Falcon turned around?

3. What steps should it take to help insure a positive say-on-pay vote if it honors Jake's demand?

4. If Falcon honors Jake's demand and then experiences a negative say-on-pay vote, will it have to take steps to reduce Jake's compensation package?

5. If Falcon honors Jake's demands and then experiences a negative say-on-pay vote, will the personal legal exposure of Falcon's board members be increased if they take no actions in response to the negative vote and continue with the current plan in hopes that Jake can reverse Falcon's course?

CHAPTER 6

PARTNERSHIP AND LLC ENTITY AND DESIGN OPTIONS

A. UNDERSTANDING ENTITY DIFFERENCES

A lawyer should know the basics of partnerships (there are four types) and limited liability companies. These entities are essential planning tools for many successful businesses and families. Although LLCs continue to grow in popularity, a partnership option still emerges as the preferred candidate in many choice-of-entity analyses. An extended choice-of-entity planning discussion is provided Chapter 9.

Since 1914, uniform acts have been developed as needed to help states enact comprehensive codes dealing with partnerships and LLCs. Although states typically modify select uniform act provisions during the legislative process, this ongoing uniform act effort has had a powerful impact in promoting consistency between the states. This section summarizes the latest uniform act provisions for LLCs and the various types of partnerships. The hope is that this summary discussion, coupled with Problems 6-1 through 6-3, will help students understand the core legal underpinnings of the various entity types and the primary differences between them.

1. PARTNERSHIPS

The partnership is the oldest form of business entity between multiple parties. Its history predates corporations and business trusts. And it is the historical foundation for all the "limited" entities: limited partnership, limited liability partnership, limited liability limited partnership, and limited liability company. Partnership statutes have existed for over 2,000 years, being tracked to King Khammurabi of Babylon.[1]

A partnership is formed when there is "an association of two or more

---

1. 1 Reed Rowley, Rowley on Partnership 2 (2d ed. 1960)

persons to carry on as co-owners a business for profit…, whether or not the persons intend to form a partnership."[2] No written document or government filing is required for the formation of a partnership. Whenever two or more parties engage in an activity in hopes of generating a profit, they may inadvertently trigger the formation of a general partnership and the application of state statutory default rules that will govern the relationship between the parties and the rights of third parties that deal with the undocumented entity.

Although broad in scope, the partnership definition requires the carrying on of a business for profit; property co-ownership alone won't satisfy the definition. Thus, a joint tenancy, tenancy in common, tenancy by the entirety, joint property, or community property arrangement generally is not deemed a partnership even if the co-owners share profits through the use of the property. Similarly, an arrangement to share gross returns, even when the sharing parties have a joint or common interest in the property that generates the returns, doesn't rise to the level of a partnership. Under the Revised Uniform Partnership Act, a person who receives a share of the profits from a business is presumed to be a partner, but not if the profits are received in payment of (a) a debt, (b) for services as an independent contractor, (c) as wages or other compensation to an employee, (d) as rent, (e) as an annuity or other retirement or health benefit to a beneficiary, representative, or designee of a deceased or retired partner, or (f) as interest or other charge on a loan, even if the amount of payment varies with the profits of the business.

Two distinct theories have forever been advanced to explain the nature of a partnership: an "entity" theory that focuses on a partnership being separate and apart from its owners, and an "aggregate" theory that views a partnership as an amalgamation of owner rights and interests and deemphasizes the separateness of the entity. Focusing on the underpinnings and reach of these theories does little to advance one's understanding of partnership law because both theories are evidenced in state statutory schemes. The reason is that all states, except Louisiana, have based their partnership statutes on the Uniform Partnership Act ("UPA"), first published in 1914. The latest version, known as the Revised Uniform Partnership Act ("RUPA"), was released in 1997 and has been adopted by 37 states. While the RUPA favors the entity theory, evidence of the aggregate theory shows up throughout the RUPA in a variety of contexts, such as an owner's liability for the partnership's debts and the impact of an owner's disassociation from a partnership.

Following Student Problem 6-1 is a recap of the key provisions of the RUPA that have been adopted in most states.

STUDENT PROBLEM 6-1

Answer the questions raised in the following three scenarios based on your reading of the partnership definition discussed above and the statutory descriptive materials that follow.

---

2. RUPA § 202(a).

Scenario One:

Doug is a civil engineer who works for a large company and lives like a hermit. On his off hours, he has developed what he calls "the ultimate bicycle derailleur." In a nutshell, it doubles the speed/effort ratio for a normal rider. Doug calls his invention "the Glide."

With a crude prototype in hand, Doug approached his rich aunt Mary for funding to refine all aspects of the Glide and produce some quality samples for testing and show. Doug had never been close to Mary, but knew she had money and was reputed to be a shrewd investor. Excited with what she saw, Mary advanced Doug $100,000 and exclaimed, "We might make a killing with this." Doug responded, "Come hell or high water, I'll get this money back to you." They signed no documents.

Doug visited Mary six months later and requested an additional $50,000. He provided a glowing progress report on the Glide's development and the patent application process as well as an accounting of how the first $100,000 had been spent. He capped his request by stating, "I guarantee that this investment is going to really pay off for us." Mary enthusiastically honored Doug's request. Again, they signed no documents and discussed no specifics of their relationship.

Four months later Doug again visited Mary and delivered a check for $162,000. The memo on the check read, "Full loan repayment of $150,000, plus interest at 12%." Doug thanked Mary and boastfully explained that he had sold Glide to a major bike manufacturer for $2.8 million. Mary was shocked and, as she threw Doug out, mutilated the check in a rage and exclaimed "my lawyers will be coming for my share."

Was a partnership formed between Doug and Mary? What additional facts might help in making such a determination? If a partnership was created, what are Mary's rights?

Scenario Two:

Same facts as Scenario One. Before Mary could marshal her lawyers, Doug quit his job and disappeared. Mary assumed that he had taken his money and skipped to another country, presumably someplace with plenty of sunshine and a low cost of living.

Five months later Walter, a 78-year-old bike fanatic, tracked Mary down. When Walter asked Mary if she had been Doug's partner in creating the Glide, Mary responded, "I sure thought I was, but the bum ended up running way with all our profits." Walter then explained that the Glide was his idea and design and that he had approached Doug fifteen months before (at the same time Doug had requested the original $100,000 from Mary) and hired Doug to produce a prototype. Walter had paid Doug $5,000, and Doug had signed a confidentially agreement acknowledging Walter's exclusive rights in the design. After spending three months on the project, Doug advised Walter that the design was flawed and a working prototype could not be built. Walter then abandoned the project.

Walter presented Mary with a copy of the confidentially agreement signed by Doug and demanded that Mary reimburse him all amounts that the bike manufacturer had paid for the Glide.

Is Mary personally liable to Walter? Would there be any personal liability issue for Mary if Doug and Mary had formed a limited liability partnership, a limited liability company, or a limited partnership with Doug as the general partner and Mary as the limited partner?

Scenario Three:

Same facts as Scenario One, except the Glide was not sold and, at the time Mary advanced the additional $50,000, Doug and Mary signed a simple document, hastily prepared by Mary, that reads, "We are now partners in the Glide Company, we will produce and sell the Glide, Doug is free to run the business, but Doug must report to Mary regularly." As to this venture:

1. Does Mary have any property rights in the Glide?

2. How will the profits of the enterprise be allocated between Doug and Mary?

3. What interests in the enterprise could Mary unilaterally transfer to her daughter Linda?

4. Will Mary bear the first $150,000 of any losses sustained in the venture?

5. Does Mary have the power to bind the enterprise to contracts with third parties? Does Doug?

6. What duties do Mary and Doug owe each other?

7. If Doug is unable to pay a personal debt that he owes a friend, what rights may the friend exercise against the partnership to recover the amount owed?

8. What would be the capital accounts of Doug and Mary if the venture loses the $150,000 advanced by Mary and then shuts down after six months because the Glide's design is flawed, marketing prospects look hopeless, and the entity has no assets? At the time of the shut-down, would Doug or Mary have a financial obligation to the venture?

9. Would Mary have any personal liability exposure if Doug borrowed $100,000 in the name of Glide Company from a wealthy bike enthusiast, the lender had no knowledge of Mary's involvement, and Mary had no knowledge of the loan?

a. The Partnership Agreement

A core feature of state partnership statutes is that they exalt the agreement between the partners as the primary governing source for the entity. With limited exceptions (all important), the agreement will preempt state statutory provisions, which kick in only when the partnership agreement does not address a specific issue.[3] This puts a premium on the development of a smart partnership agreement

---

3. RUPA § 103(a).

during the planning process. Typically, a partnership agreement may not:[4]

- Vary the statutory rights of the partnership or a partner to file a statement with the secretary of state or other designated state agency to define or limit the rights of individuals to deal with partnership real estate or take other actions on behalf of the partnership.

- Unreasonably restrict a partner's right of access to books and records.

- Eliminate a partner's duty of loyalty, but, if not manifestly unreasonable, the partnership agreement may identify specific types or categories of activities that do not violate the duty of loyalty, and the partnership agreement may provide that all of the partners or a number or percentage specified in the partnership agreement may authorize or ratify, after full disclosure of all material facts, a specific act or transaction that otherwise would violate the duty of loyalty.

- Unreasonably reduce a partner's duty of care.

- Eliminate a partner's obligation of good faith and fair dealing, but the partnership agreement may prescribe the standards by which the performance of the obligation is to be measured, if the standards are not manifestly unreasonable.

- Vary the power of a partner to dissociate as a partner, except the partnership agreement may require that a notice to dissociate be in writing.

- Vary the right of a court to expel a partner who (1) has engaged in wrongful conduct that adversely and materially affects the partnership's business, (2) has willfully and persistently committed a material breach of the partnership agreement or a duty owned to the partnership or other partners, or (3) has engaged in conduct that makes it not reasonably practicable to carry on the partnership's business.[5]

- Vary the requirement to wind up the partnership's business if (1) continuation of all or substantially all of the partnership's business is unlawful, (2) a partner seeks a judicial determination that the economic purpose of the partnership is unreasonably frustrated, a partner has engaged in conduct that makes it not reasonably practicable to carry on the partnership's business, or it is not reasonably practicable to carry on the partnership's business in accordance with the partnership agreement, or (3) a transferee of a partner's interest seeks a judicial determination that the partnership's term or undertaking has expired or that the partnership's term was at will.[6]

- Vary the manner in which the state's law is applicable to a limited liability partnership.

- Restrict rights of third parties.

b. Property Rights

Property acquired by a partnership is property of the partnership, not

4. RUPA § 103(b).
5. RUPA §§ 103(b)(7), 601(5).
6. RUPA §§ 103(b)(8), 801(4)(5)(6).

property co-owned by the individual partners.[7] A partner does not have an interest in partnership property that can be transferred, either voluntarily or involuntarily.[8] Property is presumed to be partnership property if purchased with partnership assets, even if not acquired in the name of the partnership.[9] Property acquired in the name of a partner, without use of partnership funds and a reference that the partner is acting on behalf of the partnership, is presumed to be separate property of the partner.[10]

c. Agency Authority

Each partner is an agent of the partnership with authority to bind the partnership in the ordinary course of the partnership's business or business of the kind carried out by the partnership, unless the partner had no authority to act for the partnership and the third person with whom the partner dealt knew or had reason to know that the partner had no such authority.[11] A partnership may file a statement (good for five years) with the secretary of state (or, in the case of real estate, with the county recorder) that states the authority, or limitations on the authority, of specific partners to enter into transactions on behalf of the partnership. Such grant of authority is conclusive in favor of a third party who gives value in reliance of the statement.[12] A person named in any such statement may file a written denial of the person's authority or status as a partner.[13]

d. Liabilities.

Partner-Created Liabilities. A partnership is liable for any actionable loss or injury caused by a partner while acting within the ordinary course of the partnership's business or within the partner's authority.[14] Similarly, a partnership is liable if a partner, while acting in the course of the partnership's business or within the scope of authority, misapplies money or property that the partner receives or causes the partnership to receive from a third party.[15]

Entity Obligations. Partners are jointly and severally liable for all obligations of the partnership unless otherwise agreed to by the claimant or provided by law. Exceptions apply for a newly admitted partner's responsibility for pre-admission obligations and (as described below) for the partners of a limited liability partnership.[16]

Purported Partner Liabilities. A person who, through word or action, purports to be a partner or consents to being represented by another as a partner is liable as a partner to any third party who relies on any such representation. If the purported partner representation is made in a public announcement, liability may attach even if the purported partner had no knowledge of the specific

---

7. RUPA §§ 203, 501.
8. RUPA § 501.
9. RUPA § 204(c).
10. RUPA § 204(d).
11. RUPA § 301.
12. RUPA § 303.
13. RUPA § 304.
14. RUPA § 305(a).
15. RUPA § 305(b).
16. RUPA § 306.

claimant. Personal liability under this purported liability rule is not triggered simply because a person is incorrectly named in a statement of partnership authority.[17]

e. Rights Between Partners. Unless the partnership provides otherwise, the following provisions apply to the partners:

Capital Accounts. Each partner's capital account is increased by the amount of money and the value of any property (net of liabilities) contributed to the partnership and the partner's share of any partnership profits. Each partner's capital account is decreased by the amount of money and the value of any property (net of liabilities) distributed to the partner and the partner's share of any partnership losses.[18]

Profits and Losses. Partnership profits and losses are allocated equally among the partners.[19]

Partner Advances. A partnership is obligated to indemnify a partner for payments made and liabilities incurred in the ordinary course of business or to preserve the partnership's business or property. Any such payment constitutes a loan to the partnership that accrues interest.[20]

Excessive Contributions. A partnership is obligated to reimburse a partner for any contribution to the partnership that exceeds the partner's contribution obligation. Any such excessive contribution constitutes a loan to the partnership that accrues interest.[21]

Management Rights. Each partner has an equal right to manage and conduct the partnership's business.[22]

Use of Property. A partner may use or possess partnership property only on behalf of the partnership.[23]

Partner Compensation. A partner is not entitled to any compensation for services rendered to the partnership, except for reasonable compensation for services rendered in winding up the affairs of the partnership.[24]

New Partners. A person may become a partner only with the consent of all existing partners.[25]

Dispute Resolution. A majority of the partners may resolve any dispute that involves a matter within the ordinary course of the partnership's business. A matter outside the ordinary course or any amendment to the partnership agreement requires the unanimous consent of the partners.[26]

---

17. RUPA § 308.
18. RUPA § 401(a).
19. RUPA § 401(b).
20. RUPA § 401(c).
21. RUPA § 401(d).
22. RUPA § 401(f).
23. RUPA § 401(g).
24. RUPA § 401(h).
25. RUPA § 401(i).
26. RUPA § 401(j).

In-Kind Distributions. No partner has a right to receive, and may not be required to accept, a distribution in kind of partnership property.[27]

Records Inspection Access. A partner and the partner's agents and attorneys have access to the books and records of the partnership, which the partnership is obligated to maintain and keep at the partnership's chief executive office. The same rights extend to former partners and the legal representatives of a deceased and disabled partner. The partnership may impose reasonable charges for the costs (both labor and materials) of document copies.[28]

Duty of Loyalty. A partner's duty of loyalty to the partnership and other partners is limited to (1) accounting and holding as trustee any property, profit or benefit derived by the partner in the conduct or winding up of the partnership's business or from the use of partnership property, including the appropriation of a partnership opportunity, (2) refraining from dealing with the partnership as, on behalf of, a person having an interest adverse to partnership, and (3) refraining from competing with the partnership.[29] A partner does not violate this duty or any other duty merely because the partner's conduct furthers the partner's own interests, nor is a partner prohibited from loaning money to a partnership or transacting other business with a partnership.[30]

Duty of Care. A partner's duty of care to the partnership and the other partners is limited to refraining from engaging in grossly negligent or reckless conduct, intentional misconduct, or a known violation of law.[31]

Duty of Good Faith. A partner is required to discharge duties to the partnership and other partners and exercise any rights in a manner that reflects good faith and fair dealing.[32]

Enforcement Actions. A partnership may maintain an action against a partner for violation of the partnership agreement or a violation of a duty owned to the partnership. A partner may maintain an action against the partnership or other partners for legal and equitable relief to enforce rights under the partnership agreement or state law and to enforce other interests of the partner.[33]

Partner's Transferable Interest. The only transferable interest of a partner is the partner's share of profits and losses and the right to receive distributions. This interest is personal property.[34] A partner's transfer of such interest (1) is permissible, (2) does not itself cause a dissolution or winding up of the partnership, (3) does not entitle the transferee to participate in the management or conduct of the partnership's business, to require access to information about partnership transactions, or to inspect or copy partnership books and records, and (4) entitles the transferee only to distributions and net dissolution amounts that otherwise would have been paid to the transferor partner and to seek a judicial

27. RUPA § 402.
28. RUPA § 403.
29. RUPA § 404(b).
30. RUPA § 404(e),(f).
31. RUPA § 404(c).
32. RUPA § 404(d).
33. RUPA § 405.
34. RUPA § 502.

determination that it is equitable to wind up the partnership's business.[35]

Partner's Third Party Debts. The creditor of a partner may seek a judicial charging order that constitutes a lien on the partner's transferable interest in the partnership. The court may appoint a receiver and enter other orders to enforce the charging order and may order a foreclosure of the interest. The acquirer at any such foreclosure sale receives only the rights of a transferee. Statutes usually specifically provide that this is the "exclusive remedy" of a partner's judgment creditor who seeks to satisfy a claim out of the partner's interest in the partnership.[36]

f. Partner's Termination (Dissociation).

At Will Termination. A partner may dissociate from a partnership by notice expressing a will to withdraw as a partner. When the partnership is at will, such a withdrawal will trigger a dissolution and winding up of the partnership.[37] A partnership is at will when the partners have not agreed to remain partners until the expiration of a definite term or the completion of a particular undertaking.[38]

Other Triggers. Statutes typically provide that a partner's interest also may be terminated by the:

1) Occurrence of a dissociation event specified in the partnership agreement;

2) Expulsion of a partner pursuant to the partnership agreement;

3) Unanimous vote of the other partners if (a) it is unlawful to carry on business with the partner, (b) there has been a transfer of substantially all of a partner's interest in the partnership, (c) the partner is a corporation that has filed a certificate of dissolution or has had its charter revoked or its right to conduct business suspended, or (4) the partner is a partnership that has been dissolved;

4) A judicial determination of expulsion due to the partner's wrongful conduct, willful and persistent breach of the partnership agreement or duties owed, or conduct that makes it not reasonably practical to carry on the business with the partner;

5) Partner becoming a debtor in bankruptcy, executing an assignment for the benefit of creditors, or having a trustee, receiver or liquidator appointed to handle the partner's property;

6) Partner dying, having a guardian or conservator appointed to handle the partner's property, or being judicially determined to be incapable of performing the partner's duties under the partnership agreement;

7) Transfer of the partner's interest in the partnership by a trustee or a personal representative of an estate holding the partnership interest; and

8) Termination of any partner who is not an individual, partnership,

35. RUPA § 503.
36. RUPA § 504.
37. RUPA §§ 601(1), 801(1).
38. RUPA § 101(8).

corporation, trust, or estate.[39]

Purchase of Interest. Typically, a partner's dissociation does not force a dissolution and winding up of the partnership unless the dissociation is due to the death of a partner or one of the triggers described in items (5) through (8) above and over half of the partners approve a winding up of the partnership. Absent such circumstances, the interest of the departing partner is purchased for a price equal to the greater of the liquidation value of the partner's interest or the value based on a sale of the business as a going concern. State statutes usually specify the procedures for establishing the value.[40]

Dissociated Partner's Liabilities. A dissociated partner remains liable: (1) to the partnership and other partners for any damages or losses resulting from a withdrawal that violated the partnership agreement or actions taken by the dissociated partner after the dissociation; and (2) to third parties for joint and several exposure obligations and liabilities arising prior to the dissociation. The dissociated partner's exposure on such a pre-dissociation obligation may be eliminated by agreement with the creditor and the other partners or by a material change in the terms of the obligation with the creditor having notice of the dissociation. Continued use of a dissociated partner's name in the partnership's name does not expose the dissociated partner to obligations of the partnership incurred after the dissociation.[41]

Third Party Protection. The partnership may be liable to third parties who reasonably believed that a dissociated partner was still a partner for actions taken by the dissociated partner within two years of the dissociation, provided the partnership may cut off this exposure 90 days after filing a notice of dissociation with the secretary of state.[42]

g. Dissolution and Winding Up

Triggering Events. A partnership is dissolved, and its business must be wound up when (1) a partner gives notice to withdraw in an at will partnership; (2) a majority of partners approve winding up when a partner dies or dissociates for one of the reasons described in items (5) though (8) above; (3) the partners all agree to a winding up of the business; (4) the partnership's specified term or undertaking has expired or been completed; (5) a dissolution event specified in the partnership agreement occurs; (6) an event (not curable in 90 days) occurs that makes it unlawful to carry on substantially all of the partnership's business; (7) on application of a partner, a court determines that the economic purpose of the partnership is unreasonably frustrated, a partner has engaged in conduct that makes it not reasonably practicable to carry on the partnership's business, or it is not reasonably practicable to carry on the partnership's business in accordance with the partnership agreement, or (8) on application of the transferee of a partner's interest, a court determines that it would be equitable to windup the

39. RUPA § 601.
40. RUPA §§ 603, 701.
41. RUPA §§ 702, 703.
42. RUPA §§ 702(a), 704.

affairs of the partnership.[43]

Winding Up. A partnership continues after dissolution only for purposes of winding up the business. At any time after dissolution, the partners may unanimously agree to terminate the winding up and resume the partnership's business activities.[44] Any partner who has not wrongfully dissociated from the partnership may participate in the winding up, subject to a court's power to order judicial supervision of the winding up. A person winding up a partnership may seek to preserve the business as a going concern for a reasonable time, prosecute and defend actions, settle and close the partnership's business, dispose of assets, pay liabilities, resolve disputes, bind the partnership for acts taken in connection with the winding up, and make distributions to partners.[45]

Statement of Dissolution. Any partner who has not dissociated may file a statement of dissolution which is deemed to give any third party notice of the dissolution and limitation on the partners' authority 90 days after filing.[46]

Account Settlement and Deficit Restoration Obligations. Proceeds from the winding up must first be used to discharge obligations to creditors. Remaining proceeds are distributed to the partners in accordance with the respective positive balances in their capital accounts. Any partner who has a negative capital account balance must make a contribution to the partnership in an amount equal to the negative balance. If such partner fails to restore the negative balance, any amount needed by the partnership to pay partnership debts as a result of such failure must be paid by the other partners in proportion to their loss sharing percentages, and such other partners may seek to recover such additional contributions from the defaulting partner. Any partnership obligations that surface after the settlement of all partner accounts must be paid by the partners making additional contributions in proportion to their loss allocation percentages.[47]

h. Choice of Law

State statutes typically provide that the laws of the jurisdiction where the partnership maintains its chief executive office will govern relationships among the partners and between the partners and the partnership.[48]

2. LIMITED LIABILITY PARTNERSHIPS

A limited liability partnership ("LLP") is a partnership that has filed a statement of qualification (sometimes called an "application") with the state's secretary of state and that does not have a similar statement in effect in another jurisdiction.[49] The terms and conditions on which a partnership becomes an LLP must be approved by a vote necessary to amend the partnership agreement, but if the partnership agreement contains provisions that expressly consider obligations

---

43. RUPA § 801.
44. RUPA § 802.
45. RUPA § 803.
46. RUPA § 805.
47. RUPA § 806.
48. RUPA § 706(a).
49. RUPA § 101(5).

to contribute to the partnership, it must be approved by the vote necessary to amend such provisions.[50]

a. Qualification Statement. The statement of qualification usually must state the name of the partnership, the location of a registered office, the address of its principal office, and a statement that the partnership elects to be an LLP.[51] Some states require that the qualification statement also include the number of partners and a brief statement of the business in which the partnership engages. Typically, a majority of the partners, or one or more authorized partners, must execute documents submitted to the secretary of state. The LLP's registration is effective immediately after the date the application is filed, or at such later date specified in the application.[52]

b. Name. The name of an LLP must end with the words "Registered Limited Liability Partnership," "limited liability partnership" or the abbreviation "R.L.L.P.," "RLLP," "L.L.P.," or "LLP."[53]

c. Annual Report. An LLP must file an annual report with the secretary of state and pay an annual fee. The annual report must update the contact information for the LLP's chief executive officer and registered agent.[54] Some states also require updated information on the number of partners currently in the partnership and whether there are any material changes in the information contained in the partnership's qualification statement.

d. Liability of Partners. A partner of an LLP is not personally liable for an obligation of the partnership incurred while the partnership is an LLP, whether arising in contract, tort, or otherwise, by reason of being a partner. This limited liability exists even if the partnership agreement contained inconsistent provisions before making the election to become an LLP.[55] This is the big advantage of an LLP over a general partnership.

e. Applicable Law. State statutes typically provide that the law under which a foreign LLP is formed governs relations among the partners and between the partners and the partnership, and the liability of partners for obligations of the partnership.[56] States require a foreign LLP to file a statement of foreign qualification before transacting business in the state and typically provide that such a statement does not authorize a foreign LLP to engage in any business or exercise any power that a partnership in the state could not engage in or exercise as an LLP.[57] Absent the filing of such statement, a foreign LLP usually cannot maintain an action or proceeding in the state.[58]

f. Professional Service Providers. LLPs are often used by providers of professional services. Licensed partners of a professional provider LLP may

---

50. RUPA § 1001(b).
51. RUPA § 1001(c).
52. RUPA § 1001(e).
53. RUPA § 1002.
54. RUPA § 1003.
55. RUPA § 306(c).
56. RUPA § 1101(a).
57. RUPA §§ 1101(c), 1102.
58. RUPA § 1103(a).

be liable under state law for the partnership's debts if the partnership fails to maintain professional insurance coverage required by state law.

3. LIMITED PARTNERSHIPS

A limited partnership is an entity that has one or more general partners ("GP") and one or more limited partners ("LP") and is formed under a state's limited partnership act.[59] GPs have the authority to manage and conduct the business of the partnership and are personally liable for the debts and obligations of the partnership.[60] LPs typically are investors who have limited or minimal control over daily business decisions and operations of the partnership and have no personal liability for the obligations of the partnership beyond their capital contributions to the partnership.[61] If properly organized and managed, the limited partnership form of business organization allows persons to contribute capital to a business enterprise and share in its profits and losses without having liability exposure to the creditors of the business.

Limited partnerships did not exist at common law; they are creatures of state statutory law. The Uniform Limited Partnership Act ("ULPA"), with origins dating back to 1916 and most recently revised in 2001, has served as the basic framework for limited partnership statutes in 49 states. The 2001 version of the ULPA differs from prior versions in two significant respects. First, it no longer "links" its provisions to the Uniform Partnership Act. It is a "stand-alone" act that is considerably longer than the prior versions. Second, its revisions are targeted at those situations where a limited partnership is often the preferred entity form – sophisticated, manager-entrenched commercial deals whose participants commit for the long term and family limited partnerships used for estate planning purposes. The management powers of the GPs are increased; the management role and exit rights of LPs are decreased.

Although the 2001 version is not linked to the Revised Uniform Partnership Act, many state limited partnership acts remain linked to their versions of the Uniform Partnership Act. State adoption of the 2001 stand-alone version proceeds slowly.

STUDENT PROBLEM 6-2

Assume Doug and Mary in Student Problem 6-1 (Scenario Three) form a limited partnership in a state that has adopted the Uniform Limited Partnership Act (2001), with Doug as the general partner and Mary as the limited partner. Answer the following eight questions based on your reading of the following descriptive provisions of limited partnerships.

1. Does Mary have any property rights in the Glide?

2. How will distributions be allocated to Doug and Mary if there is no specific agreement between the parties?

3. Would there be limits on the amount of distributions to Doug and Mary?

---

59. ULPA §102(11) (2001).
60. ULPA §§ 402, 404 (2001).
61. ULPA §§ 302, 303 (2001).

4. Does Mary have the power to bind the enterprise to contracts with third parties? Does Doug?

5. What duties do Doug and Mary owe each other and the entity?

6. Do Mary and Doug each have unlimited rights to inspect documents of the entity?

7. If Doug is unable to pay a personal debt that he owes a friend, what rights may the friend exercise against the entity to recover the amount owed?

8. Would Mary have any personal liability exposure if Doug borrowed $100,000 in the name of the entity from a wealthy bike enthusiast, the lender had no knowledge of Mary's involvement, and Mary had no knowledge of the loan?

a. Entity Characteristics

A limited partnership is an entity distinct from its partners and may be organized for any lawful purpose and for a perpetual duration.[62] It has the power to do all things necessary and convenient to carry on its business, including the power to sue, be sued and defend in its own name.[63] The partnership agreement governs the operation of the entity, but, as in the case of a general partnership, there is a list of statutory provisions that cannot be changed by agreement. In most states, such list is substantively identical (or nearly so) to the list applicable to a general partnership,[64] as are the provisions relating to when a person will be deemed to have constructive notice of a fact regarding a limited partnership.[65] The name of the entity must contain the phrase "limited partnership," "L.P.," or "LP."[66]

b. Formation

A limited partnership is formed by filing a certificate of limited partnership with the state's secretary of state. At a minimum, state statutes require the certificate to state: the name of the limited partnership; the street and address of the entity's initial designated office; and the name, street and mailing address of each general partner and the entity's initial registered agent for service of process.[67] A limited partnership is actually formed when the secretary of state files the certificate.[68] Limited partnerships typically are required to file annual reports with the state's secretary of state.

c. Rights and Liabilities of GPs and LPs

Agency and Management Authority. An LP has no power to act for or bind the entity.[69] A GP is an agent of the limited partnership with full authority to manage and conduct the affairs of the limited partnership and bind the entity.[70]

---

62. ULPA § 104 (2001).
63. ULPA § 105 (2001).
64. ULPA § 110 (2001).
65. ULPA § 103 (2001).
66. ULPA § 108(b) (2001).
67. ULPA § 201 (2001).
68. ULPA § 201(c) (2001).
69. ULPA § 302 (2001).
70. ULPA § 402 (2001).

Each GP has equal management rights, and any matter relating to the entity's activities may be exclusively decided by the GP or, if there is more than one GP, by a majority of the GPs.[71] A GP has the same reimbursement rights for advances and excessive contributions as a partner of a general partnership.[72] Absent a provision in the partnership agreement, a GP is not entitled to any remuneration for services rendered to the partnership.[73]

Liability for Entity Obligations. GPs are jointly and severally liable for the obligations of a limited partnership.[74] LPs have no personal liability for the entity's obligation.[75]

Fiduciary Obligations. A GP has the same duties of loyalty, care, good faith and fair dealing as a partner of a general partnership.[76] An LP has no fiduciary duties to the limited partnership or the other partners, but is subject to a requirement of good faith and fair dealing in exercising rights under the limited partnership agreement.[77]

Dual Capacity Partner. A person may be both a GP and an LP and have the rights, duties and liabilities of each of those capacities.[78]

Information and Inspection Rights. An LP typically has an unlimited right to inspect and copy select core documents (specified by statute) during normal business hours, at an office designated by the entity, and on limited advance notice (normally 10 days). Other LP document requests relating to the activities or financial condition of the entity require a written request that must state a purpose reasonably related to the partnership, describe with particularity the information sought, and demonstrate that the information sought is related to the purpose. The GPs then decide whether to honor the request and may impose restrictions on the use of the information and charge the requesting LP any cost (labor and materials) incurred in connection with the request.[79] A GP has much broader information and inspection rights and is entitled to receive all information and documents reasonably required for the exercise of the GP's management rights and authority.[80]

Contributions. A partner's contribution may consist of tangible and intangible property, including promissory notes, services performed, and services to be performed. A partner's contribution obligation is not excused by death, disability, or other inability to perform and may be compromised only be the consent of all partners. Any creditor who extends credit in reliance on a contribution obligation of a partner, with no notice that the obligation has been compromised, may enforce the original obligation.[81]

71. ULPA § 406(a) (2001).
72. ULPA § 406(c),(d),(e) (2001).
73. ULPA § 406(f) (2001).
74. ULPA § 404 (2001).
75. ULPA § 303 (2001).
76. ULPA § 408 (2001).
77. ULPA § 305 (2001).
78. ULPA § 113 (2001).
79. ULPA § 304 (2001).
80. ULPA § 407 (2001).
81. ULPA §§ 501, 502 (2001).

Distributions. Absent a contrary provision in the limited partnership agreement (which usually exists), distributions by a limited partnership are allocated among partners on the basis of the relative value of their contributions to the entity.[82] This default rule is significantly different from the corresponding default rule for general partnerships. A partner has no right to a distribution before the dissolution and winding up of the entity, nor does a partner have the right to demand or receive a distribution in any form other than cash. A limited partnership may elect to make a distribution of an asset in kind so long as each partner receives a proportionate share of the asset based on the partner's share of distributions. A partner who is entitled to receive a distribution under the partnership agreement has the rights of a creditor, subject to offset rights of the partnership for any amounts owed by the partner to the partnership. A limited partnership is prohibited from making a distribution in violation of the partnership agreement.[83]

Transferee Rights and Charging Orders. A state's limited partnership statutory provisions dealing with the "personal property" nature of a partner's interest, the rights to transfer a partnership interest, the rights of a transferee of a partnership interest, and the rights of a partner's creditors to obtain and foreclose on a charging order are usually substantially identical to the corresponding statutory provisions for general partnerships.[84] The personal representative of a deceased limited partner may exercise the rights of a transferee or the rights of an existing limited partner, as applicable.[85]

d. Prohibited Distributions

Statutory Limitations. A limited partnership usually is prohibited from making a distribution if, after the distribution, (1) the entity is unable to pay its debts as they become due in the ordinary course of business or (2) the entity's total assets have a value that is less than the sum of the entity's total liabilities plus the amount of any superior preferable distributions that would be due to other partners if the entity was dissolved and wound up. In applying this limitation, the limited partnership may value its assets based on financial statements prepared in accordance with accounting principles that are reasonable in the circumstances or on a fair valuation of the assets. Any indebtedness issued by a limited partnership to partners as part of a distribution is not considered a liability for purposes of the limitation calculation if, and only if, any payments of principal or interest on such indebtedness are to be made only if they would be permissible distributions at the time made.[86]

Related Partner Liabilities. A GP who consents to a distribution that exceeds the statutory limitations on distributions is personally liable to the limited partnership for any excess distribution if it is established that the GP violated a duty of loyalty, care, good faith or fair dealing to the entity. Any partner or transferee who knowingly receives a distribution in excess of the

---

82. ULPA § 503 (2001).
83. ULPA §§ 504 through 507 (2001).
84. ULPA §§ 701 through 703 (2001).
85. ULPA § 704 (2001).
86. ULPA § 508 (2001).

statutory limits is personally liability to the entity for the amount of such excess.[87]

e. Partner Termination (Dissociation)

Limited Partners. Limited partners generally have no power to dissociate from a limited partnership prior to the termination of the limited partnership unless they are granted specific termination rights in the limited partnership agreement.[88] State limited partnership statutes that specify the circumstances in which a limited partner's interest may be terminated usually are substantively identical to the corresponding provisions for terminating a partner's interest in a general partnership.[89] The dissociation of a limited partner's interest terminates the rights of the dissociated partner, but does not terminate the entity, the dissociated partner's duties of good faith and fair dealing, or any obligation that the dissociated partner owes to the partnership or the other partners.[90]

General Partners. A GP may choose to dissociate from a limited partnership at any time, rightfully or wrongfully, by expressed will.[91] State limited partnership statutes that specify the circumstances in which a GP's interest may be terminated usually are substantively identical to the corresponding provisions for terminating a partner's interest in a general partnership.[92] A GP's dissociation is wrongful only if it violates the partnership agreement or, unless the agreement provides otherwise, it occurs before the partnership terminates and the dissociation is due to a voluntary withdrawal, a judicial expulsion, a bankruptcy of the GP, or the GP ceasing to exist as an entity.[93] A GP who wrongfully dissociates is liable to the limited partnership for any damages caused by the dissociation. The dissociation of a GP's interest terminates all managing rights, ongoing duties of loyalty and care, and (with very limited exceptions) the dissociated GP's liability for partnership obligations incurred after the dissociation. A dissociated GP remains personally liable for partnership obligations incurred prior to the dissociation unless the dissociated partner's exposure for a pre-dissociation obligation is eliminated by agreement with the creditor and the other partners or by a material change in the terms of the obligation with the creditor having notice of the dissociation.[94]

f. Dissolution and Winding Up

Triggering Events. Statutory provisions generally provide that a limited partnership must be dissolved and wound up on: (1) the occurrence of a dissolution event specified in the partnership agreement; (2) the consent of GPs and LPs who own a majority of the distribution rights; (3) the dissociation of a GP with at least one remaining GP, and LPs who own a majority of distribution rights consent to the dissolution; (4) the dissociation of a GP with no remaining

---

87. ULPA § 509 (2001).
88. ULPA § 601(a) (2001).
89. ULPA § 601(b) (2001).
90. ULPA § 602 (2001).
91. ULPA § 604(a) (2001).
92. ULPA § 603 (2001).
93. ULPA § 604(b) (2001).
94. ULPA § 607 (2001).

GP, unless within 90 days a GP is admitted and LPs who own a majority of distribution rights consent to continue business activities; (5) 90 days after the dissociation of the last LP, unless a new LP is admitted during such period; (6) a declaration of dissolution by the state's secretary of state for failure to file an annual report or pay required fees; or (7) by order of a court based on a determination that it is not reasonably practicable to carry on the activities of the limited partnership in accordance with the partnership agreement.[95]

Impacts. The statutory impacts of winding up a limited partnership are very similar to those of a general partnership with the clarification that if the entity does not have a GP, LPs who own a majority of the distribution rights may appoint a person to wind up and dissolve the entity. A GP who causes a limited partnership to incur inappropriate obligations during a winding up is liable to the limited partnership for such obligations.[96]

g. Litigation Rights

Some state statutes specifically authorize a partner of a limited partnership to bring a direct action against the partnership or other partners for legal or equitable relief to enforce the partner's rights under the partnership agreement or applicable law. The partner must plead and prove an actual or threatened injury to the partner, not the partnership. A right to an accounting upon a dissolution and winding up does not revive a claim barred by law.[97] Such statutes also usually permit a limited partner to maintain a derivative action on behalf of the limited partnership only if (1) the partner first makes a demand on GP's to bring the action or pleads with particularity why such a demand would be futile and (2) any recovery from the litigation is paid to the limited partnership. If such a derivative action is successful, the court may award a reimbursement of the plaintiff's attorney fees and costs from the recovery.[98]

4. LIMITED LIABILITY LIMITED PARTNERSHIPS

The limited liability limited partnership ("LLLP") is to a limited partnership what an LLP is to a general partnership. Its role is to eliminate the personal liability exposure that general partners have for the obligations of a limited partnership. It's a relatively new entity form that has been adopted in roughly half the states.

The LLLP statutory provisions are additions to each state's version of the Uniform Limited Partnership Act that mirror the LLP additions to the state's version of the Uniform Partnership Act. They include statutory requirements to elect LLLP status in the limited partnership's filed certificate[99] and use of a name that includes the phrase "limited liability limited partnership," "LLLP," or "L.L.L.P."[100]

95. ULPA §§ 801, 802 (2001).
96. ULPA §§ 803 through 805 (2001).
97. ULPA § 1001 (2001).
98. ULPA §§ 1002 through 1004 (2001).
99. ULPA § 201(a)(4) (2001).
100. ULPA § 108(c) (2001).

With LLLP status, a general partner is not personally liable for an obligation of the limited partnership incurred while the partnership is an LLLP, whether arising in contract, tort, or otherwise. This limited liability exists even if the partnership agreement contained inconsistent provisions before making the election to become an LLLP.[101]

5. LIMITED LIABILITY COMPANIES

STUDENT PROBLEM 6-3

Assume Doug and Mary in Problem 6-1 (Scenario Three) form a limited liability company in a state that has adopted the Revised Uniform Limited Liability Company Act. Based on the following descriptive provisions of LLCs, how would you answer questions 1 through 8 of Student Problem 6-2 if the LLC is a member-managed LLC? How would your answers change if the LLC is a manager-managed LLC with Doug as the manager?

a. LLC Characteristics

The limited liability company ("LLC") has emerged as the most popular form of non-corporate entity. It offers limited liability protection for the LLC's members and the flexibility of having an entity that is managed by designated managers or by the members generally. The framework for state LLC laws is the Uniform Limited Liability Company Act, originally adopted in 1995 and most recently amended in 2006.

A limited liability company is an entity distinct from its members and may be organized for any lawful purpose and for a perpetual duration.[102] It has the power to do all things necessary and convenient to carry on its business, including the power to sue, be sued and defend in its own name.[103] The LLC operating agreement governs: the relations among the members as members and between the members and the limited liability company; the rights and duties of a manager; the activities of the company and the conduct of those activities; and the means and conditions for amending the operating agreement.[104]

As in the case of a partnership or limited partnership, there is a list of statutory provisions that cannot be changed by agreement. In most states, such list is similar in many respects to the list applicable to partnerships.[105] The name of the entity must contain the phrase "limited liability company," "limited company," "L.L.C.," "LLC," "L.C.," or "LC." The word "limited" may be abbreviated as "Ltd," and "company" may be abbreviated as "Co."[106]

b. Formation

A limited liability company is formed by one or more organizers filing a

---

101. ULPA § 404(c)(2001).
102. RULLCA § 104
103. RULLCA § 105
104. RULLCA § 110(a).
105. RULLCA § 110(c).
106. RULLCA § 108(a).

certificate of organization with the state's secretary of state. At a minimum, state statutes require the certificate to state: the name of the LLC; the street and address of the entity's initial designated office; the name, street and mailing address of the LLC's initial registered agent for service of process; and a statement that the LLC has no members if there are no members at time of filing.[107] If the LLC certificate states there are no members at time of filing, the certificate will lapse and be void if, within 90 days of filing, a follow-up filing is not made confirming that the LLC has at least one member.[108] An LLC is actually formed when the secretary of state files the certificate and the LLC has at least one member.[109] LLCs typically are required to file annual reports with the state's secretary of state.

c. Operating Agreement Limiting Provisions

State statutes often provide that, if not manifestly unreasonable, an LLC's operating agreement may:[110]

1. Restrict or eliminate a member's duty of loyalty.

2. Identify specific types or categories of activities that do not violate the duty of loyalty.

3. Alter the duty of care, except to authorize intentional misconduct or a known violation of law.

4. Alter any other fiduciary duty, including eliminating particular aspects of that duty.

5. Prescribe the standards by which to measure the performance of the obligations of good faith and fair dealing.

6. Specify the method by which a specific act or transaction that would otherwise violate the duty of loyalty may be authorized or ratified by one or more disinterested and independent persons after full disclosure of all material facts.

7. Eliminate or limit a fiduciary duty that would have pertained to a responsibility that a member has been relieved of under the operating agreement.

8. Alter or eliminate any indemnification rights of a member or manager.

9. Eliminate or limit a member or manager's liability to the LLC and members for money damages. Such a money-damage limiting provision may not apply to: a breach of the duty of loyalty by a member or manager; any transaction in which a member or manager receives a financial benefit to which he or she was not entitled; any liability associated with the authorization of distributions to members that violate applicable law; any liability associated with the intentional infliction of harm on the company or a member; or any intentional violation of criminal law.

---

107. RULLCA § 201(b).
108. RULLCA § 201(e)(1).
109. RULLCA § 201(d)(1).
110. RULLCA § 110.

d. Agency and Management Authority

A member is not an agent of an LLC by reason of being a member.[111] An LLC is deemed to be a member-managed LLC unless the operating agreement expressly provides that it will be "manager-managed" or includes words of similar import.[112]

Member-Managed LLC. In a member-managed LLC: the management and conduct of the company are vested in the members; each member has equal rights in the management and conduct of the company's activities; any difference arising among members as to a matter in the ordinary course of the activities of the LLC may be decided by a majority of the members; an act outside the ordinary course of the activities of the LLC may be undertaken only with the consent of all members; and the operating agreement may be amended only with the consent of all members.[113]

Manager-Managed LLC. In a manager-managed LLC: any matter relating to the activities of the company is decided exclusively by the managers unless a statute specifically provides otherwise; each manager has equal rights in the management and conduct of the activities of the LLC; and a difference arising among managers as to a matter in the ordinary course of the activities of the LLC may be decided by a majority of the managers. Also, consent of all members is required to: sell or otherwise dispose of all, or substantially all, of the company's property; approve a merger, conversion, or domestication; undertake any other act outside the ordinary course of the company's activities; and amend the operating agreement.[114]

Manager Selection and Removal. A manager may be chosen at any time by the consent of a majority of the members and remains a manager until a successor has been chosen, unless the manager at an earlier time resigns, is removed, or dies, or, in the case of a manager that is not an individual, ceases to exist. A manager may be removed at any time by the consent of a majority of the members without notice or cause.[115] A person need not be a member to be a manager, but the dissociation of a member who is also a manager removes the person as a manager. If a person who is both a manager and a member ceases to be a manager, that cessation does not by itself dissociate the person as a member.[116] A person who wrongfully causes dissolution of the company loses the right to participate in management as a member and a manager.[117]

Written Consent. An action requiring the consent of members may be taken without a meeting by use of a written consent. A member may appoint a proxy or other agent to consent or otherwise act for the member.[118]

---

111. RULLCA § 301(a).
112. RULLCA § 407(a).
113. RULLCA § 407(b).
114. RULLCA § 407(c).
115. RULLCA § 407(c)(5).
116. RULLCA § 407(c)(6).
117. RULLCA § 407(e).
118. RULLCA § 407(d).

Compensation. A member is not entitled to remuneration for services performed for a member-managed LLC, except for reasonable compensation for services rendered in winding up the activities of the company.[119]

Indemnification. An LLC must reimburse for any payment made and indemnify for any debt, obligation, or other liability incurred by a member of a member-managed company or the manager of a manager-managed company in the course of the member's or manager's activities on behalf of the LLC unless the action involved a violation of a fiduciary duty or a prohibited distribution.[120]

Insurance. A limited liability company may purchase and maintain insurance on behalf of a member or manager of the LLC against liability asserted against or incurred by the member or manager.[121]

Statement of Authority. An LLC may file a statement (good for five years) with the secretary of state (or, in the case of real estate, with the county recorder) which states the authority, or limitations on the authority, of specific persons to enter into transactions on behalf of the LLC. Such grant of authority is conclusive in favor of a third party who gives value in reliance of the statement.[122] A person named in any such statement may file a written denial of the person's authority.[123]

e. LLC Member Rights and Duties

Liability for Entity Obligations. LLC members have no personal liability for the entity's obligation, whether arising in contract, tort or otherwise. The failure of an LLC to observe any particular formalities relating to the exercise of its powers or management of its activities is not a ground for imposing liability on the members or managers for the debts, obligations, or other liabilities of the LLC.[124]

Fiduciary Obligations in Member-Managed LLC. A member of a member-managed LLC owes to the LLC and other members a duty of loyalty to: account to the LLC and to hold as trustee for it any property, profit, or benefit derived by the member in the conduct or winding up of the company's activities; refrain from dealing with the LLC as or on behalf of a person having an interest adverse to the company (subject to a defense of fairness to the LLC); and refrain from competing with the LLC. All members may authorize or ratify, after full disclosure of all material facts, a specific act or transaction that otherwise would violate this duty of loyalty. A member also has a contractual obligation of good faith and fair dealing and, subject to the business judgment rule, has a duty of care to act with the care that a person in a like position would reasonably exercise under similar circumstances and in a manner the member reasonably believes to be in the best interests of the LLC. In discharging this duty, a member may rely in good faith upon opinions, reports, statements, or other information provided by

---

119. RULLCA § 407(f).
120. RULLCA § 408(a).
121. RULLCA § 408(b).
122. RULLCA § 302.
123. RULLCA § 303.
124. RULLCA § 304.

another person that the member reasonably believes is a competent and reliable source for the information.[125]

Fiduciary Duties in Manager-Managed LLC. In a manager-managed LLC, members do not have any fiduciary duties to the LLC by reason of being a member, but do have a contractual obligation of good faith and fair dealing. Managers have the fiduciary duties of loyalty and care described above, along with a contractual obligation of good faith and fair dealing. Any approval or ratification of an act that violates the duty of loyalty requires the approval of all members.[126]

Information and Inspection Rights. In a member-managed LLC, a member typically has unlimited document inspection rights relating to the LLC's activities and financial condition. In a manager-managed LLC, such rights are reserved to the managers, and members must submit an inspection request that states a purpose material to the member's interests in the LLC, describes with particularity the information sought, and demonstrates that the information sought is related to the purpose. The LLC may then decide whether to honor the request, impose restrictions on the use of the information, and charge the requesting member the costs (labor and materials) incurred in connection with the request.[127]

Contributions. An LLC member's contribution may consist of tangible and intangible property, including promissory notes, services performed, and services to be performed. A member's contribution obligation is not excused by death, disability, or other inability to perform and may be compromised only by the consent of all members. Any creditor who extends credit in reliance on a contribution obligation of a member, with no notice that the obligation has been compromised, may enforce the original obligation.[128]

Distributions. Absent a contrary provision in the LLC operating agreement (which usually exists), distributions by an LLC prior to a dissolution and winding up must be in equal shares among the members. A member has no right to a distribution before the dissolution and winding up of the entity, nor does a member have the right to demand or receive a distribution in any form other than money. An LLC may elect to make a distribution of an asset in kind so long as each member receives a proportionate share of the asset based on the member's share of distributions. A member who is entitled to receive a distribution under the operating agreement has the rights of a creditor.[129]

Transferee Rights and Charging Orders. A state's LLC statutory provisions dealing with the "personal property" nature of a member's LLC interest, the rights to transfer an LLC interest, the rights of a transferee of an LLC interest, and the rights of an LLC member's creditors to obtain and foreclose on a charging order are usually substantially identical to the corresponding statutory

125. RULLCA § 409(a)-(f).
126. RULLCA § 409(g).
127. RULLCA § 410.
128. RULLCA §§ 402, 403.
129. RULLCA §§ 404. RULLCA § 406.

provisions for partnerships. The personal representative of a deceased member may exercise the rights of a transferee or the rights of an existing member, as applicable.[130]

f. Prohibited Distributions

Statutory Limitations. An LLC usually is prohibited from making a distribution if, after the distribution, (1) the entity in unable to pay its debts as they become due in the ordinary course of business or (2) the entity's total assets have a value that is less than the sum of the entity's total liabilities plus the amount of any superior preferable distributions that would be due to other partners if the entity was dissolved and wound up. In applying this limitation, the LLC may value its assets based on financial statements prepared in accordance with accounting principles that are reasonable in the circumstances or on a fair valuation of the assets. Any indebtedness issued by an LLC to members as part of a distribution is not considered a liability for purposes of the limitation calculation if, and only if, any payments of principal or interest on such indebtedness would be permissible distributions at the time made.[131]

Related Member and Manager Liabilities. A member of a member-managed LLC or a manager of a manager-managed LLC who consents to a distribution that exceeds the statutory limitations on distributions is personally liable to the LLC for any excess distribution if it is established that the member or manager violated a duty of loyalty, care, good faith or fair dealing to the entity. A person who knowingly receives a distribution in excess of the statutory limits is personally liable to the entity for the amount of such excess.[132]

g. Member Dissociation

Dissociation Rights. A member may choose to dissociate from an LLC at any time, rightfully or wrongfully, by expressed will. State LLC statutes that specify the circumstances in which a member's interest may be terminated usually are very similar to the corresponding provisions for terminating a partner's interest in a general partnership. A member's dissociation is wrongful only if it violates the LLC agreement or, unless the agreement provides otherwise, it occurs before the LLC terminates and the dissociation is due to a voluntary withdrawal, a judicial expulsion, a bankruptcy of the member, or the member being dissolved or terminated. A member who wrongfully dissociates is liable to the LLC and to other members for any damages caused by the dissociation.[133]

Dissociation Impacts. The dissociation of a member's interest terminates all management rights. Also, if the LLC is member-managed, dissociated member's ongoing duties of loyalty and care come to end with regard to matters arising after the dissociation.[134]

---

130. RULLCA §§ 501 through 504.
131. RULLCA § 405.
132. RULLCA § 406.
133. RULLCA §§ 601, 602.
134. RULLCA § 603.

h. Dissolution and Winding Up

Triggering Events. Statutory provisions generally provide that an LLC must be dissolved and wound up on: (1) the occurrence of a dissolution event specified in the LLC operating agreement; (2) the consent of all the members; (3) the passage of 90 days during which the LLC has no members; and (4) the entry of a court order dissolving the LLC on grounds that the LLC's activities are illegal or cannot be carried on in a reasonably practicable manner in accordance with the partnership agreement or that the managers or members in control have acted illegally or fraudulently or in an oppressive manner that has directly harmed the member initiating the proceeding.[135]

Winding Up. A dissolved LLC continues after dissolution only for the purpose of winding up. In winding up its activities, an LLC must discharge its debts and obligations, settle and close the LLC's activities, and marshal and distribute the assets of the LLC. It may deliver to the secretary of state a statement of dissolution, preserve the LLC's activities and property as a going concern for a reasonable time, prosecute and defend actions and proceedings, transfer the LLC's property, settle disputes by mediation or arbitration, file a statement of termination stating that the LLC is terminated, and take all other action necessary or appropriate to wind up the LLC. If a dissolved LLC has no members, the legal representative of the last person to have been a member may wind up the activities of the company.[136]

Notices Barring Claims. A dissolved LLC may notify its known creditors of the dissolution, specifying the required information and mailing address for a claim, stating the deadline for receipt of the claim (not less than 120 days after receipt of the notice date), and indicating that a claim will be barred if not received by the deadline. A claim against an LLC is barred if the notice is given and the claim is not received by the specified deadline. A timely received claim will be barred if the LLC rejects the claim and the claimant does not commence an action within 90 days of being notified of the rejection.[137] In addition, a dissolved LLC may publish notice of its dissolution and request persons having claims against the LLC to present the claims in accordance with the notice, stating that a claim against the LLC will be barred if an enforcement action is not taken within five years to enforce the claim. If the notice is published in accordance with the statutory requirements, an unenforced claim not previously barred will be barred after such five-year period.[138]

Enforcement of Claims. A claim that has not been barred may be enforced against a dissolved LLC to the extent of its undistributed assets and, if assets of the LLC have been distributed after dissolution, against a member or transferee, but a person's total liability for such claims may not exceed the total amount of assets distributed to the person after dissolution.[139]

---

135. RULLCA § 701.
136. RULLCA § 702.
137. RULLCA § 703.
138. RULLCA § 704.
139. RULLCA § 704(d).

Final Distributions. After discharging its obligations to creditors, a dissolved LLC must first distribute any surplus proportionately to persons owning a transferable interest based on the amount of their respective unreturned contributions and then distribute any remaining surplus in equal shares among members and dissociated members. All distributions must be paid in money.[140]

i. Litigation Rights

State statutes usually authorize a member of an LLC to bring a direct action against the LLC or other members for legal or equitable relief to enforce the partner's rights under the operating agreement or applicable law. The member must plead and prove an actual or threatened injury to the member, not just the LLC.[141] Such statutes also typically permit a member to maintain a derivative action on behalf of the LLC if (1) the member first makes a demand on the manager in a manager-managed LLC, or the other members in a member-managed LLC to bring the action or pleads with particularity why such a demand would be futile and (2) any recovery from the litigation is paid to the LLC. If such a derivative action is successful, the court may award a reimbursement of the plaintiff's attorney fees and costs from the recovery.[142] Some statutes specifically authorize an LLC to appoint a special litigation committee made up of independent, disinterested persons (who may be members) to represent the interests of the LLC in a derivative proceeding.[143]

j. Mergers

State statutes generally authorize the merger of an LLC with another LLC, a partnership, a limited partnership, or a corporation, domestic or foreign.[144] Usually such merger statutes are patterned after the state's corporate merger statutes.

Documents and Process. A plan of merger must be approved by the members. The plan of merger usually sets forth the name of each party to the merger and the name of the surviving entity, the terms and conditions of the merger, the manner and basis of converting interests in each merging entity into the surviving entity or into cash or other property, and any required amendment's to the surviving entity's organizational documents.[145] Absent specific provisions in the governing LLC agreement, the plan must be approved by all members of the LLC.[146] Following approval of the plan of merger, the surviving entity files the articles of merger with the appropriate secretary of state offices. The articles of merger set forth, among other things: the plan of merger; the date the merge is effective; a statement that the merger was approved by each party to the merger as required by its governing statute; and any other information required by the governing statute of any party to the merger.[147]

---

140. RULLCA § 708.
141. RULLCA § 901.
142. RULLCA §§ 902-904, 906.
143. RULLCA § 905.
144. RULLCA § 1002.
145. RULLCA § 1002(b).
146. RULLCA § 1002.
147. RULLCA § 1004.

Effect of Merger. Following the filing of the articles of merger, all entities that were parties to the merger, other than the surviving entity, cease to exist. Title to all property previously owned by each merged entity vests in the surviving entity, and the surviving entity is responsible for all liabilities of all other entities in the merger. If there is a legal proceeding pending against any party to the merger, it may either be continued as if the merger did not occur or the surviving entity may be substituted as the party in the proceeding. The governing instrument of the surviving entity (whether a certificate of formation, a certificate of limited partnership, or articles of incorporation) is deemed amended to the extent provided in the plan of merger.[148]

B. CUSTOMIZING THE OWNERS' OPERATING AGREEMENT

1. SCOPE AND LAWYER'S ROLE

Generally fewer organizational documents are required for an LLC or partnership entity than for a corporate entity. There is still a need for asset transfer documents, tax filings, executive employment agreements, and simple state filings for LLCs and certain types of partnerships. But for these entities, the counterpart core provisions of the other corporate documents (see Chapter Section D. of Chapter 4) are embodied in a single comprehensive operating agreement.

The primary planning challenge during the organization of a partnership or LLC is to prepare a comprehensive operating agreement that incorporates all of the essential deal points between the co-owners of the business. Often the parties are tempted to short-circuit the front-end planning effort. They perpetuate the common (but false) perception that there is a "normal" or "accepted" way of documenting issues between co-owners. The result is that, in far too many cases, the operating agreement effort is limited to filling in blanks on a stock form, and the dialogue is limited to descriptive pronouncements from the lawyers. The operating agreement looks complete and official, but does little or nothing to reflect thoughtful, negotiated deal points that the owners have resolved with the assistance of skilled planning advisors.

In nearly all situations, the lawyer must take the lead in defining the scope of the front-end planning effort. This is done by identifying key planning issues, explaining the significance of the issues, and then helping the client carefully evaluate his or her objectives or priority concerns with respect to each issue. Usually customization of the operating agreement increases as the planning effort improves. More customization leads to more complexity and, most importantly, to a better mutual understanding of the key deal points between the owners of the business.

The identity of the client affects how the potential deal points are discussed

148. RULLCA § 1005.

and analyzed in any given partnership or LLC situation. If the client will own the controlling vote in the entity, the preferred choice may be to refrain from initiating any dialogue on many deal points with the other owners. The client knows that he or she has the power to dictate the outcome of any dispute by virtue of the voting control. Typically, the burden is on the minority owners to raise any operational issues that may require special treatment in the operating agreement. Thus, the lawyer who represents the minority owners usually has the toughest job. Key issues must be identified, discussed, and prioritized. A plan must be developed for creating minority rights for those issues that are of greatest concern. Then the plan must be sold and eventually incorporated into the operating agreement.

The lawyer who is engaged to organize and represent the partnership or LLC, not a particular owner of group of owners, must be sensitive to potential conflicts between the owners. In this situation, usually the best approach is for the entity's lawyer to initiate a dialogue with all the owners in a meeting or series of meetings that addresses the most important issues, with input from lawyers representing specific owners. The process requires a modest commitment of time and expense, but it will go a long way in identifying and resolving on the front-end any fundamental differences between the parties.

Following is a brief description of certain key provisions of an operating agreement and related options for customizing these provisions. Specific references are to the LLC operating agreement in Section D of Chapter 15.

STUDENT PROBLEM 6-4

Refer to Student Problem 6-3 in which Doug and Mary form a manager-managed LLC. Doug lines up a deep-pocket investor ("Investor") who is willing to invest $1.2 million in the LLC if, and only if, the LLC operating agreement contains the following provisions:

1. Investor is the manager of the LLC and has the exclusive right to determine how the Glide is exploited, when it is sold, and the terms of any sale.

2. Investor is relieved of all liabilities to the LLC for any actions or omissions taken in good faith, even those determined to be grossly negligent or intentionally reckless.

3. All fiduciary duties of the Investor are eliminated.

4. Investor is allocated 90 percent of the losses that are expected during the first three years of operation. This is regarded as a tax benefit for Investor.

5. Investor accrues an annual fee of $100,000 for management services, to be paid when the LLC has sufficient cash flow to pay this accrued compensation.

6. Investor is allocated 50 percent of all profits realized in any year or on the sale of the Glide.

7. Available cash flows from operations or the sale of Glide are used: first, to pay any accrued management fees due Investor; second, to repay Investor's $1.2 million investment; and third, to pay Investor 50 percent of the excess and

the other members the remaining 50 percent.

Based on your reading of the following provision descriptions, what problems, if any, will the parties encounter in designing the LLC operating agreement to meet these deal-braking demands of Investor?

2. *AUTHORITY AND MANAGEMENT PROVISIONS*

Purpose of the Company (Section 5). In a partnership or LLC, the preferred choice often is to use this provision to specifically define and limit the scope of the business activities of the entity. Partners and LLC members often want the comfort of knowing that their investment will not be diverted into activities that are outside the scope of what was originally discussed. Liability exposure may also be an issue, particularly where the managers of the venture have multiple business interests. Limiting the scope of the business activities may help eliminate the business entity's liability exposure for unrelated actions of its managers. A written activity limitation also may dash any expectations other owners may have relative to their other business activities by drawing an express, unequivocal line in the sand. Some partners and LLC member may object to a written limitation on the scope of the enterprise, arguing that it restricts flexibility, creates potential confusion for third parties, and fosters notions of "separateness" and "temporariness" between the owners.

Limits on Manager Authority. (Sections 11.1 and 11.6). Often the manager of the partnership or LLC is given broad authority to administer the business affairs of the enterprise. The planning challenge is to define those situations where the manager must seek approval of the partners or LLC members before taking action and what level of approval is required. In some circumstances, majority approval may be adequate. In other situations, a unanimous or super-majority vote may be justified. It all turns on the nature and scope of the business and the expectations and goals of the partners or LLC members. These are the sections of the agreement that can be used to define and protect minority rights and often justify significant dialogue during the planning process. Provisions that often require special attention in these sections include: required cash distributions; the admission of new partners or LLC members; outside or competitive activities of partners or LLC members; related party transactions; material changes to the business plan; debt limitations; confidentially covenants of managers, partners or LLC members; tax elections; selection of professionals; and dispute resolutions procedures.

Limited Liability of Manager (Section 11.3). The key issue is whether the manager should be relieved of personal liability to the partnership or LLC for actions taken or omitted by the manager with a good faith belief that such actions or omissions were in the best interests of the entity. Resolution of the issue in the partnership or LLC operating agreement often turns on the level of culpability that partners or LLC members are willing to forgive. Ordinary negligence usually isn't enough to override a good faith exculpation provision, while willful misconduct and criminal acts often render the provision moot and trigger liability. But what about grossly negligence or intentionally reckless conduct? These are tougher issues in the planning process. Managers often do not want any liability exposure absent a showing of bad faith, willful misconduct or criminal activity. They don't want to get tangled up in line drawing between ordinary and gross negligence. In contrast, many owners want protection against a manager's gross negligence or intentionally reckless activities.

Resignation, Removal and Replacement of Manager (Section 15). This provision raises a number of potential issues in the design of the operating agreement. If a manager resigns in violation of specified conditions in the operating agreement, does the manager have any liability exposure to the entity? Will the manager be subject to any non-competition restrictions? What ongoing confidentiality covenants, if any, will apply to the manager? What level of partner or LLC member vote (majority, super-majority, unanimous) is required to remove and replace a manager? Is there any requirement to show "cause"? Is the manager entitled to any severance benefit if removed for no cause? Does the resignation or removal of a manager entitle the partnership or LLC to purchase the partnership or LLC interest of the member or give the manager a right to compel such a purchase?

Indemnification (Section 11.4). Will partners and managers who act on behalf of the partnership or LLC be protected against any personal loss, damage or liability they incur as a result of their activities on behalf of the entity? Usually an indemnification and hold harmless provision is included in the operating agreement to protect against such liabilities and any associated legal fees, but limitations often need to be worked out between the partners or LLC members. The agreement may provide that the indemnification rights are limited to assets of the entity and are not obligations of the partners or LLC members. The owners may not want any personal exposure, and the primary assets of the business may have been pledged to secure financing. The net result is that the indemnification provision, as a practical matter, may mean little or nothing if the business fails. The indemnification provision may be limited to acts or omissions undertaken in good faith and with a belief that they were in the best interests of the entity, subject to exceptions for specified levels of culpability. The operating agreement also may condition any indemnification right on a tender of the defense or resolution of the claim to the partnership or LLC so that the entity can control expenses and dispose of the matter on its own terms. These indemnification limitations often create concerns for managers. A solution to ease these concerns may be an errors and omissions insurance policy that facilitates the agreed limitations while providing an additional level of protection for the managers of the enterprise.

Compensation of Managers (Section 11 Insertion). Often there is a need to specify how those partners or members who manage the enterprise are to be compensated for their services on behalf the partnership or LLC. Absent such an agreement, the statutory default rule usually will deny any compensation for services that are not related to dissolving and winding up the entity.

Time Devoted to Enterprise (Section 11.2). For partners or LLC members who manage the enterprise, key issues often include their service commitments and their right to be involved in other activities. Are they expected to devote all of their time and energies to the enterprise? Failure to adequately clarify this issue can lead to an early showdown when the investment partners or LLC members discover that the manager spends only a fraction of his or her time looking after the affairs of the enterprise and is heavily involved in other ventures. The stock language in many forms gives the manager significant flexibility to define the service level and pursue other ventures. This language won't do the job in many situations.

3. *OWNER RIGHTS PROVISIONS*

Owner Transfer Rights (Section 14). State statutes generally permit a partner or LLC member to transfer the economic (but not voting or management rights) rights of partnership or LLC interest to a third party transferee. Often, it is necessary and smart to prohibit any such voluntary or involuntary transfer unless specified conditions exist. These conditions usually include the death of a partner or LLC member or the approval by the managers or a designated percentage of the partners or LLC members. Absent such approval, partners are unable to transfer interests in the partnership or LLC. In many situations, the operating agreement also needs to specify the procedures and conditions that must be satisfied in order for a third party transferee to be admitted as an owner with all the rights and privileges of a partner or LLC member.

Buy-Sell Rights (Section 14 Insert). In many business enterprises, the operating agreement between the partners or LLC members needs to spell out buy-sell rights that are triggered when a partner or LLC member dies, becomes disabled, just desires to cash out and move on, experiences a messy divorce or bankruptcy, or needs to be expelled. These buy-sell provisions and the associated planning may be used to accomplish various objectives, including to ensure that (1) ownership interests in the enterprise are never transferred or made available to third parties who are unacceptable to the owners, (2) there is a mechanism to fairly value and fund the equity interest of a departing owner, (3) control and ownership issues will be smoothly transitioned at appropriate times so as not to unduly interfere with and disrupt the operations of the business, (4) owners have a fair "market" for their shares at appropriate points of exit, (5) owners have the power to involuntarily terminate (expel) an owner who is no longer wanted, (6) the amount paid for the equity interest of a deceased owner determines the value of the deceased owner's equity interest for estate tax purposes, and (7) cash and funding challenges of owner departures are appropriately anticipated and covered. An extended discussion of this planning challenge is included in Section B. of Chapter 10. The substance of that discussion, including certain of the common mistakes that are often made in the buy-sell planning process, is directly applicable to partnerships and LLCs.

Major Transaction Approval Rights (Section 11.6). The operating agreement usually requires partner or LLC member approval of transactions that involve a merger of the partnership or LLC, a combination with another entity, or a sale of all or substantially all of the entity's assets. Majority approval works for many partnerships and LLCs. In some situations, the parties desire to require a super-majority vote, such as two-thirds. Often it helps to clarify if the manager's approval also is a condition to the transaction. And sometimes the often-used "substantially all" standard for determining whether an asset sale triggers owner approval rights is perceived as being too undefined or capable of manipulation. In such situations, the operating agreement may specify objective criteria (a designated percentage of assets or revenues, or both) for determining whether owner approval rights are required for a sale of assets.

Inspection Rights. (Section 13.4) Some operating agreements provide partners and LLC members with broad document inspection rights, conditioned only on reasonable notice, inspection at the location where the documents are kept, and reimbursement of any reproduction costs. Often those who manage a limited partnership or a manager-managed LLC desire to limit the inspection rights of limited partners or LLC members who have no management rights. The rationale is that broad inspection rights for such investors will not benefit the entity in any way and may create opportunities for abuse that frustrate management efforts. When limited investor inspection rights are desired, the operating agreement often requires that the requesting partner or LLC member provide a written request that specifies the entity-related purpose for making the request, the particularized list of the documents requested, and how such documents relate to the stated purpose. The manager has the final say on whether the conditions of the request have been satisfied.

Fiduciary Exculpatory Provisions. (Section 11.5 and Section 12 Insertion). Statutory provisions impose fiduciary duties of care, loyalty, good faith, and fair dealing on those partners or LLC members who have the right to participate in the management of the enterprise. As explained above, the operating agreement usually may include provisions that substantially reduce any liability for fiduciary breaches that do not involve bad faith. The only limitation in many states is that the exculpatory provision may not be "manifestly unreasonable." This presents a planning opportunity for those enterprises that want to deemphasize restrictions that come with the duties of care and loyalty.

Amendment Rights (Section 18). The power to amend the operating agreement is always an important consideration. In many situations, nothing short of unanimous consent will work. The agreement is viewed as a contract that protects minority rights. In those circumstances where ownership and management interests are separated (limited partnerships and manager-managed LLCs), the operating agreement specifies what may be amended by the approval of partners or members who own a majority or designated super-majority of the entity's interests. Also, in such situations, often the manager is authorized to amend the agreement without partner or member approval to cure technical ambiguities or inconsistencies in the agreement.

Owner Confidentiality Covenants. (Section 12 Insertion). Sometimes it is necessary to extend confidentially covenants to partners and LLC members, particularly in those enterprises where the owners may have access to trade secrets or proprietary information critical to the success of the business. Some investors may resist any such agreements or any mechanism that limits other investment options or exposes them to any future claims relating to the use of proprietary information.

Dissolutions Rights (Section 16). The operating agreement should specify the conditions for dissolving the partnership or LLC, which often track the applicable statutory provisions. A primary consideration is the approval requirement of the partners or LLC members to force a dissolution and winding up. Many require unanimous approval, while others impose a super-majority requirement. In limited partnerships and manager-managed LLCs, a dissolution decision generally always requires the consent of those who manage the enterprise.

Life After Rights (Section 12 Insertion). In professional organizations and other partnerships and LLCs where revenues are generated from the personal services of the owners, often it is advisable to spell out the "going forward" rights that each owner will have in the event there is a falling out and the group fractures. Absent such an agreement, the owners may find themselves tangled up with dissolution and wind-up issues that make it difficult to immediately shift gears and preserve the continuity of their business activities. Most professionals and service providers cannot afford a major disruption that stops their careers. Key issues include the right to engage in the same business as the fractured entity, to pursue and service clients of the entity, to hire employees of the entity, to deal with vendors and financial institutions used by the entity, to make copies of client documents, files and other important documents, to use the same personal business email addresses and phone numbers, and to disclose the prior affiliation with the entity.

4. CAPITAL AND ALLOCATION PROVISIONS

Initial Capital Contributions (Sections 7.1 and 7.6). The operating agreement should describe the initial contribution obligations of the partners or LLC members. Most importantly, the value that is going to be assigned to non-cash contributions for capital account purposes should be specified in the agreement or an Exhibit. Such contributions may include tangible property (such as land or equipment), intellectual property rights, the business plan for the enterprise, past services rendered on behalf of the enterprise, future services to be rendered, and more. The planning challenge is to clarify the expectations of the parties with respect to any non-cash assets and properly value those assets that are going to be positive additions to the capital account of the contributing partner or LLC member. The agreement should authorize the partnership or LLC to take any action to enforce the contribution obligations of partners or LLC members, to recover any associated costs and attorney fees, and to settle any such disputes with a designated approval (usually majority) of the other partners or LLC members.

Future Contribution Obligations (Section 7.4). The issue of additional capital contribution obligations of the partners or LLC members should be documented in the operating agreement. Some owners, even those with deep pockets, may want to eliminate any expectations that they will provide additional capital to keep the venture afloat or fund growth. Others may be concerned with dilution; they do not want their equity interests reduced as those with greater means continually contribute more and claim a bigger share of the enterprise. When this issue is a major concern (as it often is in start-up ventures), the owners need to talk through their concerns and, with the aid of counsel, reach an agreement that, to the fullest extent possible, addresses the objectives of the owners. One approach is to specify that each partner or LLC member must contribute his or her *pro rata* share of the capital needed to accomplish the purpose of the entity. Some owners may be unwilling to agree to an unlimited equity contribution requirement. In this situation, the agreement may have to place a cap on future required capital contributions. If there is no mandatory requirement for additional capital contributions, the operating agreement should spell out how future capital needs will be satisfied. Often this is done by specifying that owners may make additional contributions, as needed, and receive additional equity interests, while giving all partners or LLC members the right to participate in any such contributions on a *pro rata* basis.

Capital Account Maintenance (Section 7.5). The operating agreement must provide that a capital account will be maintained for each partner or member. This account ultimately determines what a partner or LLC member yields when the entity's business is sold and its affairs are wound up. The agreement should specify that each owner's account will be increased for capital contributions and allocations of income and will be decreased for distributions and loss allocations. It should also clarify the capital account impacts of contributions and distributions of non-cash assets and the rights of the partnership or LLC to restate and revalue capital account balances when a new owner is admitted and other designated conditions are satisfied. As section 7.5 illustrates, often this is accomplished by incorporating by reference the provisions of specific Treasury regulations to the Internal Revenue Code.

Allocations of Net Income and Net Loss (Section 8). The operating agreement should specify how the annual net income or net loss of the enterprise is going to be allocated to the partners or LLC members and reflected in their respective capital accounts. A benefit of partnerships and LLCs that are taxed as partnerships is that they have tremendous flexibility in structuring such allocations, far beyond that of a corporation. For example, one partner or LLC member may be allocated 60 percent of all income and 30 percent of all losses. A partnership allocation will be respected for tax purposes only if it has "substantial economic effect,"[149] three words that make section 704(b) of the Internal Revenue Code and its regulations one of the most complex subjects in the world of tax. Generally speaking (and I do mean generally), an allocation that does not produce a deficit capital account for a partner or LLC member will be deemed to have "economic effect" if capital accounts are maintained for all partners and, upon liquidation of the partnership, liquidating distributions are made in accordance with positive capital account balances.[150] In order for an allocation that produces a deficit capital account balance to have "economic effect," the partner or LLC member also must be unconditionally obligated to restore the deficit (i.e., pay cash to cover the shortfall) upon liquidation of the partnership,[151] or the partnership must have sufficient nonrecourse debt to assure that the partner's share of any minimum gain recognized on the discharge of the

---

149. I.R.C. § 704(b).

150. Reg. §§ 1.704-1(b)(2)(ii) (b)(1), 1.704-(b)(2)(ii) (B)(2).

151. Reg. § 1.704-1(b)(2)(ii) (b)(3).

debt will eliminate the deficit.[152] An "economic effect," if present, will not be deemed "substantial" if it produces an after-tax benefit for one or more partners with no diminished after-tax consequences to other partners.[153] The most common examples of economic effects that are not deemed "substantial" are shifting allocations (allocations of different types of income and deductions among partners within a given year to reduce individual taxes without changing the partners' relative economic interests in the partnership) and transitory allocations (allocations in one year that are offset by allocations in later years).[154]

Required Cash Distributions (Section 10). The operating agreement should clarify how and when cash distributions are going to be made to the partners or LLC members. Some owners want to know that the plan includes regular distributions to the owners as the business ramps up and distributions that will cover the tax burden of partners or LLC members as the entity's income is allocated and taxed to them. Others may expect that all after-tax profits will be invested to finance growth or that cash distributions will be left to the discretion of the managers. This issue usually is tied to other key factors, including the growth rate of the business and the use of debt. Often the answer is to set guidelines regarding growth and debt that, once hit, will begin to trigger cash distributions to the owners.

Cash Allocation Provisions. A related and equally important planning consideration is how cash distributions are allocated among the partners or LLC members. The most common and basic structure is to provide that any cash distributed will be allocated among the owners according to their respective percentage interests in the entity and then to insure, through forced allocations, that the respective capital account balances of the partners or LLC members at time of liquidation reflect these percentage interests. There is flexibility in structuring the distribution provisions in the operating agreement. Consider the situation where one person puts up all the capital and one provides services to the venture. The operating agreement might provide that cash distributions first will be allocated to the owner who provided the capital until that owner receives the equity contributed together with a specified preferred return. The important point is that there is flexibility in structuring cash rights among the owners, and preferences may be created in favor of certain owners.

Anti-Deficit Account Provisions (Section 8.3 through 8.8). Often the partners and LLC members want the operating agreement structured so that there is no risk that the capital account of a partner or member will have a negative balance when the affairs of the partnership or LLC are wound up. Such a negative balance would trigger an unwelcome contribution obligation to eliminate the negative balance. To protect against such a negative balance, the operating agreement often includes a number of relatively complicated provisions that limit net loss allocations, designate how net gains from non-

---

152. Reg. §§ 1.704-(2)(c), 1.704-(2)(f)(1), 1.704-(g)(1), 1.704-2(b)(1) & (e).
153. Reg. § 1.704-1(b)(2)(iii).
154. Reg. § 1.704-1(b)(2)(iii) (b) & (c).

recourse debt obligations ("Minimum Gain Chargebacks") are to be handled, force gross income allocations ("Qualified Income Offsets") in certain circumstances, authorize curative allocations and modifications, and clarify the overriding intention that no partner have a deficit capital account balance at liquidation. These provisions, illustrated by sections 8.3 through 8.8 of the form agreement, provide a multifaceted attack on the risk of a negative capital account.

CHAPTER 7

FUNDING THE ENTERPRISE

A. PUBLIC COMPANIES

Very few companies seriously consider "going public" – having their stock owned and regularly traded by a large number of public shareholders. Most businesses are just too small or not suited for public ownership and the associated regulatory hassles and horrendous expenses. The few that do succeed with an initial public offering (IPO) play in a different league and daily live with pressures, expectations and protocols that are foreign to those who run closely held enterprises.

1. PROS AND CONS OF BEING A PUBLIC COMPANY

The advantages of being a public company are compelling. The owners have liquid stock that facilitates the rapid growth and diversification of their wealth. The company has a larger, stronger capital base to fuel growth, pursue new ventures, or expand through the acquisition of other companies. The compensation paid to the corporation's executives often increases dramatically though higher salaries, bigger bonuses and stock equity incentives. There is often a perception that the prestige and presence of the entire enterprise and those who work for it has been pushed to a whole new level.

Balanced against these advantages are risks, pressures, hassles, and costs that must be carefully considered and planned for. The pressure to show strength of earnings and growth is relentless and never-ending. It's all about the short-term, the here and now. The investing public, primarily though their guardians, the brokerage community, will scrutinize results and ask the tough questions. The challenges of public disclosure and confidentiality will demand serious time and attention to avoid litigation burdens that often accompany bad disclosures or breached confidences. Accounting, audit, internal control, and regulatory reporting and compliance pressures will balloon at all levels. Management will be directly accountable to an active board of directors, partially comprising outside, independent members who will be the sole players on the all-important audit and compensation subcommittees. Sales and purchases of company stock by corporate executives will have to be publicly reported and carefully monitored to avoid securities law liability risks.

And then there are the costs – the costs to go public and the ongoing increased costs that come with being a public company. The baseline upfront costs to go public include substantial legal fees for a host of items, including preparation of the registration statement and securities law compliance, accounting and audit fees, printing costs, and various others direct fees and costs that are incurred during the launch period, which typically runs six to nine months. In a survey of 26 companies that went public during the 2009 to 2011 timeframe, Ernst & Young LLP[1] found that the companies, on average, engaged 11 third-party advisors in connection with the their IPOs, including investment bankers, attorneys, auditors, printers, D&O insurance carriers, stock transfer agents, Sarbanes-Oxley consultants, compensation advisors, investor relations firms, tax advisors, road show consultants, compensation advisors to the board, and internal audit advisors. On average, the surveyed companies spent $13 million in one-time advisory costs associated with executing the IPO. Of course, the core offering costs will typically be much less in smaller offerings. But the bottom line is always the same – the up-front costs of an IPO, which are not predicated on a successful offering, are very expensive. And beyond these direct getting-started costs are the indirect and opportunity costs of personnel and management time and the substantial commissions and expenses that must be paid to those who sell the stock in the offering.

As for the additional costs that come with being a public company, in the same survey Ernst & Young reported that new public companies, on average, incur additional ongoing costs (not related to the IPO) of approximately $2.5 million a year as public companies. Of this amount, $1.5 million is attributable to executive compensation and directors' benefits, and the remaining $1 million represents increased compliance costs.

2. *GOING PUBLIC PROCESS*

What does the process of going public involve? The starting point is a determination that the company is a good candidate for an initial public offering. This often requires discussions with consultants, underwriters, accountants and attorneys to assess the state of the market and the appeal of the company. The focus is on the proven ability of the company to maintain consistent growth, the experience and track records of the management team, the type of product or service offered by the company (the "hotter" the better), how the company stacks up against its competition, and whether the audit and internal control requirements for a public offering have been or can be satisfied.

Although the IPO process itself may run three or four months, usually it takes at least a year or two to prepare for the process. During this preparatory phase, the company must develop the capacities and tools to operate as a public company. These require a management team that instills confidence and has a demonstrated capacity to manage a public company, strong corporate governance procedures, qualified outside board members, proven internal control systems, solid accounting and audit histories, performance ratios that meet or beat established benchmarks and key competitors, reduced debt loads, and a

1. Ernst & Young IPO Cost Survey, November 2011. Ernst & Young is a global leader in assurance, tax, transaction and advisory services that employs 141,000 people worldwide.

convincing and engaging story of present and future success.

Timing is always a critical issue. Market conditions are often the most compelling factor. Smart timing creates the opportunity for an optimal yield from the offering, the development of a solid trading history after the offering, and strong upside potential for investors. Many factors can impact an IPO timing decision, including political events, interest rates, inflation projections, economic forecasts, and the performance of other companies in the same sector. Impatient gun-jumping fueled by a need for capital and an over-anxious management team can lead to poor stock prices, a disappointing or disastrous aftermarket or, in extreme situations, a complete failed offering.

A key challenge is to get an underwriter committed to the offering. Often the creditability and experience of the management team is the primary factor in attracting a quality underwriter. And, of course, size matters. Most companies who are seriously exploring a public offering have annual sales of at least $100 million. It's often impossible to reasonably justify the increased costs and regulatory burdens of being a public company when the annual sales drop much below this threshold. In select situations, an underwriter may have an interest in smaller companies that have a cutting edge product and promise sustained, extreme annual growth (say, 25 percent) for the next five years.

The registration statement is always a major challenge in an initial public offering. It must be carefully drafted to include the history of the company, details related to the market for the product or services offered by the company, how the proceeds of the offering are going to be used, the risk factors that accompany an investment in the company, the backgrounds of the officers and directors, any transactions with related parties, the identifies of any major shareholders, and more. Of course, audited financial statements must be included in the registration statement. Once completed, the registration statement is submitted to the Securities and Exchange Commission for review.

The selling begins when the registration statement is approved and the offering is effective. Usually there are multiple steps in the selling process that require constant input and monitoring from professionals who have proven IPO track records. Often a key to the sales effort is a high-quality "road show" that smartly and quickly lays out key facts and stimulates investor interest in the company. An institutional investor generally has no interest in visiting a company that it might select for its portfolio. It will want an informative presentation at a convenient (and usually private) road show meeting that gives it an opportunity to ask questions, size up management, and obtain what it needs to make an investment decision. This is the ideal time (often the only time) for the company's senior management to communicate directly with potential investors. Usually the sales presentation is carefully scripted in various formats (everything from a full-blown presentation to a two-minute pitch) to accommodate different sales opportunities.

When the offering wraps up and the money has arrived, the market reaction, governance, management, performance, disclosure, and compliance challenges of being a public company take center stage. The importance and complexity of these challenges should not be understated. They set the stage for the future and require critical advance planning.

3. PUBLIC MARKETS: FACTORS AND LINGO

A lawyer should have a basic understanding of the public markets and the terms that are commonly used to refer to various elements and strategies that are part of such markets.

a. Stock Markets

A stock market is a network of economic transactions in which buyers and sellers deal in securities that are listed on a stock exchange or that trade in private transactions. Escalating stock market prices are considered primary indicators of a strong and growing economy, an increase in business investment, and improving household incomes and consumption.

Often stock markets and the prices of specific stocks are heavily influenced by news of economic and financial developments that have no direct connection to the markets or the stocks. Rumors, press releases, announcements, political showdowns, wild speculations and many other factors can trigger massive reactions and big price swings that usually open up short-term profit opportunities for experienced investors who have the capacity and knowledge to take advantage of the situation.

A stock market crash occurs when negative economic factors precipitate a rapid loss in the confidence of the investing public, panic selling that feeds on itself, and steep declines in stock prices across the board. Famous stock market crashes include the Wall Street crash of 1929, the crash of 1973-74, the Black Monday crash of 1987, the Dot-Com Bubble Bust of 2000, and the Market Crash of 2008.

The last two crashes are painful, recent reminders of how brutal stock markets can be in destroying savings programs and retirement hopes. The Dot-Com Bubble Bust of 2000 began as some, then many, and then all concluded that the future profitability expectations of new investments were grossly overoptimistic, particularly those related to the technology and dot.com boom. Foreign capital began to disappear and stock markets crashed as spending and demand plummeted, companies quickly found themselves swimming in excess manufacturing capacity, venture capital was nearly impossible to find, and monthly investment statements became something to hide from. The tech-heavy Nasdaq Composite lost 78 percent of its value in a few short years, and even the stalwart S&P 500 got hammered, losing 49 percent of its value during the same time frame. Trillions of dollars in equity value quickly vanished in a few short years following the bubble's burst.

Slowly, the return began and then strengthened, strongly prodded by big tax cuts and the lowest interest rates most could ever remember. Foreigners fueled the recovery with serious capital, and all was back on track again until everything crashed again in 2008 and millions of investors lost big. Stock markets again recovered as the government and the Federal Reserve have kept money flowing by cutting short-term interest rates to nearly zero, driving up annual federal deficits to unprecedented trillion-dollar levels that no one could have imagined before 2009, and pumping trillions into the economy through the Federal Reserve's "quantitative easing" programs.

These measures have demonstrated that stock markets will respond to serious stimulus even as the economy continues to struggle. The big question now is whether these measures are just fueling another artificial stock market bubble that is doomed to burst and quickly wipeout major portions of all stock portfolios. What frightens many is that, as the stock market has flourished, the root causes of the 2008 crash – gross, irresponsible over-leveraging at many levels and a resulting massive drop in demand – have left us with a pitifully slow, anemic recovery, chronically high real unemployment numbers, countless business failures, no growth in real income levels, a labor force participation rate that hovers at a 40-year low, and an across-the-board loss in confidence and hope for the future.

b. Stock Exchange

A stock exchange provides a marketplace for trading securities, commodities, derivatives and other financial instruments and serves as a clearing house to ensure that shares are delivered and payments are made. The primary function of an exchange is to facilitate fair and orderly trading, the timely and efficient dissemination of pricing and other information, and the establishment of exchange rules that bind all participants. An exchange may be an electronic platform or a physical location where traders meet to conduct business on a "trading floor." Technology advances have proliferated the development of electronic exchanges.

An exchange specifies listing requirements that must be satisfied in order for a company to offer its securities on the exchange. Listing requirements can be stringent. For example, the New York Stock Exchange requires a company to have at least 1.1 million shares held by the public and a market value of public shares equal to at least $100 million and to meet specified alternative income, valuation, or asset tests. Listing requirements vary among exchanges, but significant exchanges uniformly require regular financial reports and audited financial statements.

Today, there are more than a hundred stock and derivatives exchanges, in over 140 countries. The five largest exchanges (market capitalization as of December 31, 2013) are the New York Stock Exchange (market cap in excess of $17.9 trillion), NASDAQ (market cap in excess of $6 trillion), Tokyo Stock Exchange (market cap in excess of $4.5 trillion), London Stock Exchange Group, and Euronext Exchange (market cap in excess of $3.5 trillion).[2]

c. Stock Indexes

A stock index tracks the movements of various stock values throughout

2. World Federation of Exchanges, January 2014 Report.

every business day. Usually one can't avoid hearing of the most popular three indexes: the Dow Jones Industrial Average (an index based on 30 stocks); the NASDAQ (which tracks thousands of stocks, many in the technology and communication sectors); and the S&P 500 (an index based on 500 stocks traded on the New York Stock exchange). Other less visible, but highly regarded, comprehensive indexes include the NYSE Composite Index (which includes all NYSE-listed stocks, including foreign stocks, American Depositary Receipts, and real estate investment trusts, but excludes closed-end funds, ETFs, limited partnerships and derivatives), the Wilson 5000 Equity Index (which represents stocks of nearly every publicly traded company in the United States, including U.S. stocks traded on the New York Stock Exchange, NASDAQ and the American Stock Exchange), and the Russell 2000 Index (which tracks 2,000 stocks traded on the over-the-counter ("OTC") market).

Stock market indexes are classified in various ways. A "world" or "global" index, such as the MSCI World or the S&P Global 100, includes large companies without regard to where they are domiciled or traded. "National" indexes, such as the American S&P 500, the British FTSE 100, or the Japanese Nikkei 225, are designed to showcase the stock market performance of a given nation and generally are the most quoted indexes.

d. Transaction Processing

The purchase or sale of a security often requires that an investor do nothing more than place a call to his or her broker or click a few buttons on a website. As simple as it is to initiate a transaction, the market structures used to price and process an order and promote orderliness and stability in the marketplace are quite complicated. Orders are processed one of two ways: through an exchange or over the counter (OTC).

An exchange centralizes the communication of bid and ask prices to all direct market participants through various means, which (depending on the exchange) may include a discrete electronic message, voice message, hand signal, or computer-generated command. When two parties reach agreement, the price of the transaction is communicated throughout the market to ensure market pricing transparency to all participants. Clearing facilities closely linked to the exchange handle the post-trade mechanics of securities and derivative orders traded on the exchange.

Over-the-counter markets deal primarily with securities that are not listed on an exchange. Dealers act as market makers by quoting bid and ask prices to other dealers and to their clients or customers, and the quoted prices may vary among different customers. Dealer communications may be by phone, mass e-mail messages, or instant messaging, and sometimes involve the use of electronic bulletin boards that post dealer quotes. In an OTC customer market, trading occurs between dealers and their customers, with dealers often initiating customer contact through electronic messages (called "dealer-runs") that list various securities and derivatives and the prices at which they are willing to buy or sell them. In an OTC interdealer market, dealers often have direct phone lines with each other that make it possible to quickly communicate with several dealers in a matter of seconds. In OTC markets, other market participants generally have no access to the details of a trade (although some OTC markets post execution prices and order sizes after the fact), and the clearing and settlement chores are handled by the buyer and seller firms. Compared to exchange markets, OTC markets are subject to fewer rules, are far less transparent, and are more likely to encounter liquidity or clearing problems.

Improved electronic trading platforms have enabled dealers and select nondealers in some OTC markets to submit quotes and execute trades directly through an electronic system. This exchange-like evolution may facilitate some multilateral trading among direct participants, but does not offer the access, transparency and settlement guarantees of an exchange.

Following are brief descriptions of a few common terms used in the trading process.

- **Bid vs. Ask Price.** The bid price is the maximum price that a buyer is willing to pay for a security, whereas the ask price represents the minimum price that a seller is willing to accept for a security. Since a transaction occurs when a buyer and seller agree on a price, the size of the gap between a stock's bid and ask price, generally referred to as "the spread," is a key indicator of how difficult it is to convert a security to cash; the smaller the spread, the greater the liquidity.

- **Market vs. Limit Orders.** A market order is an order to buy or sell a security at the best available price at the time the order is executed. Absent an availability or liquidity problem, fulfillment of the order is assured, but the price is not. A limit order specifies a maximum price for buying a security and the minimum price for selling a security. The price will not exceed the designated maximum buy price or be less than the specified minimum sell price, but there is no assurance that the order will be filled.

- **Round Lot vs. Odd Lot vs. Block Trade.** A round lot is 100 shares of a stock, or any number of shares that can be evenly divided by 100, and is considered a "normal trading unit." An odd lot is any order involving less than 100 shares. A mixed lot consists of both a round lot and a mixed lot (e.g. 250 shares). Commissions on an odd lot order may be higher due to specified minimums of a brokerage firm or the need to "bunch" the odd lot order with other orders to facilitate a trade. Online trading opportunities and resulting drops in trading commissions have made it easier and less expensive to fulfill odd lot orders. A "block trade" or "block order" is a large transaction (at least 10,000 shares but usually much larger) at a negotiated price between parties (usually institutional investors or hedge funds acting through investment banks or other intermediaries) outside of the open markets in order to reduce market impacts.

- **Upstairs vs. Downstairs Markets.** The upstairs market refers to the trading of securities away from an exchange, in the "upstairs trading room" of a brokerage firm. It's typically done between two brokers-dealers in an over-the-counter market transaction. The downstairs market refers to trading on an exchange or its electronic counterpart.

• **Brokerage Firm and Clearing Firm.** A brokerage firm initiates and negotiates orders and trades. The completion of a transaction requires a "clearing" process, which requires a matching of trades, delivery of the securities or book entry of ownership, and settlement of accounts between financial institutions. A small percentage of brokerage firms clear their own transactions. Exchanges and most firms use a separate clearing house to handle the clearing functions.

• **Confirmation and Settlement.** The execution of an order to buy or sell a security will trigger the sending of a trade confirmation by mail or email to the person who placed the order. This document is to confirm that the order was filled by the broker in accordance with the instructions given. The confirmation will typically include: the name of the security, applicable ticker symbol, and CUSIP number; total number of shares bought or sold; the cost or selling price per share; the commission paid; the trade execution date; the settlement date; the gross value of the transaction; the net value of the transaction after deducting brokerage commissions; the account number related to the trade; and order type (market or limit). Confirmations should be retained for tax and other purposes, and any detected error should be immediately reported to the broker. The settlement date is the date the transaction is completed and all payments must be made. The settlement date is usually three business days after the trade is executed for stock and bond transactions and the next business day for government securities and options.

e. Market Trading Breakers

Decades ago, the New York Stock Exchange put in place circuit breakers to reduce short-term market volatility by forcing a pause in trading and giving investors time to assimilate incoming information during a period of rapid market declines. In 2012, the SEC approved amendments to Exchange Rule 80B (Trading Halts Due to Extraordinary Market Volatility) that established new Level I, 2, and 3 trading breaks, triggered by declines in the S&P 500 index. A 7-percent decline between 9:30 a.m. and 3:25 p.m. will trigger a Level 1 break to halt trading for 15 minutes. Following the reopening, there can be no more Level 1 breaks during the day, but a 13-percent decline will trigger a 15-minute Level 2 halt. Following that reopening, there will be no more Level 2 breaks during the day, but a 20-percent drop will trigger a Level 3 halt in trading for the remainder of the day.

f. Derivatives

Financial instruments generally fall into one of three categories: equities (stocks), debt (bonds and mortgages), and derivatives. A derivative is a financial contract between two parties that derives its value from the performance of specified assets, which may be commodities, stocks, bonds, currencies or interest rates. The asset that governs the value of a derivative is generally referred to as the "underlying." There are various types of derivatives, which create different rights and obligations. Examples include:

- **Options**, where one party has the right, but no obligation, to buy or sell a specific security at a specified price (the strike price) on a specified future date;

- **Futures Contracts**, where a party is obligated to buy or sell a financial instrument or commodity at a specified price on a specified future date under a detailed standardized contract that facilitates trading on a futures exchange;

- **Forward Contracts**, where a party is obligated to buy or sell an asset at a specified price on a specified future date under a customized contract (any commodity, price, and delivery date) that is not suitable for trading on an exchange;

- **Swaps**, the exchange of one security, currency or interest rate for another, usually prompted by changed investment objectives;

- **Collateral Mortgage Obligations**, complicated financial instruments that enable investors to participate in the cash flow of a "pool" of mortgages through a special purpose entity that offers different "tranches" with varying repayment risks, interest rates, and maturities;

- **Warrants**, the right to buy securities, usually stocks, at a specified price within a certain timeframe that is longer than normal options periods and often attached as an enhancement to a bond or other financial instrument.

Derivatives generally are used for one of two very different purposes: as a risk-management tool to hedge against future losses resulting from changes in the value of the underlying commodity or financial instrument, or as a tool to accelerate speculation by quickly and efficiently obtaining a significant (and often high-risk) position in the underlying commodity or financial instrument.

Exchange-traded derivatives (ETDs) are traded on an exchange (e.g., the Chicago Mercantile Exchange), and over-the-counter (OTC) derivatives are traded through a dealer network.

g. Mutual Funds

A mutual fund is a pool of investment capital that thousands of investors, large and small, create by mutually contributing their savings. A professional manager then invests the funds in accordance with the stated objectives of the fund. The manager and all expenses of running the fund are paid out of the fund. A person can participate in some funds by investing a modest sum upfront and then adding as little as $50 or more to the account each month. A major advantage is instant diversification – each investor has a financial interest in every one of the fund's investments. Plus, the investor gets professional management and avoids the commissions and hassles of trading individual stocks and bonds. Mutual funds do not trigger double tax burdens like a regular C corporation (see Chapter 8), but their income from investments (interest and dividends) and capital gains (both long- and short- term) are distributed and taxed to those who own shares in the fund, and this pass-through tax consequence reduces the yield and requires planning.

In 2010, the U.S. Statistical abstract reported that there were over 7,500 mutual funds that managed more than $11.8 trillion. Today, mutual funds are the vehicles that most investors use to purchase interests in corporate stocks and bonds. Each fund is characterized by its investment objective, and the range of investment objectives is huge. There are blue chip stock funds, international funds, sector funds, asset allocation funds, bond funds – a lengthy list. There are families of funds, which are large groups of funds with different investment objectives offered by a single fund company. Examples include Fidelity, Vanguard and Dreyfus. A person who invests with such a fund family can easily move money from fund to fund within the family at little or no cost.

Mutual funds are classified in different ways:

- **Load vs. No-Load**. A "no-load" fund means that no commissions are being paid to someone for selling the fund's shares. A person can buy the "no-load" shares directly from the fund company or through a firm that offers "no-load" funds. "Load" funds use a part of the investment to pay a commission to a salesperson.

- **Open-End vs. Closed-End**. An open-end mutual fund, the most common, continually takes on new investment capital until the manager shuts off additional investments. There is no set maximum. At the end of each day, the fund's net asset value (NAV) is calculated by dividing the closing market value of the fund's investments by the shares outstanding. The NAV is the price at which investors buy ("bid price") fund shares from a fund company and sell shares ("redemption price") to a fund company. A closed-end fund has a fixed maximum amount of capital. Once the maximum is hit, no more capital flows into the fund, and the fund's shares are traded and valued like a stock. As such, the price of a closed-end fund's shares are a function of supply and demand for those shares at a given point in time and may trade at a discount or premium to the fund's NAV.

- **Managed vs. Indexed.** A "Managed" mutual fund is managed by a professional group that works to get the best possible return. Often one hears of funds boasting of beating the S&P 500 Index or the Dow Jones. An "Index" fund just mirrors an index. For example, an S&P Index Fund buys and holds the 500 stocks that make up the S&P 500. It'll never beat or loose to the index; it is the index. Why would one want an indexed fund? It offers some advantages. There's no need to fret over the fund manager's expertise, competence or track record. There are many fewer transactions in an index fund, so an investor pays fewer capital gains while in the fund. The total expenses of operating an index fund often are far less than a managed fund. And a person knows going in that he or she will never lose to the index.

h. Exchange-Traded Funds

An exchange-traded fund (ETF) typically tracks an index, a commodity or a group of assets, but trades like a stock and thus gives investors the opportunity to take advantage of price changes that occur throughout a day, sell short, buy on margin, and otherwise deal with the EFT as they would any stock. Thus, an EFT provides an active, experienced investor the diversification benefits of a mutual fund but with far more trading flexibility. Unlike an open-end mutual fund, ETF transactions that occur during a day are not priced by a net-asset-value calculation at the end of the day. In comparing an ETF to a closed-end mutual fund, both trade like a stock but EFT pricing generally is more transparent, less volatile, and typically will stay much closer (usually within 1 percent) to the net asset value of the fund.

ETFs have continued to grow in popularity since the 1993 release of the first ETF, Spider (SRDR), which tracks the S&P 500 index. The growth is attributable to professional investors and active traders who want low fund expenses and stock-like features and who can bear the significant brokerage commissions associated with ETF investing. This commission burden usually makes indexed mutual funds more suitable for small or passive investors. Although most ETFs are tied to an index, in 2008 the SEC authorized the creation of actively managed ETFs.

i. Hedge Funds

A hedge fund is a company, typically a limited partnership or a limited liability company, that uses professional management to invest and manage capital provided by sophisticated, accredited investors. A hedge fund differs from a mutual fund in various key respects: it is not sold or offered to the general public; it uses leveraging techniques; it invests in a broad range of liquid securities and employs a variety of investment techniques to generate positive yields whether markets are rising or falling; its managers often invest heavily in the fund; and it generally can avoid most (but of late, not all) of the oversight and other regulatory burdens applicable to mutual funds and investment companies. The word "hedge" refers to the techniques traditionally used by hedge funds to balance investments in minimizing (hedging) loss exposures, but today hedging is only one technique, not the primary focus, of the investment programs of many hedge funds.

Hedge funds typically are open-ended, permitting investors to make additions or withdrawals periodically. Additions and withdrawals are based on the fund's net asset value, which reflects the current value of the investment assets in the fund and the liabilities and expenses of the fund. Expenses include annual management fees, which typically are based on a percentage (e.g., 1 percent) of the fund's assets and performance bonus incentives.

j. REITs

A real estate investment trust (REIT) is a company (usually a corporation) that owns and often operates various types of income-producing real estate, including office buildings, shopping centers, apartments, warehouses, hotels, hospitals and more. Generally, a REIT is to real estate what a mutual fund is to stocks. It makes it possible for thousands of investors to pool their capital and enjoy the benefits of a diversified and professionally managed real estate portfolio. Many REITs are publicly traded and listed on stock exchanges. REITs are generally classified as equity (those that own real estate properties), mortgage (those that provide real estate financing), and hybrid (those that own equities and provide financing).

The REIT concept was pioneered in the United States, but has now been adopted by many countries. The result is a growing awareness and acceptance of global real estate securities, various REIT indexes (including the global FTSE EPRA/NAREIT Global Real Estate Index Series), and hundreds of public real estate companies in over 37 countries.

In the United States, REITs have their own tax provisions, found in sections 856 through 859 of the Internal Revenue Code. These provisions require that a REIT currently distribute at least 90 percent of its earnings to its shareholders, but provide the REIT with a deduction for all amounts distributed to shareholders. Thus, a REIT is able to avoid the double tax risks and burdens of a regular C corporation (see Chapter 8).

k. Common Trading Strategies and Related Terms

Following are brief descriptions of common terms used to describe various stock trading strategies. Descriptions of common terms related to bonds and bond investing are included in Section B of Chapter 3.

- **Buying Long or Long Position.** Investing in a security, currency or commodity with the expectation that the asset's value will increase over time.

- **Selling Short or Short Position.** Selling borrowed stock at the current market price with the expectation that the price will fall and the borrowed stock will be repaid at a cost that is less than the yield from the stock sale. The bet is on the downside. If the price drops, short selling produces a profit; if it rises, short selling produces a loss. The borrowed stock typically is provided by the short investor's brokerage firm that holds house or client shares that are available for lending to short sellers. The borrowed shares are essential to prevent illegal "naked" shorting, the selling of a shares that do not exist. An investor closes out a short position by "covering," the term used to describe the buying and returning of the borrowed shares. Short selling sometimes can be used to manipulate and drive down the price of a thinly traded security or can be used as a destructive piling-on strategy to enhance pressure on a stock whose price is falling. For these reasons, markets are subject to important restrictions that define when and how a short sale can occur, and some markets prohibit short selling.

- **Margin Buying.** Buying a security with borrowed funds on the bet that the yield from the investment will exceed the interest cost of the borrowed funds. Brokerage firms typically provide investors the option to borrow against the value of their existing portfolio account to finance margin buying activities. Regulations limit the amount of such borrowing. The maximum margin leverage permitted in the United States is 50 percent, a percentage that must be maintained if account values drop. Thus, a drop in an investor's portfolio value may trigger a "margin call," a demand that cash be added to the account or that account assets be sold to reduce the debt and protect the brokerage firm's loan position.

- **Call Option.** A contractual right, but not an obligation, to buy a security, commodity or financial instrument, at a fixed price (the "strike price") on or before a designated expiration date. An American call option may be exercised anytime before the expiration date; a European call option may be exercised only on the expiration date. Standard short-term stock options usually expire in 30 days, and long-term options may run as long as 30 months. The buyer of the option pays a premium for the option right and is betting that the price of the asset will sufficiently increase to generate a positive yield from selling or exercising the option. The seller of the option is willing to surrender any value in excess of the strike price for the premium received. A call option will not be exercised unless the price of the underlying asset exceeds the strike price. Thus, a call option is deemed to be "in-the-money" when the price of the underlying asset exceeds the strike price and is "out-of-the-money" until that point.

- **Put Option.** A contractual right, but not an obligation, to sell a security, commodity or financial instrument, at a fixed price (the "strike price") on or before a designated expiration date. It's the reverse of a call option. A premium is paid to protect against a decline in the price of the underlying asset. If the price does not fall below the strike price, the put will not be exercised. As with a call option, an American put may be exercised anytime before the expiration date, and a European put may be exercised only on the expiration date. The buyer of the put seeks protection against a price drop. The seller of the put is willing to take the downside risk for the premium received. A put option is "in-the-money" when the price of the underlying asset drops below the strike price and is "out-of-the-money" until that point.

- **Collar.** A strategy designed to lock-in existing values and protect against future price declines by simultaneously purchasing an out-of-the-money put option and selling an out-of-the-money call option. The put option protects against price declines, and the premium received from the sale of the call option covers all or a portion of the premium paid for the put option. A collar surrenders upside potential for downside protection.

- **Dollar Cost Averaging.** A strategy, often used in connection with mutual funds, that invests the same amount of funds periodically, usually quarterly or monthly. This form of automatic investing ignores market price swings and ensures over time that investment costs will reflect of average of a market's up and down movements.

- **Arbitrage.** A strategy to purchase a security on one market for immediate resale on another market to take advantage of price discrepancies in the markets. The goal of a pure arbitrage is to generate a profit without taking any risk. If, for example, a stock's price on an exchange is not aligned with a futures contract for the same stock, a short sale of the more expensive and a simultaneous purchase of the other could yield an instant profit with no risk. Market efficiencies generally make it impossible for retail investors to spot or capitalize on pure arbitrage opportunities, but market makers and investment firms often have program trading and other computerized systems that help generate small arbitrage yields from large investment transactions. The term "arbitrage" also is used to refer to quick, non-risk-free investment opportunities that surface before the market reacts to a significant development, such as an announcement of a merger or liquidation or an unexplained difference in two closely related competing stocks.

STUDENT PROBLEM 7-1

Jason is the founder and chief executive officer of TechMore, Inc. (TechMore), a rapidly growing company near San Francisco. Over the past five years, TechMore has developed a sterling reputation for designing sophisticated operating systems for select growth industries. It has a stable of talented designers and engineers that is growing weekly and continually expanding and improving its product offerings. Jason and four other key executives own 30 percent of TechMore's outstanding common stock, and the balance is owned by 38 wealthy investors, most of whom recently converted notes to common stock. TechMore has very little debt, annual sales that have passed the $60 million mark, solid profits that have consistently grown over the last 24 months, and an established and projected growth rate of 25 to 30 percent a year. The big issue now is whether TechMore is ripe for a public offering. Answer the following questions that Jason has raised:

1. What are the primary benefits that would be realized from a public offering?

2. What additional administrative and management burdens will be triggered by a public offering?

3. What governance and operating changes would be required to prepare for a public offering?

4. What are the cost factors of a public offering and operations following the offering?

5. How long does it typically take to prepare for and execute a public offering? What are the timing considerations and how important are they?

STUDENT PROBLEM 7-2

Assume for purposes of this problem that ABC Inc. is a public company actively traded on the NASDAQ. Consider which trading strategy may work best in each of the following situations:

1. Jennifer received common stock of ABC Inc. in a reverse triangular merger involving a subsidiary of ABC and a closely held corporation in which Jennifer was a major stockholder. Jennifer is restricted from selling her ABC stock and must structure any liquidation of the stock over an extended period. She wants a strategy that will protect her, at the lowest possible cost, from any serious decline in the market value of her ABC stock.

2. Pete's research has convinced him that the value of ABC's common stock will drop significantly over the next three to six months. He has just sold all of his ABC stock, but wants a strategy to further profit from his research.

3. George is convinced that the value of ABC's common stock will grow significantly over the next three to six months. He has a stock portfolio of roughly $1.2 million in his brokerage account, but no cash in the account. George doesn't want to sell any stock in his portfolio or add cash to his account, but he wants to secure a position in ABC, at the lowest cost, that will allow him to participate in the upside that he expects.

4. Luke, age 29, wants to start building capital for the future. He can afford to add $400 to an investment account each month and anticipates that this contribution amount will grow each year. He wants an investment vehicle that will facilitate monthly contributions, provide instant diversification across numerous stocks and sectors, generate returns that reflect market performance, and eliminate or minimize commissions, professional management fees, and other expenses.

B. CLOSELY HELD ENTERPRISES

1. START-UP CAPITAL SOURCES

Capital is usually the biggest obstacle for a new business. An idea has blossomed into a business plan, perhaps even a prototype or a few sales, but money is now needed to get the business started and fuel growth. Of course, the entrepreneur would love to secure the needed financing at the lowest possible cost. But, in most cases, cost isn't the driving factor. The challenge is availability or, perhaps better stated, the lack of available financing. This funding challenge often triggers the following key questions.

Is bank financing available?

Bank financing often is the key to growth for an established company that has a proven history of profitability. The business can leverage the bank debt by generating a return on its assets that far exceeds the interest cost of the debt. It is business 101 leverage at its best. The problem for a new business is that it lacks a proven income history and a solid asset base. Thus, absent a personal guarantee from a deep pocket player that trumps the company's status as a start-up, bank debt usually isn't available to a new venture.

Once the business is established, bank debt often is the best and lowest cost capital source to fund growth. A business can usually obtain asset-based bank financing for most hard assets that have a market value. It is common to secure financing for up to 85 to 90 percent of creditworthy accounts receivable, 50 percent of finished goods inventories, 80 percent of the cost of the equipment (repayable in fixed installments over a period of three to 10 years), and up to 75 percent of the value of marketable real estate. If asset-based financing doesn't work or there is a need to supplement such financing, banks often provide cash flow financing (through lines of credit or short-term debt) that allow a company to borrow against its demonstrated ability to generate sufficient cash to service and repay the financing. This ability is established through factors and ratios (debt coverage, debt-to-equity, working capital, senior debt restrictions, etc.), that are built into the loan documents as conditions that continually must be satisfied to keep the financing alive.

To assist with bank financing in select situations, the Small Business Administration, the Farmers Home Administration, and other government agencies often will guarantee a bank loan to enable a business to obtain financing that it could not obtain on its own. For SBA programs, any owner of the business with an equity stake of 20 percent or more must personally guarantee the loan. Plus, there are SBA fees that must be paid, and often banks charge a higher interest rate on an SBA-guaranteed loan. Because an SBA lender's track record is important to the lender, most banks will not lend to start-up businesses that lack financial statements for two to three years and significant owner's equity in the business.

What about angel or investment fund investors?

Angel investors range from family and friends to deep-pocket individual investors who manage their own money. They can be fertile ground for the budding entrepreneur who needs capital. Angels often are advised and heavily influenced by their accountants, lawyers and other professionals, with whom the entrepreneur must deal. Some angel investors band together to develop specialized expertise, share due diligence burdens, and spread the cost of professional advisers.

Often friends, acquaintances and advisors are the only sources for finding angel investors. Many angels are well-suited for businesses that are too small for venture capital firms, but often they are unwilling or unable to help with future capital needs and sometimes become a frustrating source of complaints and naïve questions and demands.

As compared to angels, venture capital funds tend to be more sophisticated, more expensive, more demanding, and more interested in bigger deals. They often include pension funds and endowment investors, along with wealthy individual investors. Targeted annual returns of 50 to 60 percent are not uncommon hurdles when dealing with venture capital firms. These return objectives often require a firm to negotiate tough terms that give the firm control of major corporate decisions and, in select cases, the power to dictate day-to-day operational decisions.

A venture capital firm will expend a great deal of effort investigating a potential investment. Its obligations to its investors permit nothing less. A business plan targeted at venture capital firms should be concise and attempt to stimulate further interest, rather than describe the business in exhaustive detail. The amount of needed financing should be discussed without proposing or mentioning the terms of a potential deal. Generally, information that is proprietary or confidential should be left out of the document because such documents are often copied and circulated.

Seldom do venture capital firms just purchase common stock. The preferred form of investment usually is a mix of debt and equity, convertible debt, or a convertible preferred security. The firm wants a preferred position in the event of a failure and liquidation and full upside equity benefits if things play out as all hope.

Are strategic investors an option?

In the right situation, a corporate partner or strategic investor is the best option. Such investors are becoming a popular source of growth capital for many companies. Seldom will these deals work for a fresh start-up because the unknowns and perceived risks are too high. But as the business matures and the needs and benefits of more capital are more clearly defined, strategic partners can be a good source of capital. Usually the partner is looking for something more than an investment. It may want the opportunity to get an inside track on a new or evolving technology or the first opportunity to buy the company at the right time.

What is crowdfunding?

Crowdfunding is where a group of individuals collectively contribute funds to a start-up effort in response to solicitations that usually come via the Internet. There are two kinds of crowdfunding: non-equity and equity. Non-equity crowdfunding is where the contributor does not receive any equity interest for his or her contribution to the cause. The contributor's motive may be completely charitable or with the hope of receiving a tangible item (not a security) promised by the company. Kickstarter.com is one of the leading non-equity crowdfunding sponsors. A company that has a creative idea but no money can use Kickstarter in hopes of raising money to "kick start" its business.

Equity crowdfunding is a much different, and far more controversial, concept. General solicitations in 506 private offerings (described below) represent a form of crowdfunding that may now be used to target only accredited investors. The big issue is when and under what conditions will equity crowdfunding targeted at non-accredited investors ("ordinary folks" is the term many use) be permitted. There is no question that such crowdfunding will soon be legal, but, as of this writing, nobody knows exactly when it will happen.

The JOBS ("Jumpstart Our Business Startups") Act of 2012 mandated that the SEC implement rules for a new crowdfunding securities registration exemption within 270 days of the April 5, 2012 passage date. The President heralded crowdfunding as a "game changer" for "small businesses and start-ups," stating "for the first time, ordinary Americans will be able to go online and invest in entrepreneurs that they believe in."[3] In late 2013, the SEC finally issued its proposed regulations for non-accredited investor equity crowdfunding. The comment period for these regulations closed in March 2014, and this has caused many to speculate that final regulations will be released and the crowdfunding gates will open in late 2014.

The concept of equity crowdfunding scares many. Within a short time, private business ventures of all types will be using the Internet to sell

3. President Obama's address on April 5, 2012 at signing of JOBs Act bill.

unregistered securities to "ordinary Americans" who will have no capacity to evaluate what's being offered. All the targeted investors will see are ground floor opportunities to play like the big dogs. The maximum amount that a business can raise through this crowdfunding tool in a 12-month period is $1 million – not serious money in the world of business development. Those who have an annual income and a net worth of less than $100,000 may invest the greater of $2,000 or five percent of their income or net worth. Those who exceed the $100,000 threshold many invest 10 percent of their income or net worth up to a maximum of $100,000.

Proponents of equity crowdfunding compare it positively to buying lottery tickets. Opponents claim that the securities laws should seek to promote something greater than dumb luck gambling.

Here's the feared scenario. A budding entrepreneur with a hot-sounding business idea will use the Internet to raise, say, $450,000 from 150 investors (average investment of $3,000) who have an average income and net worth of $60,000. These 150 investors will need attending to and will soon become a nuisance. They will have questions and concerns. They will want reports and information, to be assured that everything is on track. Of course, there will be no market for the stock, but some will want out anyway because of a lost job, a sickness, or a desire for a new car. A few will file bankruptcy, and their stock will end up in the hands of a bankruptcy trustee. An investor will die, and the heirs will demand the lowdown on the investment.

Meanwhile, the $450,000 will be spent on salaries, fees and start-up expenses. Soon more money will be needed to keep the plan alive. But what savvy investor will want to partner-up with 150 needy neophytes who can't bring any more to the table? If such an investor does surface, a plan will be developed to flush out the original 150 investors at the lowest possible cost. The more likely outcome is that the entrepreneur, having consumed the money, will just move on to the next deal after advising the investing crowd that there's no more money, the plan is dead, and they may be entitled to a tax deduction for a worthless investment.

Is this fraud? It might be. It might just be incompetence, stupidity or greed. Either way, the uninformed investors end up losing. Investing in unregistered securities of start-ups is a super high-risk game that always poses serious risks of fraud, abuse, and complete loss. That's why, to date, it's a game that has been off limits to general solicitation and advertising and has been limited to sophisticated investors and those with a certain level of wealth. Many believe that it's no place for unsophisticated investors of modest means.

This assessment is not unique. In commenting on the impacts of equity crowdfunding, the President of the North American Securities Administration Association (NASAA) stated, "Congress has just released every huckster, scam artist, small business owner and salesman onto the Internet." Ralph Nader claimed that it's a "return to the notorious boiler room practices" where any start-up "can sell stock to investors like the old Wild West days with little disclosure or regulation."

Will there be any serious oversight? In announcing the passage of the JOBS act, the President stated that the SEC would play an "important role" to ensure that "the websites where folks go to fund all these start-ups and small businesses will be subject to rigorous oversight." Opponents are quick to point out that this is the same SEC that failed to spot Enron, Worldcom, Madoff, the dot-com bust, the derivative showdown banking industry, the subprime mortgage lunacy, the financial meltdown, and a host of other huge messes. How about state securities regulators helping out with oversight and regulation? There is no hope there. The new law specifically provides that the federal exemption will cut off all state involvement.

Although there are now many unknowns, it appears highly likely that, at some point in the not too distant future and for better or worse, many start-up companies will be using the Internet and social media to raise capital from large groups of small, uninformed investors.

Is "do-it-yourself" start-up funding the ultimate answer for most?

It's certainly the answer for many. The owners fund their dreams with their own resources: savings accounts, 401(k)s, credit cards, second mortgages, personally guaranteed loans, gifts from family members – you name it. It's tougher and lonelier, but it ensures 100 percent ownership and freedom from investor hassles during the early life of the enterprise. And for many, there is no other viable option to capitalize the operation until the business is up and running. A study conducted years ago concluded that 80 percent of the companies on Inc. Magazine's list of the 500 fastest growing companies were started and grown with no outside capital.[4]

2. *SECURITIES LAW REGISTRATION EXEMPTIONS AND RISKS*

How much do I need? From whom can I get it? Many business owners mistakenly assume that these two basic questions sum up the capital challenges for a start-up or thriving business. But there's a third and, in many respects, a more fundamental question: How do I do it legally?

Since the immediate fallout of the great crash of 1929, our laws have recognized that there is a big difference between selling a security and selling a used car. The former is an intangible; it's not possible to get the lowdown by kicking the tires, looking under the hood, and taking a test spin. So over the past 85 years, a body of federal statutory securities laws has developed to provide special protections for those who entrust their investment dollars with others.[5]

4. Amar Bhide, Bootstrap Finance: The Art of Start-ups, Harvard Business Review (Dec. 1992) p. 109.

5. The federal securities statutes include the Securities Act of 1933 (15 U.S.C. §§ 77a et seq.), the Securities Exchange Act of 1934 (15 U.C.C. §§ 78a et seq.), the Public Utility Company Act of 1935 (15 U.S.C. §§ 79 et seq.), the Trust Indenture Act of 1939 (15 U.S.C. §§ 77aaa et seq.), the Investment Company Act of 1940 (15 U.S.C. §§ 80a–1 et seq.), the Investment Advisors Act of 1940 (15 U.S.C. §§ 80b-1 et seq.), the Securities Investor Protection Act of 1970 (15 U.S.C. §§ 78aaa et seq.) and the Sarbanes-Oxley Act of 2002 (miscellaneous provisions of 15 U.S.C.).

All states have followed suit with their own statutory schemes.[6] The purpose of these laws is to protect the public from some of the risks inherent in investing money in intangible assets. Various means are used to accomplish this overriding purpose, including mandated disclosure requirements, industry player regulation, government law enforcement, and expanded causes of action for private litigation. Very few lawyers possess the know-how or the experience to navigate a client through the SEC and state regulatory mazes to take a client public. But a lawyer should understand the basics of this all-important body of law, be sensitive to the flags that indicate that a client is near (or far over) an important line, and know how to discuss key issues with business clients. For most businesses, the three primary securities law considerations are the registration requirements, the resale restrictions, and the anti-fraud prohibitions.

Sections 4 and 5 of the Securities Act of 1933 (the 1933 Act) establish the general requirement that any security offered for sale by an issuer, underwriter or dealer must be registered with the Securities and Exchange Commission (SEC).[7] As explained in the previous section, only a tiny fraction of businesses would ever consider going through the expense and hassle of such a registration process. For this reason, the important registration issues for most businesses in need of investors are the exemptions to the registration requirement. Is there an applicable exemption that fits so that the money can be raised without enduring the burdens of registration?

There are two big statutory exceptions that become the ball game for most privately owned businesses that want outside investors. The first is found in Section 4(2) of the 1933 Act that exempts from registration any "transactions by an issuer not involving a public offering."[8] It is commonly referred to as the "private offering exemption." The second is in Section 3(a)(11) of the 1933 Act that exempts from registration securities offered and sold only to residents of a single state by an issuer who is a resident of and doing business within the same state.[9] It is commonly referred to as the "intrastate offering exemption." Of course, the challenge is to know what it takes to qualify for one of these exemptions. To this end, the SEC has published rules that set forth specific standards for meeting the exemptions. Rules 504 through 506 of Regulation D describe three private offering exemptions; SEC Rule 147 deals with the intrastate offering exemption.[10]

Rule 504 Exemption

SEC Rule 504 allows a company to issue unregistered securities with a value of up to $1 million to an unlimited number of unsophisticated investors who purchase the securities for their own account and not for resale. The offering must be completed within a 12-month period, which starts when the first

6. Most states have patterned their statutes after the Uniform Securities Act.
7. 15 U.S.C. §§ 77d and 77e.
8. 15 U.S.C. §§ 77d(2).
9. 15 U.S.C. § 77c(a)(11)
10. 17 C.F.R. §§ 230.504 thru 230.506. The definitions and other provisions of sections 230.501-230.503 should be read in conjunction with these three rules.

investment agreement is signed by an investor. The rule itself does not mandate any specific disclosures, but the issuer must satisfy the basic antifraud provisions of the securities laws (discussed below). The rule permits general solicitation, but often this is prohibited or limited by state securities laws. Securities issued under Rule 504 are not subject to certain resale restrictions because they are not considered "restricted securities." The company must comply with the securities laws of each state in which a purchaser is a resident, and usually must file a notice with that state's commissioner of corporations or similar official. Any person who purchases a security in a Rule 504 offering should sign an investment agreement as proof of his or her investment intent and other required representations. A Form D must be filed with the SEC within 15 days after the first sale.

Rule 505 Exemption

SEC Rule 505 allows a company, within a 12-month period, to issue up to $5,000,000 worth of unregistered securities to 35 unsophisticated investors plus any number of "accredited investors." Generally, an "accredited investor" is an individual with a net worth of at least a $1,000,000 (primary home excluded) or an annual income of over $200,000 ($300,000 for a married couple) for the last two years. The definition also includes: banks and investment companies; private development companies; corporations, partnerships and trusts with assets over $5 million; and company insiders (officers, directors, and promoters). There are a number of required disclosures if any securities are sold to non-accredited investors. Advertising and general solicitations are prohibited. The securities are "restricted securities" and may not be readily resold. The company must comply with the securities laws of each state in which a person who buys the security is a resident, and usually must file a notice with that state's commissioner of corporations or similar official. Any person who acquires a security in a Rule 505 offering should sign an appropriate investment agreement. The company must file a Form D with the SEC within 15 days after the first sale.

Rule 506 Exemption

Rule 506 is the most popular registration exemption because there are no dollar limitations and (this is the big one) an exemption under 506 preempts all state securities law registration requirements. This can save a great deal of time, hassle or expense for the company that intends to raise money from investors in various states. Under Rule 506, there can be any number of accredited investors and up to 35 non-accredited investors if, and only if, each non-accredited investor (or an authorized representative) has knowledge and experience in financial and business matters and is capable of evaluating the risks of the investment. Historically, all advertising and general solicitations were prohibited under 506, but the JOBS Act of 2012 (discussed below) now permits general solicitation of accredited investors in a 506 offering if all the purchasers in the offering are accredited investors and reasonable steps are taken to ensure the accredited investor status of all investors. The company must file a form D with the SEC and with the corporation's commissioner in each state where stock is sold. Any person who buys stock in a Rule 506 offering should sign an appropriate investment agreement confirming that he or she is buying the stock for investment purposes, that there are serious restrictions on the resale of the stock, and that no attempt will be made to resell the stock without the approval of the company.

Rule 147 Exemption[11]

Rule 147 exempts from federal registration a company that sells securities in an "intrastate offering" to residents of only one state. To qualify as an "intrastate offering," the principal office of the company must be located in the state, at least 80 percent of the company's gross revenues must be derived from operations in the state, at least 80 percent of the company's assets must be located in the state, and at least 80 percent of the proceeds realized in the offering must be used in the state. The company must comply with the state's securities laws. Any person who acquires a security should sign an appropriate investment agreement containing proof of residence.

Regulation A Offerings

Regulation A provides an exemption for public offers and sales of up to $5 million of securities in a 12-month period. It is sometimes referred to as a mini-registration. Investment companies and any company subject to the periodic reporting requirements of the Securities Exchange Act are not eligible. Regulation A requires the company to file with the Securities and Exchange Commission an offering statement containing disclosures similar to those made in a registration statement, certain exhibits, and financial statements prepared in accordance with generally accepted accounting principles (audited statements are not required). When the offering statement has been reviewed and qualified by the SEC, it must be delivered to prospective investors before any securities are sold. The company is required to file reports with the SEC detailing the securities sold and the use of proceeds from those sales. But once the offering is complete (and unlike all public companies), there are no ongoing reporting requirements. Securities sold in a Regulation A offering are unrestricted and may be transferred in a secondary market transaction. Regulation A offerings are seldom used because of the $5 million limitation and the amount of work they require.

The Jobs Act of 2012 mandated that the SEC issue rules that raise the limit for offerings under Regulation A from $5 million to $50 million and exempt Regulation A offerings from state securities laws so long as the securities are offered or sold over a national securities exchange or are sold to a "qualified purchaser" (a term the SEC will need to define). The revised Regulation A will require a company to file audited financial statements annually with the SEC, and the SEC is directed to develop rules relating to periodic disclosure by Regulation A issuers.

When implemented, these changes will take Regulation A offerings to a whole new level, offering a powerful money raising option for many companies. Proposed regulations were issued for comment in December 2013, and many believe that final regulations will be issued in 2014.

---

11. 17 C.F.R. § 240.147.

JOBS Act of 2012

On April 5, 2012, President Obama signed the Jumpstart Our Business Startups (JOBS) Act with strong bi-partisan support. The Act is intended to increase American job creation and economic growth by improving access to the public capital markets for emerging growth companies. Key provisions of the Act include the following:

• The maximum number of shareholders of record that a private company can have before it must register with the SEC as a public company was increased from 500 to 2,000, so long as fewer than 500 are non-accredited investors.

• The prohibition on general solicitation and advertising in a private offering under Rule 506 of Regulation D must be removed by the SEC. As a result, the SEC now has a rule that permits general solicitation and adverting if all the purchasers in the offering are accredited investors and reasonable steps are taken to ensure the accredited investor status of all investors.

• The SEC must adopt rules that permit "crowdfunding" activities so that entrepreneurs may raise up to $1 million from a large pool of small investors, subject to limitations based on investor income levels. (See related discussion of crowdfunding above.)

• The SEC must raise the limit for offerings under Regulation A from $5 million to $50 million and exempt Regulation A offerings from state securities laws so long as the securities are offered or sold over a national securities exchange or are sold to a "qualified purchaser" (a term the SEC will need to define). The revised Regulation A will require a company to file audited financial statements annually with the SEC, and the SEC is directed to develop rules relating to periodic disclosure by Regulation A issuers. As mentioned above, proposed regulations were issued for comment in December 2013.

• **A** category of issuer called an "emerging growth company" is created under the Act. This is a company that has under $1 billion in annual revenues. The regulatory burden on such companies is eased by permitting them to include only two years of audited financial statements and selected other information in their IPO registration statement, not requiring an auditor attestation of management's assessment of internal controls for financial reporting created under Sarbanes Oxley, and exempting them from certain other accounting requirements. Also, the Act eases offering-pending research disclosure rules, marketing communication conflict-of-interest rules, and pre-filing institutional investor communication limitations. Furthermore, an emerging growth company will be exempt from shareholder approval requirements of executive compensation

Antifraud Challenges

Beyond the registration exemptions are the anti-fraud prohibitions. Section 10(b) of the Securities Exchange Act of 1934 (the 1934 Act) prohibits "the use of a manipulative and deceptive device" in connection with the purchase or sale of any security.[12] SEC Rule 10b-5, promulgated under Section 10(b), makes it unlawful for any person, directly or indirectly in connection with the purchase and sale of a security, "to make any untrue statement of a material fact or to omit to state a material fact necessary in order to make the statements made, in the light of the circumstances under which they were made, not misleading."[13] This rule takes all dealings in securities to a higher level. The seller has an affirmative duty to accurately state material facts and to not mislead; the buyer has a solid cause of action if the seller blows it. Rule 10b-5 and its state counterparts keep our courts packed with countless disgruntled investors who believe they were unfairly deceived when things didn't go as planned.

In offerings that are exempt from registration, the tool that is used to protect against antifraud risks is the private placement memorandum ("PPM"), a carefully prepared document that provides the necessary disclosures. Items typically included in a PPM include:

- The name, address, and telephone number of the issuer
- A description and the price of the securities offered
- The amount of the offering (minimum and maximum amounts, if any)
- The plan and cost of the distribution of the securities
- An identification and description of the officers, directors, and advisers of the company
- A description of the company's business and products or services and any related technology
- A discussion of the market for the issuer's products and services and related competition
- A description of all risk factors, including those related to the company and those related to general market or economic conditions
- A description of how the proceeds realized from the offering will be used;
- A statement that neither the Securities and Exchange Commission nor any state securities commission has approved the securities or passed on the adequacy or accuracy of the disclosures in the PPM
- A statement describing how the offering price was determined
- A description of the company's present capital structure, prior offerings, and any outstanding stock plans or stock options
- An explicit warning that the company could become insolvent or bankrupt and any investment in the company could be a total loss
- Recent financial statements of the company (audit not required)

---

12. 15 U.S.C. § 78j.
13. 17 C.F.R. § 240.10b-5.

- Projections of future revenues, expenses, and profits or losses (optional)
- A description of the restrictions on the resale of the company's securities and the fact that no market now exists or may ever exist for the securities
- A disclosure of any contracts or agreements with management
- A disclosure of all significant contracts that the company has with third parties
- Copies of key documents related to the offering (legal opinions, Articles of Incorporation, etc.)
- An offer for investors to meet with management, tour the company's facilities, and ask questions.

Resale Restrictions

The Securities Act of 1933 does not provide an exemption for private resale of restricted securities acquired through a private placement. In order to qualify for the private placement exemption, there can be no immediate distribution or resell by the initial purchasers of the securities. For that reason, companies should take precautions to protect against resells. These precautions typically include confirming the investment intent of each purchaser, printing restrictive legends on the share certificates, issuing stop transfer instructions to any transfer agents, and obtaining representations in writing from each purchaser confirming that the security is being bought for his or her own account and not for resale or with a view to distribution.

There are options for a purchaser of restricted securities who desires to resell. SEC Rule 144[14] provides a non-exclusive safe harbor from registration for resales of restricted securities. Among other things, it imposes holding period and "dribble out" requirements. SEC Rule 144A[15] provides a separate safe harbor for resells to qualified institutional buyers. Also, the courts and the SEC have acknowledged an additional resale exception, known as the "Section 4(1 1/2)" exemption.[16] The SEC has characterized it as "a hybrid exemption not specifically provided for in the 1933 Act but clearly within its intended purpose" and has stated that it will apply "so long as some of the established criteria for sales under both section 4(1) and section 4(2) of the [1933] Act are satisfied."[17] Under this exemption, an investor holding restricted securities may resell the securities to another accredited investor who purchases them for his or her own account and not for distribution if the subsequent purchaser signs an appropriate investment letter and if the certificate issued bears appropriate legends for restricted securities.

---

14. 17 C.F.R. § 230.144.

15. 17 C.F.R. § 230.144A.

16. See SEC 1933 Act Release No. 33-6188 (Feb. 1, 1980) and Ackerberg v. Johnson, 892 F.2d 1328 (8th Cir. 1989).

17. SEC 1933 Act Release No. 33-6188 (Feb. 1, 1980). On this exemption, see Olander and Jacks, The Section 4 (1 1/2) Exemption – Reading Between the Lines of the Securities Act of 1933, 15 Sec. Reg. L.J. 339 (1988) and Schneider, Section 4 (1 1/2) – Private Resales of Restricted or Controlled Securities, 49 Ohio St. L.J. 501 (1988).

3. *DANGEROUS MISCONCEPTIONS*

The root cause of most trouble under the securities laws is ignorance. The client just didn't understand and didn't stop to think or ask for advice before charging ahead. There are many misconceptions that can get in the way. A challenge for the business advisor is to spot and eradicate these misconceptions before they become a problem. It's an ongoing educational effort with many business owners. Following is a brief summary of some of the most common misconceptions.

a. Big Guy Rules. Some business owners mistakenly assume that the securities laws apply only to public companies whose stock is regularly traded. It's the old "Why would the SEC want to mess with little old me?" notion. This misconception is supported by the little they read in the press (it's all focused on big companies), and the fact that none of their business owner friends have ever had to deal with the SEC. Although many securities law issues are uniquely directed at public companies and SEC efforts are focused on the public markets, the securities laws extend to any private security transaction between a company and individual investors. Size is not a prerequisite for Rule 10b-5. For most privately owned businesses, the fear is not a call from the SEC; it's a letter from a hungry plaintiff's lawyer who, armed with 10b-5 and a set of ugly facts, is making demands on behalf of unhappy investors at the worst possible time.

b. This Ain't a Security. The misconception is that the securities laws apply only to stocks. The term "security" is broadly defined in the 1933 Act to include, among other things, any note, bond, evidence of indebtedness, certificate of interest or participation in any profit-sharing agreement, and investment contract.[18] The Supreme Court has held that a "security" exists whenever money is invested in a common enterprise with profits to come solely from the efforts of others.[19] Applying this broad definition, courts have found a "security" in investment contracts involving worm farms, boats, silver foxes, oyster beds, vending machines, parking meters, cemetery plots, exotic trees, vineyards, fig orchards, chinchillas, beavers and more.[20] A flag should surface whenever a client claims or suggests that money can be raised by offering something that is ***not*** a "security."

c. The Safe, Dumb, Poor Crowd. Some mistakenly believe that it is "safer" to target unsophisticated investors who don't know the law and lack the means or the will to fight back if things go wrong. Plus, this group is "easier" because they don't know enough to ask the tough questions – that is, they can be fooled. This is dangerous thinking for a number of reasons. First, the most important registration exemption requires that the investors be accredited investors[21] or be non-accredited investors who are sophisticated in financial

18. 15 U.S.C. § 77b(1).

19. S.E.C. v. W.J. Howey Co., 328 U.S. 293 (1946).

20. See 2 L. Loss & J. Seligman, Securities Regulation (3rd ed. 1989-93) pp. 948-956.

21. Individuals are considered accredited investors if they have a net worth that exceeds $1 million (primary residence excluded) or an annual income of over $200,000 ($300,000 if married) for the most recent two years preceding the securities purchase. 15 U.S.C. § 77b(15) and 17 C.F.R. § 230.501(a).

affairs or have representatives who possess such sophistication.[22] Second, the company loses the opportunity to bring in savvy investors who may contribute their wisdom and experience in addition to their money. Third (and this is the crux), besides just being a bad thing to do, the whole purpose of the securities laws is to protect the naive and uninformed from those who peddle intangible investments that promise riches. The dumb, poor investors may lack the capacity to evaluate what is being promised; but after things go bad, it doesn't take much to find an aggressive lawyer who is willing to spec the case against a contingent fee because, given the undisputed limitations of the plaintiffs, it's a slam dunk. Smart business owners generally limit their offers to accredited investors who have experience in financial and investment matters and who can afford the loss of their investment. In rare instances, they might consider a non-accredited individual, but only if that individual is sophisticated in financial matters and is investing a sum that he or she can afford to lose.

d. Only "Really Important" Stuff. The misconception is that only the "really important" information has to be disclosed because Rule 10b-5 speaks in terms of "material facts." Often this misconception is aggravated by the notion that the important information is the bottom-line conclusions that support the business plan. So, they reason, there's no need to sweat details that may complicate the money raising effort. The determination of a "material" fact within the meaning of Rule 10b–5 "depends on the significance the reasonable investor would place on the withheld or misrepresented information."[23] The "material" standard will be met if the misrepresentation or omission "would have been viewed by a reasonable investor as having significantly altered the 'total mix' of information made available."[24] It's a very broad definition that presents a mixed question of fact and law in most cases; it is decided as a matter of law only when reasonable minds would not differ on the issue.[25] It's a mistake to assume that the materiality requirement eliminates the need to provide details. Plus, there is another hard reality that always supports the conclusion that more, not less, should be disclosed. If things go bad and a significant contributing factor to the failure was not disclosed up front, it may be impossible, looking back, to claim that that factor was not material and worthy of disclosure. The wisest and safest approach is to lay out all known risk factors and the related details.

e. My Successes Say It All. Many business owners focus only on past successes when talking track record. Failures or disappointments are forgotten or "amended" to look like successes. The misconception is that it is appropriate to paint the best possible track record, even when it involves a little fudging or selective editing. A key executive's track record is important to any investor. What one has done in the past often is the best indicator of what might happen in the future. If things go bad, an investor who first learns after the fact that this was not the key person's first failure may be shocked into action. The challenge

---

22. The all-important Rule 506 exemption requires that nonaccredited investors be sophisticated investors. 17 C.F.R. § 230.506.

23. Basic Inc. v. Levinson, 485 U.S. 224, 240 (1988).

24. TSC Industries, Inc. v. Northway, Inc., 426 U.S. 438, 449 (1976).

25. Id. at 450.

is to accurately and fairly summarize the background and experiences, both good and bad, of the key players in a way that suggests that they now possess the skills and abilities to successfully manage the proposed venture.

f. Good Advertising Is The Key. Some mistakenly assume that fundraising is all about advertising. They start a makeshift advertising campaign, only to learn that they have killed some of their best shots at a registration exemption. Although the JOBS Act of 2012 has opened up general solicitation and advertising in select Rule 506 offerings and presumably the crowdfunding world, usually the word of an exempt offering must be spread through friends, relatives and business associates.

g. Safety in Numbers. The misconception is that it is safer to have a large number of small investors, rather than one or two big players. It's based on the false assumption that a small investor will be more inclined to swallow a loss and less inclined to fight back. It ignores some basic realities. First, the size of one's investment does not govern the capacity to stomach a loss; many large players are better equipped to understand and suck up a loss than most small investors who have had unrealistic expectations from the get-go and can't afford any loss. Second, it ignores the capacity of many voices to stir each other up and to share the expense and burden of hiring a gladiator to fight their cause. Third, it ignores the burden, often horrendous, of having to respond to multiple ongoing inquiries all along the way from nervous, uninformed investors who just want to hear that all will pay off "as promised" and that there are "no problems." Finally, it ignores the significant value of binding a few key players to the effort. Inviting them into the inner circle gives the business the benefit of their advice and counsel and often eliminates any securities law exposure because they see it all, hear it all, and are part of it all.

h. Dodge the Downside. Some wrongfully assume that there is no need to talk about the potential of failure when trying to raise money. They figure that everyone knows there is risk. So why talk about it? The truth is that, from a securities law perspective, it is essential to spell out the risk factors in writing for any prospective investor. Nothing is more material than those factors that may potentially cause the business to fail. Thought should be given to risk factors that are specific to the business (competition, market condition changes, supply access, technology changes, skilled labor needs, capital and liquidity challenges, etc.) and the potential impact that general risks (e.g., interest rate increases) may have on the business. Often this is one of the most difficult tasks for business owners to embrace. As the risk factor list is committed to black and white, they begin to fear that everyone will be "spooked away." It helps to remind them that seasoned players are used to seeing such lists, and that they have all made money in ventures that started out with risk factor lists that were just as ugly as the one being created.

i. Projections Are Just Projections. The misconception is that since projections, by their very nature, are speculative, they create an opportunity to strengthen the money raising effort by painting the rosiest possible picture of how things might play out. It's little wonder that such projections have been the driving force behind many securities law claims. The use of projections should be handled carefully. They should not be viewed as an opportunity to oversell, but rather as a means of illustrating the business' potential under a defined set of reasonable assumptions. If overdone, they may create unrealistic false expectations that cause an otherwise good performance to disappoint or, worse yet, fuel a legal dispute when things turn sour. There are a few important precautions that can be taken. First, make certain that the projections are based on reasonable assumptions that are spelled out. The operative word here is "reasonable;" the assumptions should not reflect an ideal, unrealistic set of conditions. Second, the predictions should be accompanied by a cautionary statement that identifies the predictions as forward-looking statements, warns that conditions and risks could cause actual results to differ substantially from the projections, and lists specific risks and conditions that may have such an effect. The effort may allow the company, if necessary, to rely on the "bespeaks caution doctrine" that provides a defense against allegations of false and misleading forward-looking statements when such precautionary language has been used.[26]

j. "Puffing" Works. Some business owners believe that the key to "legal money raising" is "puffing" – making vague overstated generalizations that get potential investors excited. Often they have heard about cases where defendants escaped securities law liability because the court concluded that the alleged misrepresentations were nothing more than "obviously immaterial puffery."[27] Statements like "our fundamentals are strong," "our product is revolutionary and could change the world," and "the stock is red hot" have been dismissed as immaterial puffing.[28] The problem is when it goes too far. What may appear as harmless puffing can trigger liability under the securities laws if the speaker had no reasonable basis for making the statement. The court will examine whether the speaker really believed that the statement was accurate and had a factual or historical basis for that belief.[29] There is some room for harmless puffing, but in no sense is it a free pass without limits.

k. Let 'Em Be. The misconception is that investors, once they've bought in, should be free to deal with their stock as they see fit. As described above, the private offering exemption requires that the investors not be used as a device to disseminate the stock to a broader audience and thereby convert what would otherwise be a private offering into a public offering. This important factor, coupled with the obvious antifraud challenges, gives the company a huge interest in what the investors do with their stock. For this reason, as described above, it is common practice to ascertain the investment intentions of purchasers up front, to place resale restrictive legends on share certificates, to issue stop transfer

---

26. See, e.g., In re Worlds of Wonder Sec. Litig., 35 F.3d 1407 (9th Cir. 1994); Gasner v. Board of Supervisors, 103 F.3d 351 (4th Cir. 1996); and Nadoff v. Duane Reade, Inc., 107 Fed. Appx. 250 (2d Cir. 2004).

27. See, e.g., Grossman v. Novell, Inc., 120 F.3d 1112 (10th Cir. 1997); Raab v. General Physics Corp., 4 F.3d 286 (4th Cir. 1993); and Helwig v. Vencor, Inc. 210 F.3d 612 (6th Cir. 2000).

28. Rosenzweig v. Azurix Corp., 332 F.3d 854 (5th Cir. 2003); Vosgerichian v. Commodore Int'l, 832 F.Supp. 909 (E.D. Pa. 1993); Newman v. Rothschild, 651 F.Supp. 160 (S.D.N.Y. 1986).

29. See, e.g., Kline v. First Western Government Sec., 24 F.3d 480 (3d Cir. 1994), cert. denied 513 U.S. 1032 (1994) and In re Allaire Corp. Secs. Litig., 224 F.Supp.2d 319 (D. Mass. 2002).

instructions to those who control the stock register, and to obtain written representations from all purchasers that they are acquiring the security for their own account and not for resale or with a view to distribute the stock.

l. Cashing In Is the Easy Part. This misconception surfaces when everybody just assumes that an acceptable exit strategy will present itself at the most opportune time. Often a business plan is developed with little or no thought given to the ultimate strategy that will be used to realize a return for the owners of the business. The organizers assume if things work out and the business becomes profitable, an opportunity will surface to cash in at the best time. No serious effort is made to research the practicality and possibility of specific exit scenarios. The details of operating the business and generating revenues have been thought through, but the broader picture is left to fuzzy notions of market options and base ignorance. This gets scary when an organizer with little knowledge starts speculating on return strategies with a potential investor who has even less knowledge. The organizer often has no specific knowledge regarding the appetite others may have for the business. The sad reality is that many business owner/managers are shocked and disappointed to discover that there is little or no market for their business. This disappointment can be magnified many times for the outside investor who draws no compensation and has assumed all along that a big payday was within reach. And then there are the baseless, overstated "going public" expectations. This sounds great to the naive investor, even though the organizer has no real clue as to what a public offering entails or requires. A primary challenge for many business owners is to develop a realistic expectation of the business' capacity to create returns for the owners. Seasoned entrepreneurs do this instinctively. Experience has taught them to always have their eye on the big picture and the entire life cycle of the business. Plus, they understand that conditions can change; what is solid and profitable today can be weak and vulnerable tomorrow. So timing is often the key when it comes to cashing in the marbles. Less experienced owners, particularly those who are wrapped up in their first effort, often fail to see, let alone focus on, the broader picture and never develop such realistic expectations for themselves and those who have entrusted them with their money. As a result, they end up in a situation where they can only disappoint.

STUDENT PROBLEM 7-3

For the past three years, Judy has been the sole owner and CEO of a corporation that manufactures and distributes a relatively expensive line of fashion baby apparel, known as “Plum,” that is progressively “catching on” in more countries. The business has grown steadily, and Judy is convinced that it's time to "shoot for the stars." To make this happen, she needs $2 million of equity capital and an expanded bank line of credit that will be "doable without personal guarantees" based on the past record of the business and the new equity. Lucy is willing to give up 45 percent of the company’s equity to secure the needed capital.

Judy’s mother-in-law Diane, a wealthy divorced socialite who adores Judy and her line, is convinced that she can "rustle up the money" from her wealthy friends who live in various states and are "always looking for a great ground-floor deal." Judy is impressed with Diane's offer, but has a number of questions that have surfaced from her preliminary Internet reading. Please answer:

1. What securities law registration exemption will work best for Judy's company? What additional facts, if any, do you need to answer this question for Judy?

2. Is the wealth of those who might invest in Judy's company a factor to consider?

3. Can Judy use social media (e.g., Facebook) to prospect for potential investors?

4. Might equity crowdfunding be a partial or complete answer for Judy's company?

5. Does Judy need to concern herself with antifraud risks if she qualifies for a registration exemption? If so, how does she protect herself?

6. What is the best way to deal with investors who want to sell their investment in the company?

CHAPTER 8

BUSINESS ENTERPRISE TAXATION

A. THE WORLD TAX STAGE

Business owners need to be smart with taxes. The objective is to minimize government bites, consistent with other objectives, and to avoid costly planning blunders.

Smart tax planning requires more than just strategizing against a static set of rules. Changes in the rules must be anticipated and factored in. Tax planning has always favored those who can wisely anticipate a moving target. And there is little question that today, perhaps more than ever, the target is moving fast, and its path is hard to predict.

1. CORPORATE TAXES AROUND THE GLOBE

The importance of business and corporate taxes throughout the world cannot be overstated. They directly affect the stability and strength of nations and communities, the scope and quality of governmental services, and the growth and development of economies that provide jobs and markets for goods and services.

While many will forever debate the virtues and vices of the progressive globalization of the world's economy, it has triggered three tax consequences that no one can reasonably doubt. First, corporate tax rates generally have been descending as the world stage has shrunk and nations compete for capital and business opportunities to strengthen their economies, boost income levels, and broaden their tax bases. Second, while each nation is free to develop its own tax structure and rates, the impacts of a nation's tax changes can reach far beyond its borders as businesses around the globe engage in strategic, multinational tax planning to maximize after-tax yields for their shareholders. And third, movements by other nations have pushed the United States to the top of the list of developed countries with the highest corporate tax rates. Although many question the seriousness of the United States occupying this top slot, the unenviable position itself and a host of other factors, not the least of which is a sluggish economy for over five years, has prompted cries for lower corporate tax rates from voices on both sides of the political aisle. Many believe that lower U.S. corporate tax rates are inevitable.

The OECD. The Organization for Economic Co-operation and Development (OECD) is an international economic organization that includes 34 member countries. Originally founded in 1961 and headquartered in Paris, the OECD seeks to promote economic progress and world trade by emphasizing the values of democracy and free market forces and providing a mechanism for nations to share policy experiences, tackle common problems, identify best practices, and coordinate domestic and international policies. Member nations include the United States, the United Kingdom, Canada, Australia, many European countries (Germany, Switzerland, France, Italy, Portugal, Spain, and others), emerging countries (Chile, Turkey and Mexico), and others. Also, the OECD prides itself in working with major and emerging non-member countries, such as China, India, Brazil and economies developing in Africa, Asia, Latin America and the Caribbean. Taxes and tax policy are important considerations for OECD members. OECD members are forever being benchmarked against one another in evaluating tax trends, tax rates, and the breadth of tax bases.

Corporate Tax Rates. Corporate tax rates throughout the world have consistently dropped over the past 30 years. In 1981, the average corporate tax rate of OECD countries was 47.4 percent. That average dropped to 41 percent by 1990, to 32.6 percent by 2000, and to 25.5 percent by 2013. The policy decisions of key countries to lower their corporate tax rates have been significant. A few examples: the United Kingdom dropped its corporate rates from 33 percent in 1993 to 23 percent in 2013; Canada's corporate rates dropped from 42.6 percent to 26.1 percent over the past 20 years; Israel's corporate rates declined from 36 percent to 25 percent from 2000 to 2013; Italy's corporate rates declined from 52.2 percent in 1993 to 27.5 percent in 2013; Germany's corporate rates plummeted from 56.5 percent to 30.2 percent over the past 20 years.[1]

The global push for lower corporate rates has been fueled by competition for investment capital and business activity and a basic, proven realization that any reduction in government coffers directly attributable to lower corporate rates will be offset many times by increased revenues attributable to more capital and a stronger and broader economic base.

The corporate tax rate history of the United States has been very different than that of other countries. In 1993, the official OECD corporate tax rate of the United States (considering both the federal rate of 35 percent and state corporate income tax rates) was 39.8 percent. At that time, the U.S. corporate rate sat near the middle of the OECD pack, with over one-third of the OECD member countries having a corporate tax rate above the U.S. rate, and only three countries having a corporate rate that was at 9 percent or more below the U.S rate. As other countries have reduced their corporate rates over the past 20 years, the U.S. rate has remained constant. In 2013, the U.S. corporate rate was 39.1 percent, the highest of all OECD countries, nearly 14 percent higher than the average corporate rate of OECD countries, and more than nine percentage points higher than 29 of the other 33 OECD countries.[2]

---

1. Tax Foundation, OECD Corporate Income Tax Rates, 1981-2013, December 13, 2013.
2. Id.

Corporate Effective Tax Rates. Often the rate of income taxes actually paid by a corporation is less than the statutory corporate rate. For example, in Chapter 2 we saw that Caterpillar Inc.'s provision for income taxes in 2012 equaled 30.7 percent of its consolidated pretax net income. The difference between this percentage and the 35 percent U.S. corporate tax rate was principally attributable to non-US subsidiaries of Caterpillar that were subject to the lower rates of other countries. The term used to describe the tax rate actually paid by a corporation is the corporate effective tax rate. This effective rate often is impacted by a host of factors (often referred to as "corporate loopholes"), including deferring or eliminating taxes on controlled foreign corporations by stockpiling profits offshore, using accelerated depreciation deductions for machinery and equipment, generating tax-free interest on state and local bonds, benefiting from special deductions for domestic manufacturing, and claiming tax credits for research and development, alcohol-based fuel production, foreign taxes paid, and more. The corporate average effective tax rate (AETR) for a given country, while accepted as a conventional and useful concept, can vary widely among countries and vary significantly from year to year based on differences in the tax base that is the denominator of the equation.

Marginal Effective Tax Rates. Closely related to the AETR is the marginal effective tax rate (METR), a widely accepted analytical tool for measuring a country's corporate tax impacts on investment and capital allocation decisions. This tool is based on the premises that the increased capital mobility across borders associated with globalization enhances the relevance of tax competitiveness, and that a country's competitiveness is hurt by taxation that undermines productivity through investment. The METR compares the pre-tax rate of return on capital with the after-tax rate of return on capital for the relevant market. If the former is 22 percent and the later 11 percent, the METR is 50 percent. A high METR is indicative of a country's capital-repressive tax structure. The United States has had the highest METR of all OECD countries since 2007 by a relatively wide margin. In 2013, the METR rate of the United States was 35.3 percent, far higher than the 19.6 percent MRTR average of all OECD countries and the METR rates for other key countries: UK - 25.9 percent; Germany - 24.4 percent; Switzerland - 17.5 percent; Australia - 25.9 percent; Canada - 18.6 percent; Israel - 15 percent.[3]

Corporate Tax Contribution to Total U.S. Tax Burden. Although the U.S. corporate income tax rate and U.S. METR have topped for years the rates of all OECD countries, many are disturbed by the relatively small percentage of total U.S. taxes that come from corporate income taxes. For example, in 2013 U.S. corporate income tax collections totaled $273.5 billion, only 9.8 percent of the $2.774 trillion in total U.S. tax collections and enough to fund federal spending for only about 28 days. Individuals' income taxes and payroll and self-employment taxes exceeded by many times total corporate tax collections. A review of U.S. tax collections by source over the past 40 years confirms that 2013 was not an aberrational year for corporate income tax collections. Although the percentage of total U.S. tax collections attributable to corporate income taxes

3. Tax Foundation, The U.S. Corporate Effective Tax Rate: Myth and the Fact, February 6, 2014.

was higher in select years (e.g., 15.4 percent in 1977 and 14.41 percent in 2007), the corporate tax contribution percentage has hovered in the 9 to 11 percent range for many years and stretches of years, and there is nothing to suggest that the corporate contribution percentage will increase in the future.[4]

There are various reasons to explain this relatively low corporate income tax contribution percentage. More corporations are reducing their U.S. tax burden by taking advantage of corporate tax breaks and diversifying their operations through foreign controlled corporations that are subject to lower tax rates imposed by other countries. As explained below, many closely held businesses are able to avoid all corporate taxes by electing to be taxed as an S corporation or by operating as a limited liability company or partnership that is taxed as a partnership. Such a pass-through entity pays no entity-level taxes; its income is passed through and taxed directly to the owners of the business. And there are numerous corporations that effectively eliminate or reduce to very low levels their corporate income taxes by bailing out their earnings to owners of the business through compensation and other tax-deductible payments.

2. *ROLE AND CHALLENGES OF TRANSFER PRICING*

For the past 80 years, countries have incorporated transfer pricing adjustments into their tax structures to curb the abuse of intercompany prices by multinational companies. If Company A, a U.S. company subject to a 35 percent tax rate, provides goods or services to Company B, a U.K. company subject to a 23 percent rate, overall taxes will be reduced as the prices that A charges B are lowered. If Companies A and B are unrelated, market forces will dictate the prices between the entities as both companies seek to maximize their respective profits. But if Companies A and B are related entities owned by the same parties, market forces cease to be relevant and often the emphasis shifts to tax savings through strategic intercompany pricing. Hence, the need for transfer pricing rules.

The current, comprehensive transfer pricing rules can be traced to a white pager published by the United States that ultimately led to the adoption of detailed regulations in 1994, primarily under Section 482 of the Internal Revenue Code. Section 482 is an ominous provision that gives the Internal Revenue Service authority to "distribute, apportion, or allocate gross income, deductions, credits or allowances between and among" commonly controlled business interests "whenever necessary to prevent evasion of taxes or clearly to reflect the income" of any such businesses. In 1995, the OECD issued a draft of transfer pricing guidelines, which were expanded in 1996 and have been adopted by many countries, including European Union countries, with little or no modification.

The U.S. transfer pricing regulations and the OECD transfer pricing guidelines are similar in many respects. Members of a commonly controlled enterprise may set their own prices, but such prices may be adjusted by a taxing

4. Congressional Budget Office, The Budget and Economic Outlook: 2014 to 2024, February 4, 2014.

authority to conform to an arm's-length standard. Some countries, including the United States and Canada, impose special related-party reporting requirements to facilitate the review and adjustment process. As for the arm's-length standard determination, a price will meet this standard if falls within a range of prices that an independent buyer would pay an independent seller for an identical item under identical terms and conditions, where neither is under any compulsion to act. U.S. regulations and the OECD guidelines specify several methods for testing prices, establish standards for comparing third-party transactions, permit adjustments to a midpoint of an arm's-length range, and do not require a showing of an intent to avoid or evade taxes.

Tax authorities usually examine prices actually charged between related parties by comparison testing of such prices to comparable prices charged among unrelated parties. Some countries mandate a specific method of testing prices, but U.S. regulations and the OECD guidelines use a "best method" rule, which requires use of the method that produces the most reliable measure of arm's-length results. Factors that impact the best method determination are the reliability of available data and assumptions under the method, the comparability of tested and independent items, and validation of the method's results by the use of other methods.

Countries often impose significant transfer pricing penalties to encourage and force taxpayers to make reasonable efforts to determine and document the arm's-length character of their intercompany transfer prices. For example, the United States imposes a 20-percent non-deductible transactional penalty on a tax underpayment if a transfer price is 200 percent or more, or 50 percent or less, than the arm's-length price, and the penalty jumps to 40 percent if the transfer price is 400 percent or more, or 25 percent or less, than the arm's-length price.[5] In addition to these individual transaction penalties, U.S. statutes provide that a series of transactions may trigger a 20-percent net adjustment penalty if the net pricing adjustment exceeds the lesser of $5 million or 10 percent of gross receipts, and the penalty is hiked to 40 percent if the net transfer pricing adjustment exceeds $20 million or 20 percent of gross receipts. These penalties can be avoided only if the taxpayer demonstrates a reasonable basis for believing that its transfer pricing would produce arm's-length results and that appropriate documentation supporting such a belief existed at the time the relevant tax return was filed and is tendered to the IRS within 30 days of a request.[6]

B. U.S. BUSINESS ENTITY TAX CONCEPTS

1. *CORPORATION TAX BASICS – Q&AS*

Q.1 What is a C corporation?

A C corporation is a regular corporation that pays its own taxes. It is a creature of state law, is recognized as a separate taxable entity, and is governed

5. See, generally, IRC § 6662(e), (h) and Treas. Reg. 1.6662-6(b).
6. Id.

by the provisions of subchapter C of the Internal Revenue Code. Any corporation that does not properly elect to be taxed as an S corporation will be taxed as a C corporation.

Q.2 What tax rates do C corporations pay?

The first $50,000 of a C corporation's taxable income each year is subject to a favorable 15 percent tax rate. The rate jumps to 25 percent on the next $25,000 of taxable income. Thus, the overall rate on the first $75,000 of taxable income is an attractive 18.33 percent, far less than the personal marginal rate applicable to most successful business owners. Beyond $75,000, the rate advantage disappears as the marginal rate jumps to 34 percent. Plus, if the corporation's income exceeds $100,000, the rate "bubbles" an additional 5 percent on taxable income over $100,000 until any rate savings on the first $75,000 is lost. The impact of this 5 percent "bubble" is that any C corporation with a taxable income of $335,000 or more will pay a rate of at least 34 percent from dollar one. Earnings of a C corporation in excess of $10 million are taxed at 35 percent, and a 3 percent "bubble" applies to C corporation earnings in excess of $15 million until the rate applicable to all income is 35 percent.[7]

There are no rate breaks for a professional service organization that is taxed as a C corporation; it is subject to a flat 35 percent rate from dollar one.[8]

Q.3 What is the C corporation double tax structure?

The biggest negative of a C corporation is the double tax structure – a corporate level tax and a shareholder level tax. It surfaces whenever a dividend is paid or is deemed to have been paid. But the grief of the double tax structure is not limited to dividends; it kicks in whenever the assets of the business are sold and the proceeds distributed. It's all a result of the inherent double tax structure of a C corporation.

Q.4 What are the federal tax rates that shareholders must pay on dividends received from a C corporation?

The economic stimulus package of 2003 resulted in a compromise that reduced the maximum tax rate on "qualifying corporate dividends" paid to non-corporate shareholders to 15 percent (5 percent for low-income shareholders otherwise subject to maximum marginal rates of 15 percent or less).[9] These reduced rates applied to all dividends received from January 1, 2003 to December 31, 2012. The American Taxpayer Relief Act of 2012 (the "fiscal cliff" legislation signed into law during the final days of 2012)[10] increased this low dividend rate to 20 percent starting in 2013 for couples with taxable incomes in excess of $450,000 and individuals with taxable incomes in excess of $400,000. Plus, in 2013, the 3.8 percent Medicare tax kicked in on interest, dividends, capital gains, and other "net investment income" to the extent that this income, when added to the taxpayer's other modified adjusted gross income,

7. I.R.C. § 11(b)(1).
8. I.R.C. § 11(b)(2).
9. I.R.C. § 1(h)11(b).
10. Section 102 of the American Taxpayer Relief Act of 2012.

exceeds $200,000 in the case of unmarried individuals, $250,000 in the case of married individuals filing jointly, and $125,000 in the case of married individuals filing separately.

The net result is that a couple with an adjusted income of less than $250,000 or a single person with an adjusted gross income of less than $200,000 will continue to pay the pre-2013 dividend rates (a maximum of 15 percent).[11] Couples or individuals with higher incomes will pay a combined income and Medicare dividend rate of either 18.8 percent or 23.8 percent, depending on whether the new $450,000 or $400,000 thresholds are exceeded.

Q.5 How are C corporation dividends paid to C corporation shareholders taxed?

There is an attractive income tax deduction for dividends paid by one C corporation to another C corporation. The purpose of the deduction is to eliminate the potential of a triple tax on corporate earnings – one at the operating C corporation level, a second at the corporate shareholder level, and a third at the individual shareholder level. The deduction is at least 70 percent of the dividend paid to a C corporation shareholder, and increases to 80 percent for corporate shareholders who own 20 percent of the operating entity's stock and 100 percent for members of an affiliated group who own at least 80 percent of the operating company's stock.[12]

Q.6 How are tax losses of a C corporation treated?

Losses sustained by a C corporation are trapped inside the corporation. They may be carried backward or forward, but they will never be passed through to the shareholders.

Q.7 How much flexibility does a C corporation have in selecting a tax year?

A great deal. A C corporation may adopt any fiscal year to ease its accounting and administrative burdens and to maximize tax deferral planning.[13]

Q.8 Can a C corporation combine with other corporations on a tax-free basis?

Yes. A C corporation may participate in a tax-free reorganization with other corporate entities. It's possible for corporations to combine through mergers, stock-for-stock transactions, and assets-for-stock transactions on terms that eliminate all corporate and shareholder-level taxes.[14] This opportunity often is the key to the ultimate payday for those private business owners who cash in by "selling" their business to a public corporation. Cast as a reorganization, the transaction allows the acquiring entity to fund the acquisition with its own stock (little or no cash required) and enables the selling owners to walk with highly liquid, publicly traded securities and no tax bills until the securities are sold.

---

11. I.R.C. § 1411.
12. I.R.C. § 243(a) & (c).
13. See generally I.R.C. § 441.
14. I.R.C. §§ 368, 354, 361.

Q.9 How is the gain recognized on the sale of C corporation stock taxed?

The stock of a C corporation is a capital asset that qualifies for long-term capital gain treatment if sold after being held for more than one year.[15] The problem for planning purposes is that it is usually difficult, if not impossible, to accurately predict when stock may be sold and even more difficult to speculate on what the state of the long-term capital gains break will be at that time. Too often, planning is based on the assumption that the status quo will remain the status quo. History, even very recent history, confirms the fallacy of this assumption with respect to the capital gains tax. Just over the past few decades, we have seen the gap between ordinary and capital gains rates completely eliminated, narrowed to levels that were not compelling for planning purposes, and, as now, widened to levels that get everyone excited.

Q.10 What is the Section 1045 small business stock rollover deferral option?

Section 1045 of the Internal Revenue Code permits a non-corporate shareholder to defer the recognition of gain on the disposition of qualified small business stock held for more than six months by investing the proceeds into the stock of another qualified small business within 60 days of the sale.[16] This perk can excite the entrepreneur who is in the business of moving money from one deal to the next or the shareholder who has a falling out with his or her co-shareholders and wants to exit for another opportunity.

Q.11 How is a loss recognized on the sale of C corporation stock treated for tax purposes?

Generally, any such loss is subject to all the limitations of capital losses. Thus, the loss usually is limited to offsetting capital gains or being recognized over time at a maximum pace of $3,000 a year.

There is a limited exception under Section 1244 of the Code. This exception grants individuals and partnerships ordinary loss treatment (as opposed to the less favorable capital loss treatment) on losses recognized on the sale or exchange of common or preferred stock of a "small business corporation" (generally defined as a corporation whose aggregate contributions to capital and paid-in surplus do not exceed $1 million). In order to qualify, the shareholder must be the original issuee of the stock and the stock must have been issued for money or property (services do not count).[17] This benefit often sounds better than it really is because the ordinary loss in any single year (usually the year of sale) is limited to $50,000 ($100,000 for married couples). This serious dollar limitation, together with the fact that bailout loss treatment is not an exciting topic during the start-up planning of any business, usually results in this perk

15. I.R.C. §§ 1221(a), 1222(3).

16. Section 1045 incorporates the Section 1202(c) definition of "small business stock," which generally requires that the stock have been issued to the original issuee after the effective date of the Revenue Reconciliation Act of 1993 by a C corporation that actively conducts a trade or business and that has gross assets of $50 million or less at the time the stock is issued. I.R.C. § 1202(c), (d) & (e).

17. I.R.C. § 1244.

having no impact in the planning process.

Q.12 May C corporation shareholders who are also employees participate in a company's employee benefit programs?

Yes. A shareholder of a C corporation who is also an employee may participate in all employee benefit plans and receive the associated tax benefits. Such plans typically include group term life insurance, medical and dental reimbursement plans, section 125 cafeteria plans, dependent care assistance programs, and qualified transportation reimbursement plans. Partners and most S corporation shareholder/employees (those who own more than 2 percent of the outstanding stock) are not eligible for such the tax benefits.[18]

Q.13 May multiple C corporations that are commonly controlled file as a single entity for federal income tax purposes?

Yes. Often it is advantageous to use multiple corporations to conduct the operations of an expanding business. Multiple entities can reduce liability exposures, regulatory hassles, and employee challenges as the operations diversify and expand into multiple states and foreign countries. While there may be compelling business reasons for the use of multiple entities, business owners often prefer that all of the entities be treated as a single entity for tax purposes in order to simplify tax compliance, eliminate tax issues on transactions between the entities, and facilitate the netting of profits and losses for tax purposes. This is permitted under the consolidated return provisions of the Code.[19] The key is that the entities constitute an "affiliated group," which generally means that their common ownership must extend to 80 percent of the total voting power and 80 percent of the total stock value of each entity included in the group.[20]

Q.14 Is the tax basis of the stock owned by a C corporation shareholder impacted by the corporation's retention and reinvestment of its earnings?

No. The basis of a shareholder's stock in a C corporation is not affected by the entity's income or losses. This can have a profound impact in a situation where a profitable C corporation has accumulated substantial earnings. Assume, for example, that XYZ Inc. has always had a single shareholder, Linda, who purchased her stock for $100,000, and that the company has accumulated $2 million of earnings over the past 10 years. Linda's stock basis at the end of year 10 is still $100,000. In contrast, if XYZ Inc. had been taxed as an S corporation or a partnership from day one, Linda's basis at the end of year 10 would have grown to $2.1 million.[21] On a sale, the difference would be a capital gains hit on $2 million. This basis step-up may be a compelling planning consideration in many situations.

---

18. The benefits are available only to "employees," a status that partners can never obtain. Although S corporation shareholders may clearly qualify as "employees," Section 1372 provides that, for fringe benefit purposes, the S corporation will be treated as a partnership and any shareholder owning more than 2 percent of the stock will be treated as a partner.

19. See generally I.R.C. §§ 1501-1504.

20. I.R.C. § 1504(a).

21. I.R.C. § 1367(a). Partners experience the same basis adjustment for accumulated earnings under I.R.C. § 705(a).

Q.15 Are C corporations subject to an alternative minimum tax?

Large C corporations are subject to an alternative minimum tax. There are blanket exceptions for a company's first year of operation, for any company with average annual gross receipts of not more than $5 million during its first three years, and for any company with average annual gross receipts of not more than $7.5 million during any three-year period thereafter.[22] The alternative minimum tax applies only to the extent it exceeds the corporation's regular income tax liability. The tax is calculated by applying a flat 20 percent rate to the excess of the corporation's alternative minimum taxable income (AMTI) over a $40,000 exemption.[23] AMTI is defined to include the corporation's taxable income, increased by a host of tax preference items and adjustments designed to reduce certain timing benefits (i.e., accelerated cost recovery deductions) of the regular corporate tax.[24] The greatest impact in recent years has been the expansion of AMTI to include an amount which, roughly speaking, is designed to equal 75 percent of the excess of the corporation's true book earnings over its taxable income.[25]

Q.16 What are the disguised dividend traps of a C corporation?

Any payment from a C corporation to a shareholder may be scrutinized by the Service to see if the payment constitutes a disguised dividend. What's at stake is a deduction at the corporate level and an imputed taxable dividend at the shareholder level. Common examples of disguised dividends include excessive compensation payments to shareholder/employees or family members,[26] personal shareholder expenses that are paid and deducted as business expenses by the corporation,[27] interest payments on excessive shareholder debt that is reclassified as equity,[28] excess rental payments on shareholder property rented or leased to the corporation,[29] personal use of corporate assets, and bargain sales of corporate property to a shareholder.[30]

Q.17 What is the C corporation accumulated earnings trap?

The C corporation double-tax structure produces more revenue for the government when larger dividends are paid and less income is accumulated in the corporation. For this reason, the tax code imposes a penalty tax on C corporations that accumulate excessive amounts of income by not paying sufficient dividends. The tax doesn't kick in until the aggregate accumulated earnings exceed $250,000 ($150,000 in the case of certain professional service organizations).[31] And the penalty tax can be avoided completely if the

---

22. I.R.C. § 55(e).
23. I.R.C. §§ 55(b)(1)(B), 55(d)(2).
24. See generally I.R.C. § 56.
25. I.R.C. § 56(g).
26. See, e.g., Exacto Spring Corp. v. Commissioner, 196 F.3d 833 (7th Cir. 1999); Elliotts Inc. v. Commissioner, 716 F.2d 1241 (9th Cir. 1983); and Charles McCandless Tire Service v. United States, 422 F.2d 1336 (Ct. Cl. 1970).
27. See, e.g., Hood v. Commissioner, 115 T.C. 172 (2000).
28. See the related discussion Chapter 4. Also, see generally Hariton, "Essay: Distinguishing Between Equity and Debt in the New Financial Environment," 49 Tax L. Rev. 449 (1994).
29. See, e.g., International Artists, Ltd. v. Commissioner, 55 T.C. 94 (1970).
30. See, e.g., Honigman v. Commissioner, 466 F.2d 69 (6th Cir. 1972).
31. I.R.C. § 535(c).

corporation can demonstrate that it accumulated the earnings in order to meet the reasonable business needs of the corporation.[32] There is a great deal of latitude in defining the reasonable business needs. For this reason, the accumulated earnings penalty is usually a trap for the uninformed who never saw it coming.

Q.18 What is the C corporation personal holding company trap?

The personal holding company trap is a close cousin to the accumulated earnings trap. Its purpose is to prohibit C corporations from accumulating excess amounts of investment income, certain compensation payments (the incorporated movie star or other talent), and rental income (the corporate yacht scenario). Unlike the accumulated earnings tax, the personal holding company penalty cannot be avoided by documenting reasonable business needs. If the penalty becomes a threat, remedial actions include increasing compensation payments to shareholder/employees and paying dividends. Like the accumulated earnings penalty, it's a nuisance that has to be monitored in select situations.

Q.19 What is the C corporation controlled group trap?

This trap is aimed primarily at the business owner who would like to use multiple C corporations to take multiple advantage of the low C corporation tax rates, the $250,000 accumulated earnings trap threshold, or the $40,000 alternative minimum tax exemption. If multiple corporations are deemed to be part of a controlled group, they are treated as a single entity for purposes of these tax perks, and the multiple-entity benefits are gone.[33]

Section 1563 of the Internal Revenue Code defines three types of controlled groups: parent-subsidiary controlled groups, brother-sister controlled groups, and combined controlled groups.[34] The existence of this trap requires, as part of any business planning analysis, a disclosure of other C corporation interests owned by those who are going to own an interest in the new entity that is considering C corporation status.

Q.20 What is the section 482 trap?

Section 482 is an ominous provision that gives the Internal Revenue Service authority to "distribute, apportion, or allocate gross income, deductions, credits or allowances between and among" commonly controlled business interests "whenever necessary to prevent evasion of taxes or clearly to reflect the income" of any such businesses.

Although 482, by its terms, applies to any type of business organization, its application to related C corporations who do business with each other can trigger brutal double tax consequences. All business dealings between commonly controlled entities must be carefully monitored to avoid Section 482 exposure.

---

32. I.R.C. § 532 provides that the tax is applicable to any corporation that is "formed or availed of for the purpose of avoiding the income tax with respect to its shareholders..." Section 533(a) then provides that, unless the corporation can prove by a preponderance of evidence to the contrary, any accumulation of earnings and profits "beyond the reasonable needs of the business shall be determinative of the purpose to avoid the income tax..."

33. I.R.C. § 1561

34. I.R.C. § 1563(a)(3).

Q.21 What is an S corporation?

An S corporation is a hybrid whose popularity has grown in recent years. It is organized as a corporation under state law and offers corporate limited liability protections. But it is taxed as a pass-through entity under the provisions of Subchapter S of the Internal Revenue Code. These provisions are similar, but not identical, to the partnership provisions of Subchapter K. The popularity of S status is attributable primarily to three factors: (1) accumulated earnings increase the outside stock basis of the shareholders' stock; (2) an S corporation is free of any threat of a double tax on shareholder distributions or sale proceeds; and (3) S status can facilitate income shifting and passive income generation.

Q.22 Can any corporation elect to be taxed as an S corporation?

No. There are certain limitations and restrictions with an S corporation that can pose serious problems in the planning process. Not every corporation is eligible to elect S status. If a corporation has a shareholder that is a corporation, a partnership, a non-resident alien or an ineligible trust, S status is not available.[35] Banks and insurance companies cannot elect S status.[36] Also, the election cannot be made if the corporation has more than 100 shareholders or has more than one class of stock.[37] For purposes of the 100-shareholder limitation, a husband and wife are counted as one shareholder and all the members of a family (six generations deep) may elect to be treated as one shareholder.[38] The one class of stock requirement is not violated if the corporation has both voting and nonvoting common stock and the only difference is voting rights.[39] Also, there is an important debt safe harbor provision that easily can be satisfied to protect against the threat of an S election being jeopardized by a shareholder debt obligation being characterized as a second class of stock.[40]

Q.23 What trusts are eligible to own stock of an S corporation?

Trusts that are now eligible to qualify as S corporation shareholders include: (1) voting trusts; (2) grantor trusts; (3) testamentary trusts that receive S corporation stock via a will (but only for a two year period following the transfer); (4) testamentary trusts that receive S corporation stock via a former grantor trust (but only for a two year period following the transfer); (5) "qualified subchapter S" trusts (QSSTs), which generally are trusts with only one current income beneficiary who is a U.S. resident or citizen to whom all income is distributed annually and who elects to be treated as the owner of the S corporation stock for tax purposes; and (6) "electing small business" trusts (ESBTs), which are trusts whose beneficiaries are qualifying S corporation shareholders who acquired their interests in the trust by gift or inheritance, not

---

35. I.R.C. § 1361(b).
36. I.R.C. § 1361(b)(2).
37. I.R.C. § 1361(b)(1)(A) & (D).
38. I.R.C. § 1361(c)(1).
39. I.R.C. § 1361(c)(4).
40. I.R.C. § 1361(c)(5). To fit within the safe harbor, there must be a written unconditional promise to pay on demand or on a specified date a sum certain and (1) the interest rate and payment dates cannot be contingent on profits, the borrower's discretion, or similar factors; (2) there can be no stock convertibility feature; and (3) the creditor must be an individual, an estate, a trust eligible to be a shareholder, or a person regularly and actively engaged in the business of lending money. For planning purposes, it is an easy fit in most situations.

purchase.[41] An ESBT must elect to be treated as an S corporation shareholder, in which case each current beneficiary of the trust is counted as one shareholder for purposes of the maximum 100 shareholder limitation and the S corporation income is taxed to the trust at the highest individual marginal rate under the provisions of the Internal Revenue Code.[42]

Q.24 How does a corporation elect in and out of S status?

An election to S status requires a timely filing of a Form 2553 and the consent of all shareholders.[43] A single dissenter can hold up the show. For this reason, often it is advisable to include in an organizational agreement among all the owners (typically a shareholder agreement) a provision that requires all owners to consent to an S election if a designated percentage of the owners at any time approve the making of the election. The election, once made, is effective for the current tax year if made during the preceding year or within the first two and one-half months of the current year.[44] If made during the first two and one-half months of the year, all shareholders who have owned stock at any time during the year, even those who no longer own stock at the time of the election, must consent in order for the election to be valid for the current year.[45]

Exiting out of S status is easier than electing into it; a revocation is valid if approved by shareholders holding more than half of the outstanding voting and nonvoting shares.[46] For the organization that wants to require something more than a simple majority to trigger such a revocation, the answer is a separate agreement among the shareholders that provides that no shareholder will consent to a revocation absent the approval of a designated supermajority. The revocation may designate a future effective date. Absent such a designation, the election is effective on the first day of the following year, unless it is made on or before the 15th day of the third month of the current year, in which case it is retroactively effective for the current year.[47]

Q.25 How is the income of an S corporation taxed?

The income of an S corporation is passed through and taxed to its shareholders. The entity itself pays no tax on the income,[48] and the shareholders' recognition of the income is not affected by the corporation's retention or distribution of the income. There is only one tax at the owner level. Unlike a C corporation, a distribution of cash or other assets generally does not trigger a tax at either the entity or owner level. Since there is no double-tax structure, all the C corporation traps tied to that menacing structure, including the double-taxed disguised dividend trap, the accumulated earnings tax trap, the personal holding company trap, and the controlled group trap have no application to an S corporation. Also, the income passing through an S corporation may qualify as

41. I.R.C. §§ 1361(c)(2), 1361(d), 1361(e).
42. I.R.C. §§ 1361 (e)(1)(A), 1361(c)(2)(b)(v).
43. I.R.C. § 1362(a). See generally Reg. § 1.1362-6.
44. I.R.C. § 1362(b)(1).
45. I.R.C. § 1362(b)(2). For potential relief on a late election where there is reasonable cause for the tardiness, see I.R.C. § 1362(b)(5) and Rev. Proc. 2004-48, 2004-2 C.B. 172.
46. I.R.C. § 1362(d)(1).
47. I.R.C. § 1362(d)(1)(C) & (D).
48. I.R.C. § 1363(a).

passive income for those shareholders who are not deemed "material participants."

Q.26 How are losses of an S corporation taxed?

An S corporation's losses also are passed through to its shareholders, subject to the three loss hurdles applicable to partnership-taxed entities that are discussed in question Q.33 below. The one hurdle that is slightly different for an S corporation is the basis hurdle. Unlike the basis of an interest in a partnership-taxed entity, the basis in S corporation stock does not include any share of the entity's liabilities. The result is that this hurdle, while generally not a big deal for partnership-taxed entities, often limits the tax benefits of losses allocated and passed through to an S corporation shareholder.

Q.27 Is the tax basis of the stock owned by an S corporation shareholder impacted by the corporation's allocation of income and losses and distributions?

Yes. An S corporation shareholder's stock basis is adjusted up and down for allocable income and losses and cash distributions, much as with a partnership.[49] There is no locked-in basis, as there is with a C corporation.

Q.28 As compared to a C corporation, is it easier from a tax standpoint for an S corporation to make distributions to its shareholders?

Yes. The tax consequences of distributing money or property from an S corporation generally are much less severe than for a C corporation. Generally distributions that do not exceed a shareholder's basis in his or her stock are tax-free, and a shareholder's stock basis is continually being increased as earnings are allocated to the shareholder.

Q.29 How much flexibility does an S corporation have in selecting a tax year?

S corporations have very little flexibility, particularly as compared to the flexibility of C corporations. Partnerships, LLCs, S corporations and sole proprietorships generally are required to use a calendar year unless they can prove a business purpose for using a fiscal year (a tough burden in most cases) or make a tax deposit under Section 7519 that is designed to eliminate any deferral advantage.

Q.30 Is it costly from a tax standpoint to convert from a C corporation to an S corporation?

A C corporation's conversion to an S corporation is far easier and less costly from a tax perspective than a conversion to a partnership-taxed entity, such as a limited liability company. But there are traps even in an S conversion for built-in asset gains, accumulated earnings, LIFO inventory reserves, and excessive S corporation passive income. Usually these traps can be avoided or managed with smart planning.

---

49. I.R.C. § 1367(a).

2. *LLC AND PARTNERSHIP TAX BASICS - Q&AS*

Q.31 Are limited liability companies and partnerships taxed the same?

Generally, yes. The great bulk of partnerships and LLCs are treated as partnership-taxed entities under subchapter K of the Internal Revenue Code. However, any limited liability company or partnership may elect to be taxed as either a C corporation or an S corporation. Absent such an election, the entity will be taxed as a partnership under the provisions of subchapter K.[50] An election to be taxed as a corporation may be effective up to 75 days before and 12 months after the election is filed.[51] The election must be signed by all members (including any former members impacted by a retroactive election) or by an officer or member specifically authorized to make the election.[52]

Q.32 How is the income of a partnership-taxed entity taxed?

The income of the entity is passed through and taxed to its owners. The entity itself reports the income, but pays no taxes. The advantage, of course, is that there is no threat of a double tax. There is only one tax at the owner level. Unlike a C corporation, a distribution of cash or other assets generally does not trigger a tax at either the entity or owner level. Since there is no double-tax structure, all the C corporation traps tied to that menacing structure, including the disguised dividend trap, the accumulated earnings tax trap, the personal holding company trap, and the controlled group trap have no application to entities taxed as partnerships.

Q.33 How are losses of a partnership-taxed entity taxed?

The losses of a partnership-taxed entity also pass through to its owners. Unlike a C corporation, the losses are not trapped inside the entity.

Does this mean the owners can use the losses to reduce the tax bite on their other income? Maybe. There are three hurdles that first must be overcome, and they can be very difficult in many situations. The first and easiest hurdle is the basis hurdle – the losses passed through to an owner cannot exceed that owner's basis in his or her interest in the entity.[53] This hurdle seldom presents a problem in a partnership-taxed entity because each owner's share of the entity's liabilities, even its nonrecourse liabilities, is treated as a contribution of money by the owner for basis purposes.[54]

The second hurdle, known as the at-risk hurdle, generally limits an owner's losses to only the amount that the owner actually has at risk.[55] An owner's at-risk amount typically includes property contributed to the entity by the owner and the owner's share of the entity's recourse liabilities (those liabilities that create personal exposure for the owners).[56] Nonrecourse liabilities (those liabilities for

---

50. Reg. §§ 301.7701-2(c)(1), 301.7701-3(a), 301.7701-3(b)(1).
51. Reg. § 301.7701-3(c)(1)(iii).
52. Reg. § 301.7701-3(c)(2).
53. I.R.C. § 704(d).
54. I.R.C. § 752(a).
55. I.R.C. § 465(a).
56. I.R.C. § 465(b).

which no owner has any personal exposure) generally do not count for purposes of the at-risk hurdle, but there is an important exception for qualified nonrecourse financing that makes it easy for many real estate transactions to satisfy the at-risk limitations.[57]

The third hurdle (and usually the toughest) is the passive loss rule,[58] a 1980s creation that is designed to prevent a taxpayer from using losses from a passive business venture to offset active business income or portfolio income (i.e., interest, dividends, gains from stocks and bonds, etc.). It was created to stop doctors and others from using losses from real estate and other tax shelters to reduce or eliminate the tax on their professional and business incomes.

Losses passed through from a passive venture can only be offset against passive income from another source. If there is not sufficient passive income to cover the passive losses, the excess passive losses are carried forward until sufficient passive income is generated or the owner disposes of his or her interest in the passive activity that produced the unused losses.[59]

Whether a particular business activity is deemed passive or active with respect to a particular partner is based on the owner's level of participation in the activity – that is, whether the owner is a "material participant" in the activity. A limited partner is presumed not to be a material participant and, therefore, all losses allocated to a limited partner generally are deemed passive.[60] To meet the "material participation" standard and avoid the hurdle, an owner must show "regular, continuous, and substantial" involvement in the activity.[61]

Given these three hurdles, it is never safe to assume that use of a partnership-taxed entity will convert start-up losses into slam-dunk tax benefits for the owners.

Q.34 Are there potential passive income benefits with a limited liability company or partnership?

Yes. Generally, taxable income is classified as portfolio income (dividends, interest, royalties, gains from stocks and bonds, and assets that produce such income), active income (income from activities in which the taxpayer materially participates), or passive income (income from passive business ventures). Passive income is the only type of income that can be sheltered by either an

---

57. I.R.C. § 465(b)(6). To qualify as "qualified nonrecourse financing," the debt must be incurred in connection with the activity of holding real estate, must not impose any personal liability on any person, must not be convertible debt, and must have been obtained from a "qualified person" (generally defined to include a person who is in the business of lending money, who is not related to the borrower, and who is not the seller or related to the seller).

58. See generally I.R.C. § 469.

59. I.R.C. §§ 469(a), 469(b), 469(d)(1).

60. I.R.C. § 469(h)(2).

61. I.R.C. § 469(h)(1). Under the temporary regulations, a taxpayer meets the material participation standard for a year by (1) participating in the activity for more than 500 hours in the year; (2) being the sole participant in the activity; (3) participating more than 100 hours in the activity and not less than any other person; (4) participating more than 100 hours in the activity and participating in the aggregate more than 500 hours in significant participation activities; (5) having been a material participant in the activity for any five of the last ten years; (6) having materially participated in the activity in any three previous years if the activity is a personal service activity; or (7) proving regular, continuous and substantial participation based on all facts and circumstances. Temp. Reg. § 1.469-5T(a)(1)-(7).

active loss or a passive loss. So the passive loss rule, by limiting the use of passive losses, exalts the value of passive income. An activity that generates passive income can breathe tax life into passive losses from other activities. A C corporation has no capacity to produce passive income; it pays dividends or interest (both classified as portfolio income) or compensation income (active income). In contrast, a profitable entity taxed as a partnership or an S corporation can pass through valued passive income to those owners who are not material participants.

Q.35 Is the tax basis of the interest owned by the owner of a partnership-taxed entity impacted by the entity's allocation of income and losses and distributions?

Yes. The owner's basis in his or her partnership interest is adjusted upward by capital contributions and income allocations and downward by distributions and loss allocations.[62] Unlike stock in a C corporation, there is no locked-in basis. This can be a valuable benefit to the owner of a thriving business that retains income to finance growth and expansion. The retained earnings will drive up the tax basis of the owners' interests in the enterprise, which will result in less taxable income at time of sale.

Q.36 How much flexibility does a partnership-taxed entity have in designing special allocations among its owners?

It has tremendous flexibility. An entity taxed as a partnership may structure special allocations of income and loss items among its various owners. For example, one owner may be allocated 60 percent of all income and 30 percent of all losses. Although a C corporation has some limited capacity to create allocation differences among owners through the use of different classes of stock and debt instruments, that capacity pales in comparison to the flexibility available to a partnership-taxed entity. The same comparison holds true for an S corporation which can issue only one class of stock.

A partnership-taxed entity's allocation will be respected for tax purposes only if it has "substantial economic effect,"[63] three words that make section 704(b) and its regulations one of the most complex subjects in the world of tax. Generally speaking (and I do mean generally), an allocation that does not produce a deficit capital account for a partner will have "economic effect" if capital accounts are maintained for all partners and, upon liquidation of the partnership, liquidating distributions are made in accordance with positive capital account balances.[64]

In order for an allocation that produces a deficit capital account balance to have "economic effect," the partner also must be unconditionally obligated to restore the deficit (i.e., pay cash to cover the shortfall) upon liquidation of the partnership,[65] or the partnership must have sufficient nonrecourse debt to assure that the partner's share of any minimum gain recognized on the discharge of the

62. I.R.C. § 705(a).
63. I.R.C. § 704(b).
64. Reg. §§ 1.704-1(b)(2)(ii) (b)(1), 1.704-(b)(2)(ii) (B)(2).
65. Reg. § 1.704-1(b)(2)(ii) (b)(3).

debt will eliminate the deficit.[66]

An "economic effect," if present, will not be deemed "substantial" if it produces an after-tax benefit for one or more partners with no diminished after-tax consequences to other partners.[67] The most common examples of economic effects that are not deemed "substantial" are shifting allocations (allocations of different types of income and deductions among partners within a given year to reduce individual taxes without changing the partners' relative economic interests in the partnership) and transitory allocations (allocations in one year that are offset by allocations in later years).[68]

Q.37 How easy is it from a tax standpoint to get money out of a limited liability company or a partnership?

It's easy to get money or property out of an entity that is taxed as a partnership. The Code is structured to eliminate all taxes on distributions at both the entity and owner level. There are a few exceptions. One is where a distribution of money to an owner exceeds the owner's basis in his or her entity interest; the excess is taxable.[69] Another is where the entity has unrealized accounts receivable or substantially appreciated inventory items; in these cases, ordinary income may need to be recognized to reflect any change in an owner's interest in such assets.[70]

These easy bail-out provisions are a far cry from the harsh dividend, redemption, and liquidation provisions of C corporations, all of which are designed to maximize the tax bite at both the entity and owner levels on any money or property flowing from the corporation to its owners.

Q.38 What is the tax-free profits interest benefit available to a limited liability company or a partnership?

Often a business entity desires to transfer an equity interest in future profits to one who works for the business. An entity taxed as a partnership can do this without triggering any current tax hit for the recipient.[71] A corporation generally cannot transfer an equity interest in return for services without creating a taxable event. Note that this benefit only applies to an equity interest in future profits, not an interest in existing capital.

Q.39 What is the family partnership tax trap applicable to a limited liability company or a partnership?

Entities that are considered family partnerships for tax purposes are subject to a special trap that is designed to prevent the use of the entity to aggressively shift income among family members. If any person gifts an entity interest to a family member, the donor must be adequately compensated for any services rendered to the partnership; and the income allocated to the donee, calculated as a

---

66. Reg. §§ 1.704-(2)(c), 1.704-(2)(f)(1), 1.704-(g)(1), 1.704-2(b)(1) & (e).
67. Reg. § 1.704-1(b)(2)(iii).
68. Reg. § 1.704-1(b)(2)(iii) (b) & (c).
69. I.R.C. § 731(a).
70. I.R.C. § 751; Reg. §§ 1.751-1(b)(2)(ii), 1.751-1(b)(3)(ii), 1.751-1(g).
71. See Rev. Proc. 93-27, 1993-2 C.B. 343 and Rev. Proc. 2001-43, 2001-2 C.B. 191.

yield on capital, cannot be proportionately greater than the yield to the donor.[72]

In effect, special allocations to favor donees are prohibited, as are attempts to shift service income. Any purchase among family members is considered a "gift" for purposes of this trap.[73]

Q.40 Is it possible to convert a C corporation to a limited liability company or a partnership?

Technically it is possible, but usually it is prohibitive from a tax standpoint to convert from a C corporation to an entity taxed as a partnership. Such a change will produce a double tax triggered by a liquidation of the C corporation. The far better option (and often the only viable option) is to convert to S corporation status if pass-through tax benefits are desired.

3. SELF-EMPLOYMENT AND PAYROLL TAX BASICS - Q&AS

Q.41 What impact does the self-employment and payroll tax have on the business planning process?

The self-employment/payroll tax is a regressive tax that is easy to ignore, but the consequences of neglect can be painful. The tax is levied at a flat rate of 15.3 percent on a base level of self-employment earnings ($117,000 for 2014) and 2.9 percent above the base. Starting in 2013, the rate jumped to 3.8 percent on a married couple's earnings in excess of $250,000 and an unmarried individual's earnings in excess of $200,000, and the new 3.8 percent rate applies to any interest, dividends, capital gains, and "net investment income" received by such taxpayers.[74] A self-employed person is entitled to an income tax deduction of one-half of self-employment taxes paid at the 15.3 percent and 2.9 percent rates.[75]

Q.42 How does the payroll tax impact employees?

An employee has one-half of the tax (7.65 percent) come directly from his or her paycheck in the form of payroll taxes. The other half is paid by the employer who, in order to stay in business, must consider this tax burden in setting the pay level for employees.

Q.43 How does the self-employment tax impact high-income taxpayers?

For high-income owners, including many business owners, the personal impact of the self-employment tax often is not significant because they are able to structure their affairs to reduce or eliminate its impact, or the base amount subject to the tax is considered small in relation to their overall earnings. The tax, by design, is structured to punish middle- and low-income workers. For 80 percent of American workers, the self-employment and payroll taxes paid on their earnings exceed the income tax bite, often by many times.[76]

---

72. I.R.C. § 704(e).
73. I.R.C. § 704(e)(3).
74. I.R.C. § 1411.
75. I.R.C. § 164(f).
76. Report of the Congressional Budget Office, Economic Stimulus: Evaluating Proposed Changes in Tax Policy – Approaches to Cutting Personal Taxes (January 2002), footnote 7.

Q.44 Is the self-employment tax a factor to consider in choosing the best form of business entity to use in a given situation?

The answer is "yes" in many, but not all, situations. The form of business entity that is selected can affect the self-employment tax burden for the owners of the business. This issue is discussed in the following chapter.

Q.45 What are the self-employment and payroll tax impacts with a C corporation?

Compensation payments from a C corporation to owners or employees are subject to payroll taxes. Corporate dividends are now subject to the 3.8 percent tax to the extent a married couple's income exceeds $250,000 and an unmarried individual's income exceeds $200,000.[77] For other taxpayers, dividends are not subject to the tax. In a C corporation context, the negative trade-off is that the dividends are subject to the double income tax structure.

Q.46 What are the self-employment tax impacts with an S corporation?

The C corporation double-tax trade-off disappears for an S corporation whose earnings are taxed directly through to its shareholders. Compensation payments to an S corporation shareholder are subject to payroll taxes. But a shareholder who works for an S corporation avoids all self-employment taxes on dividends, including the 3.8 percent Medicare tax.[78] An S corporation investor who does not materially participate in the venture will also avoid any self-employment tax on dividends unless the applicable $250,000/$200,000 threshold is exceeded, in which case the 3.8 percent tax will kick in.

A question that is often asked: Can a person who is the sole owner of an S corporation and works for the entity eliminate all self-employment and payroll taxes by paying only dividends? If a shareholder renders significant services to the S corporation and receives no compensation payments, the Service likely will claim that a portion of the dividends are compensation payments subject to payroll taxes.[79] The key is to be reasonable in taking advantage of the tax loophole for S corporation dividends paid to a shareholder/employee. Set a defensible compensation level and pay payroll taxes at that level. Then distribute the balance as dividends that are not subject to any self-employment or payroll tax burden.

Q.47 What are the self-employment tax impacts with a partnership?

Section 1402(a) of the Code specifically provides that a partner's distributive share of income from a partnership constitutes earnings from self-employment tax purposes.[80] There is a limited statutory exception for retired partners[81] and a

77. I.R.C. §§ 1402(a)(2), 1411.

78. If an S corporation shareholder materially participates in the venture, dividends paid to that shareholder do not fall within the definition of "net investment income" in IRC § 1411. See IRS Guidance in Reg.130507-11 (November 30, 2012).

79. See, for example, Joseph Radtke, S.C. v. United States, 712 F.Supp. 143 (E.D. Wis. 1989), affirmed 895 F.2d 1196 (7th Cir. 1990); Spicer Accounting, Inc. v. United States, 918 F.2d 90 (9th Cir. 1990); and Dunn & Clark, P.A. v. Commissioner, 57 F.3d 1076 (9th Cir. 1995).

80. I.R.C. § 1402(a).

81. I.R.C. § 1402(a)(10).

broader exception for limited partners, but the new 3.8 percent Medicare tax will still be applicable to the extent the triggering income thresholds ($250,000 or $200,000) are exceeded.[82] Thus, the key to minimizing the tax in a partnership structure is to fit within this limited partnership exception.

Q.48 What are the self-employment tax impacts with a limited liability company?

It may be more difficult to avoid the tax for a member of a limited liability company that has no limited partners.

The Service's first attempt to provide some guidance on the issue came in 1994 when it published its first Proposed Regulations. After public comment, new Proposed Regulations were issued in 1997, defining the scope of the limited partnership exception for all entities taxed as a partnership, without regard to state law characterizations.[83] Under the 1997 Proposed Regulations, an individual would be treated as a limited partner for purposes of the self-employment tax unless the individual was personally liable for the debts of the entity by being a partner, had authority to contract on behalf of the entity under applicable law, or participated for more than 500 hours in the business during the taxable year. The 1997 Proposed Regulations also drew criticism because LLC members who had authority to contract on behalf of the entity could never fit within the limited partner exception. The result was a statutory moratorium in 1997 on the issuance of any temporary or proposed regulations dealing with the limited partnership exception.[84]

For planning purposes, where does this history leave us now with respect to entities taxed as partnerships? Any general partner under state law must pay the tax. Any limited partner under applicable state law is probably safe. As for LLC members, any member who can fit within the 1997 Proposed Regulations' definition is justified in relying on the statutory limited partner exception. Beyond that definition, it becomes more difficult and uncertain to evaluate the facts and circumstances of each situation. The risk escalates in direct proportion to the individual's authority to act on behalf of the entity and the scope of any services rendered. Note, however, that any member will now be subject to the new 3.8 percent Medicare tax to the extent the applicable triggering income threshold ($250,000 or $200,000) is exceeded.

Q.49 Is it smart to design a plan that reduces or eliminates self-employment tax burdens for the owners of a business?

Most think it is. Of course, the payment of self-employment taxes may result in higher Social Security benefits down the road. The Social Security program, as presently structured, will become unsustainable in the future. Current benefit levels can be maintained long term only if tax rates or government borrowing levels are increased to unprecedented levels. There is a strong likelihood that, at some point in the not-too-distant future, forced

---

82. I.R.C. §§ 1402(a)(13), 1411.
83. Proposed Reg. § 1.1402 (a)-2.
84. Tax Relief Act of 1997 § 935.

structural reform of the program will reduce future government-funded benefits for all except those who are close to retirement or at the lowest income levels.[85]

STUDENT PROBLEM 8-1

Linda has started a business that will generate about $200,000 of earnings each year. Linda will work full time for the business. Her plan is to withdraw $125,000 of earnings from the business each year. She will leave the remaining earnings in the business to retire debt and fund future needs of the business. Linda wants to minimize the overall tax bite on these earnings.

What will be the total entity and personal tax cost under each of the following scenarios, assuming Linda's ordinary income tax rate is 28 percent, her dividend rate is 15 percent, and the applicable self-employment/payroll tax rate is 15.3 percent on the first $117,000 of earnings and 2.9 percent on the excess? Ignore all potential state income tax consequences.

1. Linda's business is a C corporation that distributes Linda a $125,000 dividend each year.

2. Linda's business is a C corporation that pays Linda a salary of $125,000 each year for services she renders to the corporation.

3. Linda's business is an S corporation that pays Linda a $45,000 salary each year and distributes a $80,000 dividend to her each year.

4. Linda's business is a limited liability company that is taxed as a partnership. Linda owns 90 percent of the business, and Judd, an investor who does not work in the business, owns the remaining 10 percent. The LLC distributes $117,000 to Linda each year and $13,000 to Judd. Assume Judd's marginal tax rate is also 28 percent.

C. ENTITY FORMATION TAX CHALLENGES

No new business venture wants to trigger a tax hit out of the box. In most situations, the challenge is to get assets into the new entity and equity interests into the hands of the owners with as little tax damage as possible. Fortunately, the Internal Revenue Code is structured to accommodate the tax-free formation of corporations and entities taxed as partnerships. The key is to closely adhere to some relatively simple rules and avoid traps that can trigger unpleasant surprises.

A few general observations are helpful up front. First, when cash is the consideration for an equity interest, there is no threat of taxable income being recognized. The owner's basis in the equity interest is the amount of cash paid, and the business entity recognizes no taxable income.[86] Second, when property other than cash is the consideration for an equity interest, a taxable event triggering income or loss for the owner will result unless the transaction fits within a specific statutory exception that provides otherwise. So, for example, if

85. See generally The Interim and Final Reports of the President's Commission to Strengthen Social Security (August 2001 & December 2001).

86. I.R.C. §§ 721, 1012, 1032.

Linda transfers to XYZ Inc. equipment that has a basis of $100,000 and a fair market value of $300,000 in return for 100 shares of XYZ Inc. common stock in a transaction that does not qualify for nonrecognition treatment, Linda will recognize $200,000 of taxable income, the tax basis in her newly-acquired stock will be $300,000, and her holding period for the stock will be measured from the date of the transaction.[87] To avoid this distasteful outcome, Linda needs to fit within the 351 Rule, which is applicable to both C and S corporations. Finally, a corporation never recognizes a gain or loss on the issuance of its stock for money or other property.[88]

1. CORPORATE FORMATIONS

a. Non-Cash Property Transfers

The 351 Rule. No gain or loss is recognized by a shareholder on the transfer of property to a corporation in exchange for stock of the corporation if:

- Property is transferred,
- The transfer is solely in exchange for stock, and
- The transferring parties are in "control" of the corporation immediately after the exchange. "Control" means that the property transferors own at least 80 percent of the total combined voting power of all classes of stock entitled to vote and at least 80 percent of the total number of shares of each other class of stock.[89]

Example: If Linda is the sole shareholder of XYZ Inc. in the above example, the 351 Rule would apply to prevent any recognition of income because *property* is transferred *solely* in exchange for stock and Linda *controls* the corporation immediately following the transaction.

Traps. Traps under the 351 Rule surface in a number of different ways, including the following:

- **Stock for Services.** The 351 Rule may not apply if one or more of the shareholders receives stock in exchange for services. Although the term "property" for Section 351 purposes has been broadly defined to include cash, accounts receivable, capital assets, patents, licenses and even industrial know-how, it does not include services. So if one shareholder receives over 20 percent of the corporation's stock in return for services rendered or to be rendered, no shareholder can qualify under the 351 Rule because the required control was not acquired with property. Suppose the shareholder who receives stock in exchange for services also transfers some property in exchange for stock; that is, there is dual consideration. The regulations state that a dual consideration transferor will not qualify as a property transferor if the property transferred is "of relatively small value" when compared to the value of the stock already owned or to be received for services.[90] In Revenue Procedure 77-37 (here's the good news), the

87. I.R.C. §§ 1001, 1012.
88. I.R.C. § 1032.
89. I.R.C. § 351(a).
90. Reg. § 1.351-1(a)(1)(ii).

Service stated that this "relatively small value" standard can be avoided if the value of the property transferred equals 10 percent or more of the fair market value of the stock owned (or to be received for services) by the shareholder.[91] So the planning point is straight-forward: Where necessary to qualify a transaction under the 351 Rule for the benefit of all the transferors, make certain that those receiving stock in exchange for services also transfer property that exceeds this 10 percent requirement.

- **Boot Trap.** If the 351 Rule would apply to an exchange except that the corporation transfers to the shareholder other property (boot) in addition to stock, the shareholder recognizes gain equal to the lesser of (i) the fair market value of the boot or (ii) the built-in gain on the property transferred by the shareholder to the corporation.[92] Plus, the corporation recognizes income equal to any built-in gain on the property transferred to the shareholder.[93] As an example, assume Linda transfers to XYZ Inc. equipment with a basis of $100,000 and a fair market value of $300,000 in exchange for 100 shares of XYZ Inc. common stock and $80,000 cash. Linda recognizes gain equal to the $80,000 of boot received. If Linda was paid $220,000 cash with the stock, her recognized gain would be limited to her $200,000 equipment built-in gain – the excess of the fair market value of the equipment she transferred over her basis in the property.

- **Assumed Debt Trap.** A shareholder debt assumed by a corporation in a 351 exchange is not considered boot for gain purposes but does reduce the shareholder's stock basis. But if the total of all debts assumed exceeds the basis of all property transferred by a shareholder to the corporation, the excess is treated as taxable boot.[94] Plus, the debt assumed by the corporation will be treated as taxable boot if the shareholder's principal purpose was tax avoidance and not a bona fide business purpose.[95] As an example, assume Linda transfers to XYZ Inc. equipment that has a basis of $100,000 and a fair market value of $300,000 and which is encumbered by a $120,000 debt. In exchange, XYZ Inc. issues Linda 100 shares of its common stock and assumes the $120,000 debt obligation. Linda recognizes $20,000 of income (the excess of the debt over her basis in the equipment), and her basis in the stock would be zero (her $100,000 basis in the equipment, plus the $20,000 gain recognized, and less the $120,000 debt assumed).

- **Timing Differences.** Shareholders may transfer property in exchange for stock at different times. To fit within the 351 Rule, the participants who end up with control must have acted in concert under a single integrated plan. If in the example above, Linda's transfer of equipment results in her owning 100 percent of the stock following her transfer, but six months later Jim contributes equipment in return for stock in a completely separate transaction and ends up with 50 percent of the stock, Linda's transfer would qualify under the 351 Rule because she owned more than 80 percent after her transfer, but Jim's would not.

---

91. Rev. Proc. 77-37, 1977-2 C.B. 568.
92. I.R.C. § 351(b).
93. I.R.C. § 311(b).
94. I.R.C. §§ 357(a) & (c), 358(d).
95. I.R.C. § 357(b).

The transfers need not occur at the same time to be part of a single plan. What is required is that "the rights of the parties have been previously defined and the execution of the agreement proceeds with an expedition consistent with orderly procedure."[96] So if at the time Linda transfers her equipment in return for stock it is contemplated that Jim will do the same six months out, the board resolutions approving Linda's transaction should make specific reference to Jim's future transfer and leave no doubt that it is part of a single, integrated plan to form the corporation. This will help ensure that Jim's transaction falls within the 351 Rule.

- **Immediate Subsequent Stock Transfers.** Shareholders who receive stock in the exchange and constitute part of the "control" group should not dispose of their stock immediately following the exchange. If the disposition is pursuant to a prearranged or legally binding plan, it will likely kill the "control immediately after" requirement to the detriment of all those who participate in the transaction.[97] Absent a prearranged binding commitment to make such a transfer, there may still be a problem if the second transfer was expected and was dependent on the exchange transaction.[98] Gifts and other donative transfers after the exchange generally do not present a problem.[99] The planning precaution is to provide in the shareholder agreement that no post-exchange transfers will be permitted that may threaten application of the 351 Rule. Most shareholder agreements include transfer restrictions that are broad enough to provide such protection.

- **Accommodation Transfers.** Existing shareholders may choose to accommodate the admission of a new shareholder by contributing a nominal amount of property in return for more stock in order to be included in the "control" group for purposes of satisfying the 80 percent requirement. If the existing shareholders do not participate, their stock ownership does not count in the "control" calculation, and the new shareholder has no hope of qualifying under the 351 Rule. If the existing shareholders participate, all their stock counts in the control calculation. This accommodation strategy will work only if the property transferred by the existing shareholders has a value equal to at least 10 percent of the total value of the stock already owned by the existing shareholders.[100]

- **Immediate Subsequent Property Disposition.** The corporation that receives property in the exchange may trigger a 351 problem if it immediately disposes of the property. If the disposition is consistent with the corporation's ordinary business practices (e.g., inventory dispositions), there should be no problem. However, if the disposition is part of a prearranged plan that looks as if

96. Reg. § 1.351-1(a)(1).

97. See, e.g., Intermountain Lumber Co. v. Commissioner, 65 T.C. 1025 (1976) and Rev. Rule 79-70, 1979-1 C.B. 144. But see Rev. Rule 2003-51, 2003-1 C.B. 938 where a prearranged subsequent transfer did not preclude section 351 treatment when the subsequent transfer was tax-free and the overall result could have been directly accomplished tax-free.

98. See Rev. Ruling 78-330, 1978-2 C.B. 147; Rev. Rule 75-406, 1975-2 C.B. 125; and American Bantam Car Co. v. Commissioner, 11 T.C. 397 (1948), affirmed 177 F.2d 513 (3d Cir. 1949).

99. See D'Angelo Associates, Inc. v. Commissioner, 70 T.C. 121 (1978) and Stanton v. United States, 512 F.2d 13 (3d Cir. 1975).

100. Rev. Proc. 77-37, 1977-2 C.B. 568.

the corporation is being used as a conduit for disposing of unwanted assets, there is a risk that the Service may claim that the original transaction was a sham that did not fall within the scope of the 351 Rule.[101] The planning point is to avoid any such near-in-time asset dispositions that fall outside the scope of the corporation's ordinary business practices.

- **Nonvoting Stock Class.** There can be a 351 problem if immediately after the exchange, the transferors in the control group own at least 80 percent of all the voting stock and over at least 80 percent of the value of all the stock, but do not own 80 percent or more of the shares of a particular class of nonvoting stock.[102] The exchange will not qualify under the 351 Rule. The key is to make certain that the transferors meet the two-pronged control test – at least 80 percent of each class of nonvoting stock and at least 80 percent of the voting power. Only direct ownership counts; options, conversion rights, and attribution won't get the job done.

- **Loss Asset.** If a shareholder intends to transfer a loss asset (tax basis exceeds value) to the corporation in return for stock, no loss will be recognized loss on the transaction if 351 applies. If loss recognition is desired, the key is to structure the loss transaction to be after and completely unrelated to any 351 Rule transaction that may occur. Also, remember that the loss will not be allowed if the shareholder actually or constructively owns more than 50 percent of the corporation's outstanding stock.[103]

- **Nonqualified Preferred Stock.** If shareholders are issued "nonqualified preferred stock" in the transaction or such stock is outstanding at the time of the transaction, there likely will be 351 consequences. This is stock that is limited and preferred as to dividends, that does not significantly participate in equity growth, and that has one of the following characteristics: (1) the holder may require the corporation or a related party to redeem or purchase the stock; (2) the corporation or a related party is required to redeem or purchase the stock; (3) the corporation or a related party has a right to redeem or purchase the stock, and it is more likely than not that the right will be exercised; or (4) the stock's dividend rate varies with reference to interest rates, commodity prices or other similar indices.[104] Essentially, it is preferred stock that looks much like debt. For purposes of the 351 Rule, nonqualified preferred stock has a split role. Until the IRS says otherwise, for planning purposes it should be treated as stock for applying the "control" test.[105] Thus, the control group transferors had better make certain that they end up with 80 percent or more of the nonqualified preferred stock. But for applying the general nonrecognition provision of the 351 Rule, nonqualified preferred stock is not considered stock, but rather is treated as other property. If it is the only consideration received by a transferor, the exchange will be completely outside the scope of the 351 Rule and will trigger

---

101. See Kluener v. Commisioner, T.C. Memo 1996-519, affirmed 154 F.3d 630 (6th Cir. 1998); Stewart v. Commissioner, 714 F.2d 977 (9th Cir. 1983); and Hallowell v. Commissioner, 56 T.C. 600 (1971).

102. I.R.C. § 368(c); Rev. Rule 59-259, 1959-2 C.B. 115.

103. I.R.C. §§ 267(a) & (b)(2).

104. I.R.C. § 351(g).

105. See Staff of Joint Committee on Taxation, General Explanation of Tax Legislation Enacted in 1997, 105th Cong., 1st Sess. 210 (1997) and I.R.C. § 351(g)(4).

taxable gain or loss. If the nonqualified preferred stock is received along with other stock, it will constitute "boot" and will be treated as all other boot.[106]

- **Investment Company Transfer.** If the assets contributed by the shareholders qualify the corporation as an "investment company" within the meaning of Section 351(e), then the 351 Rule is out and gain or loss is recognized on the transfers.[107] For this trap to apply, two conditions must exist: (1) the transfer must result in a direct or indirect diversification of the shareholders' interests, and (2) more than 80 percent of the corporation's assets (excluding cash and non-convertible debt obligations) must consist of: stock or securities – broadly defined to include all stock and securities (not just the readily marketable); other corporate equity interests; evidences of indebtedness; options; forward and futures contracts; notional principal contracts and derivatives; foreign currencies; interests in real estate investment trusts, regulated investment companies, and publicly-traded partnerships; precious metal interests unrelated to an active trade or business; and more.[108] Real estate and tangible business assets are not included in the definition. The diversification requirement is met when two or more persons transfer non-identical investment assets to the corporation.[109] So, for example, if A, B and C each transfer a different stock to the corporation and the corporation has no other assets, the diversification requirement would be met, the 351 Rule would not apply, and each party would recognize a taxable gain on the transfer. If, however, A, B and C each contributed the same stock or identical interests in more than one stock, there would be no diversification impact and the 351 Rule would apply. Transfers that are insignificant (i.e., less than one percent) are ignored in testing for diversification.[110] Plus, diversification will not result from the transfer, and thus section 351 treatment will not be denied, if each shareholder transfers a portfolio of stock and securities that is already diversified.[111]

b. Corporate Equity for Services

Often an owner is transferred corporate stock in return for services that have been rendered or will be rendered in the future. As we saw above, such a transfer may create a section 351 problem for other contributing shareholders if too much stock is transferred to the service provider. Beyond the potential 351 risks to those who contribute property are the tax consequences to the shareholder who receives stock for services. Following are brief descriptions of three scenarios that often surface when stock is issued for services.

- **The 83(a) Scenario.** XYZ Inc. is formed by Larry and Sue transferring $900,000 of cash and property to the corporation in return for 900 shares of common stock. Linda is transferred 100 shares of XYZ Inc. common stock in return for her promise to manage the company. Assuming the stock has a value

---

106. I.R.C. § 351(g)(1).
107. I.R.C. § 351(e)(1).
108. I.R.C. § 351(e)(1)(B); Reg. § 1.351-1(c)(1)(i).
109. Reg. § 1.351-1(c)(5) & (7), Examples (1) & (2).
110. Reg. § 1.351-1(c)(5); PLRs 200006008, 200002025.
111. Reg. § 1.351-1(c)(6). The regulations adopt a slightly modified version of the 25 percent and 50 percent tests of section 368(a)(2)(f) for determining whether the contributed portfolios are already "diversified."

of $1,000 a share, section 83(a) requires that Linda recognize $100,000 of taxable compensation income in the year she receives her stock.[112] XYZ Inc. is entitled to a $100,000 ordinary business expense deduction in the year that Linda recognizes the income.[113]

- **The Deferral Scenario.** Linda does not want a tax hit on $100,000 of phantom income (income with no cash) when she receives the stock. Plus, Larry and Sue do not want Linda to keep her stock if her employment is terminated during the first four years. So the stock transferred to Linda is subject to a forfeiture restriction that kicks in if her employment comes to an end for any reason other than death or disability during the first four years. This restriction is a "substantial risk of forfeiture" that defers the recognition of any taxable income to Linda (and the corresponding corporate deduction) so long as it is in effect.[114] That's the good news for Linda. The bad news is that there is a risk that she could lose her stock via the forfeiture provision and, if she doesn't lose her stock, her phantom taxable income at the end of year four is based on the fair market value of the stock at that time. So if the value has appreciated to $4,000 a share when the restriction lapses at the end of year four, Linda will have to recognize $400,000 of ordinary taxable income, and XYZ Inc. will get a corresponding ordinary business expense deduction. A restriction will constitute a "substantial risk of forfeiture" and trigger the deferral only if it "requires future performance of substantial services."[115] A forfeiture restriction based upon the commission of a felony or some other bad act won't do the job.[116]

- **The 83(b) Scenario.** Even with the four-year restriction in place, Linda decides that she would prefer to take her tax lumps in year one so that any future growth in the stock will only be taxed at capital gains rates when she sells the stock. Linda may elect under section 83(b) to recognize the $100,000 of taxable income in year one even though there is a forfeiture restriction. If Linda makes the election, the corporation gets a corresponding deduction.[117] The election must be made within 30 days of the transfer. There is a harsh risk under this scenario; if the forfeiture provision is triggered and Linda loses the stock, she gets no deduction in the year of the loss.[118] She will have paid tax on $100,000 of phantom taxable income and received nothing of value. Despite this ugly risk, many opt for the 83(b) election when the going-in stock value is low and the prospects for significant appreciation in the early years look good.

2. *LLC AND PARTNERSHIP FORMATIONS*

A partnership or LLC that is taxed as a partnership usually can be formed

112. I.R.C. § 83(a).

113. I.R.C. § 83(h). Note, however, that if the service provided is capital in nature, the corporation will have to capitalize the expenditure. Reg. § 1.83-6(a)(4).

114. I.R.C. §§ 83(a) & (h). The restriction also must prevent the shareholder from transferring the stock free of the restriction. Reg. § 1.83-3(d).

115. I.R.C. § 83(c)(1).

116. Reg. § 1.83-3(c)(2).

117. I.R.C. § 83(b).

118. I.R.C. § 83(b).

and funded with no threat of taxable income being recognized by the partnership or its partners. Compared to the formation tax rules for its corporate counterparts, the rules for partnership-taxed entities are identical in some respects, generally more forgiving, and a bit more complicated. Care is still required to avoid the certain traps.

a. Non-Cash Property Contributions

An owner recognizes no gain or loss on the contribution of property to a partnership-taxed entity in exchange for an interest in the entity.[119] Similarly, a partnership-taxed entity recognizes no gain or loss on the receipt of money or property for an interest in the entity.[120] But any future income, gain, loss or deduction must be allocated among the owners to reflect the contributing owner's built-in gain or loss at the time of the contribution.[121]

Example: Linda contributed land to XYZ partnership in exchange for a one-third interest in the partnership. Two other partners each own a one-third interest in the partnership. Linda paid $100,000 for the land, which was her tax basis in the land at the time of the contribution. The land's fair market value was $300,000 at time of contribution, which resulted in Linda having a built-in gain of $200,000 at time of contribution. Neither Linda nor the partnership recognized any income or loss on the contribution, and Linda's $100,000 tax basis in the land carried over to the partnership. At the end of year two, the partnership sold the land for $400,000, generating a taxable gain of $300,000 (the excess of $400,000 over the $100,000 tax basis). The first $200,000 of the gain was allocated to Linda to reflect her built-in gain at time of contribution, and the remaining $100,000 of gain was allocated in equal shares to the three partners.

Corporate Comparison. This non-recognition tax rule for partnership-taxed entities is easier to satisfy up front than its 351 corporate counterpart rule. Since there is no control requirement, the corporate 351 traps relating to the "control" and "immediately after" requirements, and the associated voting and nonvoting interest issues, are of no concern in the context of a partnership-taxed entity. However, it's more complicated in the partnership context if there is a built-in gain or loss on the contributed property because the taint stays with the contributing partner. In contrast, property contributed to a corporation is not linked to the contributing owner for built-in gain or loss purposes.

Traps: Following are brief descriptions of a few of the traps to watch out for under the broad non-recognition rule of section 721 that applies to partnership-taxed entities:

- **Capital Loss Taint.** If an owner contributes property to a partnership-taxed entity that was a capital asset in the hands of the owner and the entity sells the property within a five-year period, any loss recognized by the entity on the sale will be subject to unfavorable capital loss treatment to the extent of any built-in loss (the excess of basis over fair market value) that existed at the time of

119. I.R.C. § 721(a).
120. I.R.C. § 721.
121. I.R.C. § 704(c)(1).

the contribution.[122]

- **Mixing Bowl Trap.** Partner A contributes property in exchange for a partnership interest, and the partnership then distributes the property to another partner within seven years of the contribution. Partner A must recognize at that time any remaining built-in gain to the extent such gain would be recognized if the partnership had sold the property for its fair market value on the date of the distribution to the other partner.[123] The purpose of this exception is to prevent partners from using the generous tax-free rules relating to property transfers in and out of partnership-taxed entities to structure transactions between themselves within a seven-year period.

- **Property Exchange Trap.** Partner A contributes property in exchange for a partnership interest, and the partnership distributes *other* non-cash property to Partner A within seven years. Partner A must recognize gain at that time equal to the lesser of (i) the excess of the fair market value of the distributed property over Partner A's basis in his or her partnership interest before the distribution or (ii) the pre-contribution gain that Partner A would have been required to recognize under the previous Mixing Bowl Trap if the *contributed* property had been distributed to another partner within the seven-year time frame.[124] The purpose of this trap is to force income recognition where there is exchange of properties between a partner and a partnership within a seven-year period.

- **Boot Trap.** If an owner transfers property to a partnership-taxed entity in exchange for an interest in the entity and other property (boot), the portion of the transferred property allocable to the boot will be taxed as a sale or exchange.[125] As an example, assume Linda transfers to XYZ partnership equipment with a basis of $100,000 and a fair market value of $300,000 in exchange for a one-third interest in the partnership and $75,000 cash. One-fourth of the transferred equipment ($75,000/$300,000) will be treated as a sale for cash, producing a taxable gain of $50,000 ($75,000 less one-fourth of the $100,000 basis). The remaining three-fourths of the contributed property will be treated as a tax-free contribution under section 721.

- **Entity Assumed Debt Trap.** Debt of an owner assumed by a partnership-taxed entity in a 721 exchange is treated as a distribution of cash to the owner to the extent the owner's share of the debt is reduced.[126] If the reduction in the owner's share of the debt exceeds the owner's basis in his or her partnership interest, such excess deemed cash distribution is taxed as a gain from the sale or exchange of the owner's interest in the entity.[127] As an example, assume Linda transfers to XYZ partnership land that has a basis of $100,000 and a fair market value of $300,000 and that is encumbered by a $180,000 recourse debt. In exchange, Linda receives a one-third interest in the partnership, and the partnership assumes the $180,000 debt obligation. Linda is deemed to have

122. I.R.C. § 724(c).
123. I.R.C. § 704(c)(1)(B).
124. I.R.C. § 737.
125. I.R.C. § 707(a)(2)(B); Reg. § 1.707-3(f), Example 1.
126. I.R.C. § 752(b).
127. I.R.C. § 731(a)(1).

received a $120,000 cash distribution, the two-thirds portion of the assumed debt that she is relieved of and that is allocated to the other partners. This deemed cash distribution would exceed Linda's $100,000 basis in her partnership interest (the carryover basis from the land contribution) by $20,000, and that excess would be taxed as a gain from the sale of her partnership interest. Her basis in her partnership interest would be reduced to zero as a result of the deemed cash distribution. The basis of the other partners would be increased by $120,000, their deemed cash contributions to the partnership.

- **Investment Company Trap.** The 721 rule does not apply to any gain realized on the transfer of property to a partnership that would be treated as an investment company if it were incorporated.[128]

b. Formation Equity for Services

Profits Interest Scenario. XYZ partnership, owned equally by Larry and Sue, has equity capital interests valued at $1 million. Linda is transferred a 10 percent interest in all future profits of the business in return for her promise to manage the company. Linda does not recognize any taxable income on the receipt of the profits interest (and the partnership gets no corresponding deduction) unless Linda disposes of the profits interest within two years or the profits interest relates to a substantially certain and predictable income stream (e.g., income from high-quality debt securities or a high-quality net lease).[129]

This profits-interest option creates a tax savings opportunity in a partnership-taxed entity that would never be available with a corporation. The service owner can be given an equity interest in future profits with no phantom income tax concerns and usually no need for forfeiture provisions.

Capital Interest Section 83 Scenario. XYZ partnership, owned equally by Larry and Sue, has equity capital interests valued at $1,000,000. Linda is transferred a 10 percent interest in the existing capital of the partnership (not just future profits) in return for her promise to manage the business. Linda recognizes $100,000 of income at the time of contribution section 83(a),[130] and XYZ partnership is entitled to a $100,000 business expense deduction, which is passed through to Larry and Sue.[131]

In the context of a partnership-taxed entity that issues a capital interest for services, section 83 works the same as it does in the corporate context discussed above with respect to the ordinary income recognized by a service partner on the receipt of the capital interest and the corresponding deduction for the entity. Substantial forfeiture provisions may be used to defer the recognition of income,

---

128. I.R.C. § 721(b).

129. Rev. Proc. 93-27, 1993-2 C.B. 343. See also Prop. Regs. § 1.83(l)(2005).

130. I.R.C. 83(a).

131. I.R.C. 83(h). There is a question as to whether the transaction also may be treated as a taxable transfer of the appreciated property from the other partners to Linda, followed by a contribution of such property to the partnership by Linda. If so, Larry and Sue would be required to recognize an $80,000 gain on the transfer ($100,000 less $20,000 allocable basis). Reg. 1.83-6(b). Proposed Regs. 1.83-6(b) and 1.721-1(b) (2005), if and when finalized, would not require the recognition of such a gain.

and a risk-laden 83(b) election may be made to accelerate the income recognition in those situations where it is warranted.

STUDENT PROBLEM 8-2

Larry plans to form a C corporation that will operate an Italian import supply business. The corporation will have four shareholders: Larry, Judy, Sue and Dave.

1. Larry will contribute to the corporation accounts receivable that have a value of $150,000 and a basis of zero. He has generated these accounts receivable by operating a sole proprietorship. He will be issued 150 shares of common stock in return.

2. Judy will contribute $150,000 cash in return for 150 shares.

3. Sue, a recognized expert in Italian goods, will sign a five-year agreement to manage the business. As a signing bonus, she will be issued 100 shares of stock. She will also be issued an additional 50 shares for her payment of $50,000.

4. Dave will contribute a warehouse to the corporation in return for 150 shares of stock. The warehouse has a value of $600,000, a mortgage balance of $450,000, and a tax basis of $325,000. The company will assume the mortgage.

Advise Larry on the tax impacts of his plan to capitalize the corporation. How would your answer change if Larry planned to form an S corporation, not a C corporation? How would your answer change if Larry planned on forming a limited liability company that would be taxed as a partnership and each of the owners were issued 150 LLC membership units?

CHAPTER 9

CHOOSING THE BEST ENTITY FORM

A. MOVING TARGETS AND COLLATERAL CONSEQUENCES

A primary planning challenge for all businesses is to select the best form of business organization. Too many mistakenly assume that this challenge is limited to new ventures. Many mature businesses have a need to re-evaluate their business structure from time to time to maximize the benefits of the enterprise for its owners.

Some perceive the "choice of entity" analysis solely as a tax-driven exercise. Although taxes are vitally important, there are many important non-tax factors that can impact the ultimate decision. The rules of the game have changed in recent years. Some factors, once deemed crucial, no longer impact the outcome, and often new issues must be factored in. In most situations, the analytical process requires the owners to predict and handicap what's likely to happen down the road. They need to consider and project earnings, losses, capital expansion needs, debt levels, the possibility of adding new owners, potential exit strategies, the likelihood of a sale, the estate planning needs of the owners, and a variety of other factors. The decision-making process is not an exact science that punches out a single, perfect answer. The owners need to weigh and consider a number of factors, while being sensitive to the potential consequences of each available alternative.

A choice-of-entity analysis requires a careful assessment of all relevant factors. The following section reviews 16 of the key factors, illustrated through five case studies. Each entity option offers certain benefits and traps that may pose problems down the road. The analysis should include a review of the benefits and traps to assess their relevance to the specific situation.

Although each factor may be important, they never have equal weight in any given situation. It is not a game of adding up the factors to see which form of entity scores the most points. In many cases, one or two factors may be so compelling in the particular situation that they alone dictate the solution. But even then, the other factors cannot be ignored because they help identify the collateral consequences of the decision that is about to be made.

Also, be ever mindful that taxes are a moving target. The rules often change. What works today may make no sense tomorrow. Those who watched the eleventh-hour theatrics of the Congress and White House during the closing days of 2010 and 2012 to prevent threatened tax chaos saw that it is all about politics and inherent uncertainty. We can make predictions and try hard to assess the political winds, but uncertainty is a given that makes choice-of-entity planning more challenging and exciting.

The issue of limited liability protection for the owners of the business, once considered to be the most critical factor in the choice-of-entity analysis, is no longer included in the list of key factors. It's not that insulating the owners of a business from personal liability for the business' liabilities is no longer important; it's as important today as ever. It's absent from the critical factor list because it can be accomplished in any situation. Thus, it is a neutral consideration that no longer needs to impact the decision-making process. Even a general partner can be protected by placing the ownership interest in a limited liability company or S corporation.

B. KEY FACTORS AND CONSEQUENCES

EXAMPLE CASE ONE: JASON

Jason, a seasoned entrepreneur, plans to start a new business that will offer specialized heavy equipment moving services in the western United States. Jason will own 60 percent of the new enterprise, and the remaining 40 percent will be owned equally by two investors, buddies of Jason.

Jason will oversee the business, as he does with the other businesses that he has organized. He will not be a fulltime employee of the business. The business will initially have about 30 employees. Jason anticipates that the business will be profitable by year two, and he has advised the investors that regular distributions will be made starting in year two. Plus, if things play out as planned, there might be a potential to sell the business to a large strategic player down the road.

Jason wants an entity that will minimize all tax bites, always leave him in complete control, and avoid, to the fullest extent possible, any potential hassles with the minority owners.

The best option for Jason's new company would be an S corporation. This case illustrates six key factors.

Factor 1: Earnings Bailout

In Jason's situation, an important factor in the choice-of-entity decision analysis is the tax cost of getting earnings out of the enterprise and into the hands of Jason and the other owners. Bailing out earnings in S corporations, LLCs, partnerships, and sole proprietorships usually is no big deal. Profits generated by the business are passed through and taxed directly to the owners, so the distribution of those profits in the form of dividends or partnership distributions carries no tax consequences. In contrast, bailing out the fruits of a C corporation may trigger substantial income tax consequences, because a C corporation is not a pass-through entity.

When a C corporation bails out its earnings by distributing them to its shareholders in the form of dividends, the dividend distribution is not deductible by the corporation. The corporation pays a tax on the earnings, and the distribution of those earnings to the shareholders in the form of dividends is taxed a second time at the shareholder level. This double tax is one of the negatives of a C corporation.

For some businesses, this double tax risk is more academic than real. There are often ways to avoid it. The most common is for the shareholders to be employed by the corporation and to receive earnings in the form of taxable compensation. The payment of the compensation to the shareholders is deductible by the corporation, so that income is only taxed once, at the shareholder level. But the compensation must be reasonable for the services actually rendered. If it isn't, it may be re-characterized as a dividend. In service corporations where the services are rendered by the shareholders, stripping out all of the earnings of the business through the use of compensation payments usually can be easily justified. Since Jason and his investors will not work for the new business, the compensation bailout strategy isn't an option.

Factor 2: Self-Employment and Payroll Taxes

Self-employment and payroll taxes can be an important choice-of-entity factor in some situations. In Jason's situation, use of an S corporation may create the opportunity to save these taxes and also escape double income tax treatment by virtue of the S election.

A C corporation will not help Jason on this issue. Any compensation payments to owners of a C corporation will be subject to payroll taxes. Except to the extent the new 3.8 percent Medicare tax is applicable to those with incomes above the triggering thresholds ($250,000 or $200,000), there is no self-employment tax imposed on dividends from a C corporation, but such dividends are subject to a double income tax structure.

Similarly, a partnership-taxed entity may not work for Jason on this issue. Distributions by a partnership-taxed entity, including a limited liability company, will not escape self-employment taxes unless the owners are limited partners. If the owners are limited partners of a limited partnership, there is a statutory exception that will protect them from self-employment taxes. The same exception should work in the context of a limited liability company where the owners have no management rights in the enterprise and are not personally responsible for the liabilities of the entity. The tough situation comes when a key owner, such a Jason, wants to exercise management rights. In Jason's case, reliance on the limited partnership exception in the LLC context may create an intolerable risk, given the uncertainty of current law.

For self-employment tax purposes, a much smarter option would be an S corporation whose income is not subject to self-employment taxes when passed through to its owners. Depending on the potential size of the self-employment tax in a particular situation, this factor may be the deciding issue in some cases.

Factor 3: Tax-Free Reorganization Potential

If the business succeeds and a sellout opportunity surfaces, a corporate entity will be able to participate in a tax-free reorganization with a corporate buyer. Corporations may combine through mergers, stock-for-stock transactions, and assets-for-stock transactions on terms that eliminate all corporate and shareholder-level taxes. This benefit often is the key to the ultimate payday for those business owners who cash in by "selling" to a public corporation. Cast as a reorganization, the transaction allows the acquiring entity to fund the acquisition with its own stock (little or no cash required) and enables the selling owners to walk with highly liquid, publicly traded securities and no tax bills until the securities are sold.

A partnership-taxed entity, such as a limited liability company, cannot enjoy the tax-free benefits of a corporate reorganization.

Factor 4: Control Rights

Jason wants complete control over all business decisions with as little discussion and fanfare as possible. A corporation, either C or S, or a limited partnership automatically offers this type of ultimate control in favor of the majority, absent a special agreement to the contrary. Minority corporate shareholders often have no control rights; the majority elects the board of directors, and the board has the authority to manage the affairs of the corporation. Limited partner status and the benefits associated with that status (i.e., liability protection and freedom from self-employment taxes) mandate little or no control. For the majority player who wants control of all the reins, the idea of easily getting it all "the normal way" can be appealing.

Limited liability companies and general partnerships are different only in that the control rights need to be spelled out in an operating agreement among the owners. In some cases, the fear is that the need for a single operating agreement may result in more dialogue, more negotiation, and more compromise. Minority owners may see that there is no "standard" or "normal" way of locking in voting requirements and that the agreement can be crafted to address the control concerns of all parties.

Once minority expectations are elevated, the majority players' options become more difficult. One option, of course, is to throw down the gauntlet and demand ultimate majority control. Beyond the personal discomfort of having to overtly make such demands, the demands themselves may fuel suspicions, undermine loyalties, or, worst case, trigger the departure of a valuable minority player. The alternative option is to build into the operating agreement "mutually acceptable" minority rights.

Factor 5: Sellout Tax Hit

Many who start a new business are not focused on selling out down the road. But this factor can be extremely important in selecting the right form of business organization. If this factor is neglected, a business owner may find that, when it comes time to cash in, there is an added tax burden that could have been avoided.

If Jason's business flourishes and its assets are ultimately sold within a pass-through entity, such as an S corporation, partnership or LLC, the gains realized on the sale of the assets are taxed to the owners in proportion to their interests in the business. After those taxes are paid, the owners are free to pocket the net proceeds. Bailing out of a C corporation may carry a significant additional tax cost. A simple example illustrates the impact.

Assume Jason started a C corporation with a $250,000 investment, that the assets in the company have a present basis of $750,000, and that the company is worth $3 million. It's now time to cash in. The buyer does not want to buy the stock, but is willing to pay $3 million for the assets in the business.

The C corporation would sell the assets for $3 million to the buyer, and the corporation would recognize a $2.25 million gain – the difference between the $3 million purchase price and the corporation's $750,000 tax basis in the assets. After the corporation pays a corporate income tax on the gain, the balance of the proceeds would be distributed to the shareholders, who would pay a capital gains tax on the difference between the amount received and their low basis in the stock. The threat of this double tax at the time of sale is a major disadvantage for many C corporations.

Beyond this double tax impact, other important elements of this sellout factor should be considered. First, if a C corporation accumulates earnings within the corporation over an extended period of time, those accumulations do nothing to increase the shareholders' tax basis in their stock. If a shareholder sells stock down the road, the shareholder recognizes capital gains based on the shareholder's original cost basis in the stock. In contrast, if the business organization is operated in a pass-through entity, such as an LLC, an S corporation, or a partnership, the earnings accumulated in the business will boost, dollar for dollar, the owner's tax basis in his or her stock or partnership interest. So if the owner sells the stock or partnership interest, the earnings accumulated within the enterprise reduce the tax bite to the owner. This is a significant consequence, and it should not be ignored if the business plans to accumulate earnings in anticipation of a sale at a future date.

A second consideration is that, if a C corporation already has substantial value, it is not easy to convert to a pass-through entity and eliminate the threat of double tax. The business cannot make the conversion just before the sale and expect the tax benefits of an S election. Usually, it takes a significant period of time (up to 10 years) to wind out of the double-tax threat.

When all these factors are thrown into the mix, the S corporation looks attractive to Jason with respect to this sellout factor. As a pass-through entity, it eliminates the double tax hit and provides the basis booster for all earnings that are reinvested in the business. Plus, as a corporate entity, it offers the potential of tax-free reorganization benefits.

Factor 6: Passive Income Potential

If Jason uses a pass-through entity, such as an S corporation or an LLC, the income allocated to the owners who are not material participants in the business (a given in this situation) will be passive income that can be offset by tax losses, including passive losses. Even if the income is not distributed to the owners and is retained in the business to finance growth, the owners' losses from other activities can be used to reduce the tax bite on the business income. This capacity to use real estate and other passive losses of the owners to reduce current taxes on income from profitable activities often enhances the reinvestment of earnings in a profitable pass-through entity to finance growth.

By comparison, if the business is operated as a C corporation, there is no way that the income of the business, whether retained in the business or distributed to the owners, can be sheltered by passive losses that the owners generate from other activities. The bottom line is that, for many income-producing enterprises, those owners who are not employed by the business (and perhaps the business itself) will be much better off with a pass-through entity.

EXAMPLE CASE TWO: SUE AND JOYCE

Sue and Joyce are planning to form a new business that will offer specialized catering services. They will be the sole owners (in equal shares), and they will both work full time for the business. They will start out with eight other employees, but anticipate that the employee base could grow to 50 or more as they expand into neighboring markets.

They project that the business will need to reinvest $50,000 to $100,000 of earnings each year to finance growth and expansion. They will bailout the rest of the earnings as compensation income for the long hours they both will put into the business.

Sue and Joyce can't imagine ever selling the business and doubt anyone would be willing to pay much for it. The business is a means for them to each pursue a passion and earn a nice living along the way. It will be their careers. They want to maximize any fringe benefits for themselves.

The best option for the new company that is being organized by Sue and Joyce is a C corporation. This case illustrates three additional choice-of-entity factors.

Factor 7: Owner Fringe Benefits

Sue and Joyce's desire for employee fringe benefits may be a compelling factor in selecting a business form. There are a number of fringe benefits that are available to shareholder/employees of a C corporation that generally are not available to owner/employees of a pass-through entity, such as a partnership, LLC, or S corporation.

The significance of these fringe benefits depends on their importance to the particular owners. Investor owners could care less; employee owners, like Sue and Joyce, often view them as big deals. Each owner needs to assess whether the tax advantages of the fringe benefits are attractive enough to impact the choice-of-entity decision.

The most significant fringe benefits available to shareholder-employees of C corporations include group-term life insurance plans under Section 79, medical-dental reimbursement plans under Section 106, Section 125 cafeteria plans,[1] and dependent care assistance programs under Section 129.

Factor 8: The Bracket Racket

Only a C corporation offers the potential that the tax rate applied to the net income of the business may differ from the income tax rate applied to the owners of the business. All other entities (S corporations, LLCs, partnerships and sole proprietorships) are not separate taxpaying entities. Income earned by these entities is passed through and reported by the owners in proportion to their interests in the business. A C corporation may create an income-splitting opportunity – to have the income retained in the business taxed at a rate lower than the rates paid by the owners. In Sue and Joyce's situation, the different rate structure might be used to their advantage.

C corporations have a tiered graduated rate structure. This structure imposes a low 15-percent tax rate on taxable income up to $50,000 and a 25 percent rate on taxable income between $50,000 and $75,000. So if Sue and Linda can keep the corporation's taxable income to less than $100,000 each year, these low corporate rates will produce a significant bottom line tax savings. If this reinvested income was passed through to them, it is likely that the income tax rate would be at least 28 percent and perhaps more, and payroll taxes would be on top of the income tax hit. This bracket differential can be a significant factor when the numbers are in these ranges.

Note that the potential negative consequences of a C corporation are no big deal in this situation. Sue and Joyce will avoid all double tax fears by bailing out all available earnings as deductible compensation. The C corporation accumulated earnings tax, personal holding company tax, and alternative minimum tax pose no threats. The locked-in stock basis and other sellout costs are not a factor because Sue and Joyce have no plans to sell.

Note also that this potential bracket rate advantage does not apply to personal service C corporations because they are subject to a single-tiered tax bracket of 35 percent. For this reason, a personal service C corporation usually will be better off stripping the income out as compensation on a tax-deductible basis. A personal service corporation is defined as any corporation that meets two tests: a function test and an ownership test. The function test requires that the corporation perform substantially all of its services in the fields of health, law, engineering, architecture, accounting, actuarial science, the performing arts or consulting. The ownership test requires that substantially all of the stock be held directly or indirectly by employees who perform services in one of those fields. For example, the typical medical professional corporation will be a personal service corporation. Generally, there are no tax advantages to accumulating earnings in a personal service C corporation because of the high, flat tax rate structure.

---

1. A section 125 cafeteria plan may be adopted by a partnership, LLC, or S corporation, but S corporation shareholders holding two percent or more of the corporation's stock, partners of the partnership, and members of the LLC cannot participate in the plan. C corporation shareholders may participate so long as no more than 25 percent of the nontaxable benefits selected within the cafeteria plan go to key employees. Subject to the 25 percent limitation, C corporation shareholders can take full advantage of the tax benefits of the plan.

Factor 9: Tax Year Flexibility

Most C corporations may select any fiscal year for tax reporting purposes. Thus, use of a C corporation will give Sue and Joyce an opportunity to select a tax years that simplifies and accommodates their accounting and that may provide a tax deferral potential. Partnerships, LLCs, S corporations and sole proprietorships generally are required to use a calendar year unless they can prove a business purpose for using a fiscal year (a tough burden in most cases) or make a tax deposit under Section 7519 that is designed to eliminate any deferral advantage. C corporations that are personal service corporations may adopt a fiscal year with a deferral period of no more than three months, but the minimum distribution rules applicable to such personal service corporations under Section 280H substantially reduce any tax deferral potential.[2]

The income tax deferral potential of a C corporation that is not a personal service corporation is a fairly simple concept. Consider a manufacturing corporation that is owned by its key employees and that uses a calendar year for tax reporting. Its projected taxable income for 2014, its first year of operation, will be $240,000, and it will earn that income proportionately in each month during the year. For 2014, the choice for the owners of the corporation is to either report the income in the corporation or pay all or a portion of it to themselves as deductible compensation payments. With either approach, all of the $240,000 of taxable income will be reported in the 2014 tax returns of the owners or the corporation.

If the same corporation elects to use a fiscal year ending on March 31, a one-year deferral can be achieved on $180,000 of the $240,000 of taxable income. This is accomplished by having the corporation file a short-year return ending March 31, 2014, reporting $60,000 of taxable income. The remaining $180,000 earned during the last nine months of 2014 is reportable in the fiscal year ending March 31, 2015. But during the first three months of 2015, the owners pay themselves bonuses totaling $180,000 plus any income earned by the corporation during those three months, thus zeroing out the corporation's tax liability for the fiscal year ending March 31, 2015. These bonuses are deducted from the corporation's income for the fiscal year ending March 31, 2015, but are not reported by the calendar year shareholders until they file their 2015 returns on April 15, 2016.

The ability to use this technique is limited by the normal reasonable compensation standards. Plus, the deferral impact is often watered down by withholding and estimated tax payment requirements. But the technique is fairly common and is a legitimate means of deferring taxes.

EXAMPLE CASE THREE: CHARLES

Charles plans on buying and operating a large apartment complex. Charles will put up 10 percent of the equity capital, and the other 90 percent of the equity will come from four outside investors. The business will obtain debt financing equal to nearly four times the total equity capital, and is expected to generate

---

2. I.R.C. §§ 444(b)(2), 280(H).

substantial taxable losses during the first five years of operation, fueled in large part by big depreciation deductions.

Charles wants an entity that will allocate 99 percent of the losses to the investors, award him with 50 percent of the profits after the investors have recouped their investment, and, to the maximum extent possible, free him from minority owner hassles and contractual negotiations and dealings with minority owners. He wants total control. Plus, he would like to protect the investors from any self-employment taxes.

Charles is going to need a partnership-taxed entity, either a limited liability company where he is the sole manager, a limited partnership where his investors are limited partners and his wholly-owned LLC or S corporation is the general partner, or a limited liability limited partnership (if available under applicable state law). Of these options, the limited partnership may make it easier for Charles to nail down his absolute control rights and reduce any self-employment tax risks for the investors. But any of the approaches will work with some quality planning.

This case illustrates three additional choice-of-entity factors.

Factor 10: Different Ownership Interests

As Charles' deal illustrates, often owners want to structure different types of ownership interests in the entity. Income rights, loss rights, cash flow rights, or liquidation rights may need to be structured differently for select owners to reflect varying contributions to the enterprise. With a C corporation, different types of common and preferred stock may be issued to reflect varying preferences. An S corporation is extremely limited in its ability to create different types of equity ownership interests. It is limited to voting and non-voting common stock, all of which must have the same income, loss, cash flow and liquidation rights.

Partnerships and limited liability companies offer the most flexibility in structuring different equity ownership interests. These partnership-taxed, pass-through entities can customize and define the different interests in the entity's operating agreement. Although the design possibilities are almost unlimited, all allocations of profits, losses and credits will be respected for tax purposes only if the allocations are structured to have "substantial economic effect" within the meaning of section 704(b).

In Charles' situation, there's a clear need to use one of these partnership-taxed, flexible pass-through entities to create different types of ownership interests. This is particularly true in situations where one group of owners is providing capital and another is providing management services and expertise.

Factor 11: Loss Utilization

Like many organizers of businesses that are projected to generate losses in the early years, Charles wants to ensure that such losses are funneled to the tax returns that will trigger the highest tax savings. The threshold issue is whether the losses should be retained in the entity or passed through to the owners.

Losses generated by a C corporation are retained in the corporation and carried backward or forward to be deducted against income earned in previous or future years. Losses sustained by S corporations, LLCs, partnerships and sole proprietorships are passed through to the business owners. When losses are anticipated in the initial years of a business, using a pass-through entity may generate a tax advantage if the owners have other taxable income against which those losses can be offset, within certain limitations. The advantage is that the losses may produce immediate tax benefits.

In planning to pass through losses to the owners, never lose sight of the fact that the losses, even if passed through, may produce no benefit if one or more of three loss limitation hurdles described in Chapter 8 get in the way. The at-risk and passive loss hurdles usually are not impacted by the type of pass-through entity selected.

The basis hurdle is different in this regard. The general rule is that losses generated by a pass-through entity are unavailable to an owner of the entity to the extent that the cumulative net losses exceed the owner's basis in the entity. For example, if an investor puts $50,000 into an S corporation, that owner's basis in the S corporation stock is $50,000. If the S corporation generates a loss of $150,000 in the first year and finances the loss through corporate indebtedness, the S corporation shareholder may only use $50,000 of the loss against his or her other income. The other $100,000 is suspended because it exceeds the owner's stock basis. It is carried forward to be used in future years if and when the basis is increased. In contrast, if the indebtedness is incurred in an entity taxed as a partnership, such as a limited liability company or limited partnership, the indebtedness will increase the partners' basis in their partnership interests under the provisions of Section 752, and the basis limitation will no longer be a factor in assessing the current tax value of the losses.

Factor 12: Real Estate

The choice-of-entity analysis is usually impacted by the presence of real estate. The fact that most real estate tends to appreciate over time has powerful consequences for planning purposes. First, it permits the owners to take advantage of a fiction in the Internal Revenue Code – depreciation cost recovery deductions that are based on the premise that real estate improvements lose their value over time. Second, it sometimes facilitates the use of nonrecourse debt because lenders are willing to make loans that are secured only by the value of the real estate. The nonrecourse debt eliminates the loss basis hurdle for any entity taxed as a partnership and escapes the at-risk hurdle by virtue of the "qualified nonrecourse debt financing" exception that is applicable only to real estate.[3] And third, it is never prudent to subject the appreciation of the real estate to the double tax structure of a C corporation. As a general proposition, appreciating real estate should be kept out of C corporations. Plus, income from real estate activities that is passed through to the owners generally is not subject to the self-employment tax.[4]

3. I.R.C. §§ 752(a), 465(b)(6).

4. I.R.C. § 1402(a)(1). The tax will apply to anyone who receives rental income in the course of a trade or business as a real estate dealer.

Given these consequences, real estate usually warrants its own entity, and in nearly all situations that entity should be a partnership-taxed entity.

EXAMPLE CASE FOUR: JURDEN INC.

Jurden Inc. is a successful C corporation poised to explode. It has five shareholders, all successful business investors. The plan for the next five to ten years is to aggressively reinvest earnings to create a global presence and then sell out to a strategic buyer at the right time. The shareholders want to shed the C status now. They want the future tax benefits of a pass-though entity, including the stock basis booster for all reinvested earnings and the elimination or serious reduction of double tax bites at time of sale.

Jurden Inc's only option, as a practical matter, is to covert to an S corporation. This case illustrates a controlling choice-of-entity factor for many.

Factor 13: C Corporation Conversion Flexibility

As a C corporation, Jurden Inc. has only one option that makes sense. If it converted to a partnership structure or an LLC, a gain on the liquidation of the corporation would be triggered at both the corporate and shareholder level at time of conversion – a disastrous scenario. The corporation would recognize a gain on all its assets, and the shareholders would recognize a gain on the liquidation of their stock. The tax costs of getting into a partnership or LLC pass-through entity usually are too great to even think about.

The only practical answer for Jurden Inc. is an S corporation. At the present time, a C corporation may convert to an S corporation without automatically triggering the type of gain that would be triggered on a deemed liquidation of a C corporation.

The S corporation conversion, while clearly the preferred choice in most situations, is not a perfect solution and may trigger additional tax costs at the time of the conversion and later down the road. If, for example, the corporation values its inventories under the LIFO method, the corporation must recognize as income the LIFO reserve as a result of the S election conversion. Also, the conversion will not eliminate all threats of double taxation. If a C corporation converts to an S corporation and liquidates or sells out within 10 years after the election, the portion of the resulting gain attributable to the period before the election will be taxed at the corporate level as if the corporation had remained a C corporation. If the C corporation had accumulated earnings and profits before the conversion, the shareholders may end up with taxable dividends after the conversion. A completely clean break from C status often is impossible. But in most situations, these tax consequences of conversion can be managed and do not provide a basis for rejecting a conversion to S status that otherwise makes sense.

EXAMPLE CASE FIVE: PETER

Peter has developed a business plan for creating and exploiting a series of new Internet games that promise the potential of a huge success. He has attracted the attention of various investors, none of whom want their personal tax returns exposed to any venture and all of whom want to see Peter's unique talents showcased and exploited through a public company at the right time. The plan is to reinvest all business earnings so that Peter can build the business as fast as possible.

Peter is going to want a C corporation. This case illustrates three additional choice-of-entity factors, two of which usually are controlling when they apply.

Factor 14: Going Public Prospects

When a company is funded with outside capital and the plan is to go public at the first solid opportunity, the C corporation often is the mandated choice. The interests of the outside investors and the potential of going public trump all other considerations. Usually the audited track record of the company leading up to the offering is best reflected in the same form of entity that will ultimately go public, which is a C corporation in nearly all cases.

Factor 15: The "Not My Return" Factor

This factor is a consideration that sometimes preempts everything else. It refers to the owner who has no interest in anything that will implicate or complicate his or her personal tax return. Some just cannot accept the concept of having to personally recognize and pay taxes on income from a pass-through entity that has never been (and may never be) received in the form of cash. Others are spooked by the accounting and audit risks. The thought that their personal tax return and their personal tax liability could be directly impacted by the audit of a company managed by others is too much to bear. Still others are adamant about keeping all personal matters as simple and as understandable as possible. A stack of K–1 forms flapping on the back of their returns is not their concept of simple. When this factor cannot be eliminated, the only option is a C corporation that offers the benefit of complete "separateness."

Factor 16: Reinvestment Growth

Like many, Peter hopes to grow his company by reinvesting all earnings. In recent years, the tax rate differential between individual taxpayers and a C corporation has not been significant. Both have topped out at a maximum rate of 35 percent. So the choice-of-entity analysis has not turned on the potential to reinvest after-tax earnings and grow the business.

But that all changed in 2013. The American Taxpayer Relief Act of 2012 (the "Fiscal Cliff" legislation signed into law during the final days of 2012)[5] increased individual ordinary income tax rates to 39.6 percent starting in 2013 for couples with taxable incomes in excess of $450,000 and individuals with taxable incomes in excess of $400,000. Plus, in 2013 the 3.8 percent Medicare tax kicked in for couples with a modified adjusted gross income in excess of $250,000 ($200,000 for individuals). The net result is that a successful business owner who is allocated profits through a pass-through S corporation or LLC could end up paying federal taxes at a combined income and Medicare rate of 43.4 percent. In contrast, political leaders on both sides of the aisle and the Obama administration have suggested that top corporate tax rates should be

5. Section 101 of the American Taxpayer Relief Act of 2012.

reduced to the 25 to 28 percent range to remain competitive with other countries. The result is that we could end up with a condition that we haven't had for decades – a mammoth gap between top individual rates and top corporate rates.

For a company looking to grow with reinvested earnings, such a huge rate differential between individual and corporate rates may compel use of a C corporation. The difference between reinvesting 56 cents on every earned dollar and reinvesting 75 cents, when compounded over five or ten years and adjusted for leveraging differences, may impact a business' capacity to finance growth by as much as 100 percent or more. As the push for such a rate differential intensifies, this may emerge as the newest and most dominant choice-of-entity factor for businesses that need to grow.

FACTOR SUMMARY AND CONCLUSION

A review of these 16 factors in a given situation will help in choosing the best form of business entity and understanding the primary and collateral consequences. One conclusion is fairly obvious: The C corporation is a very different creature from the other forms, all of which are pass-through entities. Therefore, often the starting point is to take a hard look at the C corporation as an alternative. If it fails to pass muster (and it will in many situations), the alternative pass-through entity forms will need to be evaluated.

STUDENT PROBLEM 9-1

Sam leads a group of five wealthy investors who are going to form a new manufacturing company. They anticipate that the company's profitability will steadily grow, starting at $350,000 in year one and growing to $2.5 million a year within five years. None of the owners will work fulltime for the company, but Sam will oversee the operations and serve as a liaison between the owners and key managers. The owners plan to reinvest all profits to quickly expand the business and then to sell to a strategic buyer as soon as possible. It's possible that any sale of the business might be structured as a tax-free reorganization that would provide the owners with stock in a public company. The owners want a structure that will fuel growth by minimizing taxes, limit liability exposure, and ensure that each owner has equal control in future decisions.

What entity form would you recommend? Explain your reasoning and any alternatives that Sam and his colleagues might want to consider.

STUDENT PROBLEM 9-2

Betty is an entrepreneur who has developed a business plan for creating and exploiting a new flash-type Internet application. Betty will be the sole owner, but will spend very little time in the business. The inspiration and driving force behind the business will be Justin. In addition to Justin, the business will have six employees who will fulfill contracts with companies that want and need the technology. Betty anticipates that the business will be profitable from the get-go and that she will withdraw profits on a regular basis. She wants to have a separate entity for business purposes that will minimize taxes and not expose her personal assets and other businesses to the risks of this business. What form of entity do you recommend? What additional facts would you like to have?

STUDENT PROBLEM 9-3

Lou has plans to form a new company that will design and build custom luxury motor coaches for celebrities, professional athletes, and wealthy couples who fear planes and want to be driven in ultimate luxury. He has secured equity financing from five wealthy investors, who collectively have agreed to put up $6 million to finance the first eight coaches. The "deal" with these investors is that (1) Lou will get a salary of $250,000 a year; (2) the investors will get their investment money back before any additional distributions; (3) Lou will then be paid the $200,000 that he has invested to develop the initial plans; and (4) profits then will be distributed 30 percent to Lou and 70 percent to the investors. Any losses will be allocated 99 percent to the investors and one percent to Lou. Lou wants to ensure that he always has complete control of all business decisions, an investor cannot get out once he or she has acquired an interest in the business, and taxes are minimized.

You represent Lou. What entity form would you recommend? Explain your reasoning and any alternatives that Lou might want to consider.

STUDENT PROBLEM 9-4

Duke, Joan and Alice are going to form a new company that will provide web and app design and construction services. They will be the sole owners and will be employed full time by the business. They anticipate adding eight to ten support employees over the next three years as the business ramps up. Projections indicate that the business will need to retain approximately $90,000 of earnings for each of the next five years to finance growth. The balance of the earnings will be withdrawn by the three owners to fund their lifestyles and capital accumulation efforts.

The owners view the business as a career income vehicle, not an entity that will be sold at some point in the future. Their primary objectives are to create a collegial working environment, maximize income and benefits for themselves, and minimize taxes. What form of entity do you recommend? What additional facts would you like to have? Explain your reasoning and any alternatives that the owners might want to consider.

CHAPTER 10

OWNERS OF CLOSELY HELD BUSINESSES

A. CO-OWNER PROTECTIONS

This chapter focuses on three important challenges often faced by owners of closely held businesses: protections from co-owners; exit strategies and opportunities for owners who want or need to sellout and move on; and optional structures for maximizing the after-tax yield from a sale of the business.

Jason, Lucy, and Sam organized a new corporation ("Newco") two years ago to develop and exploit a new product designed to make it easy to produce low-cost vinyl fencing. All three serve on the board of Newco, and Jason and Lucy are officers, employed full-time by Newco. Sam invested $1.2 million in Newco, far more than Jason and Lucy, in return for 40 percent of Newco's outstanding common stock. But as things stand, Sam is only one of three directors. Serious frictions have developed between Sam and his co-shareholders over changes in the basic business plan of Newco, incurring additional debt, paying bonuses to officers, and accelerating the growth targets of the business.

Sam feels trapped. He believes that his positions on these key issues are sound, but he is subject to the will of the majority – Jason and Lucy. At the time Newco was formed and Sam made his decision to invest, he gave no thought to affirmatively securing rights to control major operational decisions that may become a source of conflict down the road. This common failure is one of the biggest upfront planning mistakes made when colleagues come together to form a new business.

1. WHY AND HOW?

Every new venture needs organizational documents. The number, scope and complexity of the documents depend on the composition of the owners, the number and type of entities used, and the quality of the planning effort on the front end. Usually customization of the organizational documents increases as the planning effort improves. More customization results in more complexity and, most importantly, a better mutual understanding of the key deal points between the organizers and owners of the business.

An agreement between the shareholders is critically important in nearly all situations involving a closely held corporation. For planning purposes, this agreement is the most important document – by a long shot. It lays out the terms of the buy-sell agreements among shareholders and the details of those operational deal points the shareholders have chosen to document. This is not a required document, and it is shamefully ignored in far too many situations. It takes more work, more dialogue and more customization than any other organizational document.

Although the authority to manage a corporation is vested in its board of directors, state corporate statutes generally authorize the use of shareholder agreements to establish rights among the shareholders of closely held corporations (those corporations whose stock is not publicly traded) that preempt the management authority of the board. The shareholders agreement should be carefully drafted, specify how long it will remain in effect (absent such a provision, the applicable state statute may terminate the agreement after a specified term, such as 10 years), and be conspicuously referenced in written legends on all stock certificates issued by the corporation.

The initial challenge in the planning process is to identify the key operational deal points that need to be dealt with by agreement. For the majority owner or group that has voting control (over 50 percent of the voting interests), the preferred choice may be to refrain from initiating any dialogue with the other owners. This controlling person or group knows that they are in the driver's seat by virtue of their control. The burden is on the minority owners to raise any issues that may require special treatment in a shareholders agreement or operating agreement. If the minority owners do as Sam did and say nothing, the protection planning may be totally neglected as all owners get caught up in the exciting prospects of the new venture. No operational issues will be identified, discussed, prioritized, and resolved.

The lawyer who is engaged to organize and represent the organization, not a particular owner or group of owners, should be sensitive to the conflicts that various operational deal points may create between the owners. But the sad reality is that in far too many cases, the organization is formed "the normal way," with little or no dialogue on the potentially tough issues.

The far better approach is for the entity's lawyer or a prospective owner to initiate a dialogue with all the owners in a meeting or series of meetings that address the most important issues. When the necessary terms have been hammered out, they should be incorporated in the shareholder agreement. The process requires a modest commitment of time and expense, but it will go a long way in identifying and resolving on the front-end any fundamental differences between the parties. The corporation and the relationships between the shareholders will be stronger as a result.

2. *POTENTIAL BUSINESS ISSUES TO CONSIDER*

Following are brief descriptions of 20 operational deal points that often need to be discussed during the organizational process. Only a few might be of concern in a given situation and require a resolution incorporated in an agreement among the owners. But often the organizational planning process is improved and the confidence of all parties heightened by discovering through dialogue that many or most of these issues present no conflicts for the owners

a. The Scope of the Enterprise

It is often desirable to limit by agreement the scope of the business activities of the entity. Some owners may feel more comfortable about their investment in the venture if they do not have to worry about their money being diverted into activities outside the scope of what was originally discussed. Liability exposure may also be an issue, particularly where key players have multiple business interests. Limiting the scope of the business activities may help limit the business entity's liability exposure for unrelated actions of these players. And then there's the "Tag Along" problem. Often owners prefer a written activity limitation that removes any expectations that other owners may have relative to other business activities. They like the idea of an express, unequivocal line in the sand that defines the limit of their relationship with their co-owners. In contrast, some shareholders may object to a written limitation on scope of the enterprise, arguing that it restricts flexibility, creates potential confusion for third parties, and fosters notions of "separateness" and "temporariness."

b. Business Plan Changes

The issue of business plan changes raises some of the same concerns as the scope of enterprise limitation. But here the issue is not whether the corporation can venture into different directions, but rather whether it can accelerate its plan for moving in its authorized direction. Turning up the volume usually triggers more risk and requires some combination of more capital or debt. Some owners may want the comfort of a written agreement that limits the capacity of their co-owners to overreact to early success by trashing the plan they all bought into up front in favor of a new model that promises greater pressure, more risk, and a potentially faster track to the gold.

c. Debt

The first lesson of Business 101 is the value of leveraging the borrowed dollar. Most start-up operations require personal guarantees because the business operations are not mature enough to carry the debt. As the business grows, the guarantees may disappear unless a decision is made to accelerate the growth rate of the business. The big issues for the owners are: the amount of debt that is going to be incurred during the start-up phase; the guarantees that the owners are going to provide; the priority that will be given to eliminating personal guarantees in the future; and the acceptable debt level as the business grows and develops. Some owners may want a written understanding on these key issues, particularly as they relate to personal guarantees. They may want to limit expectations of others relative to their willingness to provide guarantees beyond the levels agreed to, while being assured that their colleagues will step up to the plate and provide the level of guarantees that all have accepted.

d. Additional Capital Contributions

The issue of additional capital contributions from the owners often requires dialogue and a written understanding. Some owners, even those with deep pockets, may want to kill any expectations that they will help provide whatever is needed to keep the venture afloat or fund growth. Others may be concerned with dilution. They do not want their equity interests reduced as those with greater means continually pony up more money and claim a bigger share of the whole. Preemptive rights that give all owners the right to protect their percentage interests with additional contributions are often inadequate or become obstacles to securing capital from new investors.

When this issue is a major concern, the owners need to talk through their concerns and, often with the aid of counsel, reach an agreement that to the fullest extent possible addresses the objectives of the owners. One approach is to specify that each owner must contribute his or her *pro rata* share of the capital needed to accomplish the purpose of the entity. Some owners may be unwilling to agree to an unlimited equity contribution requirement. In this situation, the agreement may have to place a cap on future required capital contributions.

If there is no mandatory requirement for additional capital contributions, the agreement may need to spell out how future capital needs will be satisfied. For example, it may permit but not require any one or more owners to make additional contributions and receive additional stock or equity interests. Another approach is to authorize any owner to make a loan to the entity if additional cash is required, and then to provide that the loan is to be paid back, with interest, before any cash distributions are made to the owners.

e. New Shareholders

The policy for admitting new owners is a critical issue in professional service and family organizations and many service businesses. It is a major event that often requires the consent of all the owners or a super-majority of owners. Often it raises the same dilution concerns as additional capital contributions. Plus, there is the added factor of a new personality. When the investors are truly passive and have no involvement in the operations, a new personality, even an unpleasant one, may be of little or no concern. But in most closely held businesses, the owners have input and the capacity to be a positive or negative force. This reality, coupled with the fear that divisive factions may develop or be fed as more bodies are added, may warrant special provisions dealing with the admission of new owners.

f. Owner Roles and Service Commitments

The roles of the owners need to be clarified in many situations. For owners employed and compensated by the venture, the key issues are the level of their service commitment and their right to be involved in other activities. Are they expected to devote all of their time and energies to the enterprise?

For those owners who are not employed by the business, the challenge is to clarify expectations. Some owners may expect that they will be entitled to serve on the board or have some other advisory role that provides an opportunity for input. Having put up their money, they want a spot in the inner circle. Some may expect that the sage advice and wisdom of a particular owner will be available when in fact that investor, although willing to put up a few dollars, has no interest in providing input or otherwise being tied to the business.

g. Owner Employment Rights

Often a need exists to clarify the relationship between an owner's equity interest in the business and that owner's employment by the business. In many organizations, the two are tied together through the agreement – no employment, no equity. The issue usually surfaces in a few different ways. A key owner may have received equity for putting the deal together or as compensation for management services rendered or to be rendered or, as is usually the case, for some combination of these considerations. Often that key owner wants assurance that his or her right to manage the business is protected and cannot be disturbed by the other owners, except under the most extreme circumstances. The other owners may want clearly defined termination rights if the key owner doesn't do the job to their satisfaction. And, to add injury to insult, the other owners may want the key shareholder to forfeit some or all of his or her equity in such an event or, at a minimum, to be obligated to sell any residual equity back to the entity at a price determined pursuant to an agreement.

h. Business Location

In select situations, the location of the business' operations or headquarters may be a concern. There have been situations where owners have frustrated the rights of a key owner/employee by proposing to move the business to a location that makes it extremely inconvenient for the key employee. Usually, such a proposed move is supported by valid business justifications, such as cheaper labor prices, lower taxes, or reduced shipping costs. The owner who has a vested interest in the business' headquarters staying in a particular city may want a contractual provision in the agreement that protects that interest. Usually it can be secured with no objection on the front end.

i. Outside Shareholder Activities

Beyond the issue of outside activities of shareholder/employees discussed previously, sometimes there is a need to consider limitations on the outside activities of other owners. Often there is a desire to restrict owners from investing in competitors, major suppliers, or important customers of the business. The fear is that such investments may create conflicts that could compromise future opportunities. Some investors may strongly resist such limitations. They may be unwilling to surrender their investment flexibility and options to a single investment, as they oppose any contractual corporate opportunity limitations. Often their willingness to participate will be conditioned on an express provision to the contrary.

j. Related-Party Transactions

Transactions with related parties often are a source of contention in closely held businesses. Examples include leasing facilities from a major owner, purchasing supplies or raw materials from a business controlled by an owner or an owner's relative, licensing proprietary rights from an owner, purchasing capital assets from an owner, and employing relatives of an owner. To avoid the conflicts and embarrassments that often accompany these situations, the parties may include approval mechanisms in the agreement that assure that any such related-party transactions are structured to include pricing terms, termination rights, and other provisions that serve the best interests of the entity.

k. Tax Elections

To avoid future conflicts, often it is advisable to document how certain tax matters are going to be handled. Examples include the selection of a fiscal year, cost recovery deductions, and inventory valuation methods. There may be the potential of a future S election, which requires the consent of all owners, or the potential termination of an S election, which requires the consent of owners owning over half the outstanding stock. In both situations, a different approval percentage may be desired and fixed by agreement. For S election purposes, the preference may be a supermajority vote that gives no single shareholder a veto power. For S termination purposes, something more than a simple majority may be warranted before the S election is discarded. An agreement among the owners is an excellent tool for nailing down how key tax elections are going to be handled.

l. Confidentiality Covenants

Employees, including owners who are employees, are often required to sign confidentiality agreements structured to protect the trade secrets and proprietary rights of the business. Sometimes it is desirable to extend these agreements to all owners of the business, particularly in those situations where the owners may have access to trade secrets or proprietary information critical to the success of the business. Some investors may resist any such agreements or any mechanism that limits other investment options or exposes them to any future claims relating to the use of proprietary information. When the issue is important and the potential investors won't budge, it may be necessary to start shopping for some different investors.

m. Accounts Payable Management

There are different perceptions about paying bills. Some see it as an opportunity to generate easy, low-cost financing by implementing a practice of delayed payment that pushes the envelope but keeps all vendors on board. Others view it as an easy way to show strength, establish an admirable Dunn and Bradstreet rating, and build vendor loyalty and confidence (which may be badly needed in rough times) by not missing a due date. Plus, with the discounts many vendors offer for prompt payment, an on-time payment strategy may add to the bottom line.

This issue can become a source of contention between owners as the business begins to mature. Some may not want to be involved with a slow-pay enterprise that always looks strapped for cash, while others may want to maximize all financing options within definable limits. An upfront discussion between the owners may result in an understanding that avoids a future conflict when the business is in full swing and the issue is hot.

n. Cash Distributions and Allocations

Are cash distributions to the owners a priority concern? Some owners may want to know that the plan includes regular distributions as the business ramps up. Others may expect that all after-tax profits will be invested to finance growth and that no cash will flow for some time. It is a fundamental part of the plan that should be clear to all owners.

The problem is that the issue is tied to other key factors, including the growth rate of the business and the use of debt. Often the answer is to set guidelines regarding growth and debt that, once hit, will begin to trigger cash distributions to the owners. Typically, a provision is structured to ensure that cash is only distributed when all other cash needs of the business have been met, including ensuring appropriate reserves for working capital and other potential future needs. Also, loan agreements with the business' bank often impose restrictions on the timing and amount of cash distributions.

An agreement regarding cash distributions is particularly important with any pass-through entity, such as an S corporation or LLC, where the earnings of the entity are not taxed to the entity but instead are passed through and taxed to the owners. The owners often want some contractual assurance that cash distributions will be made to fund their pass-through tax liabilities.

For an S corporation, it is not possible to structure such cash distributions based on the size of the respective tax liabilities of the individual shareholders. Any such attempt would likely result in a claim that the S corporation has more than one class of stock and end up killing the S election. In an S corporation, cash distributions must be allocated among the shareholders according to their respective common stockholdings. So when there is a need to contractually commit an S corporation to make cash distributions to cover the shareholders' pass-through tax liabilities, often the best approach is to specify in the agreement that a designated percentage of the income allocated to shareholders (e.g., 40 percent) will be distributed in cash to the shareholders in accordance with their respective stockholdings. Such a flat percentage approach will likely result in some individual shareholders getting slightly more or less than is needed to cover the tax bills.

o. Shareholder Compensation Benefits

In situations where certain owners are employed by the entity, there is often a need to clarify the compensation rights of those owners and how such rights will take priority over any dividends or distributions to the owners. The compensation rights may include a specified salary, period salary adjustments, cash bonuses based on the performance of the entity, deferred compensation benefits, life insurance benefits, and compensation in the form of equity. Typically, these compensation rights are spelled out in an executive employment agreement with a key owner/employee that is coordinated with the buy-out provisions of the agreement among the owners.

p. Selection of Professionals

Business entities need the assistance of outside professionals, including lawyers, accountants, appraisers, actuaries, investment firms, employee benefit firms and so forth. The method of selecting such professionals is often a potential source of conflict. Too often the organizer selects professionals who have a history with, and a loyalty to, that person. Those selected may not be the best qualified, nor the best suited to represent the interests of the entity.

Depending on the circumstances leading up to the lawyer's involvement in the start-up planning process, this may be an uncomfortable issue to deal with during the organizational effort. Nevertheless, it is often smart to do so. It makes it easy for all owners to vent any concerns, and actually may help build credibility for the lawyer. Often it leads to a procedure for selecting and monitoring the performance of all outside professionals that eliminates future concerns or conflicts among the owners.

q. Indemnifications

Will those owners or employees who act on behalf of the entity be protected against any personal loss, damage or liability they incur as a result of such activity? The answer is usually "yes." An indemnification and hold harmless provision is included to protect against such liabilities and any associated legal fees. But significant limitations are often included. First, the agreement may provide that the indemnification is recoverable only out of the assets of the entity and not from the owners. The owners usually want no personal exposure for the acts of others. If the primary assets of the business have been pledged to secure financing, the assets available for any such indemnity may be very limited. Second, the indemnification may extend only to acts or omissions undertaken in good faith and with a belief that they were in the best interests of the corporation. This places a proof burden on the employee or owner who is the target of the claim. Third, the agreement may require that the targeted employee or owner tender the defense or resolution of the claim to the company so that the company can control expenses and dispose of the matter on its own terms.

r. Dispute Resolution Procedures

An important issue that usually needs to be addressed by agreement is how disputes among owners are to be resolved. No matter how carefully the upfront planning is handled, a dispute may erupt among the owners. It's usually prudent to have all the owners agree to a method for quickly and inexpensively resolving any dispute that may surface. Absent such a mechanism, the likely result is expensive, time-consuming, and potentially destructive litigation. A common method of resolving any disputes is arbitration. The agreement lays out the necessary procedures, including where the arbitration will be held and how the costs will be shared. Everyone agrees that the decision of the arbitrators will be binding on the parties. The agreement also may require mediation before any litigation or arbitration proceeding.

s. Life-After Rights

In many businesses, particularly service and professional service organizations, it is advisable to spell out the "going forward" rights that each owner will have in the event there is a falling out and the group fractures. Absent such an agreement, the owners may find themselves tangled up with shutdown issues that may make it difficult for some to immediately shift gears and preserve the continuity of their business activities. Most professionals and service providers cannot afford a major disruption that stops their careers. Key issues include the right to engage in the same business as the fractured entity; the right to pursue and service clients of the entity; the right to hire employees of the entity; the right to deal with vendors and financial institutions used by the entity; the right to make copies of client documents, files and other important documents; the right to use the same business email addresses and phone numbers; and the right to disclose the prior affiliation with the entity. The owners often want the ability to immediately exercise these rights when things blow up, even while the affairs of the corporation are being resolved and settled.

t. Sell-Out Options

Often the owners desire to clarify how a decision will be made for the corporation to sell out and cash in down the road. Potential future transactions could include a sale of substantially all the assets and goodwill of the business, a sale of all the stock or equity interests of the business, or a merger of the corporation into a larger company whose stock is publicly traded. The owners may want to require something more than a majority vote for such a "that's-the-ball-game" transaction, and may want the assurance of knowing that all are required to play ball and go along if the requisite percentage approves the transaction.

3. *SOLUTION TECHNIQUES*

Resolving a planning issue that is of concern to the owners requires a solution. The range of potential solutions in any given situation is limited only by the imagination of the parties involved. Often a combination approach is required to satisfy the objectives of all owners. Following are brief descriptions of solution techniques that are often used.

a. Definitive Contractual Provision

The agreement resolves the issue by spelling out the "deal" and what is expected of each party. Examples: All owners must sign confidentiality agreements; accounts payable will be paid in a timely manner to take advantage of early pay discounts; an S election will be made; arbitration is mandated in the event of a dispute; each owner will be required to make additional contributions equal to 25 percent of his or her original contribution if such funding is needed; all owners will have specified life-after rights in the event of a falling out; and so forth. The parties reach an agreement that is incorporated into the shareholder or operating agreement.

b. Supermajority Vote

The parties agree that resolution of the issue will require a supermajority approval vote of the shareholders. Seventy or 80 percent will be required in order to accelerate the business plan, to incur additional debt beyond the approved limits, to trigger or revoke an S election, to approve a merger or sale of substantially all the assets, and so forth. The provision comforts both those who want something more than a simple majority and those who want the assurances that one individual cannot block certain actions, such as the making of an S election.

c. Designated Board or Management Committee

Often the solution is to delegate all future decisions regarding an issue to a board of directors that has been carefully structured by agreement to protect the interests of all parties. Assume, for example, an entity where 40 percent of the equity interests are owned by employees and 60 percent are owned by investors. The parties agree to have a four-person board, comprised of two employee-owners and two investors. Since any decision will require a vote of at least three members, all owners have the comfort of knowing that any affirmative decision on a particular issue will require the approval of at least one of their representatives.

d. Specified Conditions

Sometimes an issue can be resolved by specifying the conditions that must exist for the board of directors to act on the matter. Often such conditions are combined with a supermajority back-up provision. For example, the agreement might specify that, absent a 70-percent approval by the shareholders, the board will incur no bank financing beyond the approved limits if such financing would cause the company's debt-to-equity ratio to exceed 4-to-1.

e. Individual Veto Right

In select situations, an issue can be resolved by giving a particular owner an individual veto right. For example, a key employee who is also a shareholder may be concerned that the board will change the business plan by reducing employee health insurance benefits. The other shareholders appreciate their colleague's concern and suspect that any changes in the short term are unlikely. To resolve the issue, all agree that any reductions in employee health insurance benefits over the next five years will be subject to the approval of the specific shareholder.

f. Opt-Out Rights

Sometimes a shareholder issue can be resolved by giving shareholders the right to opt out of the effects of a decision. For example, any concerns regarding debt expansion may be eliminated by granting individual shareholders the right to opt out of any personal guarantee requirement for the additional debt. One or more individual dissenters may protect their own pocketbooks without stopping the entity from moving forward. Of course, if too many owners exercise the opt-out privilege, the additional financing becomes unobtainable.

g. Buy-Out Trigger

A buy-out trigger under the buy-sell provisions may be justified in some extreme situations to accommodate the concerns of a specific owner. For example, a shareholder may be adamantly opposed to any business plan acceleration or debt expansion changes made without his or her consent. To alleviate the concern, that owner may be given an option to trigger a purchase of his or her interest in the company under the buy-sell agreement if the others choose to move forward with such a change in the future over the objection of such owner. The concerned owner is satisfied with the exit protection, and the others are comfortable with a provision that may create an opportunity to increase their equity positions and rid themselves of a difficult colleague once things are going strong.

h. Cumulative Voting

In select situations, a cumulative voting provision may be used to give minority owners the capacity to elect an individual to the board of directors or managing committee of the organization. The provision grants each shareholder votes equal to the number of shares he or she owns multiplied by the number of directors to be elected and the right to cast those votes among one or more directors. A few states mandate cumulative voting; most states allow it if it is authorized in the articles of incorporation. The following basic formula helps in determining the number of minority shares (one vote per share) needed to elect a designated number of directors with cumulative voting, where "A" equals the total needed shares, "B" equals the total shares to be voted by all owners, "C" equals the number of directors the minority would like to elect, and "D" equals the total number of directors to be elected:

$$A = [(B \times C) / (D + 1)] + 1$$

For example, if the minority shareholders want the capacity to elect one of four directors and there are 1,000 votes outstanding, the minority shareholders would need 201 shares [((1,000 x 1) divided by 4 + 1) + 1].

For planning purposes, cumulative voting often sounds better than it really is. A single seat on the board may do little or nothing to enhance the minority's position on key issues. Plus, if the board seat is vitally important, it may be obtained by a specific agreement among the shareholders, without the complexity and arithmetic challenges of cumulative voting. But there are situations where the minority's counsel, hearkening back to his or her law school days, regards it as a big deal, and the majority concludes that it is a relatively harmless alternative to other solutions that may have more teeth.

i. Preemptive Rights

A preemptive rights provision in the articles of incorporation is sometimes used to pacify shareholders who fear that future fundraising efforts will dilute their interests in the enterprise. The provision gives each owner the right to acquire his or her proportionate share of any newly issued stock under specific conditions spelled out in the articles of incorporation or, in the absence of such conditions, according to the applicable state statute.

There are three primary concerns from a planning perspective. First, although preemptive rights may seem harmless on their face, often they can stymie a company's flexibility to move quickly and decisively in resolving its capital needs. The rights can trigger delays and uncertainties that can hurt the company and cause potential new investors to quickly lose interest. Considerable thought should be given to the use (or better yet, the nonuse) of such rights. Second, if preemptive rights are to be granted, care should be taken to structure the necessary exceptions in the articles of incorporation and not to automatically rely on the default provisions of the applicable state statute. Important exceptions may include, among others, shares issued to compensate key employees, shares issued for property other than cash, shares issued in time of financial crisis to secure important financing guarantees, and shares issued to satisfy option and conversion rights. Finally, the timing requirements of the preemptive rights should be carefully structured. The company may be stuck on hold as shareholders ponder their decision to exercise or waive their preemptive rights and consult with their financial advisors. Short time requirements will turn up the heat and help preserve the interest of potential new investors.

STUDENT PROBLEM 10-1

Five individuals are organizing a C corporation in a state that has adopted the Model Business Corporation Act. The company will develop and market a line of high-quality snowboards throughout the world. They have collectively agreed to fund the new venture with $2 million of equity capital, but the owners disagree as to the need for more capital down the road.

Linda and Dave, both deep-pocketed investors, have each committed $600,000 for 30 percent of the stock. They "feel strongly" that the group should have an understanding as to how it will raise an additional $2 million of equity if "necessary to maximize the opportunity." They have made it clear that they will contribute whatever is needed, so long as their equity increases proportionately. They do not want to use their wealth "to secure financing that just preserves the equity of the others."

Duke, an accountant with wealth but nothing close to Linda or Dave's league, has agreed to invest $300,000 for 15 percent of the stock. He is willing to "put up more to fund growth if things are going strong, but not to fund a black hole if things stall out." He contends that the company can "easily" finance any growth with "low risk" bank financing guaranteed by the owners.

Joyce and Wade, avid former professional snowboarders, have each committed $250,000 for 12.5 percent of the stock. They will play a key role in the promotion of the company's products. They have emphatically stated that they do not want to put up more capital.

The group of five needs ideas for resolving their differences on this issue. Explain how each of the techniques described in subsections a. through i. above might play a role in developing a range of solutions for the owners. Which of these techniques, alone or combined with others, might provide the best solution for the owners? Get creative.

B. EXIT CHALLENGES: THE BUY-SELL PROVISIONS

Business owners need to prepare early for the day when they will part company for whatever reason. At some point down the road, an owner is going to want or need to sell his or her equity interest in the business. Somebody is going to leave the business, die, become disabled, or experience a messy divorce. Plus, the owners should acknowledge the simple reality that no matter how good they feel about one another going into the enterprise, tough business decisions may create friction along the way. Friction often leads to a buyout or, worse yet, a legal blowup.

The answer is a smart buy-sell agreement between the owners that may define the ultimate value of each owner's equity interest in the business – what the owner will yield when it comes time to cash out. An effective and workable buy-sell agreement requires considerable thought by the business owners and guidance from their legal advisors. The owners should be encouraged to spend sufficient time to think through and hash out the issues. A careful record should be kept of the decision points in the discussions so that the agreement can be periodically reviewed to determine if the reasons for the various provisions remain or have changed. As time passes, circumstances will change that will necessitate revisions.

1. RISKS WITH NO DEAL?

Often the question is asked: What happens if a dispute breaks out and there is no buy-sell agreement? It can trigger a serious problem that tests the will of the combatants and may threaten the health or survival of the business. The minority shareholders may have no effective remedy other than a potential claim, often nearly impossible to prove, that the controlling owners have been oppressive.

As for statutory remedies, most states have corporate statutes patterned after the Model Business Corporation Act that empower a court to dissolve the corporation if a shareholder can prove that:

- The directors are deadlocked, the deadlock cannot be broken by the shareholders, and the deadlock is injuring the corporation or impairing the conduct of its business;
- The shareholders are deadlocked and have not been able to elect directors for two years;
- Corporate assets are being wasted; or
- Those in control are acting "in a manner that is illegal, oppressive, or fraudulent."[1]

As regards any oppression claim, the Official Comments to the Model Act indicate that courts should be "cautious" so as "to limit such cases to genuine abuse rather than instances of acceptable tactics in a power struggle for control of a corporation."[2]

A disgruntled minority shareholder, armed with such a statute, may have nothing more than a feeble threat to bring an action to dissolve the entity. And often there is no basis for believing that a court will go beyond the confines of the applicable corporation code. The sentiment of many courts when faced with a claim of an unhappy minority shareholder was aptly described by the Delaware Supreme Court in *Nixon v. Blackwell*[3] as follows:

---

1. Model Business Corporation Act § 14.30(a)(2). If a shareholder petitions to dissolve the corporation under the statute, the corporation or other shareholders may elect to purchase the shares of the petitioning shareholder at the fair value of such shares and, thereby, turn the proceeding into a valuation case. Model Business Corporation Act § 14.34.
2. Model Business Corporation Act Official Comment 2. B. to § 14.30.
3. 626 A.2d 1366 (Del. 1993).

> We wish to address one further matter which was raised at oral argument before this Court: Whether there should be any special, judicially-created rules to "protect" minority stockholders of closely-held Delaware corporations.
>
> The case at bar points up the basic dilemma of minority stockholders in receiving fair value for their stock as to which there is no market and no market valuation. It is not difficult to be sympathetic, in the abstract, to a stockholder who finds himself or herself in that position. A stockholder who bargains for stock in a closely-held corporation and who pays for those shares (unlike the plaintiffs in this case who acquired their stock through gift) can make a business judgment whether to buy into such a minority position, and if so on what terms. One could bargain for definitive provisions of self-ordering permitted to a Delaware corporation through the certificate of incorporation or by-laws by reason of the provisions in 8 Del.C. §§ 102, 109, and 141(a). Moreover, in addition to such mechanisms, a stockholder intending to buy into a minority position in a Delaware corporation may enter into definitive stockholder agreements, and such agreements may provide for elaborate earnings tests, buyout provisions, voting trusts, or other voting agreements. See, e.g., 8 Del.C. § 218.
>
> The tools of good corporate practice are designed to give a purchasing minority stockholder the opportunity to bargain for protection before parting with consideration. It would do violence to normal corporate practice and our corporation law to fashion an ad hoc ruling which would result in a court-imposed stockholder buy-out for which the parties had not contracted.[4]

So the planning challenge, in the words of the Delaware Supreme Court, is to use the "tools of good corporate practice" and "bargain for protection before parting with consideration."

2. BUSINESS OBJECTIVES OF THE PLANNING PROCESS

A carefully designed buy-sell agreement will accomplish many important objectives of the parties. Often, it is helpful to start the process by identifying and prioritizing the primary objectives. Key objectives of this process include:

- **Control Who Gets In.** This objective is to ensure that ownership interests in the company are never transferred or made available to third parties who are unacceptable to the owners. This objective may not be a big deal in some organizations that only have passive investors, but it usually is a top priority in all other situations. Absent careful planning, an untimely death, disability, bankruptcy, or employment termination may trigger a condition that exposes an equity interest to an unwanted third party.

- **Fairness.** This objective is to ensure that there is a mechanism to fairly value and fund the equity interest of a departing owner. The goal is to avoid the necessity of divisive negotiations at a point of crisis, where one party may be in a

4. 626 A.2d at pages 1379-80.

weak position with no leverage. The agreement should contain fair provisions that reflect the interests of all parties.

- **Smooth Transition.** This objective is to ensure that control and ownership issues will be smoothly transitioned at appropriate times so as not to unduly interfere with and disrupt the operations of the business. Unless properly planned, business ownership changes may create anxieties for lenders, key suppliers, employees, and customers of any business. The goal is to plan for a seamless transition that generates as little concern as possible for those who regularly deal with the business.

- **Market.** This objective is to ensure that all owners have a fair "market" for their shares at appropriate points of exit. Absent a well-structured buy-sell agreement, there may be no market either inside or outside the company. As a practical matter, the only viable exit opportunity for a departing owner may be an inside sale to the other owners pursuant to the terms of a carefully structured and funded buy-sell agreement.

- **Expulsion Right.** This objective is to ensure that the owners have the power to involuntarily terminate (expel) an owner who is no longer wanted. This may not be a concern in some organizations, but it is important in all service organizations, professional service organizations, and most companies that are owned by those who work in the business.

- **Estate Tax Exposure.** This objective is to ensure that the amount paid for the equity interest of a deceased owner determines the value of the deceased owner's equity interest for estate tax purposes. This can be an important consideration in many situations. Few can accept the concept of having to pay estate taxes on a value that exceeds the amount actually received for the equity interest.

- **Cash.** This objective is to ensure that the cash and funding challenges of owner departures are appropriately anticipated and covered. Often this will require the smart use of life and disability insurance. But insurance won't cover all the exit triggers. To protect the business, usually there is a need to spell out payment terms in the agreement, including mechanisms for determining the duration of the payments, the interest rate, and any special relief provisions for the company.

3. EXAMPLE AND STRUCTURAL Q&AS

ABC Inc. is a manufacturing corporation that has been in business for 17 years. The business was started by Jim and Sue Olson, husband and wife. Jim is the president of the corporation and the driving person behind its success. They have one son, Sam, age 26, who now works full-time in the business. Jim and Sue together own 60 percent of the stock of the business. The business has two key employees, Roger and Joyce. They both have worked in the business for over 12 years. Approximately five years ago, they each acquired a 20 percent stock interest in the business.

Roger and Joyce are beginning to question the value of the stock they own. There is no market for the stock; they have no capacity to initiate a sale of their stock. No dividends are paid on the stock. When one of them leaves the company or dies, what will become of their stock? As a practical matter, the company or Jim and Sue are the only potential buyers. Will they be willing to buy the stock? At what price? And on what terms?

Following is a review of some of the key planning issues that the owners of ABC Inc. should consider in structuring a buy-sell agreement and eight common planning blunders they should seek to avoid.

a. What buyout triggers should be structured into the shareholders' buy-sell agreement?

The buyout triggers are those events that give one party the right to buy out another party, obligate a party to buy out another party, or give a party the right to have his or her shares purchased by the corporation or the other shareholders. The triggering event often results in a transfer of voting shares and may result in a shift in voting control. The most common triggers in any buy-sell agreement include:

- Death of an owner
- Disability of an owner
- Voluntary termination of an owner/employee
- Divorce of an owner
- Bankruptcy of an owner
- Desire of an owner to cash out and move on
- Expulsion of an owner

Each of these triggering events creates a unique set of problems and may require a different solution.

Take death as an example. In the case of ABC Inc., it's likely that the agreement should be structured to provide that if one of the 20 percent stockholders dies, his or her stock would be purchased by the other shareholders or the corporation. Certainly, Jim and Sue, the majority owners, would want the comfort of knowing they could purchase the stock of Roger or Joyce if one of them died. Roger and Joyce also would want the comfort of knowing that the stock they own would be cashed out at a fair price in the event of an untimely death. But if Jim were to die, it's doubtful that his stock should be bought by the other shareholders or redeemed by the company. Sue may want the stock, or perhaps Jim would want the stock to be left to his son, who is moving up in the business. There's no requirement that all shareholders be treated the same under each of the various triggering events.

One of the questions often asked is: Why is it advisable to have divorce and bankruptcy included as triggering events in the agreement? The purpose of these provisions is to protect the company and the other shareholders if a shareholder's stock becomes tangled up in a messy divorce or bankruptcy proceeding. The other owners or the company are given the option to purchase that stock at a fair value to keep the company out of the mess. If the particular proceeding does not disrupt the company or pose any threat, there may be no reason for the company or other shareholders to exercise their rights under the agreement. But if an estranged spouse's attorney or a bankruptcy trustee attempts to cause problems or create uncertainty for the company by exercising control over a block of stock, the buyout rights can be effectively used to neutralize the actions of the attorney or trustee.

Expulsion usually is a difficult trigger for owners to discuss and resolve. Nobody likes to think about kicking out one of their own. But in many privately owned businesses, the owners are also the primary employees. If there are a number of business owners, usually there is a need to develop a mechanism that permits the group to discharge a colleague who is causing problems and purchase any stock owned by that colleague. The trigger usually is structured to require a unanimous or super-high majority (e.g., 75 percent) vote of the other owners.

b. What are the trade-offs between using a redemption approach versus a cross-purchase approach in structuring the agreement?

When the corporation purchases the shares of a departing shareholder, it's called a redemption. When the other owners purchase the stock, it's called a cross-purchase. Typically, whether a redemption or cross-purchase approach is used, the fundamental control results are the same. The remaining shareholders end up with the same resulting percentage ownership interests under either approach. Plus, under either approach the departing shareholder, or his or her estate, is given cash or other property in exchange for the interest in the business. But beyond these common end results, there are important factors that may favor one approach over the other in any given situation.

An important tax factor is the impact on the outside tax basis of the stock owned by the other shareholders of a C corporation. A stock redemption by a C corporation will not increase the basis of the stock held by the remaining owners. By contrast, stock acquired in a cross-purchase transaction will have a basis equal to the purchase price. This will result in a higher basis in the stock owned by the other shareholders. They will realize a lower capital gain on any subsequent sale.

Let's assume, for example, that in the case of ABC Inc., Roger, one of the 20 percent shareholders, leaves the company, his 20 percent interest has a fair market value of $400,000 at the time of departure, and his tax basis in the stock is $100,000. If ABC Inc. redeems his stock on his departure for $400,000, Jim and Sue, the original 60 percent owners, would own 75 percent of the outstanding stock, and Joyce, the other owner, would end up owning 25 percent. If Joyce's basis in her 20 percent interest was $100,000, her total basis in her increased 25 percent interest would still be $100,000. As for Jim and Sue, if their original 60 percent interest had a very low basis, say $30,000, the basis in their 75 percent interest would remain at $30,000. The stock redemption approach generates no step-up in basis for the other owners.

If the remaining shareholders acquired Roger's shares through a cross-purchase on a proportionate basis, Jim and Sue would acquire three-fourths of

Roger's 20 percent interest, and Joyce would acquire the other one-fourth. Roger and Sue would still end up owning 75 percent, and Joyce would end up owning 25 percent. But the basis in their stock would have changed. Under a cross-purchase, Jim and Sue would have paid $300,000 for three-fourths of Roger's stock, resulting in a total basis in their shares of $300,000 plus $30,000, or $330,000. Joyce will now have a basis in her shares equal to her original investment of $100,000, plus the $100,000 she would pay Roger for one-fourth of his stock. So her total basis would have increased to $200,000. On a subsequent sale of the stock or liquidation of the company, Jim and Sue have an additional $300,000 that could be recovered tax-free, and Joyce has an additional $100,000 that could be recovered tax-free.

This basis issue is not a factor for S corporations, partnerships, and limited liability companies. In these pass-through entities, the owners will receive a basis step-up whether a redemption or cross-purchase approach is used.

Does this basis difference make the cross-purchase approach the best choice for C corporations? Not always. In cases where there are many shareholders, the cross-purchase approach may be too cumbersome, particularly when multiple life insurance policies need to be reshuffled every time an owner dies or is bought out. Beyond the complexity of the reshuffling are serious transfer-for-value problems that can destroy the tax-free character of life insurance death benefits and ultimately force a conversion to a redemption strategy.[5] Also, often the shareholders do not have sufficient capital to fund a cross-purchase buyout. The capital is in the corporation, and there is no effective tax way to get the cash out of the company and into the hands of the shareholders to fund the buyout of their departing partner.

Another factor that may favor a redemption strategy in a C corporation is the deductibility of interest payments on any installment obligation paid to the departing owner or his or her heirs. Interest paid by a C corporation as part of a stock redemption is deductible as trade or business interest, whereas interest paid by the shareholders in a cross-purchase would be subject to the investment interest limitations.[6]

So in many cases, as a practical matter, the redemption approach is preferred simply from a funding standpoint.

In some situations, other factors make the redemption approach unattractive. If the C corporation is large enough to be subject to the alternative minimum tax (AMT) (annual gross receipts over $5 million during the first three years and over $7.5 million thereafter), receipt of life insurance proceeds may trigger an AMT for the corporation.[7] Plus, accumulation of funds to buy out a major shareholder may not qualify as a reasonable business need for purposes of the

---

5. I.R.C. § 101(a)(2) eliminates the tax free death benefit on life insurance policies that are transferred for valuable consideration. There are exceptions for transfers among partners, transfers to a partnership in which the insured is a partner, and transfers to a corporation in which the insured was an officer or shareholder. But there is no exception for transfers among co-shareholders of a corporation.

6. I.R.C. § 163(d).

7. I.R.C. §§ 55(b)(2), 55(e), 56(g).

accumulated earnings tax.[8] State law restrictions may limit the corporation's ability to redeem its own stock if it lacks sufficient capital surplus or retained earnings to fund the redemption.[9] At a minimum, such state law restrictions may trigger additional costs (e.g. appraisal fees) to get the deal done. Finally, restrictive covenants in loan agreements often limit a corporation's capacity to redeem stock by making substantial payments to the owners of the business. All of these factors should be evaluated in considering the redemption approach.

Note that many of these factors do not come into play with a pass-through entity, such as an S corporation, a partnership, or an LLC. As stated above, the outside basis differential is not an issue. Plus, getting money out of the entity and into the hands of the owners to fund a cross purchase usually presents no difficult tax issues.[10] There are no AMT or accumulated earnings tax issues to worry about. The deductibility of the interest on any installment purchase will turn on other factors. It may qualify as trade or business deductible interest for those who are material participants in the venture; for all other owners, it will be passive or investment interest or both, depending on the investment assets held by the entity. State law and loan agreement restrictions may be just as applicable.

c. What mandatory buyout obligations should be in the buy-sell agreement?

The business owners need to decide whether a triggering event requires a mandatory purchase or simply grants an option to purchase. And if it's optional, which party will have the option? For example, upon the death of a shareholder, the remaining shareholders typically want an option to purchase the shares of the deceased shareholder to preserve control. The deceased shareholder's heirs will want a put, which is an option to require the corporation or remaining shareholders to buy their stock, or a mandatory purchase obligation. It also is possible to give options to both the heirs and the remaining shareholders, permitting either side to trigger the purchase. Making the purchase mandatory or at the option of the heirs of the deceased shareholder puts the remaining shareholders in the position of having to come up with the purchase price at death. Life insurance often is essential.

Similar issues arise if an owner simply wants to cash out. Most owners view this event as a voluntary decision and have less concern for the cash and liquidity desires of the owner who wants to exit. The shareholders agreement may give the remaining owners the option to buy the interest of the departing owner, but

---

8. I.R.C. §§ 535(c)(1), 537; see, e.g., John B. Lambert & Associates v. United States, 212 Ct. Cl. 71 (1976); Lamark Shipping Agency, Inc. v. Commissioner, 42 T.C.M. 38 (1981).

9. In any such redemption, the applicable state corporate law must be carefully analyzed to ascertain any restrictions. Appraisals are often necessary. The Model Business Corporation Act prohibits a "distribution" (broadly defined to include proceeds from a redemption) if "after giving it effect: (1) the corporation would not be able to pay its debts as they become due in the ordinary course of business, or (2) the corporation's total assets would be less than the sum of its total liabilities plus (unless the articles of incorporation permit otherwise) that amount that would be needed, if the corporation were to be dissolved at the time of the distribution, to satisfy the preferential rights upon the dissolution of shareholders whose preferential rights are superior to those receiving the distribution." MBCA §§ 1.04, 6.40(c). These two tests, referred to as the "equity insolvency test" and the "balance sheet test," have been widely incorporated into state corporate statutes.

10. If an S corporation has accumulated earnings and profits from a prior C period, distributions that exceed its accumulated adjustment account may trigger taxable dividends. I.R.C. § 1368(c).

impose no obligation. In other situations, the owners will recognize the need for owners to come and go, particularly in service organizations and professional groups. In these cases, there is often a provision for a payout upon voluntary withdrawal, but the payment terms are usually over an extended period to avoid creating an undue burden on the cash flow of those who remain.

d. Is it advisable to tie business ownership to continued employment?

Many businesses restrict stock ownership to those who are employed by the business. For these businesses, termination of employment is an important triggering event. This is typically true for professional service corporations, as well as numerous service organizations and many companies where a portion of the stock is owned by employees. For these businesses, it's advisable to provide for a mandatory buyout upon the termination of employment of an owner. Funding is a challenge for the remaining owners. It is common for the departing owner to be paid in installments over a time frame that accommodates the cash needs of the business.

The question is often asked: What happens if one of the owners wants out and none of the other owners wants to buy that person's stock? Usually the agreement should be structured to give the parties significant time to negotiate a solution to the stalemate. If the stalemate continues for a designated time, often the owner who wants out is given the right to trigger a sale or liquidation of the business or to find an outside buyer for his or her stock.

e. What types of special exceptions should be structured into the agreement for unique shareholders?

There is no requirement that all shareholders be treated equally in a shareholders agreement. Often the expectations and the needs of the shareholders will result in different rights, particularly in organizations that have a dominant owner. ABC Inc. is an example. Upon the death of one of the primary owners, Jim or Sue, the surviving spouse will not want the two minority shareholders to have the right or obligation to purchase the stock of the deceased. Upon the death of the survivor of Jim and Sue, their stock will likely pass to their son, Sam. A similar exception may give Jim and Sue the right to transfer stock to Sam any time. They also may want the flexibility to transfer stock to a trust for the benefit of their grandchildren for estate planning purposes. In most situations, dominant owners like Jim and Sue would not tolerate the minority shareholders having similar rights.

f. How do the parties select the most appropriate method for valuing an equity ownership interest in the business?

Carefully. Often the most difficult element in a buy-sell agreement is the determination of how an ownership interest will be priced upon the occurrence of a triggering event. There are a number of options.

One common (and usually bad) approach is to use book value. Its only virtue in most cases is simplicity. The problem with book value is that it does not reflect changes in the asset values or the goodwill and going concern value of the business.

For these reasons, a modified book value approach is sometimes used. It adjusts the value of the balance sheet assets to reflect their current fair market values, but it too usually fails to adequately account for the going concern and goodwill value of an operating business.

The third common approach is to have a formula based on the recent average earnings of the business. This approach focuses on the earning capacity of the business and is used to reflect the going concern and goodwill value of the enterprise. Perhaps its biggest drawback is that it is based on historical earnings and may not fairly reflect recent changes, good or bad, in the future prospects of the business.

A fourth approach is to agree on a mechanism for having the business appraised when a triggering event occurs. The comparative advantage of this approach is that it is designed to derive the current fair market value of the business. The problem is that appraisals can be expensive, and the uniqueness of a business may prevent appraisers from accurately assessing its true value.

The fifth approach is to specify in the agreement that the price will be fixed, subject to adjustment by the shareholders at their annual meeting each year. Then each year the shareholders establish a new price that will govern any transaction for the following year. The appeal of this approach is that it requires the owners to focus on the valuation issue each year and to reach an agreement for a limited future time frame under calm circumstances unstressed by the demands of an immediate deal. A key to the approach is a specified backup valuation method if the shareholders neglect or are unable to resolve the valuation issue for a time. For example, the agreement might require that the price be re-examined each year at the annual meeting, but that if it has not been re-examined within two years of the date of an event that triggers the buy-sell agreement, the value will be determined by mutual agreement between the interested parties. If the interested parties cannot reach an agreement on price within 30 days, then each party selects an appraiser and the two appraisers jointly determine the price. This gives the interested parties an opportunity to agree on a price before incurring the expense and delay of a formal appraisal, but also provides a binding mechanism for ultimately determining the price.

A three-tiered approach of this type often is used where the owners cannot agree on a formula for valuing the business. Some may view this as avoiding the issue rather than facing it. But often the job of agreeing on a value at a given time is easier than the task of developing a formula that will work in the future, especially for a business that has not matured or that is growing rapidly.

g. Should the same valuation method apply for all triggers?

Often the owners will want to establish a different price or price formula for different events that might trigger a buyout. Mandating a discount from the regular price for a departing owner/employee who does not give the remaining owners adequate advance notice of departure can be an effective means of ensuring a smooth transition in the case of key employees. Another possible use of a discounted fair market value is the situation where the departing owner/employee may become a competitor of the business. The departing owner moves across the street and wants his or her former colleagues to help fund a new competitive business venture. A heavy discount in this situation may be justified in many cases.

h. Will the amount paid under the agreement to the heirs of a deceased owner govern for estate tax purposes?

Not necessarily. The buyout price paid under a buy-sell agreement on the death of an owner may not be the same value used to determine the federal estate tax liability of the deceased. It is possible that the IRS could determine that the actual fair market value of the interest for tax purposes is greater than the buyout price under the agreement. The owner's family would end up receiving a payment for the deceased's interest in the business that is substantially less than the value used to compute estate taxes. This could be disastrous for the family, particularly in situations where the business is the largest asset in the estate.

A buy-sell agreement often can be structured to fix the value of the transferred business interest for estate tax purposes. The difficulty of accomplishing this desired result depends, in part, on whether the business is considered a family business[111] for purposes of Section 2703 of the Internal Revenue Code.[12] If non-family parties own more than 50 percent of the equity interests in the business, the requirements of Section 2703 will not be an issue. In such a situation, the value determined pursuant to the agreement will govern for estate tax purposes if:

- The price for the interest is specified or readily ascertainable pursuant to the terms of the agreement and the price was reasonable when the agreement was entered into;

- The decedent's estate was obligated to sell at death for the price established by the agreement; and

- The deceased was restricted from selling or transferring the interest during life.[13] This third condition is not satisfied if the decedent had the right to transfer the interest by gift during life to a person who was not subject to the restrictions imposed by the agreement.

If family members control the company, then the price determined pursuant to the buy-sell agreement will govern for estate tax purposes only if the forgoing three conditions are satisfied, along with the requirements of Section 2703. Section 2703 requires that the agreement be a *bona fide* business arrangement, not be used as a device to transfer property for less than full value, and contain terms that are comparable to similar arrangements entered into by persons in arm's-length arrangements.[14] The "arm's-length" requirement is the most

---

11. Reg. § 25.2703-1(b)(3).

12. Reg. § 25.2703-1(b)(3). Family members include the transferor's spouse, any ancestor of the transferor or the transferor's spouse, any spouse of any such ancestor, and any lineal descendant of the parents of the transferor or the transferor's spouse (but not spouses of such descendants). Reg. § 25.2703-1(b)(3); Reg. § 25.2701-2(b)(5). Broad entity attribution rules are used to determine ownership, with an interest being deemed a family interest if it is attributed to both a family and non-family member. Reg. § 25.2703-1(b)(3); Reg. § 25.2701-6(a)(2)-(4).

13. Reg. § 20.2031-2(h).

14. I.R.C. § 2703(b).

difficult in almost every family situation. It requires a determination of what unrelated parties are doing in the same industry or similar types of businesses owned by unrelated parties.[15] Industry research and the assistance of a quality appraiser are often necessary at this stage of the planning process.

4. COMMON BLUNDERS TO AVOID

Blunder 1: Improper Use of the Showdown Clause

The first common blunder is the improper use of a showdown clause. A showdown clause is a mechanism that is often used in a buy-sell agreement to deal with an owner who wants to cash out.

Here's how it works. If an owner wants to withdraw from the company, that owner presents an offer to the other owners in the form of a purchase price and payment terms. The other owners then have the choice to be either buyers or sellers, at the specified price and payment terms. The showdown clause, in theory, forces the price and payment terms to be fair, since the one proposing them doesn't know if he or she is going to be a buyer or a seller.

The attraction of a showdown clause is its simplicity and apparent fairness. Many business owners and advisers wrongly believe that it is the ultimate solution to all difficult buyout situations, and, therefore, they use it as a standard in structuring buy-sell agreements. In many types of businesses, the appearance of simplicity and fairness is deceiving, and the indiscriminate use of such a clause creates opportunities for abuse.

Take, for example, a business that has a majority shareholder and one or more minority owners. The showdown clause usually gives the majority owner a huge advantage. Not only is the larger owner likely to have a bigger net worth and more capacity to pay, but he or she faces only the possibility of having to buy a minority interest in the business. By contrast, the smaller owner is not only likely to have a smaller net worth, but also has to pay a much larger price to buy out the interest of the majority owner. In this type of business, the showdown clause may be nothing more than an easy way for the majority owner to dictate price and payment terms for squeezing out the minority.

Similarly, the showdown clause can be unfair in a business where all the owners work in the business and have relatively equal interests, but one has a significantly greater net worth than the others. Again the showdown clause may become a means for the richer owner to squeeze out those who have insufficient means to be buyers in a showdown situation.

The third type of business where a showdown clause may be inappropriate is one where some of the owners work in the business and others do not. If certain owners depend on the business for their jobs, a showdown clause may force these inside owners to become unwilling buyers simply to preserve their jobs. The importance of their employment relationship with the company and the lack of other comparable job opportunities may leave the insiders no choice any time the showdown clause is triggered by one of the outside owners. For all

15. Reg. § 25.2703-1(b)(4)(i).

practical purposes, the clause may give the outside owners a put at a price and terms they can dictate.

The showdown clause works best in organizations where all the players are passive owners, no owner depends on the business for his or her employment, each owner owns roughly the same percentage interest in the business, and each owner has the financial capacity to be a buyer when the clause is triggered. Most businesses will not satisfy these conditions.

Blunder 2: Failure to Recognize the Unique Rights of the Majority Owner

The second big mistake is found in businesses dominated by a single controlling owner. The buy-sell agreement too often is structured on the assumption that all owners should be treated the same. In fact, many provisions under a buy-sell agreement should apply differently to the majority owner than to the other owners. If the owners stop to think about it and ask all the appropriate "what if" questions, they will usually see the importance of this unequal treatment.

One area where this unintended equal treatment shows up is in the control of the board of directors of a corporation. Some majority shareholders assume that they control the operations of the corporation solely because they own a majority of the voting shares. As stated above, the shareholders of any corporation, public or private, do little more than elect the board of directors. The real control of the operation of the business rests with the board. Unless the majority shareholder also controls the board, he or she does not control the operation of the business. The problem surfaces when the shareholders agreement grants certain shareholders the right to serve on the board.

Take, for example, ABC Inc. where Jim and Sue own 60 percent of the stock and Roger and Joyce each own 20 percent. If the shareholders agreement specifies a board of three members and ensures Jim, Roger and Joyce each a seat on the board, Roger and Joyce, the 20 percent owners, would control the board and the company. If Roger and Joyce are adamant about their board positions, Jim will want to restructure the board to protect control in his family. He could easily do this by expanding the board to five members. With a five-member board, Jim, the majority owner, could elect Sue and Sam to the board and thereby preserve board control in the family. A buy-sell agreement that deals with the composition of the board needs to be structured to ensure that the control of the corporation by a majority shareholder is not inadvertently forfeited.

Other buy-sell provisions that often have unintended results for a dominant shareholder involve equal application of the buyout rights that arise in certain events, such as death, disability, or retirement. In the typical buy-sell agreement, when one of these triggering events occurs, the other owners have the right, and often the obligation, to purchase the stock of the departing owner. This is appropriate and works well in an organization where all of the owners have substantially equal interests. But in an enterprise with a dominant owner, the majority owner may have never intended that he or she would be subject to the provisions. While it may be entirely appropriate to permit the majority owner to purchase the stock of a departing minority owner, it may not be consistent with the majority owner's intention that the same rights exist when he or she dies, retires or is disabled.

Blunder 3: The Constructive Dividend Trap

A mistake occurs in the context of a C corporation when the agreement imposes a primary and unconditional cross-purchase obligation on the shareholders, and the parties want to preserve the flexibility of a potential redemption by the corporation. Often the mistake is aggravated by sloppily putting ownership of life insurance policies in the corporation to facilitate the payment of premiums with corporate dollars. If there is a primary and unconditional obligation of the shareholders to purchase the stock of the deceased or departing shareholder and that obligation is paid and discharged by the corporation, all payments by the corporation to redeem the stock of the deceased or departing owners will be taxed as constructive dividends to the remaining shareholders – usually a disaster.[16]

The key to avoiding this trap and preserving flexibility is to structure any cross-purchase obligation of the shareholders as a secondary, backup obligation. This is done by first giving the corporation the right to redeem the stock, and then providing that the shareholders will purchase the stock if the corporation fails to exercise its right to purchase. It may look like form over substance, but it can be the difference between a clean deal and a costly constructive dividend.[17]

Blunder 4: Use of Inappropriate Payment Terms

A common mistake regarding the payment terms of an installment obligation provided a departing owner is the failure to provide for adequate security. At a minimum, the obligations under the installment note should be secured by a pledge of the stock or the equity interest that is being purchased. When a stock pledge is used, the buy-sell agreement should specify its terms. For example, usually it should provide that as long as the payments remain current the voting rights and the right to receive dividends and other distributions with respect to the stock are retained by the purchasers and that those rights automatically shift back to the departed owner if there is any default in the payment of the installment obligation.

Consideration also should be given to the need for other forms of security. For example, if the departing owner's stock is being redeemed by the company, should the other shareholders be required to personally guarantee the payment of the redemption price by the corporation? The issue can be very important, particularly in situations where the redemption price is being paid over an extended period. Owners sometimes, but not always, agree that it is appropriate for those who stay behind and reap the benefits of the ongoing business to personally guarantee the payment of the deferred price. Also, consideration should be given to restrictions on the payment of compensation or dividends to the remaining owners so long as the deferred purchase price is outstanding. Often this is done by requiring that the business maintain designated income levels or

16. Rev. Rule 69-608, 1969–2 C.B. 42.
17. Compare Situations 1 and 2 with Situation 5 in Rev. Rule 69-608, 1969-2 C.B. 42.

specified debt-to-equity, quick-asset, or other ratios as conditions to making distributions to the other owners.

Blunder 5: Lousy Life Insurance Structure

Another common blunder in structuring buy-sell agreements (and an expensive one) relates to the purchase of life insurance to fund a buyout obligation on the death of an owner. Most properly structured buy-sell agreements will permit the purchase of a deceased owner's stock to be made by either the corporation or the remaining owners. The surviving owners can examine the circumstances existing at the death of one of the owners and determine then whether it's most appropriate to have the corporation buy the stock of the deceased owner or to have that stock purchased by the remaining owners. As explained above, various factors may impact the decision to structure the purchase as a redemption or a cross-purchase.

A mistake is sometimes made when life insurance is purchased to fund that obligation. Because of habit, simplicity, lack of thought, or a combination of all these, the life insurance often is purchased by the corporation. The corporation pays the premiums, and the corporation is named the beneficiary. Upon the death of an owner, the corporation collects the life insurance proceeds. The mistake is that the decision relating to the ownership of the life insurance also, by necessity, decides the redemption-versus-cross-purchase issue. So even though the buy-sell agreement has been carefully structured to retain the flexibility to have either a redemption or a cross-purchase buyout, the purchase of the life insurance by the corporation forces the election of the redemption approach. The life insurance proceeds cannot be made available to the other owners to fund a cross purchase without significant adverse tax consequences.

There are two advantages of a cross-purchase that need to be carefully examined at the time the life insurance is acquired. The first is that with a cross-purchase each of the shareholders receives a stepped-up basis in the acquired stock. No such step-up occurs with a redemption by a C corporation. The second advantage of the owners owning the policies is that the risk of triggering a corporate alternative minimum tax on receipt of the death benefit is avoided.

Another life insurance structuring blunder sometimes is made in a corporation that has a dominant owner. A life insurance policy is acquired on each owner, including the dominant owner, to provide liquidity at the death of an owner. The premiums are funded by the corporation, and the buy-sell agreement is structured to require that the insurance be used to purchase an owner's stock at death. Upon the dominant owner's death, the family ends up with the policy's death benefit, subject to estate taxes, and loses all equity in the business. The minority shareholders end up with the entire business.

For many majority shareholders, an infinitely better structure would eliminate all buyout rights of the minority shareholders. The life insurance on the majority owner would be held for the benefit of his or her family in a life insurance trust that would not be subject to estate taxes. The majority owner's family would end up with the life insurance death benefit, tax-protected in trust, and still own the majority interest in the business. Most majority owners, when presented with the huge contrasts in these two scenarios, will enthusiastically opt for the latter.

Blunder 6: Misused Right of First Refusal

A common provision in many buy-sell agreements is the right of first refusal. It provides that, if an owner wants out of the business, that owner must find a third party who is willing to buy his or her interest, and then the other owners have the first right to buy the interest at the same price and terms offered by the third party. It is a method of dealing with the owner who wants out while giving the other owners the capacity to preserve ownership within the group. Each owner has the comfort of knowing that he or she will have the ability to prevent an unwanted owner from becoming part of the ownership group. In most cases, the provision just doesn't work.

The first problem with the right-of-first-refusal provision is that it assumes there is a market for the stock when, in fact, there is no market for a minority equity interest. A minority owner usually finds it impossible to locate a third party who will make a reasonable, *bona fide* offer to trigger the right-of-first-refusal provision. The result is that the provision becomes an absolute prohibition on sale. The problem with the provision is that it rests on the assumption that each owner has the capacity to liquidate his or her interest when, in fact, there is no such capacity.

The provision also may encourage individual owners to try to market their interests to uninformed third parties who know nothing about the business. It is usually not in the best interests of the company or the owners to have details relating to the business being shopped to strangers who are being invited to kick the tires. Apart from requiring executive time and expense to ensure full disclosure of all material facts, the effort may be counterproductive to the strategic development of the company's business plan. Most private business owners, if they stop to think, will quickly conclude that they want to do nothing that encourages minority owners to shop the stock to third parties.

The second problem with a right-of-first-refusal provision surfaces in the rare situation where the departing owner actually finds someone who wants to buy an interest in the business. The prospective buyer is willing to pay a premium to get a foothold in the enterprise. It may be a competitor, a potential competitor, a strategic supplier, a huge customer, an obnoxious relative of the departing owner, or some other party whom the other owners do not want. This puts the remaining owners in a tough position. They either have to come up with a large sum to match the price and terms or end up with a co-owner they don't like or want or who may pose a threat to the business.

A right-of-first-refusal provision usually gives the task of finding the new owner to the wrong person. The departing owner doesn't care who the new owner is going to be; he or she just wants the best price and terms for the stock. Yet, the provision puts the onus on the departing owner to find a candidate to trigger the provision. Those who really care about any new owner are the remaining owners, who are going to have to embrace the new owner as a colleague.

What's the alternative? It is to structure a mechanism that permits an owner to withdraw and get cashed out, without creating the problems described above that are often triggered with a right of first refusal. For example, the buy-sell agreement could provide that if an owner wants out, that owner must trigger Stage One by giving the others significant advance notice, say three months. Stage One is a reaction period for the other owners. They have a period of time to find a new owner or prepare for the purchase of the departing owner's stock. The pricing mechanism and payment terms are set forth in the agreement, but they are optional for the remaining owners.

If at the end of the three-month period the existing owners have not found an acceptable replacement owner or developed a plan to pay the price specified in the agreement, Stage Two kicks in. This is a time (say, an additional 60 days) designated for negotiation between the owner who wants out and the other owners. Everyone will have had time to ponder the realities of the situation and assess their options. Of course, the remaining owners can always buy the departing owner's interest for the price and terms specified in the agreement. But if Stage Two is triggered, the remaining owners will be looking for some concessions from the owner who wants out. If there is still no deal at the end of Stage Two, there is an additional period, say six months, for the existing owners to find a replacement owner. This is Stage Three.

During all these stages, the departing owner remains an owner and is entitled to all the benefits of ownership. If at the end of the extended period a replacement owner has not been found and the remaining owners are still unwilling to purchase the interest of the departing owner on the stated terms or mutually acceptable renegotiated terms, the departing owner has the option to force a sale of the business. This is Stage Four. If the option is exercised, any owner or group of owners may be the purchaser. Essentially, the company is put up for sale and anyone can be a bidder. If sold, the owner who wants to depart is cashed out at a price that reflects the value of the business.

As a practical matter, it is highly unlikely that the process will ever get to Stage Four. The remaining owners will have had plenty of time to find a replacement owner, secure financing to fund the buyout pursuant to the terms of the agreement, or renegotiate a more palatable deal with the departing owner. A staged-exit procedure of this type, or any version thereof, can provide the remaining owners with the time and opportunity to solve the problem of the departing owner, while at the same time providing the departing owner with a means of ultimately getting cashed out.

There are a number of variations of this approach. The important point is that the right of first refusal should not be the automatic solution to the problem of an owner who wants to depart. A better mechanism usually can be structured to provide a more realistic solution to the problem.

Blunder 7: Failure to Cover the Downside

Another common mistake in structuring buy-sell agreements is to neglect the downside – the disaster scenario. Most buy-sell agreements are entered into when all parties are anticipating a successful company. Most don't even want to think about the business failing. But it frequently happens. It helps to deal with the potential fallout up front.

The most common problem in a disaster scenario is that one or more of the owners end up getting stuck with a disproportionately large share of the liabilities because of personal guarantees or other commitments made in connection with the business. Most guarantees by multiple owners are joint and several. The lender can go after any owner to collect the entire debt. The owners should agree up front as to how they will share the debt burdens of the business. Typically, the agreement should provide that if an owner is forced to fund a company debt, the portion of the payment that exceeds that owner's percentage interest in the business constitutes a loan to the other owners, in proportion to their respective percentage interests in the business. The agreement should set forth a mechanism for the repayment of the loan and perhaps collateral to secure the obligation.

Blunder 8: Ignore S Corporation Issues

A common mistake in buy-sell agreements relates to S corporations. The mistake is the failure to address in the buy-sell agreement specific S corporation issues. The first and most obvious issue is the failure to prohibit a shareholder from making any stock transfer that would result in the termination of the S election. There are a number of shareholder requirements that must be met in order for a corporation to be taxed as an S corporation. There are limits on the number and types of shareholders. The buy-sell agreement should prohibit any transfer of stock that would terminate the S election and should provide that any such attempted transfer is void.

An S corporation also has the option of making certain tax elections, which often require the consent of all shareholders. In order to prevent a single shareholder or a minority group of shareholders from vetoing an election that the majority wants to make, the buy-sell agreement may provide that all shareholders will consent to any tax election that is approved by a specified percentage of shareholders (e.g., 70 percent). An example would be an S corporation that has C corporation earnings and profits. An S corporation may elect to treat distributions as first coming from its C corporation earnings and profits rather than from its accumulated adjustment account.[18] Many owners of an S corporation might desire such an election to accommodate their personal tax planning. This election requires the unanimous consent of all shareholders. A buy-sell agreement can soften the impact of the unanimous consent requirement.

Another important issue that usually should be addressed in an S corporation buy-sell agreement relates to the payment of dividends. It's an issue that is common to all pass-through entities, including partnerships and limited liability companies. The income of the entity is passed through and taxed to the owners, even if it is not distributed. The owners may end up with a tax bill and no cash. To ensure that the owners will be distributed enough cash to cover their tax liabilities, the shareholders or operating agreement may contain a provision that obligates the entity to distribute cash to fund the tax liabilities of the owners. In order to avoid any risk that such a provision creates a second class of stock (a condition that would kill the S election), the tax distribution to the shareholders

18. I.R.C. § 1368(e)(3).

should not be based on the specific tax liabilities of the different shareholders. Rather, the total distribution should be based on a stated percentage of the entity's total allocated taxable income for the year and be distributed to the shareholders based on their respective stockholdings in the company.

STUDENT PROBLEM 10-2

Dustin Smith, age 64, owns 60 percent of the stock of Rolling-Ball Inc., an S corporation that owns and operates a thriving chain of high-end "Bowling and Bar Hangouts." The remaining 40 percent of the stock is owned in equal shares by four key managers of the business who range in age from 39 to 46. The owners pull healthy salaries and substantial dividends from the company each year. The parties have been together for over eight years, but have never had a buy-sell agreement. The four managers are demanding a buy-sell agreement now because they openly acknowledge that one of more of them might die, retire, or just want to cash out of the business.

Justin has opined that the only fair way to deal with any buyout of an owner who wants out is a right-of-first-refusal provision that would require the departing owner to obtain a bid for his or her stock from another owner or a third party. The company or the remaining shareholders would then have a first right to match that offer. If they fail to exercise such right, the departing owner could accept the bid and sell.

The four managers believe that the best mechanism for dealing with any exit is a showdown clause that requires any departing owner to set a price and terms for the stock and then forces the other shareholders to elect to buy or sell at that price and on those terms.

1. What buyout triggers should the owners include in their buy-sell agreement? Which triggers should be mandatory and which should be optional? For those that are optional, who should have the option? Should all triggers apply to all owners? What additional facts would help you in answering these questions?

2. Evaluate the owners' respective positions on the use of a right-of-first refusal and the showdown clause. What might be motivating the advocates for each provision? What might the owners consider as an alternative?

C. BUYING AND SELLING A BUSINESS

Businesses are bought and sold every day. For most owners, it's a momentous event. They are using their power and means to grow through acquisition; or they are selling out, cashing in on a profitable adventure that may have lasted a lifetime. But whether they are buying or selling, and whether they are dealing with a business that's lasted three generations or three months, the structure of the transaction is a big deal. It sets the parameters for getting the deal done and allocates risks, liabilities, and administrative burdens. Most importantly, it directly impacts the net cost to the buyer and the net yield to the seller.

Many mistakenly assume that it's only about taxes. Tax consequences are always important and often drive the structure of the deal. But in some transactions, non-tax factors, deemed critical by one or both of the parties, will trump all other considerations and dictate whether the transaction should be structured as a sale of assets or a sale of the entity itself. In many more situations, important non-tax objectives, while not controlling, must be evaluated and prioritized against the tax consequences of alternative structures.

1. The Non-Tax Agenda

A useful starting point in any transaction is to identify key non-tax considerations that are impacted by structure and then assess their relative importance. Some of the most compelling non-tax factors that often surface are the following:

Shareholder Rights. As discussed and illustrated in Section D of Chapter 5, the structure of the sale of a business may dictate whether shareholders of the acquiring or target corporation have to approve the transaction or are entitled to dissenter appraisal rights under the applicable state's corporate statutes. In many situations, a transaction can be structured to reduce shareholder voting requirements (particularly for the acquiring corporation) and reduce or eliminate dissenter appraisal rights.

Undisclosed Liability Exposure. Often buyers fear exposure to undisclosed liabilities attributable to the operation of the business before the acquisition. Such liabilities may come in many different forms – product liability exposures; employee claims, including sexual harassment, discrimination or wrongful termination claims; environmental liabilities; unpaid taxes; contractual disputes and related expenses and exposures; regulatory violations; and many more. The buyer knows that if the entity is acquired, either through merger or stock purchase, it comes with all its skeletons. The acquisition agreement usually includes seller representations and warranties, indemnification provisions, and escrow holdback procedures, all designed to shift the ultimate risk of any material undisclosed liabilities back to the seller. But even with these, there is still the possibility – often the probability – that the buyer, as the new owner of the old entity, will get tangled in a dispute over issues that pre-date the buyer's involvement. Many buyers want a structure that provides protections greater than those offered through a contract. For them, an asset acquisition where only specific liabilities are assumed, though not completely bullet-proof from all pre-acquisition liabilities, is a preferred structure because the old entity remains with the seller.

Third-Party Disruptions. The impact of the transaction on employees, customers, vendors, and other third parties often is an important consideration. Banks and key executives usually are knee-deep in the details, no matter the structure of the deal. But an acquisition that keeps the old entity intact and functioning, just with new owners, often can be accomplished with no knowledge of, let alone any involvement with, rank-and-file employees, customers and vendors. If the business and assets are transferred to a new entity, these other players soon discover that they too are being transferred. The result may be heightened insecurities, the need for additional assurances or, worse yet, new demands.

Third-Party Consents. An asset acquisition structure usually requires many third-party consents. Typically, such consents are required for leases, licenses, permits, and contracts that the new buyer needs to maintain in order to run the business. The consent process itself may result in added costs and delays. Also, and much worse, the need for a particular consent may provide a key third party with an exit opportunity that wouldn't exist otherwise. This opportunity may result in the loss of a valuable contract right or a forced unfavorable renegotiation. Although an entity acquisition, either through merger or stock purchase, often requires some third-party consents based on the breadth of transfer-of-control provisions in specific contracts, the burden is usually much tougher with an asset structure.

Unwanted Assets. Sometimes the buyer wants to cherry-pick specific assets that are necessary for the operation of the core business. The remaining assets are left for the seller to deal with. An entity acquisition structure can work in this situation if the seller can get the unwanted assets out of the entity before the deal is done. But, depending on the nature and value of the unwanted assets, often an asset structure is preferred because the old entity remains the owner of the unwanted assets and, as a result, the seller has greater flexibility in dealing with any future transfers of the unwanted assets and the associated tax impacts.

Sales and Use Taxes. A sale of tangible assets often triggers a state sales tax or use tax, typically paid by the buyer. This is often an added expense of using an asset acquisition structure. In some transactions, it is a material cost that impacts the structural decision.

Insurance Rating. Sometimes the selling entity has a favorable historical workmen's compensation insurance rating that will be lost if only assets, not the entity, are transferred. This can be a material factor in some situations. When it is, an entity acquisition structure becomes more appealing.

Closing Complexities. The closing of an entity deal is usually much easier than an asset deal. A stock certificate or ownership interest is transferred. An asset transaction requires transfer documents (e.g. assignments, bills of sale, deeds, assumption agreements, etc.) covering the tangible assets, licenses, leases, contract rights, intangibles, and other assets being transferred and all the liabilities being assumed by the buyer. It requires more effort, more paperwork and more attention to detail. Usually this factor is less important than other considerations. Often it is cited as an added reason or excuse by a party who, for more compelling reasons, is advocating an entity structure.

Securities Law Exposures. Some sellers are spooked by the anti-fraud provisions of the securities laws. They hate the idea of being legally obligated to eliminate all misleading material facts related to a complex business operation and its potential acquisition by a buyer who may see only the surface. Often their fear is grounded in a prior bad experience involving securities. They feel safer with an asset structure that does not involve the sale of stock. Usually in any transaction, either entity or asset, the buyer will expect and demand extensive representations and warranties from the seller; and often it is standard practice to include a catchall representation that is the verbatim equivalent of Rule 10b-5, the securities law antifraud provision.[19] A seller who is spooked enough by the burdens of 10b-5 to let it influence the structure of the deal will often refuse to make such a catchall representation. This can complicate the negotiation. If the seller is adamant, the solution, in many situations, is to have the seller represent that he or she has not "knowingly misrepresented any material facts" (usually the specific "knowingly" limitation removes any objection) and to carefully design other representations and warranties to give the buyer the comfort needed to move forward.

2. *THE TAX AGENDA*

There are various tax options that are best explained with a sample case study.

Michael Manufacturing (Seller) has been in business 30 years. Its two equal owners, Larry and Sue, both age 58, have decided it's time to sell. A serious offer from a strategic, deep-pocketed C corporation buyer (Buyer) has convinced them that it is time to cash in and start enjoying the good life.

The value of Seller's equity and the price Buyer is willing to pay is $12 million, the excess of the $17 million fair market value of Seller's assets over its liabilities of $5 million. The book value of Seller's equity is $5 million, the excess of the book value of its assets ($10 million) over its liabilities of $5 million. Of the $7 million of asset value in excess of book value, $1 million is attributable to tangible assets (equipment) and $6 million to goodwill and going concern value. The company's tangible assets – primarily cash, accounts receivable, inventories and equipment – have a book value and basis of $10 million and a fair market value of $11 million.

The following sections review the tax consequences to Seller, Buyer, Larry, and Sue under different transaction structure scenarios. The first section assumes: Seller is a C corporation; Larry and Sue each have a $250,000 basis in their stock; Larry and Sue are subject to a combined federal and state marginal income tax rate of 40 percent on ordinary income and 20 percent on long-term capital gains; and the Seller and Buyer, both C corporations, are subject to a combined federal and state marginal income tax rate of 40 percent (remember, C corporations get no capital gains tax rate break).

c. Seller as a C Corporation – 11 Scenarios

Asset Sale-Liquidation

Under this common scenario, Buyer pays Seller $12 million for all the assets of the business and assumes all the liabilities. Seller pays its taxes and distributes the net after-tax proceeds to Larry and Sue in a complete liquidation of Seller. Larry and Sue pay a long-term capital gains tax on the excess of the proceeds received over their stock basis. Seller disappears. The net result is a

---

19. 17 C.F.R. § 240.10b–5.

double tax – a corporate level tax and a shareholder level tax.[20]

Here's how the numbers shake out. Seller would recognize a taxable gain of $7 million, the excess of $17 million (the sum of the $12 million received and the $5 million of liabilities assumed by Buyer) over its assets' basis of $10 million. At a 40 percent combined federal and state tax rate, Seller's tax hit would total $2.8 million. The net distributed to Larry and Sue would be $9.2 million, the excess of the $12 million paid by Buyer over the $2.8 million in taxes paid by Seller. Larry's and Sue's long-term capital gains would total $8.7 million ($9.2 million less their $500,000 combined stock basis), and their tax hit at a combined federal and state rate of 20 percent would total $1.74 million. All said and done, they walk with $7.46 million after tax ($3.73 million each). The taxes on the deal total $4.54 million – $2.8 million at the corporate level and $1.74 million at the shareholder level. See Illustration A.

Illustration A: Asset Sale-Liquidation

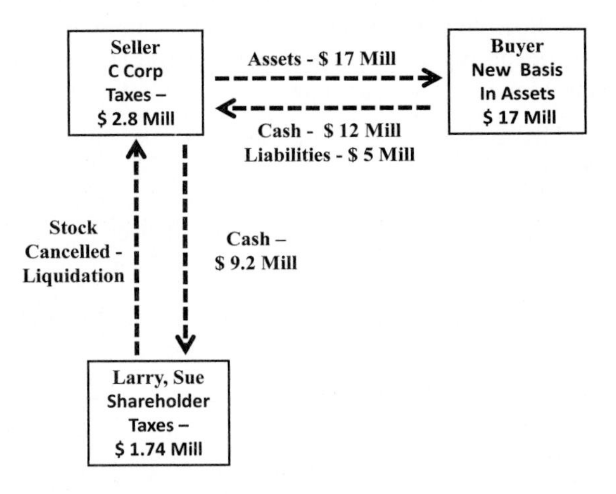

When faced with such consequences, Larry and Sue may ask: Can the $12 million paid by Buyer be allocated to reduce the overall tax bite? If it all goes to Seller, the answer is usually "No" because, as a C corporation, all of Seller's income is taxed at the same rate. The only exception is where Seller has an unused capital loss, a rare situation. In that case, care should be taken to create enough capital gain for Seller to use up any available capital loss.

Also, there may be an opportunity to reduce overall taxes by having a portion of the consideration paid directly to Larry and Sue for their personal covenants not to compete with Buyer. Assume, for example, that $1 million of the price was paid for such personal covenants. This would be ordinary income to Larry and Sue, triggering a tax of $400,000. Seller's tax bite would drop by $400,000, and Larry and Sue's capital gains tax would drop by $120,000 (20 percent of $600,000). The net result would be a tax savings of $120,000.

---

20. I.R.C. § 331.

For tax purposes, the big tax winner under this scenario is Buyer, who gets to allocate the full purchase price to the acquired assets. This results in a basis step-up that will produce larger depreciation or amortization deductions in the future. Section 197 permits a buyer to amortize intangible assets ratably over a 15-year period.[21] Such assets include goodwill, going concern value, covenants not to compete, information bases, customer lists, know-how, licenses, franchises, trade names and more.[22] No longer does the Buyer need to sweat out a fight with the IRS over how much of the price constitutes goodwill or some other type of intangible that before Section 197 produced no future tax benefit. Now there's a solid 15-year write-off period for intangibles.

So, asks Buyer, how much latitude is there in allocating the price to tangible assets that have a depreciation life of less than 15 years? After all, Seller has no interest in the allocations because it pays the same tax on all its income.

Section 1060[23] spells out the rules for allocating the total consideration paid in an asset acquisition to the various assets. It mandates a priority residual approach that breaks assets into seven classes and then requires that the total consideration (which includes all liabilities assumed) be allocated to the assets (up to their fair market value) in each priority class.[24] In this case, Buyer would allocate the $17 million total consideration ($12 million paid plus $5 million of assumed liabilities) in the following priority: cash and cash equivalents (Class I priority); marketable securities, foreign currencies, certificates of deposits (Class II priority); accounts receivable, mortgages and credit card receivables (Class III priority); inventories and other dealer property (Class IV priority); all other tangible assets, including equipment (Class V priority); intangible assets other than goodwill and going concern value (Class VI priority); and, lastly, goodwill and going concern value (Class VII priority).[25]

Seller and Buyer may, without changing the allocation priority, agree on the value of various assets in their agreement, and any such agreement will be binding on both parties for tax purposes unless the IRS determines that the value is not appropriate.[26] The IRS may use any appraisal method to challenge any allocation of value, especially in those situations (like this) where there are no conflicting interests between the parties to provide a basis for an arm's-length value negotiation.[27]

Liquidation-Asset Sale

Under this scenario, the liquidation of Seller precedes the asset sale to Buyer. Seller distributes of its assets to Larry and Sue in a complete liquidation, and Larry and Sue then sell the assets to Buyer. The bottom line tax results are identical to the first scenario, although the road traveled is different.

---

21. I.R.C. § 197.
22. I.R.C. § 197(d)(1).
23. I.R.C. § 1060.
24. I.R.C. § 1060(c); Reg. §§ 1.1060-1(a)(1), 1.1060-1(b)(1).
25. Reg. §§ 1.1060-1(c), 1.338-6.
26. I.R.C. § 1060(a); Staff of the Joint Committee on Taxation, General Explanation of the Tax Reform Act of 1986, 100th Cong., 1st Sess. 355-360 (1987).
27. Reg. § 1.1060-1(c).

The liquidation of Seller triggers a gain for Seller equal to the excess of the fair market value of its assets ($17 million) over the assets' basis of $10 million.[28] The result is a $7 million gain that triggers a corporate tax of $2.8 million that Larry and Sue must pay because Seller no longer has any assets. Larry and Sue receive assets that have a value of $17 million, and their capital gain is determined by reducing this total asset value by the $5 million of corporate liabilities they assume, the $2.8 million in taxes they pay on behalf of Seller, and their combined stock basis of $500,000. The net result is a long-term capital gain of $8.7 million that, as in the first scenario, triggers a tax of $1.74 million.

Illustration B: Liquidation-Asset Sale

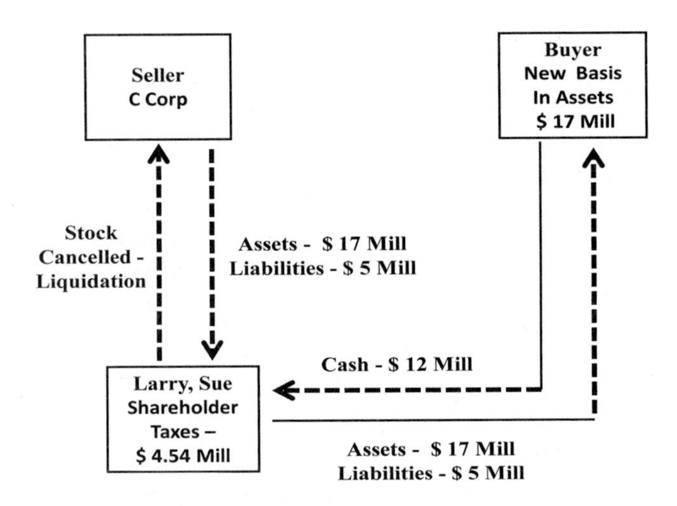

Following the liquidation of Seller, Larry and Sue have a tax basis of $17 million in the assets they have just acquired by virtue of the taxes they've paid and the liabilities they've assumed. So the sale to Buyer for $12 million plus the assumption of the $5 million of liabilities produces no gain. The end result is taxes totaling $4.54 million, the same as in scenario one. Again, Larry and Sue each walk with $3.73 million after tax.

As an asset purchaser, the consequences for Buyer under this scenario also are the same as in scenario one. Intangibles qualify for 15-year amortization treatment under Section 197, and the whole Section 1060 priority regime will apply. See Illustration B.

Cash Merger

Under this scenario, Seller is merged into Buyer or a subsidiary of Buyer in a statutory merger, and Buyer distributes cash directly to Larry and Sue. The value of the structure is that the statutory merger will automatically transfer all of Seller's assets and liabilities to Buyer or its subsidiary, thereby eliminating the

---

28. I.R.C. § 336(a).

need to document the transfer of specific assets and the assumption of specific liabilities. For tax purposes, the IRS treats this scenario the same as an asset sale by Seller followed by a complete liquidation of Seller – scenario one.[29]

Since the surviving entity in the merger (Buyer or its subsidiary) is going to have a $2.8 million tax bill as a result of the merger, the cash paid to Larry and Sue in the merger will be $9.2 million ($12 million less $2.8 million). Again, they incur a capital gains tax of $1.74 million, and they each end up netting $3.73 million. Since Buyer is deemed an asset purchaser, its tax consequences are the same as under the first two scenarios.

Installment Asset Sale – Liquidation

This scenario is the same as scenario one, with an important twist. A portion of the $12 million paid by Buyer is represented by an installment note that, with interest, will be paid off over many years. Let's assume in this case that the note obligation is equal to $7 million and Buyer pays only $5 million in cash at closing.

The tax issue is whether the note obligation will permit Seller or Larry and Sue to defer the taxes they would otherwise have to pay. There is no hope for Seller; the distribution of the installment obligation on the liquidation of Seller triggers an immediate recognition of all gain that might otherwise have been deferred for Seller's benefit under the note.[30] So Seller still owes $2.8 million in taxes that it will pay out of the $5 million cash received from Buyer.

Although Seller gets no deferred tax benefits from the note obligation, Larry and Sue will get a deferral benefit if Seller adopts a plan of complete liquidation and then sells its assets and distributes the note and any other proceeds to its shareholders within 12 months following the adoption of the plan.[13] So Larry and Sue would end up receiving $2.2 million in cash ($5 million less the $2.8 million of taxes paid by Seller) and a $7 million note issued by Buyer, for a total of $9.2 million. Their total capital gain, after subtracting their combined basis, is $8.7 million. So their gross profit fraction is 94.5 percent (8.7/9.2). Of the $2.2 million cash they receive on the liquidation, $2.079 million (94.5 percent) will be taxable as a long-term capital gain. Then 94.5 percent of all future principal payments they receive under the note will be taxable as long-term capital gain.

Asset Sale – No Liquidation

Under this scenario, Seller sells its assets to Buyer, but Seller is not liquidated. The proceeds from the sale ($12 million) are used to pay Seller's $2.8 million tax bill and the remainder ($9.2 million) are kept inside of Seller. There is no liquidation. This scenario raises two questions: Why would any shareholder want to do it? What are the tax consequences of leaving the money in Seller?

The answer to the "Why" question is found in Section 1014 of the Code. If Larry, for example, dies before Seller is liquidated, the basis in his Seller stock is

29. I.R.C. § 453(h).
30. I.R.C. § 453(h).

stepped up to its fair market value at death.[31] So if the liquidation follows Larry's death, Larry's estate or heirs will not recognize any capital gain to the extent the proceeds do not exceed the stock's fair market value on Larry's death. Plus, there is no requirement that all shareholders be treated the same with this option. Even if the liquidation of the corporation is deferred for Larry's benefit, Sue's stock could be redeemed in return for her share of the sales proceeds. The strategy makes little sense for a 58-year-old in good health. But for someone 20 years older or a shareholder dealing with serious health issues, the prospect of completely avoiding the tax at the shareholder level might be appealing, which raises the second question.

If the proceeds of the sale are maintained in Seller and invested to generate portfolio income (interests, dividends, rents, etc.), Seller will become a personal holding company subject to the personal holding company tax penalty. What this means, as a practical matter, is that Seller will need to distribute its earned portfolio income as dividend income to Larry and Sue to avoid the personal holding company penalty tax. Although this results in a double tax on the portfolio income, it may not be a serious problem if the double tax burden continues only for a short period. It might end up being a relatively small cost for eliminating a huge capital gain in the deceased shareholder's estate.

What about converting to S status after the sale in order to eliminate the double tax hit on the portfolio income as Seller holds the proceeds and waits for a shareholder to die? Won't work. Section 1375 imposes an entity level tax at the maximum corporate rate on any S corporation with C corporation earnings and profits (which Seller would have in spades by virtue of the sale) that has net investment income in excess of 25 percent of its total gross receipts. Plus, if the condition persists for three consecutive years, the S election is terminated.[32] The Code drafters saw this one coming.

Straight Stock Sale

This scenario is the easiest and one of the most popular. Larry and Sue just sell their stock in Seller to Buyer. Buyer becomes the new sole shareholder of Seller. Since Seller is not a party to the transaction, it recognizes no income. The only income recognized is the capital gain at the shareholder level – the excess of the amount Larry and Sue receive from Buyer over the basis in their stock.

The trade-off for the single tax hit is that Buyer takes Seller with its historic basis in its assets. There is no basis step-up at the corporate level for the additional value paid by Buyer. In this case, the basis loss is $7 million (the excess of the $17 million fair market value over the $10 million basis). Had the transaction been structured under any of the prior scenarios, Buyer would have received additional future tax write-offs of $7 million. Since Buyer loses this tax benefit under this scenario, it is reasonable to expect that Buyer will not be willing to pay as much.

The big question then becomes: How large of a haircut in price will the

31. I.R.C. § 1014(a).
32. I.R.C. § 1362(d)(3).

Buyer require for this structure? If we assume that Buyer's combined federal and state marginal income tax rate will remain at 40 percent, the additional $7 million in basis would produce future tax savings of $2.8 million. But this number must be reduced by two factors to arrive at a fair estimate of the value of the lost tax benefits to Buyer. First, if the transaction were structured as an asset sale under any of the prior scenarios, Buyer would have to start new depreciation and amortization periods for all assets acquired. Many of these new write-off periods may be longer than the historic write-off periods that would be inherited under this scenario. Thus, while future write-offs will clearly be less under this scenario, this scenario may result in faster write-offs (and thus faster tax benefits) for some assets.

Second, the difference in the future annual tax benefits of the write-offs under an asset scenario and this scenario, as adjusted, must be discounted by an interest factor to arrive at the present value of such benefits. Since much of the difference will be realized over a 15-year period, this present value discount often is huge. In theory, the present value of the lost tax benefits represents the additional tax cost of this scenario to the Buyer and would be the basis of any price reduction. If in this case these two reduction factors result in a present value of $1.5 million (from a starting point of $2.8 million), the price Buyer would pay for the stock of Seller would be reduced from $12 million to $10.5 million.

Note that even with such a $1.5 million price reduction, Larry and Sue net more after-tax under this scenario than under any of the previous asset sale scenarios. Their recognized long-term capital gain would be $10 million (the excess paid by Buyer over their $500,000 stock basis). Using the assumed combined capital gains rate of 20 percent, Larry and Sue's tax hit would equal $2 million, reducing their net yield to $8.5 million. They would each net $4.25 million, nearly a 14 percent increase over the $3.73 million realized under the prior asset scenarios.

Now, suppose the parties agree to a total stock price of $10.5 million, but Buyer only wants to purchase 80 percent of Larry and Sue's stock for $8.4 million (80 percent of $10.5 million). The remaining $2.1 million will come from Seller, who will pay this amount to Larry and Sue to redeem the balance of their Seller stock. Larry and Sue end up getting their $10.5 million, and Buyer ends up owning all of Seller's outstanding stock by using only $8.4 million of its cash. Of course, Seller is out $2.1 million.

The question: Will this "bootstrap" acquisition create any different tax consequences for the parties? If Larry and Sue's entire stock interest is terminated by the coordinated transactions, the redemption will qualify for sale or exchange treatment (as opposed to dividend treatment), and they will end up in the same after-tax position.[33] The only significant difference is that Buyer's basis in its newly-acquired Seller stock will be $2.1 million less. See Illustration C.

33. Zenz v. Quinlivan, 213 F.2d 914 (6th Cir. 1954); Rev. Rule 75-447, 1975-2 C.B. 113.

Illustration C: Bootstrap Stock Acquisition

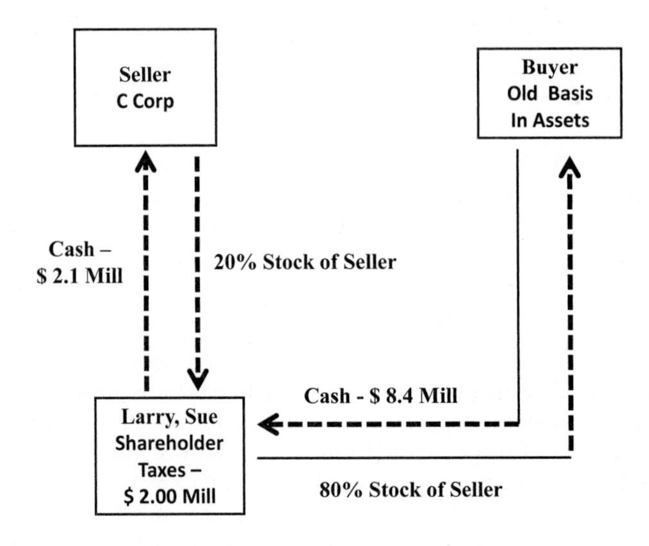

Statutory Merger

In this scenario, Seller and Buyer merge under state law and Buyer issues to Seller's shareholders, Larry and Sue, its stock as part of the purchase price.[34] The goal is to qualify the transaction as a tax-free A reorganization under Section 368(a)(1)(A).[35] Assume in this case that the consideration paid to Larry and Sue totals $10.5 million – $2.5 million in cash and $8 million in Buyer's common stock. If the transaction qualifies as an A reorganization, Seller recognizes no taxable income,[36] Buyer recognizes no taxable income,[37] and Larry and Sue recognize only $2.5 million of taxable income – the amount of cash they receive.[38] Their total tax hit, at a combined federal and state rate of 20 percent, is $500,000, a far cry from the total tax bill under any of the previous scenarios.

There are a few trade-offs for this wonderful tax treatment. First, Larry and Sue's basis in the Buyer stock they receive would equal their basis in their old Seller stock ($500,000), increased by their recognized gain ($2.5 million) and decreased by the cash received ($2.5 million).[39] Thus, in this case, their basis remains at $500,000 ($250,000 each). If either of them sells their Buyer stock before death, a large capital gain will be triggered on the sale because of the low carryover basis. If they hold the Buyer stock until death, its basis will be stepped up to its fair market value at death.[40]

---

34. See Section D of Chapter 5 for a description of different types of mergers and the related requirements for director approval, shareholder approval, and dissenter appraisal rights.
35. I.R.C. § 368(a)(1)(A).
36. I.R.C. § 361(a).
37. I.R.C. § 1032(a).
38. I.R.C. §§ 354(a)(1), 356(a)(1).
39. I.R.C. § 358(a)(1).
40. I.R.C. § 1014.

Second, Seller's basis in the assets acquired by Buyer in the merger carries over to Buyer.[41] There is no step up in basis.

And third, in select situations, the income recognized by the shareholders, Larry and Sue in this case, may be taxed as dividend income but will never exceed their gain realized in the exchange.[42] So long as the dividend rate and the long-term capital gains rate remain the same, this possibility will be of no significance to individual shareholders.

So now the big question: What does it take to qualify as an A reorganization? Four requirements must be satisfied. First, there must be a statutory merger or consolidation under applicable state law.[43] With the merger in this case, all assets and liabilities of Seller are transferred to Buyer without the need for specific asset or liability transfer documents, and Seller is dissolved by operation of law.

Second, the continuity of interest doctrine must be satisfied. In this case, the doctrine requires that the stock issued by Buyer in the transaction equal a certain percentage of the total consideration paid by Buyer.[44] How large must that percentage be? Case law suggests that 40 percent will do the job,[45] and the IRS has said that 50 percent will qualify for a favorable ruling.[46] In this case, the percentage is in excess of 76 percent ($8 million as a percent of $10.5 million). Note that the percentage requirement focuses on the nature of the consideration paid by Buyer, not the shareholder's ownership percentage in the merged entity, which often is very small. Also, this requirement places no limitation on Larry or Sue's capacity to sell some of their Seller stock to a party unrelated to Seller or Buyer immediately before the merger, nor their capacity to sell any of their Buyer stock to a party unrelated to Buyer immediately after the merger (even if prearranged).[47]

Third, the continuity of business enterprise doctrine must be satisfied. This requires that the purchaser continues the business of the selling entity or uses a significant portion of the selling entity's assets for business purposes.[48] The requirement would not prevent Buyer from transferring Seller's business or assets to a subsidiary corporation or a partnership controlled by Buyer.[49]

Finally, there must be a business purpose for the merger. In a merger designed to strengthen two corporate entities, the business purpose requirement usually is not a problem.

Stock Swap

This scenario is designed to qualify as a tax-free B reorganization under

41. I.R.C. § 362(b).
42. I.R.C. § 356(a)(2).
43. I.R.C. § 368(a)(1)(A).
44. Reg. § 1.368-1(e)(1).
45. See, for example, John A. Nelson Co. v. Helvering, 296 U.S. 374 (1935), Miller v. Commissioner, 84 F.2d 415 (6th Cir. 1936), and Ginsburg and Levin, Mergers, Acquisitions and Buyouts ¶ 610 (2004 edition).
46. Rev. Proc. 77-37, 1977-2 C.B. 568.
47. Reg. § 1.368-1(e)(1).
48. Reg. § 1.368-1(d).
49. Reg. § 1.368-1(d)(4) & (5).

Section 368(a)(1)(B).[50] Here, Buyer would transfer its voting stock to Larry and Sue in exchange for all their stock in Seller. The tax consequences for all parties would be the same as in the previous merger scenario, except that Larry and Sue would recognize no taxable income on the exchange because they would not receive any cash.

What does it take to qualify as a tax-free B reorganization? The big factor (and major difference from other reorganizations) is the "solely" requirement – the consideration paid by the purchaser must consist solely of the purchaser's voting stock.[51] Thus, Buyer could not use any other consideration, including nonvoting stock, without killing the tax-free treatment of the exchange. In addition to the "solely" requirement, the continuity of interest (a slam dunk with only voting stock), continuity of business enterprise, and business purpose requirements must also be satisfied. The "solely" requirement makes the B reorganization one of the least favored strategies.

Stock for Assets

Under this scenario, Buyer would transfer its voting stock to Seller as consideration for Seller's assets and business. Seller would then liquidate by distributing the Buyer stock to Larry and Sue. The goal would be to qualify the transaction as a tax-free C reorganization. If successful, the tax consequences to all the parties would be the same as in the previous two reorganization scenarios. One is hard pressed to imagine why this scenario would ever be preferred over a statutory merger ("A") reorganization. The execution is more difficult because specific assets and liabilities must be transferred; with a merger, this happens automatically by operation of law. Plus, as we will see, the qualification requirements are more demanding.

As for what it takes to qualify, the continuity of interest, continuity of business enterprise, and business purpose requirements must be satisfied. That's the easy part. There also is a "solely" voting stock requirement similar to the stock swap B reorganization, but it is not as strict.[52] It is not violated by the purchaser's assumption of liabilities.[53] Plus, consideration other than voting stock is permitted if (and this is a big "if") the value of the other consideration and the assumed liabilities do not exceed 20 percent of the total consideration paid. In this case, for example, Buyer's assumption of Seller's liabilities of $5 million would not violate the C reorganization "solely" requirement. But because those liabilities exceed 20 percent of the total consideration paid by Buyer ($15.5 million if Buyer issues $10.5 million of voting stock and assumes $5 million of liabilities), no other consideration can be paid. If the liabilities were less than 20 percent of the total, different consideration would be permitted up to the 20 percent mark. So, unlike the statutory merger, there is no capacity for Larry and Sue to get any cash out of the deal without killing the tax-free treatment for all parties.

There are a few additional C reorganization requirements that are not a

---

50. I.R.C. § 368(a)(1)(B).
51. I.R.C. § 368(a)(1)(B); Reg. § 1.368-2(c).
52. I.R.C. § 368(a)(1)(C).
53. I.R.C. § 368(a)(1)(C).

problem in this and many cases, but can be issues in select situations. C reorganization treatment requires that Buyer purchase "substantially all" of Seller's property, which to be safe means it must acquire at least 90 percent of the fair market value of Seller's net assets and 70 percent of the fair market value of its gross assets.[54] Finally, Seller must distribute all its assets (principally the Buyer's stock) to its shareholders pursuant to the reorganization plan.[55]

Forward Triangular Merger

Under this very popular scenario, Buyer forms a wholly owned subsidiary ("Subsidiary"), Seller is merged into Subsidiary, and Buyer's stock is issued to Seller's shareholders, Larry and Sue. Buyer ends up owning Seller's assets and business through its new subsidiary, Seller disappears, and Larry and Sue get Buyer stock. The tax consequences for all the parties are the same as under a statutory merger ("A") reorganization. The key is to qualify under Section 368(a)(2)(D), which specifically permits tax-free reorganization treatment for such a triangular merger. See Illustration D.

Illustration D: Forward Triangular Merger

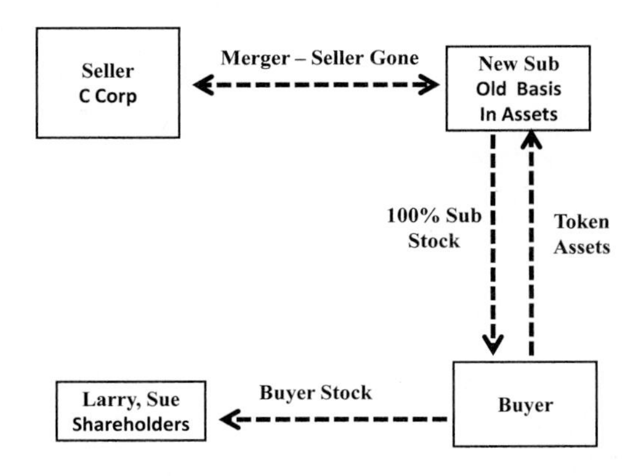

In addition to the regular continuity of interest, continuity of business enterprise, and business purpose requirements, three other conditions must be satisfied. First, Subsidiary must acquire substantially all of Seller's property.[56] It's the same "substantially all" requirement applicable to C reorganizations. No problem here. Second, none of Subsidiary's stock can be used in the transaction. Again, no problem. Third, the transaction must be structured so that it would have qualified as a statutory merger ("A") reorganization if Seller had been merged into Buyer.[57] This third condition (and here's the good news) just requires that the continuity of interest requirement for an A reorganization must

54. I.R.C. § 368(a)(1)(C); Rev. Proc. 77-37, 1977-2 C.B. 568, 569.

55. I.R.C. § 368(a)(2)(G). The statute authorizes the Treasury Secretary to waive this requirement in accordance with conditions prescribed by the Secretary. See Rev. Proc. 89-50, 1989-2 C.B. 631.

56. I.R.C. § 368(a)(2)(D).

57. I.R.C. § 368(a)(2)(D).

have been satisfied.[58] Thus, a substantial portion of the consideration paid by Buyer (50 to 60 percent) may be property other than its stock and the transaction will still qualify as a tax-free reorganization. Of course, Seller's shareholders, Larry and Sue, must still recognize income for the non-stock consideration (as in the case of an A reorganization), but otherwise the tax-free treatment applies.

The value of this strategy is that it offers the flexibility and simplicity of a statutory merger, enables the purchaser to acquire the assets in a new subsidiary, and permits the use of substantial non-stock consideration without threatening the tax-free character of the reorganization.

Reverse Triangular Merger

This scenario is a close cousin to the last. The difference is that Seller, not Subsidiary, is the surviving entity of the merger. As in the last scenario, Buyer forms Subsidiary, Subsidiary merges with Seller, and Buyer's stock is issued to Seller's shareholders, Larry and Sue. Here, Seller ends up as a wholly owned subsidiary of Buyer, and Subsidiary disappears. This reverse triangular merger[59] is attractive in those situations where Seller's continued existence is important for non-tax reasons (e.g., contractual rights, leases, licenses, franchises, etc.). The tax consequences to all parties are the same as under the prior scenario, but qualification is slightly tougher.

With one major exception, the qualification requirements for a reverse triangular merger generally are the same as a forward triangular merger. The exception relates to the amount of non-stock consideration that may be paid to the shareholders, Larry and Sue. For a reverse triangular merger to qualify as a tax-free reorganization, 80 percent of the Seller's stock must be acquired with voting stock of Buyer.[60] So the non-stock consideration cannot exceed 20 percent of the total consideration. As compared to a forward triangular merger, the reverse merger allows the selling entity to survive (which is often important in many situations for various non-tax reasons), but offers less flexibility with regard to the amount of non-stock consideration that can be used in the transaction.

b. S Corporation Scenarios

How do the structural scenarios change if Seller is an S corporation, not a C corporation? The impact of four primary factors must be assessed. First, if Seller has been an S corporation for a significant time, Larry and Sue's basis in their stock will be higher. Their basis in their S corporation stock is increased as the earnings of the S corporation are passed through and taxed to them but retained inside the company.[61] Seller's equity now has a book value of $5 million. Thus, depending on when Seller elected S status, Larry and Sue's basis in their stock may be as high as $5 million, a ten-fold increase over their $500,000 stock basis in a C corporation. This stock basis increase, a big benefit for S corporation shareholders, pays off at time of sale. Under all structural scenarios, the

---

58. Reg. § 1.368-2(b)(2).
59. I.R.C. § 368(a)(2)(E).
60. I.R.C. §§ 368(a)(2)(E), 368(c).
61. I.R.C. § 1367.

shareholders' stock basis affects the amount of gain recognized at the time of sale or, in the case of a reorganization, the amount that carries over to become the basis of the stock acquired in the reorganization.

Second, any corporate level gain triggered on the sale of assets or a liquidation of the S corporation will be passed through and taxed to the S corporation shareholders, Larry and Sue. The character of the gain is based on the assets transferred by the S corporation.[62] The real plus is that the shareholders' basis in their stock is increased by the amount of the gain.[63] As a result, there is little or no shareholder-level tax triggered on the distribution to the shareholders. Thus, the double tax hit is eliminated even in those situations where the transaction is structured to give the purchaser a basis step-up in the acquired assets.

For example, assume in this case that Buyer purchases all of Seller's assets (which have a value of $17 million), assumes the liabilities of $5 million, and pays $12 million cash (the first scenario above). As an S corporation, Seller recognizes a $7 million gain, $1 million of which is ordinary income (1245 recapture) and $6 million of which is capital gain. This income is passed through and taxed to Larry and Sue, resulting in a tax of $1.6 million (40 percent of $1 million and 20 percent of $6 million). Larry and Sue's basis in their stock also is increased $7 million. If we assume that Seller has always been an S corporation and that Larry and Sue's basis in their stock before the sale equaled the book value of Seller's equity before the sale ($5 million), Larry and Sue would have a basis of $12 million in their stock when the $12 million of sales proceeds are distributed to them. Thus, the $12 million distribution triggers no additional tax on its receipt. Plus, as a purchaser of assets, Buyer gets a basis step-up. The net after-tax yield to Larry and Sue is $10.4 million ($5.2 million each), a 36 percent increase over the $3.73 million they each would have netted after the double tax hit with a C corporation.

The practical effect of this difference is huge. No longer is there a need to balance the purchaser's desire for a step up in basis against the burdens of a double tax hit, or to hassle with a negotiated price reduction to induce the purchaser to forego the basis step-up and buy stock. Even when the transaction (for whatever reason) is structured as a stock purchase with the purchaser buying the stock of the S corporation shareholders, the parties may jointly make an election under 338(h)(10) to have the transaction treated as an asset sale followed by a liquidation.[64] The purchaser ends up with a basis step-up, and no double tax is generated.

Third, if the S corporation used to be a C corporation, the potential impacts of the built-in gains (BIG) tax must be assessed.[65] The BIG tax applies when an S corporation disposes of assets that it owned at the time of its conversion to S status within ten years following the conversion. It's an entity level tax imposed at the maximum corporate rate on the built-in gain at the time of conversion.

62. I.R.C. § 1366(b).
63. I.R.C. § 1367.
64. Reg. §1.338(h)(10-1(c).
65. See generally I.R.C. § 1374.

This tax is in addition to the tax that is realized and passed through to the S corporation's shareholders on the sale. Its purpose is to preserve, at least in part and for a period of ten years, the double tax burdens of the corporation's former status as a C corporation.

Finally, an S corporation may be a party to any of the tax-free reorganization scenarios described above. The challenge is to assess the impact of the reorganization on the corporation's continued S status if the corporation survives the reorganization. If the stock of the S corporation ends up being owned by a C corporation after the reorganization (as might happen in a B reorganization or a reverse triangular merger), the S status will be lost. If the S corporation is the purchaser in the reorganization, care should be taken to ensure that no S corporation eligibility requirements are violated (e.g., the 100 shareholder limitation, no corporate or partnership shareholders, etc.).

c. Partnership-Taxed Entity Scenarios

How do the structural scenarios change if Seller is a partnership-taxed entity? If Buyer's stock is used in the deal, the tax-free reorganization options are out. They require corporate status of all parties. So any Buyer stock used in the transaction will be treated the same as any other consideration. As for the other structural options, the partnership's presence eliminates the burden of a double tax. The basis increase on the income passed through is the same as with an S corporation – both as income is accumulated during the life of the entity and when it is recognized at the time of sale.[66] Thus, the tax consequences are similar, but not identical, to those for an S corporation.

If Seller, as a partnership-taxed entity, sells all its assets to Buyer for $12 million and Buyer's assumption of all liabilities, a $7 million gain will be triggered and passed through to the partners, Larry and Sue. The character of the gain will be determined at the partnership level; thus, $1 million will be ordinary income (1245 recapture) and $6 million will be capital gain (goodwill and going concern value). Larry and Sue's basis in their partnership interests will be increased by the $7 million pass-through gain. Thus, assuming Larry and Sue had a combined basis in their partnership interests of $5 million before the transaction, there will be no second tax on the gain when the proceeds from the sale are distributed to Larry and Sue. Buyer will get a stepped-up basis in the assets under the 1060 regime and the ability to write off intangibles over 15 years under Section 197.

Although the consequences of this asset sale scenario look just like its S corporation counterpart, there are a few potential differences. First, if Larry or Sue had contributed to Seller any of the property sold by Seller and that contributed property had a built-in gain or built-in loss at the time of contribution (that is, a fair market value different from its transferred basis), any gain recognized on the sale of the contributed property would first be allocated to the contributing partner to account for such built-in gain or loss, and the balance would then be allocated to the two partners.[67] Thus, although the total gain

66. I.R.C. § 705(a).
67. I.R.C. § 704(c)(1); Reg. § 1.704-3(a)(3).

recognized by Larry and Sue on such a sale would be the same as with an S corporation, the gain would be allocated differently among the owners.

Second, unlike an S corporation with a prior C past, a partnership-taxed entity that sells its assets need not worry about any entity-level tax comparable to the ten-year BIG tax under Section 1374. If the business had a prior C history, it would have taken its tax lumps at the time of its conversion from C status.

Suppose Larry and Sue liquidate Seller and receive all Seller's assets and liabilities and then sell all the assets to Buyer for $12 million and Buyer's assumption of the liabilities. The partnership would terminate on the liquidation, and its tax year would close.[68] Generally, Larry and Sue, as the partners of Seller, would not recognize any gain or loss on the liquidation of Seller.[69] Their basis in their partnership interests would carry over to the basis in the assets received in the liquidation.[70] Their subsequent sale of the assets would trigger a taxable gain equal to the excess of the amount they received over their basis in the assets ($7 million under these facts). The character of the gain would be based on the assets sold; thus, $1 million would be ordinary income and $6 million would be capital gain. But, again, the gain might be allocated differently between Larry and Sue if, within the seven years preceding the liquidation, one of them had contributed some of the property distributed in the liquidation.[71] Also, any attempt to allocate the ordinary income element of the gain disproportionately between Larry and Sue (if, for example, one of them was in a lower personal tax bracket) by distributing more equipment (1245 recapture property) to one partner and more of the other assets to the other partner will fail.[72] As a purchaser of the assets, Buyer would get a new basis in the assets.

Suppose, as an alternative, Buyer purchased Larry and Sue's interests in the partnership for $12 million. Seller, the partnership, would terminate for tax purposes. Larry and Sue would recognize income equal to the excess (here $7 million) of the amount received over their basis in the partnership interests.[73] But, unlike a sale of corporate stock, the sale of a partnership interest may trigger ordinary income if the partnership holds ordinary income assets (e.g., unrealized receivables and inventory items).[74] Thus, the gain represented by such assets will affect the character of the gain recognized by a partner on the sale of a partnership interest. Here, $1 million of the gain recognized by Larry and Sue would be taxed as ordinary income.

As for Buyer, the transaction would be treated as a purchase, as if Seller had made a liquidating distribution to Larry and Sue followed by Buyer's purchase of the former partnership assets – exactly as in the prior scenario.[75]

---

68. I.R.C. § 708(b).
69. I.R.C. § 731(a).
70. I.R.C. § 732(b).
71. I.R.C. § 704(c)(1)(B).
72. I.R.C. § 751(b); Reg. § 1.751-1.
73. I.R.C. § 741.
74. I.R.C. § 751(a); Reg. § 1.751-1(d).
75. Rev. Rule 99-6, 1999-1 C.B. 432.

STUDENT PROBLEM 10-3

Marble Inc. (Marble) is a calendar year C corporation that has two equal shareholders – Debbie and Joyce. Joyce, age 83, owns 2,000 shares of Marble's common stock, with a basis of $600,000. Debbie, age 34, also owns 2,000 shares, but her basis is $7 million. Debbie inherited the stock from her father. Marble's balance sheet assets and liabilities are set forth below.

Folsom Inc. (Folsom) wants to buy Marble, and Debbie and Joyce are ready to sell. Assume that Marble is subject to a combined federal and state income tax rate of 40 percent, and Debbie and Joyce's combined federal and state ordinary marginal income tax rate is 40 percent and capital gain rate is 20 percent.

Marble's Assets and Liabilities

	Book Value Basis	Fair Market Value
Cash	$ 900,000	$ 900,000
Accounts Receivable	2,300,000	3,200,000
Inventories	3,200,000	4,600,000
Equipment	1,600,000	3,400,000
Customer Lists	-	600,000
Copyrights	120,000	700,000
Goodwill	-	14,000,000
Total Assets	$ 8,120,000	$ 27,400,000
Accounts Payable	2,600,000	2,600,000

a. Marble sells its assets to Folsom for $24.8 million plus an assumption of all liabilities. Marble pays its taxes and distributes all remaining proceeds to Debbie and Joyce. Calculate the tax impacts to Marble, Debbie, and Joyce. What is Folsom's basis in the assets? Any suggestions for Debbie and Joyce?

b. Folsom buys Marble's stock from Doug and Jane for $21.8 million. Is this a sensible price under the circumstances? Calculate the tax impacts to Marble, Debbie, and Joyce. What is Folsom's basis in its Marble stock?

c. Folsom buys 75 percent of Marble's stock from Debbie and Joyce for $16.5 million. Marble redeems the remaining 25 percent of the stock by paying Debbie and Joyce $5.5 million. Calculate the tax impacts to Marble, Debbie and Joyce.

d. Folsom forms a new subsidiary (S). Marble is merged into S, and Debbie and Joyce are each issued 100,000 shares (value $110 per share) of Folsom's common stock. What are the tax impacts to Marble, Debbie, Joyce, Folsom and S in such a reorganization? If Debbie and Joyce wanted some cash out of the deal, how much cash could they be paid without destroying the tax-free reorganization?

e. Same as d. except S is merged into Marble. What are the tax impacts to Marble, Debbie, Joyce, Folsom and S in such a reorganization? If Debbie and Joyce wanted some cash out of the deal, how much cash could they be paid without destroying the tax-free reorganization?

f. Same as a. except Marble is and always has been an S corporation and Debbie's basis in her stock is $4.5 million and Joyce's basis is $9 million.

g. Same as b. except Marble is and always has been an LLC taxed as a partnership, and Debbie's basis in her partnership interest is $4.5 million and Joyce's basis is $9 million.

CHAPTER 11

FIGHTS FOR CONTROL IN PUBLIC CORPORATIONS

A. HIGH STAKES, INHERENT CONFLICTS

Public companies are "public." Unlike a closely held corporation, the management and ownership of a public corporation, at least theoretically, are always up for grabs. If someone wants to replace the board so that a new executive management team can be installed, a showdown proxy battle can be triggered to let the shareholders decide. And to hedge all bets that the shareholders will collectively approve the shakeup, the proponents of change (often a deep-pocket private equity firm or hedge fund) may use their capital to influence or dictate the vote by increasing their ownership in the enterprise. An effective tool to quickly and dramatically boost ownership in a public corporation is the tender offer – an offer made to all shareholders to buy a designated amount of stock at a price that nearly always reflects a premium over the current trading price of the stock.

Tender offers are classified and defined in different ways. A friendly offer is an offer that is blessed by the target company's management; a hostile offer is one that threatens management and, in the opinion of management, is not in the best interests of the corporation or its shareholders. A coercive offer is an offer for a limited number shares that threatens misery for the remaining shareholders of the target who are left at the mercy of the new controlling owners. Its opposite is the unlimited all-cash offer that places no limits on shareholder participation. A single tier (or one-step) offer is an offer that does not contemplate a follow-up transaction between the bidder and the target company. A two-tier offer contemplates such a follow up (back-end) transaction at some point following the successful completion of the tender offer.

Are tender offers that rattle and threaten the status quo a good thing? Some passionately argue "yes" because they promote (force?) management accountability and provide a powerful punitive incentive to keep corporate performance and stock values at high levels. The best defense to a hostile proxy battle is superior performance, and few things discourage a tender more than a strong stock price. Others argue that tender offers, on balance, are just necessary evils that provide deep-pocketed profiteers with a mechanism to leverage the capital markets with schemes that, in the end, damage multiple stakeholders – employees, creditors, communities, vendors, states and, yes, even shareholders. But, whether good or bad, two realities about tender offers are undeniable.

First, a tender offer usually drives stock prices up, at least temporarily, for the shareholders of the target corporation and often for the shareholders of the bidder. Various theories have been advanced to explain this price-escalating reality, including that a tender offer exposes the potential of stronger management in the future, the profitable synergistic possibilities between the bidder and target, the value of "bigness," the inherent market under-valuing of long-term stock values, and the impact of boosting shareholder value at the expense of other corporate stakeholders. Whatever the theory, just the mention of a tender offer often sparks shareholder enthusiasm because it suggests the opportunity for a sellout at a premium price.

Second, a tender offer can dramatically showcase the conflicts and tensions that exist between those who own the corporation and those who manage the corporation. Who should have the final say in any decision to fight or oppose a tender offer? Should management sit tight and let the shareholders play it out? Should management confine its efforts to maximizing the net yield to the shareholders? At what point does management's push to preserve the status quo violate duties owned to the shareholders? When and how can management "lock up" a friendly deal with a third party that cannot be dismantled by a hostile tender offer? Of course, these questions are often complicated by others who have a powerful, vested stake in the outcome – those who count on the corporation for a job, tax revenues, local business, community support, and long-term stability.

B. FEDERAL REGULATION

The 1968 Williams Act amendments to the Securities Exchange Act of 1934 were designed to improve federal regulation of transactions that impact corporate control. They apply to all public corporations registered under section 12 of the '34 Act. Following is a brief description of the key Williams Act provisions that are applicable in a tender offer situation.

Five Percent Notice. Any person or group that acquires beneficial ownership of more than five percent of a public corporation's outstanding equity securities must file a "Schedule 13D" disclosure with the SEC. Beneficial ownership is predicated on "voting power and/or investment power." The Schedule 13d must be filed within 10 days of acquiring the triggering five-percent interest and must include:

- The identity and background of the acquiring person or group.
- The source and amount of funds used in making the stock purchases.
- The number of the corporation's shares held by the person or group.
- Details regarding any arrangements with others relating to shares of the corporation's stock.
- The purpose of the acquisition and the intentions of the acquiring person or group regarding the corporation.

Tender Offer Notice. A disclosure document ("Schedule TO") must be filed with the SEC on the same day that a person ("bidder") commences a tender offer. The document must set forth the information required on a Schedule 13d filing, along with the terms and conditions of the tender offer, past negotiations between the bidder and the corporation, any applicable regulatory requirements, and other information that the bidder deems material. Financial statements of the bidder should also be included if they are material to the tender offer.

Mandatory Offer Terms. A tender offer is subject to the following terms:

- The offer must stay open 20 business days and at least 10 business days after any change in the offer price or the percentage of shares covered by the offer.

- Any shareholder can revoke a tender of shares while the tender offer is open.

- The tender offer must be available to all shareholders holding the same class of shares.

- All shareholders must be offered the same price and the same choices as to the form of consideration if any such choices are offered.

- If the number of tendered shares exceeds the number of shares covered by the tender offer, the bidder must purchase shares on a *pro rata* basis from the tendering shareholders.

- The bidder is prohibited from purchasing shares of the corporation's stock outside of the tender offer while the offer is open.

Target Cooperation. The target corporation must assist in distributing the bidder's tender materials to the shareholders either by mailing them or providing a current shareholders mailing list to the bidder. All expenses must be borne by the bidder. Plus, the management of the target corporation must submit a responding statement to the tender offer within 10 business days following the commencement of the offer. The statement should explain the management's reasons for opposing the offer, supporting the offer, or taking no position with respect to the offer.

Self-Tender Rules. Any self-tender offer made by a corporation to buy its own shares (usually made as a defensive move against a third party offer) must comply with the same rules that are applicable to third party offers, except (1) the corporation may purchase its stock while its self-tender offer is open, and (2) no purchases may be made by the corporation during a 10 business day cooling off period after the termination of the self-tender.

False or Misleading Statements. Tender offers are subject to the following broad antifraud provision of section 14(e) of the '34 Act:

> (e) It shall be unlawful for any person to make any untrue statement of a material fact or omit to state any material fact necessary in order to make the statements made, in the light of the circumstances under which they are made, not misleading, or to engage in any fraudulent, deceptive, or manipulative acts or practices, in connection with any tender offer or request or invitation for tenders, or any solicitation of

security holders in opposition to or in favor of any such offer, request, or invitation.

Although the language of section 14(e) is similar to Rule 10b-5, there is one major difference – 14(e) does not require a "sale or purchase" of a security. Its protection could extend to a person who elected not to participate in a tender offer. Of course, in many battles for control, 10b-5 will be applicable to disclosures that may impact stock trading, and the antifraud proxy provisions of section Rule 14a-9 will be in play to the extent proxy solicitations are made in connection with the tender offer. (See Section B of Chapter 13). The focus of section 14(e) is on false or misleading disclosures, not whether the tender offer is fair. In *Schreider v. Burlington Northern, Inc.*[1] the plaintiff alleged that management's orchestration of the substitution of a friendly tender for a more favorable hostile offer constituted an illegal "manipulation" under section 14(e). In rejecting the claim, the Supreme Court stated, "Nowhere in the legislative history is there the slightest suggestion that § 14(e) serves any purpose other than disclosure, or that the term 'manipulative' should be read as an invitation to the courts to oversee the substantive fairness of tender offers; the quality of any offer is a matter for the marketplace."[2]

Insider Trading. The SEC has promulgated a broad insider trading prohibition under Rule 14(e)(3) in connection with tender offers. This rule prohibits any person from trading during a tender offer if that person possesses nonpublic, material information about the offer that the person has reason to know was obtained from the bidder or management of the target company. Unlike normal insider trading prohibitions (see Section B of Chapter 13, Rule 14(e)(3) extends to everyone.

C. STATE ANTITAKEOVER STATUTES

States have always had a vested interest in the activities of outsiders who seek to take control of a local public company and disrupt the *status quo* by moving, consolidating or dismantling the target corporation for profit. These efforts can destroy jobs, deplete a tax base, and damage all elements of a state's economy.

1. HISTORY OF CONSTITUTIONAL CHALLENGES

State efforts to regulate takeovers initially faced constitutional challenges. The winning argument in *Edgar v. Mite Corp.*[3] was that the Illinois statute in question was preempted by the Williams Act and violated the dormant commerce clause of the Constitution by placing an undue burden on out-of-state tender offers that outweighed the state's interest in shareholder protections. The statute in *Mite*, like most first-generation state antitakeover statutes, focused on shareholder protection by requiring a 20-day preannouncement waiting period and a fairness review by state officials, and by extending its provisions to non-

1. 472 U.S. 1 (1985).
2. 472 U.S. at 11.
3. 457 U.S. 625 (1982).

Illinois companies that had significant contacts with the state. In striking down the statute, the Supreme Court stated:

> It is therefore apparent that the Illinois statute is a direct restraint on interstate commerce and that it has a sweeping extraterritorial effect. Furthermore, if Illinois may impose such regulations, so may other States; and interstate commerce in securities transactions generated by tender offers would be thoroughly stifled… Because the Illinois Act purports to regulate directly and to interdict interstate commerce, including commerce wholly outside the State, it must be held invalid…
>
> The Illinois Act is also unconstitutional under the test of *Pike v. Bruce Church, Inc.*, 397 U.S., at 142, 90 S.Ct., at 847, for even when a state statute regulates interstate commerce indirectly, the burden imposed on that commerce must not be excessive in relation to the local interests served by the statute…The effects of allowing the Illinois Secretary of State to block a nationwide tender offer are substantial. Shareholders are deprived of the opportunity to sell their shares at a premium. The reallocation of economic resources to their highest valued use, a process which can improve efficiency and competition, is hindered. The incentive the tender offer mechanism provides incumbent management to perform well so that stock prices remain high is reduced...
>
> Appellant claims the Illinois Act furthers two legitimate local interests. He argues that Illinois seeks to protect resident security holders and that the Act merely regulates the internal affairs of companies incorporated under Illinois law. We agree with the Court of Appeals that these asserted interests are insufficient to outweigh the burdens Illinois imposes on interstate commerce… Insofar as the Illinois law burdens out-of-state transactions, there is nothing to be weighed in the balance to sustain the law.

457 U.S. at 642.

Mite sent states back to the drawing board to start crafting, with the aid of pro-management advocates, a second generation of antitakeover statutes that would apply only to corporations incorporated within the state, focus on regulating corporate internal governance, and heavily target the destructive impacts of coercive tender offers. Soon Indiana's second generation version was before the Supreme Court. The statute applied only to Indiana corporations that had significant ties to the state and provided that shares acquired by a tender offer bidder could not be voted by the bidder until disinterested shareholders (management excluded) voted to authorize such voting rights. To the surprise of many, the court upheld this version of an antitakeover statute in *CTS Corp. v. Dynamics Corp. of America*[4] by stating:

> The Indiana Act operates on the assumption, implicit in the Williams Act, that independent shareholders faced with tender offers

4. 481 U.S. 69 (1987).

often are at a disadvantage. By allowing such shareholders to vote as a group, the Act protects them from the coercive aspects of some tender offers. If, for example, shareholders believe that a successful tender offer will be followed by a purchase of nontendering shares at a depressed price, individual shareholders may tender their shares — even if they doubt the tender offer is in the corporation's best interest — to protect themselves from being forced to sell their shares at a depressed price...

In such a situation under the Indiana Act, the shareholders as a group, acting in the corporation's best interest, could reject the offer, although individual shareholders might be inclined to accept it. The desire of the Indiana Legislature to protect shareholders of Indiana corporations from this type of coercive offer does not conflict with the Williams Act. Rather, it furthers the federal policy of investor protection...

The principal objects of dormant Commerce Clause scrutiny are statutes that discriminate against interstate commerce. The Indiana Act is not such a statute. It has the same effects on tender offers whether or not the offeror is a domiciliary or resident of Indiana. Thus, it "visits its effects equally upon both interstate and local business," *Lewis v. BT Investment Managers, Inc., supra,* 447 U.S., at 36.

Dynamics nevertheless contends that the statute is discriminatory because it will apply most often to out-of-state entities. This argument rests on the contention that, as a practical matter, most hostile tender offers are launched by offerors outside Indiana. But this argument avails Dynamics little. "The fact that the burden of a state regulation falls on some interstate companies does not, by itself, establish a claim of discrimination against interstate commerce." *Exxon Corp. v. Governor of Maryland,* 437 U.S. 117, 126, 98 S.Ct. 2207, 2214, 57 L.Ed.2d 91 (1978)...

Dynamics' argument that the Act is unconstitutional ultimately rests on its contention that the Act will limit the number of successful tender offers. There is little evidence that this will occur. But even if true, this result would not substantially affect our Commerce Clause analysis. We reiterate that this Act does not prohibit any entity—resident or nonresident—from offering to purchase, or from purchasing, shares in Indiana corporations, or from attempting thereby to gain control. It only provides regulatory procedures designed for the better protection of the corporations' shareholders.

We have rejected the "notion that the Commerce Clause protects the particular structure or methods of operation in a ... market." *Exxon Corp. v. Governor of Maryland,* 437 U.S., at 127. The very commodity that is traded in the securities market is one whose characteristics are defined by state law. Similarly, the very commodity that is traded in the "market for corporate control"—the corporation—is one that owes its

> existence and attributes to state law. Indiana need not define these commodities as other States do; it need only provide that residents and nonresidents have equal access to them. Accordingly, even if the Act should decrease the number of successful tender offers for Indiana corporations, this would not offend the Commerce Clause.

481 U.S. at 83 – 84.

Armed with a victory in *CTS* and guidance from the Supreme Court, states soon tackled the challenge of developing a third generation of antitakeover statutes. Today, there are various statutory schemes included in this third generation, some of which test the limits of the *CTS* holding. Following is a brief recap of the types of statutes in play today.

2. *STATE STATUTORY SCHEMES*

The Delaware Moratorium Scheme. Delaware's scheme is one of the least onerous. Section 203 of Delaware's General Corporation Law prohibits an interested shareholder (defined as one who acquires 15 percent or more of the stock of a Delaware corporation in a tender offer) from engaging in any merger or business combination ("Business Combination") with the corporation for a three-year period following the tender offer. This prohibition does not apply if (1) the corporation's board approved the Business Combination before the tender offer that triggered the 15 percent triggering threshold, (2) the interested person acquires at least 85 percent of the corporation's stock (excluding management shares) through the tender offer, or (3) the Business Combination is approved by the corporation's board and shareholders who own at least two-thirds of the other outstanding shares. So the options available to a bidder who wants to trigger a second-tier combination to terminate the interests of other target company shareholders are to wait three years, acquire at least 85 percent through the tender, secure approval of the corporation's board before the tender, or secure approval of the corporation's board and holders of two-thirds of the other shares after the tender.

Control Purchase Schemes. Under these schemes, a bidder whose holdings hit a designated threshold (such as 33 percent) of a corporation's stock is prohibited from acquiring "control shares" unless the shareholders of the corporation, at a meeting usually called no more than 50 days after the bidder's notice, approve the acquisition of control shares by the bidder. As the Court noted in *CTS*, this type of scheme protects against coercive tender offers by forcing collective action of the shareholders.

Control Voting Schemes. This is the scheme that was at issue in *CTS*. It's similar to the prior scheme, except the focus is on the voting rights of the bidder. The bidder can buy stock beyond a designated threshold, but the voting rights of those shares are contingent on a vote of the other shareholders. The potential inability to vote the shares may become an intolerable obstacle.

Fair-Price Schemes. This scheme prohibits a bidder who acquires control of a corporation though a tender offer to engage in a second-tier (sometimes called a "back-end") transaction with the corporation unless the price paid in the second-tier transaction equals or exceeds a statutorily designated fair price, which often is based on the tender price in the first-tier transaction or the market value of the stock during a designated time-frame. The objective is to ensure that the bidder does not use the newly-acquired control to force a second transaction that yields an unfair price to the other shareholders.

Combo Moratorium/Fair Price Scheme. Some state statutes incorporate both moratorium and a fair price schemes. An example is Washington State,[5] which imposes a five-year moratorium on transactions between the bidder and the corporation following a tender offer (with exceptions similar to those in Delaware) and imposes a fair price scheme on certain mergers and liquidations that fall outside of the five-year window.

Foreign Corporation Schemes. Some state statutes apply to a corporation organized in another state if the corporation meets defined criteria relative to its ties to the state: maintains its principal executive in the state; has a designated percentage (often 10 percent) of its shareholders, or a designated percentage of its outstanding shares, owned by residents of the state; has a majority of its employees in the state; and has the majority of its assets or assets with a designated value ($50 million) located in the state.[6] Other states, including Delaware,[7] limit the scope of their statutes to corporations organized in the state.

Optional or Mandatory?

Are the provisions of a state's antitakeover statute optional or mandatory? That is, may a corporation opt out of the provisions through a provision in its articles of incorporation? Delaware permits such an opt out by a provision in the corporation's articles of incorporation, provided that any opt-out amendment to the articles of incorporation is not effective for 12 months.[8] Other states do not provide for such an opt-out, but instead confirm that the statutory requirements are "in addition to, not in lieu of" other protective provisions that may be included in the articles of incorporation or bylaws of the corporation[9] – such as poison pill and staggered board provisions and specific authorization for the board to consider a broad range of corporate stakeholders (shareholders, employees, vendors, customers, creditors, employees, communities) in developing a response to an unsolicited tender offer.

D. CORPORATE DEFENSES TO HOSTILE BIDS

Corporate managers often have strong incentives to protect against the job security risks of a hostile tender offer. They know that the strength of their continued lucrative employment is tied to the stability of the board. This reality has prompted pro-management groups, with the support of many clever lawyers, to develop an arsenal of tools that can be used to fight a tender offer. Some of these defensive tools are designed to fight the offer when it arrives; others create

5. RCW 23B.19.040.
6. See, for example, RCW 23B.10.020(19(b).
7. 8 DGCL § 203.
8. 8 DGCL § 203(a)(3).
9. See, for example, RCW 25B.19.050.

obstacles that discourage tender offers by complicating or devaluing any hostile effort. It's what happens when there's a need for creativity.

In many situations, the interests of the target company shareholders are squarely aligned with the plans of a potential takeover bidder. The shareholders do not want defensive tools that entrench management, drive away bidders, and destroy opportunities for a premium yield that come when a company's true long-term value is exposed in a control showdown. Such shareholders have a few options. They can prevent a defensive tool from ever being adopted or implemented by the smart use of shareholder proposals or by putting pressure on the board. They can collectively organize (often with a bidder who owns stock) to force (via a proxy battle) changes in the board's membership that will lead to the termination or deactivation of a defensive tool. And, as discussed in the following section, they can seek injunctive and other equitable judicial relief to prevent management from protecting its interests at the expense of shareholders.

1. THE MENU: WHEN CREATIVITY AND FEAR LINK UP

It's beyond the scope of this effort to describe in any detail the breadth of the potential tools that a corporation may consider for inclusion in its antitakeover arsenal. Following is a brief description of some of the most popular tools.

Poison Pills. This defensive tool is designed to create an intolerable valuation obstacle for a hostile bidder. It can be structured in many ways, but the core feature is that shareholders of the target corporation (excluding the bidder) are given rights to buy stock at a deep discount if a triggering event occurs and the target's board does not redeem the rights and prevent release of the poison within a short time (usually 10 days) following the triggering event. A typical triggering event is that the bidder acquires a designated percentage of the target's stock (e.g., 15 or 20 percent).

The dilution risks to the bidder are prohibitive if the discounted purchase rights become effective (the poison is released). So the bidder's only options, as a practical matter, are to negotiate a deal with the target's existing management to redeem the rights (at a nominal value specified in the plan) or put an end to the rights by gaining control of the target's board.

A "flip-in" plan gives the shareholders the right to buy target shares at a deep discount. A "flip-over" plan gives the shareholders the right, usually through convertible preferred stock, to buy shares of the bidder at a deep discount in the event of a merger or other combination after the triggering event. Poison pills are very effective in preventing hostile tender offers and, for that very reason, many institutional investors and investor advisory firms oppose their use.

Some companies have "shelf poison pills," plans that have not been officially approved but that can be instantly adopted by a bylaw amendment approved by the target's board if the need arises.

Shark Repellents. These are corporate governance defensive measures that are implemented (usually by bylaw amendment) before any tender offer threat is made. The most popular repellents are:

• A ***staggered board*** provision that gives directors varying terms of more than one year and substantially lengthens the time for a successful bidder to replace the target's board,

• A ***supermajority shareholder voting*** requirement for any merger or business combination following a successful tender offer, and

• A ***"fair price" provision*** requiring that any price in a "back-end" transaction following a tender offer be at least equal to the price offered in the "front-end" tender offer.

Pacman Attack. This occurs when the target company's management reacts to a hostile takeover attempt by initiating a tender offer to gain control of the hostile bidder. For management, it's the ultimate "winner-take-all" showdown. For shareholders, it often guarantees super-escalating premiums for their stock.

White Squire Sale. This occurs when the target's management dilutes the efforts of the hostile bidder by selling additional target shares (often at a discount) to an investor ("squire") who is friendly to management. The squire is not a competitive bidder for control, but the squire's acquisition of stock makes it tougher for the hostile bidder to succeed.

White Knight Recruit. This occurs when the target's management seeks to drive up the price offered by the hostile bidder or force the hostile bidder to retreat by finding another party (a "knight" friendly to management) to engage in a competitive bidding contest with the hostile bidder.

Crown Jewel Sale. This tactic is where the target's management gives a white knight or another party a contractual right or option to purchase a valuable part of the target's business (the "Crown Jewel") at a bargain price. This is considered a "scorched earth" defensive move that is designed to make the target unattractive to any hostile bidder.

Golden Parachute Hikes. This tool drives up the costs of a takeover bid by increasing golden parachute benefits to senior executives and automatically vesting restricted stock and supplemental retirement benefits in the event of a takeover.

Greenmail Payment. This is where the target's management causes the target to purchase a large block of its stock held by a potential hostile bidder to remove the risk of a tender offer. It's akin to blackmail in that it nets the potential hostile bidder a "greenmail" price that reflects a substantial premium over the current market price of the stock. It's sometimes called a "bon voyage bonus" or a "goodbye kiss."

Macaroni Defense. This tactic involves the target company issuing bonds that come with a guarantee that the bonds will be redeemed at a substantial premium price by the target company if there is a successful hostile takeover bid. The high costs of the bonds are designed to discourage a hostile bidder. The term "macaroni" refers to the fact that the redemption price expands with the heat of a hostile bid.

People Pill. This defense is possible when retention of the target's management team is deemed essential to the success of the company. In such a situation, the management team threatens to leave *in masse* if the hostile bid is successful. The goal of the strategy is to discourage offers in those situations where the bidder needs existing management.

Share Buyback. This strategy involves the company borrowing funds to buy back its own shares in a self-tender offer that competes with the hostile bidder. It has a dual deterrent impact on the hostile bidder – it forces the bidder to pay more as the stock price is driven up by the competition, and the company gets weaker as it takes on more debt. This tactic is often referred to as a "leveraged recapitalization." When taken to extremes, the strategy can become a "suicide pill" because it can threaten the survival of the company.

Bankmail. This tactic involves an agreement between the target company and its bank to terminate any existing financing arrangements if control of the company changes as a result of a hostile takeover. It discourages hostile bids because it forces the bidder to find new financing sources for the target's business, drives up transaction costs, and gives the target's management time to implement other defensive strategies.

2. *DEFENSES UNDER JUDICIAL ATTACK*

Antitakeover defense jurisprudence has been a core challenge for Delaware's Chancery and Supreme courts for decades. The overriding question has always focused on the standard of review that a court should apply in resolving the inherent conflict between a board's statutory authority to manage a corporation and shareholder interests when actions are taken to preserve that authority in a dispute with a hostile bidder. Related questions are the role of the business judgment rule and who should bear the burden of proof when shareholders attack a management-installed defensive measure designed to deter or thwart hostile actions.

In the early days, before the creation of the present smorgasbord of defensive options, the central question was whether management could use corporate funds to end the threat of a hostile bid by purchasing the bidder's stock at a premium. There was never any question of the board's statutory authority to use corporate funds to purchase stock of the corporation. The issue was whether the board members were exercising that authority "solely or primarily" for an improper purpose – to perpetuate their position of control.[10] In *Bennett v. Propp,*[11] the court stated:

> We must bear in mind the inherent damager in the purchase of shares with corporate funds to remove a threat to corporate policy when a threat to control is involved. The directors are of necessity confronted with a conflict of interest, and an objective decision is difficult. Hence, in our opinion, the burden should be on the directors to justify such a purchase as one primarily in the corporate interest.

10. See *Kors v. Carey*, 158 A.2d 136 (Del.Ch. 1960), *Bennett v. Propp*, 187 A.2d 405 (Del. Ch. 1962), and *Yasik v. Wachtel*, 17 A.2d 309 (Del.Ch. 1941).

11. 187 A.2d 405 (Del. Ch. 1962).

187 A.2d at 409.

Given this burden of proof for directors, the Delaware Supreme Court's reversal of the Chancery Court's decision in *Cheff v. Mathews*,[12] came as a surprise to many. In that case, the directors of Holland Furnace Company ("Holland") caused Holland to purchase the shares of a shareholder ("Maremont") who had acquired a 15 percent stake in Holland and was threatening a tender offer for the balance of the corporation's stock. One director ("Cheff") was an officer of Holland and another ("Trenkamp") was Holland's attorney. The other directors were outsiders who owned Holland stock. A derivative action was brought by shareholders, claiming that the purchase was made to protect the control of the incumbent board and demanding that the purchase be rescinded and the directors be required to personally account for any damages to Holland. In reversing the lower court decision, the Delaware Supreme Court held that that the defendants, through their direct investigation, receipt of professional advice, and personal observations, had satisfied their burden of proof of showing reasonable grounds to believe a danger to corporate policy and effectiveness existed by the presence of the Maremont stock ownership.

Facts

Cheff provided a wobbly analytical framework for examining actions taken by boards to end hostile tender offer threats. The business judgment rule was in play, predicated on the board satisfying an unspecified proof burden of good faith and reasonable investigation. This framework continued to shape the law as hostile takeover bids ballooned and grabbed headlines from the late '70s to the early '90s and pro-management forces pulled out all stops to create the menu of defensive measures described above. The Delaware courts were constantly being challenged to use an undefined standard of review in high-stakes cases that posed unique facts that went right to the heart of the conflict between those who manage and those who own a corporation. Half-way through the tender offer activity surge, the Delaware Supreme Court decided the landmark case of *Unocal Corporation v. Mesa Petroleum Co*,[13] that established a standard that would be the foundational starting point for all future decisions.

a. Unocal's Two-Prong Test

In *Unocal*, Mesa Petroleum Co., a 13 percent owner of the stock of Unocal Corporation, a Delaware corporation, commenced a two-tier, "front-loaded" tender offer to purchase 37 percent of Unocal's stock for a cash price of $54 in the first tier and to eliminate the balance of Unocal's public shares with junk bonds valued at less than $54 in the back-end tier. Unocal's board and a separate board committee composed solely of outside directors, on advice of outside financial advisers and attorneys, determined that the Mesa offer was grossly inadequate and coercive. As a defensive measure, they approved a self-tender cash offer for $72 a share only to Unocal's remaining public shareholders if the first tier of Mesa's offer was succeeded. Mesa's immediate lawsuit resulted in a Chancery Court injunction to restrain Unocal's selective self-tender unless it was

12. 199 A.2d 548 (Del. Supr.1964).
13. 493 A.2d 946 (Del.Sup. 1985).

changed to include Mesa (which would destroy its purpose to stop Mesa).

The Delaware Supreme Court reversed and vacated the injunction, holding that when board-approved defensive actions to a hostile tender offer are questioned, the directors are entitled to the protection of the business judgment rule and the rule's related proof-burden shift to the plaintiff only when and if the board sustains its own burden of satisfying a two-prong test: (1) a "reasonableness" test that the directors had reasonable grounds to believe that a danger to corporate policy and effectiveness existed; and (2) a "proportionality" test that the board's responses were reasonable in relation to the threat posed. Placing such a burden on the board, reasoned the court, was justified by the inherent conflict that is created when management is threatened by a hostile tender offer.

On the facts of the case the court concluded that the board had satisfied both tests, finding that the independent committee had determined in good faith and with strong evidence that Mesa's offer was coercive, grossly inadequate, and a danger to the corporation and its shareholders, and that Unocal's selective, defensive tender offer was a reasonable response to the posed threat. The court held that the exclusion of Mesa from the defensive tender offer was not illegal or unique (referencing green mail payment ploys).

Unocal clarified the gateway to the presumption of the business judgment rule when corporate directors are challenged for their adoption of an antitakeover defense provision. When defensive actions are questioned, directors are not entitled to the protection of the business judgment rule and its related shift of the burden to rebut its presumption to the plaintiff until the board has sustained its own burden of satisfying the two-prong test of *reasonableness* and *proportionality,* as defined by the court.

Unocal involved a self-tender offer in response to a grossly inadequate two-tier coercive offer. Looking back, it was a relatively easy fact pattern for drawing lines. Its two-prong test has triggered, and continues to trigger, challenging questions in cases where the facts are tougher. What grounds will satisfy the reasonableness test? Could the interests of non-shareholders form a basis for such grounds? How will the proportionality test play out in a situation where the hostile bid is not coercive? Or how about where the board is acting to protect against an unknown potential future hostile takeover risk? Or how about the situation where the directors' objective is to "lock up" a friendly deal that might otherwise be derailed by a hostile bid? The challenge of these questions in difficult high-stakes cases has been and remains the legacy of *Unocal's* two-prong test.

In the same year the Delaware Supreme Court decided *Unocal*, it applied *Unocal's* two-pong test to a board's adoption of a poison pill rights plan in response to a coercive tender offer in *Moran v. Household International, Inc.*[14] In holding that Household's adoption of the bill satisfied *Unocal's* proportionate test, the court stated:

14. 500 A.2d 1346 (Del. 1985).

> There are no allegations here of any bad faith on the part of the Directors' action in the adoption of the Rights Plan. There is no allegation that the Directors' action was taken for entrenchment purposes. Household has adequately demonstrated, as explained above, that the adoption of the Rights Plan was in reaction to what it perceived to be the threat in the market place of coercive two-tier tender offers...[T]o meet their burden, the Directors must show that the defensive mechanism was "reasonable in relation to the threat posed". The record reflects a concern on the part of the Directors over the increasing frequency in the financial services industry of "boot-strap" and "bust-up" takeovers. The Directors were also concerned that such takeovers may take the form of two-tier offers... In sum, the Directors reasonably believed Household was vulnerable to coercive acquisition techniques and adopted a reasonable defensive mechanism to protect itself.

500 A.2d at 1356-57

Three year later, the Delaware Chancery Court decided *Blasius Industries v. Atlas Corp*,[15] 564 A.2d 651 (Del. Ch. 1988) where the court held that "when [a board] acts ... for the primary purpose of preventing or impeding an unaffiliated majority of shareholders from expanding the board and electing a new majority," its action "constitute[s] an offense to the relationship between corporate directors and shareholders that has traditionally been protected...." 564 A.2d at 652. Such disenfranchising actions, although not "invalid *per se,*" require that "the board bears the heavy burden of demonstrating a compelling justification for such action." 564 A.2d at 661.

The point at which *Blasius'* "compelling justification" standard intersects with *Unocal's* two-prong test in an anti-takeover defense battle has presented a difficult challenge for defendants and the courts. There is no denying that various popular "shark repellents" are specifically designed to create voting obstacles for those who, for example, seek to replace board members to ensure that a poison pill is never released. And there is little question that the "onerous" *Blasius* "compelling interest" standard poses a tougher burden for a board than Unocal's two-prong "reasonableness" and "proportionality" test.

The remedy sought in *Unocal* was an injunction. That is common in disputes over corporate control. The goal is to shut down the defensive strategy. The injunction request requires the court to focus on the likelihood of the plaintiff prevailing on the merits and the potential of irreparable harm. A money damage award for breach of fiduciary duties is possible, but often is rendered moot, as a practical matter, by a Delaware Code § 102(b)(7) provision in the corporation's articles of incorporation that eliminates any director liability for money absent a showing of bad faith (see Section F of Chapter 4). And although minority appraisal rights are an option in cases where the market opt-out is not applicable, they focus only on the fairness of the here-and-now value and trigger administrative challenges, costs, and inherent outcome uncertainties.

15. 564 A.2d 651 (Del. Ch. 1988).

The *Unocal* two-prong test and *Blasius'* "compelling justification" standard for measures that tamper with shareholder voting rights have created tough analytical challenges for Delaware's courts in handling disputes that involve huge sums of money and the fate of very large companies. The cases of *Unitrin, Inc. v. American General Corp.*[16] and *Chesapeake Corp. v. Shore*[17] (described below) are illustrative and instructive.

In *Unitrin*, Unitrin's board of directors (five of seven were outsiders) rejected American General's offer to purchase Unitrin for $50 3/8 a share ($2.6 billion). American General responded with a press release announcing the offer to generate interest among Unitrin shareholders and to put pressure on Unitrin's board. On advice of financial and legal advisors, Unitrin's board, convinced the press release was a hostile act to coerce a sale at an inadequate price and fearful that speculators and arbitrageurs were acquiring Unitrin stock, responded by adopting a shareholder rights plan (poison pill) and an advance notice bylaw provision, and by implementing a plan to repurchase 10 million shares of Unitrin stock, which would increase the percentage of director-owned stock from 23 to 28 percent.

American General contended that this percentage change, coupled with an existing bylaw that required 75 percent shareholder approval for any merger with a shareholder that owned at least 15 percent of Unitrin's stock, would require that American General keep its percentage ownership below 15 percent, which in turn would make a proxy contest for board control (to deactivate the pill) untenable. After expedited discovery, the Chancery Court temporarily enjoined any further stock repurchases by Unitrin, finding that there was no showing of a necessity for the repurchase plan and, therefore, it was a disproportionate response to the threat posed by American General's cash offer under the *Unocal* standards.

The Supreme Court reversed the interlocutory judgment and remanded the case. In holding that the stock repurchase program satisfied *Unocal's* "proportionality" test, the court reasoned:

1. The three actions taken by the board were defensive measures subject to the *Unocal* proof burdens placed on the board (no business judgment rule presumption);

2. The Chancery Court had properly determined that the first *Unocal* test (reasonableness) had been satisfied because the board (mostly outsiders) had determined in good faith that the price was inadequate and posed a threat to uninformed shareholders who may not appreciate the value potential of the company;

3. The repurchase program's voting impact was subject to *Unocal's* proportionality test (*Blasius'* "compelling justification" standard was discussed and then dropped from the analysis presumably because the primary purpose was not to impede shareholder voting);

4. The repurchase program satisfied *Unocal's* proportionality test because it

16. 651 A.2d 1361 (Del. 1995).
17. 771 A.2d 293 (Del.Ch. 2000).

was not inherently coercive (it did not restrict future bids or discriminate in favor of any group), was not preclusive (a proxy battle and merger approval were viable options with American General owning 14.9 percent of stock) and was within the "range of reasonableness" (it was statutorily authorized, limited in degree to the magnitude of the threat, and recognized immediate liquidity needs of some shareholders); and

5. The Chancery Court erred in requiring a showing of "necessity" and thereby improperly substituting its judgment for that of the board.

The court's "no preclusive" numbers analysis showed that, with 14.9 percent ownership and an expected 90 percent shareholder response rate, American General would have needed approval from an additional 30.2 percent of the outstanding shares to elect a new board and an additional 35.2 percent to approve a merger, both viable since 42 percent of Unitrin's stock was owned by institutions and 33 percent by only 20 institutions. The court also was unwilling to presume that the outside directors (who collectively owned more than $450 million of Unitrin stock) would summarily reject an attractive price to retain the prestige of their board position.

The outcome was very different in *Chesapeake*. When the boards of Chesapeake Corporation, a Virginia corporation, and Shorewood Corporation, a Delaware corporation, failed to come to terms on purchase offers from each party, the Shorewood board adopted defensive bylaws to supplement its poison pill and protect against a hostile tender offer or proxy contest from Chesapeake. The new bylaws eliminated the ability of the shareholders to call a special meeting, gave the board control over the record date of a shareholder consent solicitation, and (most importantly and the issue in the case) increased to two-thirds the percentage of shareholder votes required to amend a bylaw. Chesapeake commenced a tender offer, a shareholder consent solicitation, and this suit to invalidate the supermajority bylaw (which Shorewood's board reduced to 60 percent shortly before trial).

The Chancery Court enjoined the supermajority bylaw, finding that the board members had not sustained their burden under either *Unocal* or *Blasius* and that the bylaw was a preclusive, unjustified impairment of shareholder voting rights. The court reasoned as follows:

1. Delaware courts have struggled in determining whether and how the *Blasius* "compelling justification" standard is applied when voting rights are impacted by defensive measures;

2. The law, as it exists, requires that *Unocal's* standards must first be applied to the supermajority bylaw because of its defensive origin and then, if its primary purpose is to impede shareholder voting, there must be a "compelling justification" to survive the *Unocal* review;

3. Shorewood's board had sufficient, good faith reasons to believe that Chesapeake's price was inadequate (thus, satisfying the Unocal "reasonableness" test), but the threat was mild and not dangerous (still a premium price and room to negotiate);

4. The board's other "reasonable test" threat (shareholder confusion or "substantive coercion") was heavily criticized (a "slippery concept" easily subject to abuse) and was rejected in the case as a "post hoc, litigation-inspired rationale";

5. Shorewood's board failed to sustain its proof burden under *Unocal's* "proportionality" test because it did nothing to assess the preclusive impact of the supermajority bylaw (would required approval of 88 percent of disinterested shareholders with 90 percent turnout), nor did it offer any "proportionality" justification for such an "extremely aggressive and overreaching response to such a mild threat" (particularly considering the other defensive measures in place); and

6. The supermajority bylaw also violated *Blasius'* "compelling justification" standard because its purpose was to intentionally impair the voting process and the board's rationale (that it knows better than the shareholders) "provides no legitimate justification at all."

b. Revlon-Land

In *Revlon, Inc. v. MacAndrews & Forbes Holdings*,[18] the Delaware Supreme Court was confronted with the challenge of having to apply the *Unocal* tests in a case where a change of control was inevitable. In that case, Pantry Pride aggressively pursued the acquisition of Revlon, continually upping its offer while threatening a tender offer. Revlon's board considered Pantry Pride "a small, highly leveraged company bent on a 'bust up' takeover by using 'junk bond' financing to buy Revlon cheaply, sell the assets to pay the debts incurred, and retain the profit for itself."

Revlon's board initially responded to Pantry Pride's unsolicited bids by adopting a shareholders' rights poison bill and agreed to purchase 10 million shares of its own stock for notes ("Notes") that contained a covenant against any additional debt. As to these defensive measures, the court found that "the board acted in good faith, and on an informed basis, with reasonable grounds to believe that there existed a harmful threat to the corporate enterprise." Citing *Unocal* and upholding these defensive measures, the court stated, "The adoption of a defensive measure, reasonable in relation to the threat posed, was proper and fully accorded with the powers, duties, and responsibilities conferred upon directors under our law." 506 A.2d 181.

The court then focused on the steps Revlon's board had taken when Pantry Pride's offer hit $53 a share and a sale of the company was inevitable. The board authorized Revlon's management to negotiate a sale of the company to a third party. This led to a friendly agreement to sell Revlon to Forstmann for $57.25 a share and Forstmann's agreement to support the market price of the Notes. To secure the deal in the face of Pantry Pride's threat "to top" any offer, Forstmann was given "lock up" protections: a Revlon "no-shop" covenant supported by a $25 million cancellation fee, and the right to buy two Revlon divisions at a deeply discounted price.

18. 506 A.2d 173 (Del. 1986).

Pantry Pride responded by raising its offer to $58 a share and suing to nullify the rights plan, to terminate the Note's covenants, and to obtain an injunction against the lock-up provisions. In holding that Revlon's board had breached its duty of care by approving lock-up protections that shut down the bidding process, the court stated that the board's authorization to permit management to negotiate a merger or buyout with a third party changed the duty of the board from the preservation of Revlon as a corporate entity to the maximization of the company's value at a sale for the stockholders' benefit and thus significantly altered the board's responsibilities under the *Unocal* standards. The directors' role, reasoned the court, changed from defenders of the corporate bastion to auctioneers charged with getting the best price for the stockholders. The court stated:

> A board may have regard for various constituencies in discharging its responsibilities, provided there are rationally related benefits accruing to the stockholders. *Unocal,* 493 A.2d at 955. However, such concern for non-stockholder interests is inappropriate when an auction among active bidders is in progress, and the object no longer is to protect or maintain the corporate enterprise but to sell it to the highest bidder… Given the complexity of the proposed transaction between Revlon and Forstmann, the obstacles to Pantry Pride obtaining a meaningful legal remedy are immense. We are satisfied that the plaintiff has shown the need for an injunction to protect it from irreparable harm, which need outweighs any harm to the defendants.
>
> In conclusion, the Revlon board was confronted with a situation not uncommon in the current wave of corporate takeovers. A hostile and determined bidder sought the company at a price the board was convinced was inadequate. The initial defensive tactics worked to the benefit of the shareholders, and thus the board was able to sustain its *Unocal* burdens in justifying those measures. However, in granting an asset option lock-up to Forstmann, we must conclude that under all the circumstances the directors allowed considerations other than the maximization of shareholder profit to affect their judgment, and followed a course that ended the auction for Revlon, absent court intervention, to the ultimate detriment of its shareholders. No such defensive measure can be sustained when it represents a breach of the directors' fundamental duty of care. *See Smith v. Van Gorkom,* Del.Supr., 488 A.2d 858, 874 (1985). In that context the board's action is not entitled to the deference accorded it by the business judgment rule. The measures were properly enjoined.

rule
no lockups

506 A.2d at 182-185

The standards announced *in Revlon* (dubbed the "Revlon duties") have raised some tough questions. At what point in the process do the duties kick in? Does there have to be an auction for the duties to apply? What do the Revlon duties require a board to do when there are multiple potential buyers? Can a board use lockup protections in a deal the board believes is good for the shareholders? Without such lockup protections, can a potential buyer reasonably be expected to commit to a deal that can be dismantled by a competitive bid? In discharging its *Revlon* duties, can a board consider the interests of others, such as employees or creditors, or must the sole focus be short-term maximization for the shareholders? Do the Revlon duties ever apply in a stock-for-stock merger where no shareholders are being cashed out? What about a part-cash, part-stock transaction? Are the Revlon duties a special standard apart from the *Unocal* tests or are they just an example of the *Unocal* rules applied to a special fact situation? In numerous subsequent cases, the Delaware courts have struggled with these questions.

In *Paramount Communications, Inc. v. Time, Inc.*,[19] the Delaware Supreme Court helped clarify when *Revlon* duties may be triggered. Time and Warner had entered into a stock-for-stock merger. Paramount sought to stop the merger by making cash tender offers to Time's shareholders on the condition that the Time-Warner merger be terminated. Fearful that its shareholders might opt for Paramount's offer, Time restructured its deal with Warner as a cash purchase for 51 percent of Warner's stock in a transaction that would not require the approval of Time's shareholders. As a result, Time's shareholders never had a vote on the condition that would have made Paramount's offer operative. The court held that Time's outside directors had not violated their *Unocal* duties, finding that the directors had acted in good faith in determining that the Paramount offer was inadequate and that Time's shareholders may lack the capacity to appreciate the strategic benefit of a merger with Warner. The court also held that no *Revlon* duties were triggered by stating:

> Under Delaware law there are, generally speaking and without excluding other possibilities, two circumstances which may implicate *Revlon* duties. The first, and clearer one, is when a corporation initiates an active bidding process seeking to sell itself or to effect a business reorganization involving a clear break-up of the company. However, *Revlon* duties may also be triggered where, in response to a bidder's offer, a target abandons its long-term strategy and seeks an alternative transaction involving the breakup of the company... If, however, the board's reaction to a hostile tender offer is found to constitute only a defensive response and not an abandonment of the corporation's continued existence, *Revlon* duties are not triggered, though *Unocal* duties attach... [W]e decline to extend *Revlon* 's application to corporate transactions simply because they might be construed as putting a corporation either "in play" or "up for sale." *See Citron v. Fairchild Camera,* Del.Supr., 569 A.2d 53, (1989).; *Macmillan,* 559 A.2d at 1285 n. 35. The adoption of structural safety devices alone does not trigger *Revlon.* Rather, as the Chancellor stated, such devices are properly subject to a *Unocal* analysis.
>
> Finally, we do not find in Time's recasting of its merger agreement with Warner from a share exchange to a share purchase a basis to conclude that Time had either abandoned its strategic plan or made a sale of Time inevitable. The Chancellor found that although the merged

19. 571 A.2d 1140 (1989).

> Time–Warner company would be large (with a value approaching approximately $30 billion), recent takeover cases have proven that acquisition of the combined company might nonetheless be possible. The legal consequence is that *Unocal* alone applies to determine whether the business judgment rule attaches to the revised agreement.

571 A.2d at 1150 – 1151.

Paramount found itself again with a losing *Revlon* argument in a subsequent case that further clarified when *Revlon* duties may be triggered – *Paramount Communications, Inc. v. QVC Networks, Inc.*[20] Rebounding from its failed Time bid, Paramount entered into a merger agreement with Viacom, under which Paramount shareholders would receive a combination of cash and Viacom stock valued at $69 a share and Viacom was protected by a no-shop covenant, a termination fee, and unique stock option – the right to buy 19.9 percent of Paramount's stock at $69.14 per share with a senior subordinated note if the termination fee was triggered. When QVC announced a competitive tender offer for Paramount's stock at a higher price on the condition that the stock option be invalidated, Paramount's board characterized the QVC offer as "illusory" and continued to show its preference for the Viacom deal. The court held that Paramount's board had violated its *Revlon* duties with the "draconian" stock option, its refusal to negotiate with QVC, its uninformed "illusory" characterization of QVC's offer, and its unwavering allegiance to Viacom. The big issue was whether the *Revlon* duties were even triggered. In holding that the *Revlon* duties applied, the court emphasized that a change of control was inevitable in which a "fluid aggregation of unaffiliated shareholders" would sell their voting control to a single buyer. In distinguishing its holding in *Time*, the court noted that in *Time* there was no "substantial evidence to conclude that Time's board, in negotiating with Warner, made the dissolution or break-up of the corporate entity inevitable."

Application of the tough *Revlon* duties continues to be a challenge, as illustrated by the instructive, recent case of *In Re Smurfit-Stone Container Corp. Shareholder Litigation*.[21]

In that case, Smurfit-Stone Container Corp., a Delaware corporation, had emerged from a Chapter 11 bankruptcy proceeding, had a new board (primarily outsiders appointed by a creditors' committee), and had aggressively pursued (though an independent Special Committee of its board) an opportunity to sell the company that failed when the buyer (Company A) refused to pay more than $29 a share. Shortly thereafter, Rock-Tenn Company, discovering that Smurfit was an acquisition target, began negotiations with the Committee that lead to a merger agreement at $35 a share (half cash and half Rock-Tenn stock) that would result in Smurfit shareholders owning 45 percent of Rock-Tenn's stock.

The merger was protected by a "no-shop" clause (preventing shopping for a higher price), a "matching rights" provision (Rock-Tenn had an option to match any unsolicited superior bid), and a $120 million termination fee (paid if the

20. 637 A.2d 34 (Del. 1994).
21. 2011 WL 2028076 (Del.Ch. 2011).

transaction was terminated because of a superior offer or board's failure to recommend to shareholders). Shareholders of Smurfit brought this action to enjoin the shareholder vote on the merger for 45 to 60 days (time to seek higher bids), arguing that the board members had failed to maximize shareholder value under their *Revlon* duties and had breached their fiduciary duties by agreeing to the protective provisions.

The Chancery Court denied the injunction request, finding that the plaintiffs had not shown a reasonable probability that they would succeed on their claims. Noting that a pure stock-for-stock transaction may not trigger *Revlon* duties (would not amount to a change of control because the shareholders' investment opportunity would remain), the court concluded (although not free of doubt) that it is likely that the Delaware Supreme Court would apply *Revlon* duties to a transaction with a near-equal split of cash and stock because there would be "no tomorrow" for half of the shareholders' investment.

Recognizing that there is "no single path" a board must follow to maximize shareholder value and that *Revlon* imposed on the board members the burden of proving they were adequately informed and acted reasonably, the court found no threat of irreparable damage by resolving the following factual issues in favor of the directors: the process followed by Board and independent committee was not perfect, but reasonable; the board members were adequately informed, were sophisticated people, made smart use of an independent committee and financial advisor, met often, were devoid of management influence, had valuation information from the bankruptcy and the history with Company A, and had no reason to suspect higher bids; the protective provisions were relatively standard and wouldn't unreasonably inhibit other bidders; the board's advisor was a reasonable choice and the advisor's contingent fee was routine; and there was no basis to question the board's determination that the Rock-Tenn price was reasonable.

STUDENT PROBLEM 11-1

Troy Walton is the founder, chief executive officer, and chairman of the board of Kfiber Inc. ("Kfiber"), a Delaware corporation that designs and manufactures a wide broad range of synthetic fiber products. Troy, age 75, frequently talks of retiring but has done nothing to slow down. Troy's son, Julian, age 47, has made Kfiber his career and is Kfiber's executive vice president in charge of sales.

Troy is Kfiber's largest shareholder, owning 18 percent of the outstanding common stock. An additional 10 percent of Kfiber's stock is owned by key Kfiber executives (including Julian). The remaining 72 percent is owned and publicly traded by outside investors, heavily represented by institutional investors. The attraction of Kfiber has been its ever-growing profitability, its products' strategic *niche* positions in many markets, and Troy's historic *blasé* attitude about Kfiber's stock price. Troy's focus has always been on product development and operational efficiencies, not the current trading price of Kfiber stock, which currently hovers in the $20 range. As a result, many believe that Kfiber's stock is seriously undervalued in the market and that substantial values will be realized when Troy finally steps aside and the company is sold to a strategic buyer.

Kfiber has a nine member board: Troy, Julian, two other Kfiber executives, and five outsiders, all of whom are loyal friends of Troy.

Warfield Industries Incorporated ("Warfield"), a Delaware corporation, is a large diversified investment company that is forever on the lookout for undervalued companies that are ripe for a management change. It has a reputation for "busting up companies and destroying jobs." Two months ago, Warfield's CEO approached Troy about the possibility of Warfield buying Kfiber. Troy rejected the overture out of hand, stating that "Kfiber will always be run in accordance with a firmly established Walton culture that employees, customers, and shareholders all have a stake in the enterprise." Troy advised members of Kfiber's board of his short interchange with Warfield's CEO.

Troy and other members of Kfiber's board recently learned that Warfield has purchased nine percent of Kfiber's stock. They also have heard rumors that Warfield is considering a tender offer for Kfiber's stock at a price in the $32 range. It's likely that such a price would excite many of Kfiber's shareholders. It was unclear whether such an offer would be for all or only a portion of Kfiber's outstanding stock. Troy arranged a meeting with Kfiber's legal counsel and a reputable outside investment firm. After a lengthy discussion over many hours, the meeting ended with the following ideas on the table:

Recommendation A. Kfiber's board should appoint the outside members of the board as a special committee (the "Committee") to obtain an independent valuation of Kfiber's business and to consider the advisability of Kfiber taking actions to protect against the risks of a hostile tender offer that would seek to capitalize on Kfiber's undervalued stock.

Recommendation B. The Committee should consider the advisability of recommending that Kfiber's board adopt (by way of bylaw amendment) a "standard" flip-in shareholder rights poison pill plan that would empower the board to issue rights to existing Kfiber shareholders to purchase additional Kfiber stock at a substantial discount if and when a hostile bidder acquired more than 20 percent of Kfiber's stock. The board would have the right to redeem and cancel such rights at any time for a nominal consideration. The Committee was advised that, as is usually the case with a poison pill, the threatened valuation impacts of such a plan would prevent a hostile tender offer from going forward so long as there is any possibility of the rights becoming effective.

Recommendation C. The Committee should consider the advisability of recommending that Kfiber's board adopt an amendment to Kfiber's bylaws to provide that a special meeting of shareholders can be called by shareholders only if shareholders owning at least two-thirds of Kfiber's outstanding shares participate in the request.

Recommendation D. The Committee should consider the advisability of recommending that Kfiber's board adopt an amendment to Kfiber's bylaws to provide that Kfiber's bylaws may be amended by shareholders only if shareholders owning at least two-thirds of Kfiber's outstanding shares vote in favor of the amendment.

Recommendation E. The Committee should consider the advisability of recommending that Kfiber's board adopt an amendment to Kfiber's bylaws to provide that any shareholder-initiated changes to Kfiber's board of directors between annual meetings must be approved by shareholders owning at least two-thirds of Kfiber's outstanding shares.

Recommendation F. The Committee should consider the advisability of recommending that Kfiber's board approve a sale of authorized common stock to Bolton Industries, Inc, ("Bolton"), a strategic supplier of Kfiber that has always expressed an interest in owning Kfiber stock. Bolton would be loyal to Troy's interests and would have no interest in any plans of Warfield. Bolton would pay $19 a share. After the sale, Troy, existing Kfiber executives, and Bolton would collectively own 34 percent of Kfieber's outstanding stock. The capital generated from the stock sale would be used to fund a new Kfiber plant in San Diego.

Outlining the logic behind the recommendations, the advisers explained that the poison pill would stop any hostile bid until the bidder could secure enough shareholder support to trigger a shareholder-approved bylaw amendment or a change in the composition of the board. Recommendations C, D, and E would create serious obstacles to any attempts by a bidder or shareholders to eliminate the risk of the pill, particularly since the next annual meeting of shareholders wouldn't occur for 10 months. The "White Squire" stock sale to Bolton would "breathe defensive life and put strong teeth" into the two-thirds voting requirements of the other recommendations.

Please help Troy and his colleagues with the following questions that have surfaced regarding how the recommendations will stack up under *Unocal's* two-prong test (get creative):

1. What factors should be considered in assessing whether Kfiber's board can sustain its burden of proof under the "reasonableness" test? What additional facts should the Committee seek to obtain in this regard?

2. Will any of these defensive measures be considered "preclusive"? If so, what's the impact?

3. Will any of the defensive measures be subject to *Blasius*' "compelling interest" standard? If so, what would have to be shown to meet that standard?

4. What factors should be considered in assessing whether Kfiber's board can sustain its burden of proof under *Unocal's* proportionality test?

STUDENT PROBLEM 11-2

Refer to the basic facts of Student Problem 11-1. As Kfiber's Committee pursued discussions with their "white squire" Bolton, the concept of Bolton becoming a "white knight" started to take hold. Bolton would acquire Kfiber through a triangular merger in which Kfiber would be merged into a newly-formed subsidiary of Bolton and thus become a wholly owned subsidiary of Bolton. Kfiber shareholders would receive a combination of cash and Bolton stock valued at $32 a share. The mix of cash and stock has not yet been resolved, but all agree that for tax reasons the cash portion will not exceed 50 percent of the consideration. After the merger, former Kfiber shareholders would own from 18 to 35 percent of Bolton's outstanding stock, depending on the cash-stock mix. Troy and Julian would join Bolton's board, the "Walton culture" would continue at Kfiber, and no Kfiber jobs would be threatened.

Troy is "pumped" by the prospects of this merger. Bolton is willing to proceed with the transaction only if it can have comfort that "those Warfield vultures can't upset the deal or drive up the price." To protect Bolton and the strength of the deal, the Committee and Bolton have agreed to the following:

- Kfiber's board will adopt the poison pill rights plan described in Recommendation A in Student Problem 11-1.
- Kfiber will agree to a no-shop provision in its agreement with Bolton.
- Kfiber will agree to pay Bolton a termination fee equal to 4 percent of the deal's consideration (estimated at $48 million) if the deal is cancelled due to an offer from another party.
- If the conditions of the termination fee are triggered, Kfiber will sell to Bolton its Chicago and Houston plants for $325 million, a bargain price by any standard.

The overriding question now is whether Wardfield or other Kfiber shareholders will be able to enjoin the enforcement of these protective actions by successfully alleging that Kfiber's board has violated its fiduciary duties to Kfiber's shareholders. In evaluating this overall question, consider the following specific issues and what additional facts you would like to have in assessing these issues:

1. Will *Revlon* duties be triggered in this situation?

2. How can the transaction be structured to reduce the potential of triggering *Revlon* duties?

3. How do the proof and substantive challenges change for Kfiber's board if *Revlon* duties are triggered?

4. Are the interests of preserving Kfiber's culture and jobs for its workforce legitimate considerations for the board in deciding to ignore Warfield's offers?

Chapter 12

Employee Benefits and Executive Perks: The Basics

A. Benefits for the Rank and File

For most companies, a prerequisite to success is the ability to attract, retain and motivate high quality employees. Effective employee motivation often is the key to achieving the company's goals and objectives. Key challenges for most businesses today include improving employee skill levels, enhancing employee training, promoting employee stability, reducing employee turnover, and developing employees who care about the business.

Efforts to build a productive, stable workforce are affected by compensation and benefits, factors every employee cares about. It's not about spending more (something most businesses cannot afford to do) or playing hardball when a demand surfaces. It is about spending smart and creating an environment of dialogue and understanding that eliminates the need to play hardball.

Of course, the nature of the business can profoundly impact the owners' objectives regarding employee benefits. In those enterprises where the owners represent a significant portion of the total payroll, the objective may be to maximize owner benefits even at the expense of having to fund additional benefits for non-owner employees. In other organizations, the focus is not on benefits for the owners; the challenge is to maximize the value of each compensation dollar while creating a working environment that promotes and encourages loyalty, initiative, and hard work.

1. Employers and Healthcare Reform

The leading source of health insurance in America is employer-sponsored plans. Each year, researchers at the Kaiser Family Foundation, the NORC at the University of Chicago, and the Health Research & Educational Trust conduct a survey of trends in employer-sponsored health coverage. The 2013 survey showed, among many other things, that :

- Employers provided health benefits to about 149 million nonelderly people in America during 2013

- About 62 percent of workers were covered by health benefits through their own employers in 2013

- 77 percent of workers in firms offering health benefits were eligible for the coverage offered by their employers

- 80 percent of eligible workers took up coverage in 2013 when it was offered to them.[1]

No one knows how implementation of the comprehensive Patient Protection and Affordable Care Act (the "ACA") that was signed into law on March 23, 2010 will affect these numbers. It is far beyond the scope of this book to offer any specific insights into the ACA, the hottest political issue of our time. It has triggered the passage of countless "repeal" votes in the Republican-led House, a landmark Supreme Court showdown, daily surveys of every variety, administrative setbacks, delays and waivers, a push for Congress to "de-fund" the law, confusion galore, and the kind of fear and paralyzing uncertainty that often accompanies a massive change. It was a major factor in the 2010 and 2012 elections and promises to be a critical factor in future elections.

Looking ahead, business owners must assume that the ACA will be the controlling factor for employer-sponsored health plans as its provisions take effect over the next few years. Given the uncertainties and confusion triggered by the ACA, the future relevance of any words written now is unclear. And the sheer breadth of the law precludes any comprehensive review of its terms and impact. Following is a brief summary of five cornerstones of the new law.

a. The Individual Mandate. The individual mandate is a key element of the ACA. It requires individuals to purchase health insurance or pay a penalty tax. Those who are exempt from the penalty include the following:

- Individuals with religious beliefs that oppose acceptance of benefits from a health insurance policy
- Undocumented immigrants
- Incarcerated individuals
- A member of an Indian tribe
- Those whose family income is below the filing requirement threshold
- Those who have to pay more than eight percent of their income for health insurance coverage (net of employer contributions and tax credits)
- Those insured under an employer-sponsored plan, a personally-acquired Bronze level ACA plan or higher, a grandfathered employer plan, a veteran's health plan, Medicare, Medicaid, the Children's Health Insurance Program, or TRICARE (for service members, retirees, and their families).

How much is the penalty? In 2014, it's the greater of (1) $95 per adult and $47.50 per child (up to a maximum of $285 for a family) or (2) one percent of the family's income. In 2015, it ratchets up to the greater of (1) $325 per adult and $162.50 per child (up to a maximum of $975 per family) or (2) two percent of the family's income. After 2015, the penalty is the greater of (1) $695 per individual

---

1. Kaiser 2013 Employer Health Benefits Survey (Aug 20, 2013).

and $347.50 per child (up to a maximum of $2,085 per family) or (2) 2.5 percent of the family's income. Bottom line: It will very quickly get expensive for many.

When will the individual mandate really start? Its 2014 start date has been pushed back, and many believe that administrative actions will continue to trigger delays. Given the stakes of the 2014 mid-term elections, the potential political impact of this issue as the penalties kick in, and the perceived administrative chaos triggered by the ACA, further delays wouldn't come as a surprise to many.

b. The Employer Mandate. The "employer mandate" is a requirement that all businesses with over 50 full time employees provide healthcare for their employees or face a tax penalty. The penalty is officially referred to as a "shared responsibility fee." The shared responsibility fee kicks in for any business that has the equivalent of 50 or more employees who work 30 hours or more per week. The "equivalency" factor means that part-time workers are aggregated to determine if the 50-employee threshold has been met, as are workers who are split across multiple businesses controlled by the same owner.

How much is the penalty tax? The penalty is $2,000 for each employee who works 30 hours or more and who is not provided with an acceptable employer-sponsored plan. The penalty jumps to $3,000 for any employee who purchases insurance through an exchange with tax credits. The penalty does not apply to the employer's first 30 employees. Hence, an employer with the equivalent of 49 full time employees would pay no penalty, but would face a penalty of $40,000 ($2,000 for employees 31 through 50) once the full time equivalent headcount jumps to 50. The penalty does not apply to employees who work less than 30 hours, no matter how large the organization.

Small companies may have a strong incentive to stay below the 50 worker threshold, and companies of all sizes may have a strong incentive to maximize their use of employees who work less than 30 hours per week. Employers who have more than 50 employees may choose to pay the penalty tax, avoid the hassles of an employer-sponsored plan, and let their employees grapple with their responsibilities under the individual mandate.

What are the key elements of an acceptable plan that will avoid the employer mandate penalty? The plan must provide benefits equal to the minimum benefits of a "Bronze" plan on a health insurance exchange, the employer must pay at least 60 percent of covered health care costs, and an employee's share of the cost may not exceed 9.5 percent of the family's income. If the plan costs an employee more than 9.5 percent of his or her income and the employee opts for a government subsidy on a health exchange, a $3,000 employer penalty will be triggered.

When does the employer mandate take effect? The law set the effective date as 2014. In July 2013, the employer mandate was suspended until 2015. Many believe that more delays are likely.

Are penalties paid under the employer mandate tax deductible? No. This potentially may be a major cost factor for businesses that contemplate paying the penalty and not messing with a ACA-approved health insurance plan that covers their eligible employees.

c. The Exchanges. The ACA requires that health insurance exchanges be established in all states. These exchanges serve as marketplaces where eligible individuals can compare and select among insurance plans offered by participating private issuers of health coverage. The Department of Health and Human Services' (HHS) Centers for Medicare & Medicaid Services (CMS) is responsible for overseeing the establishment of the exchanges. Enrollment in the exchanges began on October 1, 2013, and the exchanges became operational on January 1, 2014.

The exchanges provide a point of access for individuals to enroll in private health plans, apply for income-based financial subsidies established under the law, and obtain an eligibility determination for other health coverage programs, such as Medicaid or the State Children's Health Insurance Program (CHIP).

The ACA directed each state to establish a state-based exchange by January 1, 2014. If a state elected not to establish and operate an exchange, the act requires the federal government to establish and operate an exchange in the state, referred to as a federally facilitated exchange. A federally facilitated exchange must carry out the same functions as exchanges established and operated by a state. Although the federal government bears responsibility for establishing and operating such exchanges, CMS has provided states the option to assist with certain operations as partnership exchanges.

Each exchange offers qualified health plans (QHP) approved by the exchange and made available by the participating issuers of coverage. The benefits, cost-sharing features, and premiums of each QHP must be presented in a manner that facilitates comparison shopping of plans by individuals. Once individuals wish to select a QHP, they complete an application (via the exchange website, over the phone, in person, or by mailing a paper form) that collects the information necessary to determine their eligibility for enrollment in a QHP. On the basis of the application, the exchange will determine a person's eligibility for enrollment and eligibility for income-based financial subsidies.

The Congressional Budget Office has estimated that about 7 million individuals will enroll in exchanges by 2014, increasing to about 24 million by 2022.[2]

d. New Taxes. The ACA contains numerous tax changes designed to generate revenues to finance the cost of the federal government's expanded role in managing healthcare in America. Some of the changes establish new taxes, such as the taxes imposed under the individual and employer mandates described above, the expanded 3.8 percent Medicare tax on investment income (applicable to married couples earning over $250,000 and single taxpayers earning over $200,000), a 2.3 percent tax on medical device manufactures, a 10 percent tax on indoor tanning services, a 40 percent excise tax on certain "Cadillac" insurance plans, and new taxes on brand name drugs and health insurers.

Other changes are designed to generate revenues by watering down tax benefits that have previously been available to assist with healthcare needs. Key examples include increasing the medical expense itemized deduction income threshold from

2. Congressional Budget Office, Effects on Health Insurance and the Federal Budget for the Insurance Coverage Provisions in the Affordable Care Act—May 2013 Baseline (Washington, D.C.: May 14, 2013).

7.5 percent to 10 percent, reducing deductible contributions to flex spending accounts from $5,000 to $2,500, providing that over-the-counter medicines no longer are qualified expenses for flex spending, health savings or Archer medical savings accounts, and increasing to 20 percent penalties for non-qualified medical expenses paid from a health savings account or Acher medical savings account.

Of course, the big concern is the impact of these tax changes in covering the direct and indirect costs of the massive changes that will flow from the implementation of the ACA. Estimates and projections are all over the board. What is clear is that the magnitude of the changes and related factors preclude projections accurate enough to provide any level of comfort. Only time will tell. Uncertainty and fear remain heightened as key implementation dates continue to be delayed.

e. Grandfather Rights. Does the ACA provide grandfather rights for employer-sponsored plans that existed before its passage? Yes – kind of. Many of the new ACA standards for employer-sponsored plans will not apply to pre-existing plans that are not substantially changed. Rules released by the Department of Health and Human Services state that a firm desiring grandfather rights cannot significantly change cost sharing, benefits, employer contributions, or access to coverage, and must maintain consecutive enrollment in the plan.

A grandfathered plan must still comply with many ACA provisions as they become effective. For example, the plan must: (1) provide a uniform explanation of coverage, (2) report medical loss ratios and provide premium rebates if medical loss ratios are not met, (3) not include lifetime and annual limits on essential health benefits, (4) extend dependent coverage to age 26, (5) not include health plan rescissions, (6) not impose waiting periods greater than 90 days, and (7) not include coverage exclusions for pre-existing health conditions.

Each company with a pre-existing plan will need to decide whether it wants to preserve its grandfather status, which severely limits future flexibility. The percentage of covered employees protected by grandfathered plans is dropping at a rapid pace. The 2013 Kaiser survey referenced above found that 36 percent of covered workers were enrolled in a grandfathered health plan in 2013, down from 48 percent in 2012 and 56 percent in 2011.

Since September 23, 2010, the ACA has required all health plans to extend coverage to a child of a covered worker up to age 26, whether or not the child is financially dependent.

The ACA requires non-grandfathered health plans to provide coverage for certain preventive services without deductibles or other cost sharing. Grandfathered health plans have the option of conforming their coverage and cost sharing for preventive care without compromising their grandfathered status.

2. *EMPLOYEE TIME-OFF BENEFITS*

a. Paid Vacations and Holidays. Nearly every business offers paid vacations and holidays as a benefit to its employees. The primary challenge of managing this benefit is to set the parameters of the benefit and clearly communicate them in writing to the employees. The written rules should indicate whether vacation benefits can be accrued and, if so, how employees can use or be paid for the accrued benefits. Some companies adopt a "use it or lose it" concept; if the vacation benefits are not used, they are lost. Other enterprises allow employees to accrue substantial benefits that are paid upon termination of employment.

Often an important consideration is the scheduling of vacation time. Some companies do not want employees using vacation time during a designated busy season or insist that vacation time be scheduled and coordinated with others to minimize any disruption to the business. For example, a department of 12 employees may allow only two members to be on vacation at the same time and may prohibit the manager and assistant manager of the department from taking vacations at the same time.

b. Sick Leave. Many companies have jumped on the bandwagon of offering paid sick leave benefits. The problem is that some of these programs backfire. The traditional sick leave program grants a unit of paid sick leave every month or pay period (e.g., one paid day for every two months). The employee is entitled to use the paid sick leave when the absence is due to an illness. The big problem with many paid sick leave programs is unscheduled absenteeism. Some studies suggest that companies with sick leave programs experience almost twice as much unscheduled absenteeism as companies without such programs. The employee reasons, "I'm going to get paid anyway, so why not take the day off?" or, "I need a mental health day" or, "They know I never get sick, so they must expect that I'll just take the days off." Unscheduled absenteeism often results in more overtime, less productivity, increased administrative hassles, and resentment by co-workers.

The challenge for many companies is to structure a paid sick leave program that discourages abuse. There are steps a company can take to help cure the problem. To prevent abuse, the program may be structured to provide no paid benefits for the first day of an illness. This discourages the one-day discretionary absence. The sick leave policy may be amended to include a well-pay bonus. The employee is paid a bonus if no sick leave is claimed for a designated period, such as a quarter. Another technique to discourage unscheduled absenteeism is the "personal time bank." The company designates a number of days during the year that an employee may use for vacation time or paid sick leave. In some cases holiday time is added to the package. The employee knows up front that there are a designated number of paid days that can be used for all purposes. The employee may choose how to use his or her own time bank. A fourth technique to eliminate abuse is the "pooled emergency account." The company adopts a plan that allows employees to contribute their accrued sick leave to a pool that participating employees may draw upon in the event they suffer a major problem that requires extended time off. Each participating employee has the comfort of knowing that he or she will be paid if a prolonged absence from work is required as a result of a major personal or family emergency. This benefit discourages employees from abusing the paid sick leave policy by increasing peer pressure against such abuse.

c. Family Leave. The Family and Medical Leave Act ("FMLA"), administered by the United State Department of Labor's Employment Standards Administration, Wage and Hour Division, is applicable to all companies that have 50 or more employees in 20 or more workweeks during the current or preceding year.[3] Companies subject to FMLA must allow eligible employees to take up to 12 weeks of unpaid, job-protected leave in a 12–month period for specified family or medical reasons.[4] To be eligible, an employee must have worked for the company for 12 months, must have worked at least 1,250 hours during the previous 12-month period, and must work in a United States location where at least 50 of the company's employees are within 75 miles.[5] The specified reasons for the leave include (i) the birth and care of a newborn child, (ii) the adoption or foster care of a child, (iii) the care of an immediate family member (spouse, child or parent) with a serious health condition, and (iv) medical leave due to a serious health condition.[6]

FMLA raises a number of issues for many businesses. First, some companies with less than 50 employees may choose to voluntarily offer the same non-paid leave benefits as those required by FMLA. This may help to bind employees to the business and discourage employees from moving to larger companies. Often it makes sense to officially adopt and implement such a policy if, as a practical matter, the company would grant reemployment rights to any employee who is forced to take time off because of a family health emergency or the birth or adoption of a child.

Second, leave for a newborn, adopted, or foster child under FMLA may be taken at any time within 12 months of the birth or placement and may be spread over different blocks of time if approved by the company. This flexibility may benefit a company that must maximize its efforts during a busy season. Although the timing of the leave is the employee's decision, approving flexible options may make it easier for an employee to accommodate the needs of the company.

Third, companies subject to FMLA should be careful not to interfere with, restrain, or deny the exercise of any right by an employee or discharge or discriminate against any employee for exercising any right. It's unlawful to do so. This can become a problem, for example, if the owners promote and encourage an environment that discourages new fathers from exercising their family leave rights.

Fourth, group health insurance benefits must be made available to an employee who is on family leave.

Many business owners feel compelled to consider the big issue: Should their employees be compensated while on family leave? It's not required by federal law, but some estimate that American employers spend over $20 billion a year on direct costs related to family leave. Various factors may impact the family leave compensation issue, including the associated direct and indirect costs, the potential of many more employees taking time off, and other ways to use available funds to provide effective incentives for all employees.

When all factors are considered, many businesses conclude that they will offer nothing more than flexible vacation and sick leave policies that allow family leave participants to use accrued vacation and sick leave benefits to soften the income loss

3. 29 U.S.C. § 2611(4)
4. 29 U.S.C. § 2612(a).
5. 29 U.S.C. § 2611(2)
6. 29 U.S.C. § 2612(a)

of a family leave.

3. TAX-FAVORED EMPLOYEE BENEFITS: THE MENU

The law encourages companies to provide certain benefits to their employees by offering tax breaks. In most situations, the company is allowed to deduct the cost of providing the benefit while the employee is not required to recognize any income. In essence, the government subsidizes a portion of the benefit. In other cases, the same result is obtained by allowing the employee to exclude from his or her compensation the cost of the benefit that the employee chooses to fund. Following is a brief description of some of the most common tax-preferred employee benefits.

a. Group Life Insurance. Many companies choose to offer a group term life insurance benefit to their employees.[7] Often the amount of the life insurance benefit is based on the size of the employee's salary. Such a plan, if properly structured, will produce a cost benefit and a tax benefit. The cost benefit is attributable to the fact that the company may be able to acquire the insurance at lower rates because it is buying on a group basis, and it likely will be able to secure insurance for individuals who might otherwise be uninsurable for health reasons. Also, with group term insurance, premiums on the first $50,000 of coverage for each employee are tax deductible to the company, but are not taxed to the covered employee.[8] If the insurance benefit for an employee exceeds $50,000, the company is still entitled to a deduction for the portion of the insurance that exceeds $50,000, but the employee is required to report taxable income for the excess coverage.[9]

The income tax benefit of a group-term life insurance plan will be available to key employees of the business only if the plan does not discriminate in favor of such employees. The benefit discrimination rules are not violated if the amount of insurance provided to the employees bears a uniform relationship to the total compensation or regular rate of pay of each employee.[10] Thus, higher-paid employees may be provided greater benefits so long as this uniform relationship standard is not violated in favor of key employees.

b. Medical Insurance Benefits. A company may deduct the cost of all premiums incurred to provide health insurance benefits to its employees. The premiums are not taxable to the employees, nor are any benefits paid by the insurance company as reimbursement for medical expenses for the employee, the employee's spouse, or the employee's descendants.[11] These tax benefits are not subject to any discrimination tests. But, as a practical matter, nearly every business must deal with the issue of health insurance coverage for its employees. Employees want access to company-wide group plans that offer benefits, premiums, and service provider discounts that are unavailable on an individual basis. As discussed above, the Affordable Care Act, its employer and individual mandates, and the new exchanges are going to require all employers to rethink their options for providing health insurance benefits to their employees. For most companies, no employee

---

7. See generally I.R.C. § 79
8. I.R.C. § 79(a)
9. See Reg. § 1.79–3(d) for the table of uniform premiums per five-year age brackets used to compute the value of the taxable benefit when an employee's term insurance benefits exceed $50,000.
10. I.R.C. § 79(d)(5)
11. I.R.C. §§ 105(b), 106(a)

benefit challenge trumps in importance the need to offer its employees health insurance coverage.

c. Medical Expense Reimbursement Plans. A commonly overlooked benefit is an uninsured medical reimbursement plan. It is a written plan under which the company agrees to reimburse employees for uninsured medical and dental expenses up to a maximum dollar amount each year. The tax benefit of the plan is that the reimbursements are deductible by the company, but not taxable to the employee.[12] Thus, the plan permits medical expenses to be paid with pre-tax dollars. Some companies use a medical reimbursement plan to help employees pay deductibles and co-payment requirements under group medical insurance programs, and to pay for services that are not covered, or only partially covered, by insurance plans (e.g., orthodontic services).

An uninsured medical reimbursement plan must not be discriminatory if it is to produce the desired tax results for "highly-compensated individuals," defined as the five highest paid officers, the highest paid 25 percent of all employees, and any shareholder who owns more than 10 percent of the company's stock.[13] As a practical matter, for most businesses this means that the plan must cover all employees except seasonal and part-time employees, those with less than three years of service, and those under age 25.[14] Also, the annual cap on the company's maximum reimbursement to any one employee in a given year is very important. This cap cannot be expressed as a percentage of pay (no uniform relationship skewing in favor of the higher-paid employees, as with group-term life insurance). It must be the same dollar amount for all covered employees.[15]

d. Dependent Expense Reimbursement Plans. A company may offer a tax-preferred dependent care assistance benefit to its employees. Dependent care reimbursement plans work much like medical reimbursement plans in that the reimbursement is deductible by the company but not included in the income of the recipient.[16] The maximum annual reimbursement amount that may be excluded from an employee's income in a year is $5,000 ($2,500 for a married separate-return filer).[17] The plan may not discriminate in favor of highly paid executives, and no more than 25 percent of the benefits under the plan may be paid to owners who own more than 5 percent of the company.[18] This type of plan may be appropriate for companies with a significant number of employees who pay day care expenses.

e. Educational Assistance Programs. A company also may offer its employees an educational assistance program that allows the company to deduct the cost of educational expenses paid on behalf of an employee.[19] An employee may receive up to $5,250 tax-free each year to assist with his or her education.[20] In order to qualify, the plan may not discriminate in favor of highly compensated employees,

12. I.R.C. § 105(b).
13. I.R.C. § 105(h)(5)
14. I.R.C. § 105(h)(3)(B)
15. I.R.C. § 105(h)(4)
16. I.R.C. § 129(a).
17. I.R.C. § 129(a)(2)(A).
18. I.R.C. § 129(d)(2) & (d)(4).
19. I.R.C. § 127(a)(1).
20. I.R.C. § 127(a)(2).

and no more than 5 percent of the amounts paid under the plan can be for the benefit of owners who own more than a 5 percent interest in the enterprise.[21] The plan may not offer the employee a choice to receive the educational assistance benefits or other remuneration included in gross income.[22] Thus, the plan cannot be part of a cafeteria plan. The plan need not be funded.[23]

f. Cafeteria Plans. Many businesses struggle with employee fringe benefits. They find that their costs for fringe benefits are constantly increasing, often faster than the general rate of wage inflation. Yet, their employees are never satisfied and have little knowledge or appreciation for the real cost of the benefits provided. To satisfy the various antidiscrimination requirements, the company often ends up paying for benefits that certain employees don't really need or value.

The solution to this challenge for many companies is a cafeteria plan or a flex plan, as it is sometimes called. It is an arrangement that allows each employee to select from a menu of benefits only those benefits that the employee wants and needs. Employees with no need for any of the tax-free benefits can elect to receive cash. Section 125 of the Internal Revenue Code essentially provides for a waiver of the constructive receipt doctrine for flex plans that meet its provisions.[24] Without this provision, the ability of an employee to select cash always would trigger taxable income for the employee. If the plan qualifies under Section 125, the constructive receipt doctrine is not a factor and the covered employees have flexibility to select from a menu of benefits that includes a cash option.[25]

A cafeteria plan offers a number of advantages. There are tax benefits; the employer deducts the cost of all amounts paid to or on behalf of the employees, and many of the benefits on the menu are tax-free to the employees. Plus, to the extent an employee selects tax-free benefits, both the company and the employee save employment taxes. Beyond the tax benefits, the company no longer pays for unneeded or undesired benefits, and employees quickly gain an understanding and appreciation of the costs and value of benefits because they are making the benefit purchase decisions. But perhaps the most significant advantage is that a cafeteria plan may be used to reduce the company's overall cost of fringe benefits. The plan can be structured so that the cost of the offered benefits is funded out of amounts presently paid employees, as each employee chooses. There are administrative costs, but often the payroll tax savings to the company more than covers the administrative expenses of the plan.

There are important decisions to be made in the design of a cafeteria plan. The company must determine whether it is going to pay for certain benefits under the plan or simply give employees the opportunity to use their compensation to pay for benefits. The menu of benefits must then be selected. Typical benefits include group term life insurance, health insurance, mental and dental expense reimbursements, dependent care expenses, enhanced retirement plan contributions, and cash.[26] The plan must specify election procedures that limit the frequency of

---

21. I.R.C. § 127(b)(2) & (3).
22. I.R.C. § 127(b)(4).
23. I.R.C. § 127(b)(5).
24. I.R.C. § 125(a)
25. I.R.C. § 125(d)(1).
26. Reg. § 1.125–2T (Q–1).

employee elections and adopt a "use it or lose it" concept — dollars an employee designates for a specific benefit (i.e., uninsured medical expense reimbursements or day care expenses) will be lost if not spent for that benefit. Elections may be changed for significant changes in family status, such as divorce, marriage, or the birth or death of a child.[27]

The tax-free benefits of a cafeteria plan are unavailable to highly compensated participants if the plan discriminates in favor of such participants as to eligibility or as to contributions and benefits.[28] Highly compensated participants include any officer, any more-than-5-percent shareholder, any highly compensated person based on a facts-and-circumstances determination, and any spouse or dependent of any such participant.[29] Plus, tax-free treatment is not available to key employees (as defined above for group term life insurance purposes) to the extent the nontaxable benefits provided to key employees under the plan exceed 25 percent of the nontaxable benefits provided to all employees under the plan.[30]

The bottom line is that a cafeteria plan cannot be used to provide extraordinary tax-free benefits to the owners or key executives of the business. Its value is not in what it offers top management but rather in how it may reduce the overall cost of benefits for all employees and, through flexibility, enhance the value of each benefit dollar spent.

4. EMPLOYEE RETIREMENT BENEFITS: BASIC CONCEPTS

Retirement planning for employees is a unique challenge, complicated by a host of issues and a hyper-technical body of law that has become a specialty unto itself. It's far beyond the scope of this work to discuss in any detail the different types of defined benefit and defined contribution plans and their comparative virtues and vices. But there are certain basic considerations and planning factors that a lawyer should know and understand in order to help business owners through the process of identifying and prioritizing objectives. As the objectives are formulated and basic trade-offs are understood, it is usually necessary to involve a specialist who negotiates this minefield every day.

Of course, all employees would prefer for someone to plan and fund their retirement three or four decades out; they just do not want to suffer any consequences now as a result. And that's the rub. Most businesses cannot remain competitive by offering what must be offered to produce results now and aggressively fund a retirement program for their employees. It's just too expensive.

The law aggravates the challenge because, except for special retirement plans for highly compensated executives (described below), it prohibits a company from cherry-picking a select group of employees (those most likely to last the duration) and providing a retirement program just for them. When it comes to rank-and-file employees, discriminatory retirement arrangements are off the table. The answer for the masses is a qualified retirement plan that mandates nondiscriminatory treatment and that, within varying limits, forces the company to offer the same retirement

27. Reg. § 1.125–4.
28. I.R.C. § 125(b).
29. I.R.C. § 125(e).
30. I.R.C. § 125(b)(2).

package to all — young and old, permanent and not-so-permanent.

There are significant benefits with a qualified retirement plan. The company gets an up-front deduction for all amounts it contributes to the plan. Contributed amounts are deposited in a tax-exempt trust that grows on a tax-deferred basis. No taxes are due until the accumulated amounts are paid to an employee during retirement, when the employee will presumably be subject to a low income tax bracket. Plus, a qualified plan for the rank and file must be formally funded along the way so that all contributed amounts are protected from the ongoing risks of the business. And there's another plus: there are many different types of qualified retirement plans to accommodate the varying needs and objectives of different businesses. That's where the complexity begins. As a business owner seeks to build an understanding that will lead to sound decision-making related to employee retirement challenges, the following basic eight considerations can help.

a. A Tax Shelter for the Owners? In many organizations where the owners work in the business, the qualified retirement plan is viewed as a tax shelter opportunity for the owners. As the company's highest paid employees, the owners may be able to eliminate any current tax hit on a substantial portion of their incomes. Plus, that income, year-in and year-out, will grow tax-free in a protected trust they manage. For many owners, it is the ultimate savings tool, particularly considering the amounts that can be stashed away tax-free each year.

With a defined benefit plan, an owner-employee may make tax-deductible contributions to a plan that, based on actuarial calculations, will fund an annual retirement benefit up to 100 percent of his or her highest three years of compensation or a designated amount ($210,000 in 2014), whichever is lower.[31] The size of the annual contributions to fund such a benefit will depend on the age of the owner when the funding starts (the older the age, the larger the contribution). But in nearly all cases, an aggressive defined benefit plan geared principally for the owners can be structured to produce huge tax-sheltered contributions every year.

Of course, the plan will qualify only if the company's other employees participate in it. Many owners view the other employees' participation as a burden that must be balanced against the benefits the plan promises to produce for the owners, both long-and short-term. If the company has many non-owner employees who are expected to make the company their career, the cost of funding a lucrative defined retirement benefit for all employees might be prohibitive and force the owners to abandon their tax shelter dreams. However, for non-owner employees in many organizations, income levels are low, ages are young, and turnover rates are high. Very few will last long enough to accrue a substantial benefit under the plan. When this situation exists, often the planning exercise quickly becomes a "we-they" game. Steps are taken to minimize the costs attributable to the non-owner employees. The accrual of benefit and funding provisions are heavily weighted to age and income levels, all of which favor the owners. Promised benefits are integrated with social security to further reduce the plan benefits for lower-paid employees. And the company maximizes its vesting options (discussed below), provisions that cause an employee who leaves the company early to forfeit all or a

31. I.R.C. §§ 415(b)(1), 415(d).

portion of his or her benefits under the plan. The forfeited amounts are recycled to fund benefits for the plan's long-term participants, principally the owners.

b. A "Do–It–Yourself" Opportunity? At the opposite end of the spectrum are those business owners who will receive little or no direct benefits from any qualified retirement plan the company may adopt. Given the size and nature of the company's workforce, broader employee concerns trump any personal benefit they may get from the plan. In this situation, often the challenge is to offer all employees a tax-favored retirement plan at the lowest possible cost to the company. The answer for most is a 401k plan,[32] an option whose popularity now causes many employees to ask during the hiring process: "Do you offer 401k benefits?"

The distinguishing feature of a 401k plan is that, even though it is usually structured as a profit sharing plan, it contains a cash or deferred arrangement (typically called a "CODA" benefit). The CODA gives each participating employee the right to divert a portion of his or her regular pay into a retirement fund that will accumulate on a tax-deferred basis for the benefit of the employee.[33] The amount diverted to the fund each year is excluded from the employee's taxable income; thus, the employee has the opportunity to fund a retirement savings with pre-tax dollars. The popularity of the 401k has caused many to view it as a valuable benefit even though for many companies its adoption is an announcement to all employees, "The Company isn't going to fund it; You're on your own."

There are some important limitations with a 401k plan. First, there are limits on how much an employee can contribute each year. In 2014, the maximum employee contribution is $17,500.[34] Second, the contribution options for highly compensated employees often are dependent on the amounts contributed by all eligible employees.[35] If the rank and file take their money home and elect to forgo the benefits of the plan, the company's key employees may be boxed out of any significant participation. Third, once an employee commits money to the plan, it may be very expensive to access that money before age 59 1/2.[36] Early withdrawals will trigger an immediate tax on the amounts withdrawn, plus a 10 percent penalty.[37] The prospect of being "worse off" if the money is needed down the road spooks many employees, particularly younger employees, away from the CODA option. A loan from a 401k plan is possible if the plan permits such loans, but it is not an easy solution. For example, the loan amount and all accrued interest must be repaid with after-tax dollars; a default is treated as an early withdrawal, triggering taxes and penalties; the loan must be repaid immediately in the event of a job change; and often fees are charged. Finally, to facilitate management of the plan, most companies limit the investment options available to employees who contribute to the plan. Although the investment menu often is broad enough to cover a wide risk-reward spectrum, the fund manager and fee options often are limited.

c. Company Matching Money? Often a company wants to sweeten the pot for employees who contribute to the company's 401k plan. This is done by the

---

32. See generally I.R.C. § 401(k).
33. I.R.C. § 401(k)(2).
34. I.R.C. § 402(g)(1).
35. I.R.C. §§ 401(k)(3) & (5), 414(q).
36. I.R.C. § 401(k)(2).
37. I.R.C. § 72(t).

company agreeing to match a portion or all of the contributions an employee makes. The company defines the terms of the match, which cannot discriminate in favor of highly compensated employees. A matching provision offers a number of benefits. Beyond encouraging participation, it is an effective pay raise for employees who elect to participate in the plan. Plus, it can eliminate any participation problems for highly compensated employees if the match equals the employee's contribution for the first 3 percent of pay and then 50 percent of the excess employee's contribution up to 5 percent of pay.[38] A plan with such a match provision is deemed nondiscriminatory and may allow contributions from highly compensated employees without regard to the participation of other employees.

d. Non–CODA Related Company Contributions? Since the CODA 401k benefit usually is part of a profit sharing plan, the company has the capacity to make contributions to the plan unrelated to the contributions made by the participants. These company contributions are allocated to all plan participants, usually in proportion to their respective compensation levels. The maximum annual amount the company may contribute for any one employee is the lesser of 100 percent of the employee's compensation or a designated dollar amount ($52,000 in 2014).[39] But the total company deductions for such contributions to a profit sharing plan may not exceed 25 percent of the total compensation paid to the plan participants.[40]

The plan may be structured to give the company complete flexibility from year to year; the board of directors each year may determine how much, if any, the company is going to contribute. Note however that if the plan requires the company to make such contributions each year equal to at least 3 percent of the participants' compensation, the plan is deemed nondiscriminatory for CODA purposes and the company's highly compensated employees may make CODA contributions without regard to the participation of other employees or any matching contributions of the company.[41]

e. Who Handles the Money and Bears the Risk? Getting money into a qualified retirement plan is only the start. Once in the trust, the money needs to be managed. This management challenge raises a number of issues. The manager of the money owes a fiduciary duty to all participating employees and will be held to a standard of care of an expert who is in the business of investing funds for others. This, plain and simple, means that a business owner should not undertake the responsibility and risk of making specific investment decisions. Pros need to be hired, and they cost money. Is the plan or the company going to pay their fees? Or should the plan be structured to offer employees a say in how their money is invested, such as through a family of mutual funds? This requires an ongoing communication and educational effort that costs money, sucks up productive time, and often creates a great deal of confusion.

And then there is the issue of who bears the ultimate risk for the investment performance. In nearly all defined contribution plans, such as profit sharing and 401k plans, the employees reap the rewards of profitable investing and suffer the

38. I.R.C. § 401(k)(12)(b).
39. I.R.C. § 415(c)(1).
40. I.R.C. § 404(a)(3)(A).
41. I.R.C. § 401(k)(12)(c).

consequences of all investment setbacks. In defined benefit plans where the company promises a specific benefit at retirement, the ultimate risk of the investment performance is on the company. In these situations, the company will want to carefully control the investment performance of the funds.

f. Reward Longevity? Often a company does not want its contributions to the retirement plan to benefit employees who have short-term tenure with the company. They want the plan to provide an incentive for employees to remain with the company, not help fund the departure for those who move on. There is no capacity to impose longevity limitations on amounts contributed by an employee under a CODA arrangement; that money came from the employee and, along with any earnings it generates, cannot be forfeited.[42] But for any amounts contributed by the employer, including matching contributions, vesting provisions can be structured into the plan that provide for a full or partial forfeiture if the employee leaves too soon.

If the plan is a defined contribution plan, such as a profit sharing or 401k plan, the vesting schedule may (i) permit 100 percent vesting after three years of service, or (ii) permit 20 percent vesting after the first two years and then an additional 20 percent each year until 100 percent vesting occurs after six years.[43] All forfeited amounts are allocated to other plan participants. These vesting provisions, if properly used, can have a powerful concentration impact over time when a significant percentage of the company's employees have tenures of less than three years.

g. Something Simpler? Many closely held business owners long for simplicity. Administrative hassles and burdensome administrative costs scare them. They turn off when they start hearing about a custom-crafted qualified plan that requires up-front IRS approval, ongoing employee communications, careful monitoring, investment trust account management and administration and the related fiduciary liabilities, employee participation tracking just to find out how much key employees can contribute, vesting provisions that promise to confuse everyone and spawn a never-ending stream of questions, and much more. They like the tax deferral benefits and want to offer their employees something. They just want a simpler plan — one that will be easier and much less expensive to administer.

In this situation, the simplified employee pension (SEP) may be the answer. With a SEP, each participating employee establishes an individual retirement account (IRA) at any institution the employee chooses.[44] The company makes contributions directly to the IRAs of its employees. The company is saved all the hassles, expenses, and fiduciary liability concerns of administering and monitoring trust accounts, investment options, and all the other trappings of a qualified plan. Plus, SEPs are easy to set up; all it takes is filling in a few blanks on a government prototype form and then sending the form to the IRS. The maximum contribution limits to a SEP are the same as for any profit sharing plan — the company deduction is limited to 25 percent of total compensation, and the annual addition to any one

42. I.R.C. § 401(k)(2)(C).

43. I.R.C. § 411(a)(2)(B). This provision was amended by the Pension Protection Act of 2006 to require such vesting for all defined contribution plans.

44. See generally I.R.C. §§ 404(h), 408(k).

employee's account is limited to a specified dollar amount ($52,000 in 2014).[45]

As with any profit sharing plan, the company has complete flexibility each year in deciding whether and how much to contribute, and the plan may not discriminate in favor of highly compensated employees. Contributions may be allocated to participants based on their compensation levels, subject to a maximum compensation factor for highly paid employees ($260,000 in 2014).[46] All employees who have attained age 21, have been with the company three of the past five years, and have earned at least $550 in a year must be allowed to participate.[47]

There are two significant disadvantages to a SEP. First, since all contributions go straight to IRAs set up by employees, no vesting provisions are allowed. All contributed amounts vest 100 percent. This disadvantage is mitigated by the three-year participation requirement. Second, a SEP may not contain a COLA feature similar to that offered by a 401k plan. Prior to 1997, a SEP could be structured as a cash or deferred arrangement. Not so now. With a SEP, the company, not the employees, must bear the cost. This factor alone forces many closely held businesses to forego the benefits of a SEP.

h. A Simpler CODA? Is there an option for a closely held business that wants to offer a tax deferred, "Do–It–Yourself" retirement opportunity to its employees, but does not want the administrative hassles and costs of a full-blown 401k plan? There is a solution if the company has no more than 100 employees who earn more than $5,000 a year and the company does not sponsor any other qualified retirement plan for its employees. Such a company may adopt a SIMPLE plan.[48]

A SIMPLE plan is similar to a SEP in that each participating employee opens and maintains his or her own individual retirement account into which all contributions are made. As with a SEP, the company is saved all the administrative hassles, expenses and fiduciary concerns of a retirement trust; and a SIMPLE plan can be easily set up in minutes. The big difference with a SIMPLE plan is that employees can be given an opportunity to contribute a portion of their pay to the plan, subject to a maximum dollar limitation ($12,000 in 2014).[49] But unlike a 401k plan that gives a company complete discretion in setting its own contribution levels, a SIMPLE plan requires the company to commit to certain contribution levels in order for the plan to qualify. The company must either (i) offer a matching contribution equal to the first 3 percent of the pay contributed by each employee or (ii) agree to make a contribution equal to at least 2 percent of compensation for each participating employee.[50] If the company elects the matching option, it may reduce the 3 percent amount to 1 percent in no more than two years in any five-year period.[51] And, of course, no vesting provisions are permitted.

Although a SIMPLE plan requires a fully vested contribution from the company, in many cases it will be the preferred option for the company that

---

45. I.R.C. §§ 404(h), 404(a)(3)(A), 415(c)(1).
46. I.R.C. § 408(k)(3).
47. I.R.C. § 408(k)(2).
48. See generally I.R.C. § 408(p).
49. I.R.C. § 408(p)(2)(E).
50. I.R.C. § 408(p)(2).
51. I.R.C. § 408(p)(2)(C)(ii)(II).

qualifies and wants to offer a CODA option to its employees. Often the savings in administrative costs and burdens will equal or exceed the company's obligations to the plan.

STUDENT PROBLEM 12-1

Bunker Industries Inc. ("Bunker") is a successful manufacturing and distribution company in a profitable niche industry. Bunker has three equal owners who compose Bunker's board. Only one of the owners, Jake, is employed by the business, serving as the president and chief executive officer. Jake courts customers, attends conventions, gives speeches, and makes pronouncements, but he does not bother himself with the details of the operation. Those are left to Matt, the executive vice president who serves as the chief financial and operating officer of the company. Matt is supported by three managers, 80 employees, and a talented group of outside vendors who benefit from Bunker's extensive outsourcing programs.

Bunker's board has tasked Matt with two challenges relating to its employees:

1. Develop a plan to provide employees with a range of tax-savings fringe benefits that will not cost the company much, force a reduction in current pay levels, or waste money on benefits that some employees neither want nor need. Bunker presently provides only medical insurance benefits. Some employees have no need for health insurance; they are covered under their spouses' plans. Others incur substantial day care expenses, and many regularly complain about uninsured orthodontic bills for their children and other uninsured medical-related expenses.

2. Develop a retirement plan for employees that will minimize costs and administrative hassles and provide tax-deferred savings and investment options for employees. Bunker presently has no retirement plan. Given the relative youth of its employees and their appetite for cash, the board has never seen a need to offer a savings program that might "cut-in" to current take-home pay. Lately, though, more employees have been asking about a retirement plan and the issue often surfaces in the hiring process.

Matt wants an understanding of the options and issues before he responds to the board or starts talking to self-proclaimed experts who want to sell a fringe benefit or retirement plan service. Please advise.

B. KEY EXECUTIVE INCENTIVES

1. EXECUTIVE EMPLOYMENT AGREEMENTS

The use of carefully crafted employment agreements in large organizations is forever expanding to deeper levels to hedge against the risk of expensive litigation and the loss or dilution of valued proprietary rights. Many businesses still resist the need to get things in writing with those who can do the most damage. The owners cling to the old notion that a piece of paper can't make a bad employee good or a good one better, so why bother?

Usually the reluctance to come of age on this issue is a result of inertia and ignorance. A program of using smart agreements with key employees takes real effort. Since many businesses lack a separate human resources person (much less a department), the burden of the effort falls on the chief executive officer or some other high-ranking officer who already has a full plate. Add to this a few common misconceptions that question the whole value of the effort and it's easy to let this "priority" drop to the bottom of the stack.

A common misconception is that the document produces more for the employee, less for the company. Why else would only a privileged few in the company have their own agreements? The truth is that nearly all of the key provisions in an executive employment agreement primarily benefit the company in a big way. Such provisions include termination rights, confidentiality covenants, post-employment competition restrictions, intellectual property protections, work effort requirements, dispute resolution procedures, choice of law designations and more. Even the compensation provisions benefit the company by spelling out the limits and defining expectations.

Another misconception is that it's counterproductive to get tangled up in legal minutiae during the courting phase with a new key executive. The focus should be on positive business challenges and synergies, not potential problems that may never surface between the company and its newest arrival. This misconception ignores a basic truth – nearly all prospective employees long for the details of the whole deal. Showing that the key issues have been fairly thought through and incorporated into a document tailored for the new executive will not be viewed as a negative or an unjustified preoccupation with the dark side of business relationships. If done right, it will confirm that the company has its act together, values relationships based on detailed mutual understandings, and regards the prospective employee as a valuable part of the management team. It can actually be an "upper" that removes uncertainties and facilitates a more complete understanding of the objectives and priorities of both parties. And if an insurmountable conflict surfaces during the process, everyone will benefit from its early detection.

A third misconception is that the details of the employment relationship with a key employee are easier to hash out after the employee has been on board for a while. Everyone knows more; expectations are clearer. It's wrong. The problem is that the job won't get done. Once the employee is in the saddle, what interest will the employee have in dealing with post-employment noncompetition restrictions, broad employer termination rights, dispute resolution procedures and the like? In most situations, the company will be left with two lousy options to push the agenda along. It can get tough and demand its agreement, which may undermine morale, mutual respect, and all the other intangibles that strengthen individual business relationships; or it can offer something more, which can get expensive. Far and away the best time to work out the details and document the deal is just before the starting gun when both parties are anxious to find common ground and move forward.

Following is a brief summary of a few of the key provisions that are typically included in an executive's employment agreement.[52]

52. For a more comprehensive discussion, see Theodora Lee and Lisa Chagala, Ten Essential Considerations for Any Employment Agreement in Business Planning: Closely Held Enterprises, Fourth Edition (West 2013), pp. 406-

a. Length of Employment. The length of the agreement – its term – is always an important issue. When it comes to the term, an agreement may be structured as "at-will," "drop dead," or "evergreen." An "at will" agreement allows either party to terminate the agreement at any time. It provides flexibility, and the opportunity for a quick exit with no showing of cause. A "drop dead" provision means the agreement will end on a given date unless the parties agree otherwise to an extension. Sometime an agreement is structured to have an "at will" deal for any employment beyond the "drop dead" date. An "evergreen" provision provides that the agreement will run for a defined period and then automatically renew for successive periods unless a party gives notice to terminate the agreement within a certain timeframe. This has the advantage of the agreement potentially continuing indefinitely, with each party having the right to jump off at key points along the way.

b. Termination Rights. The agreement should lay out how a party may terminate the agreement early. For many agreements with drop dead or evergreen terms, the company may terminate the agreement early with no adverse consequences by showing "cause" – a term that needs to be carefully defined. The employee will want the narrowest definition – perhaps limited to criminal and grossly negligent acts – while the company may prefer something much broader – perhaps including the failure to adequately perform. Hassling out the "cause" definition is a major factor in many agreements. On the flip side, the employee often is given the right to terminate with no consequence only by showing "good reason," another key definition. Here the roles are flipped, with the company preferring the narrow definition and the employee the broader. It is also important to spell out the consequences of any early termination that does not meet the requisite standard of cause or good reason. For the executive who is wrongfully terminated without cause, this often means getting paid without having to work for a period – perhaps as long as the unexpired contract term. For the company who is injured by an executive's early termination without good reason, it may mean a liquidated damage payment from the executive or other tailored restrictions.

c. Work Effort. The agreement should spell out what is expected from the executive in terms of effort. Key terms that are often used include "full time" and "best efforts." Can the executive moonlight by engaging in off-hour business activities? Limitations on an executive's off-duty recreational and political activities are usually out of bounds, but often it helps to clarify that the executive will do nothing to create a conflict of interest with the company or the appearance of such a conflict of interest.

d. Prior Commitments. A "prior commitments" provision requires the executive to certify that he or she is not subject to any contractual commitments (such as an employment agreement with a former employer) that conflict with the obligations to the company. It's pretty much a "must" in today's world to protect the company from a claim that it improperly interfered with an executive's contract with another party.

411.

e. Arbitration. An arbitration provision ensures that disputes will be resolved by binding arbitration. It offers the opportunity to resolve a dispute quickly and at minimal expense. Some fear that an arbitration clause may encourage more claims from employees because of the reduced time and expense barriers. If an arbitration clause is desired, care should be taken to ensure that it covers all disputes, binds all parties, and will stay in play even if other parts of the agreement are deemed unenforceable.

f. Protections of Intellectual Property.

The agreement must protect the company's intellectual property. Specific provisions should ensure that IP rights do not disappear with an employee's exit. Usually three elements are essential: (1) a clear definition of the company's rights with respect to existing and future IP rights, (2) a smart covenant not to compete, carefully crafted to reflect appropriate scope, time and geographic limitations, and (3) non-disclosure provisions that prohibit the executive from disclosing or making use of confidential information or intellectual property rights of the company. The agreement should be supplemented by efforts to regularly remind employees and others of confidentiality requirements and to adopt company-wide policies for trade secret protection.

g. Administration Provisions. The agreement should contain: (1) a "choice of law" provision specifying the state law that will govern the agreement and any related dispute; (2) an integration provision confirming that the agreement constitutes the complete and exclusive statement of all understandings between the parties and that no other oral or written agreements exist between the parties with respect to the subject matter of the agreement, and (3) a provision specifying how the agreement may be amended to protect against a future claim that the agreement was effectively amended by an oral statement or course of dealing.

h. Bonuses and Incentives. Of course, nothing in an executive employment agreement trumps the importance of the money provisions -- bonuses and incentives that the executive may receive under specified conditions. The perks often include cash bonuses, special life insurance benefits, a tailor-made supplemental executive retirement plan, or stock or stock rights incentives. A brief discussion of each of these follows.

2. *EXECUTIVE CASH BONUSES*

Often cash bonuses are viewed as just an expectation of the executive. Many cling to the notion that it's always smarter to not spell out the details of an incentive bonus in an employment agreement. Far too often there is nothing more than some vague bonus discussions that create expectations of more money but do nothing to perpetuate individual performance objectives. The difference between real success and baseline mediocrity in many businesses is the ability and drive of the key executives who are charged with making it happen. The ability factor is tied directly to the executive's focus on specific targets of success. The drive factor is a function of how badly the executive wants to be better than good. A smart incentive bonus often keeps the fire hot under both factors. Here are a few key issues to consider.

- **Understandable.** The executive must be able to understand all specifics of the bonus incentive. It should not be too complicated or tied to factors foreign to the executive. A smart bonus is something to work for, not just hope for.

• **Measurable.** The incentive should be objectively measurable. It should not be based totally on someone's discretion or will, although some subjectivity may be factored into the process. For example, the incentive for an accounts receivable manager may be a percentage of salary based on the percentage of accounts collected within 90 days (e.g., a bonus equal to 7 percent of salary for an 85 percent collection rate, jumping to 10 percent for a 90 percent collection rate, etc.). The plan also may give the company's CEO the discretion to increase any earned bonus by up to an additional 50 percent if the employee turnover rate in the accounts receivable department in a given year is less than 75 percent of the company's average. Such a bonus plan would be measurable and keep the manager focused on two critical success elements – collection percentages and employee turnover.

• **True Incentive.** The incentive must be large enough to matter. If the amount at stake is insignificant, the executive may pay lip service to the objectives without ever believing they are serious concerns that warrant real additional effort and commitment.

• **Calculation Factors.** The factors that impact the calculation of the bonus should be within the control of the executive. For the CEO and CFO, it may be the overall performance of the company. But there is usually a need for more specificity down the executive ladder. For the vice president of sales, it may be the volume from new customers. For a production VP, it may be the average employee cost for each unit produced. The key is to identify specific success factors that will result in the company becoming stronger as the size of the executive's bonus grows. It is the classic win-win.

• **Visible Time Monitors.** Techniques that enable the company and its executives to track and monitor progress regularly, at least once a month, are vital. This need for regular monitoring may require special periodic accounting reports or customization of the company's computer information system, but the benefits usually easily justify any added up-front effort or expense.

3. *KEY EXECUTIVE LIFE INSURANCE PERKS*

Life insurance is a key ingredient of many executive compensation packages. It provides financial protection against an untimely death. It is often structured as an integral part of the executive's long-term estate plan and as a tool to encourage the executive to remain dedicated and loyal to the company for the long term.

For example, take Joyce, a 58-year-old president of a successful company who wants a company-funded, tailor-made permanent life insurance benefit that will provide a substantial tax-free infusion of cash to her heirs at her death. She has been with the company for many years, and the company's board wants to accommodate her request to ensure her dedication to hedge against any risk of losing Joyce. Joyce's new insurance benefit may be structured in a variety of ways.

a. Executive-Owned Insurance

Joyce's benefit may be structured as a simple bonus insurance program. The company would acquire a permanent insurance policy that Joyce would own. The company would make the premium payments and realize a deduction for the payments because they would be imputed and taxed to Joyce as additional compensation income. The company could gross-up the amount of the tax-deductible payments to cover Joyce's income tax exposure on the premium payments. As the owner of the policy, Joyce would have complete control of the policy and could incorporate it into her overall estate plan as she chooses. The company would have flexibility in funding the policy; it could aggressively fund the cash value of the policy so no further funding would be required after Joyce's retirement or it could elect to fund the policy before and after Joyce's retirement.

b. Company-Owned Insurance

As an alternative, the company could choose to be the owner and the beneficiary of the policy until Joyce retires. If Joyce dies before retirement, the company would collect the tax-free death benefit and pay the proceeds to Joyce's designated heirs as a death benefit. So long as the company owns of the policy, the company would not be entitled to any deduction as the premiums are made, and Joyce would recognize no taxable income while the policy is funded. Any benefits paid to Joyce's heirs if she dies before retirement would be treated as taxable income.[53] Joyce would have no equity interest in the policy and would have no capacity to exercise any rights over the policy before retirement. This alternative may be preferred by the company if it needs a strong incentive to lock-in Joyce until a specified retirement age.

The plan likely would specify that ownership of the policy would be transferred to Joyce when she reaches a designated retirement age. Upon such a transfer, Joyce would be taxed on the value of the policy at time of transfer, and the company would receive a corresponding deduction. The company could elect to use its tax savings from the transfer to pay a gross-up cash bonus to cover all or a portion of Joyce's tax hit. Once Joyce becomes the owner of the policy, she could coordinate the policy's ownership and beneficiary provisions with the rest of her estate plan. If the policy has not been fully funded by the time of Joyce's retirement (that is, does not have enough cash value to cover all future premium payments), the company could continue to fund policy premiums following retirement through a cash bonus program.

c. Split-Dollar Insurance

A third alternative is a split-dollar arrangement. Split-dollar insurance is a popular strategy for providing a permanent life insurance benefit to select employees as an executive perk. It's a contract between an employer and an executive under which the benefits and burdens of a life insurance policy are split.[54] The classic split provides that the company will pay that part of each premium equal to the increase in cash value of the policy, and the insured executive will pay the balance of the premium. Alternatively, the company may also pay the executive's share of the premium. The major benefit of this arrangement is that the executive receives permanent life insurance protection with little or no cash outlay. There are no anti-

53. I.R.C. § 691(a)(1).
54. Reg. § 1.61-22(b)(1).

discrimination rules, so the company can selectively offer the program to only certain executives.

The split-dollar agreement also provides for a split of the death benefit paid under the policy. When the key executive dies, the company typically is the named beneficiary for that portion of the proceeds equal to the greater of the premiums it has paid or the cash surrender value of the policy. The balance of the proceeds (which is usually the lion's share) goes to the beneficiaries designated by the key executive.

There are two methods of structuring a split-dollar arrangement. The first is the endorsement method, where the company is the owner of the policy which includes an endorsement to reflect the interest of the executive. The second method is the collateral assignment method, where the executive owns the policy and "collaterally assigns" it to the corporation to secure the corporation's interest in the death benefit paid under the policy. The endorsement method gives the employer more control over the policy, including the ability to borrow from the cash surrender value.

What are the tax consequences of a split-dollar arrangement? If the endorsement method is used and the company owns the policy, the executive will be deemed to have received taxable compensation from the company for any portion of the premiums allocable to the executive's share of the policy that are paid by the company.[55] If the collateral assignment method is used and the executive owns the policy, any portion of the premium paid by the company, the non-owner, is treated as a below-market loan to the executive. The executive will be deemed to have received compensation income equal to the imputed interest on the loan and to have paid the interest to the company.[56] The death benefit ultimately received by the company and the executive's beneficiaries will not be subject to income taxes.[57]

STUDENT PROBLEM 12-2

Refer to Student Problem 12-1. Matt, the chief financial and operating officer of bunker, has been tasked two assignments from the board relating to executive compensation issues.

1. Develop a cash bonus plan that will incentivize the three managers to do a better job. The managers head up the sales, production, and accounting departments and have randomly been paid bonuses in the past. Matt's initial reaction is to pay each manager a fixed percentage of Bunker's annual earnings before taxes above a base level that would be annually established by the board. He questions whether this will do the job, and he's looking for guidance.

2. Develop a plan to provide Jake with a $3 million permanent life insurance benefit at the company's expense. Jake believes that he needs a substantial, permanent life insurance benefit that wwill protect his family in the event of an untimely death. What structural option would work best for the company? What option would Jake likely prefer?

---

55. Reg. § 1.61-22(d)(1).
56. Reg. § 1.7872-15(e).
57. I.R.C. § 101(a)(1).

3. *Supplemental Executive Retirement Plans*

Many executives rank retirement income as their number one financial concern. They want to know they are going to "have enough" and are not going to outlive their financial resources. For many executives, the solution is a special supplemental executive retirement plan (SERP) provided by their employers. The company's regular qualified retirement plan is too watered down to do the job. An old-fashioned savings program is too tough, and social security, even if available, is hopelessly inadequate.

For decades companies have recognized the value of individually-tailored retirement arrangements for their key executives. These arrangements are routinely used to recruit and retain valuable executives. The substantial benefits that accrue under the plan over time create a powerful incentive for the executive to toe the line and not even consider flirting with the competition. Plans of this type may only be offered to top executives. To avoid the regulatory burdens and rules of a qualified retirement plan, discrimination in favor of the highest paid executives is not only permitted; it's mandated.

a. A SERP Example

Peter is 55. He is the chief executive officer of a growing manufacturing company and has served in that capacity for five years. The company is privately owned, and Peter has no hope of ever receiving any equity. The stockholders consider Peter indispensable to the ongoing success of the company and want to ensure that he remains in his position for at least another 10 years. They want to bind him to the business. Peter is concerned about his retirement needs and has voiced that concern to the owners.

A deal has been worked out to provide Peter a special supplemental retirement benefit that will commence on his retirement at age 65. The benefit, equal to 70 percent of Peter's highest average salary during any remaining three-year period of his employment with the company, will be paid monthly so long as Peter or his wife is living. Peter estimates that the annual benefit should be at least $250,000 if he continues to receive salary increases as he has in the past. Absent death or disability, Peter must remain with the company to age 65 in order to receive the benefit. If he dies or becomes disabled before age 65, the benefit will commence on the second month following his death or permanent disability.

The plan accomplishes the objectives of both parties. The company and its owners are assured of Peter's continued service and loyalty, and Peter's retirement concerns are put to rest. Following are brief reviews of the tax traps, structural options, collateral consequences, and funding alternatives that often need to be considered in the planning process for such a plan.

b. SERP Tax Traps

The plan for Peter is based on the premise that no income taxes will need to be paid on any SERP benefits accrued under the plan until the benefits are actually paid to Peter or his wife. As a deferred compensation plan, a SERP is subject to tax traps that need to be carefully watched whenever income is deferred.

The Constructive Receipt Trap. Income is taxable in the year in which it is "received by the taxpayer."[58] If the constructive receipt doctrine applies to a SERP, the executive will be in the unfavorable position of having to pay taxes on money he or she has not received. The mere deferral of the actual receipt of income will not guarantee deferral for tax purposes because the phrase "received by the taxpayer" encompasses "constructive receipt" as well as actual receipt of income.[59] The constructive receipt trap can be an issue in those situations (unlike Peter's) where an executive elects to defer the receipt of compensation in order to fund a SERP benefit. The key in such situations is to ensure that the executive makes the election to defer the income before the services are rendered and the compensation is earned.[60] The constructive receipt doctrine may also become a problem if the executive at any point is given the unrestricted right to draw money out of the plan.[61]

The Economic Benefit Trap. The employee's opportunity to defer taxation may be derailed if he or she receives an economic benefit from the deferred amount that is the equivalent of cash.[62] This trap usually surfaces when the employer's obligation to pay the deferred compensation is somehow "funded" and the employee acquires an interest in the funding vehicle. Examples include an escrow account for the executive, a trust vehicle to fund benefits for an executive,[63] an annuity contract naming the executive as an owner,[64] and a life insurance policy that guarantees the executive the cash value of the policy in the event of employment termination.[65] A red flag should go up whenever an employee (1) receives a substantial economic or financial benefit from a non-qualified funding vehicle, particularly if the benefit is not forfeitable; (2) has the ability to assign his or her rights under that funding vehicle to an outside third party; or (3) has any other right or capacity to convert his or her rights under the funding vehicle to cash.

The Section 83 Trap. Section 83 of the Internal Revenue Code provides that, when property is transferred to an employee as compensation for services, the employee is taxed on the fair market value of the property at the time it is received if the property is transferable or is not subject to a substantial risk of forfeiture.[66] As regards a deferred compensation plan such as a SERP, the positive news is that the regulations under Section 83 provide that an unsecured and unfunded promise of an employer to pay deferred compensation does not constitute "property" for purposes of Section 83.[67] If the participant receives nothing more than the unsecured contractual promise of the company, there is no Section 83 problem. In all other cases where the participant is offered something extra, it is necessary to take a hard look to see whether Section 83 has been triggered. If any property right is created,

---

58. I.R.C. § 451(a).
59. Reg. § 1.451-1(a).
60. Rev. Proc. 71-19, 1971-1 C.B. 698, amplified Rev. Proc. 92-65, 1992 C.B. 428; I.R.C. 409A(a)(4)(B)(i).
61. Reg. § 1.451-2(a). See Martin v. Commissioner, 96 T.C. 814 (1991) for a discussion of the facts that impact such an application of the constructive receipt doctrine.
62. Rev. Rule 60-31, 1960-1 C.B. 174 (Example 4); Sproull v. Commissioner, 16 T.C. 244 (1951), affirmed per curiam 194 F.2d 541 (6th Cir. 1952); Rev. Rule 62-74, 1962-1 C.B. 68; Commissioner v. Smith, 324 U.S. 177 (1945).
63. Sproull v. Commissioner, 16 T.C. 244 (1951), affirmed per curiam 194 F.2d 541 (6th Cir. 1952); Jacuzzi v. Commissioner, 61 T.C. 262 (1973).
64. Brodie v. Commissioner, 1 T.C. 275 (1942).
65. See, for example, Frost v. Commissioner, 52 T.C. 89 (1969).
66. I.R.C. § 83(a).
67. Reg. § 1.83-3(e).

Section 83 will likely become a problem.

The Reasonable Compensation Trap. The company wants to secure a tax deduction when the deferred compensation is paid to the executive. If the compensation is being paid to a shareholder/employee and is determined to be excessive within the meaning of Section 162 of the Internal Revenue Code, the company will lose its deduction.[68] Reasonableness is based on the facts and circumstances that exist at the time the contract is made, not those that exist when the contract is called into question.[69] For planning purposes, the challenge in any potentially troublesome situation is to carefully document the facts and circumstances that support a "reasonableness" determination at the time the plan is adopted by the company so that, if required, a sound case can be made at a later date.

The 409A Traps. As executive deferred compensation tax traps go, the newest and toughest kid on the block is section 409A,[70] which was added by the America Jobs Creation Act of 2004. This section imposes specific statutory requirements that every nonqualified deferred compensation plan must meet. It does not replace the traps described above; it adds to them.[71] The 409A statutory requirements are not unduly burdensome in most normal situations; they are primarily designed to cause problems for those who play on the outer limits of the other traps. But they have real teeth. If a Section 409A requirement is violated, the participant is immediately taxed on all deferred income not subject to a substantial risk of forfeiture, plus he or she gets hit with an interest charge calculated at a rate 1 percent above the normal underpayment rate ***and an extra 20 percent tax*** on the deferred amount included in income.[72] Thus, Section 409A is not a "no harm, no foul" statute. It can hurt. Key Section 409A requirements generally require:[73]

- Amounts deferred under the plan may not be distributed[74] before the participant's separation from service,[75] the participant's disability,[76] the participant's death, the specified time or payment schedule in the plan, a change in the ownership or control of the corporate employer or a substantial portion of the assets of the corporate employer,[77] or the occurrence of an unforeseeable emergency;[78]

- The plan may not permit the acceleration of the time or schedule for the

---

68. Reg. § 1.162-7(b)(1).
69. Reg. § 1.162-7(b)(3).
70. I.R.C. § 409A.
71. I.R.C. § 409A(c).
72. I.R.C. § 409A(a)(1).
73. Extensive regulations to Section 409A were finalized in 2007. Reg. § 1.409A.
74. I.R.C. § 409A(2).
75. For a "specified employee," the separation from service requirement is not met if a payment is made before the date that is six months after the separation of service. A "specified employee" is a key employee (as defined in section 416(i) without regard to paragraph (5)) of a corporation any stock of which is publicly traded. I.R.C. § 409A(a)(2)(B); Reg. § 1.409A-1(i)(1).
76. Disability generally requires a condition that can be expected to result in death or can be expected to last for at least 12 continuous months and that prevents any "substantial gainful activity" or that entitles the participant to receive income replacement benefits for not less than three months under an accident and health plan covering employees of the company. I.R.C. § 409A(a)(2)(C); Reg. § 1.409A-3(i)(4)(i).
77. See Reg. § 1.409A-3(i)(5).
78. An "unforeseeable emergency" means a severe financial hardship resulting from (i) an illness or accident of the employee, a spouse or a dependent, (ii) a loss of property due to casualty, or (iii) similar extraordinary and unforeseen circumstances beyond the control of the employee. I.R.C. § 409A(a)(2)(B)(ii); Reg. § 1.409A-3(i)(3)(i).

payment of benefits, except under limited circumstances;

- The plan may not give an executive an election to defer compensation earned during a taxable year after that year begins;

- The plan may not give an executive an election to further delay the payment of benefits under the plan unless specific conditions are satisfied;[79]

- Assets held outside the United States and set aside (directly or indirectly) to pay benefits under a deferred compensation plan will be considered property under Section 83, thus triggering a recognition of taxable income for the employees, plus the 409A interest charge and the 409A extra 20 percent tax.[80]

- Employer assets that become restricted to the provisions of a deferred compensation plan as a result of a change in the employer's financial health will be considered property under Section 83, thus triggering a recognition of taxable income for the employees, plus the 409A interest charge and the 409A extra 20 percent tax.[81]

- If the company maintains a single-employer defined benefit plan that has not been adequately funded (i.e., is considered "at risk" within the meaning of Section 430(i)), any assets set aside for the payment of deferred compensation benefits to the company's chief executive officer, the company's four highest paid officers, or any individual subject to Section 16(a) of the Securities Exchange Act of 1934 will be treated as property taxable under Section 83.[82]

C. SERP Structural Basics

A SERP is a private contract between the company and the executive. The primary components of the contract are: (1) the formula or basis for determining the amount of the SERP retirement payments; (2) the circumstances under which the SERP payments will be paid or not paid; and (3) the method of payment, such as a lump-sum cash-out, monthly installments, a life annuity, or some combination of these. The contract may contain other provisions based on the circumstances and the purpose of the SERP. The company gets no tax deduction until the amounts are actually paid to the executive, and the executive realizes no taxable income until the benefits are received.

Benefit Formula. The company has flexibility in structuring the benefit accrual formula under the contract. The only limitation in structuring the arrangement is that it be reasonable. The formula may accrue a fixed sum each year, may be based on a defined monthly benefit at retirement, may be adjusted for inflation, may be based on accumulated years of service, or may consider any other factors that are reasonable. The retirement benefit accrual should be prospective, not retroactive. Typically a SERP does not involve deferral elections by the executive; it just specifies the benefits that will be paid by the company and the conditions of payment. From a tax standpoint, the safest approach is to structure the

---

79. I.R.C. § 409A(a)(4)(C); Reg. § 1.409A-2(b).
80. I.R.C. § 409A(b)(1),(3),(4).
81. I.R.C. § 409A(b)(2),(3),(4).
82. I.R.C. § 409A(b)(3).

SERP so that the supplemental retirement benefit accrues after the date the agreement is executed. And the amount of the accrued benefit under the plan each year plus the amount of the current compensation must, in combination, constitute reasonable compensation for services rendered during the period.

Elective Deferrals. A SERP benefit can be structured as an elective benefit, similar to a 401(k) plan. With this approach, the employee is given the right each year to elect to defer an amount of compensation that will be paid out at retirement or termination of employment. Alternatively, the SERP can be structured as an add-on, employer-provided benefit that doesn't involve any employee election. If the elective approach is used, the key is to make sure that the deferral election is in writing and that the election to defer compensation for any given taxable year is made before the beginning of that year. If the election to defer compensation earned during a given year is made after the year begins, the employee will be taxed currently on the deferred amount and will be subject to the interest and extra 20 percent tax provision of Section 409A.

Payout Terms and Conditions. Another issue that must be addressed in the SERP agreement is the terms and conditions for paying the benefits. Typically the payout form is described in terms of a monthly payment for life or a term of years. Often the SERP provides for a lump-sum payment upon the death of the employee prior to retirement. The key is to ensure that the payout options are definitive enough to conform to the permissible payout options of Section 409A. Another important feature of many SERPs is a provision that gives the company the option to cash out any accrued benefits if the company is sold. Such a cash-out feature will benefit the purchaser who has no interest in picking up the SERP liability or perpetuating the SERP plan. Also, a SERP can be structured to impose golden handcuffs on key employees. There are no restrictions on conditions or forfeiture limitations. The plan may provide that the benefits are reduced or eliminated if a key employee signs on with a competitor or otherwise decides to voluntarily leave the company before retirement.

Regulatory Requirements. SERPs are not subject to the same type of IRS and Department of Labor regulatory requirements that apply to qualified retirement plans. A SERP needs to steer clear of any Section 409A foul-ups and the other tax traps. ERISA regulations are no big deal so long as the benefits are unfunded at all times and are made available only to a select group of highly compensated employees.

Funding. A SERP benefit must be an unfunded obligation of the company in order to qualify for the ERISA exemption and avoid an early tax hit to the employee. This means that the company cannot set aside funds in a separate trust that is legally earmarked for the benefit of the SERP participants and is beyond the reach of the company's creditors. Although legal funding is taboo, the company can still prepare for the day when the SERP payments will commence. This is done by establishing an informal funding program. The company sets aside cash or other property to cover its future payment obligations to the executive. The key is that the assets set aside must continue to be owned by the company and be subject to the claims of the company's creditors.

FICA and Social Security. A SERP offers a potential payroll tax benefit. SERP benefits are considered earned for payroll-tax purposes when the benefit is accrued and no longer subject to a substantial risk of forfeiture.[83] So, for example, if an executive accrues a $70,000 annual SERP benefit and is already receiving cash compensation in excess of the social security taxable wage base, the additional $70,000 of SERP accrual does not increase the amount of non-medical payroll taxes either for the executive or the corporation. And since the SERP benefit was potentially subject to non-medical payroll taxes when accrued, no non-medical payroll taxes are due when the SERP benefits are paid. The other social security issue is whether the SERP benefits, when paid, will reduce social security benefits. Fortunately, SERP benefits are counted as earned income when accrued, not when paid, for purposes of determining the benefit offset. So the receipt of the SERP benefit will not reduce social security benefits if the SERP recipient is otherwise eligible.

Impact on Qualified Retirement Benefits. Another aspect of a SERP that has to be kept in mind is its potential impact on qualified retirement plan benefits. If an executive's current income is less than it would be if a SERP benefit were not being accrued, this lower income level may reduce the amount that is being accrued for the executive under the company's qualified retirement plan. It depends on the benefit accrual formula of the qualified plan.

Financial Statement Impact. A factor to consider in designing a SERP is the effect it will have on the company's financial statements. Since the accrued SERP benefit is a liability of the company, it must show up on the books as a liability. Care will need to be taken to make sure that the SERP liability does not cause the company to violate any loan-to-net-worth ratios or other covenants in loan agreements that are tied to the company's book net worth. Loan agreements should be reviewed and possibly revised to avoid this result.

The foregoing are some of the basic factors that often are considered in structuring a SERP for an executive. Since the SERP offers a nonqualified benefit through a private contract between the executive and the company, there is considerable flexibility in structuring the terms to meet important objectives.

d. The No-Fund Funding Options

Let's return to the indispensable executive, Peter, in the above example. Peter's payment rights are no better than those of a general, unsecured creditor of the company. Peter understands that if the company takes any steps to formally fund the benefit by legally earmarking a pot of money for him, the odds are that he will be taxed currently on the amount of the accrued benefit. With this understood, Peter would like to have the company take actions to start informally funding the benefit. He realizes that the benefit could represent a significant liability of the company by the time he reaches age 65. He is concerned that, as he grows older, the owners may become nervous about the size of that liability and try to renegotiate the liability or take some other action that could jeopardize his right to receive the promised benefit. Peter figures that the best way to head off any future problem is for the company to start preparing for the day when it will have to write his retirement

---

83. I.R.C. § 3121(v)(2)(A).

checks. Following are brief descriptions of four example strategies (there are more) that companies often use to address (at least in part) concerns of executives who are in Peter's position.

Company-Owned Insurance Funding. One option for informally funding Peter's benefit would a high-cash-value life insurance contract on Peter's life. The company would be both the owner and the beneficiary of the policy. Substantial premium payments would be made on the policy for the next 10 years, before Peter's retirement. The earnings within the policy would accumulate on a tax-deferred basis. When Peter reached age 65, there would be a substantial cash value in the policy that would offset, at least in part, the company's liability to Peter. The company could commence a program of borrowing from the policy the after-tax cost of the retirement payments that would be paid Peter. The company's interest deduction on such borrowings would be limited.[84] When Peter dies, the company would receive a tax-free death benefit that would reimburse the company for all or a substantial portion of its payments to Peter under the program. See Illustration A. Peter would have the comfort of knowing that the company has affirmatively taken steps to fund the program for his benefit. Although the policy would internally be tied to Peter's agreement, he would have no legal rights to the policy, and all benefits under the policy and Peter's retirement benefits might be lost if the company were to fail.

Illustration A: Corporate Owned Insurance Funding

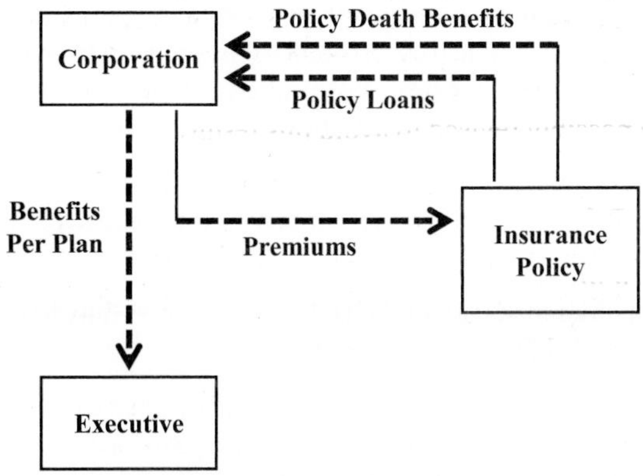

b. Rabbi Trust Option

A second option would be a "Rabbi" trust. The Rabbi trust is an irrevocable trust established by the company. The company would make periodic contributions to the trust that would be managed by the trustee of the trust. The trustee would be authorized to make investments and use the assets of the trust for only two purposes.

84. I.R.C. § 264(e)(1) limits interest deductions on indebtedness against policies insuring the lives of key employees to interest charges on $50,000 of such indebtedness.

First, the assets could be used to pay Peter's benefit under his SERP. Second, the assets could be used to pay claims of the creditors of the company if the company were to fail. Although the Rabbi trust would lock up funds for Peter's retirement benefit, it would not protect those funds from claims of the company's creditors. If the company were to experience serious financial problems, Peter's benefit might be lost.

Illustration B: Rabbi Trust Option

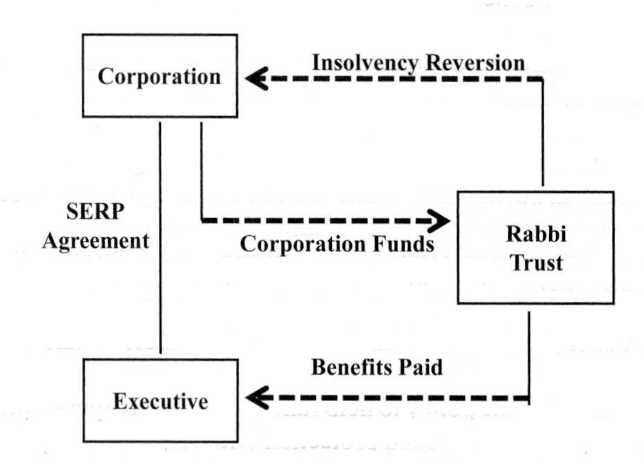

The value of the Rabbi trust is that it provides some protection to Peter while preserving the tax deferral. The trust precludes the company from using trust assets to finance other corporate priorities. For ruling purposes, the IRS has imposed a number of requirements in order for a Rabbi trust to qualify:

- Trust assets must be held for the sole purpose of paying benefits under the plan, except the assets may revert to the company if the company becomes bankrupt or insolvent;

- The company's management must have an express duty to notify the trustee of the company's bankruptcy or insolvency;

- If the trustee receives such a notice, the trustee must stop all payments from the trust and hold the assets until directed to make payments by appropriate court order;

- State law must not grant Peter any priority rights to the amounts held in the trust;

- The trust cannot be funded with securities of the company; and

- The trust may not contain an insolvency trigger or any other provision that might frustrate the rights of other creditors of the company.[85]

In addition, Section 409A prohibits use of a Rabbi trust that holds assets outside the United States or that springs into existence or becomes subject to new

85. Rev. Proc. 92-64, 1992-2 C.B. 422.

restrictions upon a change in the company's financial health.[86]

The bottom line is that the Rabbi trust strategy may provide Peter with some protection in the event of a change in control, a change in management, or a change in the company's desire to pay the benefit.

c. Rabbi-Owned Insurance Option

A third option is to combine life insurance with a Rabbi trust. Here the trust is both the owner and the beneficiary of the policy that insures Peter's life. The trust makes all the premium payments with the amounts contributed to the trust by the company. The earnings in the policy accumulate on a tax-deferred basis. When Peter reaches age 65, there will be a substantial cash value in the policy that will be owned by the trust and used to fund Peter's benefits. The trust could commence a program of borrowing from the policy to use such borrowings and other trust assets to make the retirement payments to Peter. When Peter dies, the trust would receive a tax-free death benefit that would cover all amounts due Peter's estate or heirs following his passing under the terms of the plan and potentially allow the company to recover a substantial portion of its payments to the trust.

In this situation, Peter would have the added comfort of knowing that the company would not own and control the policy, so there would be no risk of the company choosing to use the policy to help fund some other corporate priority. The Rabbi trust would provide this added protection with respect to the policy.

Illustration C: Rabbi Owned Insurance Option

Excess Proceeds
Corporation
Insolvency Reversion
Policy Loans
Rabbi Trust
SERP Agreement
Corporation Funds
Premiums
Insurance Policy
Executive
Benefits Paid
Death Benefit

d. The Guarantor Option

Another option that may be used to provide Peter with added protection is to have a third party with deep pockets guarantee the payment of the benefits due him under the plan. The third party could be a parent corporation or one or more

86. I.R.C. § 409A(b)(1) & (2).

individual owners of the company. If the company were to go under and be unable to pay the benefits, Peter could look to the third party for payment. An alternative is a surety bond that would guarantee the company's payment obligation to Peter. The IRS has ruled that if the company neither pays the premium on the bond nor reimburses Peter for the bond, the mere existence of the surety bond will not trigger tax on the deferred income, even though the employee has essentially acquired a guarantee of the payment.[87] If the company secures the bond and pays for the coverage, the likely result is that the employee would get hit with a current tax under the reaches of the economic benefit doctrine. Although a few have felt that the surety bond may be the ultimate answer for the employee who has been promised a large supplemental retirement benefit, such surety bonds are not widely available and can be very expensive.

STUDENT PROBLEM 12-3

Refer to Student Problem 12-1. Bunker's owners recently increased Matt's salary significantly and, in the process, advised Matt that they intend to sell the company within the next eight to ten years. This caused Matt to focus on his retirement needs down the road. On numerous occasions, Matt has inquired if something can be done to provide him a special retirement package. He knows that any plan adopted for the company's employees would never do the job for him.

Jake and the board are now willing to consider "something special for Matt" because they want to ensure that he will be bound to the company for the duration, and they know that other companies in the industry would jump at the chance to get Matt. Jake has many questions: Is such a plan for one person legal? How could the plan be structured to tie Matt to the company? What are the tax impacts? How would the benefits under the plan be funded? Matt has made it clear that he wants something more than just a "naked promise" down the road that a buyer of the company may have no interest in honoring. There needs to be "some teeth" to show that the benefits will be paid. Plus, Jake and Matt agree the "deal can't create a bunch of tax problems for Matt before he starts collecting following his retirement from the company."

Answer Jake's questions and advise Jake and Matt on options they may want to consider.

4. Stock and Stock Rights Incentives

Highly motivated executives often get to a point in their careers where something more than a salary and bonus is required as an incentive. They want to own a portion of the business. They want to work ***with*** the business owner – not just ***for*** the business owner. Often the executive really doesn't understand or appreciate what an interest in the business represents. All the executive knows is that he or she wants to feel like an owner and be treated like an owner.

Many employers view the challenge as a necessary evil and approach the task with suspicion, fear, and a natural propensity to drag out and procrastinate on the

87. PLR 84060022.

process. The employer usually recognizes the value of the key executive and wants to preserve loyalty and dedication. What the employer does not want is to create a structure fraught with legal and tax complexities that unduly inflates the executive's expectations, diverts the executive's commitment or, worse yet, funds the executive's departure.

a. Key Factors

Following are brief descriptions of eight factors that should be analyzed in structuring or reviewing any equity ownership incentive program for executives.

Real Cost Factor. Does the program require that the executive bear a real cost by making an investment to acquire his or her stock in the company? Most stock option programs are structured to require the executive to write a check and make an investment as a condition to acquiring stock in the company. Employers often feel that such an investment on the part of the executive is essential to accomplish the real objectives of the plan. In contrast, many executives argue that their investment has been and will continue to be quality executive services to the company and their willingness to forgo other opportunities. Whether the executive will be required to come "out of pocket" to acquire his or her interest is a threshold issue in structuring and analyzing any program.

"Value Now" Factor. Will the program be structured so that the executive is given a stock interest that has a built-in economic value to the executive at the time it is given? Many programs are structured to simply give the executive an economic interest in future appreciation that accrues in the company's stock. The emphasis is on the future, not the present. In contrast, other programs are structured to give the executive an interest in the company that has a demonstrable economic value at the time it is given. Under such a program, the executive's net worth is increased at the time he or she is granted the option or the right. Many employers are willing to part with a portion of the future value in their company, but are unwilling to simply grant the executive, free of charge, an interest in the value that has already been created.

Golden Handcuffs Factor. Is the program going to be structured to ensure that the executive can enjoy the full economic benefits only if he or she satisfies certain specified employment criteria? Many programs are structured to provide executives with significant economic benefits that depend entirely on the executive's willingness to remain loyal and dedicated to the company. If the executive prematurely terminates his or her employment with the company, fails to measure up to designated performance criteria, or elects to go to work for a competitor, the executive forfeits some or all of the economic benefits that have accrued under the particular plan.

Cash-Out Factor. This factor focuses on the mechanism that will be used to allow the executive to convert his or her stock interest to cash at an appropriate point in the future. This factor is not a consideration for a publicly held company whose stock is registered and regularly traded. In contrast, this Cash-Out Factor is particularly important to the executive of the closely held business. How is that executive going to realize a profit on the investment? A carefully drafted shareholder buy-sell agreement that specifies a reasonable basis for valuing the stock at appropriate points in time is critically important.

Phantom Income Factor. Will the program create taxable income for the executive before the program has generated cash to pay the tax liability? Many programs are structured to confer a taxable economic benefit for the executive at the time the particular option or right is granted or exercised. This can create an intolerable situation for the executive from a tax and cash flow standpoint. To remedy the situation, employers often are forced to bonus additional cash sums to the executive to cover the tax liability. As we'll see, many programs attempt to deal with this Phantom Income Factor by eliminating the Value Now Factor – that is, by granting no present economic benefit – or by maximizing the Golden Handcuffs Factor, which presents a substantial risk of forfeiture to the executive. The trade-offs can be significant for any executive.

Employer's Tax Factor. Does the program produce any tax advantages for the employer? The program may be structured to provide a tax deduction for options or rights granted to the executive, even though the employer has not expended any cash or liquid resources. Such a plan may reduce the tax liability of the employer and the overall costs of the plan. The executive, on the other hand, may request or demand that at least a portion of those tax savings be reallocated to him or her to reduce the burden of any phantom taxable income.

Fall-Out Leverage Factor. This factor focuses on the relevant positions of the executive and the company if there is a major blow-up between them. Who has the most leverage? The executive's leverage may be stronger if he or she is a shareholder of the company and can exercise the rights of a shareholder. For this reason, some employers prefer plans that grant stock equivalency rights or phantom stock rights, but never provide real stock. Carefully drafted transfer restrictions and buy-sell agreements can help mitigate the fear generated by this Fall-Out Leverage Factor when real stock is issued. Often it is difficult to get a handle on the significance of this factor in a given situation because the parties do not want to even acknowledge the prospect of a major falling-out down the road.

Real Thing Factor. As we will see, incentive ownership programs can be structured without offering the executive any real equity interest in the company. Instead, the executive receives contractual payment rights structured to produce economic benefits that are the equivalent of stock ownership. Often these programs are unacceptable to the executive simply because they do not offer the "real thing." The executive isn't satisfied with anything less than stock, even though from a tax and structuring standpoint, the executive may be better off receiving a smartly designed stock substitute.

These eight factors are important considerations in analyzing any ownership incentive program. The following planning strategies focus on these factors. It is common to find that the company and the executive disagree on the importance of a particular factor or how it should be structured into the particular program.

b. Six Strategies

(1) Incentive Stock Options

The incentive stock option (ISO) is the strategy that presents the most technical requirements. It is available only to corporate entities, not entities taxed as partnerships.[88] The ISO gives the executive the right to buy stock from the company over a designated period on certain specified terms and conditions.

With any stock option plan, there are three key points in time: when the executive is given the option, when the executive acquires stock through the exercise of the option and payment of the option price, and when the stock is sold by the executive and the sales price is realized in the form of cash. The appeal of an ISO is that the executive recognize no taxable income at the time of grant or exercise and only recognizes taxable income at the time of sale, when cash is available.[89] And any income recognized at the time of sale may qualify as capital gain income. There is one slight tax hitch. Although the executive recognizes no taxable income at the time of grant or exercise, if the fair market value of the stock at the time of exercise exceeds the option price (a circumstance that will exist in almost every case, for why else would the executive have exercised the option?), such excess fair market value at time of exercise will be treated as a tax preference item for purposes of the alternative minimum tax.[90]

What does it take for an option to qualify as an ISO so the executive can enjoy the tax benefits of ISO treatment? A number of technical requirements exist, including the following:[91]

- The plan under which the option is granted must be approved by the shareholders of the company within twelve months before or after the plan is adopted by the board of directors.

- Each option must be granted within ten years of the plan adoption.

- The option period cannot be longer than ten years, so the executive must make his or her election to exercise the option and acquire the stock within a ten-year time frame after it is granted.

- The option price cannot be less than the fair market value of the company's stock at the time the option is granted. Determining the fair market value of the stock of a closely held corporation can be a challenge. For this reason, there is a special provision that the ISO will qualify as long as a good faith effort is made to determine the fair market value of the stock.

- The option cannot be transferred, except in the case of the executive's death.

- The executive who is granted an ISO cannot own more than 10 percent of the stock of the company.

- The total fair market value of all stock subject to ISOs that are first exercisable by the executive in any calendar year cannot exceed $100,000. The fair market value of the stock is determined at the time of grant.

- To claim the capital gain benefits, the executive cannot sell the stock within two years of the date the option is granted, nor within one year from the date the stock is acquired through the exercise of the option. After exercising the option, the

---

88. I.R.C. § 422(b) requires that the recipient be an employee of a corporation.
89. I.R.C. § 421(a).
90. I.R.C. § 56(b)(3).
91. See, generally, I.R.C. § 422(a)-(d).

executive, must hold the stock long enough to satisfy these periods in order to enjoy capital gains tax treatment.

- The executive must have been an employee of the company or an affiliate of the company at all times from the date the option is granted until at least three months prior to the date upon which the option is exercised. In other words, if the executive leaves the employ of the company, the ISO must be exercised within three months of leaving in order to preserve the favorable ISO tax treatment.

The obvious question is this: Why wouldn't any executive and company only want options that qualify as ISOs? After all, there is no taxable income until time of sale. The phantom income tax risks are eliminated. Also, the ISO can be structured with Golden Handcuffs features to protect the company. Usually this is done by providing that portions of the ISO can be exercised only after the executive has satisfied certain designated employment periods with the company. And once the option is exercised, the executive acquires the real thing – stock in the company.

Although certain advantages and structural opportunities exist with ISOs, there are major disadvantages that are compelling in many situations. First, from the executive's perspective, the ISO, by definition, flunks the Real Cost Factor and the Value Now factor tests. The executive must make a real investment before getting any stock, and the purchase price of the stock, by definition, must be equal to the fair market value of the stock at the time the option is granted. The option offers only a hope of future appreciation and no existing value. Second, the employer gets no deduction for the ISO. On a net tax basis, this is a costly, inefficient approach for moving value from the company to the executive. The executive is paying a tax bill with no offsetting tax benefit to the employer. Finally, if the executive has an alternative minimum tax problem, the ISO may significantly aggravate that problem by creating an additional tax preference item at the time the option is exercised.

For these reasons, the ISO, although still a viable candidate and strategy, has lost much of its appeal. Many companies and their executives would be well advised to consider one of the less technical strategies.

(2) Nonqualified Stock Options

The second strategy is the nonqualified stock option. A nonqualified stock option is one that does not qualify as an incentive stock option; it flunks one of the technical requirements. The executive still is given the right to buy a designated number of shares of the company's stock on specific terms and conditions. However, there are no rules governing the option price, the option period, or any other items. The parties are completely free to sculpt their own deal.

Are nonqualified options taxed the same as ISOs? Not a chance. Generally, the executive will recognize no taxable income at the time the option is granted unless the option can be transferred by the executive or the option itself is tradable and has a readily ascertainable fair market value.[92] Because such options are almost never transferable by the executive and usually lack a readily ascertainable fair market values, the time of grant is not a problem.

92. I.R.C. § 83(e)(3); Reg. §§ 1.83-7(b)(1) & (2).

The tax problem comes at the point of exercise. Assume an executive is given an option to buy 100,000 shares of stock at a price of $1.00 per share (for a total of $100,000) and the executive exercises the option at a time when the shares have a fair market value of $3.00 per share (or $300,000). The executive would be required to recognize $200,000 of taxable ordinary income at the time of exercise. Yet the executive has no cash from the transaction at this point. The executive's tax basis in the stock would be $300,000. So when the stock is sold, the executive would only have to recognize income to the extent the sale price exceeds $300,000.

It's important to note that there is a tax benefit to the corporation at the time of exercise. When the exercise occurs, the corporation gets a tax deduction equal to the income that the executive is required to recognize.[93] In our example, the corporation would get a $200,000 deduction at time of exercise.

If the parties have determined they want to use stock options, nonqualified options offer great flexibility in structuring their arrangement. The option requires some investment, so there is a Real Cost Factor. But the option price can be below the existing fair market value of the stock. If, in our example, the stock has a value of $2.00 per share at the time of grant and the option price is $1.00 per share, the executive effectively would have been transferred $1.00 of real value for each share when the option was granted. From the executive's perspective, this circumstance would satisfy the Value Now Factor. Many employers have used these types of options to set exercise prices that are substantially below the existing fair market value of the stock at time of grant.

If some Value Now is built into a nonqualified option, care must be taken to comply with the requirements of Section 409A, discussed above. Under Regulation § 1.409A-1(b)(5), a nonqualified stock option will be treated as a deferred compensation plan if the option price does not at least equal the fair market value of the stock at time of option grant. Thus, a nonqualified option that has a preferred Value Now option price will lose a great deal of flexibility as to the timing of its exercise. To comply with Section 409A, the time of exercise would have to be specified at time of grant or be tied to a permissible payout event under Section 409A (separation for service, disability, death, change of control, or unforeseen emergency). In view of the penalties triggered by a violation of 409A, any company that issues nonqualified options that are not intended to comply with the exercise limitations of Section 409A should take extreme care to ensure that the option price is not less than the stock's fair market value at time of grant. In recognition of the difficulty of valuing closely held business interests (and the high stakes for Section 409A non-compliance), the regulations to Section 409A permit the use of any reasonable valuation method, describe factors that will be used to determine the reasonableness of the valuation, impose consistency requirements, create a presumption of reasonableness for a one-year period, and create a special presumption for the good faith valuation of a start-up company's stock during the first ten years of its active conduct of a trade or business.[94]

A nonqualified option does provide some flexibility. There is no limit on the

93. I.R.C. § 83(h).
94. Reg. § 1.409A-1(b)(5).

golden handcuffs feature that can be attached to a nonqualified option. From the executive's perspective, the phantom taxable income created at the time of exercise often is a real problem, but even this problem can often be resolved. Remember, the corporation is getting an offsetting tax deduction. The transaction can be structured so that the corporation transfers its tax savings to the executive in the form of a loan or cash bonus to provide a source of funding to cover all or a portion of the tax liability created at the time of exercise. If a loan is used, interest would be paid or accrue on the loan, and the loan would be paid off at the time the stock is sold.

Stock options are viable strategies in select situations, but a major disadvantage is that the executive doesn't own the stock – the real thing – until he or she steps up and pays the option price. So the benefits of actual stock ownership usually are delayed. This powerful disadvantage often triggers interest in other strategies.

(3) Bonus Stock

Bonus stock is the least technical and most straightforward strategy of all. Under this approach, the company simply transfers to the executive a specified number of its shares as compensation for services rendered. From the executive's standpoint, bonus stock offers some real pluses. There is no need to make a cash investment; there is no real cost. There is immediate value now; the existing value of the stock belongs to the executive, and the transfer of the stock is not deemed to be a deferred compensation plan subject to Section 409A.[95] A shareholder buy-sell agreement can be drafted to ensure that the Cash-Out Factor is satisfied. The executive owns the real thing now; there is no delayed enjoyment, as in the case of an option. Finally, the executive is entitled to vote the shares now and can immediately participate in all dividends and other rights.

But bonus stock also creates disadvantages from the executive's perspective. Often the executive is given fewer shares under a bonus stock plan than under some other type of plan, such as an option plan. Bonus stock also presents a major phantom taxable income problem. The fair market value of the stock is taxed to the executive at the time the stock is transferred, with the company receiving a corresponding tax deduction. As in the case of a nonqualified option, the company may find itself in the position of having to use its tax savings to fund a loan or a cash bonus to cover all or a portion of the executive's tax liability triggered at transfer.

(4) Restricted Stock

Restricted stock is bonus stock with a twist. The twist is that the stock has strings attached – restrictions. If one of these restrictions is violated, the company yanks the string and retrieves all or a portion of the stock. Suppose, for example, a company is willing to transfer to the executive $100,000 worth of stock now. No investment is required. There is immediate value now. The executive gets the real thing now. And presumably there is a buy-sell agreement to ensure the Cash-Out Factor. Further, suppose that company wants to make certain that the stock will cement the executive's loyalty and dedication to the company. It does this by placing a restriction on the stock. For example, the restriction may provide that, if the executive leaves the company at any time during the next 10 years, the executive

95. Reg. § 1.409A-1(b)(6).

will forfeit all the stock. Alternatively, it may provide that the executive's right to keep the stock vests 10 percent each year or that all or a portion of the stock is forfeited if the executive fails to hit certain sales volumes, or fails to satisfy some other objective measure of performance.

This forfeiture feature has a significant tax consequence. As long as a substantial risk of forfeiture exists, the executive does not have to pay tax on the stock that's been transferred.[96] In our example, the executive could be transferred $100,000 worth of stock and pay no tax at the time of transfer. If, after 10 years, the forfeiture feature goes away, the executive then would be taxed on the full value of the stock at that time. Often the forfeiture provisions are structured to lapse over a period of years so that only a portion of the tax liability is recognized in any year. On the other side, the company gets a tax deduction equal to the amount of taxable income the executive is required to report in the same year of the income recognition.[97]

There is a tax planning option that should be considered whenever restricted stock is used. The executive may elect to be taxed on the stock at the time the stock is received, rather than at the time the forfeiture provision lapses.[98] Why would an executive ever elect to recognize taxable income at an earlier point in time? If the stock value at the time the stock is received is very low and there is a substantial prospect that it is going to appreciate rapidly in the future, the executive may prefer to recognize the taxable income when the stock is granted at the much lower value. If the election is made to recognize income at the time of grant, there is no need to recognize any future taxable income until the stock is actually sold. The election has a disadvantage. If the executive elects to recognize the income when the stock is granted and the stock is then forfeited, the executive gets no offsetting deduction at the time of forfeiture. Thus, the executive may end up in the position of having paid tax on something that never produced value. It's a calculated risk. If the executive's choice is to make the election, the company gets a deduction at the same time the executive recognizes the income.

Restricted stock is a flexible tool that can be used in many situations. As many stock option programs have lost their appeal, the restricted stock alternative has become more popular.

(5) Stock Appreciation Rights

The next strategy is different from the four previous approaches in one significant respect: the executive never gets the real thing. There is no stock. In lieu of receiving stock, the executive is given a contractual right to compensation that is structured to provide the same economic benefits as stock. Here is how it works.

Suppose a company wants to give a key executive the right to receive the value of all appreciation that accrues on 100,000 shares of its stock in the future. The executive doesn't want stock options for a number of reasons, including the need to

---

96. I.R.C. § 83(a)(1); Reg. § 1.83-3(c). The existence of the forfeiture feature and the related tax deferral does not make the arrangement a deferred compensation plan subject to the new section 409A requirements. Proposed Reg. § 1.409A-1(a)(6).

97. I.R.C. § 83(h).

98. See, generally, I.R.C. § 83(b).

pay a real cost, option tax traps, and strict Section 409A requirements if there is any value now.

A stock appreciation right contract may be the answer. A contract is drawn that essentially states the parties will pretend the executive owns 100,000 shares of stock. The executive never really owns the stock. Usually the contract would establish a base price of the stock – say $1.00 per share – that would equal its current value. The contract would offer a number of economic benefits based on the pretend stock. It would provide that if a dividend is paid to the real shareholders of the company, then a corresponding amount of compensation would be paid to the executive on the pretend shares. It would also provide that if the company is sold, merged, or goes public, the executive would receive the excess in the value of the pretend shares, at that time, over the base value of such phantom shares at the time the contract was awarded. For example, if the company is sold at a price of $3.00 per share down the road, the executive would be entitled to receive compensation income at a rate of $2.00 per share for the 100,000 pretend shares awarded under the contract. The contract would also provide that the stock appreciation rights would be valued at the time the executive dies, is disabled, or otherwise terminates employment with the company. The excess of the value of the rights at that time over the base value of $1.00 per share would be paid as additional compensation income. Golden handcuff features may be structured into the contract to provide the executive with incentives to remain loyal and dedicated to the company. Essentially, the contract is designed to provide the executive with the same future economic benefits, in the form of compensation under the contract, that he or she would otherwise receive in the form of stockholder economic benefits if the executive owned the real stock.

What are the advantages to such a stock appreciation right arrangement? There are a number. First, there is no threat of phantom taxable income. Since all amounts paid under the contract are compensation payments, the executive will have no taxable income until cash is actually received. Second, there is no alternative minimum tax threat. Third, since all amounts paid to the executive represent compensation, the company receives a tax deduction at the time each payment is made. In many ways, a stock appreciation contractual arrangement is one of the most efficient strategies, from a tax perspective, for transferring upside stock value from a company to an executive.

Does the arrangement have any tax disadvantages? Historically, the biggest disadvantage has been the absence of any capital gains or favorable dividend tax break for the executive. Because the executive never owns any stock, there is no possibility of creating a capital gain at time of sale or receiving dividends. To sweeten the deal for the executive, an added bonus may be provided in the agreement to produce a net after-tax yield to the executive equal to the yield that would result if every payment on the pretend stock were taxed as capital gain or dividend income. Again, the company would get a tax deduction for all amounts paid. Often, this "capital gain/dividend tax equivalency bonus" can be paid with the company still incurring a net after-tax cost that is less than what would be incurred if the company used after-tax dollars to purchase stock or pay dividends under a "real stock" strategy.

A stock appreciation right arrangement provides a number of advantages.

There is no requirement that the executive make an investment in order to acquire rights to future appreciation in the stock. There is no risk of phantom income. The company gets a deduction. There is no alternative minimum tax risk. The Golden Handcuffs Factor and the Cash-Out Factor can both be accommodated in a variety of ways through the contract. The company often prefers this type of arrangement because of the Fall-out Leverage Factor. If a major problem arises between the executive and the company down the road, the executive has a contractual right to payment, but owns no stock in the company. Accordingly, the executive cannot cause problems as a shareholder.

With a stock appreciation right plan, care must be taken to ensure that it avoids the reach of Section 409A or is structured to comply with the Section 409A requirements (e.g., no executive election rights as to timing or method of payout after the grant of the rights). There is no room for ambiguity. A stock appreciation right plan may avoid 409A treatment if there is no Value Now Factor (only appreciation following the grant is considered) and the plan includes no other deferred compensation element.[99]

The biggest disadvantage from the executive's perspective is that he or she never owns the real thing. The arrangement is a fancy employment contract. The subjective desires of being viewed and treated like an owner may never be realized. Often it's possible to overcome this fear by reemphasizing that the contract is being drawn to provide a real piece of the rock by offering economic benefits that, dollar for dollar, are the same as those that would be realized if stock were actually owned.

(6) Phantom Stock

The next strategy is the phantom stock plan. This strategy is the same as the stock appreciation right strategy described above, with one significant twist. The strategy is structured to give full effect to the Value Now Factor and falls squarely within the reach of Section 409A. A contract is drawn that gives the executive the right to be compensated on the basis of certain pretend shares, but there is no existing base value price. At the time the contract is entered into, the executive is promised payments down the road based on the current value of the phantom shares, together with all future appreciation on those shares. It's as if the executive actually owned the stock now. Hence, the name "phantom stock."

An executive, for example, could be provided a phantom stock agreement that grants 100,000 phantom shares with an existing value of $2.00 per share. As the value of the company's stock increases, the value of the executive's phantom shares similarly increase. Since such a phantom stock plan is subject to Section 409A, the executive could not have any timing or payout elections after the grant of the rights. To comply with Section 409A, the time and method of payout on the pretend shares must be tied to a permissible payout event under Section 409A (payment of dividends, separation from service, disability, death, sale of the company, change of control, or unforeseen emergency).

Assuming the requirements of Section 409A are satisfied, the executive is not required to recognize as taxable income the Value Now Factor ($200,000 in our

---

99. Reg. § 1.409A-(b)(5)(i)(C)(3).

example) at time of contracting. The executive simply has the contractual right to receive compensation payments in the future based on movements in the value of the company's stock and dividend and other payments made on the real stock of the company.[100] Thus, unlike the bonus stock and restricted stock strategies described previously, the executive can receive a Real Value Now factor and avoid any phantom taxable income. The key variable is that the executive has received a contractual right to future payments, rather than a property right represented in the form of stock.

Again, the biggest disadvantage from the executive's perspective may be the lack of real stock and the perceived subjective benefits of being a shareholder. Also, because the executive never receives stock, there is no opportunity for favorable capital gains or dividend tax treatment. These potential disadvantages may be trumped by the economic benefits offered under the program and the absence of phantom taxable income problems. Plus, as described above, the plan can be easily structured to pay the executive "capital gain/dividend tax equivalency bonuses." When the plan is dolled up to include such benefits, it is sometimes referred to as a "stock equivalency plan," a term that may sound more appealing than "phantom stock."

Student Problem 12-4

Refer to Student Problem 12-3. As Matt contemplated the potential of a sale of Bunker within the next eight to ten years, he determined that he wants to participate in that sale. He wants a piece of the rock, an 8 percent interest in Bunker that would allow him to participate in the generous dividends that the owners now pay themselves and cash-in big with the other owners when the company is sold. Specifically, Matt has three requests (demands?):

1. He wants the stock now in recognition of the services he has already provided the company and will provide in the future. He doesn't want to pay anything for his Bunker stock, and he doesn't want a deal that is based solely on the future appreciation in the value of Bunker's stock.

2. He wants to pay no income taxes on the stock he receives until the stock is sold and cash is realized.

3. He wants the tax benefits of stock ownership – specifically preferred tax treatment on dividends and capital gains at time of sale.

Jake wants and needs to keep Matt happy, but has some concerns. Jake wants to give Matt nothing that is not tied to his future long-term commitment to the company. Jake has asked: What happens if we give Matt stock and he stops performing, quits, or (heaven forbid) signs on with a competitor? How do we get the stock back? Do we have to buy it back? What happens to Matt's stock if there is a falling out down the road?

Jake and the board need some answers and advice. What do you recommend?

---

100. An unfunded and unsecured right to receive money or property does not constitute "property" under the provisions of Section 83. Reg. § 1.83-3(e).

CHAPTER 13

IMPORTANT HISTORICAL AND PLANNING PERSPECTIVES

This chapter is designed to introduce students to five business-related areas of the law that regularly impact businesses and their owners and executives. The goal is to promote awareness (not expertise) and an appreciation of why the business challenges associated with these areas of the law are so important.

A. THE ROLE OF ANTITRUST

The overriding goal of our antitrust laws is to preserve, protect and maintain public confidence in our free market system by deterring and eliminating economic oppression. The post-Civil War industrial revolution quickly taught all that unrestrained free market forces can produce combinations, driven by greed and power, that will destroy the freedom of others.[1] Therefore, for the past 122 years or so, the Congress, the Executive Branch, state legislators, academic commentators, and most importantly, our courts, have wrestled with the challenge of drawing the line between good and bad competition.

Although there have been many bumps and U-turns along the way, most now agree that the social objectives of antitrust are: to promote the efficient allocation of goods and services; to prevent "deadweight loss," which results when restricted output limits access to products and services; to stop "wealth transfer," the transfer of wealth from consumers to those who exercise market power to limit or restrict competitive conditions; and to promote "dynamic efficiency," the development of new products, innovations and technologies. Of far less concern, although once deemed the essence of antitrust, are desires to decentralize power and protect market entry for individual firms. Now all have pretty much accepted the reality that big is not bad when it promotes efficiency and innovation and produces no serious signs of deadweight loss or wealth transfer. It is against these fundamental objectives that each gray area issue must ultimately be tested.

Business is all about competition. Competition is what keeps markets thriving, prices down, output up, new innovation in high gear – at least in theory, and often in practice. To stay alive and healthy in an ever-faster-paced market whose geographical barriers are being regularly shattered by new technologies,

---

1. See generally M. Josephson, The Robber Barons (Harcourt Brace Jovanovich, Inc., Copyright 1934, renewed 1962).

most businesses need to develop a competitive strategy. They must determine how they are going to meet and beat new players, products, and technologies that threaten old ways, old prices, and old market shares. It requires knowledge; competitive intelligence itself is now big business. It requires forward planning and often bold actions designed to keep barriers up and outsiders out. And sometimes it requires, in the minds of those calling the shots, coordinated efforts with others, similarly threatened, who have forever been considered the "other guys," the competition.

Not all collaborations between competitors are bad. Some lead to increased efficiencies, more output, lower prices, and innovation. But they are all potentially dangerous. The deal that promises every virtue of our competitive system may be a façade for (or soon lead to) an exercise of market power that controls output and discourages new products and innovation. The perils of getting mixed up in the wrong kind of coordinated effort, deemed smart and crafty on its face, can be severe. These perils can shake the business to its core, even threaten its survival. The fact that the line between good and bad often is fuzzy and can only be found by a court simply magnifies the danger. The business owner who perceives such uncertainty as an opportunity or excuse for boldness lacks a fundamental understanding of how a plaintiffs' lawyer earns a living. The ongoing challenge is to spot the danger flags and implement a smart competitive strategy clear of the danger zones.

The antitrust statutes themselves clarify nothing. Section 1 of the Sherman Act, the foundation for most antitrust disputes, just proscribes "any contract, combination and conspiracy in restraint of trade."[2] Section 2, dealing with monopolies, offers nothing clearer.[3] The Robinson-Patman Act's price discrimination prohibitions, although a bit more specific on their face, are just as difficult in their application.[4] The Federal Trade Commission Act outlaws "unfair methods of competition" and "unfair and deceptive acts and practices."[5] Justice Hughes characterized the antitrust statutes as a "charter of freedom," with a "generality and adaptability comparable to that found to be desirable in constitutional provisions."[6] But, according to the beliefs of most, at least the Founding Fathers had "intentions" for what they put in the constitution. No one really knows what Senator Sherman and his colleagues intended,[7] apart from their hatred of John D. Rockefeller and the deplorable tactics used by Rockefeller to build his powerful oil trust.[8] So the courts, aided by the Department of Justice, the Federal Trade Commission (FTC), hordes of commentators, and masses of private litigants, have had free reign in exercising their charter of freedom to

2. 15 U.S.C.A. § 1.

3. 15 U.S.C.A. § 2.

4. See, for example, J. Truett Payne Co. v. Chrysler Motors Corp., 451 U.S. 557 (1981) and Boise Cascade Corp. v. FTC, 837 F.2d 1127 (D.C. Cir. 1988).

5. 15 U.S.C.A. § 13.

6. Justice Hughes writing for the majority in Appalachian Coals Inc. v. United States, 288 U.S. 344, 359-60 (1933).

7. As Professor Bork wrote, "So far as I'm aware, Congress, in enacting these statutes, never faced the problem of what to do when values come into conflict in specific cases. Legislators appear to have assumed, as it is most comfortable to assume, that all good things are always compatible." Bork, The Role of the Courts in Applying Economics, 54 Antitrust L.J. 21, 24 (1985).

8. 21 Cong. Rec. 2,460 (1890).

create a body of law that is anything but clear.

Some business owners, yearning to secure what they have or to get more, are determined to push the envelope. They have an opportunity; they want to "go for it." They don't want to hear anything about dynamic efficiencies or dead-weight loss, and wealth transfer actually sounds pretty good. When faced with this situation, it often helps to reconsider the following eleven basic truths, which all lawyers should understand.

1. Who's President Often Doesn't Matter. Some think a pro-business president means no more antitrust. After all, they say, compare Microsoft's fate under Clinton and Bush. It's bad thinking. The Department of Justice and FTC always are at work. Plus (and this is what many miss), the real threat often comes from a private party who has been hurt, not the government. Or, perhaps more accurately stated, the real threat is the attorney of the private party who has allegedly been hurt. The United States is the only country that allows private parties to seek redress for their injuries under the antitrust laws. The simple truth: There are many more private lawsuits than government actions.[9] Beyond the lawsuits are those businesses (and there are many) that through calculated risk or ignorance stepped over the line, got caught, and quietly took their lumps by settling. There is no question that court decisions over the past fifteen years have created pleading and other obstacles that have made private antitrust actions tougher for plaintiffs, but a strong set of facts will transcend these obstacles and support a claim.

2. Forget the Odds. With antitrust, it's not about the odds of winning. It's the stakes of losing. Some risks with miniscule losing odds aren't worth messing with because so much is at stake. Antitrust is one of those risks. The antitrust statutes, although vague on many things, are very specific on one important detail: the plaintiff who wins is entitled to triple damages, plus attorney's fees. This provides a powerful incentive for an injured party, aided by a hungry attorney, to explore all avenues for springboarding a contract or tort claim into an antitrust claim. If successful, the potential yield triples. An owner whose business has failed sometimes longs to salvage something by pinning blame on others. When such an owner discovers a plausible antitrust claim from the "dirty pool" of others, the effort of recovering three times the business loss becomes a business venture unto itself. Just the word "antitrust" gets some lawyers excited.

3. A Criminal? Add to any civil liability exposures the ugly reality, often overlooked, that antitrust violations are also criminal. In 2004 Congress, with the support of the Bush Administration, increased criminal penalties for individuals who violate the antitrust laws to $1 million and 10 years jail time (up from $250,000 and three years) and increased corporate penalties to $100 million (up from $10 million).[10] Although criminal prosecutions are limited to the worst offenders (e.g. hard-core cartel operators), the thought of getting involved in something that is a crime, not just a calculated business risk, may prompt some to

9. Some estimate that the ratio is 10-to-1. See S. Salop & L. White, Private Antitrust Litigation: An Introduction and Framework in Private Antitrust Litigation, New Evidence, New Learning (L. White. ed. 1988), p.3.

10. Antitrust Criminal Penalty Enhancement and Reform Act of 2004, Pub.L. 108-237.

think differently.

4. Winning Is Losing. The fight itself can take an intolerable toll on a business, even when the business is declared the ultimate victor. The high stakes provide powerful incentives for all parties to fight long and hard. Often the mammoth out-of-pocket costs of the fight and the complete loss of huge amounts of otherwise productive time are too much for many businesses. Usually the essence of the claims are factual allegations that demand intense scrutiny of the business, all of which adds to the expense, discomfort, disruptions, and opportunity costs of the effort. As the dispute heats up, drags on and takes its toll, third-party observers, important to the business, may add to the mounting burdens. Key employees may become insecure and jump ship. Important customers and vendors may start looking in other directions. All these costs and burdens are known to those who are throwing the darts. Their challenge is to keep throwing and applying pressure because they know that at some point the business may conclude that winning is losing and cut its losses by settling.

5. The Plagues: Price and Output. Agreements that make it easier to control market prices or outputs are the plague. They are per se bad. Arguments about market power (or lack thereof) and anticompetitive and pro-competitive effects won't help. The challenge is to strip away all the proposed rationales and excuses for the deal and honestly answer one question: Does the company's proposed deal with its competitor make it easier to maintain or raise prices or control output of goods or services in the market? If so, run.

6. Signed Deal Not Required. A defective agreement among competitors can take many forms. It need not be in writing or be an enforceable contract. An informal understanding often is enough. [11] Coordinated actions may be all it takes.[12] Circumstantial evidence becomes the ball game. If the competitors' actions suggest some kind of agreement or understanding, the plaintiff's challenge is to present enough circumstantial evidence to get the case to the jury. Although some competitors, faced with a claim, have prevailed by refuting circumstantial evidence and proving the plausibility of their parallel conduct without any agreement or understanding,[13] the business owner who's tempted to play ball with his or her competitors by keeping prices up or output down would be foolish to bank on such an argument.

7. Beyond Price and Output. An agreement between competitors that does not affect price and output might still be out of bounds. For any such agreement, a rule of reason is applied to determine the agreement's potential for anticompetitive harm. In the words of the Department of Justice and FTC, it's a "flexible inquiry and varies in focus and detail depending on the nature of the agreement and market circumstances."[14] Translation: No certainty; could go either way. Examples of competitor arrangements tested under the rule of reason include, among others, joint agreements for marketing, production, buying,

---

11. See, e.g., United States v. Paramount Pictures, 334 U.S. 131 (1948) and FTC v. Cement Institute, 333 U.S. 683 (1948).
12. See, e.g., Interstate Circuit, Inc. v. United States, 306 U.S. 208 (1939).
13. See, e.g., Matsushita Electric Industrial Co. v. Zenith Radio Corp., 475 U.S. 574 (1986).
14. Antitrust Guidelines for Collaborations Among Competitors (April 2000), p. 10.

research and development, and shared assets and facilities. Such agreements are clearly possible, but usually it's smart to have an antitrust-savvy lawyer scrutinize the arrangement for any per se killers and rule-of-reason effects.

8. Flying Solo Can Do It. Antitrust risks are not limited to competitor collaborations. A company with dominant market power can get in trouble by itself. Being or becoming a monopoly is not illegal. But engaging in anticompetitive or exclusionary conduct to obtain or maintain monopoly power crosses the line. Any company with substantial market power should realize that it will be held to a higher competitive standard than smaller players who are struggling for market share.

9. Market Power Comes In Many Sizes. Too often, market power is confused with company size. The sole newspaper in a small town may be a monopolist with market power.[15] Market power cannot be determined without first defining the limits of the relevant market, a tough challenge in many cases. Relevant markets come in many sizes.

10. IP Not a Sure-Fire Defense. It's dangerous to assume that the exercise of valid intellectual property rights will always provide a defense to an antitrust claim of abusive anticompetitive conduct by a party with market power. In the famous Microsoft case,[16] Microsoft made such a claim, arguing that the restrictions in its Windows licensing agreements with computer equipment manufacturers could not "give rise to antitrust liability" because they were the "exercise" of "rights" that it owned as "the holder of valid copyrights legally acquired." In rejecting this argument as "bordering on the frivolous," the D.C. Circuit stated, "That is no more correct than the proposition that use of one's personal property, such as a baseball bat, cannot give rise to tort liability."[17] However, when it comes to licensing intellectual property, valid IP rights often trump any antitrust claim that the holder of the IP has a duty to deal with competitors. In *Independent Service Organizations Antitrust Litigation (CSU v. Xerox)*[18], the Federal Circuit stated, "In the absence of any indication of illegal tying, fraud in the Patent and Trademark, or sham litigation, the patent holder may enforce the statutory right to exclude others from making, using, or selling the claimed invention free from liability under the antitrust laws."[19] The historical conflicts at the intersection of IP and antitrust caused the U.S. Department of Justice and the Federal Trade Commission to jointly issue the Antitrust Guidelines for the Licensing of Intellectual Property in 1995. These guidelines have helped establish core concepts, including that intellectual property is essentially comparable to any other form of property for antitrust purposes, that there is no presumption that IP rights create market power, and that combinations of complementary IP rights may create positive, pro-competitive benefits.

11. When Rule of Reason Rules. In evaluating how any agreed restraint

15. Lorain Journal Co. v. United States, 342 U.S. 143 (1951).
16. United States v. Microsoft Corporation, 253 F.3d 34 (D.C. Cir. 2001).
17. 253 F.3d at 62-63.
18. 203 F.3d 1322 (Fed. Cir. 2000).
19. 203 F.3d at 1327.

might fare under the rule of reason, it often helps to answer key questions. The purpose of these questions is to help assess the restraint's adverse impact on market output, efficiency and innovation, and to determine whether the agreement has any pro-competitive effects not available through less restrictive means. The end result is a balancing exercise between the pro-competitive and anticompetitive effects. Some of the important questions include the following:

- Does the restraint have the potential to strengthen the market?[20]
- Does the restraint have the capacity to impact market price-setting mechanisms?[21]
- Does the restraint promote or demand exclusivity? [22]
- Is the restraint imposed by a party possessing dominant market power?[23]
- Is the particular industry susceptible to collusion?[24]
- Does the restraint help get more output to market?[25]
- Does the restraint promote efficiency-enhancing infrastructures?[26]
- Is the restraint ancillary to a broader joint venture or business arrangement?[27]
- Does the restraint have the capacity to change the character of an established market?[28]
- Does the restraint affect access to a facility essential for all competitors?[29]
- Does the restraint force a blanket license, long-term lease or boycott that forecloses competition?[30]
- Does the restraint involve the legitimate exercise of intellectual property rights or the use of such rights as a phony pretext for foreclosing competition?[31]

STUDENT PROBLEM 13-1

Business A and Business B compete in the printer cartridge replacement market for a larger manufacturer's copiers. Minor variations on copiers from

20. See, e.g., California Dental Ass'n v. FTC, 526 U.S. 756 (1999).
21. See, e.g., FTC v. Indiana Federation of Dentists, 476 U.S. 447 (1986).
22. Compare, e.g., Broadcast Music, Inc. v. Columbia Broadcasting System, Inc., 441 U.S. 1 (1979) with NCAA v. Board of Regents of University of Oklahoma, 468 U.S. 85 (1984).
23. See, e.g., Eastman Kodak Co. v. Image Technical Services, Inc., 504 U.S. 451 (1992).
24. See, e.g., United States v. Container Corp. of America, 393 U.S. 333 (1969).
25. See, e.g., Broadcast Music, Inc. v. Columbia Broadcasting System, Inc., 441 U.S. 1 (1979) and Appalachian Coals v. United States, 288 U.S. 344 (1933).
26. Med South FTC Advisory Opinion (February 19, 2002).
27. See, e.g., United States v. Addyston Pipe & Steel Co., 85 F. 271 (6th Cir. 1898).
28. See, e.g., Aspen Skiing Co. v. Aspen Highlands Skiing Corp., 472 U.S. 585 (1985).
29. Otter Tail Power Co. v. United States, 410 U.S. 366 (1973); United States v. Terminal R.R. Ass'n of St. Louis, 224 U.S. 383 (1912).
30. United States v. Griffith, 334 U.S. 100 (1948); Lorain Journal Co. v. United States, 342 U.S. 143 (1951); United States v. United Shoe Machine Corporation, 110 F.Supp. 295 (D. Mass. 1953), affirmed 347 U.S. 521 (1954).
31. See Eastman Kodak Co. v. Image Technical Services, Inc., 504 U.S. 451 (1992).

year to year require annual retooling and redesigns of printing cartridges. In order to save money and promote efficiencies, Business A and Business B have an informal understanding. Business A will retool only for even year copiers, and Business B will retool only for odd year copiers. They believe this understanding promotes efficiencies by reducing costs and risks of excessive inventories.

What antitrust risks might this understanding pose? Is there any potential of a per se claim? What additional facts would help answer these questions?

B. DEVELOPMENT OF SECURITIES LAW LIABILITIES

The federal securities laws pose ongoing risks for officers and directors charged with managing a company. Often the risks expand to others close to the organization. Key risk areas include false or misleading disclosures and insider trading. The primary statutory threat is Rule 10b-5, which Chief Justice Rehnquist described as "a judicial oak which has grown from little more than a legislative acorn."[32]

Rule 10b-5 makes it "unlawful for any person, directly or indirectly, by the use of any means or instrumentality of interstate commerce, or of the mails or of any facility of any national securities exchange, (a) To employ any device, scheme, or artifice to defraud, (b) To make any untrue statement of a material fact or to omit to state a material fact necessary in order to make the statements made, in the light of the circumstances under which they were made, not misleading, or (c) To engage in any act, practice, or course of business which operates or would operate as a fraud or deceit upon any person, in connection with the purchase or sale of any security."

1. DISCLOSURE LIABILITY RISKS

Although a private right of action by injured shareholders predicated on a violation of federal securities laws is not expressly authorized by statute, the Supreme Court held that such a right existed in the landmark case of *J.I. Case Co. v. Borak.*[33] The *Borak* holding brought federal securities laws directly into the boardroom and transformed the landscape of corporate governance litigation.

In *Borak*, the plaintiff was a shareholder in J.I. Case Co. ("Case") who brought an action to enjoin a merger between Case and American Tractor Company. The plaintiff alleged improper self-dealing by certain Case managers that resulted in the Case shareholders not being treated fairly. The statutory basis of the plaintiff's claim was section 14(a) of the Securities Exchange Act and related rule 14a-9, which makes it unlawful to use false or misleading statements in a proxy statement or solicitation. In holding that the federal securities laws provide a private right of action, the Court stated:

32. Blue Chip Stamps v. Manor Drug Stores, 421 U.S. 723, 737 (1975).
33. 377 U.S. 426 (1964).

> The purpose of 14(a) is to prevent management or others from obtaining authorization for corporate action by means of deceptive or inadequate disclosure in proxy solicitation. The section stemmed from the congressional belief that 'fair corporate suffrage is an important right that should attach to every equity security bought on a public exchange.' H.R.Rep. No. 1383, 73d Cong., 2d Sess., 13.
>
> The injury which a stockholder suffers from corporate action pursuant to a deceptive proxy solicitation ordinarily flows from the damage done the corporation, rather than from the damage inflicted directly upon the stockholder. The damage suffered results not from the deceit practiced on him alone but rather from the deceit practiced on the stockholders as a group. To hold that derivative actions are not within the sweep of the section would therefore be tantamount to a denial of private relief. Private enforcement of the proxy rules provides a necessary supplement to Commission action… We, therefore, believe that under the circumstances here it is the duty of the courts to be alert to provide such remedies as are necessary to make effective the congressional purpose.

377 U.S at 431.

Borak established the private right of action, but raised a number of key questions relating to the scope of the liability exposure risks. What should be the requisite causation link between a defective disclosure and the plaintiffs' alleged injury? What standard should be used in determining whether a specific disclosure defect is sufficiently serious to trigger liability exposure? Should substantive unfairness alone be a basis for liability? A series of key Supreme Court cases addressed and resolved these important questions. Following are recaps of some of these decisions in chronological order.

1970 - *Mills v. Electric Auto-Lite Co*[34]

In *Mills,* Mergenthaler Linotype Corporation, the owner of approximately 54 percent of Electric Auto-Lite Company shares, sought to merge with Auto-Lite. The proxy statement used in connection with the merger stated that Auto-Lite's board had recommended the merger but failed to disclose that all eleven board members were nominated by and under the "control and domination" of Mergenthaler. Minority shareholders of Auto-Lite brought both a derivative action on behalf of Auto-Lite and a direct action as a class representative of minority shareholders, alleging that the proxy solicitation was materially misleading due to the lack of information regarding the board's relationship with Mergenthaler. The district court found that the proxy solicitation was materially misleading and that because the merger agreement required an approval vote of two-thirds of Auto-Lite shares (more than Mergenthaler owned), the requisite causal connection existed between the proxy solicitation and the merger. The case was referred to a master for consideration of the appropriate relief.

The Seventh Circuit reversed on the issue of causation and remanded the

34. 396 U.S. 375 (1970).

case. Noting that an injunction would have been appropriate if the plaintiffs had timely moved to stop the merger, the appeals court held that no other relief would be available if Mergenthaler could prove by a preponderance of the evidence that the requisite number of proxies would have been tendered even with proper disclosure or (given the impracticability of such proof in a public corporation) that the merger was fair to the minority shareholders.

The Supreme Court reversed and remanded, agreeing with the district court's causal analysis and ruling that fairness is not a defense to material misrepresentations or omissions in a proxy solicitation. If materiality has been established, a sufficient causal connection exists if the proxy statement itself, not the misleading or omitted statements, was essential to the transaction. Since Mergenthaler lacked the votes needed to approve the merger, the causation element was satisfied. As for "retrospective relief" for a proxy violation, the court stated that federal courts should exercise "sound discretion," are not required to "unscramble" the transaction, and may consider the type of monetary and attorney fees relief that applies in illegality and fraud cases.

1976 - *TSC Industries, Inc. v. Northway, Inc.*[35]

In *TSC*, National Industries, Inc. (National) acquired 34 percent of the stock of TSC Industries, Inc. and nominated five of TSC's ten directors. After the stock purchase, National proposed that TSC sell its assets to National. The proxy solicitation disclosed National's ownership of TSC stock and its nominees to the TSC board, but did not specifically disclose that TSC's chairman of the board and the head of its executive committee were among the five National directors. The asset purchase was approved, and a group of minority shareholders sued, claiming that these omissions were material.

The trial court held for TSC, finding that the omissions were not material. The court of appeals reversed, holding that any facts a shareholder might consider important are material. TSC appealed.

The Supreme Court reversed the court of appeals, establishing the test for materiality as a mixed question of law and fact. The Court's test: For a fact or omission to be material, there must be a substantial likelihood that a reasonable shareholder would have considered the fact or omission important when deciding how to vote, or, "put another way," a substantial likelihood that a disclosure of the omitted fact would have been viewed by the reasonable investor as having a significant effect on the "total mix" of information available. In this case, the Supreme Court concluded that the omitted facts did not meet the definition, reasoning that an investor would not have viewed the omitted facts as important in view of the actual disclosures in the proxy materials regarding the National-nominated directors.

1977 - *Santa Fe Industries, Inc. v. Green*[36]

In *Santa Fe*, Santa Fe Industries Inc., the owner of 95 percent of the stock of Kirby Lumber Corp., a Delaware corporation, sought to integrate Kirby through a

35. 426 U.S. 438 (1976).
36. 430 U.S. 462 (1977).

short-form merger that permitted a buy-out of Kirby's minority shareholders with no vote of the directors or shareholders of Kirby and no advance notice to the minority shareholders. The minority cash-out price was $150 per share, with Santa Fe having obtained a Morgan Stanley evaluation at $125 a share. Green and other Kirby minority shareholders objected to the merger, but instead of asserting their appraisal rights (discussed in Section D of Chapter 5) under Delaware law, they commenced a federal suit to set aside the merger or to recover what they deemed a fair price for their Kirby stock (allegedly $772 per share), arguing that the merger was fraudulent under Rule 10b-5.

The district court dismissed the complaint for failure to state a claim. A divided Second Circuit reversed, holding that a breach of fiduciary duty by a majority shareholder against minority shareholders (for a merger without a business purpose and with no notice) states a valid 10b-5 claim even though there is no charge of misrepresentation or lack of disclosure.

The Supreme Court reversed and remanded, holding that a Rule 10b-5 action requires a claim of misrepresentation or lack of disclosure. The Court reasoned that the purpose of the Securities Exchange Act was to ensure accurate and complete disclosures, a cause of action for a "subsidiary purpose" should not be recognized, state corporate law should be respected, and 10b-5 should not be expanded to "cover the corporate universe."

1988 - *Basic, Inc. v. Levinson*[37]

In *Levinson*, Basic Incorporated, a public company, entered into preliminary merger discussions with Combustion Engineering, a company in the same industry. While discussions were taking place but before any deal was made, Basic issued three statements over two years denying any merger discussions. At the end of the second year, Basic halted trading of its stock and issued a press release stating that Basic had been "approached" by another company interested in a merger. Basic's board approved Combustion's offer the next day and then publicly announced a merger at $46 a share, a premium over the market price of Basic shares.

Levinson and others brought a class action suit on behalf of Basic shareholders who had sold stock during the period between the "no discussion" statements and the announcement of the merger. The suit was against Basic and its directors and argued that the merger-discussion denials were materially false or misleading statements within the reach of Rule 10b-5 that resulted in sales at "artificially depressed prices."

The district court ruled in favor of Basic on summary judgment, holding that the statements were not material because they were made before an agreement in principle as to price and structure had been reached that was "destined" with reasonable certainty to result in a merger. The Sixth Circuit reversed and remanded the case, rejecting the argument that preliminary negotiations are not material as a matter of law and holding that, once statements were made denying discussions, the existence of discussions that may not otherwise have been

37. 430 U.S. 462 (1977).

material became material because they made the statements actually made untrue.

The Supreme Court reversed and remanded, (1) adopting in the 10b-5 context *TSC's* "total mix" materiality definition, (2) rejecting the arguments that there is a bright line for materiality in the context of future contingent transactions and that information becomes material by virtue of a public statement denying it, and (3) holding that as to the potential of a transaction occurring, the materiality determination (factual in nature) is predicated on the probability that the transaction will be consummated and the significance of the contemplated transaction to the issuer of the securities. The Court also held that the fraud-on-the-market theory can support such a 10b-5 claim of market participants by creating a rebuttable presumption of reliance, with the burden of rebuttal on the alleged wrongdoers who issued the false or misleading statements. The court reasoned that such a presumption is supported by general fairness, public policy, probability, and judicial economy.

1991 - *Virginia Bankshares, Inc. v. Sandberg*[38]

In *Virginia Bankshares*, First America Bankshares, Inc. ("FABI") owned 100 percent of Virginia Bankshares, Inc ("VBI") and 85 percent of First American Bank of Virginia ("FABV"). In a freeze-out merger, FABI merged FABV into VBI, buying out the remaining 15 percent of FABV's shareholders. Before the cash-out merger, FABI had FABV valued by an outside investment banking firm that opined that $42 per share was a fair price for the minority stock. Proxy solicitations to FABV's minority shareholders encouraged approval of the merger and stated that the board believed that the $42 price was "high" and "fair" to the minority shareholders. Sandberg voted against the merger and sued to recover damages from VBI, FABI, and the directors of FABI, alleging a proxy violation of Rule 14a-9 for false and misleading statements (some board members actually did not believe the price was fair) and breach of fiduciary claims under state law. A district court jury awarded Sandberg an additional $18 a share.

The Fourth Circuit affirmed the verdict, holding that certain misleading statements in the proxy materials relating to the belief of board members were material and that the action could be maintained even though minority votes were not needed to complete the merger.

The Supreme Court reversed, holding that (1) statements of belief, opinion, or reasons may be deemed material and actionable when they are false, the maker knew they were false or had no reason to believe they were true, and they are significant enough to be important to a reasonable investor, and (2) because FABI owned 85 percent of FABV's stock and minority approval was not necessary to complete the merger, there was no "essential link" between the allegedly false statements and the transaction and, therefore, no causation. The court reasoned that the benefits of a "cosmetic" minority vote were too "hazy" and "unreliable" to support such a causal link and sustain a claim. The Court

38. 501 U.S. 1083 (1991).

also stated that the facts of the case did not require a determination of whether loss of state law appraisal rights (applicable to minority shareholders who voted for the transaction) would provide an essential link to support a 14a-9 claim based on false and misleading statements.

The issue left open by the Supreme Court in *Virginia Bankshares* – whether the loss of statutory appraisal rights could provide an "essential link" to support a claim based on the false and misleading statements – has been answered in the affirmative by lower courts. For example, in *Wilson v. Great American Industries, Inc.*[39] the Second Circuit considered whether minority shareholders who voted for a merger and lost their statutory appraisal rights could bring an action under section 14(a) based solely on the loss of such rights due to a false and misleading proxy statement. The court held that that the requisite loss causation or economic harm to a shareholder may be established when a proxy statement prompts a shareholder to accept an unfair exchange ratio for his or her shares rather than recoup a potentially greater value through a state appraisal proceeding.

STUDENT PROBLEM 13-2

Wave Incorporated ("Wave") is a small Delaware public company that designs, installs and monitors customized data and communication systems. Wave has a five-person senior management team (the "Team"), headed by Burt Rogers, age 62, who has been the President and CEO of Wave for the past fifteen years. Burt owns 10 percent of Wave's outstanding common stock, the other four members of the Team collectively own 15 percent, and the balance is owned by approximately 2,200 shareholders. Wave's stock is thinly traded over-the-counter at prices that have historically ranged from $15 to $23. The Team has never believed that these prices reflect the true value of the company.

Wave's board consists of seven members: Burt, two other members of the Team, and four outside directors (the "Outsiders"). Each Outsider owns Wave stock, has never worked for the company, has served on the board for at least five years, and considers Burt a friend.

Eleven months ago, Burt was rushed by ambulance to the hospital. A feared stroke turned out to be a false alarm, but the doctor's warning was ominous: "Slow up now or you will never enjoy your wealth or your grandkids." Burt took the warning to heart and decided to cash in, leave Wave, and move on. Burt knew that he would be able to realize a fair value on his Wave stock only if he seriously explored a sale of the company.

Burt advised the other Team members of his desire to explore a sale of the company and engaged an investment banking firm (the "Firm") to value the company and then to help find a buyer. After carefully evaluating the company, the Firm reported that the Wave shareholders could likely expect a price in the $28 to $35 range from a sale, assuming a qualified buyer could be found. Pleased with these numbers, Burt authorized the Firm to seek a buyer, with explicit instructions that Burt's ongoing personal services would not be part of

---

39. 979 F.2d 924 (2nd Cir. 1992).

the deal.

Within a few months, very preliminary discussions were underway with two potential buyers. The first candidate, Archer Inc., is a competitor of Wave that is many times Wave's size. Very interested in the strategic advantages of acquiring Wave, Archer expressed a willingness to pay up to $37 a share in a merger using Archer stock (traded on the NASDAQ). There were two problems with the Archer deal: the entire Team and many Wave employees would lose their jobs, and an antitrust hurdle would need to be cleared. Although the antitrust issue was labeled "not a big deal" by the Firm, the job cuts were a major concern for the entire Team.

The other merger candidate was a large diversified company ("Folsum") that would pay $31 a share. A Folsum deal would not threaten the paychecks of the Team or other Wave employees, nor would it present any antitrust hurdles.

The entire Team, including Burt, opted for the Folsum deal. In discussions with the board at three separate meetings, Burt laid out all the facts, provided copies of the Firm's evaluation, encouraged questions from the Outsiders, and strongly recommended the Folsum deal. Ultimately, the board unanimously approved the Folsum merger. The merger was publically announced nine months after Burt's trip to the hospital.

The merger required a majority approval vote of the Wave shareholders. The proxy statement to Wave's shareholders appropriately advised the shareholders of their dissenter appraisal rights and included the following statement: "In assessing various options, the officers and directors of Wave have relied on their knowledge of the company and advice from experts in concluding that the Folsum proposal is the best overall option for all stakeholders in the company." The proxy statement made no mention of the Firm's estimated price range ($28-$35), the potential Archer deal at $37, or Burt's health scare and his related decisions. The Folsum merger was approved by 96 percent of Wave's shareholders. The prospect of netting $31 on a stock that was currently trading at $21 appealed to everyone. The merger was quickly closed.

Shortly after the closing, certain Wave shareholders heard rumors that "Burt Rogers had rejected a $37 price from big rival Archer to protect the jobs of his four buddies." As they pursued the rumors, they learned of all the facts leading to the merger. These shareholders now seek to recover an additional $6 a share from the officers and directors of Wave, Wave, and the Firm on the grounds that the merger price was "not fair" and that the proxy disclosures to the shareholders were false and misleading.

What is the likelihood that the shareholders will prevail on their claims? What additional facts would you like to have in assessing the merits of these claims? What additional steps could the officers and directors of Wave have taken to reduce the risk of such claims?

In addition to the shareholders' claim, a class action is being threatened against the officers and directors of Wave and the Firm on behalf of all those who sold Wave stock during the period (several months) that started when Burt decided he wanted to explore selling the company (right after his health scare) and ended when the Folsum merger was publically announced. The claim is that these selling shareholders were damaged as a direct result of inadequate disclosures regarding the plan to sell Wave and the potential yield from such a sale.

What additional facts would you like to have in assessing the merits of these claims? What is the likelihood that the shareholders will prevail on their claims? What additional steps could the officers and directors of Wave have taken to reduce the risk of such claims?

2. INSIDER TRADING LIABILITY RISKS

The roots of insider trading liability risks can be traced to the SEC's 1961 ruling in *In The Matter Of Cady, Roberts & Co.*[40] In that case, the board of directors of Curtiss-Wright Corporation had voted to reduce the quarterly dividend amount by 40 percent, but the decision was not made public for slightly more than 45 minutes. During the 45-minute period, Cowdin, a Curtiss-Wright director and brokerage firm partner, advised one of his partners, Gintel, of the reduced dividend, and Gintel immediately sold several thousand shares of Curtiss-Wright stock on behalf of the firm's clients at prices in excess of $40. When the dividend-reduction information became public, trading in Curtiss-Wright stock was halted temporarily due to the high number of sell orders. Trading resumed at share prices ranging from $34 to $37 a share.

The SEC ruled that Gintel's actions and those of the brokerage firm (by virtue of Gintel's employment relationship) constituted willful violations of Section 17(a), Section 10(b), and Rule 10b-5. The SEC reasoned that the anti-fraud provisions extend to "any person," protect defrauded buyers as well as defrauded sellers, apply to impersonal market exchange transactions the same as they apply to "face-to-face" transactions, and require that one in possession of material, nonpublic information await public disclosure of the information before trading.

Cady Roberts opened the door to insider trading claims and criminal charges based on Rule 10b-5, which on its face makes no reference to insider trading and private rights of action. The case clarified that insider trading prohibitions under 10b-5 would extend to the firm and partner of a corporate director and would apply in open market transactions that involved a party who was not an existing stockholder of the corporation. But the case also triggered many compelling questions. Would liability extend to any person who trades a security while in the possession of nonpublic material information? Would liability exposure be limited only to insiders? Who qualifies as an insider? What constitutes material information? What if an insider did not know that the information hadn't been made available to the public? Is there a duty to investigate? A series of important cases have addressed these important questions in defining the scope of insider trading liabilities under 10b-5. Following are recaps of some of the key decisions in chronological order.

---

40. 40 S.E.C. 907 (1961).

1968 - *SEC v. Texas Gulf Sulphur Co.*[41]

In *Texas Gulf Sulphur*, officers, directors and employees of TGS had purchased shares of TGS stock with knowledge that recently discovered valuable mineral deposits owned by TGS had not been publicly disclosed. Kenneth Darke, a geologist in possession of the undisclosed information, was also named as a defendant because of his trading activity. The court described the essence of the insider trading rule and the options available to one who possesses nonpublic material information as follows:

> The essence of the Rule is that anyone who, trading for his own account in the securities of a corporation has 'access, directly or indirectly, to information intended to be available only for a corporate purpose and not for the personal benefit of anyone' may not take "advantage of such information knowing it is unavailable to those with whom he is dealing." Insiders, as directors or management officers are, of course, by this Rule, precluded from so unfairly dealing, but the Rule is also applicable to one possessing the information who may not be strictly termed an 'insider' within the meaning of Sec. 16(b) of the Act. Thus, anyone in possession of material inside information must either disclose it to the investing public, or, if he is disabled from disclosing it in order to protect a corporate confidence, or he chooses not to do so, must abstain from trading in or recommending the securities concerned while such inside information remains undisclosed.

401 F.2d at 848.

The court went on to explain that the "only regulatory objective" is that material information be "enjoyed equally," and that this overriding objective requires only that basic facts be disclosed to enable "outsiders" to use their own "evaluative expertise" with knowledge equal to that of the insiders. The court explained that the test of "materiality" is whether a reasonable person would attach importance to the information in making an investment decision and encompasses "not only information disclosing the earnings and distributions of a company but also those facts which affect the probable future of the company and those which may affect the desire of investors to buy, sell, or hold the company's securities." 401 F.2d at 849.

The Second Circuit reversed the lower court's ruling that geologist Darke fell outside the scope of the 10b-5 prohibition because he was not a corporate insider. The court reasoned that the inequities of "unequal access to knowledge" should "not be shrugged off as inevitable in our way of life" and that all transactions in TGS stock or calls by individuals apprised of the undisclosed drilling were made in violation of Rule 10b-5.

Two of the defendants in *Texas Gulf Sulphur* argued that they should not be liable under 10b-5 because their purchases of TGS stock occurred after the discovery was disclosed. Rejecting this argument, the court noted that the reading of a news release "is merely the first step in the process of dissemination

41. 401 F.2d 833 (2d Cir. 1968).

required for compliance with the regulatory objective of providing all investors with an equal opportunity to make informed investment judgments" and then held that the defendants "should have waited until the news could reasonably have been expected to appear over the media of widest circulation, the Dow Jones broad tape, rather than hastening to insure an advantage." 401 F.2d at 854.

These same defendants then asserted a good faith defense, arguing that they honestly believed that the news of the discovery had become public at the time they placed their orders. In rejecting this defense, the court held that due diligence, not ignorance, may be a defense to a Rule 10b-5 claim if "corporate management demonstrates that it was diligent in ascertaining that the information it published was the whole truth and that such diligently obtained information was disseminated in good faith." 401 F.2d at 860-862.

The Second Circuit suggested in *Texas Gulf Sulphur* that Rule 10b-5 may extend to any person who trades a security while in possession of undisclosed material information relating to the security. In subsequent decisions, the Supreme Court and lower courts have rejected this expansive interpretation.

1980 - *Chiarella v. United States*[42]

Chiarella was employed as a printer by a company that prepared announcements of corporate takeover bids. He used his position to discover the disguised identities of select companies and generated over $30,000 of profits trading on nonpublic information related to these companies. He was charged and convicted on 17 counts of violating section 10(b) and Rule 10b-5 for illegal insider trading. The Second Circuit affirmed the conviction.

The Supreme Court reversed, holding that the jury was improperly instructed that any party who trades with material, nonpublic information could be held liable for insider trading under Rule 10b-5. The Court held that a duty to disclose does not arise from mere possession of material, nonpublic information. Noting that an affirmative duty to disclose or not trade always applies to insiders (officers, directors, controlling shareholders, etc.), the court reasoned that such a duty will extend to another person only if that person is an agent or fiduciary of the opposite party in the transaction (i.e., selling shareholders of the companies whose stock Chiarella bought) or has been placed in a position of trust and confidence by such party. The Court stated:

> We cannot affirm petitioner's conviction without recognizing a general duty between all participants in market transactions to forgo actions based on material, nonpublic information. Formulation of such a broad duty, which departs radically from the established doctrine that duty arises from a specific relationship between two parties, should not be undertaken absent some explicit evidence of congressional intent.

445 U.S. at 223.

The court refused to consider whether Chiarella's actions could be actionable under 10b-5 by virtue of the breach of the trust owed to the acquiring

42. 445 U.S. 222 (1980).

companies as an employee of the printer because the issue had not been submitted to the jury.

The dissent argued that Chiarella misappropriated ("stole") nonpublic information entrusted to him in utmost confidence (with print shop warning signs "in the shadows") and the jury instructions, fairly read, were broad enough to include inside information obtained by such an unlawful means.

1983 - *Dirks v. SEC*[44]

Dirks was an officer of a brokerage firm. He had received information from a former officer of Equity Funding of America ("EFA") that EFA had been overstating its earnings. Dirks investigated the charges and ultimately received corroboration of EFA's fraud from several EFA employees. Dirks' investigation and his related efforts to have a Wall Street Journal article expose the fraud (which was rejected as posing undue libel risks) resulted in Dirks sharing his concerns about the fraud allegations with several members of the investment community, many of whom liquidated their positions in EFA. The SEC found Dirks (as a tippee) guilty of aiding and abetting violations of §17(a) and §10(b) of the Securities Exchange Act though his actions of disseminating nonpublic, material information to select members of the investment community. Dirks was only censured by the SEC because he played "an important role" in exposing EFA's fraud. The D.C. Circuit entered judgment against Dirks.

The Supreme Court reversed, holding that that a violation of Rule 10b-5 can exist only if there is a breach of a duty. The Court found that the persons who had tipped off Dirks had not benefitted personally in any way from sharing the information and were not in violation of any fiduciary responsibility. Thus, reasoned the Court, Dirks was under no duty to abstain from using the information. The Court held that a tippee assumes a duty not to trade on material nonpublic information only if the tipper breached a duty by disclosing the information and the tippee knew or should have known that there was such a breach. A tipper would be deemed to have breached a duty if the tipper was an insider subject to specific fiduciary duties or was a person who personally benefitted, directly or indirectly, from the disclosure.

The dissent argued that such a "personal benefit" requirement for tippee liability misconstrued the intent of 10b-5, which is to protect shareholders not just punish violations of fiduciary duties. The dissent emphasized that whether a tipper personally benefited by providing information to a tippee does not alter the fact that company shareholders are left worse off when select individuals trade on inside information. For this reason, argued the dissent, Dirks had a duty to either refrain from actions that he knew would lead to insider trading or disseminate the information publicly.

1984 - *S.E.C. v. Switzer*[44]

In *Switzer*, the question before the court was whether Barry Switzer, the famous University of Oklahoma football coach, had violated Rule 10b-5 when he

---

43. 463 U.S. 646 (1983).
44. 590 F.Supp. 756 (D.C.Okl. 1984).

traded stock based on nonpublic material information that he inadvertently overhead while sitting under the bleachers at a track meet. G. Platt, a corporate CEO, was discussing the information with another party and was unaware of Switzer's presence. In addition to trading for his own benefit, Switzer had passed the information on to select friends who he knew would trade on the information.

In holding that neither Switzer nor his buddies were liable under 10b-5, the court reasoned that Platt had violated no duty through the discussions that Switzer overheard, and therefore Switzer had not become subject to any duty that would create a basis for Rule 10b-5 tippee liability under the Dirks test.

1997 - *United States v. O'Hagan*[45]

O'Hagan was a law partner of Dorsey & Whitney, a large firm serving as local counsel to a British company engaged in merger talks with Pillsbury. Although O'Hagan never worked on the merger, he gained inside information about the merger through the firm and made personal trades and purchased call options on Pillsbury shares. An SEC investigation of O'Hagan's trades resulted in a 57-count indictment against O'Hagan, alleging he had defrauded his law firm and the firm's client by trading with material, nonpublic information. To get beyond the Court's holding in *Chiarella,* the SEC relied on the misappropriation theory that the Supreme Court expressly refused to address in *Chiarella*. The misappropriation theory holds that a person commits a fraud within the meaning of Rule 10b-5 by misappropriating confidential information in breach of a duty owed to the source of the information, even if the source is not an insider of the company whose stock is traded. The Eighth Circuit reversed all of O'Hagan's convictions, rejecting the misappropriation theory.

The Supreme Court reversed, upholding the misappropriation theory by reasoning that (1) it is consistent with its prior decisions (*Chiarella* and *Dirks)*, (2) it complements the "traditional" theory of insider trading liability for insiders and tippees, (3) it involves a "deceptive device" because the source of the information (to whom a duty was owed) is unaware of how the information is being used, and (4) it requires a purchase and sale of securities (which does not occur when the information is obtained, but when the information is acted upon by trading in securities).

The dissent argued that the "in connection with" requirement of 10b-5 should not be satisfied by the existence of a securities transaction that follows a fraud, but rather the fraud must be part of the transaction itself, noting that (under the majority opinion's reasoning) O'Hagan would have not been deemed to have used a "deceptive advice" (and thus would not have been liable) if he had disclosed his trading intentions to his firm.

STUDENT PROBLEM 13-3

Jerry, a doctor sitting in his country club's locker room, received a call from Pete, the chief financial officer of Bolton Inc, a large public company. In the call, Pete said, "I have to cancel our golf date today. Remember that potential merger that I told you about when we played last month? Well, it's happening. I am

45. 521 U.S. 642 (1997).

running in circles because it is huge. We're going to announce the merger tomorrow. There is no way that I can get away for golf today."

When Luke, a golfing buddy, later entered the locker room, Jerry said, "Pete can't make it today. He's tied up with some kind of big merger announcement that Bolton is going to make tomorrow. Being a CFO of a public company demands a lot. I'll meet you on the first tee in 10 minutes." Jerry then called his broker and bought 5,000 shares of Bolton stock. Luke did the same.

Has Jerry or Luke violated SEC Rule 10b-5 for illegal insider trading? What additional facts (if any) would you like to have in making this determination?

Roger, another club member who was unseen by Jerry and Luke, overheard Jerry's statement to Luke. Roger called his broker and bought 3,000 shares of Bolton stock. Has Roger violated SEC Rule 10b-5 for illegal insider trading? What additional facts (if any) would you like to have in making this determination?

Linda, the manager of the club, also overheard Jerry's statement to Luke. Linda called her broker Mandy and said, "I love this club job. Just learned that Bolton will have a big merger announcement tomorrow. Buy 3,000 of Bolton stock ASAP." Mandy immediately advised 50 of her best clients to buy Bolton stock.

The club's employee handbook states that every club employee "shall seek to carefully protect and not exploit the confidential information of each member."

Have Linda, Mandy or Mandy's clients violated SEC Rule 10b-5 for illegal insider trading? What additional facts (if any) would you like to have in making this determination?

C. INTELLECTUAL PROPERTY PROTECTIONS

The protection of "brain-created" rights can be traced back to the Greek state of Sybaris in 500 BC.[46] The term "intellectual property" was first officially used in the constitution of the Northern German Confederation in 1867. It was then adopted by the United International Bureaux for the Protection of Intellectual Property, the forerunner to the World International Property Organization (WIPO), a Geneva-based organization established by treaty as an agency of the United Nations in 1967. Most believe that companies in the U.S. started using the term "intellectual property" with the creation of the WIPO, but that its universal usage in the U.S. was triggered by passage of the Bayh-Dole Act in 1980, which established intellectual property protections related to research funded by the federal government.[47]

1. Role and Limits of IP Protections

Today, the importance of intellectual property rights to the economies of the

46. Charles Anthon, *A Classical Dictionary* (Harper & Brothers 1841).

47. See generally Lemley, *Property, Intellectual Property, and Free Riding*, 83 Texas Law Review 1031 (2005).

world and the United States cannot be overstated. Innovation is the key to economic growth in the U.S. and a strong competitive position throughout the world. A driving factor for such innovation is the grant of exclusive legal rights in intangible assets to those who create such assets through their mental powers and energies. Such assets include discoveries and inventions, musical, artistic and literary works, and words, phrases, symbols, and designs. Protecting rights to such assets is essential to encourage innovation, secure economic benefits for the creators, and incent investors to fund the development and exploitation of new ideas. When such protections are absent or cannot be enforced, incentives are weakened and those who seek to illegally exploit or traffic in the rights of others are emboldened.

In March 2012, the Economics and Statistics Administration and the U.S. Patent and Trademark Office jointly issued a report entitled "Intellectual Property and the U.S. Economy: Industries in Focus." The report used various "industry-level metrics" to identify the most IP-intensive industries in the U.S. economy. To the surprise of no one, the report found that the entire U.S. economy relies on some form of IP because virtually every industry either produces or uses it. The report also identified 75 "IP-intensive" industries that, in 2010, accounted for 27.1 million jobs in the United States (18.8 percent of all employment in the country) and "directly supported" another 12 million supply chain jobs. The report concluded that "every two jobs in IP-intensive industries support an additional one job elsewhere in the economy." Bottom line: approximately 30 percent of all U.S. jobs are directly or indirectly attributable to the IP-intensive industries.

The report also found that IP-intensive industries represented about $5.06 trillion in value added, 34.8 percent of the entire gross domestic value in the U.S. Exports of merchandise by IP-intensive industries totaled $775 billion in 2010, accounting for 60.7 percent of all merchandise exports by U.S. companies.

Not only does intellectual property create millions of jobs in the U.S., it creates jobs that pay well. The report found that the average weekly wages in IP-intensive industries were $1,156 in 2010, roughly 42 percent higher than the $815 average weekly wages in other private industries. This wage premium has grown to nearly twice the size of the 22 percent premium that existed in 1990. Patent- and copyright-intensive industries have been the real winners, with wage premiums in patent-intensive industries increasing from 66 percent in 2005 to 73 percent in 2010 and wage premiums in copyright-intensive industries rising from 65 percent to 77 percent. The higher wage levels, in part, are attributable to the fact that in 2010 more than 42 percent of workers over the age of 25 in IP-intensive industries were college educated, compared to 34 percent in other industries.

As important as IP-intensive industries are to the customers and employees they serve, companies in these industries operate on a world stage that is inefficient and grossly inconsistent in the protection of IP rights. The massive theft and illegal reproduction of U.S. intellectual property is now characterized as a crisis. It reaches every major business sector in the U.S., including advanced materials, aerospace, autos, biotech, chemicals, defense systems, electronics, heavy equipment, home products, pharmaceuticals, and software. Seldom does a week pass without media reports relating to stolen U.S. technologies or IP rights.

The Commission on the Theft of American Intellectual Property (IP Commission)[48] recently reported that American companies are losing hundreds of billions of dollars each year due to intellectual property theft by foreign entities. It estimates that the total revenue loss to U.S. companies each year nearly equals the value of all U.S. exports to Asia and that a substantial crack down on China thefts alone would create 2.1 million American jobs. Gen. Keith Alexander, the director of the National Security Agency and chief at the Central Security Service, claims that the ongoing theft of U.S. intellectual property is "the greatest transfer of wealth in history."[49]

While everyone acknowledges the scope and seriousness of IP thefts and reproductions throughout the world, disagreements abound as to how to deal with the crisis. Some claim it is counterproductive to attack or antagonize countries such as China that have weak IP protections but offer strong buyer-demand markets that promise to forever grow stronger. They claim that the IP theft crisis will gradually dissipate as countries with lesser-developed economies mature and discover the importance of protecting their own intellectual property.

On the other end of the spectrum are those who argue that the opportunity and actual costs of waiting for other countries to "get with it" are prohibitive and that now is the time for bold measures that "make the theft of U.S. intellectual property both risky and costly for thieves."[506] In the words of the co-chairs of the IP Commission, such measure would include: "denying products that contain stolen intellectual property access to the U.S. market; restricting use of the U.S. financial system by foreign companies that repeatedly steal intellectual property; and adding the correct, legal handling of intellectual property to the criteria for both investment in the United States under Committee for Foreign Investment in the United States (CFIUS) approval and for foreign companies that are listed on U.S. stock exchanges."[51] And, of course, there are many who advocate measures that fall between these two extremes.

2. IP Protection Tools

Patents

A patent grants exclusive rights by a country to an inventor of a product or process that helps solve a specific technological challenge. The primary right granted is the right to exclude others from using or dealing in the patented invention for a specified term (20 years from the date of filing in the U.S.). The tradeoff is that the patent must be disclosed to the world. Patent procedures, requirements and rights vary widely between countries, but generally all require a showing of novelty (new and not known), non-obviousness (differs from other items in a way not obvious to a person having ordinary skill in the area of

48. The IP Commission Report on the Theft of American Intellectual Property (May 2013).

49. Speech to American Enterprise Institute's conference entitled "Cybersecurity and American power", July 9, 2012.

50. Dennis Blair and Jon Huntsman Jr., *"Protecting U.S. Intellectual Property Rights"* The Washington Post (May 21, 2013).

51. Id.

technology related to the invention), and usefulness (must serve a useful purpose).

Patents have territorial limits, generally providing protection only in the country in which the patent is granted. The World Trade Organization has promoted the global harmonization of patent laws with its Agreement on Trade-Related Aspects of Intellectual Property Rights, which requires that patents for a minimum of 20 years be available in all WTO member states and that countries comply with the terms of the agreement as a condition for admission to the WTO.

In the United States, patents are issued by the United States Patent and Trademark Office, established by Congress under Title 35 of the United States Code. The patent application process can be slow (often two to four years) and costly. Costs vary widely depending on the nature of the required drawings and the scope and difficulty of the search required for the patent and the number of amendments during the process. Only an inventor may apply for a patent in the United States, but an inventor may assign all rights to a corporation or other business entity and may be subject to an employment or other agreement that requires such assignment. A provisional patent application may be filed before incurring the expense and hassle of a complete patent application; it establishes a priority filing date and gives the filer one year to complete and file a formal patent application.

Patents generally are enforced through civil litigation, with federal courts having jurisdiction in the United States. The patent holder has the burden of proving infringement, but is entitled to a rebuttable presumption that the patent is valid. A patent holder may seek monetary damages for prior infringement actions (based on lost profits or a reasonable royalty) and injunctive relief to prevent future infringing acts. A defendant has the right to challenge the validity of the patent through a counterclaim.

Royalties and other compensation rights often are generated through patent licensing agreements in which the patent holder grants a licensee specific exclusive or non-exclusive rights to exploit the patent and the related invention. Multiple license agreements for a single patent are common, and often companies, even competitors, cross-license their patents or "pool" their patents to maximize the effectiveness and profitability of their respective patents.

Historically, the scope of inventions that may be protected by a patent has grown to keep pace with technological developments, expanding for example to include items such as surgical procedures, business methods, asexual and select sexual reproducing plants, industrial designs, and software. Although software innovations were once considered non-patentable mathematical algorithms, a 1981 Supreme Court[52] decision upholding the patent on a computer-embedded, temperature-monitoring software program opened the door to an ever-growing volume of software patent applications. These developments put increasing pressures on the U.S Patent and Trademark Office as backlogs and time delays grew. By 2011, the backlog of patent applications had grown to over 715,000,

52. Diamond v. Diehr, 450 U.S. 175 (1981).

and the average time for approval or denial of an application was 34 months, making many patents functionally obsolete before they were granted.

The mounting patent process challenges led to the Leahy–Smith America Invents Act (AIA), which was signed into law on September 16, 2011 and has been heralded by many as the most significant change in American patent law since 1952. This law is designed to streamline the patent approval process by changing the "first-inventor-to-invent" basis of approval to a "first-inventor-to-file" (FITF) basis of approval for all applications filed after March 16, 2013. This fundamental change will eliminate many proceedings in the U.S. Patent Office for resolving priority disputes among competing applications for the same invention, but the AIA still provides for an administration "derivation" proceeding in select situations to ensure that the first person to file an application is the original inventor.

In addition to the new FITF basis of approval, the AIA makes other changes intended to improve the patent approval process. One of the most important expands the definition of actions before the filing date that may prevent patentability to include: public use; sales; publishing outside an approved grace period; and other disclosures available to the general public at any place in the world.

Disputes continue over the potential impacts of the new AIA. Many claim that the new FITI basis for approval will create a huge advantage for deep-pocket companies that have the IP expertise and resources to always file early, and that budget-conscious inventors and universities will be at a decided disadvantage. They also argue that the AIA's procedures make it easier for a well-funded patent infringer to challenge the validity of a patent. The feared result is that many inventors who lack the resources to mount a defense will be forced to abandon their patent claims. Others rebute these claims, arguing that the new provisions promote badly needed efficiencies that will benefit all who diligently seek to protect rights to their inventions.

There is no question that the new FITI approval basis and the expanded actions that bar patentability will push all inventors, large and small, to file at least a provisional patent application as early as possible. This may reduce or eliminate claims of others, hedge against the risk of knowingly or unknowingly taking a pre-filing action that cuts off any patent hopes, and permits and facilitates open dialogue and exploitation of the invention. Of course, as the dialogue and exploitation starts, the smart use of confidentiality agreements to protect related trade secrets is advisable in nearly all situations.

Copyrights

A copyright grants exclusive rights to works of authorship, such as books, movies, scripts, music, television productions, artwork, computer programs, training manuals, advertising materials, software codes, and other original works. Copyrights are not available for common items, such as names, slogans, familiar symbols, short phrases, lettering, listings of ingredients or contents, ideas, concepts, principles, and common property information (e.g., standard calendars, height and weight charts, etc.).

The owner of a copyright may prevent others from copying, using or making derivative versions of the protected work. There are various "fair use" exceptions to this blanket right for criticisms of the work, comments on the work and related news reporting, education and scholarship, research, preservation of the work, and controlled area retransmissions of the work. A copyright protects only how an idea is expressed; it does not protect the idea itself or information in the work. A copyright acquired by an individual lasts 70 years beyond the death of such individual. Copyrights may be sold, assigned and licensed.

A copyright comes into existence once the original work is written or fixed to a document, notes or other tangible medium or a performance of the work is recorded. Enactment of the Berne Convention Implementation Act of 1989 eliminated the requirement of a copyright notice, such as © with owner name and date of first publication. Most still use a notice because it informs the public that the work is protected by copyright, identifies the copyright owner, usually shows the year of first publication, and reduces the potential of a claim of innocent infringement to mitigate actual or statutory damages in a legal dispute relating to the copyright. The age-old practice of mailing a sealed copy of the original work to oneself by registered mail is still often used to establish a postmark date as proof of existence, but this practice has never been sanctioned in a published federal court opinion and the United States Copyright Office, a part of the Library of Congress, claims that this practice is no substitute for actual registration.

Although a copyright need not be registered with the Library of Congress through the United States Copyright Office, there are advantages to such registration, which may occur at any time during the life of the copyright. Such advantages include creating a public record of the copyright, permitting a federal court infringement action for works of U.S. origin, establishing prima facie evidence of the validity of the copyright (if registration occurs within five years of publication), establishing the right to statutory damages and attorney's fees in an infringement action (if registration occurs within three months of publication), and permitting registration with the U.S. Customs Service to protect against the importation of infringing works.

Copyrights are enforced through civil litigation. The plaintiff has the burden of proving ownership of a valid copyright and actionable copying by the defendant of original elements of the work. Potential remedies for the plaintiff include injunctive relief against future actions, recovery or seizure of the infringing work, and actual damages plus lost profits or statutory damages if the plaintiff timely registered the copyright. For injunction purposes, irreparable harm is usually presumed for the plaintiff's benefit once a prima facie case of infringement is established.

If statutory damages are requested by the plaintiff, the judge or jury has the discretion to award statutory damages ranging from a minimum of $750 to $30,000 for each infringed work, not the number of times a work is infringed. The maximum statutory damage award for each work jumps to $150,000 if the plaintiff can prove that the infringement was willful. Statutory damages may be reduced to as low as $200 per infringed work if the defendant can prove innocent infringement (i.e. that he or she did not know or have reason to know of the infringement).

Computer Chip Protections

A computer chip may not be protected by copyright because it is a useful product, but neither may it be protected as a patent because it lacks non-obviousness to any computer engineer. Given the universal importance of such chips (components of which are commonly referred to as a "Mask Work"), Congress enacted in 1984 the Semiconductor Chip Protection Act (SCPA) to provide mask work rights comparable to copyrights. To be protected under the Act, a mask work must be "original," which means that it must be an independent creation of an author that does not consist solely of designs that are staple, commonplace or familiar in the semiconductor industry or any combination of such designs that, considered as a whole, are not original.

Protection of rights under the SCPA requires registration with the U.S. Copyright Office within two years after the mask work is first exploited. The effective date of registration is the date on which the Copyright Office receives an application, a sample of identifying material, and the appropriate fee. Protection for a mask work begins on the earlier of the effective date of registration or the date of first commercially exploited use anywhere in the world, and the protection lasts for 10 years. Registration constitutes prima facie evidence of the facts stated in the certificate issued by the Copyright Office, gives the owner of the mask work the right to institute civil litigation to stop any infringement occurring after protection takes effect under the SCPA, and grants exclusive rights to reproduce, import or distribute a semiconductor chip in which the mask work is embodied. Use of the letter "M", often circled, is commonly used to give notice of protected rights in a to mask work.

Purchasers of semiconductor chips have the right to use and resell them freely but not to reproduce them without the permission of the owner of the mask work embodied in the products. Exclusive rights to mask works may be licensed, assigned or sold and transferred by operation of law or through intestate succession or by the terms of a will or living trust.

Trademarks and Trade Dress

A trademark includes any device, brand, label, name, signature, word, letter, numerical symbol, shape of goods, packaging, color or combination of colors, smell, or similar characteristic that distinguishes goods and services of one business from those of other businesses. Common terms to describe a trademark are "brand," "logo," or "mark." The primary federal statute governing trademarks is the Lanham Trademark Act, codified at 15 U.S.C. § 1051 et seq. which, among other things, prohibits trademark infringement, trademark dilution, and trademark-related false advertising.

A trademark must be distinctive, not be confusingly similar to other marks, and not be a generic term (e.g., chocolate bar, floor mop) that describes a type of product. It must also be capable of graphic representation and applied to the goods, or be used in connection with the services, to which it relates. Special types of trademarks include certification marks (which evidence agreements with national testing and certification organizations), collective marks (which evidence association with an industry or other group), and service marks (identifies a service, not a product). A trademark is characterized as "defensive" when an owner uses it for specific goods or services and also registers it to apply to secondary goods or services not offered by the owner in order to prevent use by others who offer such secondary other goods or services.

Closely related to trademarks is trade dress, which is the legal term generally used to refer to the visual appearance of a product or its packaging that signifies the source of the product to consumers. Trade dress will be protected only if it is distinctive and non-functional. Trade dress also is governed by the Lanham Act and generally subject to the same registration and enforcement options applicable to trademarks.

There is no requirement that a trademark be registered, and unregistered marks (often denoted by the letters "TM" for goods and "SM" for services) may be enforced. However, a mark may be registered at the state level, and federal registration with the Patent and Trademark Office (denoted by the symbol ®) is often advisable because it provides public notice of the registrant's claim of ownership, creates a legal presumption of ownership nationwide, and helps secure the exclusive right to use the mark on or in connection with the goods or services listed in the registration. Federal registration requires an intention to use the mark in interstate commerce and actual use of the mark before registration. The registration process consists of: filing of a completed application; review by the Patent and Trademark Office within three months to ensure rule's compliance and no conflicts or confusion with existing registered marks; feedback regarding any required corrections to the application; a 30-day "published for opposition" period during which third parties may file for an "opposition proceeding" to trigger a dispute to be resolved by the Trademark Trial and Appeal Board; and finally registration of the mark if there is no opposition or the case is decided in favor of the applicant.

Rights to a trademark or trade dress may be enforced through civil litigation. The basis of the complaint may be illegal infringement (unauthorized use of the mark or a confusingly similar mark), trademark dilution (loss in value or uniqueness of the mark or tarnishing the mark through its unauthorized use on non-competitive products), or false advertising (unauthorized use of the mark in false or misleading advertising). Remedies typically include injunctive relief and damages for willful misconduct. Factors that often impact the strength of the plaintiff's case are the registration of the trademark, the similarity of the trademarks involved, the nature and similarity of the products or services involved, and the popularity and strength of the plaintiff's mark. Although there is no requirement to prove that the alleged infringer acted willfully or with an intention to deceive, such evidence often is the key to a significant damage recovery.

Common defenses in trademark litigation include trademark abandonment by the plaintiff, limitations on the geographic scope of the trademark rights, and fair use by the defendant. Fair use may be established by the alleged infringer showing that the mark was used to accurately describe its own product or service ("I service only BMWs"), to identify the owner of the mark, or for comparative advertising purposes ("our used cars are better than a used Mercedes").

The Internet has spawned a slew of trademark challenges, including the registration of a domain name that incorporates a mark owned by another ("cybersquatting"), registering a domain name that slightly mistypes a mark owned by another to drive traffic to a competitor ("typosquatting"), using marks of others in hidden tags and search engine designs to drive traffic to a particular site, and using trademarks to strengthen bulk email campaigns. Internet-based trademark problems are exacerbated by the global reach of the Internet and the inherent problems of enforcement and poor or nonexistent regulation in many countries.

In the U.S., the worst Internet abuses were addressed by The Anticybersquatting Consumer Protection Act (ACPA), which was enacted in 1999 and established a new cause of action for registering, trafficking in, or using a domain name confusingly similar to, or dilutive of, a trademark or personal name. The statute is designed to thwart cybersquatters who register Internet domain names containing trademarks with an intention to sell the domain name to the trademark owner or a third party.

Under the ACPA, the owner of a trademark may bring a cause of action against a domain name registrant who has a bad faith intent to profit from the trademark and registers, traffics in, or uses a domain name identical or confusingly similar to the trademark. The statutory prohibitions extend to any distinctive or "famous" trademark and any trademark related to the Red Cross or the Olympics. A trademark is deemed famous if it "is widely recognized by the general consuming public of the United States as a designation of source of the goods or services of the mark's owner."

The term "trafficking" is broadly defined to include "sales, purchases, loans, pledges, licenses, exchanges of currency, and any other transfer for consideration or receipt in exchange for consideration." A court may consider many factors in finding a "bad faith intent to profit" within the meaning of the ACPA, including: the extent to which the mark in the domain is distinctive or famous; whether the domain name contains the mark owner's legal or common name; use of the domain name in connection with a bona fide offering of goods or services; an intent to divert customers to harm the goodwill represented by the mark or to tarnish or disparage the mark; an offer to transfer or sell the domain name to the mark owner or a third party for financial gain, without having used the mark in a legitimate site; use of misleading or false contact information when applying for registration of the domain name; and the acquisition of multiple domain names that are identical or confusingly similar to marks of others.

Trade Secrets

A trade secret is a secret owned and used by a business and is often referred to as confidential information. It might be a formula, practice, process, design, instrument, pattern, or compilation of information used by a business to secure or maintain an economic advantage over competitors. The key elements of a trade secret are: it is not be generally known to the public; it confers an economic benefit on its owner by virtue of its secrecy, not just from the value of the information itself; and its secrecy is protected by reasonable efforts of its owner. Unlike a patent, the life of a trade secret right is indefinite if the owner can preserve its secrecy.

The Supreme Court's landmark 1974 decision in *Kewanee Oil Co. v. Bicron Corp.*[53] paved the way for states to adopt their own trade secret laws. Nearly all states have now adopted some version of the Uniform Trade Secrets Act, which is designed to provide a legal framework that will better protect the trade secret rights of U.S. companies operating in multiple states. At the federal level, the Economic Espionage Act of 1996[54] criminalizes the theft of a trade secret to benefit a foreign power or for commercial or economic purposes.

Efforts to protect a trade secret often include: non-competition and confidentiality agreements with executives and employees; confidential policies for all employees; non-disclosure and confidentiality covenants in agreements, licenses and engagement undertakings with third parties; and procedures that compel employees to assign to the business all intellectual property rights related to their employment and maintain the secrecy of such rights. The owner of a trade secret may enforce such agreements through civil litigation or arbitration proceedings authorized by the agreements. Remedies often include injunctive relief (irreparable harm is usually stipulated in the agreement or covenant), accounting for profits, an award of damages, or declaratory relief that settles the respective rights of the parties.

Enforcement of trade secret rights against others who learn of and exploit the secret for financial gain, but who are not subject to any agreement or covenant with the owner of the rights, can be difficult if not impossible. In order to prevail, the owner of the rights must prove actions that establish an illegal misappropriation of the secret, such as theft, fraud, espionage, bribery, kickbacks, incentivized breaches of fiduciary duties, or other similar bad acts. An action cannot be maintained against a party who learns of the secret through lawful means, even aggressive actions related to competitive intelligence research, reverse engineering of a competitor's product, or hiring a competitor's employees.

D. EMPLOYMENT PRACTICES

Few businesses can survive without the loyal support of dedicated employees. But nearly all business owners appreciate (or certainly should appreciate) that the challenge goes beyond motivation and management. Laws have continually evolved to give employees more rights; and these rights pose risks for the uninformed business owner who is determined to run the show just as he or she did 20 years ago. Plus, because companies are responsible for the actions of their employees and the scope of potential liabilities is broad, many companies need to be proactive in minimizing their exposures for the

53. 416 U.S. 470 (1974).
54. 18 U.S.C. §§ 1831–1839.

unauthorized actions of their employees. Following are examples of steps that business owners and executives often take to minimize the risks posed by these dual challenges.

1. EMPLOYEES' RIGHTS AND BUSINESS SAFEGUARDS

Once upon a time the law was clear. An employer could discharge an employee at any time for any reason without notice. This employment "at will" doctrine was the standard.

Uncertainty and new risks have set in. While most employers believe they operate under the "at will" doctrine as regards their employees, the company takes a risk every time it terminates an employee. Wrongful discharge suits have popped up with increasing frequency throughout the country. Many employee victories have been publicized. New laws have been made in the courts and the legislatures, chipping away at the old "at will" standard. Each victory and law change has provided incentives to aggrieved, discharged employees and lawyers who are willing to fight their cases. Many companies have had to endure the pain of paying big legal fees to defend the termination, only to pay more when the employee prevails.

The operative word is "caution" when hiring and firing employees. Employment handbooks, application forms and other key documents should specifically state that the company has an "at will" termination policy. Any language that suggests that employment is "permanent" or that a discharge requires a showing of "good cause" should be deleted. It also is advisable to have each new employee specifically sign a statement acknowledging that the "at will" standard is used in the business. If the company uses a probationary employment period for new employees, great care should be taken to specifically document that completion of the probationary period of employment does not grant any special tenure rights.

Managers and supervisors should be appropriately advised of the risks involved in terminating employees. Federal laws prohibit discrimination on the basis of race, creed, color, religion, sex, national origin, citizenship status, sexual orientation, disability, and age. States have statutes that extend to most or all of these protected classes. These are high-risk areas. Any termination should be based on factors devoid of any actual or apparent prejudice or bias.

A termination decision should never be based on a desire to retaliate against an employee who has exercised a legitimate right, even if the exercise is contrary to the best interests of the company. In many states, retaliation against such an employee will be viewed as a violation of public policy and provide a basis for a wrongful discharge suit.

Supervisors and managers should be cautioned against making oral or written statements that might imply any right of permanent employment or a discharge standard of good cause. Many courts have recognized that an employee may acquire an implied contractual right to employment as a result of all the circumstances relating to the particular individual's employment. Irresponsible statements can aggravate the problem by creating a false sense of employment security.

Most companies have procedures for periodically evaluating an employee's performance and providing feedback to the employee. The procedures should be structured so they can be followed and easily implemented. If the company fails to comply with its own procedures, the employee may have a case. The key is to be realistic in drafting the procedures and tenacious in following them. It is important that managers and supervisors be candid in communicating job performance evaluations to employees. Over-sensitivity to the feelings of an employee may boomerang at a later date.

The basis for the termination should be documented in a written statement. If a fight breaks out, the company will be unable to advance grounds for the termination that were not presented to the employee at the critical time. The basis for the termination should be carefully thought out, documented and communicated in detail to the employee. There is no need to be brutal, but honesty and candor should be the primary considerations.

Terminating a difficult employee is a challenge that all business owners face sooner or later. If the task is not handled properly, the hurt and frustration of the employee will be aggravated, and the risk of a wrongful discharge lawsuit increases. Some key tips: try never to fire an employee on a birthday or some other personal date that may aggravate the situation for the employee; detail the evidence that supports the basis for the termination; carefully lay out what is going to be said to the employee in advance, do not mince words or beat around the bush, and stick to the script; select a neutral territory (e.g., conference room) that reduces the risk of a protracted discussion that cannot be comfortably terminated; identify in advance any fact that might lead to the appearance of an "ambush" and complicate the termination, such as a grievance filed by the employee against the company or a bonus that the employee is on the verge of earning; anticipate and address important collateral impacts of the termination, such as vacation time, accrued sick pay, severance pay, recommendation letters, health insurance benefits, and other items that need to be addressed; carefully listen to what the employee says in response to the termination (first reactions may be very important in any subsequent dispute) and avoid any temptation or invitation to engage in a debate; take good notes and document the entire experience from beginning to end.

Companies often work to avoid "quid pro quo" and "environmental" sexual harassment problems and properly handle any complaints. Best practices include: developing a clear, written policy against sexual harassment that forbids specific conduct directed against employees, vendors, job applicants, sales representatives and others involved in the company; repeatedly reminding all employees, especially supervisors, that both forms of sexual harassment are prohibited; adopting where appropriate a policy that prohibits supervisors from dating those directly subject to their supervision; developing procedures that encourage employees to report harassment problems, ensure timely, thorough and consistent responses, and prohibit any type of retaliatory action against an employee who has filed a sexual harassment claim, even if the claim is frivolous; regularly inspecting the workplace for potentially offensive materials; and conducting exit interviews for all employees who leave the company.

Companies should take great care in preparing an employee handbook that communicates to employees the expectations of the company, the benefits of employment, and the company's policies regarding employment and other critical issues. This usually includes: using a "no contract" disclaimer that clarifies that the handbook is intended and designed to provide information and does not constitute a binding contractual commitment between the company and its employees; eliminating any confusing or fuzzy language relating to an employee's rights to continued employment; having each employee specifically acknowledge a statement that employment is "at the will" of the company and that no supervisor or other employee has the authority to alter the "at will" termination standard; avoiding the specification of procedures the company may not be able to consistently follow or the use of statements that boast about the company; and ensuring that the handbook is broad enough in scope to addresses the important issues for the company and its employees.

2. *PROTECTING THE BUSINESS FROM EMPLOYEES' ACTIONS*

The challenge of protecting a business from acts of its employees is raised in a number of contexts. Nearly every business is dependent upon imperfect, fallible human resources. The law exacts a price for the privilege of hiring employees. Perhaps it's more accurate to say that it extracts a responsibility. In general, the company is responsible and liable for those acts of its employees that are carried out within the scope of their employment. This is a true vicarious liability. It is one of the broadest forms of vicarious, third-party liability in the law. The company may be fully liable, even though it had no direct involvement with, or knowledge of, the event creating the problem. Historically, many have simply concluded that, since the responsibility exists, there is nothing that can be done about it. But increasingly, companies are taking affirmative steps to mitigate their exposure.

The company's vicarious liability can become a reality in countless ways. In most instances, the liability pops up because an employee has committed one of four wrongs. The first and perhaps most pervasive is when an employee exceeds his or her authority in making a deal on behalf of the company, or goes beyond that authority in representing the interests of the company.

The second wrong occurs when an employee, in the process of carrying out his or her duties, negligently or recklessly injures another party. It may be an injury to the other party's person, property, reputation, career or existing contractual rights. Some third party ends up injured, and the company ends up being responsible because an employee negligently or recklessly caused the injury while acting on behalf of the business.

The third is where the employee ignores or violates a black letter law that has been established for the good of all. The employee refuses to hire someone on the basis of his or her sex, or fires someone on account of age. The employee fixes prices with a competitor. The employee ignores basic environmental regulations. The employee sexually harasses a co-worker. Whatever the event, when this condition exists, usually some combination of greed, bigotry and ignorance is at the root of the problem.

The fourth wrong is the worst and rarest. It's intentional misconduct that, in some cases, may rise to the level of criminal conduct. Fraud is probably the most common example. But there are many others: bribery, extortion, embezzlement, malicious slander, insider trading, unlawful disposal of hazardous waste and a host of others. These are the ugliest employee circumstances business owners dread having to deal with. Fortunately, most business owners never experience this dark side.

A business owner can take steps to reduce or mitigate the scope of the liability that may be created by employees. A few of the more common ones that have developed over time are described below, with no effort made to analyze the fine points of the law relating to masters and servants and principals and agents.

The whole concept of employer vicarious liability turns on the scope of the employee's authority or employment. If an employee injures another outside the scope of employment, there generally is no employer liability. But if the employee is within the scope of his or her duties, the liability will pass to the employer. Therefore, it is advisable for a business owner to define the scope of the employment for each employee. In most businesses, the best way to define the scope is through carefully prepared job descriptions. In those situations where it is impractical to fashion a specific job description for every employee, a description for classes of employees may be necessary and certain prohibitions may be included in the employee manual. A reasonable effort should be made to craft a specific job description for each key executive employee whose primary responsibility is to interface with outsiders on behalf of the company.

If an employee creates a problem by going beyond the scope of his or her authority, the business owner should act fast in determining whether steps are needed to repudiate the actions of the employee. The emphasis here is on speed. Delay and equivocation may result in de facto approval or ratification of the unauthorized act. If, for example, a particular executive makes an offer that is outside the scope of his or her authority, fast action may enable the company to revoke the offer before it is accepted and ripens into a contract. In rare situations, it may be necessary to fire the irresponsible employee to appropriately evidence the business owner's repudiation of the employee's actions, particularly if the employee has been totally irresponsible, has been compromised by a conflict of interest, or has acted in bad faith. Expulsion also may be required if the employee has demonstrated a pattern of unauthorized conduct that is likely to continue. By acting swiftly and decisively, the business owner may cut off exposure for future acts and create a basis for disclaiming some responsibility for prior acts, on the grounds that the employee was clearly acting outside the scope of his or her authority.

In business, titles go a long way in defining the scope of a particular employee's authority. Many business owners are careless with their titles. They figure titles are cheap, so they can be generous with them. The result is that many employees end up over-titled. This can present two problems from a liability perspective. First, the over-titled employee may focus on the title and start acting like a bigger deal than he or she really is. An employee who has an inflated image of his or her importance and role in the business can be dangerous. Second, it is common practice in the business world to rely on the title of an individual in assessing the scope of that individual's authority. By giving the title, the business owner may be presumed to have given the authority. It may be difficult or practically impossible for the owner to disclaim the authority on the theory that the company never intended to give the broad-based authority the title suggested.

Checking the backgrounds of prospective employees during the hiring process is a smart precautionary task in many businesses. Some employees are trouble wherever they go. They can't play by the rules. They are always looking for shortcuts. Over-reacting, overstating, and risk-taking are compulsions. Sooner or later, they end up creating a problem for the business owner. Often it is hard to get a handle on this factor. Whenever possible, prior employers (listed or not as personal references) should be contacted. Background checks can be critical in some situations, particularly where an employee is regularly exposed to members of the public. Some employers have found themselves facing a charge of "negligent hiring" made by an injured third party. The charge is that the employer should have checked and determined that the particular employee posed an undue risk because of a social, mental or physical disorder. Obviously there are limits on how far any business owner can go in checking out a prospective employee. The lesson is to be sensitive to the company's needs, to watch for danger signs in the hiring process, and to do that amount of checking that is reasonable and practical under the circumstances.

When the business owner delineates the authority and scope of activities of the employees, the word needs to be spread — not only to the employees impacted, but also to those who are responsible for supervising and monitoring the activities of the employees. Hidden, undisclosed limitations will be ineffective. In certain instances, it may even be necessary to contact parties outside the business and inform them of limitations that have been placed on certain employees or to warn prospective customers that employees and agents of the company have no authority to make verbal representations or warranties outside of those specifically provided in writing by the company. In preliminary contract negotiations, it may be necessary to advise the other side that the company negotiators have no authority to bind the company to any specified set of terms and conditions, and that another layer of review and approval exists. Spreading the word when necessary helps define the limits of the authority, reminds the employee of those limits, and puts third parties on notice.

It is helpful to periodically emphasize to all employees six things that generally should never be done.

1. Never talk or even joke about the possibility of hiring, firing or promoting on the basis of race, sex, age, national origin, disability, sexual orientation, or religion. Sensitivity is the name of the game on this issue.

2. Never discuss or attempt to resolve a conflict with the other side's lawyer.

Many lawyers develop a knack for getting others to make admissions that will embarrass them when the dispute ripens. It is generally a good idea to advise all employees that when the other guy brings in a lawyer, you bring in yours.

3. Never encourage another party to breach a contract. This one recognizes that there is a difference between healthy competition in attempting to secure a contract and new business, and openly encouraging another party to breach an existing contract with a third party. Many successful people have a hard time determining where selling ends and interference with contractual relationships begins. In some situations, the distinction is a bright light that is simply ignored. This can result in undue liability exposure. There is nothing inappropriate about hustling business from a party who is about to rightfully terminate a contract or is a party to a contract that is ready to expire. It is a different matter when that party is being encouraged and enticed to actually breach an existing contractual relationship.

4. Never sign what you do not fully understand. Each employee should be instructed against the fear of appearing ignorant for not understanding the implication of a particular document. The lesson is to seek out appropriate counsel and advice on what the document actually says. When a dispute hits, the written word becomes all-important.

5. Never discuss with a competitor or prospective competitor any matter involving prices, existing or potential market divisions, or existing or potential actions or plans to not do business with (boycott) a third party. The Sherman Act is always lurking. Lawyers love it. An aggrieved party can recover treble damages and attorney fees.

6. Never ignorantly look the other way. Some business owners have an employee who routinely breaks the rules, but who gets results. It is tempting sometimes to look the other way, take the risk of the liability exposure, and enjoy the benefits. What is important is not to be ignorant in assessing the magnitude of the risks. Look hard at the stakes before assessing the odds. There are some 2-percent risks that should never be taken because the consequences are so utterly severe that they could mean an end to the business. Other 50-percent risks can be taken all day because the consequence are not severe in light of the potential benefits to be obtained. An intelligent risk analysis is required. Looking the other way can be dangerous, particularly if it is done ignorantly.

Smart employers do not assume their employees know or appreciate basic laws or are sensitive to the risks they may create for the company. Some areas of potential liability may require special education, such as price-fixing risks, hazardous waste disposal risks, employment discrimination, sexual harassment, and the like. Other areas of potential liability require one basic reminder: stay within your authority and be careful. Some employees may need to be periodically reminded of their own personal liability if they wrongfully create a liability for the company. Many figure that since it's the company's problem, it can't be their problem also. This is faulty thinking. If an employee creates a problem, that employee will be in the middle of it all and, in most cases, will personally be on the hook.

In many situations, reducing employee turnover can be the most important step in limiting liability exposures. A stable, seasoned workforce is much safer than one that experiences high turnover rates. Many factors can impact employee dissatisfaction and turnover rates. Some, such as the nature of the work or opportunities for career advancement, may be beyond the control of the owners of the business. But other critical factors, including the company's interest in the well-being of its employees, its vision for the future, and its willingness to embrace its employees as valued teammates, not expendable commodities, are completely within the control of management. There are many important steps that management can take in setting policy and operating day-to-day to bind and motivate employees. The rewards for employees go far beyond any additional compensation they might net. The despair of complacency and an obsession to give only the minimum can soon disappear. Definable, measurable stakes in the effort can trigger an expanded purpose, a growing desire to excel and be careful, and an ongoing push to elevate the performance of the entire group.

There are three myths that often permeate discussion about a company's liability for the acts of its employees. These myths can provide a false sense of security and divert attention from the real issues.

First, some business owners believe that if they make an employee an independent contractor, they can escape liability for that employee's activities. While it is true that a business owner may have less responsibility for true independent contractors (such as outside accountants and lawyers), the answer is not to make employees independent contractors. Titles alone won't do the job. If a person is designated as an independent contractor, but the business owner retains the right to control and supervise that person's conduct, the liability will be just as great as it would have been had the person been called an "employee." There also are down sides to over-using the independent contractor title. The business owner may develop a false sense of security and end up foolishly granting the disguised employees additional rope with which to hang themselves and the company. There also may be tax problems. Independent contractors are required to pay their own income, self-employment and state business taxes. If they fail to pay these taxes and it is established that in reality they were the equivalent of employees, the business owner may end up with a serious tax problem.

Second, some wrongfully believe that liability exposure can be eliminated by immediately firing an employee who caused the problem. This is a gross over-generalization. As discussed above, there may be extreme circumstances where an employee needs to be terminated in order to protect the business against future problems. But there is no assurance that terminating the employee will absolve the business of responsibility for prior acts committed by that employee, and this myth may precipitate a needless termination.

Finally, some business owners mistakenly assume they are home free if they can demonstrate their own ignorance of the matter. It is natural for many to assume that they can't be liable for something that they did not know anything about. It's a true myth. As a general proposition, ignorance is no defense.

E. THE EVOLUTION OF ESTATE AND MULTI-ENTITY PLANNING

As the gap between the haves and have-nots has forever widened along with a growing perception that wealth-generating opportunities are becoming harder to identify and exploit, family planning has become increasingly important for business owners, executives and professionals who want to transition their wealth to future generations. The complexity of the challenge often is enhanced by the need to use multiple entities to accomplish key business and family objectives.

1. THE GOALS AND PROCESS

Smart multi-entity planning can be used to accomplish many purposes: ensure privacy; protect assets from liability exposures; fund college educations and getting-started money for existing and future descendants; limit or control value growth; scatter wealth among family members; segregate asset-based yields from operation-based risks and yields; shift or defer income; enhance tax benefits from recognized losses; facilitate business exit planning; satisfy liquidity needs; and promote a structured discipline that helps protect all family members.

And of course, such planning can eliminate or significantly reduce estate and gift taxes for those exposed to such taxes. Today, the great bulk of families need not worry about federal estate and gift taxes because the value of their estates are below the thresholds that are tax-protected by their unified credits[55] ($10.680 million for a couple and $5.340 million for an individual in 2014). But for those with estates above such thresholds (usually business owners, entrepreneurs and executives), the excess value is subject to a 40-percent tax hit at the federal level. The projected tax math often is a frightening reality for those with substantial estates. In addition to the federal taxes, 21 states have an estate or inheritance tax with (here's the bad news) a tax-protected threshold much lower than the federal threshold and (here's the good news) rates that are much lower than the 40 percent federal rate.

Multi-entity planning complicates the process, but the benefits usually far outweigh any burdens of added complexity. Often the use of multiple entities promotes an understanding of the different planning challenges and objectives because each entity is being used for specific purposes. The entity options are not limited to the business entity forms; they also include a broad menu of different trusts that can be used to promote targeted objectives.

The planning usually becomes more important and more challenging when a successful family business needs to be transitioned to the next generation. Today, family transition planning is big business. Oft quoted statistics say it all. Family dominated businesses comprise more than 80 percent of U.S. enterprises, employ more than 50 percent of the nation's workforce, and account for the bulk (some estimate as much as 64 percent) of America's gross domestic product.[56]

---

55. The estate tax unified credit under IRC § 2010 is $5.25 million for 2013 and, under the Taxpayer Relief Act of 2012, is adjusted for inflation each year.

56. See generally R. Duman, "Family Firms Are Different," Entrepreneurship Theory and Practice, 1992, pp. 13–21; and M. F. R. Kets de Vries, "The Dynamics of Family Controlled Firms: The Good News and the

And although more than 80 percent of the senior family owners claim they want the business to stay in the family, less than 30 percent acknowledge having a transition plan.[57] The result is that most family businesses remain in the family, but at a dear cost. Best estimates are that less than 30 percent of family dominated businesses survive a second generation, and the survival rate is even uglier for businesses that make it to generation three.[58]

Strategic transition planning takes time, energy, and a willingness to grapple with tough family, tax and financial issues. It cannot make a weak business strong or provide any guarantees of survival. But it can trigger an analytical process that prompts a frank assessment of available options, facilitates better long-term decision making, and saves taxes.

The plan design process for each family necessarily must be detail oriented, strategic, and forward-focused. Care must be exercised to avoid planning traps and the temptation to tack on complicated strategies that offer little or nothing for the particular family. Each situation is unique and should be treated as such. There is no slam-dunk solution; all strategies have limitations and disadvantages that mandate careful evaluation, and some pose risks or legal uncertainties that many can't stomach. Above all, the specific objectives of the family must drive the planning process. Once identified, the objectives must be prioritized to facilitate an effective analysis of the trade-offs and compromises that inevitably surface in the planning process. The ultimate goal is to design a plan that effectively accomplishes the highest priority objectives over a period of time and at a level of complexity that works for the family.

A successful business owner once explained, "It's not the hunt that excites; it's the spoils from the effort, the rewards of success." For some owners, this simple statement says it all. The prospect of acquiring "enough" personal wealth is why they put it all on the line every day to build a successful business. These individuals, the wealth managers, long for the time and freedom to enjoy their rewards with the comfort of knowing that all bases are covered and their descendants will have a substantial financial base.

On the other end of the spectrum are those who can't focus beyond the chase. For them, the real thrill is in the hunt — the challenge of first making it happen and then proving, time and again, that they still "have it." Why else would *so* many who have *so* much keep taking risks to conquer bigger prey? For these entrepreneurs, the rush is in the victory and scoping out the next target, not in figuring out how to enjoy the last kill. Personal wealth accumulation is just a wonderful byproduct of their efforts, the ultimate trophy. Their happiness is in chasing trophies. Many successful business owners, perhaps most, fall

---

Bad News," Organizational Dynamics, 1993, pp. 59–71; W. G. Dyer, Cultural Change in Family Firms, Jossey–Bass, San Francisco, 1986; and P. L. Rosenblatt, M. R. Anderson and P. Johnson, The Family in Business, Jossey–Bass, San Francisco, 1985; Arthur Anderson/Mass Mutual, American Family Business Survey, 2002.

57. Id. The survey also indicated that (1) only 56 percent of the respondents have a written strategic business plan, (2) nearly 64 percent do not require that family members entering the business have any qualifications or business experience, and (3) 25 percent do not believe that the next generation is competent to move into leadership roles.

58. J. I. Ward, Keeping the Family Business Healthy, Jossey–Bass, San Francisco, 1987. This study suggests that the survival rate to generation three is less than 15 percent.

somewhere between these extremes. The rewards of wealth management are alluring, but they have a little trophy-chasing in their blood.

Where a business owner or entrepreneur sits on this spectrum can have a powerful impact in the planning process. Nearly all can embrace planning challenges that directly impact their business interests. But big differences begin to surface when the planning extends beyond the business to matters of family and intergenerational wealth preservation. Pure wealth managers are eager for the challenge — each component is viewed as another opportunity to get to the finish line faster. Some compulsive trophy-chasers are impossible. Their potential demise isn't a possibility worthy of serious discussion. Business challenges are viewed as comfortable, exciting opportunities; family challenges are uncomfortable, impossible burdens. When they do think beyond the next deal, they figure, "If I just keep raking it in, all will work out." Sometimes they are right, even when big saving opportunities are lost all along the way. And, of course, there are all those in the middle, some with wealth manager tendencies and others who naturally shy away from anything that isn't all business.

There is no magic answer for the hardcore trophy-chaser, but there are steps that can be taken to make it easier for business owners, executives and entrepreneurs to make the all-important planning leap to issues of family and intergenerational wealth preservation.

First, this is one situation where simple, user-friendly educational tools and basic knowledge often can work wonders. The core problem in most cases is ignorance. Many owners understand complicated business issues, but really know nothing about the "estate planning malarkey" they have heard about in the past. And they figure there is no efficient, easy way to "get up to speed," let alone ponder the family dynamics that will impact tough decisions. Even modest replacements of base ignorance with simple understanding may ignite an interest that quickly shreds old barriers.

Second, often it is counterproductive to make tax fears the sole or centerpiece focus of the planning process. All business owners accept taxes as a reality. If the sole or primary focus is the potential of a smaller tax bite when the owner is gone, there may not be enough sizzle to trigger uncomfortable action now. Usually it helps to lead with business, family and charitable challenges. Taxes should be an important, but distant, priority in the process.

Third, often it helps to promote an understanding that there are options for dealing with control issues. Wealth transfer talk often induces a fear that others will have unfettered control over assets that have always been in the sole dominion and control of the business owner. The owner hatches visions of adult children buying BMWs or the owner having to ask permission to chase the next trophy. Although some recent tax trends clearly favor less owner control in select situations, many options exist for ensuring that the owner's control fears are properly addressed.

Fourth, it usually helps to make all the planning business-focused. Usually little or nothing is accomplished by acknowledging a distinction between business and estate planning — a distinction that gets very blurry and loses much of its significance with a business owner, executive or entrepreneur. It's all planning; and since the business activities are an integral part of everything, it's all about business. An integrated planning approach often helps promote understanding and keep everyone focused on the right targets.

Fifth, it helps when affirmative steps are taken to make the added complexity as understandable as possible. Usually the starting point is basis objectives. Examples: I want privacy when I die; I want to make sure my grandchildren have their college educations funded; I want to do something for my alma mater; I want my kids treated fairly; I want my business and my assets, to the extent possible, protected from unforeseen liabilities. Simplifying the objective identification process up front will allow the process to start. As it develops, specific, tougher family challenges can be tackled along the way.

Once the process starts and specific planning vehicles (e.g., family partnerships, dynasty trusts) are considered, it helps to focus first on the purpose and impacts of a vehicle, not the technical challenges of making it work. When the owner understands what the vehicle does and how it might impact future business matters, any necessary technical dialogue can occur without losing sight of the big picture.

Finally, a picture of what the plan (integrated for both the business and the family) will look like and how it will work often is used. For many business owners, this simple picture is worth many more than a thousand words. It becomes their ultimate planning cheat sheet. They have a tool that instantly reminds them of the purpose and function of each piece. Many quickly commit the picture to memory. Instead of being viewed as undue complexity, the multiple entities are viewed as tools used to accomplish specific purposes. An example of such a simple picture is included in the following section.

The purpose here is to introduce students to the concept and importance of multi-entity planning, not to present a mini estate-planning presentation. The following section presents a short case study, a brief summary of how one successful couple used multiple entities to develop a plan to meet their various business and family objectives.

2. *AN EXAMPLE OF MULTI-ENTITY PLANNING*

Duncan and Sandy Smith, both age 62, have built an estate valued at approximately $24 million. They have three children, all married and in their 30's. They have six grandchildren and hope to pick up one or two more. Duncan generates a substantial income in a consulting business ("Consulting") that he operates through a C corporation. He also is a one-third owner of a company ("Holding"), operated as an S corporation holding company that has a light manufacturing subsidiary and a distribution subsidiary. He plays an important role in the upper management and strategic decisions of Holding, but is not an employee. Sandy has always had an eye for quality real estate, principally raw land and small commercial properties. The couple owns two homes (in different states) and has significant stock and bond portfolios. The Smith's children and their spouses are all college-educated and gainfully employed; but none of them, as yet, has exhibited any of the entrepreneurial interests that have always driven

Duncan and Sandy.

The Smiths have always been planners, but their serious planning started eight years ago. They identified the following 10 objectives at that time, which remain the focus of their planning:

- Ensure that they always will have sufficient income and wealth for their personal needs, that they will never become a financial burden for their children, and that their privacy will be maintained with as little hassle as possible.
- Ensure that their estate ultimately is shared equally by their children.
- Establish a wealth accumulation program for each child that will provide a supplemental source of income and be protected from the claims of creditors and the exposures of divorce.
- Establish a wealth accumulation program for each grandchild that will help fund higher education expenses and potentially provide some "getting started" support (e.g., a home down payment).
- Provide their college alma maters with significant gifts that will fund in the future.
- Defer any estate tax liabilities as long as possible, preferably until the death of the survivor of Duncan or Sandy.
- Minimize estate taxes by leveraging their annual gift tax exclusions, unified credits, generation skipping tax exemptions, and available transfer discounts, without compromising their other objectives.
- Ensure that their estate always has adequate liquidity, including sufficient liquidity to cover all estate taxes.
- Minimize income and self-employment taxes.
- Where possible, protect assets from exposure to unforeseen liabilities.

Duncan and Sandy have implemented a plan to accomplish these objectives. A simple diagram of the plan components is set forth on the following page. Following is a brief description of each component (moving clockwise from the top of the diagram) and how it serves specific objectives.

Living Trust

The living trust is revocable. As such, it's a tax nullity. It holds title to Duncan and Sandy's assets. Its purpose is to eliminate the hassles and expense of probate (in their primary residence state and in any ancillary jurisdictions where they own real estate) and to protect the privacy of their affairs on death (with no probate, there is no public record of their holdings). The trust is established by transferring property to the designated trustees, Duncan and Sandy. Duncan and Sandy are also the initial sole beneficiaries of the trust. No probate is required if a trustee dies. The trust's terms specify who will be the successor trustee or establish a mechanism for appointing a successor trustee. The new trustee steps in and takes over the trust. No title transfer of property is required.

Key provisions in the living trust agreement include: directions on the trustees' authority and how the trustees are to manage the trust assets; designation of successor beneficiaries on the deaths of Duncan or Sandy and future beneficiaries; limited liability and indemnification protections for the trustees; trustee compensation rights; support options for future beneficiaries who are minors; accounting, reporting and other administrative matters; and the establishment of a family credit trust and an irrevocable qualified terminal interest property trust ("QTIP") on the death of the first spouse. These trusts will eliminate estate taxes on the first death, provide the surviving spouse with a regular income stream and principal invasion rights as needed, protect the deceased spouse's remainder disposition preferences, provide optional support rights for children and grandchildren during the life of the surviving spouse, and provide some creditor protection benefits.

Duncan and Sandy also each have a will that pours over to the living trust any non-trust assets they own at death.

Duncan and Sandy Smith Plan

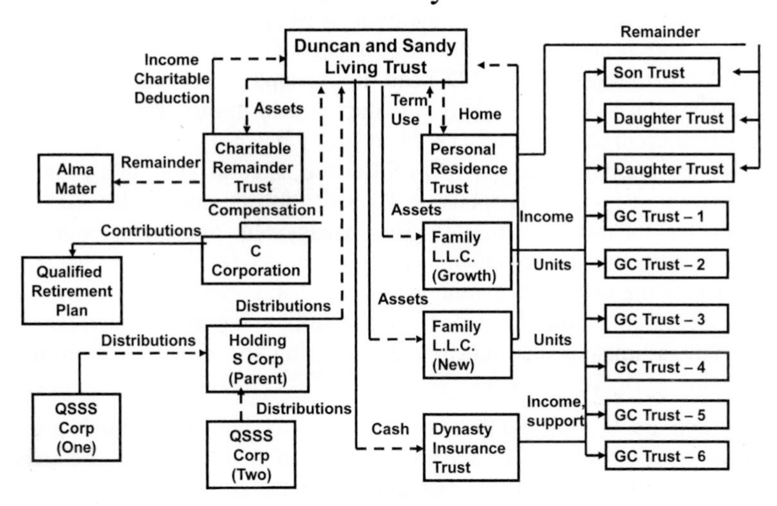

Family Credit Trust

The family credit trust is incorporated in the living trust and funded when the first spouse dies with property that equals the exemption equivalent of the unused unified credit of that spouse. This exemption equivalent (or "free amount," as some call it) for a person dying in 2014 is $5,340,000 less any prior taxable gifts that were reduced or eliminated during life by use of the unified credit. This free amount is now adjusted for inflation each year.

Property passing to the credit trust will be included in the taxable estate of the first spouse to die, but will be tax-protected by the unused unified credit. The property in the trust and all related appreciation will not be taxed in the estate of the surviving spouse. Thus the trust is used to protect and maximize the free amount and disposition rights of the first spouse to die.

Unlike the Q-TIP trust described below, the family credit trust permits income accumulations that aid in growing the trust balance and the amount that will ultimately pass to heirs free of tax. Plus, there is no prohibition on family members other than the surviving spouse receiving distributions during the life of the surviving spouse. The broad structural flexibility of a family credit trust is perhaps its most attractive feature.

The surviving spouse may be named as both the trustee and beneficiary of the family credit trust, but need not be. Distributions to the designated beneficiaries of the credit trust often are subject to an ascertainable standard to avoid tax problems that might result from a general power of appointment over the trust property. A popular ascertainable standard is "support, care, maintenance, and education according to the beneficiary's customary standard of living."

Q-TIP Trust

The Q-TIP trust incorporated in the living trust is an important planning tool for a person with a large estate who must qualify all or a portion of his or her estate for the marital deduction. If Duncan, for example, predeceases Sandy with an estate valued at $12 million (half the couple's $24 million estate) and $5.34 million passes tax-free to a family credit trust, the balance ($6.66 million) must qualify for the marital deduction to avoid estate taxes at Duncan's death. A direct transfer to the surviving spouse will qualify for the marital deduction, but often individuals want disposition control, management protections, and asset-protection benefits that disappear with such a direct transfer. That's where the Q-TIP trust enters the picture, providing a tax-eliminating marital deduction while giving the deceased spouse the right to designate how the trust property will be managed and ultimately distributed and protecting the trust assets from the creditor claims of the beneficiaries.

In order to qualify for Q-TIP treatment, the surviving spouse must be given a "qualified interest for life." This requirement is satisfied if (1) all of the income of the trust property is payable at least annually to the surviving spouse for life, and (2) no one has any power during the life of the surviving spouse to appoint any property for the benefit of any person other than the surviving spouse. So there is no capacity to accumulate income, and other family members may not receive any distributions during the life of the surviving spouse. Plus, any property remaining in a Q-TIP trust that is subject to a marital deduction on the death of the first spouse is taxable in the estate of the surviving spouse at death.

The Q-TIP trust provides the first spouse to die with a measure of control over his or her estate without giving up the benefit of the marital deduction. That spouse may specify the extent to which the principal of the trust (not income) is going to be available to the surviving spouse during the remainder of the surviving spouse's life and may specify how the trust assets are to be distributed on the death of the surviving spouse.

Children Trusts

Duncan and Sandy have established a separate trust for each of their children. These children's trusts have been funded for many years. They were used to fund the children's college educations and to help with first-home purchases. They now serve as an investment fund for each child, generating income distributions each year. All contributions to the trusts have been structured to eliminate any gift tax consequences. The trusts also provide protection from creditor claims and will help protect trust assets in a messy divorce.

Grandchildren Trusts

A separate trust has been established for each grandchild. These trusts are funded annually with gifts structured to eliminate all gift tax consequences. Each grandchild's trust will be used to fund future college and graduate school expenses, provide first-home support, and potentially serve as a long-term investment fund that generates income distributions each year.

Qualified Personal Residence Trust

The qualified personal residence trust was set up to hold title to Duncan and Sandy's personal residence, a high quality property that has appreciated in value. The terms of the trust give Duncan and Sandy use of the residence for a specified term (there are 14 years remaining). At the end of the term, the residence passes to the children's trusts in equal shares. The trust permitted a substantial leveraging of a portion of Duncan and Sandy's gift tax unified credits. When the trust was established, the value of the remainder interest (then very small) was a taxable gift that consumed a small portion of their unified credits. The benefit is that if Duncan and Sandy outlive the trust term (a probability), the home will pass to the children's trusts free of additional transfer taxes.

The technique makes it possible to transfer a valuable residence by using a small portion of the couple's gift tax unified credits. Of course, at the end of the trust term, the residence passes to the children's trusts. If at that time Duncan and Sandy want to continue residing in the home, they will lease the home from the trusts, which will create an additional opportunity to reduce future estate taxes by regularly transferring funds to their children's trusts free of any gift tax limitations or concerns.

Family Limited Liability Companies

The two family limited liability companies were established to facilitate the ownership of business and investment assets by the trusts established for the children and grandchildren. Duncan and Sandy and two of their adult children are the managers. The entities own interests in real estate ventures. The "New" LLC invests in new ventures and was funded with cash contributions from Duncan, Sandy and the children and grandchildren's trusts, with the bulk of the cash coming from the trusts. The "Growth" LLC holds seasoned investments. Duncan and Sandy are the majority owners and managers of the "Growth" LLC, but periodically gift membership interests in the LLC to the children and grandchildren's trusts.

Dynasty Life Insurance Trust

The dynasty life insurance trust is an irrevocable life insurance trust structured to provide support benefits to all of Duncan and Sandy's descendants for as long as there are assets in the trust and the law will allow (in some states, in perpetuity). Hence, the name "Dynasty." The trust owns a $7 million second-to-die life insurance policy that will pay off on the death of the survivor of Duncan and Sandy. The premiums are funded by annual cash gifts to the trust from Duncan and Sandy that are tax-protected by their gift tax unified credits. Their generation skipping tax exemption also is allocated to all gifts to the trust.

Their tax goal is to have the dynasty trust assets escape all gift, estate and generation skipping taxes – now and in the future. The proceeds of the life insurance policy may be used to help fund any estate taxes on the death of the surviving spouse by the trust purchasing assets that are included in the taxable estate of the surviving spouse.

Holding S Corporation

The operations of Holding are conducted in the S corporation that owns two qualified subchapter S subsidiaries. The separate subsidiaries protect each company's operations from any liability exposures of the other's operation and facilitate the development and compensation of separate managements. All of the operations are consolidated for tax purposes. The S structure allows Duncan to regularly receive substantial distributions free of any double income tax concerns and self employment tax burdens.

C Corporation Consulting Business

Duncan's consulting business operates through the C corporation. The company funds a qualified defined benefit plan that primarily benefits Duncan, the sole shareholder and the highest paid employee. This enables Duncan to defer income taxes on a substantial portion of his consulting income. The C corporation structure also permits Duncan and the other employees to fund medical and insurance benefits with pre-tax dollars. Duncan "zeros out" the C corporation's taxable income each year with salary and bonus payments to himself.

Charitable Remainder Trust

The charitable remainder trust was set up principally to benefit Duncan and Sandy's alma maters, but it also provides some cash flow and tax benefits for Duncan and Sandy. Unencumbered raw land with a low tax basis was contributed to the trust. The time had come to sell the land. The trust sold the land but, as a charitable remainder trust, paid no income taxes on the sale. The total sales proceeds were invested to fund a monthly annuity that is payable to Duncan and Sandy for so long as either of them is living. Upon the death of the survivor, the trust property will pass to their two alma maters in equal shares. In addition to the lifetime annuity payments, Duncan and Sandy received a charitable contribution deduction for the value of the trust's remainder interests designated for the charities.

Objectives Accomplished?

As depicted in the chart and briefly summarized above, the plan addresses all of Duncan and Sandy's objectives, at least in part. Consider:

- Duncan and Sandy receive income streams from the C corporation, the S corporation, the limited liability companies, the charitable remainder trust, and any assets owned by the living trust.

- The living trust provides probate and privacy protections.

- The children are treated equally, and the children's and grandchildren's trusts, funded via the family limited liability companies, the dynasty trust and the personal residence trust, meet Duncan and Sandy's objectives for their descendants.

- Duncan and Sandy's alma maters are taken care of through the charitable remainder trust.

- Estate taxes are deferred through the QTIP trust in the living trust and are reduced through the children's and grandchildren's trusts, the dynasty trust, the personal residence trust, and the charitable remainder trust, all of which are excluded from Duncan and Sandy's taxable estate.

- Liquidity is ensured through the life insurance in the dynasty trust, which will escape all future estate and generation skipping taxes.

- There are no double income tax concerns, payroll taxes are minimized, and taxable income can be shifted to children and grandchildren through the gifting of limited liability company units to the trusts.

- Duncan and Sandy have surrendered no control of Consulting and Holding and have the opportunity to work with (and teach) two of their children in managing the limited liability companies.

- With the exception of the living trust, all the entities (the boxes in the chart) provide some level of protection against unforeseen liabilities.

CHAPTER 14

BUSINESS-RELATED ETHICAL CHALLENGES

A. SCOPE AND SOURCES

Business lawyers often confront ethical challenges in the course of representing business clients. They may surface at the commencement of the engagement (who's the client?) and be triggered at various key points during and following the period of representation. The scope and nature of specific challenges often vary based on the depth of a lawyer's involvement with the business. The range is huge, everything from the one-time, single issue representation to a captive, in-house, fulltime employment relationship. The threshold challenge is to identify the ethical issue, smartly evaluate alternative courses of action, and choose a course that stays within acceptable ethical boundaries and promotes the interests of the client and the lawyer. Various sources may need to be considered, including state rules of professional conduct and ethics opinions, the American Bar Association's Model Rules of Professional Conduct, formal ethics opinions issued by the ABA, rules promulgated by the Department of Treasury in Circular 230 that govern practice before the Internal Revenue Service, and rules promulgated by the Securities and Exchange Commission pursuant to the Sarbanes–Oxley Act of 2002. Each of these bodies of law contains detailed rules and duties applicable to lawyers, many of which overlap and some of which conflict.

It is beyond the scope of this work to discuss in any significant depth the range of potential ethical issues business lawyers face. The following discussion by Professor Schumacher analyzes some of the common challenges.

B. COMMON ETHICAL ISSUES[1]

1. IDENTIFYING THE REAL CLIENT

The threshold question a lawyer must always answer is: who is my client?

1.The author of this section is Professor Scott Schumacher of the University of Washington School. This section is an excerpt from Dwight Drake's book, *Business Planning: Closely Held Enterprises* (West 4d Ed. 2013).

For most lawyers, the answer is obvious—it's the person sitting across the desk, asking all the questions. The answer is not so easy, however, when the lawyer is being retained to represent a closely held business. In this situation, the general rule for identifying the client is set forth in ABA Model Rule 1.13, which provides simply that a "lawyer employed or retained by an organization represents the organization acting through its duly authorized constituents." With corporations, there usually is no confusion: It is well settled that a corporation is a separate legal entity, a separate legal "person." However, the law is much less settled with regard to partnerships, limited partnerships, limited liability partnerships, limited liability companies, and all of the other related hybrid entities.

Partnerships and LLCs are creatures of state law. Under § 101(b) of the Uniform Partnership Act of 1991, the term "partnership" means "an association of two or more persons to carry on as co-owners a business for profit." Thepredominate theory in cases that have examined this issue is that partnerships, LLCs, and similar structures are separate legal entities, rather than aggregates of their owners, and the lawyer represents the entity and not the partners or owners. However, other courts have found that the lawyer did in fact represent the owners as well as the entity. Nearly every court to have addressed this issue has based its determination on the facts of the individual case. The Supreme Court muddied the water in *Carden v. Arkoma Associates*, 494 U.S. 185 (1990), where the Court held that, for purposes of diversity jurisdiction to permit a suit in federal court, the citizenship of an unincorporated association is to be determined by the citizenships of all its members. Thus, the Court in essence held that a partnership or other unincorporated entity should be treated, at least in some instances, as an aggregate of its individual members.

The ABA has attempted to set forth a bright-line (or at least a brighter-line) rule on this issue of client identification in situations involving a partnership or a limited liability company. Model Rule 1.13(a) provides simply that a "lawyer employed or retained by an organization represents the organization acting through its duly authorized constituents." In ABA Formal Opinion 91–361 (1991), the ABA held that a partnership is an "organization" within the meaning of Rule 1.13, and that, generally, a lawyer who represents a partnership represents the entity rather than the individual partners. This rule would also be applicable to LLCs. Nevertheless, the ABA acknowledged that despite this general rule, an attorney-client relationship may nevertheless arise with the individual partners or owners, depending upon the facts of the case. Thus, while the ABA has clarified the issue as to whether an attorney represents the partnership as an entity (rather than an aggregate of individuals), the facts of any given case may well show that the attorney also represents one or more of the partners or owners.

2. DEFINITIVELY RESOLVING CLIENT IDENTITY

The way in which nearly every ethical duty must be discharged will depend upon who the client is, that is, to whom the duties under the various ethical rules are owed. And yet, this most fundamental question often is unanswerable in the absolute when dealing with certain entities. While the inconsistent treatment of entities and owners is bad enough, what is especially troubling is that the determination of who the client is may in some cases be based on the subjective beliefs *of the clients*. ABA Formal Op. 91–361 provides that whether a relationship between a lawyer and one or more of the partners has been created almost always will depend on an analysis of the specific facts involved, including "whether there was evidence of reliance by the individual partner on the lawyer as his or her separate counsel, or of the *partner's expectation* of personal representation."

It is therefore imperative that a lawyer (1) determine as many facts as possible about the case and the parties (partnership and partners); (2) decide which of the parties he or she will represent; (3) clearly communicate to all parties involved (whether being represented or not) who the practitioner will be representing; and (4) to the extent possible, obtain consents or acknowledgements from all of the parties as to the extent and limitations of that representation.

In ABA Formal Opinion 91–361, the ABA stated:

> Lest the difficulties of representing both a partnership and one or more of its partners appear impossible to overcome, however, Rule 1.7(b)(2) and, to a lesser extent, Rule 1.13(d) suggest a procedure that may be helpful in many situations. If an attorney retained by a partnership explains at the outset of the representation, preferably in writing, his or her role as counsel to the organization and not to the individual partners, and if, when asked to represent an individual partner, the lawyer puts the question before the partnership or its governing body, explains the implications of the dual representation, and obtains the informed consent of both the partnership and the individual partners, the likelihood of perceived ethical impropriety on the part of the lawyer should be significantly reduced.

In his *Ethics Chat* Newsletter (Issue 2, Vol. 7, Spring 2003), Professor Walter W. Steele, Jr. sets out two clauses to be used in retainer agreements in order to avoid the common misunderstandings about whom the lawyer represents:

Suggested Clause for Initial Retainer Letter to Entity Organizers

> It will be necessary to discuss numerous issues with each of you as the process of forming [name of entity] takes place. I have already advised you that I have agreed to serve as the lawyer for the entity—I am not the lawyer for any of you in this transaction. As I told you during our initial conference, you have the right to engage another lawyer of your choosing to represent your personal interests in this matter. The fact that I discuss issues with you during the process of forming [name of entity] must not be interpreted by you as any indication that I am your lawyer or that I am guarding your own individual interest in this matter. Because I am not your lawyer, I have the right, and perhaps the obligation at times, to share any information

you provide to me with the other entity organizers.

Suggested Clause for Affirmation by Organizers—Post Entity Formation

We, the undersigned organizers of [name of entity] hereby ratify and confirm our agreement not to be represented personally as set forth in the retainer contract attached to this document, and we now confirm that at no point during the process of organizing [name of entity] did [lawyer] form an attorney-client relationship with any of us. Each of us were free at any point during this process to retain a lawyer to guard and protect our own personal interests, and the fact that we chose not to do so is not any evidence that we relied on [lawyer] for that purpose.

3. Representing Both Entities and Owners

Even though the general rule is that a lawyer represents the entity and not the individual owners, the situation routinely arises in which the lawyer may be asked to represent one or more of the owners in addition to the entity itself. In addition, lawyers representing an entity will inevitably develop a relationship with one or more of the owners and, if the lawyer has been effective on behalf of the entity, an owner may wish to retain the services of the lawyer in an unrelated legal matter. Is it acceptable under the rules to represent an owner while also representing the entity? Rule 1.7 sets out the rules governing a lawyer representing more than one client:

Rule 1.7 Conflict of Interest

(a) Except as provided in paragraph (b), a lawyer shall not represent a client if the representation involves a concurrent conflict of interest. A concurrent conflict of interest exists if:

(1) the representation of one client will be directly adverse to another client; or

(2) there is a significant risk that the representation of one or more clients will be materially limited by the lawyer's responsibilities to another client, a former client or a third person or by a personal interest of the lawyer.

(b) Notwithstanding the existence of a concurrent conflict of interest under paragraph (a), a lawyer may represent a client if:

(1) the lawyer reasonably believes that the lawyer will be able to provide competent and diligent representation to each affected client;

(2) the representation is not prohibited by law;

(3) the representation does not involve the assertion of a claim by one client against another client represented by the lawyer in the same litigation or other proceeding before a tribunal; and

(4) each affected client gives informed consent, confirmed in writing.

Under Rule 1.7, a lawyer may represent parties with potential conflicts of interest, but only if the lawyer believes his or her representation will not be affected, and each client consents in writing. It is therefore essential that the lawyer do a full conflicts check at the outset, obtain as many facts as possible, and secure written consents from each of the clients.

As in the case of any potential conflict involving multiple representations, a lawyer may represent an entity and one or more of the owners. However, Rule 1.13(g) imposes the additional requirement that the consent on behalf of the entity that is required by Rule 1.7 must be given by an owner other than the owner who will be represented by the lawyer. Accordingly, if a lawyer will be representing both a corporate client and one of the shareholders or a partnership client and one of the partners, it is essential that the lawyer obtain written consents from both the entity and the other individual to be represented, with the consent on behalf of the entity from an owner other than the one to be represented. It may be advisable, if the number of owners is sufficiently small to make it practicable, to have each of the owners who will not be represented by the lawyer consent to the dual representation.

4. DUTIES OWED TO FORMER CLIENTS AND PARTNERS

Another common conflict of interest involves former clients. For example, a lawyer represents an entity with several owners and, during the course of the representation, the lawyer learns information about one of the owners. Later, that owner is an opposing party in another case. Can the lawyer represent his client against the former owner? This issue is governed by Rule 1.9.

Rule 1.9: Duties to Former Clients

(a) A lawyer who has formerly represented a client in a matter shall not thereafter represent another person in the same or a substantially related matter in which that person's interests are materially adverse to the interests of the former client unless the former client gives informed consent, confirmed in writing.

(b) A lawyer shall not knowingly represent a person in the same or a substantially related matter in which a firm with which the lawyer formerly was associated had previously represented a client

(1) whose interests are materially adverse to that person; and

(2) about whom the lawyer had acquired information protected by Rules 1.6 and 1.9(c) that is material to the matter; unless the former client gives informed consent, confirmed in writing.

(c) A lawyer who has formerly represented a client in a matter or whose present or former firm has formerly represented a client in a matter shall not thereafter:

(1) use information relating to the representation to the disadvantage of the former client except as these Rules would permit or require with respect to a client, or when the information has become generally known; or

(2) reveal information relating to the representation except as these Rules would permit or require with respect to a client.

This is yet another reason to make sure about the identity of "the client." If the lawyer is not careful, numerous owners could be considered to be clients, thereby increasing the list of "former clients." Thus, Formal Opinion 91–361 opines that "a lawyer undertaking to represent a partnership with respect to a particular matter does not thereby enter into a lawyer-client relationship with each member of the partnership, so as to be barred, for example, by Rule 1.7(a) from representing another client on a matter adverse to one of the partners but unrelated to the partnership affairs."

Nevertheless, Rule 1.9(c) prohibits a lawyer from revealing "information relating to the representation" except as otherwise permitted by the Rules (e.g., Rule 1.6). This prohibition is absolute and is not waivable. Given the breadth of the attorney-client privilege and the inclusion of partners as agents of the partnership for purposes of the privilege, a lawyer should be extremely careful about using facts learned from or statements made by an owner during the course of the lawyer's representation of the entity against the owner in a later proceeding against the owner.

5. LAWYER AS A DIRECTOR

It has long been accepted practice for corporations to ask their outside counsel to serve as a director of the client. The practice is common among closely-held businesses, as well as public companies. However, merely because it is common practice does not mean it is a good idea nor free of ethical dilemmas. Among the problems associated with a lawyer serving his or her client as a director are the possibilities that the attorney-client privilege will be jeopardized, the lawyer's independent professional judgment may be hindered, and the lawyer may be disqualified due to a conflict of interest.

Most of the issues surrounding the lawyer as director must be analyzed under Rule 1.7, which governs conflicts of interest. In short, Model Rule 1.7(a) provides that a lawyer may not represent a client if the representation of one client will be directly adverse to another client, or if there is a significant risk that the representation of one or more clients will be materially limited by the lawyer's responsibilities to another client or other third party. There is nothing in Model Rule 1.7 prohibiting a lawyer from representing a client of which he or she is also a director. Nevertheless, given the numerous ethical pitfalls, members of the profession sought guidance from the ABA on this question.

In Formal Opinion 98–410, the ABA addressed whether it would be appropriate for an attorney to act as a director for a corporate client. Formal Opinion 98–410 enumerated the steps attorneys must take to mitigate the problems inherent in this dual role.

At the beginning of the relationship, the lawyer should take steps to ensure that the corporation's management and the other board members understand the different responsibilities of outside legal counsel and director. For example, management and the board must understand the importance of, as well as the limitations of, the attorney-client privilege, and that in some instances matters discussed at board meetings will not receive the protection of the attorney-client privilege that would attach to conversations between the client and the lawyer *qua* lawyer.

The client should also understand that conflicts of interest may arise that would require the lawyer to recuse himself or herself as a director or to withdraw from representing the corporation in a matter. The lawyer should also ensure that management and the other board members understand that, when acting as legal counsel, the lawyer represents only the corporate entity and not its individual officers and directors.

The Formal Opinion goes on to advise that during the course of the dual relationship, the lawyer should exercise care to protect the corporation's confidential information and to confront and resolve conflicts of interest that may arise. The opinion noted that it is essential that the lawyer be particularly careful when the client's management or board of directors consults him for legal advice. If the purpose of the meeting or consultation is to obtain legal advice from the lawyer in his or her capacity as lawyer, the lawyer-director should make clear that the meeting is solely for the purpose of providing legal advice, and the lawyer should avoid giving business or financial advice, except insofar as it affects legal considerations such as the application of the business judgment rule.

If during the course of the discussions the lawyer's presence and opinion is needed in his or her role as director, the lawyer should have another member of the firm present at the meeting to provide the legal advice. Vigilantly segregating the two roles of lawyer and director will provide the best support for a claim of privilege.

Formal Opinion 98–410 advises lawyers to "[m]aintain in practice the independent professional judgment required of a competent lawyer, recommending against a course of action that is illegal or likely to harm the corporation even when favored by management or other directors." It then advises the lawyer to "[p]erform diligently the duties of counsel once a decision is made by the board or management, even if, as a director, the lawyer disagrees with the decision, unless the representation would assist in fraudulent or criminal conduct, self-dealing or otherwise would violate the Model Rules."

Lawyers must also avoid conflicts of interest that may arise as a result of the insider status he or she enjoys on the board of directors. For example, a lawyer should recuse himself or herself as a director from board deliberations when the relationship of the corporation with the lawyer or the lawyer's firm is under consideration. Likewise, Formal Opinion 98–410 points out that a lawyer should decline any representation as counsel when the lawyer's interest as a director conflicts with his responsibilities of competent and diligent representation. For example, a lawyer should not represent a client matter if the lawyer is concerned about potential personal liability as a director resulting from a course approved by the board. *Id.; see also* Model Rule 1.7(a)(2).

Finally, Formal Opinion 98–410 points out what may be an unavoidable conflict: A director, who also is the corporation's lawyer, may be under a duty to disclose information to third parties that, in his role as attorney for the corporation, he could not disclose without obtaining consent from the client. In this situation, the lawyer-director's knowledge as a director may prove inseparable from the lawyer's acts and knowledge as outside legal counsel. The lawyer may have to resign his or her role as director in order to protect client confidences.

6. Lawyer as an Officer

An officer, depending on the duties assigned, could be everything from a figurehead who performs ministerial functions to an officer involved in every aspect of the corporation's day-to-day operations. Depending upon the nature and extent of the duties performed by the lawyer, acting as an officer may violate the rules of professional conduct if the lawyer undertakes legal representation of the entity. While it may be appropriate for a lawyer to act as corporate secretary and receive all legal documents served on the corporation, in most situations it would not be appropriate for a lawyer to represent a corporate client while serving as its chief financial officer. The ethical issues applicable to the lawyer-director are equally applicable, if not more so, depending on the duties of the lawyer-officer. A lawyer should keep each of the potential problems in mind when considering service as an officer of a corporate client.

7. Ethical Issues in Investing with a Client

May an attorney properly invest in a business with a client, either as payment for services or as an independent investment? The general rule on conflicts of interests with respect to current clients is found in Model Rule 1.8, which provides:

Rule 1.8: Conflict Of Interest: Current Clients: Specific Rules

(a) A lawyer shall not enter into a business transaction with a client or knowingly acquire an ownership, possessory, security or other pecuniary interest adverse to a client unless:

(1) the transaction and terms on which the lawyer acquires the interest are fair and reasonable to the client and are fully disclosed and transmitted in writing in a manner that can be reasonably understood by the client;

(2) the client is advised in writing of the desirability of seeking and is given a reasonable opportunity to seek the advice of independent legal counsel on the transaction; and

(3) the client gives informed consent, in a writing signed by the client, to the essential terms of the transaction and the lawyer's role in the transaction, including whether the lawyer is representing the client in the transaction.

Thus, a lawyer may invest in a venture with a client or may take stock in the client's business in lieu of fees only if the terms of the deal are fair and reasonable, the client is fully informed in writing about the terms of the deal, the client consents in writing to these terms, and the client is advised to seek independent legal counsel on the deal and is given the opportunity to seek that advice. Comment 1 to Model Rule 1.8 explains the reasons for this rule: "A lawyer's legal skill and training, together with the relationship of trust and confidence between lawyer and client, create the possibility of overreaching when the lawyer participates in a business, property or financial transaction with a client." If the transaction with the client involves one in which the lawyer will actually be advising the client, the risks highlighted by Comment 1 are even greater, since the knowledge, trust, and confidence that creates the risk of overreaching are even greater under these circumstances.

The ABA weighed-in on this issue in Formal Opinion 2000–418. First, the ABA answered what should be an obvious question by holding, "In our opinion, a lawyer who acquires stock in her client corporation in lieu of or in addition to a cash fee for her services enters into a business transaction with a client, such that the requirements of Model Rule 1.8(a) must be satisfied." After reviewing the requirements of Model Rule 1.8, the formal opinion then outlined situations where, despite satisfying the literal requirements of Rule 1.8, the transaction, and the lawyer's role in representing the client, may raise other ethical issues not contemplated by Rule 1.8. The opinion notes an example where the lawyer might have a duty when rendering an opinion on behalf of the corporation in a venture capital transaction to ask the client's management to reveal adverse financial information even though the revelation might cause the venture capital investor to withdraw. Under those circumstances, an attorney must evaluate his or her ability to exercise independent professional judgment in light of the adverse impact the advice may have on his or her own economic interests.

Formal Opinion 2000–418 notes that one way of reducing the risk that the stock-for-services fee arrangement will be deemed to be unreasonable is to establish a reasonable fee for the lawyer's services based on factors enumerated under Rule 1.5, and then accept an amount of stock that, at the time of the transaction, equals the reasonable fee. The difficulty of course, especially with start-up companies, is to determine the value of stock of the company. The opinion nevertheless encourages the stock to be valued at the amount per share that cash investors have agreed to pay for similar stock.

Joseph F. Troy has written a "Best Practices Checklist" for firms to follow when taking stock in clients, which is published in *Representing Start–Up Companies*, by Lee R. Petillon and Robert Joe Hull. Among the "Best Practices" Troy lists are:

- Impose firm control of all investments by lawyers in client's stock. Do not allow individual lawyers in the firm to make these investment decisions.

- Invest through a firm vehicle, and avoid direct investing by firm attorneys.

- Strictly limit the size of investments and the percentage of ownership. Troy lists a maximum of $25,000–50,000 or 1–2% of the company as typical or safe investment levels.

- Obtain a third-party valuation of the stock.

- Take all or the bulk of fees in cash.

- Do not take stock for future services without including vesting provisions and an express right of the client to terminate.

- Avoid flipping (immediate resale) of stock, and impose a voluntary lock-up.

- Impose strict insider trading rules.

- Require stock be held for investment and not with a view to resale. Do not permit trading of client stock.

- Disclose the stock ownership to third parties when appropriate.

- If you cannot fully and zealously represent your client on a matter because of your stock ownership, either do not invest or decline the representation.

- If your investment would compromise your independent professional judgment, either do not invest or decline the representation.

- Schedule a regular review of the conflicts and, when necessary, get a revised consent.

- Make a detailed and comprehensive disclosure of the conflicts; do not rely on boilerplate disclosures.

8. General Duties Owed to Business Owners

The general rule is that a lawyer who is retained by a corporation, partnership, or LLC, represents the entity itself and not the individual owners. A lawyer may also represent an individual owner in the same matter or in an unrelated transaction, as long as he or she satisfies the requirements of Rule 1.7, dealing with conflicts of interest. The next question is what ethical duties are owed to the owners who are *not* clients? In one sense, the owners are merely third parties, and they are entitled, at a minimum, to the same treatment as other third parties. Model Rule 4.1 governs the treatment of third parties:

Rule 4.1: Truthfulness in Statements to Others.

In the course of representing a client a lawyer shall not knowingly:

> (a) make a false statement of material fact or law to a third person; or
>
> (b) fail to disclose a material fact to a third person when disclosure is necessary to avoid assisting a criminal or fraudulent act by a client, unless disclosure is prohibited by Rule 1.6.

Thus, Model Rule 4.1 requires at a minimum that a lawyer may not knowingly make a false statement of material fact or law to third persons, nor may the lawyer knowingly fail to disclose a material fact when disclosure is necessary to avoid assisting a criminal or fraudulent act by a client, unless disclosure is prohibited by Model Rule 1.6.

In addition, since many owners will not have their own representation, the lawyer may be required to treat the owners as "unrepresented persons" and comply with Model Rule 4.3:

Rule 4.3: Dealing With Unrepresented Persons

> In dealing on behalf of a client with a person who is not represented by counsel, a lawyer shall not state or imply that the lawyer is disinterested. When the lawyer knows or reasonably should know that the unrepresented person misunderstands the lawyer's role in the matter, the lawyer shall make reasonable efforts to correct the misunderstanding. The lawyer shall not give legal advice to an unrepresented person, other than the advice to secure counsel, if the lawyer knows or reasonably should know that the interests of such a person are or have a reasonable possibility of being in conflict with the interests of the client.

Ideally, the lawyer will have set out in the engagement letter that he or she represents the entity and not the individual owners. As a result, there should not be a misunderstanding as to the lawyer's role in the matter. However, Rule 4.3 imposes a continuing duty to correct any misunderstanding that a third party (i.e., partner/member/shareholder) may have. Moreover, Model Rule 1.13(f) reinforces the requirement that the lawyer representing an entity must ensure that the owners are reminded of where the lawyer's duty of loyalty lies:

Model Rule 1.13(f)

> In dealing with an organization's directors, officers, employees, members, shareholders or other constituents, a lawyer shall explain the identity of the client when the lawyer knows or reasonably should know that the organization's interests are adverse to those of the constituents with whom the lawyer is dealing.

The Rules and comments make it plain that when dealing with owners, lawyers should ensure that there is no confusion as to who the lawyer represents.

9. THE ATTORNEY-CLIENT PRIVILEGE

One of the most common issues in representing a partnership, corporation, or other entity involves the application of the attorney-client privilege. During the course of representing an entity, a lawyer must routinely determine whether statements by officers, directors, partners, employees or other "constituents" are subject to the attorney-client privilege. Privilege issues also may impact what a lawyer may disclose to individual owners and what the lawyer may refuse to disclose to owners. Whether a lawyer may refuse to divulge a given statement under the attorney-client privilege will depend upon (1) the identity of the declarant (i.e., his or her role within the entity); (2) the identity of the person seeking to obtain the statement (i.e., whether the person is also an owner of the entity or and outsider); (3) the purpose for which the statements were made to the lawyer; and (4) whether the privilege has been waived.

The general rule in dealing with confidences is found in Model Rule 1.6, which provides that "a lawyer shall not reveal information relating to the representation of a client unless the client gives informed consent, the disclosure is impliedly authorized in order to carry out the representation or the disclosure is permitted by paragraph (b)." The exceptions of 1.6(b) include: (1) To prevent reasonably certain death or substantial bodily harm; (2) to prevent the client from committing a crime or fraud that is reasonably certain to result in substantial injury to the financial interests or property of another and in furtherance of which the client has used or is using the lawyer's services; (3) to prevent, mitigate or rectify substantial injury to the financial interests or property of another that is reasonably certain to result or has resulted from the client's commission of a crime or fraud in furtherance of which the client has used the lawyer's services; (4) to secure legal advice about the lawyer's compliance with these Rules; and (5) to establish a claim or defense on behalf of the lawyer in a controversy between the lawyer and the client. How is this rule applied in the context of an entity client?

The seminal case in this area is *Upjohn Co. v. United States*, 449 U.S. 383, 101 S.Ct. 677 (1981), in which the Supreme Court adopted a fairly broad application of the attorney-client privilege in the corporate context, holding that where communications were made by corporate employees to counsel for the corporation acting at the direction of corporate superiors in order to secure legal advice from counsel, and the employees were aware that they were being questioned so that the corporation could obtain advice, these communications were protected. Thus, the Court in *Upjohn* examined the purposes for which the attorney obtained the statements from the employees. Since each of the disputed statements was elicited pursuant to the attorney's representation, the statements were protected by the privilege. While this is certainly the general rule, the *Upjohn* test has not been uniformly adopted. Accordingly, whether statements made by an employee or other constituent of an entity-client will be subject to the attorney-client privilege may depend upon the law of the jurisdiction involved.

In addition, whether a lawyer can refuse to disclose statements obtained from an owner or other constituent will depend upon who is seeking disclosure. In Formal Opinion 91–361, which is the Formal Opinion declaring that the partnership is the client, the ABA stated that "information received by a lawyer in the course of representing the partnership is 'information relating to the representation' of the partnership, and normally may not be withheld from individual partners." The ABA went on to explain its opinion as follows:

> The mandate of Rule 1.6(a), not to reveal confidences of the client, would not prevent the disclosure to other partners of information gained about the client (the partnership) from any individual partner(s). Thus, information thought to have been given in confidence by an individual partner to the attorney for a partnership may have to be disclosed to other partners, particularly if the interests of the individual partner and the partnership, or vis-a-vis the other partners, become antagonistic.

According to the ABA, since the partnership is the client, and not the individual partners, information received from the partners cannot be a "client confidence," at least with respect to the other partners. As a result, information received from a partner may not be withheld from other partners. Although the fiduciary duties owed by partners to their fellow partners are somewhat unique among business entities, the logic of Formal Opinion 91–361 would appear to apply equally to other entities types, and thus, in dealing with an entity and its owners, a lawyer may not normally refuse to disclose facts learned during the course or representing the entity. It is essential that the owners understand this and do not mistakenly make statements to an attorney, believing that the statement will be held in confidence. A lawyer should make this clear at the outset of the representation and remind owners of this during the course of the representation, if it appears that an owner may be mistaken as to the application of the attorney-client privilege…

On the other hand, Model Rule 1.13 suggests that statements by an owner or employee of an entity may be subject to attorney-client privilege if the person seeking disclosure is an outsider. Hence, the application of the privilege appears to depend upon who the declarant is, the declarant's role in the entity, the circumstances under which the lawyer sought and obtained the information and statements from the declarant, and who is seeking access to the statement or information. The lawyer must keep each of these factors in mind when dealing with owners and employees of the entity client in a situation that is or might soon become a sensitive or controversial matter. The problem, of course, is that statements are often obtained when neither the lawyer nor the client has any inkling that a controversy might soon erupt. The specific issue of an attorney's ethical duties when he or she learns of client misconduct is discussed in the following section.

Another common ethical issue concerns the situation where the lawyer learns that one or more of the owners, employees, or other constituents has done something that is either illegal or contrary to the best interests of the entity. As has been established, a lawyer represents the entity as a separate entity. Yet, entities can only act through individual owners and employees. Who speaks for the entity when there is a dispute and who should the lawyer listen to? Model Rule 1.13(a) provides that an organization acts through its "duly authorized constituents." However, particularly in the case of closely held businesses, it is not always clear who the duly authorized constituents are.

Comment 3 to Rule 1.13 emphasizes that the actions and decisions of the duly authorized constituent must generally be respected by lawyer: "When constituents of the organization make decisions for it, the decisions ordinarily must be accepted by the lawyer even if their utility or prudence is doubtful. Decisions concerning policy and operations, including ones entailing serious risk, are not as such in the lawyer's province."

One of the most difficult ethical issues a lawyer can face occurs when, for example, the general partner, who is the duly authorized constituent of the partnership, has taken some action that is either illegal or contrary to the interests of the partnership. Technically, the lawyer represents the partnership, not the general partner. However, in reality, the lawyer is retained by, paid by, and is answerable to a real person—the general partner. Lawyers must therefore resolve the inherent conflict in their duty to protect the "real" client (i.e., the partnership), not reveal confidences of a duly authorized constituent of the client, and still ensure that the best interests of the client and the other constituents are defended. Model Rule 1.13(b) sets out the basic rules on how the professional should act in these circumstances:

> Rule 1.13(b) If a lawyer for an organization knows that an officer, employee or other person associated with the organization is engaged in action, intends to act or refuses to act in a matter related to the representation that is a violation of a legal obligation to the organization, or a violation of law that reasonably might be imputed to the organization, and that is likely to result in substantial injury to the organization, then the lawyer shall proceed as is reasonably necessary in the best interest of the organization. Unless the lawyer reasonably believes that it is not necessary in the best interest of the organization to do so, the lawyer shall refer the matter to higher authority in the organization, including, if warranted by the circumstances to the highest authority that can act on behalf of the organization as determined by applicable law.

Thus, Rule 1.13(b) reemphasizes that the lawyer's primary duty is to act in the best interest of the organization. In addition, the lawyer must, if the circumstances warrant, report the misconduct to the "highest authority" within the organization. However, this does not answer the situation where the malevolent actor is the general partner who *is* the highest authority within the partnership.

Model Rule 1.13 was substantially revised in August of 2003... Under the revised version of Rule 1.13(c), a lawyer may reveal information about the organization's (or constituent's) misconduct, even though revealing that information would not normally be permitted by Rule 1.6. Thus, if the lawyer knows that an owner or employee is engaged in action in a matter related to the representation that is a violation of a legal obligation to the entity, or that the action is a violation of law that reasonably may be imputed to the entity and that will likely result in substantial harm to the entity, then the lawyer shall proceed as is reasonably necessary in the best interest of the entity. The lawyer's action will be determined by the circumstances, but ordinarily this means referral to a higher decision-making person or group within the organization. The lawyer may, but is not required to, reveal facts relating to the representation, even if not expressly permitted by Rule 1.6, but only if and to the extent the lawyer reasonably believes necessary to prevent substantial injury to the organization.

A common area of the law about which business lawyers routinely give advice involves the client's tax liability. Business lawyers can give prospective tax advice as to how clients should structure certain deals, provide advice on reporting positions for tax returns that are to be filed, and represent clients in tax disputes with the IRS. A significant issue in these contexts is whether statements between a client and its lawyer are subject to the attorney-client privilege.

The attorney-client privilege is affected in the tax area by how "legal advice" is defined. If the advice is considered "accounting advice," the privilege does not apply. This can include preparation of tax returns. The privilege does not apply to return advice because there is no expectation that communications from the client would remain confidential, given that the communications were made for the purpose of reporting transactions on a tax return. Hence, to the extent the privilege may have attached to any of the communications, it was waived when the return was filed. However, if there is an expectation of confidentiality and that confidentiality is not later waived, an attorney's tax advice is privileged if client confidences would be revealed by disclosure of the attorney's advice. The line between what is privileged and what is not has never been clear. As a result, a lawyer providing tax advice should assume that all communications may be discoverable by the IRS.

When a lawyer gives tax advice, the client's accountant often is involved in the conversations as well. In 1998, Congress enacted new § 7525 of the Internal Revenue Code that extends the attorney-client privilege to all authorized tax practitioners. Section 7525 extends the same common law protections of confidentiality that apply to communications between a taxpayer and an attorney to communications between a taxpayer and an accountant. However, the privilege may only be asserted in a non-criminal tax matter before the Service, and in non-criminal tax proceeding in Federal court brought by or against the United States.

Given the limited scope of the accountant-client privilege, an attorney should be careful in retaining the services of an accountant in certain tax matters. If the case involves a dispute with the IRS and has a potential for a criminal prosecution of the client, a lawyer must only employ the services of an accountant under certain conditions. While the client will most likely wish to use its current accountant, the lawyer should insist on retaining a different accountant because of the difficulty in segregating the non-privileged tax return advice from the later privileged communications. Accountants retained under these circumstances are known as "Kovel" accountants, from the case *United States v. Kovel*, 296 F.2d 918 (2d Cir. 1961), where the court held that the attorney-client privilege extends to communications made by a client to an accountant *employed by the lawyer*, as part of the client receiving legal advice from the attorney. It is therefore essential that the *lawyer* retain the accountant directly and not have the client retain the accountant. In addition, all bills for services rendered by the accountant and all work-product produced by the accountant should go through the attorney before being distributed to the client.

PROBLEM 14-1

Four years ago, you represented Jason, then age 28, in the implosion of a start-up venture. Four deep-pocketed investors had funded a new company and selected Jason, boy wonder engineer, to be its president. Jason was given a "dream" employment contract that promised big riches if all played out as expected. Within six months, the investors were thoroughly dismayed with Jason's alleged incompetence, bizarre temper, and propensity to shade the truth.

Jason was dismissed for cause and a brief legal battle ensued. You succeeded in quietly and quickly getting Jason out of the mess with a few bucks in his pocket.

Jason now has asked that you represent Lucy, Sam, and himself in organizing a new corporation ("Newco") that will develop and exploit a new product that is designed to make it easy to produce low-cost vinyl fencing. All three will serve on the board of Newco, and Jason and Lucy will be officers, employed full-time by Newco. Jason indicated that Newco may need your help in resolving a "frivolous" sexual harassment claim that likely will be triggered as a result of his efforts to recruit an office manager for the new venture.

Address the following:

1. May you collectively represent Jason, Lucy and Sam in the organization of Newco? Should you?

2. May you represent just Newco?

3. What precautions should you take in connection with your representation of Newco or any of its owners?

4. Must you or should you advise Lucy and Sam of your prior experiences with Jason?

5. May you invest $100,000 in Newco for six percent of its stock? Jason promises that, if you make such an investment, you will be guaranteed a position on the board, will be elected secretary of the corporation, will be assured all of the corporation's legal work, and will realize a great return on your investment. If you can do this, should you do it?

CHAPTER 15

FORM EXAMPLES

A. RISKS AND REWARDS OF FORMS

A good form library is a blessing for any lawyer. It's a necessity; no one has the time or the competence to start from scratch with every important document. A quality form jumpstarts the drafting process and becomes a valuable aid in the planning process. The competent lawyer knows his or her forms—what they say and, far more important, what they do *not* say. The limitations, shortcomings, and imperfections of each form (they all have them) are well understood. A form never becomes a tool for short-circuiting or cheating the planning process.

Forms become risky when they are misused. They make it possible for the lazy or ill-informed to create complete, official-looking documents without ever embracing the planning process. Often the form's misuse is rationalized by perpetuating a dangerously false notion that there is a "standard" or "normal" way of doing things. The perpetrator sometimes lacks a thorough knowledge of what the form really says and usually has no clue as to the form's flaws or shortcomings. The foolishness of such a practice should be obvious to anyone who has read the foregoing pages.

Sample forms are included in the following sections of this chapter. They were taken directly from the form file of one of the top Seattle-based firms.[1] As forms go, they are fine but nothing special. They are offered here not as examples of extraordinary quality, but rather as tools to assist the learning effort.

The educational value of analyzing a form is in identifying and understanding its limitations and shortcomings. You will discover that the following forms, like all their counterparts, contain limitations that a quality lawyer will spot and a phony will often miss. The hope is that your review of each form will be educational and promote a healthy respect for the value and limitations of all forms.

---

1. The forms in this Chapter, included for educational purposes only, are from the form files of Foster Pepper PLLC, a Northwest-based firm with regional and national practices.

B. FORM: ARTICLES OF INCORPORATION

Articles of Incorporation

OF

____

__________ hereby executes these Articles of Incorporation for the purpose of forming a corporation under Title 23B of the Revised Code of Washington, the Washington Business Corporation Act.

ARTICLE 1

Name

The name of this corporation is:

____

ARTICLE 2

Capital Stock

☐This corporation has the authority to issue __________ shares, the par value of each of which is $_____________.

☐This corporation has the authority to issue __________ shares, and each share shall be without par value.

☐The shares shall be classified as follows:

**** Insert Text ****

ARTICLE 3

Preemptive Rights

☐The shareholders of this corporation have no preemptive rights to acquire additional shares of this corporation.

☐The shareholders of this corporation shall have preemptive rights to acquire additional shares of this corporation.

ARTICLE 4

Cumulative Voting

☐The shareholders of this corporation shall not be entitled to cumulative voting at any election of directors.

☐Shareholders entitled to vote at any election of directors are entitled to cumulate votes by multiplying the number of votes they are entitled to cast by the number of directors for whom they are entitled to vote and to cast the product for a single candidate or distribute the product among two or more candidates.

ARTICLE 5

Action by Consent

Any action required or permitted to be taken at a shareholders' meeting may be taken without a meeting or a vote if either:

(i) the action is taken by written consent of all shareholders entitled to vote on the action; or

(ii) so long as the Corporation does not have any capital stock registered under the Securities Exchange Act of 1934, as amended, the action is taken by written consent of shareholders holding of record, or otherwise entitled to vote, in the aggregate not less than the minimum number of votes that would be necessary to authorize or take such action at a meeting at which all shares entitled to vote on the action were present and voted.

To the extent prior notice of any such action is required by law to be given to nonconsenting or nonvoting shareholders, such notice shall be made before the date on which the action becomes effective. The form of the notice shall be sufficient to apprise the nonconsenting or nonvoting shareholder of the nature of the action to be effected, in a manner approved by the board of directors of this Corporation or by the board committee or officers to whom the board of directors has delegated that responsibility.

ARTICLE 6

Approval by Majority Vote

Unless these Articles of Incorporation provide for a greater voting requirement for any voting group of shareholders, any action which would otherwise require the approval of two-thirds (2/3) of all the votes entitled to be cast, including without limitation the amendment of these Articles of Incorporation, the approval of a plan of merger or share exchange, the sale, lease, exchange or other disposition of all, or substantially all of the Corporation's property otherwise than in the usual and regular course of business, and the dissolution of the Corporation, shall be authorized if approved by each voting group entitled to vote thereon by a simple majority of all the votes entitled to be cast by that voting group.

ARTICLE 7

Limitation of Liability

A director of this Corporation shall not be personally liable to the Corporation or its shareholders for monetary damages for conduct as a director, except for liability of the director *(i)* for acts or omissions that involve intentional misconduct by the director or a knowing violation of law by the director, *(ii)* for conduct violating RCW 23B.08.310 of the Act, or *(iii)* for any transaction from which the director will personally receive a benefit in money, property or services to which the director is not legally entitled. If the Washington Business Corporation Act is amended in the future to authorize corporate action further eliminating or limiting the personal liability of directors, then the liability of a director of this Corporation shall be eliminated or limited to the full extent permitted by the

Washington Business Corporation Act, as so amended, without any requirement of further action by the shareholders.

ARTICLE 8

Indemnification

The Corporation shall indemnify any individual made a party to a proceeding because that individual is or was a director of the Corporation and shall advance or reimburse the reasonable expenses incurred by such individual in advance of final disposition of the proceeding, without regard to the limitations in RCW 23B.08.510 through 23B.08.550 of the Act, or any other limitation which may hereafter be enacted to the extent such limitation may be disregarded if authorized by the Articles of Incorporation, to the full extent and under all circumstances permitted by applicable law.

Any repeal or modification of this Article by the shareholders of this Corporation shall not adversely affect any right of any individual who is or was a director of the Corporation which existed at the time of such repeal or modification.

ARTICLE 9

Directors

☐The initial board of directors shall consist of ____________ (_______) directors. The names and addresses of the persons who are to serve as initial directors are:

____

____

____

____

____

____

____

____

____

☐The initial board of directors shall consist of one director. The name and address of the person who is to serve as the sole initial director is:

____

____

____

Except with respect to the initial board of directors, the number of directors constituting the board of directors shall be determined in the manner specified in the bylaws. In the absence of such a provision in the bylaws, the board shall consist of the number of directors constituting the initial board of directors.

ARTICLE 10

Registered Office and Registered Agent

The street address of the initial registered office of this corporation is:

☐ 1780 Barnes Blvd. S.W.
Tumwater, WA 98512-0410

☐ 1111 Third Avenue, Suite 3400
Seattle, WA 98101-3299

☐ ______________________
____
____
____

and the name of its initial registered agent at that address is:

☐National Registered Agents, Inc.

☐FPS Corporate Services, Inc.

☐[Client]

ARTICLE 11

Incorporator

The name and address of the incorporator is:

☐ ______________________
1111 Third Avenue, Suite 3400
Seattle, WA 98101

☐ ______________________
____

Executed this ______ day of ________________________, __________.

________________________,
Incorporator

CONSENT TO SERVE AS REGISTERED AGENT

National Registered Agents, Inc. ("NRAI"), hereby consents to serve as Registered Agent in the State of Washington for ____________________________________ (the "Corporation"). NRAI understands that as agent for the Corporation, it will be its responsibility to receive service of process in the name of the Corporation; to forward all mail to the Corporation; and to immediately notify the office of the Secretary of State in the event of its resignation, or of any changes in the registered office address of the Corporation for which it is agent.

NATIONAL REGISTERED AGENTS, INC.

By:_____________________________

Name: _________________________

Title: __________________________

NAME OF REGISTERED AGENT: National Registered Agents, Inc.

ADDRESS OF REGISTERED AGENT: 1780 Barnes Blvd. S.W.

Tumwater, WA 98512-0410

ARTICLE II

TEXT INSERTS

[**INSERT:** Voting and Non-Voting Classes of Common Stock.]

The shares consist of ___________ shares designated as "Class A Common Stock" and ___________ shares designated as "Class B Common Stock". Each share of Class A Common Stock shall have unlimited voting rights. Class B Common Stock shall have no voting rights, and no separate vote of the holders of Class B Common Stock as a class shall be required for any purpose except as may be required by law. Other than with respect to voting rights, Class A Common Stock and Class B Common Stock shall have identical rights.

[**INSERT:** Special Class of Stock to Elect Designated Directors.]

The shares consist of ___________ shares designated as "Class A Common Stock" and ___________ shares designated as "Class B Common Stock". With respect to the election of directors, the holders of Class A Common Stock shall have the sole and exclusive right to elect ___________ director(s), and the balance of the directors will be elected by the holders of Class B Common Stock. The holders of each class of stock shall have the sole and exclusive right to remove at any time the director(s) elected by such holders. The election and removal of the director(s) to be elected by the holders of any class of stock may be effected by unanimous written consent of all such holders, at a special meeting of such holders called for that purpose, or at an annual meeting of shareholders. Any vacancy with respect to a director elected by the holders of any class of stock shall be filled by a special election by the holders of that class, and not by a vote of the remaining directors. Other than with respect to rights relating to the election and removal of directors, Class A Common Stock and Class B Common Stock shall have identical rights.

The Board of Directors shall consist of not less than ___________ directors.

[**INSERT:** Special Class of Stock to Elect Designated Directors. [All stock to elect balance of directors.]]

The shares consist of ___________ shares designated as "Class A Common Stock" and ___________ shares designated as "Class B Common Stock". With respect to the election of directors, the holders of Class B Common Stock shall have the sole and exclusive right to elect ___________ director(s), and the balance of the directors will be elected by holders of all shares. The holders of Class B Common Stock shall have the sole and exclusive right to remove at any time the director(s) elected by such holders. The election and removal of the director(s) to be elected by the holders of Class B Common Stock may be effected by unanimous written consent of all such holders, at a special meeting of such holders called for that purpose, or at an annual meeting of shareholders. Any vacancy with respect to a director elected by the holders of Class B Common Stock shall be filled by a special election by the holders of Class B Common Stock, and not by a vote of the remaining directors. Other than with respect to rights relating to the election and removal of directors, Class A Common Stock and Class B Common Stock shall have identical rights.

The Board of Directors shall consist of not less than ___________ directors.

[**INSERT:** "Blank Check" Stock Authorized.]

The shares consist of ___________ shares designated as "Common Stock" and ___________ shares designated as "Preferred Stock."

Except to the extent such rights are granted to Preferred Stock or one or more series thereof, Common Stock has unlimited voting rights and is entitled to receive the net assets of the corporation upon dissolution.

The preferences, limitations, and relative rights of Preferred Stock are undesignated. The Board of Directors may designate one or more series within Preferred Stock, and the designation and number of shares within each series, and shall determine the preferences, limitations, and relative rights of any shares of Preferred Stock, or of any series of Preferred Stock, before issuance of any shares of that class or series. [Preferred Stock, or any series thereof, may be designated as common or preferred, and may have rights that are identical to those of Common Stock.]

Shares of one class or series may be issued as a share dividend in respect to shares of another class or series.

OPTIONAL PROVISIONS

[**INSERT:** Simple Majority Vote to Amend Articles, etc.]

ARTICLE ____

Amendment of the articles of incorporation, approval of a plan of merger or share exchange, authorizing the sale, lease, exchange, or other disposition of all, or substantially all of the corporation's property, otherwise than in the usual and regular course of business, and authorizing dissolution of the corporation, shall be approved by each voting group entitled to vote thereon by a simple majority of all the votes entitled to be cast by that voting group.

ARTICLE V

TEXT INSERTS

To the maximum extent allowable bylaw, any action which may be authorized or approved by a vote of the shareholders at a meeting thereof at any time prior to the registration of any Corporation securities under the Securities Exchange Act of 1934, as amended, may be taken with the written consent of shareholders holding that number of shares as could authorize or approve the action at a meeting of all shareholders entitled to vote on such action. Except as otherwise provided by law, a notice describing the action taken and the effective date of such action shall be provided to each nonconsenting shareholder no later than ten (10) days prior to the effective date of any action approved pursuant to the preceding sentence

C. FORM: BOARD OF DIRECTORS' ORGANIZATIONAL CONSENT RESOLUTIONS

**CONSENT IN LIEU OF
ORGANIZATIONAL MEETING
OF [SOLE] DIRECTOR(S)**

OF

____

The undersigned, being [all the] [the sole] director(s) of ________________________, a Washington corporation (the "Company"), pursuant to Section 23B.08.210 of the Washington Business Corporations Act (the "Act") hereby consent(s) to, and by this action approve(s) and adopt(s) the following resolutions:

FORMATION

WHEREAS, the original Articles of Incorporation of the Company were filed in the office of the Secretary of State of Washington on ________________________; therefore it is

RESOLVED, that a certified copy of said Articles of Incorporation be inserted in the minute book of the Company; and

RESOLVED, that all the acts of the incorporator of the Company in forming and organizing the Company are hereby approved, ratified, and adopted as valid and binding acts of the Company.

BYLAWS

RESOLVED, that the Bylaws, consisting of fifteen (15) pages inserted in the minute book following the Articles of Incorporation, are hereby adopted as the Bylaws of the Company.

AGENT FOR SERVICE OF PROCESS

RESOLVED, that the appointment of ________________________ as the Company's registered agent for service of process in Washington is hereby ratified, approved and confirmed.

FISCAL YEAR

RESOLVED, that the Company's fiscal year shall end on ________________________ each year.

PAYMENT OF ORGANIZATIONAL EXPENSES

RESOLVED, that the officers of the Company or any of them be, and each hereby is, authorized and directed to pay the expenses of incorporation and organization of the Company.

DIRECTORS

WHEREAS, the Bylaws of the Company allow for the number of directors to be set by the Articles of Incorporation or by resolution of the board of directors; therefore it is

RESOLVED, that the number of directors of the Company be fixed at ____________ (______) until such time as such number is amended by action of the Board of Directors or the shareholders of the Company.

OFFICERS

RESOLVED, that the following persons be, and they hereby are, elected, effective immediately, as officers of the Company to serve until the next annual meeting of directors and until the election and qualification of their successors:

Name	Title
________________________	President
________________________	Vice President

__________________________ Secretary

__________________________ Treasurer

FORM OF STOCK CERTIFICATE

RESOLVED, that the form of stock certificate attached hereto be, and the same hereby is, approved and adopted for use by the Company.

ISSUANCE OF SHARES

WHEREAS, the Company is authorized to issue up to __________________________

(_________) shares of Common Stock, [no] [$_________] par value, and none yet have been sold or issued;

RESOLVED, that the board of directors hereby determines that $_________ per share is adequate consideration to be received by the Company for its Common Stock;

RESOLVED, that subject to compliance with the applicable state securities laws and the Securities Act of 1933, as amended ("1933 Act"), the Company shall issue shares of its Common Stock to the persons listed below at a price of $________ per share, in cash, and for the number of shares set forth opposite their name:

Name	Number of Shares
__________________________	______
__________________________	______
__________________________	______

RESOLVED, that upon receipt of the stated consideration and payment in full of any amounts payable pursuant to the terms thereof, such shares shall be duly and validly issued, fully paid and nonassessable.

RESOLVED, that the appropriate officers of the Company are hereby authorized and directed for and on behalf of the Company (i) to take all action necessary to comply with applicable state securities laws and the 1933 Act with respect to the above offer and issuance of shares, (ii) to thereafter issue shares on behalf of the Company pursuant to the above authorization, and (iii) to take such other action as they may deem appropriate to carry out the offer and issuance of shares and the intent of these resolutions.

BANK ACCOUNT

RESOLVED, that the officers, or any of them, be, and each of them are hereby authorized to execute on behalf of the Company any and all forms of bank resolutions dealing with corporate banking matters, including the establishing and maintaining of corporate bank accounts, which in their judgment from time to time may be required for the proper fiscal management of the Company, including the designation thereon of such authorized signatures of corporate officers or other agents as may to them seem appropriate. Such officers may execute such banking resolution or resolutions as if authorized to do so by a specific resolution of the board of directors adopted on the date this resolution was adopted by the board. A copy of any such banking resolutions shall be placed in the corporate minute book.

REGISTRATIONS AND LICENSES

RESOLVED, that the officers of the Company are hereby authorized and directed to cause the Company to be registered with federal and state taxing authorities, to obtain all necessary business licenses, and otherwise take all actions that are necessary or appropriate to enable the Company to commence business.

* * * [S CORPORATION OPTION] * * *

S CORPORATION ELECTION

RESOLVED, that for the first taxable year that is hereby designated to end on December 31, ______, the corporation shall make an election pursuant to Section 1362 of the Internal Revenue Code of 1986, as amended, to be treated as an "S corporation." The shareholders shall execute such consents as are required thereby and the corporation shall timely file Internal Revenue Service Form 2553 and the required consents.

OMNIBUS

RESOLVED, that any and all actions heretofore taken by the incorporator and/or officers of the Company resolutions are hereby ratified and confirmed as the acts and deeds of the Company; and

FURTHER RESOLVED, that the officers of the Company be, and each of them hereby is, authorized, directed and empowered to do all such other acts and things and to execute and deliver all such certificates or other documents and to take such other action as they deem necessary or desirable to carry out the purposes and intent, but within the limitations, of the above resolutions.

DATED this ______ day of __________________________, __________.

DIRECTOR(S):

____

____

____

____

D. FORM: LIMITED LIABILITY COMPANY OPERATING AGREEMENT

OPERATING AGREEMENT OF

_________________ _________________

A Washington Limited Liability Company

This Operating Agreement (the "Agreement") is made and entered into as of the ___ day of _______, 2011, by and between _______ ("_______") and _______ ("_______") (the "Members"). The parties agree to operate as a limited liability company under the laws of the state of Washington as follows.

The parties hereto agree as follows:

1. DEFINITIONS. The following terms used in the Agreement shall have the meanings specified below:

1.1 "Act" means the Washington Limited Liability Company Act, as amended from time to time.

1.2 "Adjusted Contribution Amount" with respect to each Member means the Capital Contributions pursuant to Sections 7.1 and 7.4, as reduced from time to time by distributions pursuant to Section 10.

1.3 "Agreement" means this Operating Agreement of the ABC, LLC as it may be amended from time to time.

1.4 "Assignee" means a person who has acquired a Member's Interest in whole or part and has not become a Substitute Member.

1.5 "Capital Account" means the account maintained for each Member in accordance with Section 7.5. In the case of a transfer of an interest, the transferee shall succeed to the Capital Account of the transferor or, in the case of a partial transfer, a proportionate share thereof.

1.6 "Capital Contribution" means the total amount of money and the fair market value of all property contributed to the Company by each Member pursuant to the terms of the Agreement. Capital Contribution shall also include any amounts paid directly by a Member to any creditor of the Company in respect of any guarantee or similar obligation undertaken by such Member in connection with the Company's operations. Any reference to the Capital Contribution of a Member shall include the Capital Contribution made by a predecessor holder of the interest of such Member.

1.7 "Cash Available for Distribution" means all cash receipts of the Company, excluding cash available upon liquidation of the Company, in excess of amounts reasonably required for payment of operating expenses, repayment of current liabilities, repayment of such amounts of Company indebtedness as the Manager shall determine necessary or advisable, and the establishment of and additions to such cash reserves as the Manager shall deem necessary or advisable, including, but not limited to reserves for capital expenditures, replacements, contingent or unforeseen liabilities or other obligations of the Company.

1.8 "Code" means the United States Internal Revenue Code of 1986, as amended. References to specific Code Sections or Treasury Regulations shall be deemed to refer to such Code Sections or Treasury Regulations as they may be amended from time to time or to any successor Code Sections or Treasury Regulations if the Code Section or Treasury Regulation referred to is repealed.

1.9 "Company" means the Washington limited liability company named ABC, LLC governed by the Agreement.

1.10 "Company Property" means all the real and personal property owned by the Company.

1.11 "Deemed Capital Account" means a Member's Capital Account, as calculated from time to time, adjusted by (i) adding thereto the sum of (A) the amount of such Member's Mandatory Obligation, if any, and (B) each Member's share of Minimum Gain (determined after any decreases therein for such year) and (ii) subtracting therefrom (A) allocations of losses and deductions which are reasonably expected to be made as of the end of the taxable year to the Members pursuant to Code Section 704(e)(2), Code Section 706(d) and Treasury Regulation Section 1.751–1(b)(2)(ii), and (B) distributions which at the end of the taxable year are reasonably expected to be made to the Member to the extent that said distributions exceed offsetting increases to the Member's Capital Account (including allocations of the Qualified Income Offset pursuant to Section 8.7 but excluding allocations of Minimum Gain Chargeback pursuant to Section 8.6) that are reasonably expected to occur during (or prior to) the taxable years in which such distributions are reasonably expected to be made.

1.12 "Interest" or "Company Interest" means the ownership interest of a Member in the Company at any particular time, including the right of such Member to any and all benefits to which such Member may be entitled as provided in the Agreement and in the Act, together with the obligations of such Member to comply with all the terms and provisions of the Agreement and the Act.

1.13 "Manager(s)" means those Member(s) and other persons who are appointed in accordance with this Agreement to exercise the authority of Manager under this Agreement and the Act. If at any time a Member who is a Manager ceases to be a Member for any reason, that Member shall simultaneously cease to be a Manager. The initial Manager of the Company shall be [________].

1.14 "Mandatory Obligation" means the sum of (i) the amount of a Member's remaining contribution obligation (including the amount of any Capital Account deficit such Member is obligated to restore upon liquidation) provided that such contribution must be made in all events within ninety (90) days of liquidation of the Member's interest as determined under Treasury Regulation Section 1.704–1(b)(2)(ii)(g) and (ii) the additional amount, if any, such Member would be obligated to contribute as of year end to retire recourse indebtedness of the Company if the Company were to liquidate as of such date and dispose of all of its assets at book value.

1.15 "Member(s)" means those persons who execute a counterpart of this Agreement and those persons who are hereafter admitted as members under Section 14.4 below.

1.16 "Minimum Gain" means the amount determined by computing, with respect to each nonrecourse liability of the Company, the amount of gain, if any, that would be realized by the Company if it disposed of the Company Property subject to such nonrecourse liability in full satisfaction thereof in a taxable transaction, and then by aggregating the amounts so determined. Such gain shall be determined in accordance with Treasury Regulation Section 1.704–2(d). Each Member's share of Minimum Gain at the end of any taxable year of the Company shall be determined in accordance with Treasury Regulation Section 1.704–2(g)(1).

1.17 "Net Income" or "Net Loss" means taxable income or loss (including items requiring separate computation under Section 702 of the Code) of the Company as determined using the method of accounting chosen by the Manager and used by the Company for federal income tax purposes, adjusted in accordance with Treasury Regulation Section 1.704–1(b)(2)(iv)(g), for any property with differing tax and book values, to take into account depreciation, depletion, amortization and gain or loss as computed for book purposes.

1.18 "Percentage Interest" means the percentage interest of each Member as set forth on Appendix A.

1.19 "Substitute Member" means an Assignee who has been admitted to all of the rights of membership pursuant to Section 14.4 below.

2. FORMATION. The Members hereby agree to form and to operate the Company under the terms and conditions set forth herein. Except as otherwise provided herein, the rights and liabilities of the Members shall be governed by the Act.

2.1 Defects as to Formalities. A failure to observe any formalities or requirements of this Agreement, the articles of organization for the Company or the Act shall not be grounds for imposing personal liability on the Members or Manager for liabilities of the Company.

2.2 No Partnership Intended for Nontax Purposes. The Members have formed the Company under the Act, and expressly do not intend hereby to form a partnership under either the Washington Uniform Partnership Act or the Washington Uniform Limited Partnership Act or a corporation under the Washington Business Corporation Act. The Members do not intend to be partners one to another, or partners as to any third party. The Members hereto agree and acknowledge that the Company is to be treated as a partnership for federal income tax purposes.

2.3 Rights of Creditors and Third Parties. This Agreement is entered into among the Company and the Members for the exclusive benefit of the Company, its Members and their successors and assigns. The Agreement is expressly not intended for the benefit of any creditor of the Company or any other person.

Except and only to the extent provided by applicable statute, no such creditor or third party shall have any rights under the Agreement or any agreement between the Company and any Member with respect to any Contribution or otherwise.

2.4 Title to Property. All Company Property shall be owned by the Company as an entity and no Member shall have any ownership interest in such Property in the Member's individual name or right, and each Member's interest in the Company shall be personal property for all purposes. Except as otherwise provided in this Agreement, the Company shall hold all Company Property in the name of the Company and not in the name or names of any Member or Members.

2.5 Payments of Individual Obligations. The Company's credit and assets shall be used solely for the benefit of the Company, and no asset of the Company shall be transferred or encumbered for or in payment of any individual obligation of any Member unless otherwise provided for herein.

3. NAME. The name of the Company shall be ABC, LLC. The Manager may from time to time change the name of the Company or adopt such trade or fictitious names as they may determine to be appropriate.

4. OFFICE; AGENT FOR SERVICE OF PROCESS. The principal office of the Company shall be ______________. The Company may maintain such other offices at such other places as the Manager may determine to be appropriate. The agent for service of process for the Company shall be _______ at the above address.

5. PURPOSES OF THE COMPANY. The Company shall be in the business of providing _______ marketing products and services. In addition, the Company may engage in any other business and shall have such other purposes as may be necessary, incidental or convenient to carry on the Company's primary purpose or as determined by the Manager and Members from time to time in accordance with the terms of this Agreement.

6. TERM. The term of the Company shall commence on the date of the filing of the Articles of Organization for the Company in the office of the Washington Secretary of State, and shall continue until dissolved, wound up and terminated in accordance with the provisions of this Agreement and the Act.

7. PERCENTAGE INTERESTS AND CAPITAL CONTRIBUTIONS.

7.1 Initial Capital Contributions; Percentage Interests. The Members shall make the initial Capital Contributions to the Company in the amounts set forth on Appendix A for the Percentage Interests in the Company as shown on Appendix A.

7.2 No Interest on Capital. No Member shall be entitled to receive interest on such Member's Capital Contributions or such Member's Capital Account.

7.3 No Withdrawal of Capital. Except as otherwise provided in this Agreement, no Member shall have the right to withdraw or demand a return of any or all of such Member's Capital Contribution. It is the intent of the Members that no distribution (or any part of any distribution) made to any Member pursuant to Section 10 hereof shall be deemed a return or withdrawal of Capital

Contributions, even if such distribution represents (in full or in part) a distribution of revenue offset by depreciation or any other non-cash item accounted for as an expense, loss or deduction from, or offset to, the Company's income, and that no Member shall be obligated to pay any such amount to or for the account of the Company or any creditor of the Company. However, if any court of competent jurisdiction holds that, notwithstanding the provisions of this Agreement, any Member is obligated to make any such payment, such obligation shall be the obligation of such Member and not of any other Member, including the Manager.

7.4 Additional Capital. Except as otherwise provided for herein or mutually agreed upon by the Members, no Member shall be obligated to make an additional Capital Contribution to the Company.

7.5 Capital Accounts. The Company shall establish and maintain a Capital Account for each Member in accordance with Treasury Regulations issued under Code Section 704. The initial Capital Account balance for each Member shall be the amount of initial Capital Contributions made by each Member under Section 7.1. The Capital Account of each Member shall be increased to reflect (i) such Member's cash contributions, (ii) the fair market value of property contributed by such Member (net of liabilities securing such contributed property that the Company is considered to assume or take subject to under Code Section 752), (iii) such Member's share of Net Income (including all gain as calculated pursuant to Section 1001 of the Code) of the Company and (iv) such Member's share of income and gain exempt from tax. The Capital Account of each Member shall be reduced to reflect (a) the amount of money and the fair market value of property distributed to such Member (net of liabilities securing such distributed property that the Member is considered to assume or take subject to under Section 752), (b) such Member's share of non-capitalized expenditures not deductible by the Company in computing its taxable income as determined under Code Section 705(a)(2)(B), (c) such Member's share of Net Loss of the Company and (d) such Member's share of amounts paid or incurred to organize the Company or to promote the sale of Company Interests to the extent that an election under Code Section 709(b) has not properly been made for such amounts. The Manager shall determine the fair market value of all property which is distributed in kind, and the Capital Accounts of the Members shall be adjusted as though the property had been sold for its fair market value and the gain or loss attributable to such sale allocated among the Members in accordance with Section 8.1 or 8.2, as applicable. In the event of a contribution of property with a fair market value which is not equal to its adjusted basis (as determined for federal income tax purposes), a revaluation of the Members' Capital Accounts upon the admission of new members to the Company, or in other appropriate situations as permitted by Treasury Regulations issued under Code Section 704, the Company shall separately maintain "tax" Capital Accounts solely for purposes of taking into account the variation between the adjusted tax basis and book value of Company property in tax allocations to the Members consistent with the principles of Code Section 704(c) in accordance with the rules prescribed in Treasury Regulations promulgated under Code Section 704.

7.6 Default. In the event any Member shall fail to contribute any cash or property when due hereunder, such Member shall remain liable therefor to the Company, which may institute proceedings in any court of competent jurisdiction in connection with which such Member shall pay the costs of such collection, including reasonable attorneys' fees. Any compromise or settlement with a Member failing to contribute cash or property due hereunder may be approved by a majority by Percentage Interest of the other Members.

8. ALLOCATIONS.

8.1 Allocation of Net Loss from Operations. Except as otherwise provided in this Section 8 and in Section 16.3, the Company shall allocate Net Loss to the Members in proportion to each Member's Percentage Interest.

8.2 Allocation of Net Income from Operations. Except as otherwise provided in this Section 8 and Section 16.3, the Company shall allocate all Net Income as follows:

1. First, to the Members in proportion to the aggregate distributions of Cash Available for Distribution made to the Members in the current year and all prior years pursuant to Section 10 until such time as each Member has been allocated Net Income pursuant to this Section 8.3 in an amount equal to the excess of (i) the amount of Cash Available for Distribution distributed to such Member for the current year and all prior years pursuant to Section 10, over (ii) the amount of Net Income previously allocated to such Member pursuant to this Section 8.3; and thereafter, all remaining Net Income shall be allocated in proportion to each Member's Percentage Interest.

8.3 Limitation on Net Loss Allocations. Notwithstanding anything contained in this Section 8, no Member shall be allocated Net Loss to the extent such allocation would cause a negative balance in such Member's Deemed Capital Account as of the end of the taxable year to which such allocation relates.

8.4 Minimum Gain Chargeback. If there is a net decrease in Minimum Gain during a taxable year of the Company, then notwithstanding any other provision of this Section 8 or Section 16.3, each Member must be allocated items of income and gain for such year, and succeeding taxable years to the extent necessary (the "Minimum Gain Chargeback"), in proportion to, and to the extent of, an amount required under Treasury Regulation Section 1.704–2(f).

8.5 Qualified Income Offset. If at the end of any taxable year and after operation of Section 10, any Member shall have a negative balance in such Member's Deemed Capital Account, then notwithstanding anything contained in this Section 8, there shall be reallocated to each Member with a negative balance in such Member's Deemed Capital Account (determined after the allocation of income, gain or loss under this Section 8 for such year) each item of Company gross income (unreduced by any deductions) and gain in proportion to such negative balances until the Deemed Capital Account for each such Member is increased to zero.

8.6 Curative Allocations. The allocations set forth in Sections 8.3, 8.4 and 8.5 (the "Regulatory Allocations") are intended to comply with certain requirements of the Treasury Regulations issued pursuant to Code Section 704(b). It is the intent of the Members that, to the extent possible, all Regulatory Allocations shall be offset either with other Regulatory Allocations or with special allocations of other items of Company income, gain, loss, or deduction pursuant to this Section 8. Therefore, notwithstanding any other provision of this Section 8 (other than the Regulatory Allocations), the Manager shall make such offsetting special allocations of Company income, gain, loss, or deduction in whatever manner they determine appropriate so that, after such offsetting allocations are made, each Member's Capital Account balance is, to the extent possible, equal to the Capital Account balance such Member would have had if the Regulatory Allocations were not part of the Agreement and all Company items were allocated pursuant to other provisions of this Section 8.

8.7 Modification of Company Allocations. It is the intent of the Members that each Member's distributive share of income, gain, loss, deduction, or credit (or items thereof) shall be determined and allocated in accordance with this Section 8 to the fullest extent permitted by Section 704(b) of the Code. In order to preserve and protect the determinations and allocations provided for in this Section 8, the Manager shall be, and hereby is, authorized and directed to allocate income, gain, loss, deduction or credit (or items thereof) arising in any year differently from the manner otherwise provided for in this Section 8 if, and to the extent that, allocation of income, gain, loss, deduction or credit (or items thereof) in the manner provided for in this Section would cause the determination and allocation of each Member's distributive share of income, gain, loss, deduction or credit (or items thereof), not to be permitted by Section 704(b) of the Code and Treasury Regulations promulgated thereunder. Any allocation made pursuant to this Section 8.9 shall be made only after the Manager has secured an opinion of counsel that such modification is the minimum modification required to comply with Code Section 704(b) and shall be deemed to be a complete substitute for any allocation otherwise provided for in this Section and no amendment of this Agreement or approval of any Member shall be required. The Members shall be given notice of the modification within thirty (30) days of the effective date thereof, such notice to include the text of the modification and a statement of the circumstances requiring the modification to be made.

8.8 Deficit Capital Accounts at Liquidation. It is understood and agreed that one purpose of the provisions of this Section 8 is to insure that none of the Members has a deficit Capital Account balance after liquidation and to insure that all allocations under this Section 8 will be respected by the Internal Revenue Service. The Members and the Company neither intend nor expect that any Member will have a deficit Capital Account balance after liquidation and, notwithstanding anything to the contrary in this Agreement, the provisions of this Agreement shall be construed and interpreted to give effect to such intention. However, if following a liquidation of a Member's interest as determined under Treasury Regulation Section 1.704–1(b)(2)(ii)(g), a Member has a deficit balance in such Member's Capital Account after the allocation of Net Income pursuant to this Section 8 and Section 16.3 and all other adjustments have been made to such Member's Capital Account for Company operations and liquidation, no Member shall have any obligation to restore such deficit balance, as provided in Section

8.9.

8.9 Deficit Restoration Obligation. No Member shall have an obligation to restore a deficit Capital Account balance upon liquidation of the Company or liquidation of its interest in the Company.

9. COMPANY EXPENSES. The Company shall pay, and the Manager shall be reimbursed for, all costs and expenses of the Company, which may include, but are not limited to:

9.1 All organizational expenses incurred in the formation of the Company and the selling of interests in the Company;

9.2 All costs of personnel employed by the Company;

9.3 All costs reasonably related to the conduct of the Company's day-to-day business affairs, including, but without limitation, the cost of supplies, utilities, taxes, licenses, fees and services contracted from third parties;

9.4 All costs of borrowed money, taxes and assessments on Company property, and other taxes applicable to the Company;

9.5 Legal, audit, accounting, brokerage and other fees;

9.6 Printing and other expenses and taxes incurred in connection with the issuance, distribution, transfer, registration and recording of documents evidencing ownership of an interest in the Company or in connection with the business of the Company;

9.7 Fees and expenses paid to service providers, including affiliates of the Manager;

9.8 The cost of insurance obtained in connection with the business of the Company;

9.9 Expenses of revising, amending, converting, modifying or terminating the Company;

9.10 Expenses in connection with distributions made by the Company to, and communications and bookkeeping and clerical work necessary in maintaining relations with, Members;

9.11 Expenses in connection with preparing and mailing reports required to be furnished to Members for investment, tax reporting or other purposes that the Manager deems appropriate; and

9.12 Costs incurred in connection with any litigation, including any examinations or audits by regulatory agencies.

10. DISTRIBUTIONS OF CASH AVAILABLE FOR DISTRIBUTION. At such times and in such amounts as the Manager in its discretion determines appropriate, Cash Available for Distribution shall be distributed in the following order of priority:

10.1 First, among the Members in proportion to their Adjusted Contribution Amounts until such balances are reduced to zero; and

10.2 Thereafter, among the Members in proportion to their Percentage Interests.

11. POWERS, RIGHTS AND OBLIGATIONS OF MANAGER.

11.1 General Authority and Powers of Manager. Except as provided in Section , the Manager shall have the exclusive right and power to manage, operate and control the Company and to do all things and make all decisions necessary or appropriate to carry on the business and affairs of the Company. All decisions required to be made by the Manager or action to be taken by the Manager shall require the approval and action of only one Manager, acting alone, except as otherwise specifically provided in this Agreement. The authority of one Manager, acting alone, shall include, but shall not be limited to the following:

(a) To spend the capital and revenues of the Company;

(b) To manage, develop, and operate the business of the Company and the Company properties;

(c) To employ service providers to assist in the operation and management of the Company's business and for the operation and development of the property of the Company, as the Manager shall deem necessary in its sole discretion;

(d) To acquire, lease and sell personal and/or real property, hire and fire employees, and to do all other acts necessary, appropriate or helpful for the operation of the Company business;

(e) To execute, acknowledge and deliver any and all instruments to effectuate any of the foregoing powers and any other powers granted the Manager under the laws of the state of Washington or other provisions of this Agreement;

(f) To enter into and to execute agreements for employment or services, as well as any other agreements and all other instruments a Manager deems necessary or appropriate to operate the Company's business and to operate and dispose of Company properties or to effectively and properly perform its duties or exercise its powers hereunder;

(g) To borrow money on a secured or unsecured basis from individuals, banks and other lending institutions to meet Company obligations, provide Company working capital and for any other Company purpose, and to execute promissory notes, mortgages, deeds of trust and assignments of Company property, and such other security instruments as a lender of funds may require, to secure repayment of such borrowings;

(h) To enter into such agreements and contracts and to give such receipts, releases and discharges, with respect to the business of the Company, as a Manager deems advisable or appropriate;

(i) To purchase, at the expense of the Company, such liability and other insurance as the Manager, in its sole discretion, deems advisable to protect the Company's assets and business; however, the Manager shall not be liable to the Company or the other Members for failure to purchase any insurance;

and

(j) To sue and be sued, complain, defend, settle and/or compromise, with respect to any claim in favor of or against the Company, in the name and on behalf of the Company.

11.2 Time Devoted to Company; Other Ventures. The Manager shall devote so much of its time to the business of the Company as in its judgment the conduct of the Company's business reasonably requires. The Manager and the other Members may engage in business ventures and activities of any nature and description independently or with others, whether or not in competition with the business of the Company, and shall have no obligation to disclose business opportunities available to them, and neither the Company nor any of the other Members shall have any rights in and to such independent ventures and activities or the income or profits derived therefrom by reason of their acquisition of interests in the Company. This Section 11.2 is intended to modify any provisions or obligations of the Act to the contrary and each of the Members and the Company hereby waives and releases any claims they may have under the Act with respect to any such activities or ventures of the Manager or other Members.

11.3 Liability of Manager to Members and Company. In carrying out its duties and exercising the powers hereunder, the Manager shall exercise reasonable skill, care and business judgment. A Manager shall not be liable to the Company or the Members for any act or omission performed or omitted by it in good faith pursuant to the authority granted to it by this Agreement as a Manager or Tax Matters Partner (as defined in the Code) unless such act or omission constitutes gross negligence or willful misconduct by such Manager.

11.4 Indemnification. The Company shall indemnify and hold harmless the Manager from any loss or damage, including attorneys' fees actually and reasonably incurred by it, by reason of any act or omission performed or omitted by it on behalf of the Company or in furtherance of the Company's interests or as Tax Matters Partner; however, such indemnification or agreement to hold harmless shall be recoverable only out of the assets of the Company and not from the Members. The foregoing indemnity shall extend only to acts or omissions performed or omitted by a Manager in good faith and in the belief that the acts or omissions were in the Company's interest or not opposed to the best interests of the Company.

11.5 Fiduciary Responsibility. The Manager shall have a fiduciary responsibility for the safekeeping and use of all funds and assets of the Company, and all such funds and assets shall be used in accordance with the terms of this Agreement.

11.6 Restrictions on Authority of Manager.

(a) Except as provided in Section 11.6(b), the following Company decisions shall require the written consent of the Manager and Members holding a majority of the Percentage Interests in the Company:

(i) The dissolution and winding up of the Company;

(ii) The sale, exchange or other transfer of all or substantially all the assets of the Company other than in the ordinary course of business; or

(iii) A change in the nature of the business of the Company.

(b) Notwithstanding the provisions of Section 11.6(a), no consent or approval of the Members shall be required prior to a transfer of the Project or other Company property for no consideration other than full or partial satisfaction of Company indebtedness such as by deed in lieu of foreclosure or similar procedure.

(c) Notwithstanding the provisions of Section 11.6(a)(i), the dissolution and winding up or insolvency filing of the Company shall require the unanimous consent of all Members.

12. STATUS OF MEMBERS.

12.1 No Participation in Management. Except as specifically provided in Section 11.6 above, no Member shall take part in the conduct or control of the Company's business or the management of the Company, or have any right or authority to act for or on the behalf of, or otherwise bind, the Company (except a Member who may also be a Manager and then only in such Member's capacity as a Manager within the scope of such Member's authority hereunder).

12.2 Limitation of Liability. No Member shall have, solely by virtue of such Member's status as a Member in the Company, any personal liability whatever, whether to the Company, to any Members or to the creditors of the Company, for the debts or obligations of the Company or any of its losses beyond the amount committed by such Member to the capital of the Company, except as otherwise required by the Act.

12.3 Death or Incapacity of Non–Manager Member. The death, incompetence, withdrawal, expulsion, bankruptcy or dissolution of a Member, or the occurrence of any other event which terminates the continued membership of a Member in the Company, shall not cause a dissolution of the Company unless such Member is a Manager of the Company. Upon the occurrence of such event, the rights of such non-Manager Member to share in the Net Income and Net Loss of the Company, to receive distributions from the Company and to assign an interest in the Company pursuant to Section 14 shall, on the happening of such an event, devolve upon such Member's executor, administrator, guardian, conservator, or other legal representative or successor, as the case may be, subject to the terms and conditions of this Agreement, and the Company shall continue as a limited liability company. However, in any such event, such legal representative or successor, or any assignee of such legal representative or successor shall be admitted to the Company as a Member only in accordance with and pursuant to all of the terms and conditions of Section 14 hereof.

12.4 Death or Incapacity of a Manager Member. The death, incompetence, withdrawal, expulsion, bankruptcy or dissolution of a Member that is a Manager, or the occurrence of any other event which terminates the continued membership of such Member in the Company, shall cause a dissolution of the Company, unless the Company is continued in accordance with Section 16. If the Company is continued in accordance with Section 16, the rights of such Member to share in the Net Income and Net Loss of the Company, to receive distributions from the Company and to assign an interest in the Company pursuant to Section 14 hereof shall, on the happening of such an event, devolve upon such Member's executor, administrator, guardian, conservator, or other legal representative or successor, as the case may be, subject to the terms and conditions of this Agreement, and the Company shall continue as a limited liability company. However, in any such event such legal representative or successor, or any assignee of such legal representative or successor shall be admitted to the Company as a Member only in accordance with and pursuant to all of the terms and conditions of Section 14 hereof.

12.5 Recourse of Members. Each Member shall look solely to the assets of the Company for all distributions with respect to the Company and such Member's Capital Contribution thereto and share of Net Income and Net Loss thereof and shall have no recourse therefore, upon dissolution or otherwise, against any Manager or any other Member.

12.6 No Right to Property. No Member, regardless of the nature of such Member's contributions to the capital of the Company, shall have any right to demand or receive any distribution from the Company in any form other than cash, upon dissolution or otherwise.

13. BOOKS AND RECORDS, ACCOUNTING, REPORTS AND STATEMENTS AND TAX MATTERS.

13.1 Books and Records. The Manager shall, at the expense of the Company, keep and maintain, or cause to be kept and maintained, the books and records of the Company on the same method of accounting as utilized for federal income tax purposes, which shall be kept separate and apart from the books and records of the Manager.

13.2 Annual Accounting Period. All books and records of the Company shall be kept on the basis of an annual accounting period ending December 31 of each year, except for the final accounting period which shall end on the date of termination of the Company. All references herein to the "fiscal year of the Company" are to the annual accounting period described in the preceding sentence, whether the same shall consist of twelve months or less.

13.3 Manager's Reports to Members. The Manager shall send at Company expense to each Member the following:

(a) Within seventy-five (75) days after the end of each fiscal year of the Company, such information as shall be necessary for the preparation by such Member of such Member's federal income tax return which shall include a computation of the distributions to such Member and the allocation to such Member of profits or losses, as the case may be; and

(b) Within one hundred twenty (120) days after the end of each fiscal quarter of the Company, a quarterly report, which shall include:

(i) A balance sheet;

(ii) A statement of income and expenses;

(iii) A statement of changes in Members' capital; and

(iv) A statement of the balances in the Capital Accounts of the Members.

13.4 Right to Examine Records. Members shall be entitled, upon written request directed to the Company, to review the records of the Company at all reasonable times and at the location where such records are kept by the Company.

13.5 Tax Matters Partner. Should there be any controversy with the Internal Revenue Service or any other taxing authority involving the Company, the Manager may expend such funds as they deem necessary and advisable in the interest of the Company to resolve such controversy satisfactorily, including, without being limited thereto, attorneys' and accounting fees. _______ is hereby designated as the "Tax Matters Partner" as referred to in Section 6231(a)(7)(A) of the Code, and is specially authorized to exercise all of the rights and powers now or hereafter granted to the Tax Matters Partner under the Code. Any cost incurred in the audit by any governmental authority of the income tax returns of a Member (as opposed to the Company) shall not be a Company expense. The Manager agrees to consult with and keep the Members advised with respect to (i) any income tax audit of a Company income tax return, and (ii) any elections made by the Company for federal, state or local income tax purposes.

13.6 Tax Returns. The Manager shall, at Company expense, cause the Company to prepare and file a United States Partnership Return of Income and all other tax returns required to be filed by the Company for each fiscal year of the Company.

13.7 Tax Elections. The Manager shall be permitted in its discretion to determine whether the Company should make an election pursuant to Section 754 of the Code to adjust the basis of the assets of the Company. Each of the Members shall, upon request, supply any information necessary to properly give effect to any such election. In addition, the Manager, in its sole discretion, shall be authorized to cause the Company to make and revoke any other elections for federal income tax purposes as they deem appropriate, necessary, or advisable.

14. TRANSFERS OF COMPANY INTERESTS; WITHDRAWAL AND ADMISSION OF MEMBERS.

14.1 General Prohibition. No Member may voluntarily or involuntarily, directly or indirectly, sell, transfer, assign, pledge or otherwise dispose of, or mortgage, pledge, hypothecate or otherwise encumber, or permit or suffer any encumbrance of, all or any part of such Member's interest in the Company, except as provided in this Section 14. Any other purported sale, transfer, assignment, pledge or encumbrance shall be null and void and of no force or effect whatsoever.

14.2 Withdrawal of Member. A Member shall have no power to withdraw voluntarily from the Company, except that a Member may withdraw upon written approval of a majority of the non-withdrawing Members voting by Percentage

Interests, which approval shall include the terms for redemption by the Company of the Interest of the such Member.

14.3 Transfers by Members.

(a) Subject to any restrictions on transferability required by law or contained elsewhere in this Agreement, a Member may transfer such Member's entire interest in the Company upon satisfaction of the following conditions:

(i) The transfer shall (A) be by bequest or by operation of the laws of intestate succession, or (B) be approved in writing by the Manager, which approval shall be withheld only if the proposed transfer does not comply with the requirements of this Section 14.

(ii) The transferor and transferee shall have executed and acknowledged such reasonable and customary instruments as the Manager may deem necessary or desirable to effect such transfer; and

(iii) The transfer does not violate any applicable law or governmental rule or regulation, including without limitation any federal or state securities laws.

(b) At the time of a transfer of any Member's interest, whether or not such transfer is made in accordance with this Section 14, all the rights possessed as a Member in connection with the transferred interest, which rights otherwise would be held either by the transferor or the transferee, shall terminate against the Company unless the transferee is admitted to the Company as a Substitute Member pursuant to the provisions of Section 14.4 hereof; provided, however, that if the transfer is made in accordance with this Section 14, such transferee shall be entitled to receive distributions to which his transferor would otherwise be entitled from and after the Effective Date. The Effective Date shall be the date that is the later of the following dates: (a) the effective date of such transfer as agreed to by the transferee and transferor and set forth in writing in the transfer documentation, or (b) the last day of the calendar month following the date that the Manager has received notice of the transfer and all conditions precedent to such transfer provided for in this Agreement have been satisfied including receipt by the Manager of all documents necessary to comply with the requirements of Section , provided that the Manager, in its sole discretion, may agree to an earlier effective date if an earlier date is requested by the transferor and transferee. The Company and the Manager shall be entitled to treat the transferor as the recognized owner of such interests until the Effective Date and shall incur no liability for distributions made in good faith to the transferor prior to the Effective Date.

(c) Notwithstanding any other provision of this Agreement, a Member may not transfer such Member's interest in any case if such a transfer, when aggregated with all other transfers within a twelve (12) month period, would cause the termination of the Company as a partnership for federal income tax purposes pursuant to Section 708 of the Code, unless such transfer has been previously approved by the Manager.

(d) A change in the custodian or trustee of a Member that is a IRA, Trust, or pension or profit sharing plan, will be reflected on Appendix A in connection with an amendment completed in the first quarter of each year following notification to the Company of such change by the Member and the new custodian or trustee. The IRA, trust or pension or profit sharing plan shall pay the costs incurred by the Company to amend the Company documents to reflect the change in custodian or trustee.

14.4 Admission of Transferees as Members.

(a) No transferee of a Member shall be admitted as a Member unless all of the following conditions have been satisfied:

(i) The transfer complies with Section 14.3;

(ii) The further written consent of the Manager, to such transferee being admitted as a Member is first obtained, which consent may be arbitrarily withheld;

(iii) The prospective transferee has executed an instrument, in form and substance satisfactory to the Manager, accepting and agreeing to be bound by all the terms and conditions of this Agreement, including the power of attorney set forth in Section 17 hereof, and has paid all expenses of the Company in effecting the transfer;

(iv) All requirements of the Act regarding the admission of a transferee Member have been complied with by the transferee, the transferring Member and the Company; and

(v) Such transfer is effected in compliance with all applicable state and federal securities laws.

(b) In the event of a transfer complying with all the requirements of Section 14.3 hereof and the transferee being admitted as a Member pursuant to this Section 14.4, the Manager, for itself and for each Member pursuant to the Power of Attorney granted by each Member, shall execute an amendment to this Agreement and file any necessary amendments to the articles of organization for the Company. Unless named in this Agreement, as amended from time to time, no person shall be considered a Member.

(c) In the event of a change in the custodian or trustee of a Member that is a IRA, trust, or pension or profit sharing plan that complies with Section hereof, the Manager, for itself and for each Member pursuant to the Power of Attorney granted by each Member, shall execute an amendment to this Agreement to reflect such change.

14.5 Assignment as Security Permitted. Notwithstanding any other provision of this Article 14, a Member may assign, as security for a loan or other indebtedness incurred by such Member, such Member's right to receive distributions from the Company, and the Manager, upon receipt of notification of any such assignment, shall acknowledge such assignment and shall agree to pay or distribute proceeds in accordance with instructions from such Member subject to such conditions, including indemnification, as the Manager may reasonably require; provided, however, that such lender shall acknowledge in writing to the

Manager that such assignment of proceeds shall not entitle such lender to foreclose or otherwise acquire or sell the Company Interest and that the only right acquired by such lender shall be the right to receive distributions of cash and property, if any, made by the Company to the Members in accordance with this Agreement.

15. RESIGNATION AND ADMISSION OF MANAGER.

15.1 Resignation of Manager. A Manager shall be entitled to resign as a Manager 120 days after delivery of written notice to the Company and the Members of the Manager's intention to resign, or upon such earlier date as the Manager's resignation is accepted by Members holding a majority of the Percentage Interests in the Company. Resignation of a Manager, who is a Member, pursuant to this Section shall not affect its interest as a Member of the Company. Notwithstanding the foregoing, the transfer by a Manager, who is also a Member, of its Interest in the Company, shall constitute a resignation by such Member as a Manager, which resignation shall be effective as of the date of such transfer.

15.2 Death or Incompetency of Manager. A Manager who is a Member in the Company, shall cease to be a Manager upon the death, incompetence, bankruptcy or dissolution of such Manager, or any other event which terminates the continued membership of the Manager as a Member of the Company.

15.3 Removal of a Manager. A Manager may be removed as a Manager upon the written approval of Members holding a majority of the Percentage Interests of the Company. Removal of Manager who is a Member of the Company, pursuant to this Section shall not affect such Manager's interest as a Member of the Company.

15.4 Appointment of a New or Replacement Manager. A new or replacement Manager may be appointed with the written approval of Members holding a majority of the Percentage Interests of the Company.

16. DISSOLUTION, WINDING UP AND TERMINATION.

16.1 Events Causing Dissolution. The Company shall be dissolved and its affairs shall be wound up upon the happening of the first to occur of any of the following events:

(a) Expiration of the term of the Company stated in Section 6 hereof;

(b) Entry of a decree of administrative or judicial dissolution pursuant to the Act;

(c) The sale or other disposition of all or substantially all of the assets of the Company;

(d) The death, incompetence, withdrawal, expulsion, resignation, removal, bankruptcy or dissolution of a Manager, who is a Member, which is the last remaining Manager of the Company, unless (i) within 120 days of such occurrence, Members owning at least a majority of Percentage Interests in the Company, consent to the appointment of a new Manager(s) in accordance with Section 15.4, in which case the business of the Company shall be carried on by the newly appointed Manager(s), and (ii) the conditions of Section 14 are also satisfied;

(e) The death, incompetence, withdrawal, expulsion, bankruptcy, resignation, or dissolution of a Manager, who is a Member, or any other event that terminates the continued membership of such Manager unless at the time of the occurrence of any of such event there are at least two other Members, and within 120 days of such occurrence, remaining Members owning at least a majority of the Percentage Interests in the Company (or, if greater, remaining Members owning at least a "majority in interest" in the capital and profits of the Company as such term is used in Treas. Reg. Section 301.7701–2(b)(1)), consent to the continuation of the Company, in which case the business of the Company shall be carried on by the remaining Manager(s); or

(f) The unanimous vote of Members.

16.2 Winding Up. Upon dissolution of the Company for any reason, the Manager shall commence to wind up the affairs of the Company and to liquidate its assets. In the event the Company has terminated because the Company lacks a Manager, then the remaining members shall appoint a new Manager solely for the purpose of winding up the affairs of the Company. The Manager shall have the full right and unlimited discretion to determine the time, manner and terms of any sale or sales of Company property pursuant to such liquidation. Pending such sales, the Manager shall have the right to continue to operate or otherwise deal with the assets of the Company. A reasonable time shall be allowed for the orderly winding up of the business of the Company and the liquidation of its assets and the discharge of its liabilities to creditors so as to enable the Manager to minimize the normal losses attendant upon a liquidation, having due regard to the activity and condition of the relevant markets for the Company properties and general financial and economic conditions. Any Member may be a purchaser of any properties of the Company upon liquidation of the Company's assets, including, without limitation, any liquidation conducted pursuant to a judicial dissolution or otherwise under judicial supervision; provided, however, that the purchase price and terms of sale are fair and reasonable to the Company.

16.3 Allocation of Net Income and Net Loss Upon Termination or Sale. All Net Income and Net Loss upon dissolution of the Company or from sale, conversion, disposition or taking of all or substantially all of the Company's property, including, but not limited to the proceeds of any eminent domain proceeding or insurance award (respectively, "Gain on Sale" or "Loss on Sale") shall be allocated as follows:

(a) Loss on Sale shall be allocated among the Members as follows:

(i) First, proportionately to those Members having positive Capital Account balances until all positive Capital Accounts have been reduced to zero; and

(ii) Thereafter, among the Members in proportion to their Percentage Interests.

(b) Gain on Sale to the extent available shall be allocated among the

Members as follows:

(i) First to those Members having negative Capital Account balances in proportion to such negative balances until they are increased to zero; and

(ii) Thereafter, any remaining Gain on Sale shall be allocated to the Members in proportion to their Percentage Interests.

16.4 Distributions. Prior to making distributions in dissolution to the Members, the Manager shall first pay or make provision for all debts and liabilities of the Company, including payment of any Manager Loans, and other loans to Members and their affiliates, and all expenses of liquidation. Subject to the right of the Manager to set up such cash reserves as it deems reasonably necessary for any contingent or unforeseen liabilities or obligations of the Company, the proceeds of liquidation and any other funds of the Company shall be distributed in the following order of priority:

(a) First, to Members in proportion to their Capital Account balances as adjusted by the allocations provided for in Section above; and

(b) Thereafter, the balance, if any, to the Members in proportion to their Percentage Interests.

It is intended and anticipated that the amount of cash distributable upon a termination or dissolution of the Company should equal the sum of the Members' Capital Accounts, after adjustment of such balances in accordance with Sections 16.3(a) and 16.3(b), and that therefore all cash will be distributable under this Section 16.4.

16.5 Certificate of Cancellation; Report; Termination. Upon the dissolution and commencement of winding up of the Company, the Manager shall execute and file articles of dissolution for the Company. Within a reasonable time following the completion of the liquidation of the Company's assets, the Manager shall prepare and furnish to each Member, at the expense of the Company, a statement which shall set forth the assets and liabilities of the Company as of the date of complete liquidation and the amount of each Member's distribution pursuant to Section 16.4 hereof. Upon completion of the liquidation and distribution of all Company funds, the Company shall terminate and the Manager shall have the authority to execute and file all documents required to effectuate the termination of the Company.

17. SPECIAL AND LIMITED POWER OF ATTORNEY.

17.1 The Manager, with full power of substitution, shall at all times during the existence of the Company have a special and limited power of attorney as the authority to act in the name and on the behalf of each Member to make, execute, swear to, verify, acknowledge and file the following documents and any other documents deemed by the Manager to be necessary for the business of the Company:

(a) This Agreement, any separate articles of organization, fictitious business name statements, as well as any amendments to the foregoing which, under the laws of any state, are required to be filed or which the Manager deems it advisable to file;

(b) Any other instrument or document which may be required to be filed by the Company under the laws of any state or by an governmental agency, or which the Manager deems it advisable to file; and

(c) Any instrument or document which may be required to effect the continuation of the Company, the admission of a Manager or Member, the transfer of an interest in the Company, the change in custodian or trustee of any IRA, trust or pension or profit sharing plan Member, or the dissolution and termination of the Company (provided such continuation, admission or dissolution and termination are in accordance with the terms of this Agreement), or to reflect any increases or reductions in amount of contributions of Members.

17.2 The special and limited power of attorney granted to the Manager hereby:

(a) Is a special and limited power of attorney coupled with an interest, is irrevocable, shall survive the dissolution or incompetency of the granting Member, and is limited to those matters herein set forth;

(b) May be exercised by the Manager (or by any authorized officer of the Manager, if not a natural person) for each Member by referencing the list of Members on Appendix A and executing any instrument with a single signature acting as attorney-in-fact for all of them;

(c) Shall survive a transfer by a Member of such Member's interest in the Company pursuant to Section 14 hereof for the sole purpose of enabling the Manager to execute, acknowledge and file any instrument or document necessary or appropriate to admit a transferee as a Member; and

(d) Notwithstanding the foregoing, in the event that a Manager ceases to be a Manager in the Company, the power of attorney granted by this Section 17 to such Manager shall terminate immediately, but any such termination shall not affect the validity of any documents executed prior to such termination, or any other actions previously taken pursuant to this power of attorney or in reliance upon its validity, all of which shall continue to be valid and binding upon the Members in accordance with their terms.

18. AMENDMENTS. Except as otherwise provided by law, this Agreement may be amended in any respect by a majority vote of the Members voting by Percentage Interests; provided, however, that:

18.1 This Agreement may not be amended so as to change any Member's rights to or interest in Net Income, Net Loss or distributions unless (i) such amendment is made in connection with an additional capital contribution to the Company or an additional guarantee of Company indebtedness, (ii) each Member is given the first opportunity maintain its Percentage Interest by participating in such contribution or guarantee in proportion to their existing Percentage Interest, and (iii) the amendment is approved by a sixty-six and two-thirds (66 2/3) of the Members voting by Percentage Interests;

18.2 Without the consent of each Member to be adversely affected by the amendment, this Agreement may not be amended so as to increase the liability of or change the capital contributions required by a Member;

18.3 In the case of any provision hereof which requires the action, approval or consent of a specified Percentage Interest of Members, such provision may not be amended without the consent of the Members owning such specified Percentage Interest; and

18.4 In addition to any amendments otherwise authorized herein, amendments may be made to this Agreement from time to time by the Manager without the consent or approval of the Members, (i) to cure any ambiguity or to correct any typographical errors in this Agreement or (ii) to correct or supplement any provision herein which may be inconsistent with any other provision herein.

19. MISCELLANEOUS.

19.1 Notices. Any notice, offer, consent or other communication required or permitted to be given or made hereunder shall be in writing and shall be deemed to have been sufficiently given or made when delivered personally to the party (or an officer of the party) to whom the same is directed, or (except in the event of a mail strike) five days after being mailed by first class mail, postage prepaid, if to the Company or to a Manager, to the office described in Section 4 hereof, or if to a Member, to such Member's last known address or when received by facsimile if to the Company or Manager to the facsimile number for the office described in Section hereof, or if to a Member, to such Member's facsimile number. Any Member may change such Member's address for the purpose of this Section 19.1 by giving notice of such change to the Company, such change to become effective on the tenth day after such notice is given.

19.2 Entire Agreement. This Agreement constitutes the entire agreement among the parties and supersedes any prior agreement or understandings among them, oral or written, all of which are hereby cancelled. This Agreement may not be modified or amended other than pursuant to Section 18 hereof.

19.3 Captions; Pronouns. The paragraph and section titles or captions contained in this Agreement are inserted only as a matter of convenience of reference. Such titles and captions in no way define, limit, extend or describe the scope of this Agreement nor the intent of any provision hereof. All pronouns and any variation thereof shall be deemed to refer to the masculine, feminine or neuter, singular or plural, as the identity of the person or persons may require.

19.4 Counterparts. This Agreement may be executed in any number of counterparts and by different parties hereto in separate counterparts, each of which when so executed shall be deemed to be an original and all of which when taken together shall constitute one and the same agreement. Delivery of any executed counterpart of a signature page to this Agreement by facsimile shall be effective as delivery of an executed original counterpart of this Agreement.

19.5 Governing Law. This Agreement shall be governed by and construed in accordance with the internal laws of the state of Washington.

IN WITNESS WHEREOF the parties have executed this Agreement as of the date first hereinabove written.

MANAGER/MEMBER:__________________________________

MANAGER/MEMBER:__________________________________

MANAGER/MEMBER:__________________________________

SPOUSAL CONSENT

The undersigned acknowledges that she has read the foregoing Agreement, knows and understands its contents, and has had ample opportunity to consult with legal counsel of her own choosing. The undersigned is aware that by its provisions, her spouse agrees to hold their Percentage Interest in the Company subject to certain restrictions. The undersigned hereby approves of the provisions of this Agreement and consents to the imposition of certain restrictions on any interest he may have in the Percentage Interests, and agrees that she will not make any transfer of, or otherwise deal with, the Percentage Interests or with any interest she may have in the Percentage Interests except as expressly permitted by such Agreement.

DATED:_______________

____

APPENDIX A

Member	Cash Contribution	Percentage Interest	
	$	______	%
	$	______	%
	$	______	%
TOTAL	$	100	%

E. FORM: CORPORATE SHAREHOLDERS AGREEMENT

SHAREHOLDERS AGREEMENT of

____

This Agreement dated as of _______, _______, is made by and among _______, a corporation (the "Company"), and the shareholders set forth on attached Exhibit A (the "Shareholders").

RECITALS

This Agreement is intended to set forth the restrictions to which any transfer of any or all of the shares of the Company's capital stock now or hereafter outstanding ("Shares") will be subject. The Shareholders together own all the currently outstanding Shares as set forth in attached Exhibit A.

AGREEMENT

1. RESTRICTIONS ON TRANSFER

1.1 Transfers by Shareholders. No Shareholder may transfer any Shares except as expressly permitted by this Agreement. For purposes of this Agreement, "transfer" is intended to be construed as broadly as the law allows and to include any change of legal or beneficial ownership with respect to the Shares or the creation of a security interest by any means. Any transfer made in connection with the foreclosure of a security interest will constitute a separate transfer.

1.2 New Stock Issues. The Company may not transfer Shares by new issue to anyone (including a Shareholder or an outside party) or permit anyone (including a Shareholder or an outside party) to subscribe to a new issue of Shares without the prior written consent of all Shareholders [or, if that consent cannot be obtained, without first offering to the Shareholders the right for a period of _______ days to subscribe to the proposed issue in proportion to the Shareholder's respective interest at the time of issue].

2. PERMITTED TRANSFERS

2.1 With Consent. A Shareholder may transfer Shares at any time with the written consent of [all] the other Shareholders [who hold at least _______ percent (_______) of the Shares of the Company at the time of the proposed transfer].

2.2 Without Consent. A Shareholder may transfer Shares to trusts created by the Shareholder for the Shareholder's benefit or for the benefit of family members of the Shareholder. For purposes of this Agreement, "family members" means lineal descendants of the Shareholder.

2.3 Binding on Transferees. No permitted transfer may be made unless the transferee (and, if applicable, the transferee's spouse) executes a document substantially in the form of attached Exhibit B evidencing the transferee's agreement to be bound by the provisions of this Agreement, as amended.

3. PERMITTED LIFETIME TRANSFERS. Any Shareholder desiring to transfer Shares in a bona fide voluntary transfer not permitted by Section 2 must first give written notice to the Company and the remaining Shareholders of the Shareholder's intention to do so. The notice ("Transfer Notice") must name the proposed transferee and the number of Shares to be transferred and, if the transfer constitutes a sale, must specify the terms of a bona fide offer, including the price per Share, and the terms of payment.

3.1 Company Option. The Company will have the option, exercisable within _______ days after receiving the Transfer Notice, to purchase the Shares. To exercise the option, the Company must give written notice to the offering Shareholder. Subject to Section 3.4, the Company must pay the purchase price on the same terms and conditions set forth in the Transfer Notice.

3.2 Option of Remaining Shareholders. If the Company does not exercise its option as to all or any of the Shares set forth in the Transfer Notice, then the Company must so notify the remaining Shareholders.

(a) The remaining Shareholders will each have the option, exercisable within _______ days after receiving notice from the Company, to purchase any Shares not purchased by the Company. To exercise the option, a Shareholder must give written notice to the Company and to the offering Shareholder specifying the number of shares the Shareholder wishes to purchase.

(b) If the total number of Shares specified in the notices of election exceeds the number of offered Shares, each Shareholder will have priority, up to the number of Shares specified in the notice of election, to purchase the Shareholder's Proportionate Share of the available Shares. Proportionate Share means that proportion determined by dividing the number of the Company's Shares that the electing Shareholder holds by the total number of the Company's Shares held by all Shareholders electing to purchase as of the date the offer was made.

(c) The Shares not purchased on a priority basis will be allocated to those Shareholders that elect to purchase more than the number of Shares to which they have a priority right, up to the number of Shares specified in their respective notices of election to purchase, in the proportion that the number of Shares held by each of them bears to the number of Shares held by all of them as of the date the offer was made.

(d) Promptly after receiving the written notices of election of the remaining Shareholders, the Company must notify each Shareholder of the number of Shares as to which the Shareholder's election was effective and must provide to the offering Shareholder a notice summarizing these elections. Subject to Section 3.4, each Shareholder must pay the purchase price on the same terms and conditions set forth in the Transfer Notice.

3.3 Conditions of Transfer. If the Company and the Shareholders elect not to purchase all the Shares set forth in the Transfer Notice, then all those Shares may be transferred subject to the satisfaction of all the following conditions:

(a) Within thirty (30) days after receiving notice from the Company, the offering Shareholder must transfer the Shares to the transferee identified in the Transfer Notice at the price and on the same terms stated in the Transfer Notice; and

(b) The transferee (and, if applicable, the transferee's spouse) must execute a document substantially in the form of attached Exhibit B evidencing the transferee's agreement to be bound by the provisions of this Agreement, as amended.

(c) If all of the above-conditions are not satisfied, the offering Shareholder may not transfer the Shares under this Section 3 without giving a new written notice of intention to transfer and complying with this Section 3.

3.4 Right to Purchase Pursuant to Agreement. Notwithstanding any other provision to the contrary, the Company or the remaining Shareholders, or both, will be entitled to purchase all the Shares specified in the Transfer Notice at the price and on the terms set forth in this Agreement (and not at the price and on the terms set forth in the Transfer Notice), if any of the following occur:

(a) The price stated in the Transfer Notice is greater than the price set forth in this Agreement;

(b) The offering Shareholder has included in the Transfer Notice the terms of a gift, pledge, or other transfer not constituting a sale; or

(c) The terms of a bona fide offer in the Transfer Notice provide for the payment of nonmonetary consideration, in whole or in part, and the offering Shareholder and the Company or remaining Shareholders, or both (as applicable), are not able to agree on the equivalent cash value of that consideration.

(d) If appraisal is required to determine the value of the Shares under Section 8, the Transfer Notice will be deemed to be given on the date that the Company receives notice of the appraisal determination.

4. OBLIGATIONS OF TRANSFEREES. Unless this Agreement expressly provides otherwise, each transferee or subsequent transferee of Shares, or any interest in those Shares, will hold those Shares or interest subject to all the provisions of this Agreement and may make no further transfers except as provided in this Agreement.

5. PURCHASE ON DEATH

5.1 Mandatory Purchase on Death by Company or Shareholders

(a) Upon the death of a Shareholder, the Company must purchase all the decedent's Shares and all Shares that have been transferred to third parties under Section 2.2, and the decedent Shareholder's estate and any such third parties must sell those Shares, at the price and on the terms provided in this Agreement. Subject to Section 9.1, the purchase must be completed within a period commencing with the death of the Shareholder and ending sixty (60) days following the qualification of the Shareholder's personal representative.

(b) If the Company is not legally able to purchase all of the decedent's Shares and all Shares that have been transferred to third parties under Section 2.2

under applicable law, the remaining Shareholders must purchase all of the decedent's Shares and all Shares that have been transferred to third parties under Section 2.2 that the Company is legally unable to purchase at the price and on the terms provided in this Agreement.

(c) The obligation of the remaining Shareholders to purchase those Shares will be [joint and several] [several and not joint and will be prorated based on their respective shareholdings in the Company].

5.2 Insurance: Corporate Buyout. The Company [may] [must] apply for a policy of insurance on the life of each Shareholder to enable the Company to purchase the Shares of that Shareholder. Each Shareholder agrees to do everything necessary to cause a policy of life insurance to be issued pursuant to that application. The Company must be the owner of any policy or policies of life insurance acquired pursuant to the terms of this Agreement. Each policy, and any policies hereafter acquired for the same purpose, will be listed on attached Exhibit C.

6. DISABILITY

6.1 Optional Purchase on Disability. If any Shareholder who is then an employee of the Company becomes disabled, the Company and the remaining Shareholders will have the option, for the periods set forth below, to purchase all or any part of the Shares owned by the Shareholder and all or any part of the Shareholder's Shares that have been transferred to third parties under Section 2.2.

6.2 Exercise of Option

(a) To exercise its option, the Company must give written notice to the disabled Shareholder within _______ days after receiving notice of the determination of disability under Section 6.3.

(b) If the option is not exercised within that _______ -day period as to all Shares owned by the disabled Shareholder, the remaining Shareholders will have the option, for a period of _______ days commencing with the end of that _______ -day period, to purchase all or any part of the remaining Shares owned by the disabled Shareholder, at the price and on the terms provided in this Agreement. To exercise the option, a Shareholder must give to the disabled Shareholder written notice of election to purchase a specified number of the Shares.

(c) If the notices of election from the other Shareholders specify in the aggregate more Shares than are available for purchase by the other Shareholders, each Shareholder will have priority, up to the number of Shares specified in the notice of election, to purchase the Shareholder's Proportionate Share of the Shares. Proportionate Share means that proportion determined by dividing the number of the Company's Shares that the electing Shareholder holds by the total number of the Company's Shares held by all Shareholders electing to purchase as of the date the offer was made.

(d) The Shares not purchased on a priority basis will be allocated to those Shareholders electing to purchase more than the number of Shares to which they have a priority right, up to the number of Shares specified in their respective notices of election to purchase, in the proportion that the number of Shares held by each of them bears to the number of Shares held by all of them as of the date the offer was made.

(e) If this option is not exercised as to all the Shares owned by the disabled Shareholder, the disabled Shareholder will hold the remaining Shares [subject to] [free and clear of] the provisions of this Agreement.

(f) For purposes of this Agreement a Shareholder will be deemed to be "disabled" if one of the following conditions is satisfied:

(i) Under the terms of a bona fide disability income insurance policy that insures the Shareholder, the insurance company that underwrites the insurance policy determines that the Shareholder is totally disabled for purposes of the insurance policy.

(ii) A physician licensed to practice medicine in the state _______ of or _______, who has been selected by the Shareholder (or agent) and the board of directors of the Company, certifies that the Shareholder is partially or totally disabled so that the Shareholder will be unable to be employed gainfully on a full-time basis by the Company for a _______ -month period or more in the position that the Shareholder occupied before the disability. If the board of directors of the Company and the Shareholder (or agent) do not agree on the choice of a physician, these parties must each choose a physician who must in turn select a third physician. The third physician will have the authority to determine the Shareholder's disability. If the Shareholder refuses to choose a physician, the determination made by the physician selected by the Company will be conclusive. The Company must pay for the costs and expenses of the physician. As used in this Section 6.3(b), "agent" means, if applicable, the conservator of the Shareholder's estate or a person duly granted power-of-attorney to act on behalf of the Shareholder.

(iii) The Shareholder and the board of directors of the Company agree in writing that the Shareholder is partially or totally disabled so that the Shareholder will be unable to be employed gainfully on a full-time basis by the Company for a _______ -month period in the position that the Shareholder occupied before the disability.

7. TERMINATION OF EMPLOYMENT

7.1 Option to Purchase on Termination of Employment. If any Shareholder who is an employee of the Company [and who has not attained age _______] voluntarily terminates employment with the Company [or is discharged for cause], the Company and the remaining Shareholders will have the option to purchase all or any part of the Shares owned by the Shareholder and all Shares transferred to third parties pursuant to Section 2.2. The option will be exercisable first by the Company and thereafter by the remaining Shareholders, and the price, terms of purchase, and method of exercise of the option will be the same as are provided in Section 6.2. If this option is not exercised as to all of the Shares, the Shareholder and any third party to whom Shares were transferred under Section 2.2 will hold the Shares [subject to] [free and clear of] the provisions of this

Agreement].

8. VALUATION

8.1 Agreed Price With Arbitration. The purchase price to be paid for each of the Shares subject to this Agreement will be equal to the agreed value of the Company divided by the total number of Shares outstanding as of the date the price is to be determined.

(a) The initial agreed value of the Company is $ _______, and, at regular intervals hereafter, but no more often than quarterly and no less often than annually, the Shareholders to this Agreement will review the Company's financial condition. The Shareholders will at that time determine, by a vote of two-thirds of [the outstanding shares held by the Shareholders] [Shareholders (each Shareholder having one vote)], the Company's fair market value, which, if so voted, will be the Company's value until a different value is so determined or otherwise established under the provisions of this Agreement.

(b) If the parties are able to determine the value by that vote, they will evidence it by placing their written and executed agreement in the minute book of the Company. However, if the Shareholders have been unable to establish a value by that method within _______ years after the date on which the Shareholders last agreed on the value of the Company, the purchase price for each of the offering Shareholder's Shares will be determined by appraisal, in accordance with Section 8.2.

8.2 Appraisal. If required under Section 8.1(b), promptly after the occurrence of the event requiring the determination of the purchase price under this Agreement, the Company will appoint an appraiser to determine the fair market value of the Shares.

(a) If the Company and the offering Shareholder fail to agree on the identity of the appraiser, they will each appoint an appraiser to determine the fair market value of the Shares. If the appointed appraisers are not able to agree on the fair market value of the Shares, the appraisers will appoint a third appraiser, and the decision of a majority of the three appraisers will be binding on all interested parties.

(b) If a party fails to designate an appraiser within fifteen (15) days after receiving written notice from the other designating an appraiser and demanding appointment of the second appraiser, the first appraiser appointed may determine the fair market value of the Shares.

(c) The appraisal must be completed and communicated to the relevant parties not later than sixty (60) days after appointment of the first appraiser. [The appraisal fees must be paid by the Company.]

(d) Among other things, in making the appraisal, the appraiser must value real estate at fair market value; machinery and equipment at replacement cost or fair market value, whichever is lower; goods in process at cost, using the cost accounting procedures customarily employed by the Company in preparing its financial statements; receivables at their face amount, minus an allowance for uncollectible items that is reasonable in view of the past experience of the

Company and a recent review of their collectibility; all liabilities at their face value; [bank orders]; good will based on probable future work; and must establish a reserve for contingent liabilities, if appropriate. The appraiser must also consider the value of other comparable companies, if known.

9. PAYMENT TERMS

9.1 Terms. Unless otherwise agreed, the purchase price for Shares purchased under this Agreement must be paid as follows:

(a) If the purchase price is $ _______ or less, the purchase price must be paid in full within ninety (90) days after the offering Shareholder receives notice of the mandatory or optional purchase of the offering Shareholder's Shares.

(b) Subject to Section 9.2, if the purchase price is greater than $ _______, a down payment of _______ percent (_______) of the purchase price must be paid within ninety (90) days after the offering Shareholder receives notice of the mandatory or optional purchase of the offering Shareholder's Shares.

(c) Subject to Section 9.2, the balance of the purchase price must be paid in _______ equal monthly installments, including interest at the prime rate announced from time to time in the Wall Street Journal, plus two percent. The installment payments must commence on the first day of the month next following the date on which the Company or the remaining Shareholders or both purchase the Shares, and like payments must be made on the first day of each month thereafter until the purchase price is paid in full. All or any part of the unpaid balance of the purchase price may be prepaid without penalty at any time. The purchase price for the Shares must be paid to the offering Shareholder or the offering Shareholder's estate, as the case may be.

9.2 Insurance. The purchase price for the Shares must be paid as follows if the Company has insurance under Section 5.2 on the life of a deceased Shareholder whose Shares are purchased in accordance with Section 5.1.

(a) If the purchase price for the Shares is less than or equal to the amount of the proceeds received by the Company or the remaining Shareholders or both from the insurance on the life of the deceased Shareholder, the purchase price for the Shares must be paid in cash on the date of the purchase of the Shares.

(b) If the purchase price for the Shares of the deceased Shareholder exceeds the amount of the insurance proceeds, an amount equal to the proceeds of the insurance on the life of the deceased Shareholder must be paid in cash on the date of the purchase of the Shares, and the balance of the purchase price must be paid in accordance with Section 9.1(b).

(c) The Company must file the necessary proofs of death and collect the proceeds of any policies of insurance described in Section 5.2 outstanding on the life of the deceased Shareholder. The decedent's personal representative must apply for and obtain any necessary court approval or confirmation of the sale of the decedent's shares under this Agreement.

9.3 Documentation

(a) The deferred portion of the purchase price for any Shares purchased under this Agreement must be evidenced by a promissory note executed by the Company or all the purchasing Shareholders or both (as applicable) substantially in the form of attached Exhibit D. Except to the extent otherwise provided under Section 5.1(c) (but in that event only with respect to purchases under Section 5.1), the obligations of the Company or the Shareholders or both (as applicable) under the note will be [joint and several] [several and not joint prorated based on the number of Shares that each purchaser is purchasing]. If the obligation is several and not joint, each purchaser must sign a separate promissory note substantially in the form of attached Exhibit D. If the obligation is joint and several, all purchasers must sign the same promissory note, substantially in the form of attached Exhibit D but appropriately modified to reflect the joint and several obligations of each.

(b) The note or notes must be secured by a pledge of all the Shares being purchased in the transaction to which the note or notes relate [and of all other shares owned by the purchasing Shareholders], as set forth in the promissory note attached in Exhibit D and must contain such other provisions as set forth therein.

9.4 Payment of Consideration; Procedures for Transfer. Upon the exercise of any option under this Agreement and in all other events, consideration for the Shares must be delivered as soon as practicable to the person entitled to it. The Company must have the certificates representing the purchased Shares properly endorsed and, on compliance with Section 11, must issue a new certificate in the name of each purchasing Shareholder.

10. ADMINISTRATIVE REQUIREMENTS

The Company agrees to apply for and use its best efforts to obtain all governmental and administrative approvals required in connection with the purchase and sale of Shares under this Agreement. The Shareholders agree to cooperate in obtaining the approvals and to execute any and all documents that may be required to be executed by them in connection with the approvals. The Company must pay all costs and filing fees in connection with obtaining the approvals.

11. SHARE CERTIFICATES

On execution of this Agreement, the Company must place the legend set forth in Section 12 on the certificates representing the Shareholder's Shares. None of the Shares may be transferred, encumbered, or in any way alienated except under the terms of this Agreement. Each Shareholder will have the right to vote that Shareholder's Shares and receive the dividends paid on them until the Shares are sold or transferred as provided in this Agreement.

12. LEGENDS ON SHARE CERTIFICATES

Each share certificate, when issued, must have conspicuously endorsed on its face the following legend:

> SALE, TRANSFER, PLEDGE, OR ANY OTHER DISPOSITION OF THE SHARES REPRESENTED BY THIS CERTIFICATE IS SUBJECT TO AND RESTRICTED BY THE TERMS OF A SHAREHOLDERS AGREEMENT DATED _______, _______,

BETWEEN THE COMPANY AND ITS SHAREHOLDERS. A COPY OF THE SHAREHOLDERS AGREEMENT IS AVAILABLE AT THE OFFICE OF THE COMPANY. THE SHARES REPRESENTED BY THIS CERTIFICATE MAY BE SOLD, TRANSFERRED, PLEDGED, OR OTHERWISE DISPOSED OF ONLY UPON COMPLIANCE WITH THE SHAREHOLDERS AGREEMENT.

On the request of a Shareholder, the secretary of the Company must show a copy of this Agreement to any person making inquiry about it.

13. TERMINATION OF AGREEMENT. This Agreement will terminate upon the occurrence of any of the following:

(a) As to each Shareholder only, the transfer of all Shares held by that Shareholder pursuant to the provisions of this Agreement;

(b) The written agreement of all parties who are then bound by the terms of this Agreement;

c) The dissolution [,or] bankruptcy, [or insolvency] of the Company; or

(d) At that time, if ever, that only one Shareholder or other transferee who is subject to the terms of this Agreement remains.

14. SHAREHOLDER WILLS

Each Shareholder agrees to include in his or her will a direction and authorization to the Shareholder's personal representative to comply with the provisions of this Agreement and to sell the Shareholder's Shares in accordance with this Agreement. However, the failure of any Shareholder to do so will not affect the validity or enforceability of this Agreement.

15. EQUITABLE RELIEF IN THE EVENT OF BREACH

The Shares of the Company subject to this Agreement are unique and cannot be readily purchased or sold because of the lack of a market. For these reasons, among others, the parties will be irreparably damaged if this Agreement is breached. Any party aggrieved by a breach of the provisions of this Agreement may bring an action at law or a suit in equity to obtain redress, including specific performance, injunctive relief, or any other available equitable remedy. Time and strict performance are of the essence of this Agreement. These remedies are cumulative and not exclusive and are in addition to any other remedy that the parties may have.

16. SUBCHAPTER S ELECTION AND STATUS

If all the Shareholders elect (or have elected) for the Company to be taxed as an "S Corporation" pursuant to Code Section 1362, then the Shareholders and the Company and will maintain that status until the Shares representing percent (_______ %) [NOTE TO DRAFTER: more than fifty percent (50%)] of the outstanding shares of Company are voted to terminate this election. Any provision of this Agreement is void that would prevent the Company from being able to make an effective election to be classified as an S Corporation once the decision has been made to elect S corporation status or that, once the Company becomes an S Corporation, would cause that status to be involuntarily terminated.

17. LEGAL LIMITATIONS

The obligation of the Company to purchase Shares under this Agreement is in all respects limited and by the ability of the Company to draw upon a legal source of funds from which to pay the purchase price. If the Company is legally unable to purchase and pay for any Shares that it is required to purchase under this Agreement, the Shareholders must promptly vote their respective Shares to take whatever steps may be appropriate or necessary to enable the Company to lawfully purchase and pay for all of the Shares.

18. MISCELLANEOUS PROVISIONS

18.1 Deletion and Addition of Parties. The secretary of the Company may add as a party to this Agreement any transferee of Shares or delete as a party any Shareholder who transfers all of the Shareholder's Shares. The secretary may take this action without the need for any further action by the board of directors of the Company or the consent of any party to this Agreement or of their respective heirs, personal representatives, successors, or assigns and regardless of whether or not a counterpart of this Agreement has been executed by that party. The Secretary may do so by amending the Shareholder list attached as Exhibit A.

18.2 Extension of Time for Closing. If in the opinion of legal counsel, additional time is needed in order to comply with applicable securities laws, the time of the closing of any sale or other transfer hereunder may be extended for a reasonable period not to exceed sixty (60) days.

18.3 Authorization. The Company is authorized to enter into this Agreement by virtue of a resolution duly adopted at a meeting of its Board of Directors dated effective _______ .

18.4 Employment Not Guaranteed. Nothing contained in this Agreement nor any action taken hereunder is intended to be construed as a contract of employment or to give a Shareholder any right to be retained in the employ of the Company in any capacity, or to be a director or officer of the Company, or to be retained by the Company as any type of independent contractor.

18.5 Notices. Any notice or other communication required or permitted to be given under this Agreement must be in writing and must be mailed by certified mail, return receipt requested, postage prepaid, addressed to the appropriate party or parties at the address(es) set forth in attached Exhibit A. Any notice or other communication will be deemed to be given at the expiration of the _______ day after the date of deposit in the United States Mail. The addresses to which notices or other communications are to be mailed may be changed from time to time by giving written notice to the other parties as provided in this Section.

18.6 Attorney Fees. If any suit or arbitration is filed by any party to enforce this Agreement or proceedings are commenced in bankruptcy or otherwise with respect to the subject matter of this Agreement, the prevailing party will be entitled to recover reasonable attorney fees incurred in preparation or in prosecution or defense of that suit or arbitration as fixed by the court or arbitrator, and if any appeal is taken from the decision of the court or arbitrator, reasonable attorney fees as fixed by the appellate court.

18.7 Amendments. This Agreement may be amended only by an instrument in writing executed [by all the parties] [by the Company and by Shareholders holding at least _______ (_______ %) of the Shares as of the date of the Amendment, except that, if another provision of this Agreement specifically requires the consent or vote of a lesser or greater percentage with respect to a particular action, that provision will control as to that action].

18.8 Headings. The headings used in this Agreement are solely for convenience of reference, are not part of this Agreement, and are not to be considered in construing or interpreting this Agreement.

18.9 Entire Agreement. This Agreement (including the exhibits) sets forth the entire understanding of the parties with respect to the subject matter of this Agreement and supersedes any and all prior understandings and agreements, whether written or oral, between the parties with respect to that subject matter.

18.10 Counterparts. This Agreement may be executed by the parties in separate counterparts, each of which when executed and delivered will be an original, but all of which together will constitute one and the same instrument. Signature pages may be detached from the counterparts and attached to a single copy of this Agreement to form an original document.

18.11 Severability. If any provision of this Agreement is held to be invalid or unenforceable in any respect for any reason, the validity and enforceability of that provision in any other respect and of the remaining provisions of this Agreement will not be in any way impaired.

18.12 Waiver. A provision of this Agreement may be waived only by a written instrument executed by the party waiving compliance. No waiver of any provision of this Agreement will constitute a waiver of any other provision, whether or not similar, nor will any waiver constitute a continuing waiver. Failure to enforce any provision of this Agreement will not operate as a waiver of that provision or any other provision.

18.13 Further Assurances. From time to time, each of the parties agrees to execute, acknowledge, and deliver any instruments or documents necessary to carry out the purposes of this Agreement.

18.14 Time Is of the Essence. Time is of the essence for each and every provision of this Agreement.

18.15 No Third–Party Beneficiaries. Except as may be expressly stated herein, nothing in this Agreement is intended to confer on any person, other than the parties to this Agreement, any right or remedy of any nature whatsoever.

18.16 Expenses. Each party agrees to bear its own expenses in connection with this Agreement and the transactions contemplated by this Agreement.

18.17 Exhibits. The exhibits referenced in this Agreement are a part of this Agreement as if fully set forth in this Agreement.

18.18 Governing Law. This Agreement will be governed by and construed in accordance with the laws of the state of _______.

18.19 Venue. This Agreement has been made entirely within the state of . If any suit or action is filed by any party to enforce this Agreement or otherwise with respect to the subject matter of this Agreement, venue will be in the federal or state courts in _______, _______.

18.20 Arbitration

(a) Any claim between the parties, under this Agreement or otherwise, must be determined by arbitration in _______, _______ commenced in accordance with applicable law. All statutes of limitations that would otherwise be applicable will apply to the arbitration proceeding. There will be one arbitrator agreed upon by the parties within ten (10) days before the arbitration or, if not, selected by the administrator of the American Arbitration Association ("AAA") office in _______, or failing that, the nearest AAA office. The arbitrator must be an attorney with at least fifteen (15) years' experience in commercial law and must reside in the _______ area. Whether a claim is covered by this agreement will be determined by the arbitrator. At the request of either party made not later than seventy-five (75) days after the arbitration demand, the parties agree to attempt to resolve the dispute by nonbinding mediation or evaluation or both (but without delaying the arbitration hearing date).

(b) The arbitration must be conducted in accordance with the AAA Commercial Arbitration Rules in effect on the date hereof, as modified by this Agreement. There will be no substantive motions or discovery except that the arbitrator may authorize such discovery as may be necessary to ensure a fair hearing, and discovery may not extend the time limits set forth in this Section. The arbitrator will not be bound by the rules of evidence or civil procedure.

(c) The arbitrator must hold a private hearing within one hundred twenty (120) days after the arbitration demand, conclude the hearing within three (3) days, and render a written decision within fourteen (14) calendar days after the hearing. These time limits are not jurisdictional. In making the decision and award, the arbitrator must apply applicable substantive law and must make a brief statement of the claims determined and the award made on each claim.

(d) Absent fraud, collusion, or willful misconduct by the arbitrator, the award will be final, and judgment may be entered in any court having jurisdiction thereof. The arbitrator may award injunctive relief or any other remedy available from a judge, including the joinder of parties or consolidation of this arbitration with any other involving common issues of law or fact or which may promote judicial economy, and may award attorney fees and costs to the prevailing party but will not have the power to award punitive or exemplary damages.

18.21 Legal Representation. Each of the undersigned recognizes and acknowledges that the law firm of _______("Counsel") has represented _______ with respect to this Agreement and no other party and that Counsel has advised each of the undersigned to obtain independent legal counsel.

DATED this ___ day of __________, _______.

COMPANY: ____________________________

By: ________________________________

Its: ________________________________

SHAREHOLDERS:

____

____

SPOUSES:

1. I acknowledge that I have read the foregoing Agreement and that I know its contents.

2. I am aware that by its provisions my spouse agrees to sell all of my spouse's Shares of the Company (including, if applicable, my community interest in them) on the occurrence of certain events.

3. I hereby consent to the sale, approve the provisions of the Agreement, and agree that those Shares and my interest in them are subject to the provisions of the Agreement and that I will take no action at any time to hinder operation of the Agreement on those Shares or any interest in them.

4. In the event of a dissolution, divorce, annulment, or other termination of marriage of my spouse's and my marriage other than by reason of death, I hereby agree to release or transfer (or both) whatever interest I may have in the Company (including, but not limited to, any interest as a Shareholder or creditor, or interest in the Stock or debt of Company) to my spouse on the termination of our marriage.

5. As part of any property settlement of our marital assets, my spouse must compensate me for my interest. In the event the parties cannot agree as to the value of my interest or upon terms of payment, the value of any Shares in which I have an interest will be determined and will be paid to me in accordance with the terms and conditions of the Agreement.

6. If my interest in Company is in the nature of debt, the value of that debt will be deemed to be its outstanding principal balance plus any accrued and unpaid interest thereon and compensation therefore will be provided as agreed by the parties.

7. I acknowledge that I have been advised to consult with independent legal counsel regarding this Agreement and this provision and, further, expressly acknowledge the provisions of Section [18.21] regarding legal counsel and conflicts of interest.

____

____

____

____

EXHIBIT A

LIST OF SHAREHOLDERS SUBJECT TO SHAREHOLDERS AGREEMENT

Dated _______

[Company name and address]

Shareholder Name	Address	Number of Shares Held

EXHIBIT B

LIFE INSURANCE SCHEDULE

Name of Insured	Insurance Company	Policy Number	Type pf Policy	Initial Cash Benefit	Death Benefit

EXHIBIT C

PROMISSORY NOTE

$__________

1. For good and valuable consideration, the undersigned promises to pay to the order of _______ ("Holder") the sum of _______ ($ _______), together with interest thereon, in monthly installments of not less than $ _______. The first installment is due on _______, _______, and a like installment is due on the same date of each successive month thereafter until _______, at which time the entire unpaid balance of this Note, any accrued but unpaid interest, and any other amounts payable under this Note, must be paid in full. The unpaid balance of this Note will bear interest at the rate of _______ percent (_______ %) per annum.

2. The undersigned may prepay a portion or all of the balance at any time without penalty.

3. With respect to any payment not made within ten (10) days after it is due and without waiving any other remedy the Holder may have under this Note or otherwise, the Holder may charge the undersigned a late payment charge of five percent (5%) of the unpaid amount.

4. If any payment required by this Note is not paid within fifteen (15) days after receipt by the undersigned of notice of nonpayment from the Holder ("Event of Default"), at Holder's option, the unpaid balance will bear interest at a default rate of fifteen percent (15%) per annum from the date the payment was due until paid in full.

5. As security for the obligations of the undersigned evidenced by this Note, the undersigned hereby grants to Holder a security interest in _______ shares of the common stock of _______, (the "Shares") issued under certificate number _______ (the "Certificate"). The undersigned has delivered to the Holder the Certificate, together with a stock power endorsed in blank, to hold subject to the terms of this Agreement. Holder agrees to take reasonable care in the custody and the preservation of the Certificate. On payment in full of the principal and interest on the Note, Holder must deliver the Certificate to the undersigned, together with the stock power endorsed by the undersigned in blank.

6. The undersigned irrevocably appoints Holder as attorney-in-fact and grants Holder a proxy to do (but Holder shall not be obligated and shall incur no liability to the undersigned or any third party for failure to do so), after and during the continuance of an Event of Default, any act that the undersigned is obligated by this Note to do and to exercise such rights and powers as undersigned might exercise with respect to the Shares. With respect to voting the Shares, this Section 6 constitutes an irrevocable appointment of a proxy, coupled with an interest, which shall continue until the Note is paid in full.

7. Upon the occurrence of an Event of Default under this Note, the Holder may, in the Holder's sole discretion and with or without further notice to the undersigned and in addition to all rights and remedies at law or in equity or otherwise (a) declare the entire balance of the Note immediately due and payable, (b) register in Holder's name any or all of the Shares, (c) sell or otherwise dispose of the Shares, or (d) exercise Holder's proxy rights with respect to all or a portion of the Shares. In such event, the undersigned agrees to deliver promptly to Holder further evidence of the grant of such proxy in any form requested by Holder.

8. The undersigned hereby waives demand, notice of default, and notice of sale, and consents to public or private sale of the Shares upon the occurrence of an Event of Default, and the Holder will have the right to purchase at the sale.

9. If any action, suit, or other proceeding is instituted concerning or arising out of this Note, the prevailing party will be entitled to recover all costs and attorney fees reasonably incurred by such party in such action, suit, or other proceeding (including all bankruptcy courts), including any and all appeals or petitions therefrom.

____

Signature

F. NED'S AMORTIZATION SCHEDULE (Section B of Chapter 3)

	Beginning Balance	Interest	Principal	Ending Balance
1	$200,000.00	$1,166.67	$2,793.57	$197,206.43
2	$197,206.43	$1,150.37	$2,809.87	$194,396.56
3	$194,396.56	$1,133.98	$2,826.26	$191,570.30
4	$191,570.30	$1,117.49	$2,842.75	$188,727.55
5	$188,727.55	$1,100.91	$2,859.33	$185,868.22
6	$185,868.22	$1,084.23	$2,876.01	$182,992.21
7	$182,992.21	$1,067.45	$2,892.79	$180,099.43
8	$180,099.43	$1,050.58	$2,909.66	$177,189.77
9	$177,189.77	$1,033.61	$2,926.63	$174,263.14
10	$174,263.14	$1,016.53	$2,943.71	$171,319.43
11	$171,319.43	$999.36	$2,960.88	$168,358.56
12	$168,358.56	$982.09	$2,978.15	$165,380.41
		year 1 end		
13	$165,380.41	$964.72	$2,995.52	$162,384.89
14	$162,384.89	$947.25	$3,012.99	$159,371.89
15	$159,371.89	$929.67	$3,030.57	$156,341.32
16	$156,341.32	$911.99	$3,048.25	$153,293.07
17	$153,293.07	$894.21	$3,066.03	$150,227.04
18	$150,227.04	$876.32	$3,083.92	$147,143.13
19	$147,143.13	$858.33	$3,101.91	$144,041.22
20	$144,041.22	$840.24	$3,120.00	$140,921.22
21	$140,921.22	$822.04	$3,138.20	$137,783.02
22	$137,783.02	$803.73	$3,156.51	$134,626.52
23	$134,626.52	$785.32	$3,174.92	$131,451.60
24	$131,451.60	$766.80	$3,193.44	$128,258.16
		year 2 end		
25	$128,258.16	$748.17	$3,212.07	$125,046.10

26	$125,046.10	$729.44	$3,230.80	$121,815.29
27	$121,815.29	$710.59	$3,249.65	$118,565.64
28	$118,565.64	$691.63	$3,268.61	$115,297.03
29	$115,297.03	$672.57	$3,287.67	$112,009.36
30	$112,009.36	$653.39	$3,306.85	$108,702.51
31	$108,702.51	$634.10	$3,326.14	$105,376.37
32	$105,376.37	$614.70	$3,345.54	$102,030.82
33	$102,030.82	$595.18	$3,365.06	$98,665.76
34	$98,665.76	$575.55	$3,384.69	$95,281.07
35	$95,281.07	$555.81	$3,404.43	$91,876.64
36	$91,876.64	$535.95	$3,424.29	$88,452.35
		year 3 end		
37	$88,452.35	$515.97	$3,444.27	$85,008.08
38	$85,008.08	$495.88	$3,464.36	$81,543.72
39	$81,543.72	$475.67	$3,484.57	$78,059.15
40	$78,059.15	$455.35	$3,504.89	$74,554.26
41	$74,554.26	$434.90	$3,525.34	$71,028.92
42	$71,028.92	$414.34	$3,545.90	$67,483.01
43	$67,483.01	$393.65	$3,566.59	$63,916.42
44	$63,916.42	$372.85	$3,587.39	$60,329.03
45	$60,329.03	$351.92	$3,608.32	$56,720.71
46	$56,720.71	$330.87	$3,629.37	$53,091.34
47	$53,091.34	$309.70	$3,650.54	$49,440.80
48	$49,440.80	$288.40	$3,671.84	$45,768.97
		year 4 end		
49	$45,768.97	$266.99	$3,693.25	$42,075.71
50	$42,075.71	$245.44	$3,714.80	$38,360.91
51	$38,360.91	$223.77	$3,736.47	$34,624.45
52	$34,624.45	$201.98	$3,758.26	$30,866.18
53	$30,866.18	$180.05	$3,780.19	$27,086.00

54	$27,086.00	$158.00	$3,802.24	$23,283.76
55	$23,283.76	$135.82	$3,824.42	$19,459.34
56	$19,459.34	$113.51	$3,846.73	$15,612.61
57	$15,612.61	$91.07	$3,869.17	$11,743.45
58	$11,743.45	$68.50	$3,891.74	$7,851.71
59	$7,851.71	$45.80	$3,914.44	$3,937.27
60	$3,937.27	$22.97	$3,937.27	$0.00
		year 5 end		

INDEX

References are to pages.

A

B

C

D

E

F

G-H-I

J-K-L

M-N-O

P-Q-R

S-T-U

V-W-X-Y-Z

†